ALSO BY HELEN GARNER

The Children's Bach
This House of Grief
Monkey Grip

HOW TO END A STORY

HOW TO END A STORY

Collected Diaries, 1978–1998

Helen Garner

Foreword by Leslie Jamison

Pantheon Books
New York

FIRST U.S. HARDCOVER EDITION PUBLISHED BY
PANTHEON BOOKS 2025

Pantheon Books,
A Division of Penguin Random House LLC
1745 Broadway, New York, NY 10019
www.penguinrandomhouse.com
www.pantheonbooks.com

First published by The Text Publishing Company Australia, in three volumes,
in 2019, 2020, and 2021.

Library of Congress Control Number 2024950305
ISBN 978-0-553-38749-0
ebook 978-0-553-38750-6

Printed in the United States of America

2 4 6 8 9 7 5 3 1

The authorized representative in the EU for product safety and compliance
is Penguin Random House Ireland, Morrison Chambers, 32 Nassau Street,
Dublin DO2 YH68, Ireland. http://eu-contact.penguin.ie

'We are here for this—to make mistakes and to correct ourselves, to stand the blows and hand them out.'

PRIMO LEVI, *The Periodic Table*

Contents

Foreword by Leslie Jamison

What secret desires and resentments are tucked inside the people we love? A little girl's diary, with its tiny lock and key, testifies to the impulse to keep parts of ourselves hidden, but it's impossible to look at a locked diary without imagining breaking it open.

What to do then, with the published diary? With its lock removed, its interior offered to the world not only as exposure but as *form*: a genre beholden to the insight that rises from immediacy rather than retrospection. Many writers' diaries have been published, but far fewer have been published in their lifetimes—and none carry the singular acuity, wit, and electric grace of Helen Garner's. An Australian national treasure known for her novels of domestic nuance and entanglement (*Monkey Grip, The Children's Bach*) and journalism of grand sorrow and fierce controversy (*The First Stone, This House of Grief*), Garner has given us diaries that read like they are inventing a new language made from utterly familiar materials: fresh, raw, vibrating with life. "Like being given a painting you love gleaming with the still-wet paint," as the writer Helen Elliott put it. They are seductively loose and nimble, delivering shards of experience rather than an overdetermined narrative, pivoting from sharpened skewers of observation ("The writers' festival. It's like being barbecued") to a clear-eyed claiming of pleasure ("tear meat off a chicken and stuff it into her mouth"), swerving from deep reckonings with romantic intimacy and dissolution to sudden, perfect aphorisms hidden like Easter eggs in the grass: "Sentimentality keeps looking over its shoulder to see how you're taking it. Emotion doesn't give a shit whether anyone's looking or not."

The writer Catherine Lacey once brilliantly described the difficulty of writing about experiences you're still living as "trying to make a bed while you're still in it," but as I read Garner's diaries, I kept thinking that perhaps not every bed needs to be made. Sometimes we want the *un*made beds, with messy sheets and sprawled-out bodies stretching and spooning, the fossils of curled hairs on the pillow, the faint salt of dried sweat.

Far from reading like B-roll footage, these diaries feel magnificent and sui generis, beholden to no rhythms or logic but their own, simultaneously seductive and staggering, a blend of pillow talk, bar gossip, and eavesdropping on therapy. They offer an intoxicating, astute account of the deep emotional movements of Garner's life over two decades—two marriages and divorces, the flowering of her literary career, and her daughter's coming-of-age—but they always live in the weeds, built of the grain and texture of her days. No small part of their brilliance stems from their faith that there is no meaningful separation between these realms of inquiry: that reckoning with human purpose and the anguished possibilities of human love always happens within, and not above, the realm of "trivial" daily experience. Which is to say: in their form as well as their content, they reveal where meaning dwells in our lives (everywhere), and how we might excavate it. "In my heart," Garner has said, "I always liked my diary better than anything else I wrote."

Between entries, Garner pivots deftly and unapologetically from interior to exterior, gravity to banality, existential rumination to lively anecdote: love affairs and therapy sessions, but also hot wind, big moons, salt air, a sunset cloud "ridged as neat and fine as salmon flesh," and "the rodent flowing of squirrels" across grass; the sting of a terrible review, the satisfactions of friendship, the beautifully naked bodies of aging women at bathhouses. In these pages, we find all the facets of living beautifully juxtaposed, as they are in life: gossip, sex, parenting, plate-smashing rage, trips to the dentist. "Crazy about the way Proust uses physical objects to keep his huge, billowing sentences grounded," she writes, and her prose does the same. We are returned to the concrete stuff of life: the single pubic hair she finds in the quiche at a dinner party, and politely tucks away; the half-dead tree carved up for a bonfire; the copy of *Paradise Lost* stashed in her outdoor toilet; a friend describing his wife's homemade bread: "the sort of bread you want to peel open and lie down in." Even her description of a Thai meal on her fifty-fifth birthday is a minor revelation, and an ode to the pleasures of surprise (Garner loves surprise as a daily, creative, and even ethical force): "just as you think you know the taste, a note of some other herb or spice breaks through, as clear as a beam of light through a cloud."

When people talk about personal narrative as a literary form, there is almost always a bias toward the insights made available by hindsight. But what can you see as you are coming down the road? "Story is a chunk of life with a bend in it," Garner has said, inviting us to consider the possibility that there's not necessarily a direct correlation between time passed and insight gained, as if you will necessarily "know" the most about your own life at precisely the moment just before you die. You know things as you move through experience, and sometimes the fervent immediacy of this sort of knowing actually diminishes across time. Once you know how things play out, you cannot absolutely re-create all you felt inside of them: that sensation is gone for good. Garner's diaries are full of this intimate entwining of knowing and feeling, like two lovers tangled up in the sheets of an unmade bed.

*   *   *

Yellow Notebook begins in 1978, when Garner's daughter, M, is just nine years old, still living at home. Garner's first novel, *Monkey Grip,* has just won a major prize, but Garner is wrestling with whether her writing is too "small" in its scope. "Everyone's talking about *Apocalypse Now,*" she laments. "My work seems piddling, narrow, domestic." This first volume tracks the disintegration of her volatile relationship with F, her second husband, and the beginning of her affair with a married writer she calls V (the novelist Murray Bail) who will eventually become her third. "One day I'll have to burn this book," she writes. "I use as buckets of cold water thoughts of his wife's preparations for Christmas."

One Day I'll Remember This tracks Garner's deepening affair with V, as well as Garner navigating M's leaving home: "This state is like a second labour. I'm struggling to let her be born," she writes. A friend tells her, "A brand-new abyss. I envy you. Don't fill it up with old things." Eventually V leaves his marriage to be with Garner, and she leaves her life in Melbourne to live with him in Sydney. At their wedding, her father predicts trouble: "They're both writers, though," he says, predicting one of the major subplots of the pages still to come. Things are already bumpy, but V and Garner are still allies through the bumpiness: "When we see couples who are cheerfully loving we exchange sad, wry glances." Resilience shows up like a glimmering, essential thread through all three volumes: coming back to art, and to herself as an artist, through the frustrations of the process, the daily trials of love and grief, and the slings and arrows of critical reception—at one point Garner girds herself to "accept that I have enemies, and be robust about it."

The title of Garner's third volume, *How to End a Story,* refers not only to its place as the final movement of a triptych, but to its account of the prolonged and messy dissolution of Garner's third marriage. By this point, the diaries have come to assume the velocity and integrity of a novel. Two of the major forces pressurizing the end of their marriage are V's relationship with X, a painter, and Garner's relationship with her analyst, who points out that she often lies on the couch in a fetal position, sometimes clutching her scarf "like a comforter, or a bottle." V worries that analysis will threaten her artistic life, that it promises to too neatly solve or defuse the "family unravelling" that fuels her work. But he need not have feared: there is plenty more unraveling ahead. (And eventually, delightfully, Garner manages to claim her therapy expenses as "professional development" on her taxes, her triumph at this accomplishment so fervent it gets italicized, *"they allowed it!"*)

We meet X at her fortieth birthday party: "She uses her body expressively, in ways that are un-Australian—turns of the head, graceful arm and hand gestures." Earlier in the diaries, Garner has wondered if the world is made of triangles rather than couples, and X will eventually become the third point in the triangle of Garner's marriage—X and V develop a consuming friendship that Garner suspects has become an affair: "If you're a man's second wife you know for a fact that he's capable of anything."

One of the great hardships of V's intimacy with the painter X is not just the sting of romantic betrayal but the fact that jealousy obstructs Garner's relationship with her own powers of observation: "I didn't know any more how to be happy or to enjoy, for example, the glorious beauty of the ocean and the summer sky." But her jealousy eventually becomes an artifact to be investigated, an object on which Garner can train her furious insight, and an enemy to be subdued by "turning away to something more interesting." In their constant pivots, the diaries often offer a version of this relief from claustrophobia, turning from domestic conflict to the world outside—the city, friends, work, daughter—like opening a window in a dim, stale room and letting in fresh breeze, oxygen, sunlight or moonlight, or the smell of rain.

As ever, Garner is attuned to both the existential depths of romantic conflict and the banal surfaces of how these conflicts play out. "Since we were writers, each of us had a horror of being engulfed by the other," she writes, "and had to fight against it." But so often these deep conflicts express themselves through the materials of petty grievances: "Contest between me and V about what each of us has done to keep the soap from going mucky in the bathroom." There's catharsis in the moment when Garner finally discovers the draft of a love letter to X, confirming all her suspicions of an affair. She documents the wild scene with vigorous specificity: smashing V's espresso machine onto the floor, grabbing his expensive cigars from the humidor and jamming them into the beetroot soup she made for him, stabbing a draft of his novel with his Mont Blanc fountain pen until the nib is smashed and bent. (Later, she feels solidarity with a schoolgirl who has cut the laces of her brother's expensive new running shoes. "I long to say, 'Sweetheart, I have cut up a straw hat with scissors and drowned cigars in soup. We are sisters.'")

Garner takes her heartbreak with her to Buenos Aires ("I trudge up and down the avenidas lugging my smashed and bleeding heart") and then to Antarctica for a travel piece: "I wish I could have a clean heart. Mine's like an ashtray. Full of Cohiba butts and spit"—where she finds the air so clean and cold it's like a numbing agent: "inside of my head is an ice landscape, an element of brutal clarity, like the first snort of cocaine," and a sense of wonder and gratitude in pushing her face into the "tight, springy moss-pads" left in the wake of an ancient glacier: "The concrete inside me started to soften and give way."

*   *   *

The *Künstlerroman,* a bildungsroman that focuses on the development of an artist, is a genre traditionally associated with youth and coming of age, but anyone who has ever tried to make art knows the process of becoming an artist never ends. In Garner's diaries, we find, among other things, a stunning *Künstlerroman* of middle age. Here is an artist expanding and evolving across the middle of her life, in thrilling and unexpected ways. Over and over again, we witness Garner reaching through various kinds of grief and frustration (divorce, artist's block, maternal guilt) to keep falling in love with daily life, her family, her city, strangers on the streets and in the baths, finding in her art a well of power that cannot ever be taken from her. "Nothing can touch me," she writes, in the midst of fighting with her second husband, because she feels close to "the power of *work*. Art, and the huge, quiet power it gives."

We also watch the emergence of Garner as a journalist, starting to investigate extreme manifestations of human darkness and tragedy. After an interview with an arsonist, she writes, "I begin to think of violence, death, burning, what people do to each other, to their children. And to think that I need to find out about these things." In toggling back and forth so dynamically between her own interiority and other peoples' lives, these diaries give lie to the assumption that being interested in yourself necessarily means you are less interested in other people. Garner's diaries—indeed, the arc and range of her entire career—suggests another truth entirely: that deep introspection and outward curiosity are often symbiotic.

Garner writes with vivacity and precision about the process of writing itself, a subject that often drives writers into the clutches of self-referential tedium. (She is also wonderful on her own dreams, another thematic Bermuda Triangle, describing a dead body stuffed full of pens, or nursing a large red bell pepper: "A slit opened in the capsicum's side and it began to suck voraciously.") She nails the frustration of unproductive sessions ("now that I'm sitting up in bed, pen in hand, on a rainy Saturday afternoon, all my little stored-up treasures turn their backs and hide in the shrubbery") and confesses the sting of not being included in the Oxford book of Australian literature, but she gives us the good stuff, too, like the triumphant sensation of finding the right place in a novel for a detail that's been "dogging" her for a decade. If Horace coined the term *ars poetica* to describe a poem that explains the art of poetry, then perhaps Garner has given us an *ars diarium*—insofar as these diaries skillfully, glintingly, make a case for their own mattering, a quicksilver manifesto sewn like a glimmering thread through these pages: "Meaning is *in* the smallest event," she reflects. "It doesn't have to be *put* there: only revealed."

At one point near the end of their marriage, Garner writes, "V says that women's writing, 'lacks an overarching philosophy,'" and records her own brisk reply: "I don't even know what this means. Also, I don't care." Tonally, this is pure Garner: colloquial and self-possessed, jaunty and winking, supple and wry—but not huffy. And while it's true that there's nothing I would call an "overarching philosophy" spanning these diaries, they give us something far better, with a slyer and more inviting architecture: not overarching but subterranean, deftly emerging from the rough terrain of experience.

What are the tenets of this subversive, subterranean philosophy? It has more to do with cleaning the dishes, or making breakfast for a grandson, or sitting down for tea with a friend, than it does with the utterly silent lunches Garner recalls the composer Igor Stravinsky demanding from his family. At its core, this subterranean philosophy believes that the obligations and distractions of daily life are not distractions at all: they are the conduits through which we arrive at profundity; they are midwives of grace and insight. It believes that humility and surprise are the cornerstones of both rigorous self-knowledge and moral action. The more willing we are to be surprised by ourselves, other people, and experience, the more we are capable of honesty, discovery, care, and transformation. Garner feels a deep kinship with the nun who says, "I love intellectuals who *hesitate*." She is fascinated by a man who keeps but doesn't read his parents' letters to each other: "Perhaps he doesn't want to lose the state of having a secret from himself; or to reach the end of the mystery, the bottom of the bag." One senses Garner doesn't really believe in the bottom of the bag; instead, she believes in the generative understanding that she can't ever fully understand herself. "What is the point of this diary?" she asks. "There is always something deeper, that I don't write, even when I think I'm saying everything."

These diaries are not only generous with the soaked sponge of daily life, they are also generous with the *reader,* inviting and rewarding many different modes of reading. You can disappear into them for hours, like swimming deep into the ocean of another person's life. But you can also read them in tiny doses—just a few entries at a time, in moments stolen from precisely the kinds of obligations and relationships the diaries document—without feeling you are betraying them. Moving in and out of the diaries, tunneling into them for a few rapt moments, then being called out again feels like inhabiting their native ecosystem. I found myself reading the entirety of 1983, the year of my own birth, in stray moments on a weekday afternoon, waiting for the results of a strep test at an urgent care clinic, and then curled in a corner of the living room while my daughter played a game that involved laying out an imaginary banquet for fairies who were deciding what ages to remain for the rest of their lives. "Ludmilla will be forty-nine forever!" she cried. These diaries do the incredible thing that great literature can: they create a mood and a field of resonance that reaches far beyond the act of reading them. They offer to return us to our own lives with more curiosity and keen attention.

Yellow Notebook

Diaries

Volume I

1978–1987

1978

Maybe it'd be a good idea to start another diary, just to cream it off. I bought this yellow book today.

———

Man in the metro, a 1950s relic but *real*, not an affectation—untidy, perfectly period clothes—lumber jacket, tight trousers, big, worn, nondescript shoes. He was playing an exquisite basic rock-and-roll guitar and singing 'Corinna' through a little amp that looked like a white Daisy Duck radio.

———

Monkey Grip appears to have won the National Book Council Award. Letter from T in Melbourne: 'Sometimes I fall into the trap of thinking that jobs and money and grants are luck instead of recognition for talent and hard work. Do you feel that still?'

———

I know what the matter is. I haven't got any women friends here. I miss, I miss. I feel crazy and weepy.

———

F says he's not really French: that he comes from the south, that it's different there. He says if you don't turn a mattress it starts to smell bad. He sings to himself as he works. If he looks over my shoulder at this I'll start screaming.

Actually, I don't care if he reads this. I'm protected by the fog of incomprehension that's always between us unless we work single-mindedly at *direct contact*.

M and I work to wall off a sleeping space for her at one end of the living room. We stretch a length of unbleached calico tightly over the back of the high, open shelf we bought at Habitat, stand it at right angles to the wall, then lie side by side on her little bed and gaze at the tent-like structure. A bottle of Scotch on the living-room side picks up the light and shines a brown glow through the fabric. When we do a task together she turns me into a better mother. She's a witty person, companionable and kind. 'Got any idea how to draw a hamster?'

Rilke wrote that when people know your name they 'scatter your forces'. He suggests changing your name as soon as they get hold of it.

I must disabuse myself of the illusion that I once sat down and wrote a novel. I am not good at constructing major pieces of work. I have a short concentration span. I can work only in small, intense bursts. I don't seem to work consciously. I write to unburden myself, to amuse myself, to arrange in order the things that bulge in my head, to make myself notice things.

Jerzy Kosiński's absolutely unemotional style. As clear as crystal, as objects arranged in a line. Whenever the lost child in *The Painted Bird* approaches a farm to ask for work or for shelter, the peasants 'consult their neighbours'.

At Cap Fréhel F tried to stop me from tackling the cliff. 'Don't climb!' he cried, white-faced, seizing my ankle. So as not to watch me, he went to prise mussels off the rocks with his knife. I climbed. His fear had infected me. The void sucked at my back.

———

I have a lot of trouble with self-disgust. It disgusts me that I repeat things in this book that I have already written in letters. It disgusts me that I am so lazy.

———

A critic in Melbourne writes that 'some people consider *Monkey Grip*'s subject matter distasteful'. Someone else said I was a traitor to my class. I now grasp the meaning of the term *provincial*.

———

Cure for homesickness and ennui: walk. I must have walked ten kilometres yesterday. Bought two jumpers and a pair of red shoes, which are perfect.

———

I went to shake hands with Solange. She laughed and went 'Oh!' as if to say 'Come off it!' and kissed my cheeks instead.

———

M didn't understand the information the teacher gave about the week's holiday for Toussaint: she thought it was a school camp, and tried to ask if she was supposed to bring her sleeping bag and something to eat. The teacher had no idea what she was talking about. M gave up and came home bewildered. She cried when she tried to explain to me what had happened.

———

Drank some kir and this and that. In Charlie Hebdo I read: 'BOUM! = NO FUTURE x 7.' I laughed and laughed. I don't even know why it's funny. If I lived alone with my leedle cassette player and idiosyncratic assortment of tapes, I'd probably drink myself stupid.

———

F took an old wooden-handled hammer out of his briefcase this morning and laid it on my desk. It's still there.

———

How he pronounces VAPORUB.

———

We went walking in the cold, up to Place Clichy and rue Joseph de Maistre etc. He put his hand through my arm and I was happy.

———

The visitor on his way to London—'It's my spiritual home!'—spoke about his poems as being ahead of their time. 'In ten years people will see what I was trying to do.' I doubt this. Also, he was too cheap to pay fifty centimes to use the toilet at Parc Monceau.

———

I wish I lived peacefully somewhere. I wish I had a shit job involving physical exertion.

———

In Toulouse our hostess made a dormitory of her bedroom and she, M and I slept comfortably in a row. All the sheets and towels, from her trousseau sixteen years ago, are embroidered with her initials. At about 4 pm I remembered that it was my birthday. She took us out of the city to stay with some friends in a village. On the drive she told us that the husband had had an affair. The wife had fought it, or sat it out. He had returned to her. 'So,' she said with a satisfaction that did not quite convince me, 'she won.' The air in the house was thick. The husband and wife did not look at each other. In the afternoon we walked halfway up a small mountain. An easy track. Chestnuts still bright with yellow leaves. At night the darkness and silence around the house frightened me.

———

A drunk black man in a cobbled street yelled at us that we were '*de la pourriture*'.

———

Tweezers. Wool. Needles. Pencil sharpener.

———

A certain graciousness of manner; a deep courtesy.

———

'I'll be the toughest kid in the whereabouts,' says M.

———

'The fact that the glass is raised to the lips without being smashed into the face is a tribute to the subtle weighing abilities of the outstretched limb. And the fact that the glass remains at the mouth while losing weight as it is emptied shows how punctually the news is updated: without this information the glass would levitate as it was drained.' —Jonathan Miller

———

Some teargas got in my eyes at the demo. It was my first dose, unbelievably confusing and painful. I was surprised at how philosophical people were about it. They covered their noses and mouths. '*Aii!*' said F's friend. 'It hurts your eyes! Well, that's what it's for, I suppose.' Everyone around him laughed.

———

Despair and sadness and fear are easier to write about than hope, happiness, confidence.

———

Middlemarch. A substance smooth of surface but containing firm lumps of foreign matter.

———

The famous publisher and his translator took me to lunch at Brasserie Lipp. I am sure they will not want my book. They addressed me in perfect English. They were unbearably chic. When I offered my hand to the translator, all she gave me was her little finger. My cheeks were red with awkwardness. She worked hard, I suppose:

'See the man with the moustache? That's Romain Gary.'

'He looks sad,' I said.

'He's been looking like that ever since Jean Seberg left him.'

———

F is sick. I'm looking after him. He hates to be '*dépendant*', but he appears to have abandoned attempts to fight it and is sitting up in my bed reading *Playboy France*.

———

M cries because I get eight letters and she gets only a postcard. She refuses to speak to me, then bursts into tears, casts herself on to my lap, and sobs: 'I had a sudden feeling of meanness.' In the afternoon we sit together knitting. She is so thrilled about her new cherry-red knee-high boots that she can hardly sleep. Soon after midnight I wake to find her standing beside my bed, fully dressed for school: 'I thought it was morning!'

———

I quarrelled with F because I wouldn't show him a fan letter I was writing to Woody Allen. He says that he and his former girlfriend used to show each other everything. He says I'm secretive. It's strange to realise that I am a very different person from the one I thought I was.

———

Siouxsie and the Banshees at l'Empire. They were revolting.

———

Divorce papers came today from Australia. I was sad, remembering that failure, afraid of another one, of being unable to go on loving someone eminently worthy of love. 'Love is your last chance. There is really nothing else on earth to keep you there.' —Louis Aragon, quoted by Patrick White in *A Fringe of Leaves*

———

It was snowing at Père Lachaise. My sister in a pink beret, long blue coat, pink scarf. We picked our way between the graves looking for Proust's. A frozen jonquil lay on his shiny black tombstone. A dark day, very still and cold. Tomorrow she's taking M home to Melbourne.

―――――

We didn't cry at the airport. She was excited to be travelling home to her father with her groovy aunt. I got back to the dark apartment and tidied up her belongings. That's when I howled, finding the dozens of little half-used notebooks in which she had been obliged to amuse herself drawing and writing because she had no playmates. My girl, stuck in a foreign country with her cranky mother. Is there any point to this guilt? What she learned from being here I can only guess at.

―――――

I read the paper and doors open in my head like those in a cuckoo clock. I had forgotten why people read papers. You learn things. Ideas come to you. Connections strike off each other with ringing blows or slot together like carpenters' joints.

―――――

Everyone's talking about *Apocalypse Now*. My work seems piddling, narrow, domestic.

―――――

I helped F's journalist friend spackle the walls in his new apartment. I was afraid he'd scorn me for my ignorance of politics but when I happened casually to mention Ibsen he looked embarrassed and said, '*Qui ça?*'

―――――

At the Parc de Bagatelle we had to pay to get in. One franc, fifty. It was worth it. Crocuses and daffodils.

―――――

M rings from Melbourne: 'Me and my best friend did a show, and the kids applaused really really loudly. Louder than for the other kids who did a play.'

———

Postcard from my sister, a Renoir pencil drawing of a heavy-bodied, half-naked girl reading. A thought balloon: 'Will my shape still be fashionable in the 1970's? Probably not.'

———

F and I took our bikes on the train to the forest of Compiègne and rode along the paths and avenues. Only one squabble. Pale green leaves everywhere. Blue flowers like cloud shimmered in the clearings. A deer bounded across the road in front of us—it came flying from nowhere, struck the ground a single blow with its dainty hooves, and took off again into the trees. In a cafe we raved about it to the barman. He was too bored even to fake interest. We felt foolish and urban; drank up and pedalled away.

———

The film-maker's blue jumper and bright blue eyes. He says that at Cannes people took him for Mick Jagger and asked for his autograph. I never noticed till today that he's rather beautiful. I say 'rather' because he is *affected*, physically. I wonder what he's like when he's alone.

———

I think all the time about the thing I'm supposed to be writing, that I've got a *grant* to be writing. I've found a library to work in. Rue Pavée. If I write what I want to, about the people I know at home, I'll never be able to live in Melbourne again. About the woman who always sang in a register too high for her voice, and that wasn't the worst of it. Lazy, charming G in his band, all the girls hanging round him waiting to be fucked. I don't even do the dishes or cook. I change the position of my bed. I buy huge sheets of drawing paper, pin them to the bedroom wall, cover them with diagrams of characters and their inter-relating. I play the High Rise Bombers tape full-blast and dance by myself, jumping high in the air. Then I crash into appalling bouts of self-doubt, revulsion at my past behaviour, loathing for my emotional habits and the fact that I still feel the need to expose, thinly disguised or barely metamorphosed, my own experience. In the metro this morning, on my way to the library, I felt grey and shrivelled, watching the tunnel lights slip past in their rhythm, wishing that I spoke French twice as well as I do and had a real job with people I didn't particularly like, so I wouldn't have to produce my own raison d'être every day, like a spider yanking thread out of its own guts, or wherever the hell they pull it from.

1979

I've found a workroom I can rent, over a dress shop in Moonee Ponds. It looks north towards a low mountain very far away. In a corner, a hand basin. Its drain is clogged and it's full of old brown water. Maybe mozzies will breed in it. I don't care. I'm writing three sentences a day. Wretched, ill-tempered, nervous, unbearable. Maybe I'm a one-book woman.

———

M brings home a note about the school concert: 'Children should come dressed to the hall. Boys to come in pyjamas. Halos and Wings will be put on by teachers.'

———

HG: (*getting out of the car at 2 am*) 'There's the saucepan.'

    F: 'What?'

    HG: 'See that first star? Go up from there, and further, and there it is.'

    F: 'That is *not* the saucepan.'

    HG: 'For thirty-seven years I have called that star formation "the saucepan". When I was a little girl my father took me by the hand and pointed up and said, "That is the saucepan." You can't *tell me* that's not the saucepan.'

———

M ate a real egg from my sister's chook. It was so rich that she retired to bed groaning and sobbing, and couldn't go to school till 10.30: 'I feel all eggy inside.'

―――――

M and F found a brown pup at the market. Beautiful, but dumb. Our training methods don't work on her. This morning she took off at the front gate. With me in hot pursuit she bolted, trailing her lead, across four lanes of traffic on Mt Alexander Road. She made it unscathed and wound up cringing on her back under a palm tree, shivering and pissing. As I thundered up to her I realised that what she was running from was *me*.

―――――

The Italian girl who works in the dress shop is engaged. She tells me that for her trousseau her grandmother has given her a quilt that's 'stuffed with duck leaves'. When she talks I feel like swooning. I could stand on the bottom step and listen to her rave all day.

―――――

At the Kampuchea Benefit I saw half a dozen people I knew at a table and I was too shy to walk over and say hello. I was *scared* to.

―――――

'F is very funny,' said one of the guys in the band. 'He's got such a fantastic delivery that you laugh even if you don't understand what he's said.'

―――――

There was a bird singing in the garden. When I opened the back door it was sitting on the chimney trilling away, but as soon as I appeared it flipped across the vegetable patch to a tree on the other side of the fence, where it threw back its head and sang tune after tune, its little beak open like a pair of scissors.

―――――

Riding round the corner on to Brunswick Road I change gear

clumsily and the whole bike locks. I get it on to the footpath (F already a yellow dot half a mile away on the freeway bridge) and crouch beside it, helplessly regarding the hub and sprockets. A well-dressed pedestrian in her forties stops beside me. 'Got troubles?' 'It's jammed.' She takes one look and points: 'There—it's stuck there.' The chain is wedged between the smallest sprocket and the white frame. I poke my finger in and wiggle. I seize the chain and yank at it. To my surprise it's got give, and spring—so that's how it works! I jerk it free and fit it on to the correct sprocket. A bunch of tissues appears near my face. 'Thankyou!' 'That's all right,' she says with a cheerful, impersonal smile, and strides away. I wipe my hands on the tissues and shove them into my pocket. Now I know I'm home. My country, right or wrong.

———

Memo: do not drink coffee. It makes me uselessly nervy, even trembly, and engenders baseless optimism about my powers of creation.

1980

I met Frank Moorhouse today in Tamani. He remarked that 'organisation of energy' was a crucial matter. A very nice man. Greying curly hair, massive head—a bullyboy in form but sharp and reserved and intelligent in expression. Very careful about wiping his lips while eating. Two blokes I vaguely knew came in and sat with us. They turned on a Carlton performance: rapid-fire wisecracks about Chomsky, war, politics and corrupt journalism. I wanted to scream. Later Frank bought a bottle of 'good bourbon—seeing as I can afford it'. I walked with him (having trouble keeping up) to his office at the university.

HG: 'I can't stand it when blokes talk like those two. I just wish they'd *shut up.*'

FM: (*mildly*) 'They were high on caffeine, weren't they. It was a coffee thing.'

———

I passed through the kitchen and saw N at the table with my huge galleys on her knee. She looked up with a laugh and said, 'You're going to be hung, drawn and quartered.' I went away in a panic. This morning she said, 'It's delightful to read. I kept laughing. But you're very hard on the character who's partly you.'

———

M's entrance exam at University High: a hundred and fifty frightened kids being harangued by an old fart in an academic gown. I saw that her face was white. I was ready to kill. I cried all the way home on the bus and walking down our street. She did not look well as she came out of the exam: strained, pale and slightly vague. She told me all about it, with seriousness. I looked at her skinny little leg muscles in fawn tights and wanted to do terrible violence to someone. She said, 'The maths was *really hard*—you know—"If n equals m times 2", that kind of thing. I nearly cried when I saw some of the questions.' She made a trembling gesture with out-stretched arms. 'I just thought, Oh, no!'

———

A perfect spring morning: colourless clear sky, luminous at the horizon, faint roar of distant traffic, car window pearled with condensation, power lines and antennae sharply defined in pure air. A tall tree behind the house opposite is thick with creamy blossom. A rooster crows far away towards Westgarth Street. Nothing moves except the odd passing bird.

———

I was cooking dinner tonight while a couple of hard-line leftie visitors raved on at the kitchen table about an academic they knew who was writing a book on Indo-China.

'In Bangkok,' said the woman, 'he got up to all sorts of stuff he could never do in Australia.'

'What, like fucking prostitutes?' I asked.

'Oh, worse. You know—twelve-year-old virgins.' She laughed. 'The kinds of things he shouldn't really be into, considering where he's at.'

I turned back to the stove.

'Actually,' she went on, in a voice softened by affection, 'he fell in love with the first prostitute he got involved with. He wanted to bring her back to Australia. It was a tragic story, really. He spent a fortune getting her papers and everything, and then she didn't want to go.'

Smart girl.

———

'Once you've used your experience to make something,' said T, 'it takes on a life of its own. It's a bit silly to keep dragging it back to its source.'

———

When I read the writers, particularly the Jews, in *Best American Short Stories* I feel lazy, weak and lacking in *skill*. They will drive and drive, these blokes. What does this mean, for me? It means I must push myself outside what I'm sure of. Take risks.

———

Spring night: black sky speckled with stars, air cool and thickly scented with grass, and the odours of things growing.

———

She says she's writing an essay on the nature of art as myth, myth as the expression of male dominance, myth as *useless to women*.

———

Honour will be out in two weeks. It has several fairly serious typos. I resolve not to look at it any more.

———

Yesterday I felt like burning all my old diaries. I spoke about it to two people, a writer and a photographer. Each replied to this effect: 'You'll be the same person, with the same past, whether you burn them or not.' I decided not to burn anything, but to pack them up and store them somewhere where I can't *get at* them.

———

My eyes are sore, and yesterday my front tooth got chipped while I was eating a Butter Menthol, but is now fixed.

1981

Finished rereading E. M. Forster's *Where Angels Fear to Tread*. I'm sure he had never seen a real baby when he wrote it, but this doesn't matter, it's still marvellous. He is one of the writers I long to meet or write to, and this is one way in which I grasp the fact of death: because I can't. Virginia Woolf is another, despite Pamela Brown's insistence to me that Gertrude Stein was greater.

––––––

Went to the State Library looking for *Mourning Becomes Electra*. It wasn't where it should have been so I flipped through V. S. Pritchett's *The Working Novelist*. Fabulous, intelligent, witty without even a tinge of the smartypants. 'The cork-pop of the easy epigram.'

––––––

To Dallas Brooks Hall to hear Roger Woodward play Chopin. A stiffly dramatic performance: some very controlled throwing up of the hands. I liked the music but his presence was so intellectual and contained that one might as well have been watching a movie. Little warmth; but in certain pieces his control seemed less rigid, and the left hand rolled almost sexually. In a cafe afterwards a man greeted two guys sitting at the other end of my table. He leaned over them with both hands on the table edge, stiff-armed as a detective, and said that he hadn't liked the concert.

HG: (*butting in*) 'Why?'

Him: 'Because it was *bad*.'

HG: 'Yes, but in what precise ways?'

Him: 'Too many wrong notes. Memory lapses, which offended me. And too cold. Very *Polish* interpretation: holding the beat over into the next bar. When *he* does that it's no good because— Rubenstein, for example, when *he* does it he's still in contact with the basic human thing—Claudio Arrau, too, he messes with things, but you always know he's still really *feeling*.'

Finally he left.

'What a bloody bore,' said one of the men. 'Some people have no an*tenn*ae.' He wriggled his hand in the air above his left ear.

The other said, very politely, 'I was quite interested in what he was saying.'

––––––

Rumour reaches me that H in Prahran has 'joined the born-again Christians'. This does not surprise me. I rang him tonight. After a relaxed twenty-minute conversation he said, 'Can you keep a secret?'

'Yes.'

'Can you really?'

'Of course.'

'I've gone back to Jesus.'

He said it completely without irony or defence. With gladness, really. 'I used to act proud,' he said, 'as if the things I'd hung on to from the New Testament were really things I'd made up myself. I was taking the credit for them.'

––––––

The *Age* asks me to review Beatrice Faust's book *Women, Sex and Pornography*. I file a piece in dialogue form that I really enjoyed writing. They reject it. Would I please rewrite it as a straight review.

Rage and contempt. Cutting potatoes and onions, I reflect on the pain of rejection, and on how little of it I've had to endure. I think of my CAE students and the way I cheerfully rip into their precious work. I could try to learn a lesson from their humility. I agree to rewrite.

———

Reagan gets shot, but not killed. On TV, the high, thin voice of the gunman crying, 'President Reagan! President Reagan!' The shots. In seconds the gunman is buried in men's bodies against a brick wall.

Next morning I said to the librarian, 'Did you hear about Ronald Reagan?'

'Yes, I did,' she said. 'I've been thinking about how clearly I remember exactly what I was doing when I heard that Kennedy had been shot. And this time I just thought, Ho hum.'

———

Dreamt I travelled a long way on a rickety train with slatted sides. I got off at a country station and saw a wonderful house that backed on to the platform: faded green corrugated iron walls, dirt floors inside, no doors; on the lower part of the roof a thick strewing of peppercorns and gum twigs; the area surrounding the house clear, uncluttered; gum trees, three or four, standing on a slight angle as in a Hans Heysen painting.

———

Australian journalist: 'Why do Americans *want* to carry guns in such large numbers?'

American politician: 'They want to carry guns because...to them...it's the symbol of life itself.'

———

Having had a child when I did has been one of the major strokes of good fortune in my life.

———

The woman calls me. Why? I hardly know her. 'I read *Honour* and I just burst into tears. It was such a relief.' She talks, through bursts of bitter laughter and occasional weeping, of her impossible marriage. I suggest timidly that she might consider leaving the whole box and dice. 'I'll never leave my children, *never*—do you understand?' she shouts. She invites me to her house for lunch. I accept out of curiosity. She is out. A maid lets me in: she *has a maid.* Soon she returns with food in white plastic bags. In her elegant clothes and high-heeled black sandals she takes awkward strides, throwing her arms around pointlessly. Chin always lifted and thrust forward in defensive posture. Her hair cut to shoulder-length, swept away to the left in a movie-star style. She's always fiddling with it but not tentatively—rather she will seize the comb that's holding it off her face, bunch the hair up at the back of her head and thrust the comb into it again, thus creating an entirely new hairdo. She did this at least ten times while I was there. Something shocking about her relationship with inanimate objects. She moved around the kitchen with violence: open a cupboard door, look inside, slam it again with a loud report. She did not seem to know where anything was. I cut up some vegetables: first I wasn't cutting fine enough, then I cut too fine, but it didn't matter, she didn't 'give a damn' how I cut them, it wasn't important to her at all. She sliced up fish and flung the whole collection of cut matter into an extremely hot wok. Trying to make conversation I mentioned a woman I did not know she hated. This drove her into a frenzy. Even trying to write this down is making me sick. We sat at the bench with our plates of food. It was delicious but I couldn't get past the brutality of its preparation. She kept jumping up to feed the cat, to push its three bowls about on a sheet of newspaper. Once she went to the back door and opened it. The autumn wind blew in and she banged it shut with a muttered word.

I call him. From the first moment I hear his voice I know that all is lost. I am once again the terrified, plain eighteen-year-old on the green telephone chair in the hall, having done the unforgivably forward thing and *rung up a boy*. The sensation is *exactly the same*. He is surprised. He draws back infinitesimally, there is a yawning gulf. Perhaps he is not even alone. I am humiliated. I hear the drawl in his voice. I am shaking with fear.

————

If it does nothing else, this whole business will turn me into a feminist again. I was about to write, 'I am terribly unhappy.' And then I thought, That is not even true.

————

After the phone call I worked on bitterly, trying to finish my review of the University of Queensland Press short story collection: the only woman in it is the naked one on the cover. I had to work very hard indeed to hold the bitterness out of my writing, while at the same time keeping criticism sharp. I think I succeeded. It's quite funny, and not particularly punishing.

————

The letter comes at long last. He plays certain notes, knows what their effect will be. I know, myself, that when I am able to write a charming letter, neither too short nor too long, striking just the right balance between literary stylishness and spontaneity, I am writing falsely, and perhaps even lying.

————

I am about to make a colossal fool of myself. I am breaking a decent man's heart. 'What can I do for you?' says F. 'Trust me,' I say, 'and leave me alone.' In case anyone should want to know, I'm crying because I was born in Australia and not in Europe, and because I'm tired and sick, and because in the taxi I read Kafka, *At Night*: 'Why are you watching? Someone must watch, it is said.

Someone must be there.'

My intellectual equipment has gone rusty. And has never developed to its full strength in the first place. I get frightened when I think it might be too late.

Yesterday M sat happily at the piano in the kitchen, playing the simplified 'Moonlight Sonata'. She had been working away at it for half an hour or so, completely absorbed, when a woman from the circus wandered in. She listened for a moment in her stoned, distracted way, then said very loudly, in a harsh voice, 'Can she play rock-and-roll as well?' 'Oh yes,' said someone hastily, 'she plays a mean boogie.' The child, oblivious, laboured on.

Got up at 6.30 to work. A fat, bone-coloured moon was sinking into a sky streaked pink and lavender, between the rabbit hutch and the fig tree.

Letters are too slow; the telephone is too fast.

Romantics are dangerous. They will not give up the privileges of childhood. They save up little secrets for themselves, which can become lies. Sometimes, if surprised, they turn a cold face.

'...Thus it is that egoists always have the last word; having laid down at the start that their determination is unshakeable, the more the sentiment in them to which one appeals to make them abandon it is touched, the more fault they find, not with themselves who resist the appeal but with those persons who put them under the necessity of resisting it, with the result that their own firmness may be carried to the utmost degree of cruelty, which only aggravates all the more in their eyes the culpability of the person who is so indelicate as to be hurt, to be in the right, and to cause them thus treacherously the pain of acting against their natural instinct of pity.' —Marcel Proust, *The Guermantes Way*

———

I feel like a bombed city. All the remaining life is underground.

———

I have to go right to the end of the story.

———

'What's attractive about you is a very charming…nastiness,' said the journalist. 'It makes you able to squeeze through cracks. Suddenly a brick is thrown, and you're gone.'

———

About writing: meaning is *in* the smallest event. It doesn't have to be *put* there: only revealed.

———

Bobby Sands died today in the Maze. There is fighting in the streets of Belfast. These things I heard on the car radio as I mastered the lane system of Sydney's streets. Will he go to hell? Is starving yourself to death counted as suicide?

———

At their table sat a wild child. A boy, androgynous (M swore he was a girl but something in his cheek-line was masculine to me) with an expressionless face, eyes slitted over high Russian cheekbones, blond hair chopped short and dyed in a skunk-like streak from brow to nape. He did not speak at all, but shovelled down a plate of soup, listening warily to the grunts and cries of what passed for conversation among the young men at his table. By the time we got to the register he was at the counter ordering a coffee. He carried it carefully to a table and drank it by lowering his face to the cup, in which still stood a spoon.

Suddenly the editor turns to me where I'm sitting behind him on a couch. 'You know what I liked, in an interview with you that I read? The way you said you write by hand. I reckon handwriting's bloody dying out.'

'Good, sensible people often withdraw from one another because of secret differences, each becoming absorbed by what he feels is right and by the error of the other. Conditions then grow more and more complicated and exasperating, until it becomes impossible to undo the knot at the crucial moment on which everything depends.'
—Goethe, *The Sorrows of Young Werther*

Small boy: 'We've got—well, him and my mum aren't married yet. A boarder. He hit her one night when he was drunk!'
    HG: 'I hope she gave him a couple of good ones back.'
    Boy: 'She was *unconscious*! She sat up and said, "What was *that* about?"'

The people next door were celebrating something with fireworks. Each of them was waving a sparkler. Their faces were soft with excitement and pleasure. M and I got hold of a cracker ('Trilogy Ground Type') and took it out to the car park to let it off. We were so busy running away, glancing back over our shoulders, that we saw only the very beginning of the explosion, and the cloud of smoke left hanging over the bare concrete. As we came back to the house, hand in hand up the lane, an answering rocket shot into the balmy air a hundred yards ahead of us, above some houses. We screeched in fright and both instinctively stepped sideways as if to press ourselves against the smooth white side wall of the house next door.

'When you're young,' said C's wife, 'you really believe that two people can make some kind of dream together; but you try it, and you get older, and you come to realise that all there is is *you*, finally.'

———

What is the point of this diary? There is always something deeper, that I don't write, even when I think I'm saying everything.

———

At 6 pm S came to pick me up and we ran through the park, across Heidelberg Road and the freeway, and all the way to the river, in tides of warm air and under an apricot sky. We squatted at the water's edge and watched the daylight fade and the wind stream through the gum-tree tops. A half-moon was out, high up. We walked back along the fence of the football ground. A soccer team was doing sit-ups in the dark. A parked car flicked its lights at us: a grinning, stupid face behind the windscreen.

———

B comes home from Italy. Her boyfriend in Bologna calls her. I hear her laughing and chatting with him: '*Il cielo è molto diverso. E bellissimo.*'

———

'It was only a joke.'
   'Jokes don't come from nowhere!'

———

I got a cheque for $80 for a theatre review. A few months ago I was getting at least $100. Better investigate this.

———

A piece of S's husband's childhood is for sale: thirty-five acres on a mountain out past Healesville, and on it the guesthouse, long ago closed down, that his parents used to take him to in the fifties. He drives us to see it on a windy morning. 'Out on this lawn was where they set up the cane chairs,' he says in a dreamy voice. 'The tartan rugs. The tam-o-shanters.' He is in a trance, glazed and smiling like a simpleton. We peer through the windows into tiny cabins with dark panelling and heavy furniture.

———

'I told her,' said F, 'it was not a matter of choice. That one's main relationship was the meal, and the other person was the condiment. If you ever had to choose, for nourishment, between a chop and some mustard, you would always choose the chop.'

———

I dreamt I saw myself from behind. I was wearing a top without shoulders or sleeves, and my bare back rippled with hard, glossy muscle.

———

B and I rode to the Fitzroy Gardens to watch the wedding parties having their photos taken. We leaned on our bikes for a long time, half hidden by vegetation, greedy for detail. Flashes of colour behind shrubbery. In the distance, great heavy elms with dark trunks, and at their base a tiny froth of white: a hurrying bride. The young Italian and Greek men wear their silly top-hats shoved to the back of the head, ears sticking out of thick hair, like louts from Eton. The Australian bride runs her day with an iron fist: her harsh, humour-less voice giving orders. Australians have no sense of occasion. They stand about with shy faces that look mean. The Mediterraneans dress with unselfconscious flamboyance and play their roles with gusto.

———

How we fight, tooth and nail, against gaining real insight. Against letting go of what makes us suffer.

———

'...We know from the testimony of the Russian conspirators the incomparable feeling that overcame them in that moment of utter solitude when they reared back to throw the bomb. With the bomb they simultaneously took their own fate, that of their victim and that of their entire cause into their hand. This moment lifted them outside themselves and above everyone else...' —Hans Magnus Enzensberger, *Dreamers of the Absolute*

––––––

Derby Day at Flemington. Five hours of pure pleasure. The vast expanse of grass that made a sky-ey silence under the murmurous voices of the crowd; the women's and men's pipe bands full of children and fat-legged ladies; the horses which despite their thunder seem not to touch the ground; a strapper of ten or eleven who, leading the huge animal with its rider, has to throw his head and shoulders desperately into the neck of the horse to keep it from walking astray; the hooked, witch-like faces of the jockeys; the way the roar of the crowd travels along parallel with the horses until it reaches you and swallows you up and you're helping to make it. Two old ladies stood beside us, laughing like schoolgirls at the fashionable people inside their wire enclosure, the merciless women with hard, thin lips and ambitious eyes. 'There's two or three centuries in there,' said B. 'There are *no reference points*.' 'Look at that white dress!' said one of the old ladies. 'Those dangly bits are like albs. What bishops wear.' 'And her head-dress is like what Arabs wear,' I said. We all doubled up, hanging on to the green railing, keeping our hands carefully between the very sharp green spikes.

––––––

In fifteen minutes I'll be thirty-nine years old.

––––––

In any interlocking group of three, information flows in and out, like tides, and at any given moment no one person is in possession of a fair share of it.

––––––

The kitchen in the house we've rented: as soon as I walked through the back door I knew that someone had been happy in it. Something to do with yellow light, or cream walls, or a plenteous sense of organisation. At my old ladies' writing class we chanced to talk about this instinctive certainty. Every one of them agreed vehemently that it was a power of reception found almost exclusively in women. 'We had a fight about a house once,' said one of them. 'My husband was looking at timber and windows and measurements, but I said *no*. I couldn't live here. He was furious.'

———

A sign on the wall at the Learning Exchange: a bloke is seeking someone who'd like to 'engage in non-competitive fencing bouts'.

———

Walking the dog in the old, forgotten parts of the cemetery. Milk thistles stand as high as your shoulder, dry grasses bend in the wind between the slabs of grey stone. In pockets, among the Emma Elizas and Charles Edwards, lie Panagiotis, Ahmed, Julio. Huge sky. Rain threatening.

———

'Can I come in here and hang around you? I just want to be near you.'

———

On community radio, the young announcer's voice was deep with outrage: 'For those listeners who wondered why, instead of last week's anti-uranium show, there was half an hour of the Beach Boys, it was because *somebody* "mislaid the tape"—what's that phone ringing? They're trying to stop this one too.' *Oooh*. A conspiracy. Still, we went to the demo. It was quite big. A man near us said he wished there were more 'ordinary-looking people from the suburbs. Remember the Moratorium marches?' B says demos are a waste of time, and that she is thinking of joining a party. She was talking about the ALP. Surely that would complete her disillusionment?

———

The old historian rang. We met at a weird place in Swanston Street called Cafe Nostalgia, furnished with old dining-room tables of the massive, polished kind. He is a gossip. Mostly I listen. He'll never get it, about women. When I ironically used the expression 'according to the orthodoxy of the women's liberation movement', he jumped in his seat as if he'd been shot.

———

I was invited to a 'come as your heroine' party. I wore cream clothes and a surgeon's mask: Sister Vivian Bullwinkel. No one but the oldest woman present recognised the name. She herself was dressed as Boadicea. I looked up Boadicea later in the encyclopedia and was astonished to learn of her exploits.

———

A man is being tried for allegedly stabbing to death a five-year-old boy in a school dunny. The child and his eleven-year-old companion had been sent to the corner shop. On their way home they threw a stone at the accused, who took them into the dunny, 'indecently assaulted' one or both of them, then said he would have to kill them because they would tell on him to the police. The eleven-year-old escaped when the murderer heard voices approaching and hopped up to look over the wall. Later the five-year-old's body was found, full of stab wounds. The eleven-year-old said in court that the dead boy had offered the man a dollar to spare his life.

———

Jessye Norman at the Town Hall. Big as a haystack, with a small, dramatic head, tiny hands and immense, slow, graceful gestures. She strolled, like the mountain coming to Mahomet, from the wings to her work position beside the Steinway, at which crouched the wizened, bent-backed Félix Lavilla, and then stood quite still for a good three minutes, gaze lowered to her clasped hands, composing herself after that exertion. Her voice I cannot describe. She ended each song with mouth wide open, an expression of ecstatic delight, eyes up-turned to the balcony.

———

I can't bear it when people I know haven't *become happier.*

———

My short story was rejected by the *Bulletin* because it contained four-letter words. A letter from Geoffrey Dutton: 'It pains me to have to knock this back…It's you at your best.' Thanks a lot. I suppose he's a skilled writer of rejection letters.

———

Mansfield Park. She never tells you anything about the appearance of her characters. As if they were moral forces. I love it.

———

Another friendship murdered in the name of sexual freedom and sexual fidelity. Jammed in the middle and squashed till blood came out of its eyes and ears.

———

On TV I saw the Pope touching people and speaking to them. He was wearing a little silk cap. He moved along a row of people, stretching out his hands in a quiet, formal manner, smiling and nodding, leaning to them. Someone held up a child and out came his hand, fingers spread star-wise, like a blind man's, to touch the child's cheeks and temple. His movements were so extremely slow (as if the film were being run at half speed, though the movements of people around him were normal) that I wondered if this were not the source of the extraordinary power of the little scene, although it was on the screen only a few seconds.

———

The young woman talks relentlessly, her pretty, broad-mouthed face lit with intelligence, her permed brown hair quivering. So eager to impress.

1982

Two young girls write a story and run outside, leaving the page on the table: 'Sorrow, destruction, riots, death, starvation, wars, depression, unhappiness, poverty, black market, slaves, civil wars, battles, ghetto's, racism, predudice, bigots, suffering, crime, generation gaps, sadness, hopelessness and 10 000 000 other tradgedies would evolve when he was gone.'

———

S rang to say her husband was ill and in pain: she took him to the doctor who found a little lump in his groin and sent him straight to the Alfred. 'He dropped his bundle,' she said. 'He was all cold and white and shivering.' She went to Dimmey's and bought him a pair of cotton pyjamas, fawn with a maroon pattern.

———

I dreamt that the Russians surprised everyone by invading Czechoslovakia again.

———

B and I tried to do the *National Times* 'Great Literary Quiz' and got about one in ten. So what, I say, ashamed. She's always told me she doesn't know anything about poetry but I never believed her till she failed to recognise *'There was movement at the station…'*

———

Circus Oz is loading itself into its prepared vans, trucks and cara-
vans, ready to depart for good from the Pram Factory tomorrow,
they say. I hang around upstairs in the Tower watching people busily
come and go. One of the oldest performers stops to speak to me.
She seems cheerful but suddenly turns her face away and covers it
with one hand. Past her bowed shoulders I see that huge chest-high
weeds have forced their way unchallenged between the terra cotta
tiles of the patio at the end of the hallway.

————

Apparently I am bossy, impatient, ill-mannered and a hypocrite. I
also don't like the way I look, much. It's probably mostly the haircut.
The waiters at l'Aquila obviously think B and I are lesbians.

————

The hottest night that's ever been recorded: still 32 degrees at 6 am.
I lay all night with my feet pointed towards the window through
which poured a stream of anti-human wind, hot and dry, straight off
a desert. A glaring moon. The only way to fall asleep was to have a
cool shower and lie, still wet, on a towel with a damp nightie spread
over me. But as soon as the water evaporated I woke.

————

I am teaching myself to embroider. I stitched three little fish on
the edge of a pillowcase. 'The iron and the damp cloth,' says the
neighbour. 'Everything will become smooth and flat.'

————

Sometimes ideas for stories surface as if from a muddy pond. I'd like
to write about a young savage. I would need an older sister character,
rather shadowy. Could the elder sister and another woman be in
conflict for the savage's…what? Allegiance? Certainly not mind.
Possession. I don't know.

————

In the cafe we were talking about coprophagy. A woman went to say 'fetish' but stopped at 'fet—', realising it was the wrong term. One of the men saw the moment of hesitation and went in boots first. 'I know it's not the right word!' she yelled. 'I was trying to think of the correct one! Can't anyone make a mistake?' 'It's as if you called a chair a table!' he shouted, seizing a chair, banging the flat of his hand on the table.

At the music school I felt like bawling with envy as I walked along a wet path between two buildings in which children practised in small rooms: oboes, strings. The way M bows with her skinny brown arm, jumps her fingers up and down the strings. Her eyes stare at the music without blinking, like a surgeon's when he operates, cuts flesh.

Now I'm making a living from freelance journalism I keep having an irritable feeling that newspapers are hysterical and silly; that the rush to fill their pages, especially the magazine sections in which stuff like mine is published, is bad for people, bad for the newspaper, bad for *me*.

I asked my sister to show me her caesarean scar. It was less drastic than I'd imagined: horizontal, slightly curved upwards like a faint smile, neatly cut near a natural wrinkle in the skin of her belly. It was healing beautifully. Really it's a wonder that people ever die. The other day I read about Vivian Bullwinkel and the bullet that the Japanese shot into her at the massacre of Banka Island: it went straight through her from back to front, and missed her vital organs—and the wound never became infected, though they were in the tropics. She put this down to the length of time she spent in salt water, in the hours and days after the massacre.

I heard third-hand from New York that a 'very famous old woman writer' had read *Honour* and wanted me to come to Columbia for a term to teach in her course. My informant had left at home the piece of paper with the old writer's name on it. It turned out to be Grace Paley. Surely this can't possibly be true. I called my sister and told her about it. 'Wow!' she said. 'But I hate her stuff.'

———

The chiropractor had gone quite grey since the last time I saw him. His hands were shockingly strong. He put me on my back and pulled my head towards him: a crack, and a distinct ripple right down my spine, as of beads on a string jerked out straight. 'Ah, lovely,' he said to himself.

———

G told me about a place he went to in London called the Comedy Store. 'There was this line-up of comics, breaking their necks to get to the mike. One would get booed, the gong would go and he'd get hustled off—another would be pushing forward to take his place. The audience was full of people with really developed consciousness. Any hint of sexism and he wouldn't just get abuse—there'd be a torrent of hamburgers, and rubbish. It was as if the audience was dragging the comics up to its level.'

———

Today I saw a US review of *Honour*. 'Drably clinical', 'hang-loose, dreary, quasi-commune living', 'with some mirthless humour', 'lacking in narrative shape and occasionally over-written'...; however, 'these vignettes of disordered domestic life are fleetingly affecting...all in all, promising glimpses—more so than in *Monkey Grip*—of a limited but tangible talent.' It's probably true that my 'talent' is limited. My range is, anyway. Or so I am always being told.

———

As dark fell, a faint light glimmered on the undersides of the eucalypt branches. It slithered between their narrow leaves, making them strongly three-dimensional. A young man remarked to me, as I stood sober in the middle of the garden, 'Have to get 'em dancing soon, over there on the grass. They're too bloody arrogant to dance unless we make 'em.' 'Oh, they're probably just shy.' '*Shy?*' He turned his head away in irritation, then whirled back: 'Shyness and arrogance are two sides of the same coin.'

————

'He panicked,' she said. 'It was like going out with a trainee priest.'

————

Our friend is only part way through the surgery, but one is already to use the word *she*. This is not difficult. Late in the afternoon we all drove to Bronte and swam in the surf. A light mist of spray hung over the water. The sand was extraordinarily clean and pale. She wore pink bathers with bra cups and a little skirt. She has narrow hips and long thighs like a man, but a woman's skin: white, smooth, and rather tender. When we came home she left her hair messy and it dried curly. She tied a bright red scarf round her head in a band, and black curls escaped over her neck and forehead so prettily that I kept glancing at her. Her beauty was touching, somehow; the result of drastic decisions, yet vivid and spontaneous. We got talking about modes of greeting in different languages and cultures. 'I like it in France,' I said, 'the way when you go into a shop they just say "*m'sieu*" or "*madame*"—they greet you according to your sex.' At this she pulled a face of comic dismay so exaggerated that we all burst out laughing.

————

First old lady in writing class: 'What does everyone do on Sunday mornings?'

Second old lady, like a shot, with a smug smile: '*I* go to church. What do *you* do?'

'Probably writes in her diary,' I refrained from saying, 'which is witty, unlike the "poetry" and "natural description" that *you* turn out.'

———

I don't know much about getting on with people. I'm as selfish as a cat. I don't like cats and I never have. I would like to write about dominance, revulsion, separation, the horrible struggles between people who love each other.

———

The play veered between being really funny and wallowing in embarrassing sentimentality. 'There's nothing wrong with sentiment, as long as it's not masquerading as real feeling,' said Professor Maxwell at Melbourne University twenty years ago. But in this case it *is* masquerading. Sentimentality keeps looking over its shoulder to see how you're taking it. Emotion doesn't give a shit whether anyone's looking or not.

———

The young savage is wearing a very small, bright blue bikini made of three ruched hearts. She bounds up the concrete steps to kiss me. 'It's my birthday! I'm twenty-two and I'm *so drunk*!' We watch her skip away and plunge into the pool. The mother next to me lets out her breath: 'It hasn't even got a strap to hold it up.'

———

The naturopath said my blood pressure was low. This surprised me. I always imagine it's so high that the top of my head is about to blow off.

———

My sister comes to stay while she does a training course at a big hospital. I have the annoyance of new Levis. Stiff, biting at the waist. 'I look awful in these jeans. All out of shape.' 'Listen,' she says, 'I'll take you out to the Austin and show you some *really* misshapen bodies.'

M went to a farm and had her feet stepped on by two horses. One at a time.

'I therefore advise young people to adopt the practice of beautiful women and *to care for their line*, to prefer the lean to the fat. And not to look at themselves in a mirror, but simply to look at themselves.'
—Jean Cocteau, *On Line*

Girl: 'Why do you have to go to Adelaide for ten days?'
    Mother: 'It's a writers' festival. It's work.'
    Girl: 'But I can't live without you.'
    Mother: 'Oh, you can so.'
    Girl: 'Well of course I *can*. But I hate it.'
    Mother: 'Why don't you like it?'
    Girl: 'I like it when you get up in the morning and I like it when you're there when I get home from school. And no one will kiss me goodnight.'
    Mother: 'Somebody else could.'
    Girl: 'Yes, but it's not the same.'

As I approached the back gate I could hear The Police, very loud. I expected to see M and her friend dancing, but when I got to the kitchen door I saw two neat little lassies sitting opposite each other at the table, doing their homework.

In the bus full of writers, an Englishman takes the seat beside me: 'Do you mind my talking to you?'

'Course not. What'll we talk about?' 'Shall we get right down to it and talk about sex?' We laugh. 'Why don't you describe your wife?' 'Okay. She's got a naughty face. Now, your husband.' 'He's got a big round head and he's very funny.' Behind us is sitting a quiet New Zealander, a Maori. The Englishman invites her into our game: 'What does your house look like?' 'Well, it's made of asbestos. It's behind my brother's house, so we had to build up higher to get a view over his place to the sea.' 'What are your ambitions?' asks the Englishman, 'and don't ask me mine, 'cause I don't know.' 'I want to live a long time,' says the Maori woman, 'because I've got a lot of things I want to write.' I say, 'I want to stay married.' I start to feel carsick from turning around in my seat.

––––––

At the mighty fireworks display a little girl sobbed desperately, clinging to her father's leg, while her younger brother gaped upwards, silent with wonder, one fist firmly attached to his father's trousers. An Italian man standing near us, distressed by her panicky weeping, murmured furtively to the little girl: 'Are you scared?' 'What do you want me to *do*?' said the father to the girl, bemused and cross. Pick her up, you moron.

––––––

The English writer believes in turning the other cheek. 'A magazine I knew was going out of business published a harsh attack on me, so I sent them a cheque for twenty-five quid. In the following issue they ran an even worse one, so I sent them a second cheque for the same amount. After that, it stopped.'

––––––

The way people with terrible hangovers feel obliged to think up an entrance line at breakfast. 'Anyone get the number of that truck that hit us?' 'Kindly explain why you punched me last night.'

––––––

HG: 'What's it like when your children grow up and move out?'
    Japanese writer: 'Merit is greater than sadness.'

––––––

The academic talked to me about teaching: 'I realised I was wasting a lot of time making sure that all the students *liked* me.'

Ka-blam. So that's why I'm always exhausted after a class.

'Charming people is very tiring, isn't it,' I said.

'Not only charming them, but constantly checking to see if it's working.'

———

I stick my head out the window and bang! A fat sun, gold as gold, hits me full in the face. I walk down the stairs into a well of yellow. The sun is bursting through any crack it can find. The air itself is shining. I come upstairs again, carrying two cups of coffee and the hem of my nightie. The closed door of F's room is a rectangle of wood barely holding back the eastern light. It is rimmed in gold, and through the keyhole shoots a narrow bolt of sun.

———

With a pair of short-bladed scissors the Chinese street-artist cut out a rooster from a small piece of paper. The only hint of expression in his face as he worked was a slight knotting or bulging of the flesh between his eyebrows; this was also his only mark of ageing. He seemed to keep the scissors still, and to move the paper.

———

When we walk down the street I notice G's eyes following a certain kind of woman. It's a game with me to '*suivre son regard*', to pick which ones he'll like the look of. I usually get it right. I enjoy watching his senses register. I don't know if he knows I'm doing it and I don't care. He's making a mess of his life. I don't think I'm much good to him as a friend. Maybe he likes to be with me because he can talk about writing, which seems to be the rock he's standing on in the rising flood.

———

The harpsichordist was wearing a very attractive dress with a belt and a collar and a lot of skirt, and long sleeves which she had unbuttoned at the wrist and rolled up to the elbow. Her thick, frizzy hair was pulled into a knob on top of her head. She had a perfect pink and white complexion. After the first piece she took a tissue out of her sleeve and blew her nose, which turned a darker pink and then faded.

———

B and I went to see *As You Like It* at the Melbourne Theatre Company. We laughed so much in the first half that tears ran down our cheeks. There were two empty seats in the front row so at interval we went down and sat in them. A man behind us: '*Tsk*. I can't *bear* it when people take seats they've got no right to.' His female companion: 'Do you want to move?' 'I certainly *do*.' Tomorrow I have to write my review. Wish I could write about the snotty couple and leave the play alone.

———

Indian summer. Mild air from the north, dust rises, skies at night are velvet. In the park the ground is hard: cracks have appeared, whiskers of grass tinge dry earth with green where yesterday, perhaps, a hose sprinkled.

———

F gets four days off work and becomes very cheerful and entertaining. His teeth flash at the table. He walks around the house singing a phrase or two like Teresa Stratas: falsetto, quite pure and clear, and true.

———

Something in the snubbed shape of the woman's nose makes me suspect trouble—or maybe it's the stuff she comes out with. She declares that a menstruating woman can prevent plants from growing merely by walking through a garden. 'What is the reason?' I ask. 'Well, I know that just before my period my energy field is in such a mess that it could easily affect another one nearby.' When I approach the table carrying three apples and a knife she cries out: 'You're not going to *peel* them, are you?' She is trying to finish her university degree: she says she's always stopped before, 'to go and look at clouds for a while', or 'because the pressure on me was too much'.

————

Everyone at the table longs to pull the whining, manipulative child into line. His mother is at his mercy. 'I've heard,' she says helplessly, 'that it's safe to hit them just here, on the side of the thigh.' F remarks that his parents used to hit him across the face. His father's blow would leave a hand-shaped mark with a red ridge around it.

————

New director of the museum: 'Like to come and see our Fred Williamses?'

HG: (*nervously*) 'Yes please.'

Director: (*striding through the glass and china section*) 'Got to change all this.'

HG: 'Why? I quite like it.'

Director: 'Too samely. Too bland. We'll rip out all this and make—you know, the silver all together in one place—darker—so people get that secret feeling that they've found the treasure themselves.'

We arrive at the Fred Williams paintings. I stand in front of them blind with nerves and ignorance. Away he goes, telling and showing in his red-and-white striped shirt and red velvet bow tie and black suit. As I look and listen, the responsibility for speech having been deftly removed from me, I begin to see the things he speaks about: warm or cold surfaces, smooth or roughened; lumps of paint, the suggestion of a grid; 'the essence of the country—repetitive marks on a huge emptiness—but fleeting, fleeting'. I'm breathless, dizzy:

being offered the gift of sight. I would have followed him all over the gallery. In front of one painting, having made a few remarks, he says, 'Do you like it?' 'Oh yes! It's *beautiful*!'

———

G's daughter pulls an office chair up to the piano and sprinkles her fingers over the keyboard. Her father speaks to her in the middle of the piece, which she is rendering in a slummocky manner. She looks up at him and answers, swivels the chair towards him, but continues to play, as if her mind and her hands had nothing to do with each other.

———

'Oh, Helen!' says M. 'I'm in love with Tom Burlinson!'

'Who?'

'You know! In *The Man from Snowy River*! Dee and I played all day, pretending we were in a movie and at the end we were having a party for the cast and crew. We had this disconnected old black phone, and rang up all the famous people we knew and invited them. And when we finished the game we felt really awful.'

———

My scary auntie tells me about seeing a ninety-year-old woman neglected by the staff in a nursing home: 'Stupid goats—they didn't see she was euchred. A bit light-on. Not the full bob. She had that gurgling business you get with pneumonia.'

———

'Wanna hear something terrific?' I squatted beside the stereo and put on a track of Sviatoslav Richter playing *The Well-Tempered Clavier*. G stood in the middle of the room. As the music ran, bounced and thickened he gave a few little grunts of pleasure, then threw back his head and laughed out loud.

———

'We don't really know it, but we sense it: there is a sister ship to our life which takes a totally different route. While the sun burns behind the islands.' —Tomas Tranströmer in *The Blue House*

———

How it's done. 'At that party I had,' said G, 'the big new Carlton dealer came sidling up and slipped me a little bit of heroin. I laughed and put it into a cigarette and smoked it. Later he slid up to me again and said he had a lot of it to unload and did I want to buy some. I said I had no money. But he sort of nodded round the room and said, "Look—there's at least five people here who use—why don't you just do a whip-around? You'll get the price of a deal." I said I didn't want to.' G spoke with a kind of disgust, putting it on for my benefit.

———

I was practising the piano, rather sloppily I suppose, while F washed the dishes. He came in when I'd finished and said, 'I think what you should do is play the piano when I'm not here. It's pretty annoying.'

———

Two buses crash in France and forty-four children die. One report says the drivers were racing, flicking their lights on and off, and hit a broken-down car with no lights. Everything and everyone burned except one boy, who was later found wandering nearby, shocked out of his mind. On TV, forty-four coffins made of pale, polished timber are lined up in what looks like a school gymnasium. Outside, banks of flowers. On one coffin—and surely many more—a hand-lettered card: ENFANT NON-IDENTIFIÉ. A cavalcade of square, glass-sided hearses winds up a hilly road with houses on one side and a high brick wall on the other.

———

We found a place to park the Kombi—up behind Lorne where the ground fell away on all sides and huge, pale-trunked gums, with strips of bark lying about their feet, soared up into a night sky absolutely milky with stars. We lit a fire. Wind rushed through the tops of the trees, and sometimes rushed also on ground level: I had to hold down the lighter bits of my fire with a stick. Odd sounds. I was scared. A bird whipping a hundred metres away in the dark.

_____

When the woman speaks at length she slides her eyes away to the left and rattles out her clever, well-expressed thoughts with a constant smile, as if amused by something she sees over your shoulder. And she grimaces and distorts her features while she thinks and talks, trying perhaps to distract attention from the un-beauty of her face by keeping it in motion.

_____

At the pub B wrote herself off. She was too drunk to take her contact lenses out—she passed out, mumbling, 'All I want is to be *warm*.' So I put her into her bed and covered her up, and hoped the lenses wouldn't bore their way into her eyes during the night.

_____

G said he learnt how to stand, at parties and clubs, from black men he saw in London: 'back to the wall *but not leaning*; head up, eyes narrowed.'

_____

Virginia Woolf, in her diary, often writes that she's not up to the job of recording her encounters with her friends, but she launches on it anyway and is soon merrily swimming along. Very sharp, especially about other women.

_____

On the other side of the river is New South Wales. I wish this fact had greater significance, or that I could write, 'On the other side of this river is Spain, or the Sudan. Or Brazil.' Always wishing for romance, ho hum, and anyway I can't speak Spanish. Or Portuguese.

_____

In *The Aunt's Story* he says, about Theodora, that she is not creative, that she has not got 'the artist's vanity'.

———

Waxworks, in Echuca. I'd never seen one before. B and I got the giggles, being the only people there. We noticed that the most obvious failures were two modern characters, John and Robert Kennedy. In their suits, with their anxious, businessmen's faces, they could have been anybody. Nasser and King Hussein were terrific. Funny how they can't get the feet to look real. They should get worn-out shoes and polish them, instead of using stiff, new ones.

———

The biographer came for a cup of tea and played some Bach on our piano. She coaxed me to play and I did, and when I got lost she was just *friendly*. She said, 'I love Bach's resolutions', and simple things that seemed important to say. I told her I'd been asked not to play when anyone else is home. She laughed, but she was shocked.

———

I could develop a real passion for Graham Greene: 'Even at night the air was so humid that it broke upon the cheek like tiny beads of rain.'

———

This is my fifth day without coffee, tea or alcohol. I have still got iron bars in my shoulders, but I am not full of mad haste to nowhere. I notice that a glass of water is sufficient, in conversation, for something to raise occasionally to my mouth.

———

At the Last Laugh I met a boy called Noah Taylor. His face was smooth, round-cheeked, absolutely unmarked, solemn, thoughtful, weird. A round forehead, above which rose a peculiar black beret.

———

I really like reviewing plays. What I love about it is the necessity to think back to, and formalise, what I really felt or thought in the theatre.

————

In the Kombi on the way home M used the word *pedantic* in its correct and appropriate sense. 'Where'd you pick that up?' 'At school. Miss Saunders taught it to us.' 'It's got a rather negative connotation, hasn't it.' 'What's that mean?' 'Well, it's never a compliment.' 'I see. Maybe I should try to use it in the exam, if it fits.' Days later she reports that she got it into her essay at the MacRob entrance exam.

————

The horrible saga of a breaking marriage. The child tells his father, innocently, that the other man has been in the house. The father goes berserk: 'It's territorial. He's been in my *house*.' I am drawn to the drama. At first I thought he had it coming to him. Now I see how he's suffering. And she reminds me of myself. Behaving with a queenly, detached selfishness that shocks and enrages people. 'Matilda told such dreadful lies,/It made one gasp and stretch one's eyes.' Well—I was never much of a liar. I tended rather to tell the truth and expect people to cop it.

————

I rode my bike to my piano lesson. I'm not so afraid of making a fool of myself now. As I merrily tinkled away, saying 'Oh shit' whenever I made a mistake, she said, 'I think you should do an exam. You'd be sure to get an A. You're very, very musical. You notice things in the music that others don't see.' Bathed in joy, I nonetheless thought, Tell that to the people I live with.

————

I make up my bed every night as deliciously as if for a sick person I was looking after.

————

Man behind the counter in the post office, to his colleague: 'It took her quite a while to calm down, after I slapped her face, Frank. Yes, I've always told her that if there's one thing I won't allow it's telling me what to do when I'm driving. I just reached across and hit her. Because we were passing the spot where a few years ago I was nearly involved in a very serious accident.'

A girl waiting for the lights in Bourke Street last Tuesday. A perfect example of how I would like to look: not her face, but her way of dressing: practical, comfortable, colourful, not fashionable. Straight black skirt just below the knees, a mauve-ish jumper, red stockings, brown flat shoes, green gloves, and a little red knapsack on her back. She looked *terrific*. M teased me for turning back, again and again, open-mouthed, to stare after her.

A reviewer of a collection of women's diaries from the late eighteenth century is surprised to find that they're about family affairs and do not mention the French Revolution. I don't find this at all surprising. But now that I'm sitting up in bed, pen in hand, on a rainy Saturday afternoon, all my little stored-up treasures turn their backs and hide in the shrubbery.

The man at the meeting had a tense and rather sexual presence. I mean, he couldn't seem to look at a woman in an ordinary way. A challenging sexuality was behind his eyes. A slightly pugnacious way of tilting his head back to look at you.

In the magazine the subs once again make me look an idiot. All my jokes cut out, the tone violated, the central argument truncated. I cry over it. I feel like resigning. I've felt like this a hundred times before and haven't done it. Oh, if only I knew I had a grant I'd tell the *National Times* to cram it.

———

M and her teacher play a little duet on their cellos. Sight-reading. How the hell do they do it? The note on the page, move fingers to prepare strings, keep the bow moving—up or down as indicated— no wonder musicians' eyes are so staring and fixed. 'Look at ya thumb!' cries the teacher. 'Ya thumb's like a crippled crab crawling!' They tackle a piece called '*L'Orientale*'. He shouts at her: 'You sound as if some Arab had stabbed you and you'd fallen across the strings!'

———

The boy is skinny, with a pale, fine-boned, waxy-skinned face, a kind of manic energy, a loud, shrill voice, obsessive behaviour. He loves matches and fire.

———

Why I like the English language: because it contains words like *cup*. Fat, short and stumpy, and rather optimistic.

———

I got a one-year grant. I rented a room in the Nicholas Building. Ninety dollars a month. It faces north. A fair amount of sky hangs outside its windows. Faintly, from the City Square nine floors below, a brass band. I will get curtains. I will get a weekly tram card. I will be a working woman.

———

I'm supposed to be interviewing the composer. But I'd rather just sit and watch the way he unobtrusively smokes a little rounded wooden pipe with a curved stem and a fine silver joint. Between puffs he cradles it in his half-closed hand, which rests palm-up on his long thigh. Later I type up my notes and find them curiously flat. All the magic I thought was in what he said must have come from something other than his words—his manner of speaking, his very calm solid presence. I don't *think* I invented him.

I feel like sending the writer who got a harsh review a letter of encouragement. But I haven't read his books and I probably never will.

I turn forty. M gives me a pack of cards and an American book of rules for card-games written in clear and simple prose. We're sitting on my bed at seven in the morning, slowly and carefully teaching ourselves draw poker, when F comes to join in and does what my father would have done: gets himself dealt into the game, grasps the rules at once, and then with a challenging grin refuses to abide by them. It's a birthday, we don't want to fight. So we do what women do: we fade away. We put down the cards quietly and go about our business.

I lay on my bed and read the *Paris Review* interviews. I kept dozing off. Nabokov: too clever and nasty. Kerouac: vain and noisy, a show-off. Eudora Welty: a nice, dear old lady full of respect and modesty.

HG: 'What are you working on?'

Sydney writer: 'I'm doing a dramatisation of the Azaria Chamberlain case. It has all the elements of Greek tragedy.'

HG: 'What are they?'

SW: 'Oh…rural setting. Baby. Sacrifice…'

HG: '…Intervention by an animal…'

SW: '…Religion…the pitting of man against circumstance or…'

HG: '…Fate…'

SW: 'A chorus.'

HG: 'Who's the chorus?'

SW: 'The press.'

HG: 'Oh, yes! How did you find out about Greek tragedy? Did you already know a lot about it?'

SW: 'No. I looked it up.'

HG: 'Do you mean you read some?'

SW: 'No. I looked it up in the *Oxford Companion to Ancient Literature*, and they had it all set out.'

———

At three in the morning the wind got up and blew everything about in my room but it smelled so sweet of the coming rain that I couldn't shut the window. I just bunched up the curtain and thrust it through the gap and now it's damp.

———

'No one was allowed to leave the theatre during his recitals, however pressing the reason. We read of women in the audience giving birth, and of men being so bored with listening and applauding that they furtively dropped down from the wall at the rear, since the gates were kept barred, or shammed dead and were carried away for burial... To destroy every trace of previous winners in these contests he ordered all their statues and busts to be taken down, dragged away with hooks, and hurled into public lavatories.' —Suetonius, about Nero, in *The Twelve Caesars*

———

On TV I saw the Queen Mother leaving a hospital. She had been rushed there to have a fishbone removed from her throat. As she emerged to her limousine, dressed in sky blue with one of those terrible turned-back hats in the same colour, cries arose from people in the small crowd that had gathered: 'How are you feeling? How are you *feeling*?'

———

A letter comes from the West Australian writer. What an unusual character he is! Four pages numbered in the Roman style, full of encouragement, embarrassment for presumption, reports on his progress. I feast on it, an intelligent and enthusiastic mind all optimistic.

———

At the meeting a new person entered, one of those balding men in their fifties with alert eyes that fix the women present in an eager stare. I felt riveted by him and had to drop my gaze. To hide this response I kept glancing at a vulgar chain bracelet of heavy silver that he wore on his left wrist. I can't take seriously a man who would wear such a thing. And yet I noticed him, and he knew that I did, and this made me furious.

———

The little boy's mouth is so stiff that he can hardly speak. When I greeted him he pointed his lips in and out, like a fish. Poor little fellow. He is wretched and whiny and hard to love. Even within his hearing she can't stop talking about her controlling husband, telling and retelling the story of their escape from him. The child stands there listening with a white face, hands at his sides like a ghostly little soldier.

———

F offered to pay some of my expenses so I could stop doing journalism and concentrate on my own work. I felt a stab of panic at the thought of being dependent.

1983

'They asked me if I went out much,' B reports. 'I said no, that I'd like to go out dancing more often but I had no one to go with. And *then* they asked me why I didn't go to places like Inflation! *Inflation*! It's only one step up from a singles' bar.'

———

M comes back from the toilet at Notturno and tells me she's seen some graffiti of mine in there. 'What did it say?' 'I don't remember, but I recognised your writing.' I go out there to check. Someone has written, 'What happened to the graffiti? Nobody writes it any more.' Underneath it, in my neat teacher's printing: 'It was fun for a while, but it got too personal.'

———

Two new teachers at the gym. Country-and-western women with mountains of teased bleached hair. One was wearing a leotard with a fringe up one arm, across the body and down the other leg. She looked like a kid who lies down in the shallow surf and stands up with a long strand of seaweed draped over one shoulder.

———

'I met a woman who says she lives in the room where *Monkey Grip* was written.'

'Bullshit. I wrote it in the State Library.'

———

The beginner will cling and cling to her thin first draft. She clings to the coast and will strike out into the ocean only under extreme duress.

———

At the Carlton baths, mothers as massive as sea lions lie about in groups with numerous kids under ten, at whom they squall and grunt. Also present are girls in their late teens, several of whom are pregnant. They eat hot chips out of white paper, and drink can after can of Tab. They don't have much of a handle on language. In fact they seem almost brain-damaged.

———

Flickers of a dream I once had are flashing in the corners, today. About a building, that's all I can get hold of. Must be just chemicals shunting around up there.

———

She went off to MacRob for the first time this morning, looking like a pretty insect in the uniform, her skinny brown legs ending in enormous new black shoes. 'Perhaps I'll get a nickname for having big feet!' she said with an excited laugh. 'From my *friends*!'

———

D. H. Lawrence uses the same word over and over till he makes it mean what he needs it to.

———

At Tamani I ran into a guy I used to know. He was with a friend. He told me he was getting married.
    HG: 'Oh, good! Who to?'
    Him: 'To a girl called—' (*goes blank*)
    HG: (*shocked laugh*)
    Friend: 'Stella.'
    Him: 'Oh, yes. Stella.'

HG: 'How did you meet?'

Him: 'I met her at a party. She took me home to bed, and the next morning she said, "Let's get married."'

———

I went with G to the post office so he could send some cocaine in an envelope marked WIZO—Women's International Zionist Organisation—to his friend in Sydney. The jolly lady behind the counter felt the envelope and tried to pass it through the testing slot. It wouldn't go: it would cost forty cents instead of twenty-seven. At this point I did not know what was in the envelope, although, while the friendly woman palpated it, I was beginning to guess. I concealed my dismay. G was absolutely relaxed. He smiled at her and said, 'Too thick, is it? Oh, I'll just pay the extra.'

———

Riding home, I passed the flats just as a car parked inside the fence caught fire. Thick flames wriggled out of its windows, and smoke rolled away to the north-east through the traffic on Princes Street. A young girl with a plait down her back was in a phone box barely six feet away from the burning car. The branches of an overhanging tree began to crackle and snap, right above the box, but she calmly finished her call, opened the door and walked away without a glance. The car was gushing flame. Its back windows were closed but they melted and flames flowed out through them, and through the windscreen. A wild-looking man with a carton of beer in his arms stopped near me to watch. We exchanged awed looks. 'I don't want to sound cynical,' he said, 'but my guess is that somebody lit it on purpose.'

———

Tears came to B's eyes. Suddenly her face lost its guarded, ironic look and became beautiful. I had forgotten that her eyes were such a vivid blue.

The Jungian says that dreams are messages to the conscious mind from the unconscious, which has picked up a vibe that the conscious mind is unable to perceive. He also says, I think, that the people we dream of often represent aspects of ourselves we would prefer to ignore or suppress. I wonder if it's possible to analyse one's dreams in any useful way.

At 8.30 pm I took the dog for a walk. The temperature was 42 degrees and it was dark because of a thick layer of dust in the air. I was halfway down McPherson Street when a great wind swung around behind me, coming from the south-west. The temperature dropped ten degrees in seconds. Dust flew. I had to cover my eyes. The air stank of burning and was full of smoke, the small trees whipped about. I kept walking, excited and scared. Down a lane behind a car a huge sheet of paper rose vertical into the air and danced there. People ran to their gates. 'Where's the fire?' 'Outside the city.' In another house the front window was closed tight but the curtains were open. I saw a table set formally for a dinner party, white cloth and red candles, and a beautiful young woman with thick black hair, wearing a red dress, standing at the table talking to her husband who was only a shoulder in a brown suit, half out of the room.

B describes Luciano Pavarotti's mouth, when he sings, as 'pastie-shaped'. He doesn't move his lips to shape the sound. It's all controlled elsewhere.

I've started to write, without thought of form: it keeps coming, I am happy and no longer straining after effect. But each morning I set out for my office weak with fear. I will never be a great writer. The best I can do is to write books that are small but oblique enough to stick in people's gullets so that they remember them.

―――――

The mountains were almost hidden in cloud. The sun rose between two dunes, huge and orange, I couldn't look at it, it was so bright. I felt like prostrating myself.

―――――

The woman at the next table appeared to have been crying for hours: there was something odd about her eyes under the wavy fringe. The man, who had an RAF moustache, talked a lot, with a smile, insisting gently on her attention. She asked him to buy her some matches, and he jumped to his feet. I thought they were a couple breaking up, but one of the others suggested she might have lost someone in the bushfires.

―――――

F came after work to inspect the house I had found. It was a terrifically hot day. He walked very slowly from room to room. The estate agent, a tactful old man, sat on a chair and took off one of his shoes. I suppose he guessed he would not be making a sale.

―――――

I spent only three-quarters of an hour at my office, because of agitation, too much coffee, lateness, distractions and so on, but I felt it was time well spent, for I can see 'dimly-lit pathways' into the forest of a book. I've got Alexander, Athena, Philip. They are established and already their names belong to them. Now I must take charge of them, lead them away from the literal past, start to snip and pin and stitch my SEAMLESS GARMENT.

―――――

G came into the cafe with his black guitar case. I introduced him. He shook hands with many nods and smiles. He almost bowed. It made me think of a Japanese woman I once saw near the Louvre asking directions of a local. When the Parisian had finished his explanation, the woman put her hands together at the waist and bowed low in gratitude. I was as shocked as if I'd seen someone walking down the street in a suit of armour.

―――――

HG: 'I saw your ex last night at a party. I went up to him and we shook hands. I realised I didn't hate him as much as I thought I did.'

Ex-wife: 'Huh. You'd hate him all right if you heard what he said to me yesterday. He said he was going to destroy my life.'

―――――

Labor got in. Fraser wept. As if to enlighten or celebrate, the ABC ran *The Dismissal* on TV. How weird, the shadowy resemblances of actors to real people. They're a stiff-faced, stiff-necked mob, Australian politicians. Bill Hunter as Rex Connor, minister for minerals and energy—his stolid bitterness after a political life in Opposition, his grinding determination, his unpolished speech and crude social manner, his slow, sour bulk. Fraser—it's all in the way he tilts his head back and looks down his nose.

―――――

I watched the beginning of *La Règle du jeu* on video. It's marvellous but I've never been able to sit still long enough to get to the end. Renoir's love of people, that unfashionable thing: the sense of a rich, three-dimensional, teeming life away there beyond the flat screen and spreading out from it in all directions. A kind of fizzing and bubbling that goes on. Everyone busy living.

―――――

At three in the afternoon the Vietnamese schoolkids sail past my window on bicycles. 'How, how,' they cry, with their singing intonation. I can't see them but their voices float between the high houses.

―――――

Two wretched little urchins of eight or nine, in the doctor's rooms, one of them waiting for an X-ray. They charged in and out, communicating in grunts and foul language. A young woman came in with a tiny girl, just learning to stumble about in her nappy, knitted dress and topknot ribbon. The boys went quiet at once and approached her reverently. 'Dad-da,' she said. 'Da-da!' they repeated, beaming round at the other patients. They passed her smooth, blocky little body from one to another, tenderly helped her to walk and to get up when she fell. Everyone in the room became happy.

———

Barry Dickins made us sick with laughter remembering Lou Richards on TV. 'Some vain young footballer's up there, from Geelong probably, talking about his future, and suddenly in comes Lou Lou and whacks this great packet of bacon down on the table and yells out, "Here's some bacon for ya, compliments of Huttons— and some pantihose for the missus!"'

———

Mum had seen *Staying On* before, and was keen for me to watch it with her. Scenes of Trevor Howard and Celia Johnson sitting at a table on a terrace with their backs to mountains so wondrous… Their terrible emotional strangulation, his, in particular; she, at least, used to dance and twirl about the house, when he went out.

———

My father drove at speed along the Great Ocean Road. I hunched in the back seat, expecting to be steamrolled with horror at the sight of the burnt-out landscape, but like all such perverse hopes it was disappointed. Perhaps we were moving too fast. Perhaps I'd already seen too much of it on TV while it was actually happening, or it was too long after the event. Perhaps it had nothing to do with me and I didn't really care. The thing that did strike me was the apparent deadness of the soil itself between the black, leafless trunks. Like radioactive dust.

I spoke at the anti-nuclear rally. I hated it, felt awkward, had no idea whether the crowd could even hear me. Somewhere a jackhammer was going rat-a-tat-tat. Whenever I looked up from my notes I saw thousands and thousands of faces turned in my direction, as small as mushrooms and completely unreadable. I was boring them. My tone was pitched wrong. I became very flushed. I scrambled down off the truck. An Aboriginal bloke in dark glasses hugged me and hopped up to go next. He stuck his hands in his pockets, thrust out his chin, and became a demagogue. He laid out a series of positions and gave cues for rousing applause, which he got. I skulked away, envious but also relieved, as if let off from future duty: I'll never have to do *that* again—'climb on a wagonette to scream'.

The GP told me about a post-mortem done on some kids killed in a car smash. The pathologist had been astonished at the number of intestinal parasites they were carrying. While she was telling me this story my eye wandered to a framed photo on the wall behind her: a class of forty white-coated medical students in rows, each one holding a tiny, swaddled baby.

In *Paris Review*, an interview with James Thurber. He talked about a bulldog he once had, which used to drag rails around, six, eight, twelve feet long. He loved to get the enormous thing by the middle and try to haul it through the garden gate—'everything finely balanced, then *crash*, he'd come up against the gate posts'. This, said Thurber, was the feeling he got when reading Henry James.

The fat man in the cafe saw through the window that his Citroën was about to be booked. He sprang up, lumbered to the door, and tried to clown his way out of it. He advanced towards the parking attendant with his hands clasped behind his back and a bouncing, knee-bending gait, like a naughty child faking repentance. She looked up at him with a stony face. He dropped it and started to argue. She ignored him and kept writing. He got into the car and made as if to drive off. She tried to push the ticket through the half-open window, but he screwed it up, shoved it back at her and roared away, leaving the pink leaf fluttering on the road at her feet. 'Why should he be able to bludge in a cafe,' said F, 'while she has to work all over Easter?'

———

I feel, when I'm with him, that I'm holding myself lightly in check.

———

A wonderful night out dancing. 'As soon as they started to play,' said B, 'you knew why they existed. Every band's up there for a different reason—they were up there because they can really play guitar.' We drank whisky and champagne, and threw up on the way home. I wasn't too far gone to hold her hair.

———

Walking up Bourke Street past the Southern Cross we passed a youthful couple engaged in a fight. The bloke had his back to us but the girl was turned our way, sobbing out loud, completely without shame. Her face was distorted and tear-stained. One felt immediately on her side, that she was a good person. 'Why do you have to tell me on a fucking *street corner*,' she cried out, 'that you're—' We passed at speed. We heard a light scuffle behind us, and then a blow. We thought she'd struck him across the face, but it might have been an open hand hitting a raincoat sleeve.

———

I ripped through Katherine Mansfield's journals and letters. Flashes of rage at her for being so *cute*—the nursery tone, the sugary 'my mountains'—it turns my stomach. But it's only a protective layer over the real stuff, which is sheer muscle.

———

When I was not yet 'a writer' I used to write colossal, twenty-page letters to people. Now I communicate on the backs of postcards. This thought made me feel quite cheerful, as if I had imperceptibly, over years, and not by the exercise of will, rechannelled wasted energy into a more useful course—but now I mess with the taps, I keep them turned off, or let just a tiny trickle escape. I'm terribly restless and cranky, unable to be calm enough to think properly about the matter in hand, which is Philip and his daughter in the cafe.

———

Tiberio came into the cafe and reported that Mario in the pasta shop had just cut the top of his finger off.

———

Goodness I am *drunk*. Can hardly write. And while I danced I felt so *sensible*! A BOY of twenty or so and I exchanged looks as we danced beside each other. He was six foot tall with short-cropped hair and a white T-shirt. When the music was over he said to me, 'See you!' I saw Paul Madigan leaning against a speaker box at the back. I approached to shake his hand. He had not shaved.

———

I went to the dentist. Perhaps it was the hangover but I felt my jaw and mouth trembling with the strain of gaping. Although I didn't suffer actual pain, I felt violated, and upset.

———

The magazine editor damns my story with faint praise: 'Yes…I quite liked it actually…the dialogue works…in parts…' I hung up the phone in embarrassment and confusion. And then I wrote him a letter that was like a hard kick in the arse.

———

I hereby resolve to refuse all social engagements on weekdays (before evening) from now on. I am completely out of synch and it'll take me weeks to get back in.

———

People sometimes talk about their boredom and I don't know what they mean. But this afternoon I had a nap, longer than necessary, and woke to find it was raining and no one had brought the clothes in off the line. I went downstairs and began to do the ironing. On the radio was some oboe music, full of formal resignation, and I started to feel those old waves of sadness, as if outside the house were nothing but grey wet fields and other buildings made of grey wet stone and people in clumsy, ugly clothes and strange hats.

———

In the car on the way to the restaurant last night with the visiting American lefties, I heard myself talking smoothly, putting on an effortless, tailored, hard-nosed little performance for their benefit. Disgusted, I fell silent. At the table I mentioned the name of Italo Calvino. Everyone looked at me blankly. I sat there full of anxiety. I'm finished as a writer, irredeemably bourgeois, my concerns so small (waiters in a cafe, a girl kneeling on a bed singing 'Lush Life'). All I've got are those ten pages in my room. This morning I got to my office and took it into my head to make a plan. What a sudden revolution then occurred! I rushed out and bought some system cards, wrote a character's name on each one, and pinned them up in a horizontal row. I thought very hard, pacing up and down and dashing off notes and reassuring statements, for an hour. Then, just as suddenly, the rush faltered and was over. I locked the door and went to see *Sophie's Choice*. Too pretty. Two prams exquisitely arranged by the railway tracks. And don't people vomit when they've taken cyanide?

———

'I have spent an hour cooking this meal. I would like you to eat it with a less foul-tempered look on your face.'

———

I saw Princess Diana go past in a Rolls-Royce. Such a *pretty* girl.

———

I hadn't seen the former actor for a couple of years. In the cafe he told me he was in love. 'Because I'm a fairly gentle sort of bloke— because I've been thoroughly trained by feminists—well, I've got this power to really *blow people away*.' He smiled, breathing out audibly through his nose. 'What do we all look like?' he went on luxuriously. He glanced down at my sober, dull clothes. 'You—you could be a school teacher. *I*—'

   'You look like what you are,' said another man at the table. 'A fucking arts bureaucrat from Sydney.'

———

The impervious self-confidence of the upper-middle-class educated young Frenchman. That smooth, slightly bilious skin, the narrow, pretty mouth, the small chin, the bony nose, the large intelligent eyes. He talks and talks, completely unaware that his concern at having reached the age of twenty-five is of no interest to anyone.

———

The bitter, sadistic-looking waiter in Notturno approached me today and said, 'I think I wrote something beautiful. Will you pass judgment on it for me?' He had recorded it on cassette, and gave it to me to take away. It consists largely of philosophical dissertations of a nebulous kind. The effect of his badly recorded voice is distressing, almost moving, because the pauses and silences are so eloquent.

———

In a caravan park on the western outskirts of Sydney some people noticed a dazed-looking man standing by his caravan in blood-soaked clothes. They called the police. He has been charged with the murder of a man found clubbed to death with a hammer—and with frightful attacks on three young teachers, women, who worked at a school for retarded children and were asleep in their quarters. He broke in, forced one of the women to tie up the other two, and made them torture each other, then hacked two of them to death. The third one survived to tell the tale. On TV, very sober, quiet shots of what looked like a small country town: a road leading to a building with a faded green corrugated-iron roof.

————

I can't write any more. I'm clumsy. Outside my window a fine rain is falling, perfectly vertical.

————

An article about different translations of Baudelaire's poem *La Cloche fêlée*. I read the poem out loud to myself and got one of those shocks that only poetry can deliver: a violent shiver, a rush of tears. I took off my hat to Richard Howard who, in his urge to render the last three lines, shows the poet in himself with a string of verbs: 'the gasping of a wounded soldier left/ beside a lake of blood, who, pinned beneath/ a pile of dead men, struggles, stares and dies.' But of course the original is somewhere else, that last line so strange and horrible: '*Et qui meurt, sans bouger, dans d'immenses efforts.*'

————

The biographer came over. We talked about writing. She said she'd started reading *The White Hotel* but when she got to a description of an old woman in a ditch having a bayonet shoved up her cunt, she closed the book. 'These days,' she said, 'it's considered a mark of moral superiority to contemplate the most horrible things. *I* think it's a sickness, the mark of an inadequate intellect. That's why I'm *sick* of Tolstoy, and think he's inferior to Henry James—because he won't admit the possibility of freedom.' He won't? I had nothing to say about this. I realise that I accept blindly what I read.

Three young men, whose catamaran was wrecked on the North
Queensland coast, struggled for three days through mangroves so
thick that it took them two hours to go two hundred yards.
Woman interviewer: 'But you had no water.'

Man: 'We licked dew off leaves.'

Interviewer: 'How did you have the energy to keep going, with
no food?'

Man: (*with a small snuffle of laughter*) 'Aw, I dunno. Hope...I
s'pose...'

After dinner the power went off and the house was dark. We sat
quietly by the fire talking about syntax and whether it was snobbery
and a misuse of power to criticise the mangling of it. She opined
that Murray Bail did not put that split infinitive in the first line of
Homesickness on purpose. He didn't even know, she said.

'*Tsk*. Why are you crying?'

'In Blanche d'Alpuget's book someone is crying and a kid asks
why. The mother says, "Because there is bitterness in life." That's
why I'm crying.'

'*Pfff*. That's just literature. I'm cold.'

'You're saying cold things. That's why you're cold.'

'I'm cold because I'm thinking.'

'Can't you think and feel at the same time?'

'No.'

G talks about telling his daughter he's leaving. 'I'm grief-laden,' he
says. 'I walk round laden with grief.' He's standing very straight,
with his back against the street window of Notturno, like a man
facing a firing squad.

———

Within two minutes I was sobbing and F was out of the room. I wanted to punch my hand through the window, smash up the house, I wanted to hurt myself, I couldn't feel it enough, I was looking for pain. I bashed the wall with my fists. He heard my racket and came back, put his arms around me stiffly, made me get into bed and tucked me in, kissed my cheek and left quietly like a mother hoping a sick kid is about to drop off to sleep and give her some peace. He had put the doona on sideways. My feet were sticking out. When the door closed I had to get out of bed, snivelling, and turn the whole thing around.

———

I have decided to smarten up my appearance. I bought some pretty earrings, and I now have two dresses. With woollen tights and my ankle boots from Paris I feel a killer of style.

———

'What's the matter?' Nothing major, but I don't like being reminded of the fact that I don't look happy.

———

I wonder if I could write a play. I can *imagine* a play. It will be about different points of view of exactly the same event. She comes in and they're at the kitchen table drinking. 'Do you want a sherry?' 'Yes.' 'There isn't any left.' 'Well why the fuck did you ask me then?' There would be different starting points, e.g. the boot-throwing scene.

———

Mount Buffalo. Folds and folds of 'armèd hills', blue after blue, and a cold wind rushing up from a deep gorge as it got dark—a roaring which might have been air in leaves or else a white, thin, steep torrent that I thought I saw half a mile below. A lyrebird strolled past me on its large feet, among the granite boulders. I shuffled, to alert it, but it glanced up casually and kept walking.

———

I tried to buy a coat. The only one I liked was Italian, marked down from $999 to $333. But it did not fit me. I bought a slip, a pair of black tights, a ream of A4, some carbon paper, and two pencil sharpeners.

———

My old teacher invited me to lunch at University House. He is tiny, plumpish, pink and grey, silver-haired, with soft, unwhiskered skin on his cheeks, as if he never needs to shave. He is a keen talker, a skilled and funny storyteller, a gossip, I suppose—not exactly malicious, but hard: 'They were tough with him and he went to water. I rang him up. I said, "What do you want done?" He said, "No, nothing. It's all right." He was going to get back in their good books by showing them he was a good boy.' Ouch. 'She must have known when she married him that she was condemning herself to the six kids, the whole family thing.'

———

The famously gloomy Stalinist had cut his hair very very short and 'started a new relationship'. He looked almost cheerful.

'What's your book about, Hels?'

'Oh…love, pain…'

'Interview *me*.'

'Everything you know about pain, my dear, you have already told me.'

'I've learnt something else.'

'What?'

'I've learnt that some things are beyond words.'

'Didn't you always know that?'

'No. I thought everything could be intellectualised.'

'Well, that's an advance, isn't it?'

'Except that it can make a pessimist even more pessimistic.'

'But if all that was standing between you and sheer pessimism was a false belief, isn't it better to—'

He laughed and turned away. 'Yeah, yeah, course, it's better.'

———

I made a plan: in the mornings I'll try to write my book, and in the afternoons I'll work on the translations of the Malraux programs for SBS. I started this morning at 8 am. I loved it in my room, quiet all around, barely even properly light. I rewrote Vicki and Elizabeth, the very beginning of the book. I worry that I ought to pour out a whole draft and then go back and rewrite. What I do is write a page, then fix it up straight away and go back to the beginning to see if everything fits. So my progress is slow. But the work is solid. After lunch I sat at my desk with the big dictionaries, the mild afternoon sun on my back through the window, and wrestled away. Writing in the morning is battling through jungle. Translating in the arvo is riding along a flat country road on a bicycle.

———

These mornings we see the most dazzling sunrises: the five cypress trees I can see from my bedroom window point like a raised hand in front of a broad band of clear sky with dove-grey cloud, pink-tinged, above it. Birds sing loudly. I don't know where they are.

———

Every day when I sit down at the desk I wonder if there will come a certain moment when, with a pop, each character will attain physical reality in my imagination, quite separate from its worldly model.

———

We used to be friends but now I'm afraid of him. The photo on the back of his new book shows him black-faced, black-browed, his shirtsleeves rolled up to show strangler's arms, all muscly and hairy.

———

How am I going to survive this? I have a lemming-like urge to dash off the cliff now, instead of waiting till he leaves. It's like the urge to punch walls: 'Look how you hurt me. I am acting out a little play of pain.'

———

I like making cosmic observations, e.g. the power enjoyed by those who ride in the back seats of cars.

———

The only way I can keep a rhythm going is to keep off booze, go to bed early, and not drink too much coffee. 8.30–12.30 work on novel in office. 2.00–4.00 translate at home. 7.30–10.00 read Vogel Award manuscripts at home. Most of them are unbelievably terrible. One was like a black hole in space: all my energy was sucked into it, it drained and sucked and gave back no spark. It scared me.

———

I went to a union meeting. God, it was boring, stacked with old dead-heads obsessed with procedure. A man I used to teach with in the seventies shyly expressed to me his disappointment: he had expected the meeting to be 'about literature'.

———

O was down from Sydney. We went for a long walk in the cemetery. I asked him about a woman we knew at university. He told me that she had jumped off a building. He said she had remade herself, after a terrible car crash in which she had sustained brain damage, but it wasn't good enough for her and it wasn't going to get any better. So she jumped. We agreed that this was consistent with her whole life and personality: reckless courage.

———

G wrote to me, speaking of heroin, coke, a 'suicide' attempt by his girlfriend. She scratched her wrists with a pin, 'then asked me to hit her up with heroin. I did, then had some myself.' Disgusting confidences. Nothing he can do will surprise me, but I thought she was tougher, clever, going somewhere.

———

'I met a man,' said U, 'and we talked about you. He said that he found you a very interesting person; that he thought you were shy; and that you were not going to let people waste your time.' I wondered what she had said in reply, but did not ask.

———

'When you say you cough blood, what do you mean exactly? Is it just a pinkish tinge, or—you don't mean actual gouts, do you?'

'Yeah, gouts,' said G. 'Black. Especially in the morning.'

———

We fought about housework. I saw red and smashed a plate and a bowl.

'There are more plates here. Why don't you break them as well?'

'Shut your face.'

He went upstairs and turned the TV on full blast. I swept up the mess. I bawled a lot as I swept, and then as I washed my plain, spotty, forty-year-old face and looked at it in the mirror and thought that I couldn't bear having to go through another bout of this BATTLING. I also thought, I am about to get my period. It absolutely *shits* me that this should explain anything. I objectively do most of the housework and it's NOT FAIR. After I'd washed my face I took off my pants and they were stained black with blood.

———

This flaming book is jammed again. I feel my ignorance and fear like a vast black hole.

———

Heading for Griffith University in the Kombi. At nightfall I walked down the main street of Gundagai eating hot chips out of newspaper. The lumpy little hill straight ahead of me was dead black, its silhouette fringed with the odd gum. The fading light behind it, airy, mauve and pure, seemed to be projected upwards towards two horizontal streaks of grey cloud. In my motel room the double bed sank in the middle before I even got into it. A deep sleep. Dreams of Paris: climbing flights of stairs. I peeped out at dawn and saw darkness, and thick frost on the Kombi's windscreen. How comforting it is to write in this notebook, in an awful room so far from home. I write, and become lord of all I survey.

———

She kissed me goodbye. Her firm cool cheek: still a child's slight plumpness. Poppy's will be like that, to Elizabeth. I thought a lot on the Hume highway about how to make Elizabeth an unlikeable character but still interesting.

———

Woman in the hippie gift shop. About fifty, blonde, a weatherbeaten, upper-class face with piercing blue eyes. 'I'm asexual,' she announced. 'I've been wanting to talk to someone about this. I don't have a relationship with a man, and I *love* my life.'

———

ABC radio is a wonderful institution for travellers and other solitary people: those soothing talk programs full of information about echidnas. Apparently the echidna, the hedgehog and the porcupine each evolved quite separately.

———

In the restaurant it was 'go to the counter and get it yourself'. I was out of place, the only solitary among the families and the groups of young people hardly out of childhood, smoking desperately between mouthfuls. Perched on bar stools four women in their late twenties were sipping wine and smiling, smiling, smiling at each other as their conversation went. I wondered whether my loneliness made me want to take notes, or vice versa: how is a writer made?

_____

R says that in reading she is always looking for the moral voice of the writer. She says she never feels better after having committed violence—not even after smashing a plate.

'I do,' I said defiantly.

'I don't,' she repeated. A pause.

'I'm not sure if I do or not,' I said. 'I feel humiliated when I have to sweep up the pieces.'

_____

The seven-year-old is a jolly, endearing boy. He described someone as 'greedy and boastful'. I said, 'Is it boastful to tell about one's successes? I remember you boasting once that you were the second-best runner in your school.'

'Second-best _long distance_ runner! And that wasn't boasting! That was a _success_!'

_____

I dreamt that my publisher told me my novel was bad. 'Bad? Why?' 'Oh yes. It's terrible.' Through my waking mind ran escape clauses: I'll do short stories instead; she mustn't have liked the trimmed-back style; I'll take out the old man's hairy hands. I was panicking, but deep down I was not surprised.

_____

D, who I'm billeted with, seems to believe, as do many people who are fully-fledged examples of their type, that she is 'not like' the others: 'I can't stand academics,' she says. 'I was born not standing academics.' And yet she has their brittle manner, their tendency to monologue, their habit of irony, of picking up words in tweezers. I'd better look out. No one's safe, once they've been inside a university.

_____

Awfully homesick. I walked for miles along a beach. On my way back I saw a foreign man who had found an orange fish floundering in the shallows, and was trying to flip it into deeper water with his thong. I ran forward and picked it up by the tail, but it flipped strongly—I'd never picked up a live fish before and was astonished by its muscle—I had to seize it in two hands and fling it out to sea. 'Sank you, sank you,' cried the man and his two female companions.

———

I went to a lecture on realism. A lot of detached, ironic descriptions were offered, in a tone that seemed to assume that realism is historically discredited now and rather dull. I don't know if I'm a realist or not. I don't think it's a good idea to sit around in a university trying to categorise myself. The lecturer said twice that words signify reality but don't represent it. I'd quite like to find out what this means, but I'm not breaking my neck.

———

I worked all morning, slipping myself slowly back into the world of the book. I love Athena. She is rather stern. I'm dying to make her meet Philip. They will have dry kisses that lead nowhere.

———

In the campus bookshop I accidentally stole something. The woman at the register was cold and rude to me, quite unnecessarily, and I left the shop in irritable confusion. Halfway back to the Humanities building I realised I was still carrying Elizabeth Bowen's *The Last September*. Fuck you, I thought, and kept walking.

———

In this town the rubbish man comes right into the backyard, finds your bin wherever it may stand, and heaves its contents into another bin that he carries on his shoulders.

———

An Englishman invited me to a class about technique. 'You're a writer. You might be interested.' He gave me the course outline and said to come at four. I read it and was alarmed to see that it had nothing whatsoever to do with any sense of the word *technique* that I'd ever heard of. I had no idea what he was getting at. I went, miserably, to his class. He talked for an hour and I still had very little clue. It all seemed so cloudy, so full of terms I did not know. My spirits sank and sank. Later I tried to explain my response to two academics I met at dinner. They were amused and encouraging. I said, 'I feel inadequate, and as though I'm under attack.' 'You probably are,' said the man. 'Not in a personal way, but your assumptions are being challenged.' I suppose it's good for me, but I still don't see any link between the lecturer's 'technique' and what I do in my notebook.

————

Another Englishman (the place is swarming with them) lent me some Roland Barthes: 'to show you he's weally about w'iting'. I read a little piece called *La Lumière du Sud-Ouest*. It was beautiful. Hills *'toutes proches et violettes'*.

————

The Italian academic said she hated this town and had not gone to any other places in Australia, although she's been here nearly four years.

HG: (*shocked*) 'But why?'

Woman: (*with an eloquent grimace and a sideways flicking gesture*) 'Every time I had holidays I just couldn't *stand* it here, so I'd go back to Rome.'

I found this so mortifying I almost burst into tears. I was the only Australian at the table and I was terribly offended.

————

On many mornings in this house a radio alarm clicks on in the kitchen at 6.30. No one ever gets up in response to it. I feel guilty, as if I had set it myself. I get up and stand on the cold floor, unable to decide whether I should switch it off or not.

————

F calls me from his parents' house, where he's taken M on a visit. 'I suddenly understand,' he says, 'why I get so mad with you when you're bossy. It's *very* bossy here.'

―――――

A long interview-documentary with Billy Wilder, a charming and likeable old rogue who, in the final ten minutes, turned on the interviewer, a humourless French film buff with the appropriate name of Michel Ciment, and made gentle mockery of him: 'The only thing worse than not being taken seriously, Michel, is being taken too seriously. As long as I can make movies, I don't give a shit.'

―――――

My sister told me that a young man had come off his motorbike last night outside her holiday apartment at Surfers. In the paper this morning his death was reported. 'I heard the crash,' she said, 'and I ran out to see if it was the girls. He was lying with his helmet near him, it had flown off, and his head was right up against the gutter. There was quite a bit of blood. As soon as I saw it wasn't the girls I thought, There's plenty of people looking after him, and I went inside and got back into bed.'

―――――

Up here I'm little more than a machine that records horrors and small dismays.

―――――

'The best thing you can do as a Creative Writing teacher,' said a man who had been one for four years, 'is to put tight fences around them. I used to tell them I was absolutely not interested in their outpourings. It's worth it. At the end you say, Well, X came in here a verbal cripple, and he's walking out the door without crutches.'

―――――

'I love you,' said G on the phone, vaguely, as if wanting to register a small fact while the occasion presented itself. I knew that already.

It's part of what I know about the world, but it's never steady, it flickers and disappears, and I would only feel this as painful if I'd been steering myself by its unreliable light. This metaphor will stand, if I don't try to develop it any further.

———

The Vogel judging in Sydney was pure pleasure. We were put in an office high above bits of harbour, with windows that didn't open. It seemed that I hadn't laughed out loud in the company of others since I left Melbourne. (Frank Moorhouse: 'Beware of committees that laugh too much.')

———

In the pub, as the priest waited for me to finish with the public phone, he took a few steps back into the lounge where a jukebox was playing some loud rocking thing. He turned his back to me, unaware that I was watching him through the glass door, and took three big steps in time to the music, swinging out his arms in a large, free gesture, embracing the world. I like men. I just *like* them. (But not Norman Mailer.)

———

If I lived in Sydney perhaps these people, and the women they know, would be my friends. Perhaps this is just a provincial fantasy. Perhaps their lives are as closed as mine sometimes seems to be, in Melbourne.

———

I wiped myself and saw blood. Days early. Cynicism says: a disease. Romance says: weeping.

———

I wondered, seeing the state G was in, whether I did agree after all with his remark about the attractiveness of other people's unhappiness. I wanted to sweep out his head with a straw broom, wash out his mouth with soap, put him across my knee and spank him with a rolled-up newspaper, and then fuck him silly, just to cheer him up. Instead we walked along a path in a park, looked at the Opera House gleaming in the sunshine, and felt extremely patriotic.

———

Frank O'Hara is a ratbag, so likeable, and what a voice. 'Love's life-giving vulgarity,' he says in his ridiculous Manifesto.

———

A house! The sun comes in/ Through small surprising windows./ The occupants left for the coast/ early this morning in an old car./ 'Sleep in our bed,' they said,/ and I will: I've made it up already/ with thin blankets out of a cupboard./ I've turned back the top corner/ And placed the pillow;/ But that's for later. Now/ I cut my fingernails to the quick/ And sit down at the piano, giddy,/ The child all secret left alone/ With bare board and kitchen jars,/ Doors that don't lock, And ragged bleached towels/ Which have drunk water off those/ Travelling bodies that I love.

It took me an hour and a half to write that. The whole time I was reworking it I was thinking I should be doing something else. I'll never be a poet! But it's more fun than prose, that's for sure.

———

Opposite the bedroom window stands a church. The morning light brightens its sandstone steeple. Pigeons swagger along its edges.

———

'Want to come with us to see *Flashdance*?'

'Love to! Only one problem—if it's tomorrow I might be going to the Opera House to see *The Cherry Orchard*.'

'It's fabulous! You'll cry! No, you won't *cry*…'

'Yes I will. You should've seen me at *Three Sisters*.'

———

'I saw she had been writing you a postcard,' wrote B, 'and I was full of jealousy. I thought, Well, if everyone else is going to write to her,

I'm not. These feelings must be hounded out and whipped like a thieving servant boy.'

———

The young girl's confident vocabulary: 'If you look at her hands fleetingly you don't even notice; but if you examine them properly…'

———

Been drinking again. But all I had was three margaritas and one very watered-down scotch. So I am all right.

———

Missed the plane. Do not care. Walk with slow steps in my pink high-heeled sandals. The muzak in the airport sounds as if it's being boiled, or percolated. One is not sure what tune it is, though it causes a familiar feeling.

———

A student brought me a poem she had written. She asked me to correct her punctuation. The first line: 'A, TV reporter came up to him.'

———

One of the Englishmen grumbles fiercely to me at lunch about the 'theory' people in the department. He's furious because they make their students read theory of literary criticism without reading the novels first. 'I was interested when they said they were going to teach *Lady Chatterley's Lover* and the trial. I thought, They'll have to read the novel. But they didn't. They studied the transcript of the trial.' I'm listening, agog, but just as what he's shouting becomes really interesting, he breaks off mid-sentence. 'Why did you stop talking?' 'I've got high blood pressure.' 'What? Don't be silly.' 'No, it's true. And there are better things to get worked up about.'

———

While the GP was writing out my prescription, she was breast-feeding her baby.

We lay on the couches in his living room, gossiping about musicians.

'She's got no studio manners,' said G.

'What's that mean?'

'Okay. We're in this very small room. She's holding a guitar, I'm not. I'm in there trying to tell her how to do it. The guitar is connected. The slightest flutter she makes on the strings makes a tremendous noise. I say, "How about trying it like this?" She goes chucka-chucka-chucka—gets it wrong—and in her frustration she *whacks* the strings, really hard. The noise it makes is like being punched in the head! I nearly have to cover my ears! It *hurts*! And she does this ten, fifteen times!'

The evening comes down. A postcard I'd left on the bed in the morning was bent in a curve. Crickets make their soothing, reliable rhythm. A visible mistiness fills the valley. The house is like a ship: riding high in damp air.

On TV, riot police in Santiago, Chile charge a peaceful sit-in against the military regime: they savagely attack students with their nightsticks. A witness says, 'They fell to the ground, blood gushed from their heads, the man was screaming in agony, his head was dented like a ping pong ball.' People all over the city toot their car horns in protest, and people inside their houses, when night falls, begin to beat spoons against saucepans. The whole city is in uproar.

I'm worried about art, what it's for, whether what I do is any use to anyone, whether I've been kidding myself all these years that I'm any good at it, that I've got anything at all to offer the human race, whether I should just chuck it in and look for a job.

I was astonished at the violence of the short story. The control the writer thinks he has of it is the control that a furiously angry driver has of a car, a person who ought to be kept from the wheel until he recovers his temper: the narrative voice makes grinding changes, throws itself into sickening halts and turns. The last few sentences are a head hitting the windscreen.

―――――

When the Englishman washes the dishes he splashes water all down his front in great slops that soak his shirt and trousers. He is perfectly oblivious, for he is singing to me, in a sweet and cultivated light tenor, a song to illustrate why he loves Berlioz. We show each other photos of our children, whom we painfully miss. 'She looks wise,' he says, looking at M, and she does: thin arms folded over the sinewy torso, the straight line of the mouth, the eyes with their reserved, humorous expression.

―――――

The student and I sat together at the kitchen table, sewing. She was taking in a pair of trousers; I was mending the sleeve of a dress.

'This is nice, isn't it,' I said. 'Reminds me of that scene in *Gone With the Wind* where the women sit sewing while the men are out getting into trouble.'

'And,' she said, 'one of them is reading out loud from *David Copperfield*. "Chaptah One. Ah am bawn."'

―――――

At the hippies' house for dinner, I find in my slice of quiche two foreign items: a dead match and a pubic hair. I hide them under a lettuce leaf and we go on talking.

―――――

At the prize-giving I stretch out my legs and rest my feet on a kind of wooden pew. A journalist from Sydney called K introduces himself, sits on my feet and tells me several gaudy tales of his emotional life:

various insane behaviours. I feel like taking the cheeky-faced fellow by the hand, leading him into a dark hallway, and saying, 'Let's kiss.' I discipline myself by planning a Schnitzler-style short story about the waxing and waning of a flirtation. By the time I get home I have forgotten it.

———

A Christian student came to see me and talked at length about her decision to leave university. 'I'd been praying about it for a long time. In church last Sunday I got an answer. I knew that I had to leave. The Lord spoke to me. He said, "Well, are you going to serve me, or aren't you?"' I was interested in what she said. I did not think it was silly. I imagine that if one became a Christian one could not do otherwise than to proselytise. Anything else would be inconsistent.

———

My predecessor in the department talked to me in confidence about D. He has known her for many years. Everything he said confirmed my own doubts and suspicions. Still, I feel an allegiance to her which makes this disloyal scribbling seem treacherous—a cold, slightly sickened sensation of curiosity which, when I pick up the pen and the diary, presents itself almost as a duty: isn't this what writers *do*? Can a writer be a loyal friend? To be a loyal friend I'd have to mark off a distinct line past which I decline to make mental notes, to probe or observe.

———

The dog in the house over the back has been circling it for an hour or so, barking to be let in. I can feel my shoulders going rigid. I wish I could make a tremendous *noise*. If I had a gun I'd fire it into the air until they came out and shut him up.

———

Before dinner, three little boys of charm and vigour clumsily handed round plates of biscuits and pâté. Their father winced and flinched

at their awkwardness. He made them go to their room. Twenty
minutes later the middle one came out in tears. He stood on the
lounge-room carpet in his cotton shortie pyjamas and absolutely
howled. 'What's the matter?' said his mother. 'Dad won't let me
out!' he bawled, fat tears bouncing off his cheeks. 'Oh, let him out,'
she said to her husband. 'He's *so* sociable.'

———

Two men listen to Strauss's *Four Last Songs*.
   'I hate sleep,' said one. 'Sleep is death.'
   'That,' said the other, 'has something to do with why your
marriage broke up.'

———

My clever student has the 500-watt blue eyes, black-lashed and set
ever so slightly too close together, that cause the person on whom
they rest to feel a significance he almost certainly does not intend.

———

I've started a story called 'Postcards from Surfers'. If I can maintain
the tone, and keep it all small and bare, it will be good. I know I'll
never write anything that could be called 'great'. I suppose for that
you have to have a big idea. All my ideas are small and the best I
can do is cobble them together.

———

My sister told me that being with our parents made her cry. When
she woke in the morning after their visit her eyes were so puffy that
she looked 'like a cane toad'.

———

The board member astonished me by her vehemence against the
funding of poets. She went right overboard, deckchairs and all,
laughing as she spoke. She said she rarely read poetry and that most
poets were full of shit, posturing and squabbling among themselves.
I thought of R, the only poet I know, quietly and patiently spinning

away in secret, and wondered if the board member had any idea (or if I did myself) of the length of that process, compared with the job of prose. She seemed to think that poetry could be dashed off in the gaps between real activities. Well, perhaps it can, but what about the long, slow formation of something big, or pure?

G asked me to visit him at the studio. He kept me waiting for half an hour, then told me a tale of how he'd behaved on Saturday night: 'I made a real animal of myself.' I listened, with the weary, unjudging curiosity his stories provoke in me. He had locked himself in a bedroom at a party with the wife of his friend; not only was his official girlfriend also at the party, the one he'd left his wife for, but some other 'new girlfriend' with whom, unbeknownst to the official one, he had just spent the afternoon. Having related this to me, he went to a different part of the building and didn't come back. I finished reading the paper, listened to a small orchestra in the next studio, and left without saying goodbye.

I'm scared to go to my office in case I can't make things up.

I wrote two or three sentences about Vicki waking up. Vicki is the only character who is almost completely invented. I love to let her float around in my mind, bumping up against things that are in there: views, articles of furniture.

I would like to make Elizabeth *hard*. She is already but I have this sneaking romantic duty to show a soft side to her—as if she is 'really' just as 'vulnerable' as anyone else, only hides it better. A scene where she will shock Athena with her bitterness and pessimism.

Dreamt that G betrayed me. He robbed me of my bag, and blatantly admitted it. I woke from this dream knowing, before I even opened my eyes, what it meant: that I felt *I* was betraying and robbing *him*, by writing a character that's based on him. But I can't stop now.

———

'Your school shoes are disgusting. Why don't you clean them?'

'It's fashionable to have dirty shoes.'

———

F buys a house, a tiny dump, all crooked but nice. He is going to live in it by himself. He has doubts. 'What will I do after work?'

Me: (*briskly*) 'You'll drive home to your place, have a sleep and a wash, then you'll ring us and say, "Can I come over?" and I'll say, "Do you want to come for tea?"'

———

I loved the scene in Syberberg's film of *Parsifal* where Klingsor summons Kundry from sleep and urges her to try to seduce Parsifal. He asks her what she wants and she cries out, 'Sleep! Everlasting sleep!' Each time one of these bloody men revives her or drags her out, she opens her eyes in a kind of horror, like a failed suicide who comes back to consciousness, looks around and says, 'Oh *no*—I'm *still alive*.'

———

I don't enjoy the way the therapist fixes me with her unblinking gaze. She seems to want to urge me to undertake a search and reconstruction of myself such as the one she herself is attempting. When I think of her ugly clothes and the quite stunning, almost deathly ugliness of the inside of her house I shiver. She is trying to get me to face the most difficult area in myself. I don't have the courage to do it. Not now, anyway. Thinking about it is like contemplating a mountain range in winter.

———

I do feel sad though at the way the sun passes unobstructed through his empty room.

On the tram home M and I examined together the intro to a book of Scarlatti sonatas. It quoted a sentence in archaic language. I began to read it out loud (not very). 'Helen!' she said, twisting her shoulders. '*Shhhh*!' I felt, as always when she is embarrassed by my public demeanour, stabbed to the heart. I turned my face away and sat very still. 'What's the matter?' 'I hate it when you tell me to shut up. It makes me feel awful.' 'I didn't tell you to shut up!' In the house later each of us went about her business, but I noticed that when our paths crossed she smiled at me, instead of walking around in a dream as she normally does these days. When she left for her friend's place she kissed me goodbye. And last night at dinner, she actually *sat on my knee* and leaned against me for at least *ten minutes*.

A woman on the Lygon Street tram was afraid that her four- or five-year-old son would fall out through the open side of the middle section. She gripped his wrist.

'But I want to walk around.'

'No, Sam, you can't. It's dangerous.'

He bursts into a roar: 'But I *want* to!'

'You *can't*, Sam. It's *dangerous*.'

'Please let me go! Oh, please! Let me go! Let me out! *Please*!'

'No! Look! If you fell out there you'd be under those wheels and you'd be dead! *Dead*!'

'No I wouldn't! Please let me go, please, please!'

'No! I don't trust you, Sam. I don't trust you not to do something silly!'

'I won't do something silly!'

'You've been silly all morning!'

'No I haven't! I haven't been silly!'

'I don't trust you, Sam! I *don't trust* you!'

It was a neurotic drama conducted at top volume, utterly without abashment of any kind.

————

I was alone in the house late on a summer evening, playing the piano with all the windows open. Somebody knocked at the front door. I was seized by fear. But when I looked out the window I saw the bearded Greek. We sat at the table and drank some wine. He read me his new poems. I liked best some short ones about a Gertrude Street cafe he worked in: 'A woman crosses the road and becomes a waitress.' As he read, I watched a small moon, in a dark blue sky 'seeded with stars', sail with surprising rapidity across the uncovered window behind him.

————

I flipped through *The Horse's Mouth* and found a message to me: 'What I say to an artist is—WHEN YOU CAN'T PAINT, PAINT. But something else.'

————

I think about my characters, and their world is real to me.

————

I lay around all evening in my cotton nightie and watched TV by myself. The dog dreamed in her beanbag. Every now and then I got off the sofa and sprayed myself with Yardley's Lily of the Valley.

————

Now G tells me he's left his girlfriend and fallen in love with a woman who's 'a cross between Marilyn Monroe and…'

'Are you in the shit?'

He nods.

'What happened?'

'It's like having lived with the moon for four years, and the sun comes out.'

1984

We talked about A. S. Byatt's novel *The Virgin in the Garden*. B said she hadn't liked or been convinced by the sex between the older sister and the plump curate. 'I've never felt anything like that,' she said rather testily. I was astonished to hear this: it was the first time I'd ever read an account of those profound wanderings of the imagination that have occurred in me while I was fucking—as if my own body, blood vessels, my inner hollowness were a whole country in which I slowly and dreamily travelled—along rivers, in endless gardens—like a stage set or a mighty reddish-lit cavern.

I have drunk three glasses of chablis and feel tiddly. But I am not drunk. I know this from the fact that I have just sewn on the Singer two calico cushion covers. And they fit.

'He's mixed up with a twenty-five-year-old,' says U miserably. 'She has a Playboy body and eyes that are blue. But without depth.'

He snored, so I crept out and slept on the hard fold-out couch, wrapped in a cotton blanket. I dreamed I was in a Dickens novel, that I was happy and that I laughed and laughed. Another character 'tortured water' in his experiments. I wore a pretty muslin dress and I was in love with someone, a funny and clever man who was also kind. When I woke up my eyes were puffy and my nose was blocked, as if I had been crying for a long time.

———

The gum-tree boughs are so flexible, they toss like heads of hair.

———

Sunbaking with my sister in her garden. 'Look out, Helen, there's a very bad worm just near your foot.'

———

At the Greek restaurant our table was in a kind of annexe with a canvas roof stretched over it, filled with small flourishing trees, which dropped little mauve flowers on to our dinner. I went looking for the toilet. The upper floor was like a cheap hotel in Teheran or Cairo: an air of something sinister having just happened; rooms emptied very recently of personal belongings but still holding their former occupants' presence, like an agitating gas.

———

I'm often surprised to find, when I reread an article for which I have been criticised as harsh or unsympathetic, that my tone in the piece is quite courteous and benevolent. Even mild.

———

I thought that I ought to do more planning for this book—never leave my office without having made solid notes for the next day's work. Today I did plan, and now I feel curious as to what will surface when I sit down tomorrow and follow my own orders: 'Philip, Poppy and Elizabeth go to dinner at the Foxes' in Bunker Street'. Philip will have a very small butterfly tattoo. I want him to talk about watching a science program on TV: 'that acidy little zing'. Dexter won't know what he means by 'acidy'. I also have *major* decisions to make about *who* Athena is going to *get off with*. I can't believe she'll have enough money to go to Europe.

On the other hand, who does? Mustn't let this realism business get on top of me.

———

When we got to the biographer's house she spoke with exaggerated care. The grinding deliberateness of her manner was really just her ordinary tone intensified a great deal. The penny didn't drop for a while that she was profoundly drunk and trying to pretend she wasn't. To kick things along I talked about the Florence Nightingale biography I've been reading. She asked whether Nightingale remained a virgin all her life. 'I think so,' I said. 'She seems to have decided against anything other than work. Oh—she did receive several good offers of marriage—' At this she burst out laughing and turned her head away. '*Good* offers of marriage?' she repeated, with the grating bitterness she always shows whenever marriage is mentioned favourably. She went very slowly upstairs and returned a long time later with some poems, which she read to us. She said no one would publish them. If I'd been frank I'd have said, 'You're not a poet. Your poems are really prose. They're plodding, and lecturing. You haven't got a poet's imagination.' People can't *say* that kind of thing, I think.

———

Today I worked in a trance for nearly four hours. I did the dinner scene at the Foxes' place. I even got to the very end, when Poppy says on the way home, 'Athena's perfect, isn't she.' Dexter sings his hymn, is crossed by Vicki, falls off his chair and breaks it. They drink a whole bottle of gin. Athena and Philip notice each other. I cobbled together that scene out of elements so disparate that only a compulsive note-taker like me could have had the raw material at her disposal. Whacko! I could have gone on all day but didn't want to push my luck.

———

From reading Doris Lessing I saw how I might one day *dare* to exaggerate the surreal aspects, e.g. the Paradise Bar...but I let myself be distracted and did not go to my office.

———

My friend goes into her fourteen-year-old daughter's bedroom in the morning and finds her sitting up in bed with a boy, a girl in the other bed, all three of them naked and chattering away, the daughter with love bites all over her neck. 'What's going on here?' The answer to this was not reported to me.

———

I am learning not to round a scene off. I like to leave the reader with one leg hanging over the edge—like E. M. Forster: 'but her voice floated out to swell the night's uneasiness.' I am trimming so close to the bone that a reader will require either good will or sensitive nerves. Naturally I would prefer the latter.

———

At a table near me sat three or four couples in their early thirties, bogging into their lunch—the men in shorts and T-shirts, the women with neat haircuts and modest clothes. There appeared in the cafe doorway two teenaged girls, one tiny and slim, the other plumper, taller, blonder, wearing on top of her head a flamboyantly tied pink bow. One of the men spotted the bow-girl. He gaped, caught the eye of another man at his table and gave a high-pitched, exaggerated laugh, dropping his face towards his plate. His companions, both women and men, looked up and followed suit. Their mockery was so loud, so rude, so uncalled-for, that I felt a burst of furious anger. I sat there staring at them with hatred. I thought I should have walked over to the first man who had laughed and said, 'What makes you think you've got the right to mock her? Quite a few people in this restaurant, if they didn't have better manners, might well point and laugh at *you*, for wearing those shorts and combing your hair into a fringe and holding your knife pencil-grip and drinking a *milkshake* with a *meal*.'

———

I'm not very skilful. I don't know, intellectually, what I'm trying to do. I want it all to be fast and light but to echo, and yet I don't want to be trapped in speed.

———

If I were a man of a pre-feminist generation, with a wife to provide my meals and clean my house and bring up my children, perhaps I would have a free mind for the large thought, the unlimited plan; and free time for night work, for hours without the necessity to think ahead about trivia—will we have veal for dinner or will I send the girls out for Lebanese take-away? Will the dog be lonely all day? Why didn't I defrost the fridge before I went to the market? Or is my mind slack and small for other reasons?

———

Flipped through an old poetry collection. Michael Drayton (who?): 'this ill-fac'd Munky'. I also read again *To Penshurst*: 'The blushing apricot and woolly peach', which for some reason brought up a sob.

———

Oh, frustration and despair, and last week I thought I was getting somewhere. I'm just a middle-level craftswoman. Saw a doco on TV about James Joyce. His vast reading, his intellect, his disorderliness, etc etc. Pooh, pooh, I cry, then the voice-over reads a paragraph from *The Dead* and I'm gasping with tears in my eyes.

———

I feel, when it goes badly, resentful and alarmed at the thought that I must spend the rest of my working life in this discomfort, inadequacy and grief. Grief is not too strong a word for what one feels before one's own weakness and mediocrity.

———

Virginia Woolf in her diary, about trying to write 'the mad scene in Regent's Park. I find I write it by clinging as tight to fact as I can, and write perhaps fifty words a morning…One feels about in a state of misery—indeed I made up my mind one night to abandon the book—and then one touches the hidden spring.'

———

I wish I knew some jolly intellectuals. Well, I do know U. She came over and stayed all arvo. She looked very pretty, with her thick curls well cut. She's lost a lot of weight but when I hugged her I felt the softness of flesh on her torso and realised with pleasure that I am, by comparison, hard and muscular. So I should be, with three aerobics classes a week. She talked endlessly about her husband. 'He was laughing as he played cards and sang along with the radio.' On the beach at night they fought. She hit him. He picked her up and flung her down on her back. 'He tells me terrible things about myself. And I can't help wondering if he's right.'

———

Went to work and fiddled round for half an hour, then began properly to feel it come, and got Athena and Philip into the cafe and the two girls with blood-sucking lipstick walk in, and THEN, oh joy, I swung into the first Poppy-and-Elizabeth scene, also Poppy alone with her school uniform: great, long sentences, one of them at least half a page! Delirious I ran downstairs and bought myself a pastie from the San Remo Bakery.

———

A visitor passed me a joint, also I drank some wine and some pernod and some port. (Only a little of each.) I want to read Freud's *Civilization and its Discontents* but I'm too stoned.

———

Musician: 'Do you ever find that you're working on some piece of art, and all it needs is one final leap to grasp it, but that in order to do it you're going to have to be not a nice person?'

Me: 'Yes. Every day.'

———

Each morning M comes into my room and gels her hair in front of the mirror. I love to watch her preen and skip. Her legs are long and brown in her gingham school dress—she's grown an inch since November. At the Vic Market she took me to see a certain pair of boots: little flat black suede ones, pointy like witches' shoes, that tied at the ankle. She obviously had no hope that I'd buy them. In a rush of generosity I said, 'Try them on.' She did. 'They fit!' she cried in a trembling voice. I bought them with a cheque. She was so excited I thought she'd burst into tears. 'I can't *believe* it!' she kept saying.

———

A big dry wind blew all night from the north. The street has been swept clean, and things have a dry sparkle. The eastern sides of chimneys are sharp and white. The air hisses along our house-side and buffets the small protuberances.

———

I went to work and broke through a brick wall or went round the side of it or dug under it or something: Athena's moral crisis and flight. The pace picked up incredibly. Present tense. A weaving and twining of many a disparate thread. All these years of note-taking, of being what Joan Didion calls 'a lonely, anxious re-arranger of things', are now paying off. I even got in the skier on the colour TV in the Italian cafe! That image has been dogging me for ten years at least.

———

T showed me two drawings of windows, each one with a different weather outside it.

'They're beautiful,' I said.

'Should I put them in the show?'

'I would.'

'But they don't sort of make any social or political comment, do they.'

'For God's sake, woman! They're windows! What more do you want?'

———

I admired some little dark blue lace-up leather boots K was wearing. He immediately took one off and suggested I try it on. Its slightly damp warmth.

———

P invited me to come to the framer and see her big pastels: she was showing them to some distant relatives who were interested in buying. The pictures were in a pile on a table, interleaved with tissue paper, waiting to be put into the dusty gold frames she had chosen for them. The ones I saw were striking. I liked them very much. She was asking $650 and I thought that was a fair price. One of the women was so antipathetic I could hardly believe it—an abrasive manner with the subtext 'Nobody makes a monkey out of *me*.' 'You're selling yourself short,' she said harshly, 'by showing us these unframed. I know for a *fact* that there's no point asking my husband to look at things flat out on a table. I know there's no *way* he'd be interested when they're not in frames.' At least a novelist doesn't have to provide decoration for people's new houses.

———

Will I ring up K and say, 'I like you; I am interested in you'? Or will I do the safe, housewifely thing, that is, nothing?

I will *go to work*.

———

And after that I went to my office and wrote, without fuss, in an hour and a half, the story the magazine asked me for. It's short, a piece of fluff somewhere between journalism and fiction, but it's nice, it's clean, and I like it. And I know today why people write short stories: because they are *short,* because your imagination can encompass the entire thing all in one go: whereas a novel will hang and hang over you, for a year at a time, like a mountain right behind the house blocking out the sun.

———

Reading Nadine Gordimer's *Selected Stories.* So marvellous, sensible, confident, modest-toned, informative, decent. I can't put it down. I read between putting on one item of clothing and the next. She *knows* a lot. 'She runs a tough line, in her introduction, on writers using other people's lives,' I say to B at Notturno; 'she says of *course* writers have to use other people's lives.' B gives me a wry look: 'Does she?' I take these remarks and glances of hers as reproaches, even warnings.

———

They lowered her coffin into the grave. The rabbi took out a little manila envelope full of fine dirt and sprinkled it over her. Across the heap of clayey soil that had been dug out of the hole lay four or five long-handled shovels and a rake. People (only men) from the watchers approached and took it in turns to scoop up spadefuls of the dirt and throw them in on top of her. When each had done his share he passed on the shovel to the next man, wiped his hands on his trouser thighs and stepped neatly out of the way. One man's pencil fell out of his shirt pocket on to the clay when he bent over to dig. He picked it up quickly, without looking round. They filled the grave right up to the top: they buried her. Put her to sleep. Tucked her into bed and drew the covers up over her—not leaving this last job to strangers. When it was done the rabbi said, 'If you would like to wash your hands, there are several taps over near the gate. Please be careful not to walk on the—please be careful not to walk on the—' He pointed to the sheets of corrugated iron that covered the nearby, freshly dug, empty graves.

———

At dawn I looked out my bedroom window and saw the dog trotting down the street towards the back gate with a huge knobby bone between her jaws: its knuckle shone white.

———

I didn't go to work today. But I did *work*. I wrote the account of the Jewish funeral. In other words, I practised. I took notes. I practised. I did not perform.

———

'He can't stand me when I sob and become abject,' says U. 'I repel him as Jews and homosexuals repel one.' Seeing my jaw drop she adds suavely, 'I know some people would think I was being anti-Semitic, but I'm not.'

———

The young tram conductor wore an earring that represented a Marmite jar, and several cheap silver rings, one a writhing snake. He did small dead-pan performances from time to time. 'Keep your legs apart,' he said to a woman who was standing near the door, holding a shopping bag between her ankles. '*What?*' she said. 'Keep your legs apart and you'll be able to balance better.' All the women within earshot glanced at each other and laughed. 'I thought for a minute he was going to say something else,' murmured the gap-toothed one beside me. 'Okay, gang, come on,' he called to a group of passengers in a corner. 'I used to say, "Fares please",' he said to his colleague out of the corner of his mouth, 'but that was bloody ridiculous.'

———

On the Overland to Adelaide I read on in *The Way of All Flesh*. It's quite leisurely, but full of the most shrivelling hatred and bitterness. Dawn. We stopped for a few minutes at Tailem Bend. Now the day is clear, the sky pale blue. The hills are bald and rounded. A triangular dam is so still that I can see the ripples on its floor.

The line swings south and sun bursts into my 'roomette'.

———

Elizabeth Jolley, in her dutiful way, tried to inform me of the literary status of a woman in an ugly flowered dress and thick pancake make-up to whom she was introducing me. The woman cut across her: 'I've published two novels,' she said, 'and countless stories in the US.' *Countless* was the word she used.

———

Elizabeth read shyly from a prepared speech full of enjoyable quotations from Tolstoy and Kleist. I love her careful old-fashioned manners. She paused at one point and said into the microphone, 'I'll just have a drink of…this delicious…' She sipped from a plastic glass of mineral water. 'Ah, yes. Lovely.' I wanted to rush up and cast myself at her sandalled feet.

———

I was astonished when O said to me yesterday in the street, 'I've changed my mind about clothes. I used to think they weren't important and had no meaning, but now I see they're a way of making statements about yourself—even, if I can say it, an attempt to communicate.' This is a huge concession, from a man who once said to me irritably, '*You* make judgments about people based on what *shoes* they're wearing.' (Which is true.)

———

The married couple argue in their bedroom. Even with the door closed I hear her shout in a rough, angry voice, 'Look! I didn't put *any* bloody Milo in your coffee!' A moment later she passes my room with a histrionic sigh.

———

When I listen to other writers reading from their work, I sometimes try for a moment to examine, before I give in to it, the way my mind is developing its visual response to the tale. And I realise with a joyful feeling that the same miraculous thing might happen to people who hear me reading from *my* book.

————

After the panel session J and I went, shivering as the day grew cooler, to the piano bar and had some bad coffee and an extraordinary conversation. It went on for at least an hour, and involved what I suppose was me questioning him closely about the way he lives his religion. He had already, in answer to questions by mail, written me an enormous letter, setting it out and also making apologies (as if I'd think he was proselytising) for 'boring' me 'with this stuff'. He talked about wanting to live like Christ, a life of 'submission and humility'. (I'm striking a false note, somehow—like many very important conversations it exists in my memory as a particular kind of mood or emotional state and not as precise dialogue.) He talked a great deal about his father, whom he loves and admires, but also in answer to my awkward questioning about their use of the Bible etc: 'How do you…sort of…organise your approach to it?' 'I go to it for…enlightenment, or information on a particular point, or for entertainment. And I write with a Bible beside me and on top of that a bloody great Concordance.' He told me about the book he's writing, and how it comes from his own childhood. It sounds beautiful, and I think very good, and daring—a cloud stands over the house, and at the end it comes down and fills the house as the boy goes for oil to anoint his father. I was very moved by this story. And I thought again, *I* want to write like that—to have people doing huge things of symbolic meaning.

By the time we left the bar we were blue with cold and shivering. I took his arm and said, feeling shy but that it was necessary, 'I'm really glad we're becoming friends.' 'Oh, so am I!' he said, and tried to put his arm around my shoulders. We were laughing and embarrassed, almost tearful, handicapped by our heavy bags of books, making clumsy movements of affection. He said that when I'd started asking him about Christianity he'd been afraid it would be the end of the friendship: he said he was used to this happening, to being teased and laughed at.

'In the bar,' I said, 'I kept thinking I was going to keel over. I don't know if it's the cold, or if it's a spiritual crisis!'

'Oh, I'm used to it,' he said, making a two-fisted pounding gesture. 'Working out what I think about things.'

As we approached the other writers at the tent we walked more and more slowly.

I said, 'I think there's something huge, and one day it's going to roll over me.'

I don't even know what I meant by that. But I've known it in some secret part of myself for years. As if I have a puny, tenacious little ego, which is straining at holding back a *mighty force*.

———

I was awake most of the night. At nine in the morning I finally passed out and slept till noon. When I saw J at the tents I felt shy. I didn't know how to follow up the shocking intimacy of the conversation. But he greeted me simply and asked how I was. We sat on the rim of the grassy slope and watched the world go by. An academic I had met once or twice came scrambling up the rise towards us. She said hello to me, and then, while her smile faded, she stared right into J's face and up and down his body, in the most blatantly curious and speculative fashion. It was as if she were raking him with her nails and could not wait to get away and examine them for clues. She moved on and he turned to me. Under the freckles his face had gone white: 'Did you see that?' 'Yep. They'll all be saying we're having an affair. That's how they think.' He dropped his forehead against my shoulder: 'I think that's *rude*. I think that's really *rude*.'

———

Why do I write down this stuff? Partly for the pleasure of seeing the golden nib roll over the paper as it did when I was ten.

———

Home. My lovely bed. My bright room.

———

I wrote, straight after the scene in the topless bar, a scene between Athena and Dexter in the lobby of a hotel. It made my skin stand up, the cruelty and honour that emerged between them in about a hundred and fifty words.

———

Yesterday F and I went to a lecture by a man who worked with Einstein and is renowned for his ability to explain his theories to laypeople. But it had been advertised in the paper and by the time we got there, five minutes before it was to start, it was so packed that crowds were shoving at each door and people who looked faint were stumbling out gasping, 'I can't stand it in there.' Disappointed, we drove to a swanky bar in Fitzroy and had a cocktail. We were happy. I thought, How lucky I am to be married to this lovely guy!

———

Two people driving at night. On the radio comes a song by Mondo Rock: 'Come, Said the Boy'. One person thinks, 'That song was on last time we drove somewhere together. But I won't mention it, for fear of appearing sentimental.' The other person says, 'This song came on last time.'

———

The day I realised my novel was going to be a short one, and that its domestic subject and setting were quite proper, I walked home from work and passed a print shop, in the window of which stood a copy of that van Gogh painting of the inside of his bedroom: floorboards, a bed, two cane-bottomed chairs, a window. I thought, That's a beautiful painting. And it's only the inside of a room.

Was bound, but now am free.

Two good rousing hymns were sung at the wedding. But why was she marrying this man, who is plainly unworthy of her?

To Paul Crossley's piano masterclass at the Con. After three hours of intense concentration I was completely exhausted. His teaching was very challenging. He was not a giver of praise or even of encouragement, except to one girl who played Ravel; everyone else played Debussy. I loved the language he used: not only because it was clever and striking but because it showed me that the way I have been trying to write about music is not, as I had feared, hopelessly romantic or amateurish. 'A furtive texture,' he said. 'A harmonic wash in the left hand. Then he clears the texture. Let the harmony settle again, before we take off. *Hover* above what you're going to do.' The concept of *phrasing* began to have meaning for me, not to mention *texture*. And now I know what the pedal is for: to 'avoid breaking the sound'.

Paul Fussell, in *Abroad: British Literary Travelling Between the Wars*, quotes Evelyn Waugh: 'Conversation seriously pursued...consists of narrative alternating with "comment".'

A tremendous wind, cold, gritty and in powerful, frightening gusts, blew all day from the north. Then, late in the afternoon a heavy, soaking rain fell. I went to the gym. B was there. She said, 'I'm lonely.' Her face seemed to quiver. I didn't know what to say.

As I approach the end of the novel I can feel it pulling itself into shape, as if I were only a secretary. Never had this experience before—the characters getting the bit between their teeth.

———

B and I saw Robert Meldrum and the magician Doug Tremlett in *The Tempest*. They brought such delicacy, humour and wonder to Prospero and Ariel that I was on the verge of tears. Tremlett, it having been established from the start that Ariel was in bondage to Prospero through gratitude, fear and love, seemed to be holding himself back from evaporating. No chiffon, no light-footedness—he was a solid presence in well-filled white overalls, a turquoise T-shirt and clean runners, his hair cut short with one tiny curved lock on his forehead. He did it all by the extreme slowness of his movements, his density, his powerful focus. His magician's tricks were graceful, breath-taking, yet anything he picked up—a hat, a cane, a scarf—he imbued with a vital importance. What a play! Virginia Woolf's right—Shakespeare is 'incandescent'.

———

And this morning, Sire, I, your handmaiden, *l'umile ancella*, wrote eight pages, and was content.

———

G came in with his pockets sprouting contracts. We talked about good deals; how to be paid what one is worth.

———

The prostitutes are small-mouthed girls who call to a man, 'Wanna girl?' 'No.' 'Sure?' Not many of them about in the morning. I saw a man of twenty-five or so standing at a rubbish bin. His movements, even as he stood still, drew my attention, and when I glanced at him I saw something dreadful in his face: a thuggish thickness in the mouth and jaw, eyes oppressed by a great, dense knot of anguish between the brows. He continually clasped his hands and flicked up his elbows like a boxer loosening up before a fight. He uttered wordless sounds, strangled grunts, as if he were trying to speak but, like Caliban, were only earth.

———

T wanted to come with B and me to aerobics. From the lobby we could see a man inside the gym doing those repetitive jumps where you keep both hands on the floor. 'Seems a bit *funny*,' said T, 'doing that kind of thing on the *carpet*. Wearing it out.' I shudder with secret pleasure at her criticisms. On our way out afterwards the dopy girl at the desk called to her, 'How'd you go?' 'Oh,' she said grimly, 'okay. I suppose. But I thought it was a bit masochistic.' '*Good!*' cries the girl, beaming.

———

U commented on 'Postcards from Surfers'. 'Terrific writing. Especially the opening.'

I wonder if one day I'll ever be able to present such a surface that nobody will be able to say '*especially* the…'

———

At Castlemaine it was very warm. Even the night was milder than I'd expected. Discouraging memories presented themselves as I roved about the slopes picking up firewood. What does this almost-finished book say about men and women? There doesn't seem to be a way of planning this. My attitude emerges as the story tells itself. I couldn't help agonising over it, thinking of the smallness of my scope, the ordinariness of it, its bourgeois nature. What critics will say. What my friends will think and not say. How I will appear before the world. Oh *shut up*.

We stood on a slope and watched the moon rise: up it came, round as a drawing. We saw how the stars became brighter, sat deeper in space. M and her friend struggled to philosophise. They laughed, and were excited. 'I can't sort of *grasp*,' said M, 'what there is *beyond* the universe.' We all played the ukulele when we felt like it. She made up a song called 'In the Paradise Cafe'. The boy read

Tom Sawyer aloud: he couldn't restrain his laughter. I woke at two in the morning, lay there filled with a kind of shame. Looking out at the moonlit bush, silver by night, grey by day. Don't be so proud. Accept criticism, accept editing and guidance. No one will think less of you. I got up at dawn. There were tasks and I did them: finding wood, making a fire, boiling water. The sky became more orange and the wind began to stir. The coming light. It creeps across the dull grass and pinkens it, between the thin trunks. My panic left me. The problem becomes merely the work I still have to do, rather than an indictment of my whole personality and talent and social position.

———

I feel scraggy-haired, thin-cheeked, masculine. At the service station I saw myself drop into a masculine mode: 'talking to a mechanic'. I did not like this but it seemed to happen spontaneously: my hands went into my trouser pockets, my utterances came out sideways in laconic, deprecating half-sentences. I felt like my father.

———

Loneliness without the pleasure of solitude. What will become of us. Awful tension. Shoulders like iron bars. F doesn't like me. Why doesn't he like me? Am I so unlikeable?

———

'Ah well, you can be optimistic and totally without hope. One's basic nature is totally without hope, and yet one's nervous system is made out of optimistic stuff.' —Francis Bacon in *Interviews with Francis Bacon,* David Sylvester

———

T's house is being painted. I love the way she sees colours and shows them to me: the room that looks white until you've been in it for five minutes and then you start to notice that it's grey. The 'teal green' corduroy she's going to make into curtains.

———

I rewrote the dinner scene, tried to convey the flippancy and darting of their conversation by a careful series of non sequiturs.

———

An old friend came over for dinner and I was full of dislike for her. She was passive and idle in company, spoke sharply in a 'doesn't suffer fools gladly' manner, offered nothing, and when the meal was over put her booted foot on the corner of the table.

———

Spectacular dawns I see from my bedroom window. Sometimes I look out at this richness of sky—layer after layer of colour rising from a bed of dove-grey cloud—and I think, This is a rich person's view, or an adult's view. As if I were not entitled to it, or had it only temporarily, or on sufferance.

———

M comes in from playing hockey with her friend.

'How did you get home?'

'We went to Lygon Street and got a free meal at Tiamo, then we—'

'How did you get a free meal at Tiamo?'

'We just begged and begged. We said, "Oh, go on—give us one," and they did.'

———

I typed THE END. I rushed home 'dizzy with unconsumed excitement'. Could not seem to get much of a response from the people present. 'I've finished. I've typed the words THE END.' 'What—again?' 'Guess what, I typed THE END.' 'You'll have more to do.' But then someone went out to get champagne and they made a fuss of me, which embarrassed me, for I felt I should have been mature enough and tactful enough to have demanded less of them. I will never get this right.

———

Is this 'the artist's' fate? Always to be loved less than I need; or somehow to repel love, or what is seen in the myth or dream of our society as normal marital love? I feel I'm reaching my strength, in my work, but there's a corresponding falling-away…It's terribly sad.

———

T rang to ask me to go to a film with her. 'It's a twelve-minute short at the festival. It's called *Passionless Moments*. As soon as I saw the title I went to the phone and rang you.'

———

I'm worried about my clothes: that they will be too informal for Japan. But I've just thought, If I have to put up with 'the artist's loneliness' I will take 'the artist's prerogative', i.e. looking slightly peculiar.

———

I had never before seen a diplomat go into action. She held a glass in her hand, and smiled, and out of her mouth poured a stream of bland, silly, obvious, trivial clichés, while her face was lit by the same expression of warmth and intelligence that appears on it when she is conversing with her friends.

———

'And when I got back to Canberra,' said the Japanese professor, 'I found that four out of my five colleagues had divorced and remarried.'

'Had they married younger women?'

'Yes. Students. Graduate students.'

We laughed.

'Sad, isn't it. Pathetic.'

'One professor had gone to marriage counselling. The counsellor was a woman. She advised him to get a divorce. Now *they* are married.'

We laughed again, looking away from each other.

I said, 'It's almost immoral.' By then we were both doubled up.

This is what will happen to me. He will leave me and go off with someone younger. In a novel I read by Fumiko Enchi, mention was made of terrible revenges that scorned women wreak on men (spirit possession for example), and of women who 'dissolve their whole beings in the anguish of forgiving men'.

———

'How should I approach Bartók, or Webern, or Schoenberg?'

'Immersion,' says the South African. 'Repetition. But if on a particular day you don't like it, stop listening. That's how I learned.'

———

The huge salesman in the hotel bar mentioned where he came from in an apologetic tone. 'Queens. In Nyork. Have you heard of it?'

'Course I've heard of it! There probably isn't a single place in the USA that I haven't heard of!'

'How about Boise, Idaho?'

'I've seen it written, but never heard it said.'

———

In my dream someone said to me, 'I want to look for some graves.' I said, 'So you can desecrate them?' Even in my sleep I was laughing.

———

I'm starved. Of love.

———

The chief attraction at the reception was a fourteen-year-old wunderkind of the piano in connection with whose name Mozart has been mentioned. He was a pale, soft, neurasthenic creature with feverish eyes set close together, and a lisp. I looked at him with distaste and remembered something Nabokov said about youthful prodigies: 'their sad, pear-shaped bottoms'. He kept rushing up to his guardian (a New York Jewish lawyer who was entertaining me and

the diplomat with stories of the young man's successes and talents)
and chattering in an oddly child-like way about Maria Callas, whom
he ostentatiously admired. After one of his excitable approaches, he
dashed away and the lawyer turned to us with an expressive look.
The diplomat said, 'Is he always like this?' 'Worse,' said the lawyer.
'He's a pain in the ass.'

————

The diplomat and her daughter were yelling at each other about
leotards. The daughter went for the jugular: they were nothing
but vanity; the sporting activity is the point; what you looked like
while you were doing it was irrelevant. 'That seems to me a rather
puritanical position,' I said, dexterously wielding my chopsticks. 'I
like extreme positions,' shouted the girl. 'I *hate* middle positions.'
The wind went out of the mother's sails and she sat there looking
at her plate.

————

'What sort of a life did you have in Paris?' asked the old Japanese
scholar.
      'I was lonely in Paris.'
      A smile cracked his severe professorial face. '*Everybody* is lonely
in Paris!'

————

Yesterday the diplomat asked me if I'd like to have my hair cut at her
hairdresser, 'so you won't have to worry about it.' I politely declined,
but I knew she really meant, 'Your hair looks awful.' I remembered the Frenchwoman in Toulouse who put kohl round my eyes,
stood back, and said, 'You look *much* better like that.' I can't bear
this kind of thing, it makes me feel quite mortified with shame,
ugliness and self-consciousness. Like when Whatsername said,
with that smile she gets when she's about to be daringly frank, 'I like
your hair when it's pushed back at the sides.' I felt like screaming,

'*I* like my hair when it's all shaved off! So get fucked!'

Four groups of firemen in mediaeval-looking costumes walked, one after another, on to the bare, dimly lit stage, and chanted. At first, when I realised that nothing else was going to happen, I imagined that I would soon become bored, but I didn't. The chanting produced a peculiar feeling of being outside time. They did dangerous stunts: one man would shin up a ten-foot bamboo ladder that was held upright by a dozen or more of his colleagues, and would cast himself into impossible positions by twisting his closely trousered legs round the top of the ladder and balancing; then, tapping one palm against the bamboo as if to attract attention, he would extend his torso in a graceful posture. The old woman beside me turned to me in excitement and we laughed together and clapped wildly. People played tiny breathy flutes, a drum, and something I couldn't see in the half-light that sounded like a harmonica but was held perpendicular to the mouth. A great crowd of men, dressed in ordinary trousers, shirts and street shoes, walked slowly on to the stage and made a rhythmic *shh-shh-shhh*, like water squirting. The little flutes wailed above the shh-ing. This went on, crescendo and decrescendo, for what must have been five or ten minutes, but it never occurred to me to look at my watch. Just when I thought I couldn't endure the stillness and the rhythmic sound another second, the musicians began to walk very slowly in a big circle, single file, round the shh-ing men, still playing, and returned to their positions behind. The meaning of all this I could not begin to guess at. At the very end the entire company stood massed in curved rows at an angle to the audience, and the four leaders, older men, sang a song. A very old man, thickset, with an almost shaven grey-stubbled head, was ushered on from the wings and stood in front while the chanting started again. Then one of the four leaders cried out something to

the audience and everyone in the theatre clapped their hands—
two, three, four, in unison—and shouted out a word, and it was
over. Everyone applauded and sprang up smiling and laughing and
poured out of the building.

'What did he say at the end?'

'He said, "Now let's all do something together!"'

———

Back in my hotel room I put 100 yen into the TV and saw: a car
crash, the dead man's formal headshot; a conference of world
leaders, Thatcher, Mitterrand, and Nakasone; two huge guys arm-
wrestling; and a modern soap in which a man in a suit hit very hard
in the face, knocking her to the floor, a woman dressed in a kimono;
this scene occurred in a restaurant—something I cannot *imagine*
happening here.

———

A visiting Australian professor lightly suggested that when I give
my 'lectures and seminars' I should speak slowly, enunciate clearly,
and keep my vocabulary down to about a thousand words. Oh, why
did I come? I long to go to Kyoto and stand in a peaceful garden. Do
they have gardens in Tokyo? I miss my girl. The schoolgirls here
have small waists, slightly bowed legs, rounded cheekbones, thick
swinging hair. I ate a delicious breakfast: rice, pickles, miso soup,
two slices of cold omelette, and the front half of a dried fish.

———

A long, absorbing documentary at a cinema in Roppongi—old
people in a mountain village talking straight to camera about their
lives and families, their occupations (charcoal burning; silkworm
farming), and *the war.* Many black-and-white still photos, riveting.
Their handsome, sober, tender faces, as youths, as soldiers. A man
told how his regiment was dumped in New Guinea unarmed and
unprovisioned. They buried unripe bananas in the sand. They died

of dysentery and malnutrition. He was the only one of his mates who survived. 'I was ashamed to go home. I didn't know where the ship was going. I saw the pine trees. "There are no pines in the tropics. It must be Japan! *Tadaima*!"' An old woman spoke in an artlessly poetic way about a fireworks display in her village, how people came from further down the mountain and sat in her garden to watch. 'And the most beautiful were flags that waved and fluttered as they fell. There were red ones among them.' Gracefully flexing her wrists she swooped her wrinkled hands back and forth in front of her face, down and down and down. A soldier told how his superior officer made him polish boots so much that he had no time to polish his own. '"Stick out your tongue," he said to me. "You can lick them clean." So I did. I licked and licked. *Erghh*. They were covered in dung. But I was a farmer, it wasn't dirty.'

No wonder they lost the war.

It's raining. They have laid the garden chairs on their sides in the bar under my window.

A bunch of small boys in school hats like inverted pudding bowls was scuffling on the pavement in play. One of them stepped back and accidentally trod on my foot. He turned his face up to me with an almost cringing expression, bowed and said, '*Sumimasen*!'

K is very forward with me, but always with the shy person's glossy and frightening barrier of witticisms. He's small and clever and furious. He has bees in his bonnet. He talks a lot, likes talking about himself. An interrupter, an earbasher. I have to push for my share of airtime. I'm not tough enough to fight off his cross-cutting technique. He asks for, and expects in quite a bare-faced way, a great deal of my time: he's lonely, unable to be on his own, demanding, nervous, depressive. He says he likes my work. He says it's 'fabulous'. I can never accept that kind of comment. I just can NOT accept or compute it.

––––––

I now have two weeks to absolutely *currycomb* the tics and adverbs and adjectives-in-pairs out of this goddamn novel.

––––––

P lay on her bed and wept. She was grieving over her isolation as an artist. 'I'd like to talk about things with other painters, the men, but they know so much, and I feel sure they'd realise how ignorant I am of all the things they know, and they won't think I'm worth talking to.' This sense of herself as a charlatan or a phoney is something I am all too familiar with. But I don't feel anguished about lack of contact with other writers. I must be more secretive than she is. I hide to work and I have nothing to talk about. Chatting with some smart-arse about semicolons and long sentences is all very well, but it's no more than chat.

––––––

A man once told me, years after we broke up, that he had built a little shrine inside himself, and that I had got in and kicked it all to bits. At the time I had no idea what he meant. But now I get it, watching another man hovering reverently over the little altar of his sufferings, wanting me to approach and genuflect.

––––––

Culture Club is in town. Boy George is a plain-looking lad, though journalists go on about how 'pretty' he is. He'll have a double chin in a couple of years, and he has large, white, soft-looking hands, but his voice is gorgeous and there's something good-natured and undramatic about his personality in interviews that makes me like him. He relaxes all the time into a vague cheerfulness, and so does the viewer. When he talks I feel like laughing in a drippy kind of way.

———

At home we played General Knowledge. F got out his guitar and made up a song about the answer to each question. He was so clever and imaginative, parodying styles and making up rhymes, we were in fits.

———

We heard about a boy who lit some gunpowder. It exploded and skinned his face.

———

'He's reading your manuscript. He says it would be better if it had chapters.'

———

Why married people have affairs: you feel luckier, with a happy secret place in your imagination in which to refresh yourself. My mistake in the past has been to keep it on the front boiler, cooking briskly, instead of turning off the gas and letting it go cold.

———

I'd like to go to Sydney. Visit my friends. Loll on G's couch in Elizabeth Bay, listen to *La Cathédrale engloutie*, look out the window at the masts, ask him why he wants to get married in a church. Lean on R's cupboard-front in Newtown and watch her dealing quietly with her kids, listen to her light, quick, self-effacing voice, her slight lisp; be near her barely glimpsed and brilliant inner life. Walk in the Botanic Gardens and see the Opera House eggshells shine, water and ships sparkle.

———

'I've got no friends,' sobbed P.

I roared at her. 'What are you TALKING about? You've got DOZENS! You're just too lazy to go and see them! Look in your fucking address book!'

———

'This is going to sound very reactionary,' says K, ' but I don't think women should smoke in the street.'

'*I* don't think they should *eat* in the street,' I say. 'I don't think *anyone* should.'

———

F so rarely buys clothes that he can barely bring himself to be polite to shop assistants.

———

But I don't like lying.

———

Some men were loading sheets of building material on to a skip. I walked past and seconds later heard a colossal crash. I ran back. The sheets had toppled and pinned a workman's lower leg against the side of the skip. He was dangling upside down, leg caught, knee bent, head and shoulders and arms resting in crucified position on the pavement. He was uttering strange cries—not harsh, not screams, but light, rhythmic, descending moans, like the sound of someone making love. His Italian workmates were calling out. A shop assistant ran back into the jeans store to call an ambulance. A small crowd gathered. 'Lie 'im down!' called a woman. I walked away.

———

She wrote that my comments on her manuscript were 'like a refreshing breeze blowing into a stuffy room'. How generously people other than me can accept criticism!

———

G called about the book. His voice sounded very close and warm, as if he'd been laughing. 'Hel? I loved it. I laughed, I cried, I shivered, I hugged myself.'

———

It's raining silver and the sky to the east is blazing with a vivid double rainbow, a fatly arched one. Mad spring.

———

'I used to hit her,' says the man in the bar.

'What sort of hitting?'

'Up against the wall. Backhander across the face. That sort of thing. And it would turn into a fuck. Because there are some women who goad a bloke into violence. It gives them the moral advantage. Years later, after I'd gone away lacerating myself for having been a violent, woman-bashing pig, she came to see me and said, "I wanted to tell you that I see now that I provoked you all those times, that I goaded you into hitting me."'

'Wow. That was honest. How did you feel then?'

'*Furious.* That she hadn't told it to me years earlier, and let me go on punishing myself all that time.'

'Maybe it took her that long to understand it about herself. I think it was big of her.'

He goes silent. Flicks me a complicated look.

———

M has her school friend over for the night. Together they enter an element quite separate from ordinary life—male and female characters, invented accents, vast fantasies, paroxysms of malicious laughter. There's something terrifying about them.

———

I love F and I want him to be joyful. I'd like to say to him, 'Let's chuck the whole jigsaw up in the air and see what comes down.' But he wants to hash things over, to make sardonic remarks, to criticise again my horrible personality. The love and attention I have to give him wither on the vine. A line from some forgotten book: 'We always want those we are hurting to be gay.'

———

A visit from the new parents. She feeds the baby from her enormous breasts, so big she has to lie on her back and lay him belly down across her bosom like a tiny mountaineer.

———

The Cuban author Guillermo Cabrera Infante says that the writer is important not because he can write but because he can listen. His job is 'to catch the human voice in flight'.

———

Sex fades, and if one has chosen the right person something else comes to fill the space it leaves. Maybe one day I'll read this over and be overwhelmed with *bitter laughter*.

———

In the library I sat down with three translations of Rilke's *Duino Elegies*. Translators are a mob of cheats, vain and attention-seeking. An impossible profession. So I stumbled from word to word in the original, without a dictionary. I wanted to groan and weep with frustration. All that knowledge I once had, dissipated through lack of use.

———

Stranger at the lunch table: 'This is the day after my husband walked out. He came home on my wedding anniversary and said he'd reached a stage in his life where he didn't want the responsibility of a family. I've taken some tranquillisers. That's why I'm not having any wine.' Her elder boy, she said, took to his bed, then asked her, 'What did I do wrong?' The younger boy cried for a quarter of an hour, then came out of his room and said, 'Why don't we all have a game of cards?' Maybe it was the tranquillisers, but something about her calm chilled me. I sat beside her, aware that I was gazing carefully and curiously into her face as she talked. She was very good-looking, with eyes set in deep sockets. 'I'm a pretty tough lady,' she said. 'I'll survive.'

———

A little girl today at the lolly shop. Seven or so. Silvery blond hair pulled into wispy pigtails. Jeans rolled to the knees, and the most extraordinary legs and feet. Her calves were as developed as a dancer's, slim and with muscles clearly outlined, almost squared. She sprang and leapt about with her sister. She crept after a bird that had hopped under the table looking for crumbs. Something heart-breakingly strong about her legs and high-arched feet.

———

The mother asked the father to go to the counter for an ice cream. He turned to go, then flung himself back to her with a grimace of discontent and said, '*You* go. I feel an idiot, holding your purse.'

———

'Marriage *is* a kind of…mystical union,' said the new father. 'You're not only you any more.' Mystical union. I stared at him. The size of the statement, the theological term, dropped casually at the table. I have never, ever felt any such thing, and do not expect to. Like R, I feel that 'in the end, there's only you'.

———

The newspaper interviewer, young and intelligent and pretty, with a thick plait, seemed disappointed that I was not 'rebellious'. 'Did you have a message?' she asked. 'Were you trying to criticise middle class values?' 'No. I was just trying to tell a story the best way I could.'

———

Young male photographer: 'Come on. Big smile. Love those big smiles.'

'Please don't tell me to smile.'

'You look starched.'

'I *am* starched. I am a starched *person*.'

———

Peacocks in the courtyard outside my office window engage in what looks like mating preliminaries: the male puts up his splendiferous tail and strolls about, stretching it forward, curving it over his head, bowing and turning and preening like a Brazilian drag queen. I have a powerful urge to run out there and sink the toe of my boot into his fluffy arse.

———

We rode together into the big park. Spring flowers everywhere— freesias in throngs, and startling growths of kangaroo paw with its dark red, *vividly* red stalks. From an eminence I saw a vast cloud of rain moving in from upriver. It hit us and she fell off her bike—came off slowly and gracefully into a patch of thick grass. It cushioned her. The rain poured down and we were doubled over with laughter. She was too weak from laughing to get up. She knelt there in the undergrowth bowed over with her palms on her thighs.

———

'I burnt all your letters,' he said. 'The postcards exploded. I thought that was significant.'

———

First student: 'That's a cliché.'
    Second student: 'I put it there on *purpose!* To *disorient* people!'

———

The strange couple arrived late at the dinner party. She paraded in, chin high, teeth blazing. She had skinny little legs and a short dress that barely reached her knees. No sooner had they sat down than she said to her husband, whose little legs were as stumpy as hers were stick-like, 'Dougal, would you go out to the car and get my bag?' He sat still. We all looked at him. 'I won't be able to find it,' he said sulkily. 'Oh, just run out and get it,' she said, as if brushing aside a child's objection. And he did. She spoke with a kind of serene boastfulness: 'One of the reasons why I know more than many people is that we had servants, a butler, a boy—and I read a great deal.' Throughout the meal she was always moulding her husband: 'Dougal. Tuck your serviette into your belt, so you won't keep dropping it and having to hunt for it. *That's* better.' I worked hard for hours, asking questions to keep myself awake. Late in the evening her husband turned to me: 'So. What's s' special about *you*?' I surprised myself by saying calmly, 'Why are you speaking to me like that? I don't know how to answer.' He backed down at once. He said he had taken up golf, and played by himself at the crack of dawn.

––––––

Eduard Limonov, in *It's Me, Eddie*, describes a thirty-year-old woman as 'ageing', 'in the autumn of her life'.

––––––

Elizabeth Jolley spoke about the huge hotel the Toronto festival had put her in: 'The first night, there was a white flower in the bathroom. The second night, a scarlet flower. Of course this sort of thing is completely wasted on someone of my age.'

––––––

'He's a sweet bloke, isn't he.'

'He is. Adorable. But with such vast areas of ignorance! Not knowing what ravioli was!'

––––––

I came out of the Arts building this evening after my class and saw a huge, pale-orange moon rising out of the Swan River. It was so big that for a moment I didn't know what it was. And then I wanted to shout to people passing, 'Why aren't we all standing still gazing at it? Or down on our knees praying to it?'

––––––

She had long smooth dark hair drawn back off her ears and temples by two combs, and skin that at first I thought was made-up; as the evening progressed and we struck up conversation, she came and sat beside me and I saw that her skin was bare, and quite perfect.

I liked her. She was extremely slim, and was wearing a cobalt blue jumper with shoulder pads. Once, in an absent moment, she pushed her left sleeve up past her elbow. This gesture made her seem less perfectly presented; it was the moment at which her beauty ceased to repel me. I looked happily at her lovely face while she talked.

————

'Some people are Christians,' said J, 'some people are atheists or agnostics, and some people agonise about it. They're sub-Christians. I think that's what *you* are.'

————

The house: an uncertainty of taste, a bit too cluttered, furniture not quite the right shape for the room that contains it; but pleasant, light and clean. If I owned a house I would always be getting rid of things.

————

Homosexual man ten years older than I am: 'My parents always took care to teach us that we mustn't show our emotions—that they are tedious, and a bore and a nuisance to other people. I learned this lesson so well that as an adult I have found myself in a situation where someone will leave me because he thinks I don't need him.'

————

At dinner the surgeon asked me why I write with a pen rather than using a dictaphone or a word processor. 'Why would I?' 'Because it's faster and more efficient.' 'But it's my life's work. I'm not in a hurry.' I was surprised to hear myself make that answer.

————

When I play the piano I have a lot of noble and generous thoughts. Moral thoughts. Correctives to what I actually *do*. In my life I have gone round hurting people. I would like to ask everyone I know: On what basis do you make moral decisions? I know what they'd say: 'You've always been good at getting what you want.' But now

I can't, and I don't like it.

———

A dream about a heap of old fans that I found on the floor behind a couch. They were all made of ivory and clearly of value. I picked them up, one by one. They were heavy, smooth and very beautiful. One of them consisted of so many slats that I couldn't open it right out: as if it were a full circle of slats, and not in a fan form at all—I could not handle its richness. Another had too few slats, only two or three, and even those were so loosely connected that they flopped in the hand, like keys on a ring.

'What could a fan represent?' I asked my hostess.

She looked slightly panicky: 'Fresh air?'

———

The only passionate love that can co-exist with civilised daily working life is the love we have for our children. The other sort either loses its madness and becomes something else, or blows everything sky-high.

———

I opened the front door. It was the professor. He handed me the cheque for the week's work, and said without preliminary, 'What's speed?' His son had rung him from Sydney, asking for money 'for a ticket home'. He showed me a photo of a gaunt, good-looking boy of twenty or so, dressed in fashionable rags, his hair with that gelled, torn-out-by-the-roots look. Thank God for Javo. My girl sees no romance in *that*.

———

'I should tell you I've read your book in proof,' said the visiting writer. 'Brendan had it at his place. He was sure you wouldn't mind.' He added, in a light, dismissing tone, 'I rather enjoyed it.'

Is that *all* you feel about it? Is that *really* all?

———

With the drawing pens K gave me I begin to understand the limitations of the rapidograph: so rigid, the line unvarying. With the dip pen you get thick and thin, and curlicues, and the way you can draw a striped jumper is absolutely *voluptuous*.

———

The new parents were moving house and I went to give them a hand. I helped them carry boxes and cartons for an hour or so. Eventually I said, 'Well, I'm off now.' He looked at me with an expression I couldn't read. His face was white, even strained. 'You were mad to come,' he said. 'Dunno why you stayed so long.' I cried on the way home.

———

'Did you get my letters?'

'Yes. It's the problem of timing. When I needed the letters they didn't come, and when they came I didn't need them.'

———

In the roadhouse the food was what you'd expect and I loved it. I ordered a nut sundae. 'What flavour topping?' asked the lacklustre waitress. 'Chocolate,' I whispered, flooded with bliss.

———

I'd go outside except that a large Alsatian is loose in the motel compound, roaming about in that smooth, low-backed way they have; I heard deep barking first, then looked out and saw the dog, posing like a dingo against the swimming-pool fence, favouring one hind leg and dragging its lead.

———

One of Elizabeth Jolley's stories starts: 'Every small town has some kind of blessing.' And so does every blighted motel. The tiny room, the sagging bed, but when I climbed up and cranked open the bathroom window, what I saw was a sunny morning and a big paddock full of what I ignorantly imagined was wheat. Something yellow.

———

Rereading my letter I saw I had smudged the ink while turning a page, at such a point that he'd think it was the blot of a tear. Oh *no*. I threw it in the bin.

———

'If I asked you now to drop everything and run away with me,' said K, 'you wouldn't, would you.'

(*Hangs her head*) 'No. But I would've. Once.'

'What changed?'

'I started thinking.'

———

Peter Handke's notebooks, *The Weight of the World*. Intense pleasure at the tininess of his observations. Actually, they're not observations so much as junctions between moments. When I read them I feel that I am not after all crazy or even weird. I feel strengthened, *private*, encouraged. I feel the worth of very small things. The whole cast of his mind is familiar to me.

———

Indira Gandhi has been assassinated.

'They got her and missed Maggie,' said F.

'Only just.'

'She'd finished cleaning her teeth only a few moments before.'

'It's because those idiots mess around with bombs,' I said. 'Guns are more accurate.'

As if we were professionals, or had considered such actions ourselves.

———

P wheeled her bike towards me across the grass. Her shirt was the colour of the grass, her bike basket that of the daisies. It was spring.

———

When people have been drinking they taste of wood.

A young man sings tunefully and wordlessly in the street: 'dada–*da* da–*da*dad*a*.' Writing those sounds, a blast of memory—being taught to write. At Manifold Heights State School. A flash of the old building. The objective correlative is the loop loop loop action of dadadadadadada.

I love to make F laugh. How handsome he looks when his face is filled with teeth.

'"I want you to go on living for many years." I was glad to hear her say that. It was a bright, pure, friendly night, reasonable through and through.' —Peter Handke, *The Weight of the World*

'*Faut pas contrarier les fous.*' In French cartoons a mad person is drawn with a funnel as a hat.

'Do you think there's anyone in the world who doesn't like Bach?'

He shrugs, fills his cup with strong tea. 'I don't know. It'd be like not liking water.'

When the English teacher got a posting to Inner Mongolia she took a whole suitcase full of sanitary pads and tampons—'They stuff themselves with rags, or, out in the country, leaves'—but her menopause came, and she's never had a period since.

'Writing: safe again.' —Peter Handke. He's more brutal with himself than I have ever been. He inspires me to try to be more truthful in this book. It's hard, for I am always hiding something, either from myself or from the person who may or may not, today or on some future day, read this and be inclined to think less of me.

K calls from some hotel, to tell me, thick-voiced from crying, that his friend, whom I didn't know, has killed himself. With pills. 'He set it up. He told his girlfriend to go away for the weekend, said he was going to work; didn't turn up at work but when people went to his place there was no answer and his car wasn't there. After a couple of days they broke in. They found his little body in there.' He was crying; so was I. 'He wasn't a close friend of mine. But he was one of the pure ones. He wasn't one of the guilty ones. It's the dirty, gritty ones who survive.'

Next day he calls to tell me he's bought me a couple of Exacto cotton jumpers.

HG: (*thinks*) I *hate* Exacto jumpers and they are *not cotton*. (*says*) 'That'll be a nice surprise—thanks.'

I make myself *sick*.

The gardener tells me I must see Sissinghurst before I die.

I ask, 'Why aren't Australian gardens as wonderful?'

'Because we don't believe in straight lines.'

Handke: 'I thought of art as a parachute that would stop me from falling.'

Last night I turned out the light and lay on my bed. Warm night. I was awake. I remember now that I said out loud, 'People need to be loved.' I found that my hands were near each other, and clasped them. Then I said the Lord's Prayer, very slowly, not sure after each line that I would remember the next. And when I got to the end I felt better, so I went back to the beginning and said it again. I tried to think, with each phrase, of its practical application to my life.

'Forgive us our trespasses, as we forgive those who trespass against us.' I thought of F, of my anger and harshness. I thought it would be better to be firm, and not to try to save myself by hatred. This morning, having remembered the prayer, I feel as if I've stumbled on something useful. A technique.

———

K was walking in front of me along a narrow, overgrown track between two rows of graves. I said to his back, 'Sometimes I think I might become a Christian.'

His face appears, over his right shoulder, in a slow, firm, dramatic movement. He keeps walking, still looking back at me. His look, how can I describe it? Partly for comic effect, as if to say, 'Oh, come off it.' But also a flash of incredulity that his sophistication cannot quite conceal.

I laugh: 'You bit.' Protecting my flank, instantly.

People don't respect each other's serious dilemmas as much as they respect, for example, each other's tastes in food.

———

Morning, at the bathroom mirror. 'How did I get such a good-looking daughter? And I so plain.' 'He-*lern*.' (Carefully combing her wet fringe into one eye.)

———

I feel I've been dragged into secrecy, and I hate it, I never wanted to, I think it's wrong and it makes me terribly unhappy. I dread *bitterness*. I must be careful of my *tone*. And not to speak as if all pain should now END instantly.

———

When people came to look at the suicide's body, his sister said, 'Doesn't he know he'll have to go through it all over again?' Belief in reincarnation as a deterrent to suicide.

———

The GP told me I was too thin. She said to drink milkshakes or I would get wrinkled. I said, 'I am already.'

———

My sister's elegant dress and grey boots, her intelligent, rapid gathering together of points and insights about Dad: '*That* must be why he keeps buying new houses and shifting Mum around—he doesn't want her to stay anywhere long enough to develop friendships that might exclude *him*. His mother died. All his daughters have grown up and gone. He lost his sister—' We stared at each other in horror as she fitted the pieces together.

———

A letter from a friend. '*Dear* Helen,' he writes. Surely if *he* likes me I can't be such a monster.

———

On the way to the cinema T said, 'I must get some petrol.' After the movie, which we hated and walked out of early, we set off up the Nepean Highway. I remembered her remark about the petrol but, fearing to be thought bossy, said nothing. Halfway up the St Kilda hill we ran out. We crossed the road to a hamburger shop to ask where the nearest petrol station was. We *had a hamburger*. It was early evening, still light. The Greek woman squeezed lemon juice on to the meat. Our food was delicious. We carried the jerry can up the hill to the petrol station, eating as we walked and talking happily. We filled the can, took it back to the car, did the necessary and drove calmly home.

———

I answered J's letter. 'Something is "travelling furiously towards me". I don't think it's God. It's some sort of force, and it's inside me, and I've been feeling it coming for a year or more, and now I feel its *might*, and it's a force of immense good, and it will connect me with the oneness of things, it's coming through my dreams, and what I'm having to do is clear the decks so that it can be unobstructed.' And he replied, patiently, 'It hurts to be quickened.'

———

I feel I'm fighting for my life. Walking down Rathdowne Street to collect a mended shoe I have a large, painful lump in my throat. I'm engaged in some colossal moral struggle. Am I trying to bargain with God? That is not good enough. I try to think of someone wise I can go and talk to. Names occur but none of them will do. I'm aching all over, all the time. Bleeding too. Muscles like rocks. Fallopian tubes in pain. Left thumb joint swollen and sore. I was so unhappy, yesterday, that I thought, Maybe I'm the sort of person who will go mad. Things I looked at had no meaning. The sky was dull with clouds.

———

It is perhaps always hard to find a person who will play out a drama with you right to the end, and not stroll off the stage before the killing starts.

———

'When I get garrulous in restaurants,' carolled U, 'my daughters get more and more remote and aristocratic.'

———

School holidays and M comes down with a bad cold. I put her into my bed and 'tickle her face with a particularly nice feather' until she falls asleep. Then I lie down beside her and read Jung until I fall asleep too, at which point the phone begins to ring.

———

K says he feels 'glum' that it's over. And I'd been thinking of broken hearts and madness!

———

F and M played a card game last night of such ferocious competitiveness that it made me nervous to be in the same room. I liked being with them, though: they were on the bed and I was at the table writing letters, and on the cassette player was a tape of gospel music from a radio show. Room full of light and noise and laughter and cries of outrage from the card game, while I was permitted to be present and yet absent. Between songs the singer gave a mild little account of himself: 'I believe in Jesus. I'm really into it, actually.' The card players looked up with grimaces, but I kept on listening. On the bottom of a letter I wrote, 'Do you believe in God, Herbert?' It could be a terrific opening scene in a movie. A lot is happening.

———

5 am. The air is pink and the moon is squashed and pale. A small, steady breeze is running smoothly up the street from the east.

———

I thought my head was going to burst, I felt so interrogated and observed. Bashed my head against the wall. He cried and tore his hair, hit his forehead with his palms.

———

At the wedding I saw a row of people snigger when the vicar earnestly invited Jesus to come into the new couple's home, and to stay. Then the passage from Corinthians about *what love is*. How wonderful—but secretly I bet that they're thinking of it as a tribute to their own romantic and sexual infatuation.

———

I dreamt that I went back to our old house and found that a beautiful archway had been constructed, a high, curved, classical one, halfway down the short path to the front gate. Its purpose was to bear climbing roses, of which only the strong twisted stems were already there—no leaves or flowers.

———

One of life's great pleasures: using my pen when I have just put a new nib in it.

———

On the beach a beautiful Weimaraner had found a dead bird and was tearing it apart, spitting out mouthfuls of feathers. We bought mediocre fish and chips in Fitzroy Street and ate them shuddering in the doorway of a closed shop.

———

'What's the matter?' says M.
   'Hopeless love.'
   'Oh, you talk like a book. Which one of them do you prefer?'
   'It's not that simple.'
   'Yes, but which one *do* you?'
   'Really it's not that *simple*.'
   'It's just *silly*. It's like one of those love comics I've been reading.'

———

The old Vietnamese man was full of anti-Communist bitterness. He said that before the French came Vietnamese society had no classes. I found this hard to believe, especially when he then began to speak of kings, princes and dukes.

———

There they sat in the cafe, two tall fair blessed ones, at a table halfway back, drinking mineral water. They showed me their jewellery: her rings, one with a diamond; his Russian one, three rings entwined; her pearl ear-studs, his black and gold watch, her black pearl double-strand necklace. I found this naïve display piercing to the heart and tear-ducts. But then they spoke disobligingly of someone I'm fond of, and lost my sympathy.

1985

'Have you been in my room?'
  'No. Downstairs.'
  'Listening to us fighting?'
  'Yes.'
  'Where were you?'
  'Under the stairs, near the telephone.'
  'Did you hear everything?'
  'Yes.'
  (*Hand over mouth*) 'Was I awful?'
  She laughs slyly.

———

The two bodies found in the tray of a ute. Decomposing corpses. The girl. I knew her. I can grasp this fact intellectually but in no other way.

———

'People who've had something dreadful happen to their children seem to have a glass wall around them,' said U. 'Ordinary people can never really contact them again.'

———

I sat down and made a list of people I knew, of my age or younger, who had died. There were fifteen. And I'm only forty-two.

———

Sergei Bondarchuk's *War and Peace* on SBS. How Tolstoy does those moments where a character for a split second gets everything wrong: Prince Andrei, waiting outside the bedroom while his wife is in labour, hears a baby cry and says, 'Why on earth have they brought a baby in here?' And when he's lying wounded after the battle of Borodino and sees the man next to him having his leg amputated, hears him sobbing, then recognises him as Kuragin, the man he hates who tried to elope with Natasha: 'Oh, why does *he* have to turn up here?' Crying over all this I kept thinking of the two kids in the ute, the bludgeoning and shooting. Their funeral tomorrow.

———

'Usually,' said the priest beside the two flower-loaded coffins, 'I wear white vestments at a funeral, when the person who's died was old. Today I almost decided not to vest at all.' His voice was trembling. 'But then I decided to wear red. Red is a vibrant colour. And it's the colour of martyrdom.'

———

How the men carried the coffins: each locked his free arm round the next one's waist—a gesture of tender, manly comradeliness.

———

At the wake the murdered girl's stepfather stood with his friends. We were telling old stories, making each other laugh. Once he put his hand over his face and wept silently; tears poured down his cheeks. I kept my arm around him. After a moment he took his hand away and resumed his part in the conversation.

———

I read through the first draft of my story and saw immediately the point at which it goes off the rails. It gave me great satisfaction to know that my critical apparatus is in working order.

———

When I've written something strong that's on the right track I have an urge to get up from the table. I leave the room, walk to the shop, have a coffee. And when I come back, confident that I've got something solid to build on, I reread the last phrase and find it *better than I had remembered*.

———

I called P in Paris, and heard $29.30 worth of information about her vaginal infection.

———

I read a short piece in French by Roland Barthes, about how he guessed Proust had changed his thinking and his behaviour in order to write *À la Recherche*. Now I understand why people love Barthes. His tone is friendly, he is quite at ease with the simple, he says things that many another would have considered beneath his notice because someone else would already have thought them. He is really tackling the subject, not trying to impress anyone. Completely charming, direct and comradely with the reader.

———

I still have a 'secret life' in my mind. But who doesn't? And it only troubles me when I'm in a mood to trouble myself. I'll use anything that's available at such times.

———

Bushfires. Three people burnt to death at Kilmore. One of those mouth-of-hell days, air that dried the skin in seconds, north wind. The light an ugly dull yellow. When we sat in the garden to eat our dinner the wind dropped and a coolness came. But flakes of ash fell from the sky and gathered on our clothes and our plates.

———

Saw two Truffaut movies: *La Peau douce* and *Baisers volés*. One thing he's really good at is the tiny encounter with the nutcase. The student ex-friend who runs into Doinel on a flight of steps and tells him a string of obvious lies about a TV channel having accepted his scripts. The stranger in the cream raincoat who approaches the heroine, declares his love for her and his determination to devote the rest of his life to being in her company, then walks away, saying over his shoulder, *'Je suis très heureux.'* The girl says to Doinel, *'Il est complètement fou, ce type-là.'* This is the last line of dialogue in the movie. *Wah.*

––––––

It's ten years since I heard from him but now he calls from Sydney to tell me his mother's got pancreatic cancer. A year to live. When she opened the door to me she looked very small, and younger, as if her face, which I had never before seen without pancake make-up, had softened and lost its social mask. We stood with our arms round each other and she cried. She took me into the bedroom and sat me on the bed and began to talk very rapidly about some baby clothes she'd bought at a sale, years ago, and stashed for the birth of grandchildren. She wanted her son to know where they were, for later. 'We've loved each other for a long time, haven't we,' she said. Surprised, I realised that I had loved her much less than she had me; that I must represent something about her son's past that she did not want to lose. That night she was in my dream. She burrowed her head under my clothes and began to suck on my breasts, one after the other.

––––––

At the Carlton Baths B and I saw an African man set upon by some horrible very young teenage girls from the flats. We were frightened of them.

On the grassy area their group, scarcely out of puberty, emitted a disturbing erotic vibe. He must have made the mistake of speaking to them flirtatiously. He asked them for a drink. They laughed, and cursed him. He said, in his slow English, 'Are you not even a little bit kind?' They walked on his leg, poured cordial on his body, stole his watch, cigarettes, shirt. Throughout their attack he never raised his voice, and this was his only remaining scrap of power.

'Girls are worse than boys,' B remarked on our way home. 'You feel there's no end to their cruelty and malice.'

———

One thing I know I will never receive due credit for, EVER, and that is the amount of cleaning I do in this house. I am the *only one* who ever cleans the lavatories. Sweeps the stairs. Scrapes food dribbles off the cupboard doors. I clean the bathroom basin every other day. I sweep the kitchen, I sweep the yard, I defrost the fridge, I iron the tablecloths, I tidy the benches, I put away the newspapers. I do this work, mostly, without thinking. But when F tells me he works harder than I do, the household jobs come to my mind with *force*.

———

The old writer lives alone in a high, airy apartment with pretty furniture and a cheerful orderliness. She says that married people have affairs *only* to hurt the other. She says that spouses are jealous of writers, artists etc because we have this area to function in where they can't go, and where they can't hurt us or punish us, i.e. where we are free.

———

Three jolly plumbers came and fixed the blocked toilet. In the backyard a minor but sudden unblocking sprayed one of them with shit. Until he laughed we didn't dare to. He shook himself and hopped around on one foot, flapping his hands. His teeth were very white, his eyes bright blue.

———

'What a hot night!'
    'It's not a very hot night. I don't feel much heat.'
    'I didn't say "very hot". I just said "hot".'

'To me a hot night is over thirty degrees. I'm even going to put my doona over me.'

―――

It seems I am a really awful person. Pushy, aggressive, demanding, always wanting everything to be clear, worked out, resolved. Also I have bad table manners: I was the first to put out my chopsticks at Brilliant's when the food was served. My enthusiasms, my expectation that others will follow me, lead people to do so against their will: apparently I phrase suggestions in a way that brooks no refusal. When I said 'Let's go to the nude beach on Sunday', my manner made him say, 'All right' instead of what he really felt which was 'Maybe'. Growing more pathetic, dismal and contemptible every minute, I tried to explain my feeling that there is a link between my 'enthusiasms' and the bluff that's needed to be a writer. No, no—many writers are quite introverted. I will have to tone myself down. I couldn't help crying. Silent sobs, with a lot of tears running out. I despised myself for giving way to a spasm of self-pity. I wish I could bawl out loud, get some voice into it and *howl*.

―――

I have read in feminist literature about women who could not handle their own talent: who were ashamed of it, or tried to hide it. I never thought I would become one of those. But one comes under certain subtle pressures that are unforeseeable in their form, direction and detail.

―――

I dreamt I went to a party in a garden. Bikies were there. I left my old green shoulder bag in an unattended room and when I went back to find it, it had gone. I was scared of the bikies who looked as if they might turn nasty, so I didn't complain about the bag, but moved quietly round the party on my own, looking for it in every conceivable place, without luck.

I made some curtains for my room and they are a disaster.

The women talked about 'spiritual' things and how sad it is that our husbands are afraid of them, or scornful, and cannot share them.

The prisoners in the film about Uruguay, when guards were present, were obliged to stand with their heads bowed. Lined up against the cyclone wire fence they looked, from a distance, like a row of hanged men.

I watched Q, the dressmaker, waiting at the cash register to buy a big slice of watermelon. I saw the graceful angle of her leg and I thought, She's beautiful and full of grace; she likes me; she does not defer to me, nor does she need to undermine me; she has a private mind and a private life; we are not in competition; her areas of competence are so different from mine that we never clash. I envy—or rather *intend to be*, one day—a woman like her. Or those older women writers I've met, who at sixty live alone in a lovely flat, work calmly and with recognition, *have friends*.

Bumped my head hard on the window frame. Wanted to cry; gave a few sobs and gasps, sitting at my table; but realised, as I heard myself beginning, that I *must not*; because I have a day of social duty ahead and must hold it together. I was also shocked and alarmed, even as I controlled myself, by the immensity of sadness that I need to cry about: like glimpsing a grey ocean. I quickly closed my eyes. I sat there with my hands over my face and my elbows on the table and thought, I am desperate. At the same time I thought, And I must write this down. Virginia Woolf and Guy de Maupassant on this subject. What sort of a creature am I?

———

Damp sand. Flat water, pale silky grey with tints of mauve and pink if one looked very carefully. Hundreds of seagulls circled above the beach. I noticed many moth-like insects in the air and tried to see if they were being hunted by the birds. The life of a wild animal: the basic element must be HUNGER. How many small moths would it take to fill a seagull's stomach?

———

F says we are 'like adolescents'. He tilts back his head and howls like a dog at the moon: '*Oooooooooooooooo*.' I can't help laughing.

———

Days of bitter fighting. Sometimes we seem to get somewhere, and emerge sobered, chastened. Then we treat each other with quiet respect. At these times I feel like a human being again, instead of a very bad and wrong person, a sack of different sadnesses being hauled around by a skeleton.

———

In Emma Jung's essays, *Animus and Anima*, I find that the animus presents itself in many guises, and that one of these is 'a pseudo-hero who fascinates by a mixture of intellectual brilliance and moral irresponsibility'. Surely this is a description of the character called Philip who keeps turning up in everything I write.

———

F's workmate brought his girlfriend to dinner and we had a wonderful time. She is a young woman who manifests the opposite of what is meant by the phrase 'full of shit'. She was wearing a little green hat in a wartime style, soft material made into a turban. I watched her dancing with him to a Billie Holiday record: that clear blankness of concentration that comes over a dancing woman's face, the readiness to respond in a formal way to whatever might be asked of her legs and torso. The hem of her green crepe dress was down and I sewed it up for her. She kissed my cheek by way of thanks.

———

The teenage girls, going out to Johnny's Green Room in their clever, bright, improvised clothes: scarves artfully tied, an orange suit from the sixties, a battered golden bag. So fresh and pretty. Full of hope. Their eyes were shining. Not children any more, but only just starting to be adults.

———

At the dinner we drank tequila and exchanged tales of weak people enabled by fury to stand up against tough ones. A man had made three big teenagers clean up a kids' playground he had come upon them smashing. A woman saw a kid walking down the street carrying an axe. 'Every time he passed a tree he chopped a big chunk out of it. So I went up to him and shouted, "You do that once more and you'll get that axe in your *head*."' 'What did he do?' She shrugged. 'Ran home.'

———

A woman in Brisbane reviews *The Children's Bach*: apparently it is 'written with great cynicism towards human nature—a more unlovable bunch of characters would be hard to find'.

———

I see that compared with Doris Lessing I am lazy and a spendthrift.

———

The sick woman, in her retirement village, talked without stopping for hours. I made myself stay three, then four. I thought, Go the extra mile. You are healthy and young. She is lonely and sick, and she needs you. The cancer management man, she said, had asked her if she could remember any shock in her life, any grief or anger. She told him she'd always been angry about 'what men do to women'; and then she remembered to mention that twenty years ago her daughter had been murdered.

———

In the cafe this morning a grey-haired old man came in, wearing a fawn safari jacket and shirt, polished brown shoes and socks, and no trousers. As he walked you could see his red underpants flash in the vent of his jacket. The Italian waiters accepted this strange fellow with an impressive nonchalance. He went to the toilet and back, sat at his table, and was brought his coffee just like everyone else.

———

I feel great relief that I did not conduct my side of the thing secretly. I did my cleaning-up and straightening as I went along, like a brutal sort of housework; but on his side K let the dirt accumulate, and now the rotting things and dried chop bones are being found behind the piano. 'It was always easier for me than it was for you,' he said. Yes, because he lied. But the law of karma is reasserting itself. 'Want some advice?' I said. 'Stay off the piss. You won't want to be handling this kind of thing with a hangover. And drunk people say things they regret later.'

———

TV interview with the Aboriginal girl who is Penthouse Pet of the Year.

'You must be very excited. Did you get much sleep last night?'

'No. I was awake half the night looking at my diamond watch!' She holds it out to the camera. 'It cost four and a half thousand dollars!'

Her eagerness, her naïve pleasure in the $80,000 worth of prizes and rewards, cuts no ice with the disapproving woman interviewer, who proceeds to guilt-trip her about feminism and her Aboriginal blood and responsibilities.

———

The surrogate mother was asked on TV how she had arrived at the price she charged her couple. 'Well, I asked myself how much

I could earn if I was fully employed for nine months, and I worked it out at $6000.' The paltriness of this sum was not remarked upon. 'And if you did it again, how much would you charge?' She thinks, then gives a daring little smile and a sideways glance. 'Ooh...I'd charge...ten thousand?'

'What about labour?' said T crossly. 'Surely that'd be overtime?'

———

Sunset last night was like a swap card I once had of a pirate ship: torn clouds, dramatic perspective, orange, gold and green. And now a dawn sky of delicate purity, and a smell of eucalypts. Maybe a marriage can get up again and walk, after a terrible beating.

———

'What've *you* been up to?'

'Nothing I wouldn't talk about if the right person asked me in the right tone of voice.'

———

'It is when one's talent has been recognised that the great misery of the creator begins.' —Camus

———

I met Raymond Carver in Sydney and he signed a copy of *Will You Please Be Quiet, Please* and gave it to me. I wanted to tell him how much his work has meant to me but there was only time to shake hands.

———

In the street, noticing that as usual B was dragging two paces behind me and to one side, I slowed down, again and again, to see if it was *me* doing it; but no, each time she slowed down as well, so I was always in front, no matter how I tried to walk beside her.

'You mean,' said the Jungian, 'that if you put down the reins she doesn't pick them up—they just lie there?'

———

Someone got into the Adelaide zoo and slaughtered sixty animals. Stabbed them, cut their throats, sliced out their entrails.

———

Went to *Die Walküre* last night. I loved the way a character would sing a very long *story*.

———

The French tutor said she had been very anxious before the surgery; that it was hard to submit to the fact that she was obliged to put total faith in the anaesthetist (she could not pronounce the word, and made a gesture of poking something into the back of her hand). 'But,' she said, 'when I thought that otherwise I might die, I found it easier to…get more philosophical.' At these three words, so characteristic of my serious, thoughtful teacher, I was moved, and grabbed her hand. She said that since the operation she has been less bothered by the small anxieties of ordinary life.

———

The dreams: so dense.

———

For twenty-four hours I had nausea and diarrhea. It was a hot autumn day with a dry wind pouring in through the window. M looked after me nobly, without signs of revulsion, even when she came in and found me on my hands and knees over a bowl on the bedroom floor, spewing bile. It was Palm Sunday. They say there were 120,000 people at the anti-nuclear rally. I read some Jung, some of *The Waiting Years* by Fumiko Enchi, bits of *A Passage to India* and stories from David Malouf's *Antipodes*.

———

Dreamt that in a house on stilts, above water, I was laid up and then found I was ill and soon to die. I looked at objects with regret and longing. I was lifted by people not quite strong enough and dumped on to a stretcher.

I wish I could get this tone, and pace, in fiction.

―――――

A 'bloodless coup' in the Sudan. The president goes to Washington, and as soon as his back's turned nine army officers take over. He ends up stranded in Cairo.

'Imagine,' says F. 'He can't go back. All his things…'

―――――

Last night, Greek Good Friday, a thousand people passed under my bedroom window in the almost-dark, each one holding a burning candle. I leaned out to watch them. Our street was packed to the gutters with slowly stepping, murmuring Greeks, whole families, a bearded patriarch. A mass of flowers, like a huge cake, was borne along by a group of four. A brass band quietly played a hymn I remembered from school. No one was singing but as I watched the stream flow by, the words of the hymn came back to me: 'casting down their golden crowns around a glassy sea'.

―――――

In the Fitzroy Gardens I made it clear to K. 'It's like carrying a wardrobe. We have to put it down and walk away.' We stood in the middle of the huge lawn with our arms round each other. He stepped back. I saw that his glasses were fogged up. 'Sorry about that,' he said.

―――――

'Why don't you *like* me?'

'What *is* this question? Why do you ask this question?'

'What do I *do*, that makes you not like me?'

'You're *there*. That's all.'

On my way home I bought a 'couple self-help' book at Readings and ripped through it greedily. It suggests very practical ways of breaking destructive patterns of behaviour. I cried over it because its examples were so petty, so familiar, and so utterly convincing.

———

'My husband and I have agreed to part,' said the woman in the post office to her friend. 'My presence is inhibiting his creative development.'

She said this without irony or apparent animus.

———

I held their Airedale puppy in my lap. I tickled it and it groaned.

———

A young girl was found dead, naked except for a pair of underpants, in a St Kilda gutter. Dumped there after she had overdosed. What savagery. To leave your friend in a cold gutter without even covering her—not a sheet, a rug, an old coat.

———

In the bookshop I picked up the new *Oxford Anthology of Australian Literature*, a book whose existence was unknown to me. I knew I could not be represented in it because they would have had to ask my permission. I examined its index. No, I wasn't there. I felt the world seesaw. I walked to the tram stop wretched. I am full of shit. I am crude, a beginner. People must laugh at me behind my back. I posture as a writer and at forty-two I can't even get into the Oxford book.

———

He seems to be full of anger towards me. The slightest misstep on my part brings out a jet of it.

———

A couple passed us on the beach. We guessed they had met through a dating agency. I said the man couldn't find a woman because he talked all the time and expected her to listen. F said the woman couldn't find a man because she listened all the time with her head on one side and made attention-murmurs, and was 'limp'.

———

'The deeper you go,' said the Jungian, 'the more sceptical you must become.'

———

B was so sick of me that when she saw my writing on the envelope she tore it up unopened and threw it away. Later, she learned it had contained a publisher's cheque for several hundred dollars, for a job we did together. She had to call me and eat crow.

———

I'm so tired, even after all that sleep. My head and body are full of lead.

———

In the Exhibition Gardens I saw a man walking with a bitch and her pup at his heels. The bitch ran smoothly, smiling, but the pup kept stumbling and tumbling in his eagerness to keep up. He rolled right on to his back in the dry plane leaves, scrambled to his feet and galloped on.

———

J and I walked in the cemetery with the dog. A grey afternoon. He felt the cold. Sometimes we walked with our arms around each other. He said I was skinny. He said he had lost a stone. I think he was still in shock from the media attention he got in Sydney for the big prize. He spoke rapidly, almost gasping. I saw that my job was to give him my full attention, to ask questions and listen to the answers. I asked him if his ego was swollen. No, he said, the opposite: he felt he was small, he was nothing. He told me about his church, how it 'goes back to the time before there was a pope'.

———

The way M answers the phone: with a rising intonation, a little breathless—'Hello?'—as if to say, 'I'm ready for whatever this is and I think it's going to be good.' How will I live without her, when she grows up and moves away?

———

The AA meeting at the health farm. I said the truth at the door, which was that I had an alcoholic friend and wanted to know how to be useful, but they looked at me with crooked smiles of scepticism and said, 'Come in.'

'The wife was home by herself, wonderin' where I was. I was down the river drinkin' and doin' wheelies with my brother's apprentices. They were the only blokes who'd drink the way I wanted to drink. I was thirty.'

'I didn't know what love was. I got married for the convenience. To have someone to wash my clothes and cook a meal and be there. I can remember the first time I ever sat on the couch with my wife and held her hand. We already had three kids.'

The way they talked frankly about disgusting things: 'spewin' blood, piddlin' in the bed'.

'Once they go to Al-Anon they start kickin' the props out from under you. Before my wife went, if I was sick in the bed she used to clean it up and wash the sheets. But after she started goin', if I was sick she'd pick up me head and drop me face in it.'

At the end of the meeting they all sprang to their feet and recited the prayer.

———

On French TV at F's parents' place we saw an old man who had invented an alarm clock that didn't bother to go off if it was raining (he produced a large plastic bottle with a spray top and squirted it) and a hammer that dispensed bandaids. Another man had devised a toilet seat that weighed you if you sat on it and raised your feet off the ground.

———

Siena, the trattoria, the rain, the free glass of grappa, the cherry red suede shoes I bought him.

———

In the guest room of the Tuscan house where I lay reading, a small bat clung to the ceiling. Every time I turned a page its ears stood up.

———

Very early evening. Fifteen or so people in the grassy courtyard outside the Romanesque church. A mild little wind. People's faces softened by the singing of four young monks (three of them wearing glasses). The long grass full of wildflowers, the valley behind, the thin rows of cypresses, some as thin and pointed as sharpened pencils; poppies in a wandering line that followed a broken fence. Sometimes we would turn a corner and see a whole field of them, tilted, casual, like a red dress thrown out to dry. A German boy passed, looked at us with open face, smiled, we said good evening in our various languages, his girlfriend came behind, a sweet and pretty face. Later a full moon. Fireflies. Our host knows the names of flowers.

———

I am getting better at playing pétanque and even quite enjoy it. I never can care about winning but I like the effort of getting the boule up to the bouchon. I must be a boring opponent. Glenn Gould says that competition rather than money is the root of all evil.

———

He said that since his first short story had been accepted by a magazine he didn't need to go on writing: he had proved that he was capable of having his work published.

'Proved to whom?' said his friend, looking shocked. 'To yourself, or to the world?'

'It's the same thing, isn't it?'

———

When I got home the house was dirty and disorderly. I went straight out and bought four nice towels, soap, toothpaste, and a new rubbish bin to replace the green one, which had been stolen *without anyone noticing*. I also called a mechanic and had the leaking washing machine fixed. Today's great achievement: I scrubbed the kitchen walls. They look wonderful, all cream and smooth.

———

He sent me a postcard from Amsterdam: a Daumier drawing from a series called *Moeurs Conjugales*, a man and a woman in two armchairs, their faces distorted by huge, ugly yawns.

———

I showed B my short stories in manuscript. She flipped through it, and remarked on the plastic folder the stories were in, but said nothing about the stories themselves.

———

C and I drove to the Botanic Gardens. I took her arm and we strolled around. I mentioned the Penguin cocktail party and she was mortified that she hadn't been invited. She thought it might cheer her up to see the cactus garden. For the first time, in a real gardener's company, I was able to *look* at these plants, which had always left me cold: their extraordinary obsessive patterns, their shocking excrescences and sudden colours, the subtlety of their black tips and serrated edges.

———

'They asked me,' said P, ' "How do you like the picture of yourself in Helen's story?" They were pushing me to outrage.'

I lost my temper. I kicked a tree, a rubbish bin. They think of themselves as artists, as writers. What do they think artists DO? She was laughing; she had seen it before it was published, and had liked it. But I suppose seeing the story in print causes a different kind of pain about oneself from simply reading it in manuscript. Am I a kind of monster? If I am, then Frank Moorhouse and Nadine Gordimer and Raymond Carver are monsters too: 'It's a jungle out there.' I resolve not to defend myself, not even to indulge my rage and fear in coldness.

———

The Children's Bach is shortlisted for the Victorian Premier's Award. It's a lot of money, fifteen grand or so. I don't know who I'm up against but *I want that prize.*

'Don't get too hopeful, though, Helen,' says M earnestly. 'Just in case.'

———

K and I ate room service food, sitting on the edge of the single bed like two good children.

———

M goes to the Melbourne High social, all chic in black.

'You look as pretty as a picture.'

'Thank you, Helen.'

———

I went and had my hair absolutely CHOPPED.

———

A tremendous cold northerly blew all day. We drove to St Kilda and walked out on the pier. The air was so clear it was almost frightening: distance had ceased to exist. Closeness of the city buildings, iron grey, all their detail visible.

———

He'll be like the Russians: he'll retreat and retreat and retreat until I freeze to death.

———

'After this she was born and re-born with incredible swiftness as a woman, as an imp, as a dog, and finally as a flower. She was some nameless, tiny bell, growing in a stream, with a stalk as fine as hair and a human voice. The water flowing through her flower throat made her sing all day a little monotonous song, "*Kulalla, kulalla,*

kulalla, ripitalla, kulalla, kulalla, kulalla, kulalla, kulla".' —Antonia White, *Beyond the Glass*

———

Thought I'd finished my *Postcards* manuscript and drove over to McPhee Gribble to deliver it. I hung around their pleasant office for an hour, fiddling with the pages, not wanting to part with them. I became dissatisfied with one of the Paris stories and saw it would not do. Deflated, I went home, where I rummaged through an old folder and found a sheet of paper with one sentence scribbled on it: 'We heard he was back.' Ooh, that Sydney wedding—a story about gossip, about someone who leaves his social group behind. It came pouring out, as short stories sometimes do. I tried to abstract it, to smash it into sharp pieces. I kept thinking of Ania Walwicz's broken sentences, the shock and wit of them.

———

My problems are never syntactic.

———

Clear statement: I have very strong urges (irresistible urges) towards some kind of religious or, rather, spiritual experience. This frightens me, not because the spirituality in things is so inscrutable but because I don't know what it will do to my ordinary life arrangements, my friendships, my attitude towards my work, if I turn around and acknowledge something I privately refer to as 'the mighty force'. It's there behind me, and in me, all the time. It's benevolent, it's totally *good*—not morally—I mean that it only wishes me well. But I'm afraid to find out what I'll become if I stop running away from it. It's as if I were always swimming against a tide. How do I turn round and face it? How's it *done*?

———

My sister talked about reading the Gospels again. The woman at the well was the first person to whom Jesus revealed himself as Messiah.

Women were at the foot of the cross. Women entered the empty tomb. 'It's *all there*,' she said, 'and we've let ourselves be talked out of it.'

But I can't go to church. It would be like going back to Dad, to being an angry daughter.

———

'Solitude is not something you must hope for in the future. Rather, it is a deepening of the present, and unless you look for it in the present you will never find it.' —Thomas Merton

———

This morning, between waking and waking, while sun and wind blew into my room, I dreamt I was going to move to another room in this house. A room I didn't know existed before, although it turned out to be the little white one I had at Capel Street. I was going to have nothing in it but my bed.

———

Finished *Wise Blood*, which I do not understand, and which began somehow to sicken me, all its characters warped and ugly, twisted with ignorance and bad motives and sin.

———

Got proofs of the short stories. Proofs always disappoint me: I hope for beauty, or enlightenment, but it's the same old *matter*.

———

On TV a doco about black gospel singers in Alabama. The old men teaching the young ones the dense harmonies *by ear*, taking them over and over it; the very old men's faces shiny, hard-skinned, reserved, almost noble. A group of women in robes with hoods hanging down their backs—the weirdest singing, with a kind of free, tense rhythm, wild-sounding yet perfectly controlled—the story of the TEW little fishes and the FAHVE loaves of bread.

———

'You're very calm today,' said Q.

   'It's false.'

————

I'm more anxious about what I'll wear to the prize dinner than about whether I'll win or not.

————

The winner must have known: as soon as his name was read out, a door at the back of the hall burst open and a trolley loaded with copies of his book was trundled in. After the announcement, one of the women judges was nice to me in a way I privately found humiliating. The former ambassador, his devilish good looks somewhat the worse for wear, put his arm across the back of my chair, looked right into my face with an expression of sparkling, malevolent curiosity, and said, showing all his teeth, 'And how are *you* feeling?' It was hard to keep smiling but I hope I managed it. And in my heart I knew that even one of the winning stories knocked my dry, sparse tale into a cocked hat. I know I'm good, but I'm not in his league. Not yet, anyway.

————

A man tells me he has cards and letters his parents sent to each other. He says he doesn't feel like reading the letters. Perhaps he doesn't want to lose the state of having a secret from himself; or to reach the end of the mystery, the bottom of the bag.

————

'Oxford Street's Babylon, mate,' says the born-again. 'It's the pit.'

————

I agree to take part in an ABC radio discussion about 'the future of personal relationships'. 'But why did they invite *you*?' says F. 'What do *you* know about the subject? What made you accept?' He goes to work. I call him and we discuss it further. My voice is shrill and trembly. His is small and vague, as if he were really not all that interested and were even reading something as we spoke.

———

In the discussion I ran the line against possessiveness that we thought was so cool in the seventies: 'Jealousy is a completely useless emotion.'

Psychoanalyst: 'On the contrary. I think jealousy is at the cutting edge of the psyche.'

Me: (*riveted*) 'What do you mean?'

Psychoanalyst: 'It's painful, but it shows us in no uncertain terms that we are not rational beings. That our lives are not under our conscious control.'

———

I went outside. I thought wildly of going back to Melbourne, to Geelong, anywhere, hitch-hiking, but it was 10 pm, dark and clouded, and a dog was barking next door. I could hear his heavy boots, he seemed to be walking from one end of the house to the other. I was scared even of walking to the road overlooking the water. I stood with my hands in my pockets and then I came back inside.

———

He tells me that the vision of life that's in my work is not real; it's much less bad, dark, mischievous, painful etc than real life. It holds out some belief in the essential goodness of people. It is a picture of the way I'd like life to be rather than the way it really is.

'I'm afraid your pessimism will contaminate me,' I say.

'If you believe in good, why are you afraid that bad will contaminate you?'

It's like arguing with the devil.

———

'She was scarcely still for ten minutes at a time and appeared to have excellent control of her high and hard temper.' —Christina Stead, *Letty Fox, Her Luck*

———

'That was nice soup we had, wasn't it.'

   'Yes but I didn't like the salad.'

   'But did you *like* the *soup*.'

   'I *said yes*.'

———

I tried to be ordinary but everything I said sounded false.

———

'You won't tell me what's wrong. I keep asking, and you won't *tell* me.'

   'But that's the problem. You keep *asking* me. You don't ask the right question—you push, push, push, all the time.'

———

At least I wore my white shoes all day.

———

The hush of attention, at the literary conference, that comes when someone reads a poem. Everyone is still, even those who have fidgeted during the paper's argument. I love this silence and feel it to be precious.

———

'I should have gone out,' said the poet casually, 'and found myself a man or two, to make me feel better about myself. But the few I liked were unavailable. So I had to get better by myself. It took longer.'

   I said I thought it was probably a more lasting recovery, 'like a very long diet instead of a series of crash ones'.

———

The barman was a middle-aged Chinese man in horn-rimmed spectacles. We asked for margaritas. He said he didn't know how to make them—did we? One of the academics did, and told him. 'This is inter-esting,' said the barman, keenly following instructions, having a bash at salting the rims. I thought him a remarkable person.

F brings home a video of a wonderful concert in Managua. We sit in a row to watch it. He leans forward eagerly. A handsome woman with a black chignon and blazing white teeth all the way down her throat sings in a wild, flamboyant voice a song about revolution. If we'd been alone I would have said to him, 'According to your picture of the world and of art, the only song worth her singing would say "Fight as you may, peasant comrades, you will be crushed like beetles between the super-powers. Your land will be defoliated and your children slaughtered."'

Why do I persist? I have no hope left. I conclude that I persist out of fear.

A stranger actually writes me a letter urging me not to become a Christian. I throw it in the bin.

In the kitchen at the publisher's party the novelist talked about a movie he wants to write. I sat and listened to him talk himself into being too scared to do it and then out again.

The African-American feminist's announcement that she would read last was brought to us by one of the organisers as we milled about before the session began. We all deferred without a murmur, though I had read enough of her work to know it was plod-dingly didactic. She assumed that we were ignorant of terms such as 'mortar', 'pestle', 'gay', 'Lucky Strike': before enlightening us she would make a little fence over her mouth with one hand and murmur, 'Culture break'. But when she spoke to me, down in the seats, she seemed an ordinary human being, likeable and warm.

Trucks rush past outside the motel on the Western Highway. An orange sunset impressed my father. He leaned his elbows on the metal rail and stared at it, then returned to his room to tear another handful of flesh off the cold chicken he had brought with us from Highton. He flips the bones over the railing into the carpark. Next day, as we drive on, he says, ''Member those chicken bones I chucked over the rail? This morning they were all gone. Must be cats. Or rats.'

———

I turned on the TV and saw a woman having her baby delivered by caesarean. I burst into tears when they lifted the tiny thing out: a girl, her head covered in that grey waxy stuff, her legs bent and weak. They weighed her, cleared out her breathing passages—a close-up of the little head in profile, eyes stuck down tight, mouth gaping, the plastic tube being pushed down her throat by two huge hands in surgical gloves. They put a white cotton cap on her head and wrapped her in silver paper, exactly like a fish fillet for the oven.

———

My father describes a woman we know as 'a very attractive girl, a very *precise* girl, with a polished voice'. Delighted with these adjectives, I look away. Next he uses the expression 'not privy to'. Maybe, if I lie low and listen, he'll let out a grand vocabulary that he's been hiding all his life.

———

When he addresses a stranger he uses no preliminary attention-getting phrase like 'Excuse me'. He just walks up behind them and starts talking. 'Where would the supermarket be?' 'Take long to walk into town from here, does it?' 'Got any orange squeezers?' His voice seems very loud and deep in public places.

'This is the worst town I've been in for—'

'*Shhh*! Lower your voice!'

I'm surprised to find he has strong views on the treatment of Aboriginal people. 'See? *Aboriginal Reserve*,' he says, with his big flat fingertip on the map. 'Right up north. Where it doesn't rain.'

On the Ghan, an endless night of trundling, rattling, bumping, shivering of fittings, and occasionally, between fitful periods of sleep, sightings of tremendous, dense panoplies of stars. At dawn horizontal stripes of morning sun run brokenly along the bushes. In the night I finished *Seven Poor Men of Sydney*. I'm shocked. I never knew Stead was a visionary. (What does that word mean?) Beside her I am a dwarf, scared, narrow, a timid shallow burrower.

The timidity, the ugly clothing of the travellers on the train. Cheap, gristle-soled shoes, home-made cardigans in a variety of browns and oranges and beiges. To see a decent pair of old brogues or proper leather shoes is a reprieve from murderous contempt. I'm poised to despise; my smiles are false. A man walked through the bar carrying a copy of the *Age Monthly Review*. I longed to run after him and his wife and kid.

On the platform at Port Augusta, a big group of black women with their children. Their stick-like legs, some marked with ulcers and scabs, their big runners and tennis socks pulled up, their loose synthetic dresses and football beanies, their large stomachs, their big breasts that hang down over their bellies, their straw-like curly hair. The babies' top lips gleam with silver snot. They were going to sit up all night in economy.

My father is incapable of conversation. His speech is almost rhetorical: he speaks very slowly, with the emphases of someone giving

important information to a listener whose understanding he has
no faith in. Any topic that comes up is quickly put aside as soon as
his opinion has been delivered. If I try to keep it going he makes no
response. I wonder if my tone becomes hectoring. We batted ideas
(dull lumps, but all we had to play with) across the table for an hour
or so. I felt by comparison quite light on my feet, whereas usually in
argument I am blurred, slow, opinionless. I brought my case around
in a big circle and closed it; I felt the satisfaction of form. I felt also
unscrupulous, even ashamed.

———

He doesn't like my driving. When I stalled on a stony rise near the
ochre pits, he clicked his tongue and took the wheel. The gorge:
beautiful white gums, slate-green water riffled by a strong dry
northerly. No one in sight. Sandals, two big pairs and two small, in
a neat row on the bank, like the remains of a family suicide.

———

He says his father was one of thirteen children. Various tales of wills
capriciously changed, or changed under malicious influence. The
cousin whose father wouldn't let her marry the man she loved, and
who would have been a Lady by now. The aunt who's weak and
whose children and grandchildren sponge off her. Fascinating but
drily told, not in the juicy way one longs for—no sense of the real
lives of people, just wooden figures being moved about on a board.

———

Why am I here? I thought it was to find my father, but maybe it's
to connect with a power so much bigger than he is that it will free
me from him.

———

I dreamt about a new house. In the room that was to be mine I found
a dead body lying on its back in a long cardboard carton under
the table. I pulled it out by its ankles. Its leg bones were split open

lengthwise and in their furrows lay, end to end, dozens of brand-new biros, Bic medium-point, the transparent plastic sort. They rattled around and tipped out when the body was moved.

I told Dad the dream. At the bit about the biros we laughed, and he said, 'How many did you take?'

I climbed the rock at dawn with a London barrister who arrived at the base on a motorbike just as I got out of the car. One of those floppy-haired Englishmen with pink cheeks and fine features. Hurray! The first person I'd met in a week with whom small talk was not necessary. It was a hard climb and I started along the chain too fast. I tasted blood. 'We'll take plenty of rests,' said the barrister. The wind was powerful and very cold and I didn't have enough clothes on, but my heavy boots were suited to the job. The two Japanese kids coming down, gasping with wonder: 'We—saw—many stars! We—saw—*comets*!'

You can't write about this stuff. I met my Mighty Force on top of the rock and it played with me.

'She's got a season ticket,' said Dad. 'She likes to go to concerts. She likes classical music. Oh, I like it too, but—I reckon you can have too much of that sort of thing.' The idea of excess; how he hates it. I walked out to see the sun go down, and passed the bar, from which poured loud music and voices, like the noise of a party. I glanced in, saw dimness, many men in working clothes, some bending over pool tables. I loved the noise. I thought gladly that somewhere people were shouting, talking to each other, *over-doing it*. I looked round and saw a clapped-out Valiant with two mattresses and some bendy strips of building materials strapped to the roof. In the front seat sat three men in singlets, dust-coated, sunburnt. I smiled and waved, and so did they. The driver planted his foot and the car took off in a plume of dust. The motor sounded sick, the man was laughing, I laughed too and off I went, running and jumping and swinging my arms. 'Ratbags!' I shouted to myself, a tribute to maniacs and excess.

———

Corny, mediocre country-and-western songs that touch on painful truth.

———

My father lives on meat.

———

At the base of the rock the silence plugs my ears. There are no sounds. Then a little tuft of grass behind me rustles. I jump round. Other clumps hiss and move, it is a sudden rush of wind, my skin stands up.

———

Oh, how we hang on to that last prison! Even though it's ugly and damaging.

———

I felt stranger and stranger. I took a cab to North Sydney. In the hotel a strange wind whined at the window and what water I could see was mistral-coloured. I sat looking out at the warm evening, the sparkling towers, and thought in a stunned way, This is a very peculiar moment in my life.

———

I could say to him, 'I would get a broken heart if you left. But it's been broken before, and has healed.'

———

In the funding meetings they probably think I am 'tough and ruthless', but they are mistaking for ruthlessness a spontaneous following of my shit-detector, which is the only part of me that functions confidently in this impersonal world.

———

A poem translated from the Arabic called *Homesickness*. Words to the effect of 'Once again you take out your knife and stab me', and then this: '*Nobody knows whether I am dancing or staggering.*'

———

'There is something between me and her.'
　'Since when?'
　'Two weeks.'
　I keep walking but put my hands in my pockets.
　Nobody knows whether I am staggering or dancing.

———

It is night. Perhaps it is raining, or has been. He stands with my suitcase in his hand, and looks wildly for his car. The car park is half empty, but he cannot see it. 'I think it has been stolen,' he says. 'Look again,' I say. 'It must be here.' And it is, white and long, slightly closer to the building than he has remembered.

———

He has been tormented for a long time by childlessness.

———

I'm split in two: the shocked, stunned part which will suffer when feeling returns, and another part which examines and censors certain urges that rise thickly and clumsily from the stunned part: no, that is a cheap shot; no, there you are drawing attention to yourself as suffering; no, it would not be just to say that, and so on.

———

I slept about two hours, woke at 5.30 in my room and watched the curtains get whiter.

———

'You never made concessions to me, in the way you lived your life.' This I cannot deny.

———

Downstairs M and the two girls from Ballarat have set up their music stands and are playing eighteenth-century music with sweetness and confidence. I love their straight backs, their gay clothes, their lovely concentration. 'Again? Two, three, *four*.'

———

I was hard inside, bitter and cold, wanting to hurt her: 'If you'd been fifty-three, ugly and stupid, this wouldn't have happened.' But she went on being humble. She turned the other cheek, is that it? She went on standing there, presenting herself, not running away.

———

'People who are jealous,' he said, 'ask questions whose answers will hurt them. That's why I lied.'

———

'I'm sorry,' I said. 'I've hurt you terribly.'
    'But I have hurt *you* much worse than that.'
    'Let's forgive each other.'
    'I forgive you for everything.'
    'I forgive you too, for everything.'
    All this through sobs, and floods of tears. And then we went out into the kitchen and started drinking.

———

The girls played, and I washed the dishes, wearing the grotesque rubber gloves my sister brought me from New York, with the silver ring and painted nails. I finished the scotch. I went to bed. I read a poem by Alison Clark called *Credo*: 'I *am* chained, but I have a soul...' And then I went to sleep.

———

M's father, F and me walking in the cemetery with the dog.
    Now I have two ex-husbands.

———

Strange images of loneliness: a bathroom that's *clean*, with a hollow sound because it contains only two towels, hers and mine.

―――――

In the old woman's calm flat, full of her quiet, idiosyncratic, practical objects and things of unusual colour, she too was calm. Women who live alone and like it have a rested, full look. I told her everything. 'It seems,' she said, 'that when you are successful you need to have someone near who will undercut you. As if you will not allow yourself to flower fully.'

―――――

In the wine bar F put to me his proposition. I stayed firm, but felt inside the small screaming sadness of having to reject something you long for but which is offered in a wrong spirit.

―――――

I need to find out why I so often get myself into situations where people have to symbolically murder me.

―――――

My little niece's collection of matchboxes, full of obsessively modelled plasticine objects. Each box has a label: 'CONTAINS: Carrot. Guitar'. I want to burst out laughing with each treasure she unveils, her intricate inspirations. I long to make a little movie, to show her absorbed expression, the way her head comes forward on her neck to peep into the next container.

―――――

'My experience tells me that marriage does not make one happier. It takes away the illusion that had sustained a deep belief in the possibility of a kindred soul.' —Paula Modersohn-Becker in her diary, 1902

―――――

'...Layers, or strata, or veils; an indefinable looseness or flexibility of handling; windows; autobiographical content; animals, flowers; a certain kind of fragmentation; a new fondness for the pinks and pastels and ephemeral cloud colours that used to be tabu unless a woman wanted to be accused of making "feminine" art…' —Lucy Lippard on recurring elements in women's art, in *From the Center*

———

Leave me alone. I'll get over you if you'll just leave me alone.

———

A drunken, filthy old man walked straight off the street into R's house. He thought it was *his* place. We pushed him gently out the front door. He sat on the pavement shouting: 'I kill. I kill every-thing.' After half an hour he got up and walked away.

———

A voice almost oily with the desire to appear co-operative.

———

'When my husband and I split up,' the woman told me, 'he suddenly wanted to talk at great length about himself. He used to invite me over and cook a meal and have a bottle of wine, and start pouring out streams of stuff. I used to feel so terribly tired, and bored, that I'd fall asleep at the table.'

   'Because it was too late?'

   'Yes—and because instead of tinkering all along, the way women do with their friends, he wanted to produce one great dollop, and expected me to pick it up and carry it. And I couldn't, and didn't want to.'

———

Traces of his presence: large, hacked scraps of toenail on the bedcovers. I picked them up with care. Lucky for him I'm not a witch.

———

Fresh morning. I went for a jog in Princes Park. Elms still fluttering and shedding those very pale green seedpods: they make a tiny rustle on the ground when a breeze moves them. Near the football ground a black man, a Pacific Islander I think, was doing stretch exercises after a run. His body was thick, dark, packed solid, shining, in green shorts and a tracksuit top. I *think* that's what he was wearing. How on earth do people give evidence in murder trials?

———

A houseful of sleeping teenage girls. Bleached hair sticking out of twisted doonas.

———

I told Z that we'd split up. His reaction was what I'd expected—a rapid drawing-back, a look that said, 'I don't want you to tell me about it, I don't want to know the emotional stuff.'

———

At Tarrawarra the brown river ran by. In an outside corner of the abbey there was an arsenal of anti-magpie sticks, leaning against the white weatherboards. Each of us carried one in rifle position on the shoulder. Every now and then we would pause and stand still. Always traffic noise, but also the twittering of swallows. The soft, heavy air that hangs over rich farmland. Wheel marks in the grass—on each blade a glossy sheen of light.

———

The interviewer asked me a strange question: 'In what ways are you a different person from the one you were ten or twenty years ago?'

I could have bawled, but I thought for a long time and then said, in a low voice, 'I know now that people will do anything. They will do *anything*.'

———

At the Harbourfront International Literary Festival in Toronto I am mistaken by three separate male writers for a staff helper. 'How many buses do you *have*, in this organisation?' 'I've no idea. I don't work for it.' Stanley Elkin, an American writer of 'extravagant, satirical fiction', is offended when I say I have to go straight home after the festival. 'Nobody *has* to do anything.' 'Yes, they do.' 'Why can't you stay a couple of weeks and go to New York?' 'I'd have liked to. But I have to go straight home.' 'But why?' 'Because I split up with my husband just before I came away, and I've got a daughter at home.' That shut him up. But when he found out that my daughter was sixteen he renewed his attack. He moves about on two sticks and has the bitter look of someone in pain.

––––––

In the gallery I liked humble paintings of interiors. A bedroom, a strip of light across a chest of drawers. It becomes clear to me that middling art comforts, while very good art challenges and unsettles. The Henry Moores, though, do something else: they make you *still*. Your breathing slows down.

––––––

Two gay shop assistants saying goodbye. The black one says, 'Touch you later.'

––––––

At Niagara Falls, Kenzaburō Ōe told me a little story. 'A Japanese man came up to me, back there. He said, "Are you Japanese?" I said, "Yes." He showed me his camera and said, "Japanese camera." Then he said, pointing at the falls, "Are you surprised?" I said, "Yes." He turned to his wife and said, "This man is Japanese, and he is surprised."' We laughed so much, we could not stop.

––––––

The timelessness of a long flight. I gazed down on the land we were passing over. An immensity of absolute flatness, divided by humans into a regular pattern of squares, and planted and cropped. It spread away in every direction for thousands of miles. I was frightened. Every now and then a small town would cluster at an intersection of roads, or in the bend of a river. I thought, Each of these settlements has a name, a social fabric, a *feel* to it all its own which its inhabitants consider to be unique. This thought made my heart ache. We passed over snow-sprinkled mountains, then a wide valley, then a grey, bare wilderness through which twisted seaweed-shaped rivers or dry watercourses.

———

At 3 am I woke, and came to very gradually. My eyes focused on the top shelf of a bookcase. I thought, 'That looks just like my bookcase at home.' I let my glance roll sideways and down. I saw a planet lamp, a mirror, all these minor, still objects in the faint light from outside the curtains. I was astonished. 'This room, in Canada, is exactly like my room in Melbourne.' Then I woke properly. I was at home, in my own bed. A moment of absolute happiness.

———

The Exhibition Gardens are thick with new leaves and lovers lying in sexual postures.

———

The woman at the wedding who told me about the months, even years, after her husband was killed in a car accident. 'Nothing that should have been good was. I'd look out the window in the morning and see the sun shining, but it wasn't good.' Is that what grief is?

———

On the phone K told me some true-life stories about swords and rings. They were wonderful. I said, 'Why aren't you writing all this down? Without trying to be funny?'

———

Imagine living in a city beside an OCEAN.

———

At the pub reading, the lights shone in my eyes and I saw nothing but one young woman's face, right at the back. She was smiling, rapt. It unnerved me. I felt I could not read well enough, had not written well enough, to justify her undefended openness.

———

I saw the mad one. His face is triangular, like that of a knight in a painting. His eyes slide away.

———

I wonder if what we see as a world full of couples is really a world of triangles.

———

The dream where someone gave me three Swiss knives, big, middle-sized, small.

———

I get no pleasure out of drinking. I feel blurred, stunned, disconnected, after even the tiniest quantity. I've got pains. Shoulders stiff as coathangers. My neck is rigid. My ovaries hurt. My tubes hurt. The twinges are tube-shaped.

———

The meeting at the Goethe-Institut. Openable windows, huge pale green leaves thickly massed outside the glass. The motherly woman stood next to me with her hand on my shoulder. Her kindness made my self-control almost impossible to maintain. I longed to burst out sobbing, to lean my face against the arm of the tall man beside me, and for people to go on talking quietly and let me be weak. But *the show had to go on*. She pointed to my head and said, 'You've got a real little puritan in there, haven't you!'

———

I dreamt I saw a white bird, like a pigeon, waddling along a path with a smaller white bird riding on its head, and the second white bird had an even smaller bird perched on *its* head, a bird that was of a striated appearance, black and white, like a stone or a streaky opal. People watched and laughed indulgently, as at a clever circus trick or a childish antic.

———

It is always me who ends our phone calls. Sometimes I feel boredom creeping over me, but K could chatter on till nightfall.

———

I feel: disgusted. Angry, jealous, tired. Bored. But all in quantities so small as to make action or even statement too much of an effort.

———

Dreamt I was in India, in a room full of children. The window was open. A jeep full of soldiers drove past. One of them stood up and threw a hand grenade into the room. I turned away and covered my head. One of the older boys picked up the grenade and threw it back out. A close-up of the grenade as it lay on the floor: it looked black and greasy, and its surface was divided into those raised squares one sees in cartoon drawings of such manly objects.

———

M got 97% for French. She's going to Paris next week. In the park she left her coat on a rail and did cartwheels and somersaults on the grass.

———

'Perhaps it is better that men don't grow up,' said the Polish doctor. 'When they do they become sad, and serious.' Is this why women are sad? Because they are obliged to grow up? They have children, they shoulder the emotional responsibility and let the men go free?

———

A letter comes. Another description, from someone I love, of me as too big to handle.

———

I dreamt I went to the doctor complaining of a nasty discharge. She approached me with a pair of scissors. 'You're not going to cut my hair, are you?' I cried. She insisted, good-humouredly, and I let her. I shut my eyes while she clipped. When I opened them and looked in the mirror I was surprised to find I looked all right. Fragile, almost pretty, like someone recovering from a dangerous illness.

———

The old writer read a story full of flip stuff, lists of expensive things—cars, furniture, whisky—and tales of faithless wives. I watched two women in the front row. As he read, their faces registered a polite distaste.

———

The way P had put watercolour on the paper made tears of respect come to my eyes. A picture of a centaur in a ring of moonlit trees had the same effect on me as a book I remember reading as a child, illustrated by Edward Ardizzone: some children in a moonlit garden, silvery and mysterious and terrifying.

———

I have stopped cracking hardy. I cry, I shout. Last night I reached the lowest moment. I went into the kitchen, I didn't turn on the light. I stood at the sink and ran myself a glass of water, but I was crying so hard my mouth was too stiff to drink. I was full of shame and cheapness and misery.

———

The painter told me that when she finished the portrait she 'sat down in the lumpy chair and cried'. The miracle of making something that wasn't there before. Pulling something out of thin air.

———

I cried a bit more and then I ate my breakfast and read the paper. A stubborn optimism came creeping into me as I climbed the stairs. I went and had a healthy shit. I got out my new Hermès and set it up with pleasure.

———

I pulled the petals off the pink roses, which were almost dead. I seized each bloom with my fingertips and pulled: they came away with a little fleshy helpless resistance.

———

I dreamt of a church. A spiritual possibility in living alone, with children but without a man. I ate about a kilo of cherries, all by myself, without having to feel guilty for *not sharing*.

———

I wanted to say, 'Can I come over?' But I was too proud.

———

I am by myself. I think I like it but I'm not sure. It's 'good for me'.

———

It is always worse to see your mother lie down and take it than to see her stand up and start yelling.

———

The old woman showed us a photo of herself on holiday in America, standing on a country road in summer wearing a dress that reached halfway down her calves—an abundant skirt, a loose blouse and flat sandals. Her legs were comfortably spaced, her feet planted firmly. 'It's *you!* You look wonderful. You look like a peasant woman.' She simpered, back home in her Melbourne eastern suburbs outfit of a neat-cut synthetic frock, sheer stockings, and prissy little high-heeled sandals that made her stance like that of a bird gripping a twig.

———

Went to Communion. The Mighty Force is not there. Or it doesn't stand near me. The bread and wine don't seem to have anything to do with it. Or maybe it's me, awkward on my knees, anxious about doing or saying the wrong thing among those pretty, slender, grey-haired ladies who genuflect.

———

Twenty years ago, at uni, but I knew her at once. The long Italian boots, the brown wool dress. The face: closed, dark, in pain. The hands in pockets, the fast, absorbed walk, head down.

———

We say hurtful things that are not quite true. Such a war. Ammunition to hand in any situation. Any memory can be distorted at will.

———

He drove away. I stood at the gate. His face remained turned towards me until he was swallowed up in the dark.

———

They told me that no English publisher is interested in my work. A bloke with a hyphenated name said, having read *The Children's Bach* and *Postcards from Surfers*, that he 'just didn't like the stuff'. Why does this make me cry? Why should I *care*?

———

The doctor's kindness and intelligence make his face attractive. He said that the medical politics surrounding AIDS was 'disgusting'. He said that at the hospital they got attached to the AIDS patients. 'It's awful. They *all die*. Every one of them. Young men, never had a day's sickness in their lives. It's sad. It's as if your brothers and sisters kept on dying.' He said the gay men in the AIDS task force 'had a hidden agenda: basically, underneath, they claim it as a right that they should be able to fuck any man they choose. That's all right, except when you've got a fatal disease.'

———

I read in the *New Yorker* that Rosario Godoy, a member of an organisation of women searching for 'disappeared ones' in Guatemala, was found dead in a car that had crashed over a cliff. Also in the car were her brother and her infant son, both dead. It might have been passed off as an accident but for one thing: the baby's fingernails had been pulled out.

———

K calls and wants to change all the arrangements.

  'We've had our deadlines brought forward. They sprang it on us at the weekend.'

'Why didn't you ring up at the weekend and tell me?'

'I had all my *shopping* to do,' he says irritably, 'and then I was at a *party*.'

———

A strange little orgasm, a keeping-still orgasm, brought about by a sudden mind-sight of a museum, an art gallery, a wall filled to the sides with a rapid series of intense and highly-coloured paintings. All this, however, as if experienced by someone else, which explains my reluctance to use 'I' in an account of it. Now that K's gone, and I'm in the hotel room by myself, I can't find any trace of his having been here: as if the hours of his visit existed in some element other than the time which is now in force.

———

A rainstorm, with hail and thunder, passed over. It blotted out the harbour entirely. It was strange to see the raindrops from this far (eleven storeys) above the ground: they fell past the window in an apparent order, each in its own column of air, not jostling or swerving. I fell asleep watching a tap-dancing movie on TV.

———

I'm scared.

———

I'd like to be able to accept my physical self as it is. I resist being looked at. I want to be the controlling one, the one who looks.

———

The harbour pool, Balmain, with two women, a producer and a director, who want to make a movie with me. Grey water slapping, a salty smell like Eastern Beach in Geelong. We swam about, calling to each other and laughing. From the dressing sheds, if we stood on the seats, we could look out through louvres and see the low port buildings all peaceful in the grey rainy evening. We walked up the steep hill under the trees. A strong smell of moss.

I remembered my body, that I was alive in the physical world.

———

'Gosh, you're prolific, aren't you!'

'Lately I am—but I'm always lashing myself for being lazy.'

———

I told the Jungian about Dad, his mother dying when he was two. 'A child who loses his mother,' he said, 'is often unable to trust anyone, ever again.'

———

Wonderful landscapes, full of grain—shades of blond—and tremendous clouds, richly shaped, with dark floors and boiling white tops. Sometimes a split, through which a clear blue would show or, further west, a paler pastel greenish-blue.

———

She saves used teabags. She uses every teabag twice. I refuse to believe she's that poor.

———

A horrible dream about sex with a man whose face as we fucked turned beast-like: the eyes sank into the skull, moved closer together, burned with a red light. I knew that this creature wanted to murder me, and that I had some secret power which could hold its savagery under control as long as I went on *believing* I had this power.

———

The student told me about speed, cocaine.

'Do you mean snorting?'

'No. Hitting. My boyfriend was dealing, he had enough money for us to *go right down*. I went right to the bottom, really quickly. And came up again. I feel I've got that stuff out of the way.'

'Do your parents know?'

'I told Mum. She said, "Should I be worried?" and I said, "No, you shouldn't."'

I was getting dressed after my swim when I heard the woman on the turnstile say, 'He's got all his clothes on!' Running steps, the PA hissed, and a scornful, angry male voice, highly amplified, said, 'Will that man in his clothes *get out of the water. GET OUT NOW.*' I came out to look. A sodden man with thick dark hair, in jeans and a shirt and shoes, was sitting in the posture of Rodin's Thinker on a starting block, with his back to the water, passing one spread hand back and forth across his forehead. 'He's a flip,' said the woman at the turnstile. 'He's a flip. He's got something wrong with him.'

Could I write a story without any characters? Only objects?

I bought some red leather sandals and some pink ballet shoes.

'Cod seemed a suitable dish for a rejected one and I ate it humbly without any kind of sauce or relish.' —Barbara Pym, *Excellent Women*. This is Elizabeth Jolley's tone and it made me laugh out loud.

At Parsley Bay I hit my right knee very hard against an underwater concrete step. It hurt so much that things went colourless.

T and I agreed that we liked having short hair, and didn't feel very female. She told me she had read a Jungian book about goddesses, and bought herself some skirts. 'But in a while I got sick of them. They don't have pockets. And what are you supposed to wear on your feet and legs?' I lent her the Kombi. She stole some bricks in it, went home and built a barbecue, then rang and asked me to dinner. She cooked two trout on the coals.

———

Q's patient demeanour makes me ashamed of the pleasure I take in complaining, in being aggrieved.

———

The murdered girl's stepfather told us that at the committal hearing the two accused were sitting right in front of him. 'They were holding hands and giggling. All my principles about capital punishment went out the window. Immediately. *Straight away.*'

Another friend at the table said, 'Do you want to get inside their heads?'

A long pause.

'No. I've never wanted that. Because it might make me feel—'

'Merciful?'

'No! Not merciful. I'm afraid it would be like going through the gates of hell. I'm afraid that if I found what violence and cold-bloodedness there was in *their* heads, I might find the same thing in myself.'

The other man tried to argue with him about this—to comfort him, to reassure him that he could never be as bad as that. But he would not be persuaded. Secretly I admired him for it.

'Everybody in my position,' he said, 'wants to be asked the questions we can't ask ourselves.' He said they want to be *pushed*, but they are concerned not to tell people things they might not be able to handle. 'You're scared you'll make them feel worse than you do yourself.'

I asked him if I could come to the trial.

'Why do you want to?'

'First because I thought you might like people to be with you. And second because I'm curious.'

The real truth would be in reverse order. In fact the real truth is part 2. The first is cosmetic, though it *is* true also, in another way.

Each of us sat with her chair turned slightly towards the open back door. The baby is due in five weeks. Upstairs I saw the baby's things. I loved the singlets best of all: white cotton, size 000, with a rib. Something in Elizabeth Jolley about the pangs caused by the sight of a baby's shoulders. I remember the shoulders, and the pangs.

Someone's applied to rent our spare room, a law student, and M's school friend's big brother.

'Is he a spunk?'

'Not when you first see him. But then you realise he is.'

'What's their family like?'

'A bit like us. They eat crude things. Nobody's much of a cook. Once I asked her if she wanted some pastrami and matzos, and she looked blank. I showed her what it was and she said, "At our place we call that meat and bread."'

C calls me from a restaurant in St Kilda. 'My father's just told me: a nudnik is a bore. A shlemiel is an idiot. And a shmendrick is a born loser.'

I told the Jungian how I hated and feared the kind of privilege claimed by beautiful women.

'And how have *you* claimed attention, Helen?'

I did not like being asked this question.

'Sex. Using my brains.'

Swimming laps at 8 pm. The cold, when I get out of the water, makes my jaw go up and down like that of a ventriloquist's dummy.

Tenant number 2. A, a born-again, from Sydney. Heavy eyelids, hair that grows in points in front of his ears, a slow naughty wit and an old-world turn of phrase: 'Don't give 'em too much leeway or they'll skin you.' The girls ask what makes black bread black. 'It's probably got molasses in it,' he says. I inspect the packet. 'There's no mention of molasses on this list of ingredients.' He snatches it from my hand with a snarl: 'Gimme a look at that label.' I seize the uke and defiantly play *There Is a Fountain Filled with Blood.* Maybe this could become a household.

———

I reviewed Spalding Gray's one-man show. Last night he came up to me in the lobby and shook my hand, asked for my phone number. Up close his eyes looked unnaturally wide apart, as if they didn't focus or as if he'd had something to drink, or smoke. The audience loved him and I felt proprietary.

———

Space Shuttle Challenger blew up just after blast-off. The 'first school-teacher in space' was thus vaporised before the eyes of her pupils, parents, husband and children. The strange shape of the exploded stuff—white smoke etc. It was pretty horrible but I felt revolted after a while by the emotional tirades the US media carried on with.

———

The woman's husband, whom she deeply loved, has died. She wrote: 'I feel I have been reborn without skin on an alien planet.'

———

The teenager told us that when she heard that her parents were going to separate, she pulled the new wallpaper off her bedroom walls. 'I tore it all down with my fingernails. I didn't even know I was doing it. I suddenly saw—' She mimes waking up and looking at her outstretched hands as if they held strips of paper.

———

The mind of A, the born-again, has several gears: dreamy and disconnected; witty and on the ball; plodding with difficulty from point to point in some long internal argument of which only the iceberg tips emerge in speech: 'There's worse things than war.'

———

The gist of it is, I guess, that I wasn't vulnerable, or feminine. F says that I didn't need him enough, that I barged straight through him. I have to accept this in silence. Because it is true.

———

I am a forty-three-year-old woman, a mother, healthy, reasonable-looking; I am in my own city; I am able to make a living; I am sometimes sad or frightened, and recently I have been hurt; but I am also learning to examine myself and my crimes less defensively; the Mighty Force has not lately come to me in the form I was expecting; but it does not abandon people, and it won't abandon *me*.

———

Spalding Gray, the monologist. He talks *all the time*. But since he is never boring, one is never bored. His voice is 'soft, pleasant and emphatic'. He has a strange face, rather like a dog's: big-mouthed and snubbed. He says he is very drawn to the neuroses of women: 'I'm always acting out stuff with my mother, who killed herself in 1967.' A woman approached him in Sydney. 'It was getting too much for me so I left the bar without saying anything. Next morning she left a note in my box: "That was a pretty tacky thing to do." She even came to my hotel when I wasn't there and asked the clerk for my *key*.' He gave me a copy of his book and wrote in it, having to ask me to check his spelling: 'Thank you for shinning your lights on me.' I suppose he meant what I wrote about him in the newspaper. We talked for several hours. I've never met a more fully and richly self-obsessed person in all my life.

———

I listened and listened. Did I hear? Maybe not what the man was telling me, or wanting to impart; but something.

————

The law student washed the dishes last night, without speed, enthusiasm or skill.

————

A day at the murder trial, in the Supreme Court. At first bored with the nit-picking and the slow pace, but after a while we became accustomed to the rhythm and entered into the case's *world*. The feast of human types dragged in as witnesses: two junkies; a man from Glen Waverley; a union official and his wife, a toughie with a cigaretty voice, long perfect silver nails which she tapped loudly on the witness stand, a carefully tended tan, long arms and legs, slender, very well-preserved (younger than me, no doubt). After this I was terribly tired, almost ecstatic with fatigue. And I was only *watching*.

————

They have found at Ayers Rock the body—partly eaten by 'dingoes, birds or goannas'—of a young English tourist who had fallen; and beside or near it *a baby's matinee jacket*.

A told me about his father and his brother. 'I felt that if they couldn't get themselves together they should *die*.' He said it harshly, with a sharp pushing-aside gesture of one hand. Then, of course, they did, and the girl killed herself. 'I just went to bed. I was completely undone. And I prayed. I didn't believe, but I prayed.'

'What did you say?'

'I said, "If there's anybody who can take away this load of guilt, please will you."'

———

'You seem happy lately, sweetheart. Singing round the house, always in a good mood.'

'Yes, I am. It's so much nicer around here. You used to fight *all the time*.'

———

In the cathedral, fifteen minutes before the communion service was to start, a bloke got up and said, 'As we feared, someone has rung a TV station and said there's a bomb in the building.' A boy of five or so was sitting beside me with his mother. At the word 'bomb' he looked up at me with an expression of intense and comical puzzlement, and said, as if trying to nut out a problem, 'Well, it can't be the Americans, because—'

'It's not a bomb from a plane,' I said. 'It's only a stupid joke—somebody's told the police that there's a bomb under a seat.'

He sprang up like a scalded cat, would not be reassured that it was a hoax, and dragged his mother off down the aisle at a fast clip.

———

Another day in court. Fascination seized me. An unflappable pathologist read out her description of the injuries and wounds on the girl's body. The shock of detail.

———

They rang and told me I'd won the festival award. Ten grand. I began to tremble at the knees.

———

I woke and heard the north-westerly rushing the dead leaves past our house: thousands and thousands, an unending supply, a people going into exile. Now the sky over the low mountains is dusty orange.

———

While we were in the Twins it began to thunder and lighten and pour with rain. The dog, chained to the post outside the shop, barked and whined. She did not have the nous to stand under the veranda.

———

P called in at dinner time and ate with us. She spoke about Halley's Comet and suddenly the wonder of its colossal journey struck me. Surely God exists? Can such a phenomenon have no meaning?

———

Dreamt I went to church and sat in a pew. I felt calm, and waited for enlightenment which I knew would come: I didn't have to *do* anything in order to be enlightened, just sit quietly and be ready. A feeling of quietly simmering expectation. Something good and right coming, if I could be patient.

———

The woman accused of the murder must have learned her evidence by heart. Would a girl who says 'somethink' and 'anythink' also say, 'And I think on the odd occasion another female' or 'prior to reaching the service station' or 'the matter that I'd been taken into custody for'? She said she was 're-luke-tant' to do something and her barrister had to correct her. The frightful pathos of this. I would say they were done like a dinner.

––––––

The man was found guilty. And the judge directed the jury to acquit the woman because the charge against her could not be proved. We all stood up, incredulous. But then came to me a sharp flash of illumination: what we were bowing to was not this thin, tough-faced man in a red robe, but to the power that he exercised, that passed through him, that our society gives him. I felt the spirit of the law—something tremendous restraining itself by reason. *They really do have to prove it.*

––––––

The class reunion, in a suburban backyard. People had brought their husbands. Nobody told me we could, and just as well, for I no longer have one. The men must have been very bored. They barbecued a creature on a spit and stood about drinking. A woman whose quiet, intelligent manner and thick fair hair I vividly remembered told me she was a hypnotherapist: 'I like depressives. Suicides. People in extreme fear states. Schizophrenics.' The woman who was head prefect the year before me, a powerful hockey player, seized my arm: 'I read your book. Saw it on TV. Bloody awful. Sorry. Hated it. Not trying to be rude, but it was bloody awful. You won't get any false praise from *me*.' I shrugged, and folded my arms. She immediately folded hers. It was cold in the garden. Someone passed round an exercise book and we wrote our names. When I saw the way one woman wrote—left-handed, a thin brown claw—I felt a small rush of emotion: 'Oh—the way you hold a pen—I remember it!' People burst into shrieks and cries. I suppose we spent all our school lives together with pens in our hands.

———

Marcos flees the Philippines. Photos of him, mouth agape, orating into a microphone on the palace balcony, and behind him, plump and coiffed and upholstered, the repellent Imelda, her face casting a slanted glance past him as if towards a mob.

———

Pulling on his steel-toed boots, A sings to himself softly, tunefully and correctly, 'Blame It on the Boogie'.

———

The husband talks as if the wife were not present. He considers himself the main act and will cut across her quite ruthlessly, not even noticing he's doing it, in the middle of her sentence. She neither objects nor submits, but lowers her voice slightly and goes on speaking as a subtext to *his* discourse, even though each of them might be talking about something quite different.

———

J's put on a lot of weight and looks brown, smooth and solid. I was so happy to see him, I wanted to curl up under his arm and stay there all day. We lay on the grass listening to the speakers. When I got up I had green duck shit on my linen jacket, and I did not care.

———

They gave me the prize. I had to make a speech. My new black shoes were giving me terrible blisters. Thea Astley gave me some bandaids. She hugged me and said, 'You can write about all those tiny household things, like scraping the food off the cupboard fronts, and *validate* them.' Quite a few people told me that *The Children's Bach* is 'so small that it's hardly even a novel at all'. One bloke remarked in a classic backhander that he liked me and Frank Moorhouse because neither of us was any good at writing novels.

———

A hard-faced, blue-eyed poet in a singlet and jeans gave me tips on how to teach writing in Pentridge: 'Take a packet of Camel. Camel plain. Chuck 'em on the table and say, "Help yourselves."'

———

I was the only woman writer at the dinner. As the evening progressed I felt the foreign writers' egos balloon and take up even more air than did the pall of cigar smoke that issued thickly from their lips. Everybody deferred to the French *nouveau romancier*. He was actually rather pleasant. The Cuban big-shot avoided meeting my eye at all. I sneaked away into the garden after dessert. His glamorous wife, also Cuban, came out and sat beside me in the dark. I asked her, 'What is your work?' She looked at me with a blank surprise. 'I don' *work*. I maarried to berry fah-mous wriiiter.'

———

The ravaged beauty takes me to her newly renovated pied-à-terre close to the city. We drink tea and coffee. She is charming in the way that women (especially beauties) of her age and class can be: 'How *dreadful*! That must have been *ab*solutely *dev*astating!' etc—those phrases of the consummate listener, women's expressions that mean simply, 'I am paying attention to your tale', but which probably serve, as well, to conceal boredom and the fact that she is thinking of something else, something private, paying attention to her own silent story.

———

I was taken to visit a high school. Some students read out their stories. I loved this and was able to show it. Afterwards their teacher and I laughed happily together about the frequent theme of shit. One girl's story was even entitled *The Droppings*.

———

At 4 am someone opened my door and walked in. Waking in the dark, I thought, 'Oh no—I must have gone to sleep in somebody else's room by accident.'

'W-who's there?'

'Security. I can smell smoke. Is everything all right?'

'It must be my mosquito coil.'

'Sorry! Goodnight.'

When my heart stopped thumping I thought, 'Well, at least somebody's looking after me, even if I don't know who he is and will never see him again.'

———

In the long-term carpark at Tullamarine, waiting for the bus, sitting on an old hunk of timber against a cyclone-wire fence through which the morning sun is carefully warming my back. Birds. A phone ringing in the Budget office. Cars close and distant. Men's voices shouting, a hose squirting air. A small, cool breeze. A smell of grass.

———

My little niece gives me, Christmas-wrapped, a beautiful seaside stone, exactly the size to fit the palm.

———

After a warm night: rosy sky; remaining darkness clustering inside trees; pale objects drawing the new light towards them.

———

A party for Laurie Anderson in a beautiful gallery in the Domain. Arty people: some whose gender was not immediately apparent, others wearing exaggerated outfits—one bloke in a kind of helmet with shiny metal objects attached to it.

———

The biographer is going to AA. She told me she realised she had spent a lot of her life feeling envious and jealous, but censoring these emotions and denying to herself that she felt them. And I remembered—but did not speak about it, for she seemed to need to be the one doing the talking, though I could see that it was tiring her—a day when she came to my house, sat down opposite me at the table, and said, in her determined, dangerously smiling way that used to make me shiver at what she was about to hit me with, 'I've noticed that you use the word "envious" a great deal more than anyone I know.'

————

I wonder if I will ever meet a man I can love. Love, let alone live with. At my age is this such a tall order? Yes, it is. In a shop window I saw a poster of a naked man in profile holding a naked baby. The photo was cropped at the point of the man's torso where his cock began to be visible: I saw with a shock the stiff little bush of pubic hair. I had forgotten that such intimate sights existed. If I'm not careful I will forget my own body, too. Well—I may be lonely, but at least I'm not bored, and neither am I being hated by someone who is supposed to be loving me.

————

The movie I wrote is going to Cannes. Fear of the pincer action: on one side, public attention, on the other, the rage of people who see themselves portrayed.

————

In the Botanic Gardens A and I lie on two blankets that he's spread on the Oak Lawn and read *The Europeans* aloud. The bliss of being read to. The speckled shade, small children shouting and running across the grass. We take it in turns, chapter by chapter. The long sentences tax our powers of forward-seeing, but our skills develop as we warm to it. My crabby temper evaporates in the beautiful autumn day. The leaves are hardly brown, let alone on the ground.

————

The ex-junkie borrowed $68 off me ten days ago and has not been seen since. I thought I'd wait another week before I made inquiries. Then he called.

'Sorry I haven't paid back the money you lent me.'

Silence.

'But I—umm—well, I need to borrow some more. I need $80.'

Pause.

'No. I don't want to lend it to you.'

Pause.

'I'm crook and I need to go to work.'

'No. I don't want to lend you any money.'

'Oh. All right.'

'OK?'

'Yeah. Bye.'

So the gossip is true. I didn't hesitate, or feel guilty, or even give a reason. I must be making progress.

———

Cool, cloudy day at Anglesea. They took us for a swim. Everyone was leaving the beach for lunch and it started to rain lightly. The water was green and the sky was grey. Big, cold, slow swells that didn't break. P turned blue: 'My teeth are what you call chattering!' After five minutes it was no longer cold. We were all laughing and shouting—blasts of intense joy. On the way back to the house I looked around me at the low scrub and the greyish air and the massed tea-tree in a sort of bliss.

———

A movie about war crimes in Poland. A small crowd had gathered to watch the exhumation of bodies from a mass grave. Two men at the very edge of the trench slipped on the crumbling soil and fell in among the blackened, rotting remains. Their frantic scrambling to get out was frightful.

I thought my ladder had been stolen, but it turns out F had come over and taken it. What is the actual *process* by which one separates oneself from another person?

I bought a cassette of Maria Callas and played it in the car. When she sang *Io son' l'umile ancella* I amazed myself by bursting out sobbing. Not just a few tears but real weeping. All kinds of good and comforting thoughts rushed through my head. *I* want to be 'the humble servant-maid'.

I dreamt that someone threw blood on my long skirt. I took it off and wrapped myself in a towel while I washed out the blood. A young Eastern European man was anxious that someone would come in and suspect indiscretion. He stood in a corner with his finger across his lips. I couldn't convey to him that there was nothing to suspect. Someone was playing a piano for children to dance to.

The surgeon's wife actually considered buying a watch that cost $700. The courteous young man serving her kept his face blank while she loudly bashed my ear about Australia's descent into the maelstrom of unionism, high taxation and welfare. 'Workers are bludgers,' she said with scorn. 'Rostered days off, one a fortnight.' 'What's wrong with that?' I said, really wanting to know. She didn't have an answer.

The law student came downstairs to tell me something he'd read in a judgment he's studying. 'This judge reckons the law says that as much responsibility is to be expected of a twelve-year-old as of a twenty-one-year-old.' I noticed how white his face was, mauve shadows under his eyes. I said, 'Do you feel sick? You've gone very pale.' 'No—it's just the shock of the judgment.' His emotions often show in the colour of his face. When his girlfriend was coming back from overseas his skin was green.

———

The prisoners in the Pentridge writing group liked gasbagging about families, about touching people while you're talking, and whether this habit came from your parents. One bloke said, 'My family's very close, always huggin' and that. When my mum comes in here she throws her arms round me and starts bawlin'. I could've started meself—but *you* know—you have to—' He mimes himself darting embarrassed, tiny glances to left and right. Imagine if everybody in Pentridge started bawling at once, screws and all. The tears would rise up and spill over the curved top of the bluestone walls.

———

We walked out to Princes Park to look for the comet. A found it and I saw it, very blurred, six times as big as a star, like a headlight in a very thick fog.

———

Walked to the shop. Picked a twig of bottlebrush with three flowers on it. Looked at it with extreme pleasure. At home I noticed a shifting and saw that a praying mantis was hiding among its spiky leaves. 'Poor thing. Poor thing.' I took it out the front and held the twig against the wisteria: it stepped across and, adjusting its camouflage, disappeared.

———

M read me some Banjo Paterson poems. 'Where the breezes shake the grass.'

———

Peggy Glanville-Hicks was interviewed on TV.

'You love it, don't you—music?' said the interviewer, in a shy, humble voice.

'Well,' said the old woman, holding a whining black poodle in her arms, 'it's international. It can go anywhere. It doesn't need translation. And its manifestation is the displacement of air.'

_____

Once I accepted F's analysis, in his letter—that we'd never really committed ourselves to each other as married people do—all my victim feelings and anger fell away. All that was left was a terrible sadness. Days of crying at the slightest stimulus.

_____

'Afterwards she repented it bitterly, but she was hopeless at apologising: instead of retracting her feelings, what she always did was to say that she was sorry for expressing them, a kind of amends that costs nothing and carries the built-in rebuke that the other person is unable to bear the truth.' —Penelope Gilliatt, 'The Redhead', in *The Transatlantic Review*

_____

Sick in bed. My sister came round and told me the latest family gossip. We laughed and laughed. I thought of a little movie about how information passes round a family—very sternly structured, solely in the form of two-way conversations—all in dialogue, clothes and body language. 'And I said, "*Look*, Mum, there are dead letters in dead letter offices all over the *world*."' When I get better from this I'm gonna WORK. I'm going to make fur and feathers fly, I'm gonna ATTACK IDEAS and *let the chips fall where they may.*

_____

If I had a little boy I'd call him Angelo.

_____

'What I missed,' said the law student about the time his girlfriend was away, 'wasn't so much getting love as giving it. I just wanted to—I wanted to cover her with love.'

A said that anger ruled my life. Which of course made me furious but I tried not to be. Once again his humility and ability to accept criticism took away my weapons. He was washing up while we talked. When he got to the saucepan he turned aside and left it lying in the water. All the while, as the talk went to and fro, I was looking at the saucepan in the water, congealing with fat, bobbing in the sink, and I was thinking, 'Can't you finish a job? *That's* what makes me angry with you. You're sloppy.'

———

Dreamt I was doing an English exam and making a mess of it. I had missed one of the essay questions. I panicked, and began to give up. I looked out the window. A bird flew away. I felt sad and hopeless, as if all were lost. A woman supervisor looked at me through a grille. Suddenly I laughed and said, 'I'm a famous novelist! I don't *need* this exam!' She laughed too but still I felt ashamed, as if a necessary step were missing in my self-preparation for life.

———

A horrible nuclear disaster, a meltdown, at Chernobyl in the Ukraine. Nobody knows how many people have died.

———

Dinner with the famous ones. Among men, as usual, I became aware that I have no subject on which I can deliver quantities of information, facts etc. Savage gossip. I wondered how many knives would be quivering in my back after the door had closed.

———

All day at the Royal Women's birthing centre. I longed to watch a birth but of course this was out of the question, though I did glimpse, through opening doors, several cunts—one bloody, with a doctor sitting at it sewing it up. A huge placenta in a metal dish, the young nurses examining it bloody to the wrists. The matter-of-fact calm of midwives. The premature babies, their shuddering and gasping, their appalling tininess, I wanted to sob out loud. As if a nose were not made for anything but to have a tube shoved up it.

———

The nurse's husband, in a letter: 'Geez you women cry a lot but yer as tough as nails. I walk around feeling limp and inferior in the face of that iron-hearted sex you belong to.'

———

I drove her to school at 7 am for camp. We laughed all the way at I have forgotten what. She's had a dramatic, rather sixties haircut. 'It makes you look older,' I said. 'At least eighteen.' Her face burst into a joyful smile. I love her as one is afraid to love, through superstition. Even having written that...

———

A letter from the American. 'I swim beside you in spirit.'

———

Dreamt I was to be ordained and to give the sacrament. Anxious because I hadn't studied the liturgy. I woke thinking that if I were ordained I would be qualified to bury the dead. And the part I want to lay to rest is the girl I was in the 1960s. Who thought she was free but who was in fact chained. Who had two abortions and was not loved or respected by the men she slept with, although she believed she was, through inability to see the facts and insufficient imagination about what went on in men's minds and hearts. Cruel to herself without realising it.

———

Two people told me they'd seen me on TV. The man said, 'You looked sad.' The woman said, 'Your eyes were twinkling, as if you were about to laugh.'

I suppose being sad and laughing are not mutually exclusive.

———

The psychotherapist talks about 'men in suits' who come to him.

'They think they can hand me their problem and get me to fix it for them. They're so blocked. It's sad.'

'They must be terribly lonely?'

'And frightened. At some stage they always cry.'

———————

Up at Primrose Gully with Y. We're both scared of snakes. And we're ignorant of electricity, and how to use the car battery for power in the house. The neighbour from down the road: plain, with a mouth that's drawn in, watery eyes, filthy farmer's clothes, a loud, rather harsh voice—but a lively mind, witty turn of phrase, a tough and cheerful friendliness. He called each of us by name once or twice, as if to fix us in his mind. He offered to help with buying a chainsaw. I liked him very much, and felt lucky to have met him. He mentioned in passing that one of their children had died.

———————

Dreamt I was to sleep in a borrowed room. I asked the woman, 'What's in that drawer?' 'Maps,' she said. I looked at her with happy respect, knowing that she was a traveller, someone who'd been to strange, distant and perhaps dangerous places and who had returned. She seemed a calm person, the kind who makes plans and fulfils them with steady application.

———————

A hawk on a tree. We saw its shoulders.

———————

I *dread* having to *become a Christian*.

———————

A beautiful letter came from J. He said he loved my work, and that though I may not define goodness as he does, I was 'searching for a language of grace'. I went stumbling out on to the footpath still reading, and when I glanced down, the pebbles sprang into such bright relief that I had to look again. I had the dog with me and we walked slowly round the big block. It was a windy, sparkling afternoon.

———

'People who can't accept a gift,' said the Jungian, 'often feel a need to wound the giver.'

———

The biographer does that maddening thing of asking, 'Am I boring you?' at the exact moment when I am most deeply attentive to what she is saying: thus she breaks my concentration. It's as if she's jealous of her own discourse: when I'm paying total attention to *it*, she needs to force on me the distinction between *what she is saying* and *her*.

———

A Giuseppe Bertolucci movie, *Segreti Segreti*. I was struck dumb by its sophisticated structure and the deep sense of the society it emerges from. The final scene, where the terrorist sits opposite the woman judge and begins to reel off the names of her comrades, made me want to get down on my knees and grovel. Why can't Australian films achieve that density? It must be because our society is so porous.

———

At Primrose Gully the grass is stiff with frost. Feet aching with cold. The clear patch on the window where I wiped it to see out has refrozen in prettier patterns.

———

I saw a big fat koala fall out of a tree. It sloped off towards the road with a sulky look over its shoulder. I laughed out loud and clapped my hands but it paid me no attention. Its victorious rival, clinging to a tall slender trunk, had what looked like a bloody wound on its chest. Life is carnage up here.

———

Census night. The law student and I were filling out the form. He

had to say what he was in relation to the head of the household. I
expected him to write 'tenant' but he put 'friend'. I think of this on
and off all day and it comforts me.

———

Hannah and Her Sisters. Too close to the bone. Oh, it hurts so much
to look back. I rode over him roughshod. Impatient, vain, self-
important, and then abject. No wonder he can't stand me. I can
hardly stand myself.

———

House full of music. The law student and his huge friend roaring
away upstairs on amplified bass and guitar. The girls downstairs
singing Schubert at the piano.

———

The I Ching says that flight means saving oneself under any circumstances, whereas retreat is a sign of strength. Voluntary retreat.
Friendly retreat. Cheerful retreat. That's what I'm after.

———

As the afternoon was ending my friends took me for a walk along the
Glebe waterfront. The sky was quite black in parts, then streaked,
swirled and plumed like a Turner painting. A strong, warm wind
blew. The evening star shone steadily between rents in the cloth.
'Australians are hopeless with land use,' said the Cretan. 'In Europe
there'd be a couple of little restaurants along here.' He showed me
some photos he'd taken of me last year and I was shocked by my
ugliness: spotted skin, lined face, ugly haircut, dark expressions. I
mean I was *shocked*. I quailed at the possibility that I will be alone
now for the rest of my life. That I will never turn back into a
womanly being but will find myself stuck here in between, plain and
dry in my manly or boyish little clothes. I was afraid of my ugliness.
I thought, I will go on getting older. This is not a temporary phase. I
am moving slowly and surely on towards decrepitude. But walking

with them I became happy. I picked wattle, bottlebrush, Geraldton wax. The Cretan poured out so much botanical information that we teased him and called him Professor. They asked me if I would ever consider moving to Sydney. 'I feel,' said the Cretan, 'that you're on the verge of plunging into a pool of clear water.'

Up here, among kind friends, I forget my troubles.

———

How the nun says goodbye: 'Go in peace.' 'You too,' I say, without having to think. Afterwards I felt her little blessing and was grateful.

———

F says I ought to get a regular job, so as to be less 'frantic'.
  'What could I be?'
  'A teacher. A publisher's reader.'

———

The historian who came to my reading at Monash. She told a little anecdote, with gestures, about using the expression 'phallische Symbolen' to some visiting German friends of her age: to her astonishment they had never heard the term. She was speaking about a row of carrots standing on a shelf in a juice shop.

———

I like it when my sister talks about nursing. She told me about nasogastric tubes and how to insert them. And about colonic irrigations.

———

Les Murray's wonderful poem 'When Bounty Is Down to Persimmons and Lemons'. The infuriating accuracy and simplicity of his images—birds that 'trickle down through' foliage. *Of course*, I think, that is what they *do*—why didn't *I* know how to say it? '*Women's Weekly* summer fashions in the compost turn blue.'

———

Evil Angels—its marvellous combination of tenderness for the characters with an awesome ability to handle masses of factual material. And the delicacy of its emotional texture. The whole thing is buzzing with life.

———

At the school concert a girl's proud father says, 'I *love* you!' and squeezes her in his arms. She shrieks, '*Ewww*, YUCK!' and fights to break free. He grips tighter with a demonic grin.

———

To the dentist for a crown preparation. He stuck the needle twice into my lip, babbling rapidly, '*Oooh*, yes you're a good girl a brave girl a very very good girl a brave girl.' Almost two hours of grinding, drilling, injections, string, blood, impression taken twice, post screwed in. As the time went on I became weakened by attrition. His waggish, chatty spiel, his way of addressing me as if I were a child and stroking my face while the impression set, caused a regression which reached its peak when I told him, after he'd cemented the temporary crown on, that it felt big in my mouth. He snapped at me: 'I *asked* you before! And you *said* it wasn't touching!' To my horror I burst into tears. 'I'm sorry! I'm so tired! I didn't understand exactly what you were asking—oh, boo hoo!' He was astonished, and embarrassed: 'WHY are you so tired?' 'I've had my mouth wide open for TWO HOURS!' He put me back in the chair and drilled off a bit more. I tried hard to control myself, for fear that if I jerked he would puncture my already bloody gum, but I couldn't stop my quivering sobs, like a child's, and tears ran off my face. He and the nurse acted soberly. The nurse didn't look at me again. It was awful. His falsely cheery goodbye. I stumbled off down the hallway. Before I reached the street I had recognised it: Dad territory. His baby talk had lulled me, and then the shock of his anger—a sudden withdrawal of approval. At the traffic lights I met Mum's brother. He didn't even notice I was crying, so I quickly stopped.

I lie in bed thinking voluptuously of the stories I'm going to write.

'I think,' says R, 'that people who "long to have children" are just being romantic.'

The bloke next door shows me the room with bunks that he says his children will sleep in, if he ever finds anyone to have them with. I forbear to point out that any child who sat up in the top bunk would be beheaded by the ceiling fan.

The plane lurched in the air and was lit by lightning, but in Melbourne the land was sunlit and the air was crisp.

I entered the living room and found Mum sitting alone on the couch, looking elegant. During our short conversation I had one of those moments of disconnection from myself: looking at her face I felt strongly that I both knew and did not know this person.

The high-school drama night. M's house did Molière, *Le Médecin malgré lui*, which she had directed. It ripped along, seductive, hilarious. Her fleeting bit-part as the passing stranger who tries to stop Sganarelle from beating his wife—she was a flash of lightning, her face white with righteous anger and then with alarm and apology— people shouted with laughter. This skinny little trouper of mine. Not mine much longer.

Raymond Carver called collect when I wasn't home, and the law student, confused, caused him to hang up.

Out near the rubbish bins I ask my neighbour if she knows anything

about Melanie Klein. 'I absolutely *detest* psychoanalysis,' she snaps.
I bet you do. Look at your life.

―――――

A woman reviews my postcards book in *Meanjin*. Covers it
with praise. 'Artful.' 'This brilliant story.' 'Consistently good.'
'Outstanding.' I'm glowing, defences down. Then on her way out
she flicks me with her tail: 'She is at her best, so far, when dealing
with…middle-class, contemporary living and relationships. This
is her great talent. It remains to be seen whether this is also her
limitation.' What do they WANT from me?

―――――

Visconti's wonderful movie *Bellissima*. We writhed with laughter
in our seats: the comedy of the child's suffering. How there's often
a secondary activity in the background of the main action: a line of
tiny distant dancers rehearsing on an outdoor stage: '*Uno! Due! Tre!
Quattro!*' A man on a high scaffold banging in a nail with tremendous arm movements. Layer after layer of life.

―――――

Afterwards at the Rialto A ordered another beer when everyone else
was ready to go home. Three quarters of the way down it he went
off to the lavatory. T seized his glass and swigged a large mouthful,
to speed up his painful slowness. 'Here he comes,' she hissed. 'Is
there foam on my lips?'

―――――

I want to write a story called 'The Punishment for Not Being
Beautiful'.

―――――

I shot off a whole roll of colour film in our house while everyone
was out. First I took one of each bed as it had been left; then I
crammed myself into corners, set things up, crouched, stood on
chairs, screwing up my face, framing things—to take photos you

must have to relearn to *look*. Filled with respect for people who do this difficult thing beautifully. I loved trying. Thought of writing a story with no characters in it, called 'Four Beds', and even began it, but put it aside, out of fear I suppose.

————

At their house we ate barbecued chicken out of a paper bag and listened to Nat King Cole.

————

Dreamt I was a teacher and there was one uncontrollable boy in my class. I sent him to the principal. I said, 'I'm not stupid, you know, no matter how much you dislike me. What *do* you think of me?' He replied frankly, 'I think you're *awful*.' At that moment I saw a close-up, near my face, of a bush covered in pretty little flowers, in the front garden of our old house at Ocean Grove.

————

Outside the post office the dog shat out a tapeworm. It trailed behind her and I had to put my foot on it to snap it off.

————

In Readings I picked up a novel about a sadomasochistic affair. I read it in furtive bursts, in case someone looked over my shoulder. It was frightening. I realised I am very much a moralist: afraid of the tremendous power of sex when it's let loose from love and social restraints.

————

'There are people,' a reader writes to me reproachfully, 'who have their babies at home, get married with flair, and get buried in triumph.'

————

After the funding meeting comes a surprising letter from the old poet who worked with us, a small, gentle, mildly spoken, slightly trembling woman with long white hair in a French roll: 'You will never be in need of friends. I mean of all sorts and degrees—and whatever your own personal uncertainties may be.' The extraordinary kindness of this. She mothered me. I'm not used to it.

———

Spring comes. People fall in love—or they will, when the sunny breezes blow and exams are soon and cafe tables are put out on the pavements. Will I? I can't imagine who with.

———

On a sparkling morning, windows wide open, Crowded House on the stereo, the law student and I wrestle with a lamb shank. He twists and wrenches with the rubber gloves on, I hack with a big blunt knife, so he can make stock and cook us some soup. Carnage over the trough. Blood splatters his front. 'Take your shirt off and soak it.' 'I wouldn't have known about doing that.' 'Women know a lot about blood.' He's the closest I'll ever get to having a son.

———

Primrose Gully with T. There's a star beside the moon that neither of us has ever noticed before. Star and moon are both reflected in the dam so vividly that it's unnerving—as if we were suddenly seeing everything upside down.

———

A big dry wind roars all night. Stars brilliant. Several are yellow. 'Look at them,' says T. 'Aren't they queer. They make the others look really *blue*. They look like electric bulbs.' She messed around with some grass and rags and came up what she called a 'pagan bride', a little straw doll in a dirty cloth dress and hood. She called me to look at it and I got a funny feeling, seeing it leaning against a small bush. It looked primitive, mysterious and powerful. Maybe I could write about A's panic when I said I was going to get my palm read. His refusal to tell me his astrological sign. Can I use the Cathedral Tearooms? The women's ordination?

Ayers Rock? It could be a novel. Oh, calm down.

———

I sat at the table working away with the Faber Castells while the law student played his Jazz Originals book on the piano. Drawing beats colouring-in hands down.

———

In a magazine a sketch of three women sitting at a table, and on it, in the foreground, a crudely drawn pistol and a very high-heeled shoe. The artist does people with hardly any lines: women with funny little bobbed haircuts and sober faces.

———

'I saw how beautiful she was,' said the bridegroom in his speech, 'and I saw that a man'd be a fool not to want to share his life with her.'

———

The things men say to me sometimes at public gatherings. In a strange, jesting, almost pugnacious tone they say that they like my work, and then they tell me what bugs them about it. This one couldn't stand the way I 'talk about Bach and popular music in the same breath. That's an *abomination* to me.'

———

They must have seven kids by now, the youngest only a few months old. Felt a longing to visit them, to see them all thronging, hear their family language and songs, jokes at the table, the *noise* of it.

———

The academic was wearing a little pale satin shift to mid-calf, like a pretty nightie. Watched her in the line for food, saw how large her head looked, pale and tired, well-set on her slimmed-down body.

———

Should the law student write his new almost-girlfriend a letter? If so, what sort? My tactician's idea: a postcard. What'll he write on it, though? Something short. What about 'Dear X, Come back quick. Love—' and sign? Perfect! But should he put some kisses? Just put one. OK—he doesn't want to be *heavy*.

―――――

Dream of a court case. A report typed on a typewriter that made small plants grow out of the page. I had to push the little stalks and leaves gently aside so I could read the print at their roots.

―――――

A visitor from Circus Oz. Her grey hair, flamboyant comfortable clothes. In the kitchen we talked with urgency and uttered screams of laughter.

―――――

My mind is full of stories but I lack the nerve to catch one and try to pin it down.

―――――

After the concert of mediaeval music the academic said she had seen the counter-tenor walking down the street with his little drum over his shoulder on a leather strap. We thought that he probably slept under a hedge.

―――――

We quarrelled. M spoke sharply to me. I suppose I was being silly and middle-aged. I was embarrassed that her rebuke had hurt me. She gave me a perfunctory hug which I accepted. I drove off to review a play, alone in my car and my clip-on earrings. Walking in the dark down Queensberry Street I felt quite desperate. I thought, 'This far down is when you ought to pray.' I didn't know how, but the thought presented itself like a reminder of a *practical technique*.

―――――

A thunderbolt struck me—*a character*. Ideas and plans flooded in and out of my mind all day. Such a richness of material that I hardly dare to look straight at it: I have to keep looking in the other direction. Surges of excitement and confidence, which suddenly ebb away and leave me panicking: *can I do this? Can I find out what I need to know?* By this I mean that a creature is beginning to exist which will lead me into a story. All I had to do was wait for my guide. I stepped out the back gate, my head bursting with this, and remembered that state where one lives night and day in the world of the novel and one is NOT AVAILABLE. No wonder men don't stick around.

———

A Russian cruise liner crashes into a tanker and sinks in 'the warm waters of the Baltic Sea'. Three hundred die. 'Those who had retired for the night would have had little chance of escape.'

———

Dreamt I cooked a meal and put those green anti-slug pellets in it. We all ate it before the terrible truth was revealed; and yet we agreed that its flavour had been delicious, with a hindsight tinge of horror.

———

A spiteful review of a friend's novel. I ask the magazine editor what the critic looks like. 'Oh,' he says, 'she's one of those Australian women with thin faces and black hair who remind you of Heckle and Jeckle.'

———

Primrose Gully. My sister comes down the track from the car, all in black, sunglasses, white-faced, like a refugee. Very upset and weeping. The married man she's having an affair with, his coldness in public, his failure to turn up, she lay awake all night waiting. Disgusting memories of my own. I talked at length about humiliation, low self-esteem, self-punishment etc. I must learn to shut up. Talking loosely and inefficiently is an indulgence. We went for a walk to look at the river, and back across the gully under the big pine tree. We picked up firewood. In the morning she said, 'I woke up once in the night and looked out the window.

The sky was full of stars. I thought I must be in heaven.'

_____

Against Z's back door jamb, after the *Rigoletto* rehearsal, leaned a small, white-faced, long-headed, warped figure. Weird, like something that had crept out of a dark hole where it had been lying for a long time in a tense and twisted position. 'This is V,' said Z. When the others went out of the room I felt nervous, like a schoolgirl having to entertain a grown-up. As we walked away from the house R said, 'Just as well neither of us is married to *him*!'

_____

Later, a dream: some kind of dark, dumb attraction between V and me.

_____

My sister breaks it off with the guy. 'I felt really happy for two days, and I still feel good. But sometimes I get very *sad*.'

'Sadness is better than wretchedness though, isn't it. It's more dignified.'

I felt very proud of her. As if she'd dragged herself out of a swamp in front of my very eyes.

_____

We walked the dog round Princes Park and kept noticing a strong smell of animal shit. We inspected our boot soles—nothing. 'It must be a circus,' said A, meaning it as a joke, but then I remembered that there *is* a circus on the other side of the footy ground—I saw the two camels, tall and lonely away from their desert.

_____

A doco about Berlin after the war. Footage of a boy of eight or so picking his way across a huge pile of building rubble, cap on head, pack on back, bare knees, boots—answering the questions of a disembodied voice: 'Where are you going?' 'I've lost my family. I'm looking for them.' 'How long since you saw them?' 'Six weeks. Goodbye!' He smiles, turns and walks away, a man with a mission—then a few yards further on turns again, waves, calls out 'Goodbye!' and goes on his way. I stood at the sink dumbly washing and stacking, despairing of ever having anything worth saying. I know nothing of what is savage and cruel in life. My work is as ignorant as I am. *I don't know anything.* But maybe it's the devil talking when we get the idea that someone who knows no savagery knows nothing—as if only evil were real and the rest weightless.

———

Near us, after midnight in the piano bar, sat an old man with a carnation in his buttonhole. He clapped his square hands in time to the music in such a way as to let it be known that he was with the band. Behind us a woman knocked over a stemmed glass. It smashed. She moved off to the dance floor without a backward look. A Japanese tourist at a third table bent down, picked up the glass, stem and base from the carpet, and placed them reverently on the glass-smasher's table. The only person who observed the Japanese woman's act, and her low bow, was a half-drunken young man, the gooseberry left at the dropper's table: he stared at her, loafing back in his chair, and made no sign.

———

The worst moment at the funding meeting was rejecting the application of a man who wanted to write a novel about the Kampuchean bloodbath. I looked at his file and thought, This guy's seen people suffocated in plastic bags and I'm sitting here telling him he can't have money to tell his story. I tried to make a coherent statement but felt heavy and desperate. I wanted to say that our procedures were inadequate and frustrating, but all that came out was, in a dull voice, 'He used to be a journalist and now he's a labourer.' 'It's a tough world,' said the chair, and on we went.

———

'He became a Roman Catholic after his son died of a drug overdose,' said the journalist. 'Course, being a Catholic in the right wing of the Labor Party isn't exactly a disadvantage…'

———

L, an unfairly handsome guy who was at the festival. I like him more than I'd expected to. Rather soft, talkative, an enthusiast, the sort of person who gives your forearm a little push as he approaches the punch-line of his story. I suspect a series of terrific emotional crashes in his past. Why does a man like this attract me? Don't be silly. Because he's *gorgeous*.

———

The student asked me if I thought love could connect people across boundaries of class. 'Of course.' He said he'd been convinced by Communism, then felt its rigidity: 'It dropped off me like a shell.'

———

At lunchtime I sat in the gallery beside a large, flat, shallow body of water in a pebble-bottomed bed. It quivered like the water in my best dream: trembled with inner life. A girl beside me on the couch, wearing modern clothes, was deep in a serious paperback novel. I sat there and thought, *I am happy*.

———

Fay Zwicky on the effect of Les Murray's work: 'Why then, after wrestling long and hard with many poems in this book, have I come away feeling excluded, mystified and defeated?' *Excluded* is the word I had been using.

———

My sister got some freebies to Mondo Rock. In the hour of waiting she took us to a new place called the Hyatt on Collins. A noisy palace in pink marble. A very amateurish singer and pianist, both boys, murdered certain innocent classics. '*Tsk*,' she said, tossing back a glass of terrible Australian champagne. 'That's a very pedestrian version of "Walk On By".' Next morning the law student sneered but I thought Mondo Rock were quite good. During one old-fashioned guitar solo I found I had tears in my eyes. I thought, I've been lonely for a year. I can still *like* this music. I will spend the summer dancing. I will have fun.

————

A house I like. Full of light. A backyard full of bull-dozable sheds. A huge park in front, and behind, a view over to Mount Macedon. Do people like me buy houses?

————

V's proprietary tone when he speaks of the high priests of European literature—'Yes, they are peculiar titles,' he says about Canetti's autobiography—reminds me of the German poet who boasted to me about how he had once sat up all night reading Chekhov's letters. As if no one else had ever done this.

————

The movie I wrote was screened on TV. I felt a waning of enthusiasm in the room as it progressed. All I saw were its faults and crudities—points at which it was rushed—big, far-off images instead of the small, intimate ones I had wanted. I felt tired, foolish, somehow ashamed. When it was over I hoped someone might ring me, but O, who was staying the night, went straight to the phone and made shouting interstate calls for an hour. I was too deflated to object. Then, very late, the old woman in Queensland who likes my work rang and said, 'I know I'm biased but I loved it. I cried.' I heard the sweetness in her voice and thought, She has been a pretty woman.

————

At the dinner table the law student's eyelids kept falling. He had plainly been at the pub all afternoon. The dainty Japanese backpacker looked at him carefully and said, 'Have you been drinking? Because there is strong smer of arcohor.'

———

L shows me a list he's typed up, of adjectives and epithets used by reviewers about his novel. An A4 page and a half. He read it out to me and we laughed and laughed. The whole range, from 'meaningless and pretentious' to 'brilliant', was covered.

———

Woken pleasantly from a nap by Bach on the piano downstairs, those powerful patterns flexing their muscles through the afternoon when no one's home but me and my daughter.

———

'I always thought that when we accepted things they overpowered us…This turns out not to be true at all, and it is only by accepting them that one can assume an attitude towards them.' From a letter by one of Jung's patients. —Peter O'Connor in *Understanding Jung*

———

Girls pass in the street, clapping a fast rhythm and singing a vigorous song.

———

In the pub after Carlton lost the Grand Final, the table of roaring, bellowing brothers. 'This is going to be one of those *nights*,' I muttered to one of their young wives, 'and I'm fucked if I'm going to put up with it.' She laughed in a comradely way and said, 'Aren't they terrible!' How come these yobs all end up with fabulous women?

———

V wrote, 'I wanted to see you again straight away.' So I was not imagining it. A gong of terror sounded in the bottom of my stomach. Something chilling in him. His intellect.

———

While I was asleep the Japanese girl got stranded in North Melbourne at 2.30 am and called our place for help. The Sydney visitor answered, told her he couldn't do anything for her and she should call a taxi—leaves her to her fate in the dark. She gives up and sleeps at the Youth Hostel. I know nothing of this till eight in the morning when she calls me. Furious and ashamed I drive over and collect her. When the law student hears that she had thought the rude visitor was him, he is strangled with distress: 'If it'd been me I'd've *run* to North Melbourne. I'd've piggybacked her.' 'I know you would, you darling,' I say fondly. 'Oh *yuck*,' says M with a grimace.

———

I walk down the street in bright lipstick and light-coloured clothes. People look into my face and smile. I've got seven-league boots on. I'm alive again.

———

Bulletin review of our movie. So splenetic it's embarrassing: apparently all my characters, in everything I ever write, are 'renowned for their unlikeableness', and the director has taken cinema back to a primitive stage before cameras could move. 'If Ms Campion is to be hailed as the new empress of Australian film...' Wonder what made *him* so crabby.

———

'Your daughter's terrifically striking-looking, isn't she,' says L. 'Boys must be swarming round her, I suppose.'

'Well, not really. She knocks around with a rather blue-stocking crowd. They repel boys with contemptuous stares.'

———

At the party a clean and bright young man in a striped shirt and little round tortoiseshell spectacles, with a flamboyantly Hungarian name, told me he'd read only one of my books and thought I ought to 'broaden my range' and 'write about the proletariat'. I was a bit drunk and said, 'What bullshit. *Why?*'

'Because the middle class is boring. It's narrow, small, confined, a minority.'

His wife or girlfriend, a striking dark woman, said, '*I'm* from "the proletariat". He's got a thing about it.' She looked at me in a friendly way and laughed. I wandered off, shaken by his challenge.

———

Rain is falling softly and steadily. This is comforting. What do I need comfort for? Being a member of the middle class. Not writing. Being forty-three and three-quarters. Being a solitary woman. Only no. 2 is a painful thing. All the rest often give me extreme pleasure.

———

Constant struggle between money and time: will I waste an hour going into town to Bell's Discounts to get the skin cream cheap, or will I waste a couple of extra dollars at the corner chemist and save the hour?

———

L hasn't answered my letter. The sense of having lost something, that his silence provokes. Remember that always, when a horror balloons in my memory around something I've written, a calm re-examination of the thing itself reveals a lightness of tone that saves it from being the crusher I have let myself imagine. Do my duties, try to get more sleep, drink less, try to keep this feeling of *worth* alive.

———

The American poet at the festival dinner meets my eye from the opposite corner of the long table and *holds it*, almost aggressively, with a small smile on his very wide, very smooth face. He holds my gaze for such a long time, smiling like a little brown Buddha, that I laugh out loud in a spasm of embarrassment. Later, I move to his end of the table, where a woman is declaring that feminism has caused an increase in male homosexuality. The poet says he thinks most people are sexually 'much more timid' than our society allows them to be. A bunch of us talk for a long time about sex and love. The young editor says he has never slept with anyone he hasn't 'got to know really well first'. The poet says he's always felt he was 'just as eager for love as women are supposed to be'; that he has 'never been interested in sex without love'. I opine that people organise their emotions to accord with their sexual interests, 'so that what you get is emotional rather than sexual promiscuity'. 'Love,' says the young editor, 'just *comes*.' 'Does that mean,' I ask, 'that you can't seek it, then?'

———

I am the only person in the world who carries round an inventory of my crimes. Everyone else is busy with their own.

———

The poet comes up to me in the lobby and says, 'I get consolation from seeing your face.'

———

Today I'll get up, have a shower, see how my period's going; make my bed; wear something clean and comfortable; go to the last day of the festival; maybe walk across the river and look at the water; and come home.

———

Mum comes to stay a night. I'm so tired. I ask her if she'll 'look after me'.

'Is there anything in the kitchen?' she asks. 'Any…eggs?'

'The trouble is, Mum, I haven't been here for days. There's no food.'

'I'll go to the shop.'

'Do you know what I'd really like? Chicken noodle soup out of a packet, and a boiled egg, and some fingers of toast.'

She laughs and looks pleased. The law student is playing 'My Funny Valentine' on the piano. My sister calls to tell me she's met Cyndi Lauper at a party: 'She's just a regular woman. She's *great*.' I go upstairs and lie down.

Mum returns. She brings my meal upstairs, sits on my bed and chats to me. I lie here bathing in her wandering tales. Sometimes my eyes close, but I don't have any trouble staying awake. I feel loving and thankful towards her. She kisses me goodnight at nine o'clock and goes downstairs with my tray. On my way to the bathroom I glance into the mirror. My face is young and smooth, exactly as it was after my crack-up two years ago when I dropped my bundle and slept for twenty-four hours.

————

One of these days I'll meet a man to whom I'll be circumstantially free to say, 'Do you want to get in the car with me and drive to Darwin?' and he'll say, 'Yes,' and we'll do it.

————

The poet Rosa Cappiello. Her terrifying sadness. Her clumsy questions: 'Helen, are you happy?' and statements: 'I want someone who is clean inside.' She asks me to read out her paper, for the panel 'Why I Write'. It's full of her awkward passion. Her poems terrify me too—I read the translations for her, trying to be only a vessel or a conduit for the rage and disgust that's in them: 'Lie down, man'—wanting to ravish, to 'breathe into his lap' a sexual fury that would set the world of gender right—but I felt very Presbyterian— restrained, small, neat, quiet. One of the poems was simply too much for me and I didn't even attempt it. But the American poet took her aside and spoke to her urgently in a low voice. I heard him as I passed: 'You are really, really good. You must practise and *practise*.' She seems to have no friends, or very few, and to spend her time alone, waiting for her dole cheque. When she received her pay for the festival session she was staggered. I said, 'You must apply for a fellowship—$25,000.' She gave a strange laugh: 'I can't ask for so much money.' She is lost between Italy and here, stuck in her terrible English. She seemed a member of another species, wild, in pain, knowing things I could barely dream of—humiliations, violence, disgust, loneliness, fear. She's got a wild animal's face—although she's my age she has smooth skin, her eyes narrow and lying on high cheekbones, mouth that is generous like all Italian mouths, with a pretty top lip that doesn't move much when she speaks. Her legs are slim. Beautiful hands, small, narrow and slender; very small feet in distorting, ugly, very high-heeled sandals—her toes pinched lumps, curved in and under as if trying to hold themselves back off the pavement—squirming back to stay on the inadequate leather. 'I've suffered too much,' she said to me. 'I can't change now.' Her weak, reedy voice. When she read her poems in Italian it was barely audible. I could see her skirt quivering as she stood whispering and gabbling at the lectern.

———

On my way out of the Athenaeum, so tired I could hardly speak, I was approached by a young woman.

'I heard you read that story about the friend. The painter. It made me very angry. I thought it was a *cruel* story,' she said, clenching her hands. 'You took all the little illusions that people use to make life bearable, and you *stripped* and *stripped* and *stripped* them away. I'm trying to be a painter, and I—'

Exhausted, looking at her smooth pale skin, her items of silver jewellery here and there, I thought, Come back in twenty years, sweetheart, and tell me about your little illusions then.

I walk away, get into my car, drive home, and go straight to bed, at five in the afternoon. What I could have said to her was, 'Listen. *There is no comfort*. And if you think there is, then maybe you're not really an artist.'

———

Walking with C in the Botanic Gardens. Rain. Our shoulders were damp. We talked about our lives, our loneliness; how we are

tempted to invite unwanted men back into our lives just in order
to feel less alone.

———

The reason, says T, why house-hunting is so tiring: because you have
to move, in fantasy, in and out of every house you look at—shift all
your furniture and arrange it, and cook and eat several meals; and
carry out the rubbish. Yes, and you have to *part from your daughter*,
and leave your piano behind. Half of me will be with her always,
longing to care for her and make a life for her.

———

Dinner at Toki with T's son. At sixteen, the pure lines of his face,
those marvellous bones, the *strain* of youth in a face. His lively
company, tales of bashings, school wars, 'rumbles' etc. On the way
home we stop for a coffee at Notturno. A hulk with a five o'clock
shadow enters, runs him through the soul handshake, and engages
him in urgent conversation about someone called Eddy who is
going to bash him. '*Eddy?* Oh, man.' The hulk wears a jumper
with the sleeves rolled right up past his biceps. He leaves, upon being
summoned by his scrawny mate outside.
    'Who was *that?*'
    'Hassan. He's so cool.'
    'He sure is. How do you know him?'
    'From school.'
    'But he must be twenty-five!'
    'He's the same age as me.'
    'Sixteen? *Him?*'
    'I bet he only shaved an hour ago. Once, he decided to grow a
moustache. Next day, he had one.'

———

Spring. The curtain moves all night on fitful streams of air.

———

The house auction. My father bid for me, late, twice, and with contemptuous authority. His astonishing exhibition of cool. A merchant in his element. A life of buying and selling. 'Gawd. What a lotta mucken around. We'da bought a million dollars wortha wool by now.' My sister stood beside me uttering a stream of hard-nosed opinion and theory. I sank down on to the asphalt with my knees up and my back against the fence and stared at the ground. The agent, a blue-eyed Greek called Koletsos, jogged back and forth between us and the vendors who remained inside the house: '*He'd* sell. It's his wife.' Dad refused to raise, shrugged and turned away. So we lost. My sister drove away to Kew. I trailed him back to the car. 'Don't worry, Miss,' he said. 'They'll be in touch. My bids were the only two genuine ones they had.' *How could he tell?* 'What'll I say if they ring?' 'Push the faults forward at 'em. The rotten roof on that loose-box. The kitchen. The bathroom.'

———

I cook dinner for M and serve it. 'To think that this time last year I had a broken heart. Do you remember how we used to eat together and play Aretha Franklin records?'

She looks blank, and slightly embarrassed. 'No. I don't remember.'

———

Randolph Stow, *To the Islands*. He wrote it when he was twenty-three. It's a man's book, a young man's book—about the Big Things—death, trying to die, murder, wanting to murder—the land; myth—actually it's brilliant, but there's something grim about it, and deathly serious; he's got no lightness in his personality. There's almost a kind of grinding quality. It's an Important Book. Maybe he's been mad, or something terrible happened to him that crushed all lightness, airiness, wit. Maybe people are born without these.

———

Ran, Kurosawa, with the born-again. As usual in these manly dramas I feel distant and excluded. But a fabulous spectacle.

———

'If you *do* meet someone you like,' says the tough Polish GP, 'for goodness' sake *use condoms*.'

———

I'm supposed to send a story to an anthology. I haven't written a word. I was in that intolerable state of having cleared the decks and finding how far inside me all the real obstacles are. But this morning an hour's work. Two typed pages and the tremulous sense of having hit a vein—that sensation of recognition—as if it were all formal, I mean as if all one were seeking was *form*, and the rest came after.

———

School concert. M played with plenty of attack, rhythm and *feel* the prelude from Bach's Unaccompanied Cello Suite No. 3 in C major. So difficult—she made a lot of mistakes and was white, but there was guts in her playing and I was proud of her.

———

Another ratbag from the seventies comes to visit. 'Remember when—remember how—' His memories of me seem skewed and even invented, though this of course is the Rashomon principle. 'Remember when I told you I went to bed with X *and* Y, the three of us? And you acted not jealous, but for tea you gave me two burnt chops?'

———

When I have begun to carve out the little country of a story in which I will make my home for the next few days (or months, if it should be a novel) I feel a secret power. I don't need to chatter.

———

There's no romance going on with L, just a kind of racketing friendliness. Or maybe it's a smokescreen of shyness.

Darryl Emmerson's *The Pathfinder*—John Shaw Neilson's poems set to music. His sweet tenor, so lovely. Most of the audience was old. I found the story of the poet's life, his lonely struggles, terribly moving. A woman near me pushed up her glasses and wiped her eyes with a shuddering sigh. Her husband saw she was crying and put his arm round her shoulders. Thinking of Neilson's solitariness I wondered if I would be solitary for much of my life from now on, and whether I would find the comfort he did 'in song'.

I dreamt that a man whose beauty was gone—his face had been burnt—brought me a present. I opened it and found first one pigskin glove, then two, as if it had doubled in my hands. They were brown, flexible, seemingly worn in but with the price tag still on them. I slipped my hands into them. They were a perfect fit. The man walked me across a deep meadow, French, high green grass, bordered by a line of poplars.

'I had a dream last night,' said T, 'about cocks. There were three. And I was testing them, to compare and contrast. And the one I chose was the one that went best with its own body.'

At Primrose Gully, a night visitor: a bloke from up the road. Unblinking eyes, ocker manner. Glad not to have been alone when I saw his tall figure stooping to come under the creepers. Q and I tried to hide our boredom, tried to be sociable, while a splendid silver moon rose over the gully and moved steadily up into a cobalt sky through cloudbanks and then wraiths of gossamer. We kept exclaiming; he showed no interest.

A letter from V. Charming, I suppose. He says my handwriting is 'nicely childlike, and yet not'.

———

I read his first novel again. Before I'd heard his voice I never got it, or saw what the fuss was about. It never made me laugh. But now I can hear its tone, and it's so funny that waiting in the foyer of the Con while M does her cello exam I keep giving grunts of laughter and having to sink my mouth into my jumper neck. My response to this is a kind of panic. Why would anyone so brilliant (and giving the appearance of *casual* brilliance) want to have anything to do with *me*?

———

She comes out of the exam all flushed. 'Guess what happened! I had to *sight-read* a Bach *sarabande*! The teacher told me the prelude was all I had to do—but they pointed to the syllabus! And it said "TWO pieces"!' In the evening the teacher rang to apologise. His voice was trembling. I was astonished by his distress. I said, 'Look—she came through it all right. If she'd come home in dark despair maybe I'd feel differently—but she handled it well—and it's the quality of the teaching she's had over the past four years that *enabled* her to handle it.' He seemed relieved, and calmed down. Later she told me about the ambitious mothers of many of the music students: 'They live through their daughters. I *hate* them.'

———

Stomach cramps, attributable only to the fact that L is speeding down the Hume in my direction. I'm jumpy, I can't hide it. I'm a free woman. He's a free man. I like him. He likes me. What am I complaining about?

———

I wake up early to get M off to school. When I return L is sleeping soundly—'sweetly', I think, looking at his head of brown curls half buried in the yellow sheet. I stand by the door and watch him with that respect one feels for completely silent, still slumber.

———

'God,' says the law student, 'he's a hunk, that guy. I saw him coming out of the bathroom'—he makes a two-handed gesture from shoulder to waist—'and I wanted to say, "You can be in my video clip! You can mime *my* part!"'

———

I manoeuvre the complicated intersections that lead off the Westgate Bridge and listen with a burning curiosity to L's tale of heartbreak. 'I can't even use her name! I've had a terrible year. Probably the worst year of my life. Thousands of dollars worth of phone calls. Always rushing from one country to another. The strain of everything. The language problem. The only happiness I've had this year's been with you.'

I look up sharply. *Me?* Have I got the dates wrong?

He's addicted to drama, glamour, pain. He's almost totally un-self-examined, at least in the sense in which I mean it.

———

I sneaked a look in his address book when he was out of the room. There she was. I had expected beauty but was shocked by what I saw in her face: a delicacy of emotional tone that was almost frightening. Wide face, wide-set eyes, an enormous mouth that still looked child-like—it was the mouth that was terrifying—it looked as if it was quivering, the shape of its top lip was irregular in a way that was too sensitive for life. I felt a stab of fear—I mean for *her*—and for him too because he's put what happened in a little shrine, with a candle burning in front of it, and he worships it.

———

He wakes panting from a dream. He's had a phone call. It's her; but her voice fades away and is disconnected—it's a nightmare,

I feel the shock of it, how it hurts him.

I see that I've actually lived a quiet life.

In the restaurant he asks me how my marriage ended. He shudders with horror, picks up a knife and mimes operatically stabbing himself in the heart.

'If something like that happened to me I'd—I'd—I'd never have *seen* them again—I'd have wiped them out of my life! I'd have—'

'You'd have to kill something in yourself, to achieve that. That's revenge. That's useless.'

'But you can't be an emotional *wimp* about it. You've got the right to *feel* things.'

'Are you kidding? Do you think I didn't *feel* anything? I was wounded. I was bleeding.'

With him one can use that sort of language.

He leaves me a Gilberto tape. I play it over and over, in the car. What on earth can come of this? Nothing but the pleasure of what it is. Let it be what it is, then. And be grateful.

————

Deeply embedded in V's novel are turns of phrase of an Australianness I've never before seen on paper. Someone describes a collection of railway stations, of which one was 'completely rusty. The platform, benches, even the ticket office…were all made from old railway track. Passengers would always *come away with orange hands*.' 'Come away with.' This could be my mother speaking. I laugh again and again, and at times shudder at what awfulness he sees in people.

————

Having a beer in the kitchen with the law student while I cook dinner. We talk about falling in love.

'Do you learn how not to,' he asks, 'as you get older?'

'You learn what the process is, and you recognise its stages.'

'Do you mean you can *stop* yourself?'

'You can discipline yourself. You can feel the moment at which it would be possible to let go another string of yourself, and you can choose whether to or not.'

'I've said "I love you" about a thousand times.'

'So have I.'

'*Have* you?'

'Of course,' I said. 'A million times.'

'And I always mean it.'

'Me too. Or—hang on—I've probably had to force it out two or three times.'

'*Force* it out?'

'I mean I said it when it was no longer true. Just to make someone feel all right.'

'I know exactly what you mean. When Donna used to come round here, remember? All I had to do was say "I love you" and she'd stop crying. It was the only thing that'd make her stop.'

———

Three teenage suicides in the news: a boy hangs himself after an argument about eating too many biscuits; a boy shoots himself because he wasn't allowed to have a motorbike; a sixteen-year-old girl shoots herself with a shotgun and they don't know why. 'Don't anyone out there even *think* of doing it,' said the mother of one of the boys on TV. 'You don't know what you leave behind.'

———

A sunny day. I am wearing a floppy skirt with hyacinth and white stripes. The psychological effect of wearing stripes. They move, and cross each other, with an audible whirr.

———

Dreamt I was wheeling my bike towards the uni through an unfinished two-storey building. I was wearing a thin white nightie but also a black jacket that meant I was reasonably modest. Workmen whistled at me but in imitation because I was singing as I went along. In a garden I asked a man, 'How deep is that compost heap?' The compost heap was beautiful. It had a coating of green moss and did not look ugly or messy: it contained a *substance*, it seemed, already smooth and broken down.

———

I thought of volunteering at the Children's Hospital. But there are huge nurses' strikes on.

———

Watching 'experimental' movies is terribly cheering—makes one feel more *daring*.

———

Lying in despair on the couch in my work room I noticed in the wire shelf a forgotten notebook. Pulled it out. It was a sort of diary I had kept back at the beginning of writing *The Children's Bach*. At first I thought, I'll be able to sell this one day. Then I read it and saw with astonishment and relief the HOPELESS MESS my mind was, back then. I thought of the shapely thing *The Children's Bach* is, and remembered that writing a novel is a process of refinement. Out of chaos comes the fine thing; out of chaos comes *form*.

———

In an essay Fay Zwicky quotes Germaine Greer about Henry Handel Richardson's 'provincialism' in being unable to see that *The Getting of Wisdom* is superior to *Maurice Guest*: '…for in a country which is utterly philistine, people who are genuinely excited by the arts tend to distrust any art form which seems close to ordinary life and to adopt paranoid, overblown concepts of the artistic personality'.

———

Worked on the bandaid story, wept over it a bit—it's still lumpy and clumsy, but I am *working* on it.

———

The house vendors have accepted my offer. I signed a contract.

———

I used the expression 'a beachhead' about the steadiness I've worked out for myself over this year. The Jungian sat up. He quoted Freud— 'Where id is, there ego shall be'—and said he thought 'beachhead' was a better image than the strict idea of the ego descending right over the id (he made a covering, seizing movement from above with one claw-like hand). 'The ocean's still there. Nothing's permanently reclaimed. It can all be washed right back in.' He said, 'Now you're back in contact with that part of yourself you'd lost, you must feel reluctant to lose it again in a big projection—which is what falling in love is—letting your whole peace of mind be dependent on someone else.'

———

My forty-fourth birthday (and La Stupenda's sixtieth, I heard on the radio on my way to the pool). M won't come out with me for breakfast. The law student, embarrassed perhaps, offers himself as company.

———

I told L my husband gave me a lemon tree for my birthday.

'A lemon? Sour fruit. Couldn't he have chosen a peach?'

———

Dreamt I was standing on a bridge over a canal, looking down into the water. A black, hairy, slimy creature surfaced and swam away down the canal. I screamed, 'A rat!' but it was too big to be a rat. I watched with revulsion as it swam away from me, its shoulders working, and then dragged itself up on to the bank. I saw it wasn't a rat, it was as big as a cat and had a thickness at the root of its tail that made it unidentifiable.

Trigger for this: a dead thing near the tram stop the other day when the law student and I were driving.

HG: 'It's a rat. It's huge.'

LS: 'I don't think it is a rat. Go back, let's have another look.'

U-turn.

HG: 'You're right, it's a baby possum.'

We both made sentimental noises. Whereas when it was a rat we thought, Good riddance.

———————

Clowning with M on the couch, actually having her in my arms and making her laugh by teasing her about the trumpet player in the band, who is six foot three, pale-skinned, handsome, with a WWI face and brow, hair pulled back in a ponytail.

———————

V's piece about Borneo in the *National Times*. An efficient piece of writing without any sign that his emotions had been engaged. And why should they? It's only journalism.

———————

Dreamt my sister and two other women gave me, in a huge cinema, baskets of flowers and herbs to plant in the garden of my new house. In exchange I wrote out for them the words of 'Praise My Soul the King of Heaven'.

———————

Went to work and wrote a short story about a 'luminous boy'. It poured out in a rush and then I spent a timeless couple of hours fiddling with it, changing this and that, cutting, shaping etc— utterly enjoyable. Now I must discipline myself not to spoil it with my cumbersome afterthoughts.

———————

R rang and offered me their house in Sydney for three weeks while they're down the coast.

———————

M came home from her HSC English exam in excellent spirits. Her father called her at dinnertime from America and after this she was radiant with happiness.

———

A cheque arrived from the lady in Queensland. Stunned, I accepted. I gave half of it to my sister so she could see a shrink.

———

L sends me an account of his latest struggles to extract himself from emotional entanglements ('you must think I'm a walking basket case'), plus a drawing of his just-planted garden. I wrote back, taking a breezy tone: 'You are much too charming and good-looking for a tranquil life, and in this respect we belong to different species.' Told him I'd be in Sydney in summer. 'But you're overloaded. The last thing you need is more female attention. You sound like a man who's going down for the third time in a sea of consequences.'

———

Mass-murderers of girls arrested and charged in Perth. A married couple in their thirties. Shallow bush graves. Stranglings, suffocations, sexual assaults. What does this *mean*? The devil, A would say. The rottenness in people.

———

While M slaves in her room for tomorrow's exam the law student and I drink beer downstairs and listen to Miles Davis and Mink De Ville. I'm fascinated by the power that beauty has over him. 'On the beach, Helen, I'd look at this creation—the *colour* of her, and the skin of her arms—and I'd be nearly passing out—thinking, How can God have made something this *perfect*?'

———

At Brunswick Baths I was alone for an hour against a brick wall in the sun reading J's new stories in proofs. His terrifying prolificness. I read until I felt trembly, hypoglycaemic, and had to go home.

———

L grumbles on the phone: 'I watched that show on Brazil—God, why do I live in this country? It's so self-satisfied here. In Brazil there's so much *energy*—' etc etc, ho hum, but underneath is fear: the first draft of his novel is 900 pages long, 'a mess'. He says, 'I was reading *Postcards from Surfers* again the other day and I could see how it's made up of notebook things—it's terrific, how you do that?' I bet he really thinks, She hasn't got an imagination as big and creative as *mine*. Heh heh. Polished up my little story and sent it to the *Adelaide Review*.

———

At the baths I lay on a wonderful foam rubber object I bought en route at K-Mart, fount of all goodness. Creamed my skin, put on my sunglasses, and just as I was about to lie down I glanced towards the northern end of the pool and saw four people, a group, of different sizes and ages, sitting on the rim. Something in their postures, their groupness, the angles of their spines filled me with a rush of bliss so intense that my eyes ran with tears. How could I have forgotten this *simple joy*? Available to any moron with the money to get past the turnstile. The sky was pure blue, and in it sailed great galleons of cloud, white with blue-grey floors. I felt my skin begin to burn. I swam a length in the cold water, shuddering, in my goggles. Two rough girls near me kept giving me friendly looks and smiles. God, I was happy, I was content!

———

I'm shortlisted for the *Age* book of the year, which I have never won or even, I think, been shortlisted for. I look at the list of judges and think, I haven't won. I feel nothing. I determine not to go to the presentation. Never again, that shameful public torment.

———

Dancing in Lygon Street to Venetta Fields and her band—the wonderful power of gospel, its shouts of joy. Five minutes of that music does more to convert a person than six months of solemnity from a born-again in your house. Just before the last song she said, 'That lady in the blue dress who's been clappin' and singin'—maybe you'll know this song—"Steal Away to Jesus!"' People looked around. She meant *me*. I blushed. Two men dancing—Aussie crim types—one a stumpy pale little fellow with very muscly legs bared by rude torn-off denim shorts, the other tall and limp-backed in a Hawthorn beanie and cheap fawn trousers. They seemed to know each other and danced in a way that was distressing—tensely, with clenched arms and bent knees and no fluidity of spine, all aggression. A black American danced right in front of me, a great hunk of a man with massive hips, bum, thighs—his relaxed authority— nothing flashy or even skilful, just easy in his body and glad to be moving. Everything he did originated in his hips, completely centred there and at ease.

———————

Roland Barthes, in *A Lover's Discourse*, on dedicating a book: 'Writing is dry, obtuse; a kind of steamroller, writing advances, indifferent, indelicate, and would kill "father, mother, lover" rather than deviate from its fatality (enigmatic though that fatality may be). When I write, I must acknowledge this fact...: there is no benevolence within writing, rather a terror: it smothers the other, who, far from perceiving the gift in it, reads there instead an assertion of mastery, of power, of pleasure, of solitude. Whence the cruel paradox of the dedication: I seek at all costs to give you what smothers you.'

Hmmm. I see it's a proper noting and working out of the tiniest flickers of consciousness, a teasing out of their meanings i.e. (like Handke) he is using the same raw material that I use, and his field of operation is home to me, but we perform different acts/actions upon it.

———

I wonder if I will become one of those women in their forties who have affairs with married men. No! I will not. Full of curiosity about this one, though—V. I read an interview with him and see his alarming statements and concerns—how he is 'horrified' by the idea of the 'erosion of his standards'. This is real, stern, rigid animus talking. But I can't say he hasn't warned me—describing his own hand-writing as 'cramped, tight, stilted and jerky, and this nib can't be blamed'.

———

The *Adelaide Review* paid me $200 for my story. Now I'm working on the opera one. Something improves in it every day, and I get more control over it. Today I fiddled with the river and water imagery.

———

Meeting at the Windsor about some film festival I'm invited to. Two cups of tea and a glass of orange juice cost *$11*. We nearly fainted.

———

A critic, writing about Elizabeth Jolley: 'Compared to Garner, who was once presented to us as the *enfant terrible* of Australian fiction—'

———

Reading Elizabeth Bowen, very good of course in an infuriating English way. Full of depths, if not widths.

———

Three mothers of teenagers laughing together at the dinner table. Two of us talk about how sexy the son of the third one is. I jokingly offer to take him to live at my place. 'Take him,' she says. 'I bet he'd be the perfect gentleman at your place. To me he says "Fuck up and die."'

———

I spent an hour standing on a high stool at the cupboard reading old diaries. My bare feet were blue with cold. Pain of those years, when I read them without the filter of previous ignorance. Why didn't I see that the marriage was already done for? The soul was not itself.

———

A woman's tinkling showers of laughter.

———

Dad came to Primrose Gully, taught me to use the motor mower. A wheel came off, twice, and he showed me how to fix it with a piece of wire. I was impressed with his competence, patience and ability to improvise. He went home. I cut the grass on my own. Now I understand why he used to be so single-minded about it. It's positive destruction. You're obsessed, walled in by the tremendous noise, faced with a design problem—the pattern of the strokes. You can't hear voices speaking to you, the phone has no hope of being heard, you have the luxury of being incommunicado. You see an immediate result. After mowing, I raked.

———

The native tree outside our back gate is thickly covered in cream-coloured flowers. The street is lined with these trees, but none of the others has more than half a dozen blossoms. Ours is the only one that is riotously flourishing. The law student and I noticed this on our way back from the shop. I said, 'It must be because we have such a happy household.'

———

The law student has found a room in a student house and will leave in ten days.

———

'I've got many *things*,' says L. He wants to show me his life. His sweet-smelling skin, his thick curls. The bedroom is in the very centre of his house. The streetlight is blocked by curtains. We make love in pitch blackness. He is generous with the bed: leaves plenty of room for me. We sleep, or rather he sleeps, and I drift all night just below the surface, with occasional brief dives deeper.

———

'They arrested a bloke in Brisbane who had a bomb to blow up the Pope. He was from a lunatic asylum.'

'Was he making *purposeful strides* towards the Pope?'

We fall about at this but she was not trying to amuse.

———

'I love talking to girls,' says the law student. 'I *need* to. I feel as if I need to release something in me.'

———

At the lunch table I can't help staring at V, the married man. I want to let my eyes wander freely. A plain man. A very white neck. Old, soft, faded Levi shirt, jeans, horrible old seventies boots with heels, black corduroy jacket. He's the flipside of L, the curly-headed, laughing one. He is very *male*. Something very definite and uncompromising about him. Do I mean 'rigid and inflexible'? I don't know, yet.

———

At Toki I tell the law student about the two men. He listens with bated breath, groans and shouts. When I start to *compare* them he twists in his chair and cries out as if in pain.

———

The law student stumbles in after a night at a party and the Users' Club. 'This guy called Daniel says to me, "Hey! Come upstairs! There's this fabulous guitar!" So I go up to a bedroom and we play this steel-string guitar, and he plays some blues and I play some blues, and I show off; and whenever I do anything on the guitar that I—see, he's not very *musical*—he's a really nice guy but he—so if I do something that I just *feel*, he says, "Oh! How'd you do that? Show me! I wanna learn! I wanna learn!" And I feel like saying, "Go and listen to this record. *I* can't teach you."'

L took me to his friends' house for lunch. We sat at the table in the sun, drinking and talking *as people do*. We all got on merrily. I sat beside him, liking him and liking everything. I saw his lovely sociability, his readiness. When people spoke he listened, and when it was his turn he spoke. One of the women was very pregnant. The pure skin of pregnancy. Her dainty ankles and sparkling eyes. I felt very drawn to her, wanted to stroke and pat her and admire her radiance, and I did.

After dinner the waiter brought L the wrong coffee, was corrected, went away. Time passed. He realised he'd been forgotten and from that moment the evening was lost. He went dark and stiff with rage. Anger spread into the air around him. A grille clanged down between him and the world. I panicked. All the air went out of me. I felt my face drop on its bones. He noticed and said, 'What's up?' I said, in a small voice, 'I feel sad. And scared.' 'Sorry,' he said, 'I just hate it when things like that happen, when people treat you like—' I wanted to say, 'He doesn't scorn you, or hate you—he just made a mistake.' But his whole ego was bound up in it. My own iron grille came down. I missed the chance to level with him. From then on we were both deep in reticence but keeping the superficial intimacy going. In the morning, a shyness. I like him. I envy his beauty and I hate the way it distorts his life. He is all split and troubled; and his loneliness is as bad as mine. We would wear each other out.

'You can feel Patrick White in your own writing, can't you,' says the man. 'Sometimes you look at a sentence and you can see where it comes from—completely unconsciously. That's his power.'

'Yes,' says the woman gaily, 'even in someone like me who's hardly even *read* him.'

―――――

Two actors walk into Pellegrini's, the wife more famous and highly regarded than the husband. He walks very close behind her, shepherding her through the crowd, chin high and wearing the look that says, 'I am famous and I am only looking at you for two reasons: (1) to check briefly whether I shall greet you if by chance you too are famous and (2) to repel your eager glance if you are not.' Her skin is white white *white*: the whiteness (1) of the redhead and (2) that says 'I work indoors', bounces back light and makes her photogenic.

―――――

Outside the university college, in the dark garden, a huge magnolia tree held out its opening buds, and in the street some night birds were singing, one in one tree, one in another. I remembered a French essay I wrote in 1961 about those birds, which I heard near the Union sandwich bar on an early summer night just before my first uni exams.

―――――

I dreamt that my nutty old boyfriend from the other side of the river was near me, singing sweetly.

―――――

I stood.

'Why do you have to go now?' said V.

'Because I have to do something in Melbourne at six o'clock.'

We were looking each other right in the eyes. Not a romantic or soft look, but a direct, hard challenge, straight out of the hard self.

―――――

P walked with me at Primrose Gully. We took sticks against snakes. Grass very long, with beautiful russet tips.

―――――

I dreamt of a yellow object. I forget what it was. Was it thickly coated in perfect duco? About the size of—what? Even that's gone.

It gleamed, it was bright, smooth, it made the heart glad.

———

At the launch the writer kissed me on the cheek and gave me a cassette of her work. Her bright make-up, narrow fox-like face, her straw-dyed and square-chopped hair, and a little black fez.

———

Damn it. There's an opening in me towards where V is. If we lived in the same town I would write and say, 'Tonight, grave sir, both my poore house, and I,/ Do equally desire your companie…' —Ben Jonson, *Inviting a Friend to Supper*

———

After I'd signed a paper agreeing to pay the house loan back 'on demand' should anything 'go wrong', Dad became expansive and made orotund pronouncements on matters of family finance, saying each thing several times in several different ways. We had steak, perfect boiled potatoes, peas they'd picked at Portarlington, and strawberries ditto, with King Island cream. A fabulous, classic lunch in our mother's tradition. He put a spoonful of tomato sugo on my steak, reaching over my shoulder with a flourish deft enough to get him a job at the Italian Society. Driving home with my brother: warm wind, the huge, low horizon of that plain, streaks of grey cloud and a hot-looking sunset.

———

On the phone Y and I went through my story line by line and raked all the lumps out of it, cut off the last sentence, fixed misleading punctuation etc. Of course I'm anxious about it. Is she really telling the truth when she says it's 'lovely' and 'fine' and that she 'loves' it?

———

Speech Night. Hundreds of brown-legged girls in those ugly, bag-like uniforms. Nothing can make a young girl less than lovely. The steadiest, quietest, most faithful, least ambitious, least flamboyant thing in the world is the alto voice in a girls' madrigal group. The law student and I whisper across each other, 'It's so *quiet*.' 'It's so *calm*.' When the choir sings an Elgar song, 'The Snow', with two violins, a father on my other side cries openly, tears collecting in the creases under his eyes; then, between items, he opens a business magazine and reads on. '*C'était un peu sucré*,' says F. The law student and I, both tear-stained, are pained by his refusal '*d'être ému*'. A professor of economics gives a rousing feminist speech: 'It's all out there waiting for you—you can have a *wonderful life*.' On the way home I mention this admiringly. M is less impressed: 'We get told that kind of stuff every week at assembly.'

———

The man's clothes are very expensive, and look it—suits obviously Italian, shoes of the fashionable clod-hopper kind. His ex-wife's are well-chosen, stylish, fashionable, but when seen close up are of cheap cut and material. She puts her money elsewhere, I guess. She is potentially beautiful. What stops her is unhappiness, anger, resentment.

———

Dreamt I was a police cadet. I was lonely and a bit scared in the building where we were being trained. I made friends with a young bloke, not my type at all, curly-haired and beefy, not all that bright. We were issued with a kind of yearbook, containing a page about each of us. My page said that he was my friend and I was embarrassed.

———

L wants worldly esteem. I know that feeling. I hope he'll get it because it means so much to him that if he doesn't it will deflate him and make him sad and bitter.

———

What am I setting up for myself, here? Some happiness, perhaps.

I'm calm, and in good spirits, quietly, as if something important and good were about to happen. I'm not scared or nervous. I can't even imagine it, how it will be, what it will look like, what felicities or clumsinesses either of us will commit. Bucket of cold water: he's married. He is an intellectual and *I am not*. 'He lives,' said Z, who introduced us, 'almost entirely in the world of books and ideas. I imagine that's why he didn't want to have children.' Maybe he's in the habit of having quick, harsh, demanding affairs. Or maybe this will be an important relationship, for both of us.

————

At the peace vigil a pastor gets up and says, 'The most important thing I've written in the last year is some remarks I made at a meeting about trying to re-unite North and South Korea. You'll hear the emotion and the politics in it.' He then proceeds to read, in a wooden voice, an interminable sermon. He stood with his heels together and his feet in a broad V. At the end he said, 'Amen.'

————

Went to Borsari's and bought a new bike, a Puch 5-speed, big and female and reliable as a pram. With girl's handlebars and a skirt guard. Flew home up Lygon Street, sitting up with straight back, not angled forward as on the too-racy Hillman which I now pass on to M.

————

At Heide I liked the paintings very much. Arthur Boyd bridegroom pictures. Bouquets sprouting from people's ears. In a frame, several pages torn from the artist's notebook, from the early fifties, pencil scribbles on yellowing paper. He can't spell at all—very endearing. *'Cresent moon always looks like this…dingoe's sniffing bone's.'*

————

The enclosed garden, full of flowers, very beautiful. V is botanically even more ignorant than I am. At the bottom of it an extraordinary vegetable—is it a turnip? A betterave like on the French kitchen poster? It's mauve and green, as big as a cantaloupe, touches the earth on a lower point, and is held vertical by flying buttresses of long, muscular-looking leaves. It is split, and looks dry and woody inside.

————

V doesn't like his name. 'Why don't you change it?' 'If you change your name you have to change your surname as well, don't you? 'Cause that's what you *are*.' 'Most women change their surnames at least once in their lives.' He's surprised—never thought of this before.

————

In the warm and windy night streets, kids stumble about in gangs or alone. A chubby girl carrying her shoes and smoking stops me and asks me the time.

'Five to eleven.'

'Oh! I thought it was later.'

Her face is smeared, somehow—she is drunk and unhappy, perhaps has been humiliated. She tries to smile at me. Her features aren't anchored in place, they slide on her face. I feel a pang for her. She stumbles away up Russell Street.

V says, 'Why's she got her shoes off and her shirt hanging out?'

''Cause she's unhappy, and her feet hurt 'cause she's a fat girl. And some man's probably just been cruel to her.'

'For sure. At the bottom of every bit of trouble there's always a man.'

'Yes. You only have to look, and there is.'

This banter, which to me is flippant, is perhaps less so to him.

He presses: 'Do you think that's true?'

'Oh, I don't know.'

'See, I think what women don't realise is that men like to be with other men.'

'That shouldn't cause problems necessarily, should it?'

All evening I am dodging and feinting, to avoid being pinned down.

———

'What did you do in the fifties?'

'Lay on my bed and read. Listened to Little Richard records and danced. Mucked around with my family. What did you?'

'Cars,' says V. 'I was crazy about speed. I drove an MG, stripped down, no floor.'

'Where'd you put your feet?'

'Well, there was a *bit* of floor, on the driving side. But in the rest you could see the ground going past.'

———

Me: 'What's your house like?'

V: 'You should come there one day.'

Me: (*thinks*) 'What? Don't be ridiculous.'

———

'You know how marvellous it is,' says the woman in Notturno, 'to be with another writer. They don't get bored or think you're mad.' But this stuff I'm writing in here will embarrass me later when V ceases to be a MYSTERIOUS STRANGER and reveals all his meanness and weakness (and I mine).

———

Thelonious Monk playing 'Ruby My Dear'. Over and over. On the cover: 'He had evolved an unorthodox approach to the piano, involving crushed notes and clusters, and left-hand chords made up of seconds and sixths instead of conventional triadic jazz harmonies.' They're only technical terms but I wish I'd made up 'crushed notes and clusters'.

———

V turned away from me, while we were looking in a shop window, and I caught a whiff of him—only faint—but it was a *plain* smell, unadorned and unperfumed (not like that of L, who's all fresh and herbal)—a smell of wool, of ordinary skin—*not young*—a smell that reminded me of my father and *my grandfather*—I was jolted by the connection—and I thought, If I do know you when you are old, it will have been a plain life indeed.

————

Gloomily coming into my bedroom I stump towards the bed and see the mess of *New York Reviews* beside it, and a copy of Joan London's stories that are so beautiful, and I think, Whatever happens, I've got this one little *power*—I'm a writer. I can use everything that happens, I can use it and shape it and in that way I can get control of it.

————

It has been discovered that humans emit certain smells or substances which cause *health* in the opposite sex. Men can only pass on their health-giving substances by sex. Women's, however, can be conveyed over distance and even tend to permeate the atmosphere—and women's, also, work on other women. *Really?*

————

I see that what I am doing, in this diary, is conducting an argument with myself, about these two men, and myself, and men in general.

————

Family lunch at the Latin. Just as my sister is getting red-faced and shrill about the nurses' strike, two men rush through the room, one cringing under the blows of the other who is covered in a white mess of food and roaring in a fury: 'How *dare* you! You're only a waiter!' They roll on to the street and disappear. 'You can tell it's a joke,' says my sister, 'because he said, "How *dare* you?" No Australian would say that. He'd say, "You bastard!" and punch him in the face.' 'Aww, I dunno,' says our father. 'I reckon if one of 'em had had a knife there'da been real trouble.'

———

In the shack I get up to take the kettle off the fire and see through the narrow window a pretty sight: a blue wren flirting with his own reflection in the outside mirror of my car. He flips up, whirring his wings like mad, performs a caracole and a pirouette in mid-air before the glass, then perches on the mirror's rim and looks around in confusion—then back he goes and does it all again.

———

'Most people are not aware of such a call' (to the numinous) 'yet they may feel the strongest attraction to make some sense of the "God-feeling" within them, and be overwhelmed by feelings of sickness, sadness, depression and despair if they suppress it because they disagree with conventional kinds of religious belief, or are afraid that others will think them mad or odd...They will find it painful to begin with to admit to being driven by such an improper longing, but if they can get past this stage they will discover that most people have a very good idea what they are talking about and are repressing similar longings and experiences of their own...We are all contemplatives to a greater or lesser degree, and we all need, to the limit of our capacity, to admit the experience which we may, or may not, call God.' —Monica Furlong, *Contemplating Now*

All this is true, and it is what my novel should be about. The spirit comes to an unhappy woman. She denies it. It departs. I'm frightened of all this, I think.

———

Fear—of being drawn to another man whose phlegmatic nature will limit and distort mine—or for whose sake I will limit and distort *myself*. And yet I am so much stronger, now.

———

The only way I can have anything to do with him is by (a) lies and (b) hurting someone. Am I prepared to do this?

———

Annie Gottlieb's dream that when she began to enjoy her 'powers as a writer', her mother had her sterilised. The terrific jolt of this: *I* didn't simply *dream* being sterilised. In the year between the writing of *Monkey Grip* and its publication, I had it done to myself.

———

The university year ends. Our law student is moving out.
    Me: 'How will I live without you?'
    Him: 'Who'll I talk to?'

———

'There are virtually,' says V, 'only two things that go wrong with a car engine. Petrol, or—far more likely—spark.'

———

The window is open, the curtains lift and drop on a warm breeze that smells strongly of dry grass.

———

Went and had a little haircut. I think the hairdresser's freaking out. He cut it dry, a thing he's never done before. He was late. He looked pale, distracted; is going to France on Thursday. Has moved out of his house and is sleeping in the salon.

———

The biographer talks about her progress. 'I didn't *want* to write another book about a put-upon woman. At first I was full of admiration for her. I thought she was a heroine. Then I saw what really happened, and I was angry. And then I sulked.' She gives her tuneful laugh. 'Yes—I *sulked*. And now I know that if it *has* to be a book about an oppressed woman, that's what it'll be.'

———

Because I know that someone finds 'almost everything about' me 'interesting', I am walking round in a cloud of power.

———

In an old diary I find this exchange between me and Y:

Me: 'I'd like to have a man in another city. I'd like him to be crazy about me, and for him to write me wonderful letters, once or twice a week, and to come to me every now and then, and me to him—a real passion—but for him not to want to make me his wife.'

Y: 'Now you're talking.'

I forgot to mention that *I* would like also to be crazy about *him*.

———

Invited to eat with two high-powered academics, philosophers. I'm happily surprised by their worldliness. While she works in the kitchen she has the radio on low and I hear her singing along to the Bangles: 'Walk like an Egyp-she-an.' She tells a tale of drunkenness, of 'calling for a bucket'. Feel no longer shy of asking them what, for example, Heidegger was on about. Rain fell, quiet and vertical, at dinner.

———

A letter I can't quite bring myself to write to L:

'I'm no good at these reticent, half-hearted affairs. I thought for a while it was what I needed, in my awkward, bruised convalescence; and because you seemed to be in a similar state I felt it all to be appropriate. But I feel your wariness and it's brought out all my own: it made me grow a thicker skin. And now you're on the outside of it and voilà.'

If I told the whole truth I would have to say: 'I think I've fallen in love with someone else.'

———

A woman has reviewed *Postcards from Surfers* and *The Children's Bach* in the *New York Times Book Review*: '…lit by a kind of eerie, slanted light, reminiscent at times of Jane Bowles's work, as are

Ms Garner's sharp, strange images and the dense, rich texture their layering creates.'

I know it's dangerous to dwell on praise but allow me a little moment of delight at being mentioned in the same sentence as Jane Bowles.

———

I am mean to our dog. I ignore her when she casts herself at my feet. I must be in love.

———

Dreamt I sat on a couch beside another person, a cheerful man I knew to be a semi-reformed crim. From the floor a dog, hairy and importunate, wormed its way between us. We went to a strange house, where in a derelict room with no furniture a fire was only just alight in a big, empty fireplace. While I waited for him to come into this room (were we going to make love?) I took the poker and moved the fire around, grouped its fallen parts and tried to make it burn properly. There was no wood, the room was quite empty and dark, and the fire was almost ashes, but still gave out a little bit of warmth if not a clear flame.

———

Sun came out of the clouds while I was in the pool. Water suddenly full of little yellow feathers.

———

The Polish philosopher said she had found Stendhal's *On Love* attractive and relevant 'as an adolescent', but that now she considers love to be 'a cancer of the mind—you pick a man out of the crowd, and you demand that he should play a part, that he should be this, and that—it's grotesque! It's ridiculous!' I came away rather sobered. Fortunately I was *en vélo* and this always cheers me up in doubtful moments.

———

An Italian photographer from a magazine. He reminded me of the one who said to me meanly in the seventies, 'Your profile, it is not the best.' But this one ended up charming me into smiling and laughing. He even laid his palm against my cheek.

———

'All the kids in maximum security,' says the poet, 'have read your book. And they *love* it.' Am I supposed to believe this? His alarming gaze. He can fix you for up to five minutes without blinking. Is that a jail thing? His hard, forceful presence, his hard talk and anecdotes, his need to *keep talking*, his discourse of violence—what he said to men who crossed him, what he said he'd do to them, what he in fact *did* do to them. 'I jumped up and down on his arm, I was yellin', "Ya cunt, if you break *her* arm I'm gunna break yours."' I kept thinking, must I take account of this? Is it *middle class* not to want to? 'I was bored with m' wife,' he says. 'I kept saying, "Here, go and buy yourself a nice dress or something." But she wouldn't. She'd wear a tracksuit, 'n' ugg boots.'

———

Out all day with the jaws of my purse straining wide. Horror of Christmas. But I exchanged friendly looks with many strangers...I like people when they are in a great mass, thousands of lonely or rather solitary blobs, each one with '*le front barré de souci*'.

———

The barrier of shyness that attacks us both (and especially V) when we're together. I mean sexual shyness. As if we were learning each other by some more decorous means. An inversion of the modern order.

———

One day I'll have to burn this book. I use as buckets of cold water thoughts of his wife's preparations for Christmas.

———

The landlord comes to examine the cracked wall and the powerful wisteria on the house-front. F is visiting. I set up the ironing board and say to the girls, 'Sing to us.' One plays the piano, the other sings: *An die Musik*. While I work, F sits quite still with his forearms on the table. I don't dare look at him; it's a song that brings such painful memories of the music we discovered together. *'Du holde Kunst, in wieviel grauen Stunden...'* They sing other less poignant songs, and shift into carols. We join in. Meanwhile the landlord wanders up and down the stairs. I pass him in the hall. He's standing still, listening to the girls' voices: 'Isn't it lovely!' Later, in the kitchen, he tells me a story: 'When I was a kid I had a really good voice. I sang all the time, in choirs. I was good, and I loved it. My father—he was a wonderful man—used to get me to sing for him when we were going along together in the car. Then one day I overheard him talking to another bloke, someone he knew, a neighbour or someone he worked with. He was saying, "Some blokes have sons who are footballers. Some have sons who are runners. But I've got a son who's a singer." I thought he was ashamed of me. So I stopped. Gave it up. Never sang again. And years later he said to me, "I've never understood, John—why'd you stop singing?"'

On the doorstep he pauses. It will be fine with him, he says, if the four girls live here when I move out.

———

Maybe he's the kind of man who conducts flirtations with women in such a way as to allow his wife to find out; she then puts a stop to the developing affair and, though he grumbles etc, *this is what he wants, and needs.* No idea why I thought of this. Just running through the painful possibilities.

———

On TV a dramatised life of Freud. Very enjoyable. Did he really have a black lower lip, like a dog's? The madwomen in the hospital:

raving, twitching, and nothing that could be done.

———

'You look well. You look happy. Are you?'

'Yes, I am happy.' Feeling my flesh light on my bones.

———

The visiting German editor wants me to write a big piece about Melbourne. Though his monthly circulation is 250,000 he offers me only $1200. I make a series of small sounds meant to indicate slight interest in the piece but lack of excitement about the money. We agree to write to each other. Before my foot hits the pavement outside I have lost interest.

———

'I'm a woman now,' says M, pirouetting at the kitchen door.

'How do you mean?'

'I got my learner's permit. I'm allowed to drive a car. *I can drive a car.*'

We laugh so madly we have to lean on the walls. Fact: I love her more than anyone in the world.

———

Whenever I start worrying about not being beautiful and young, I try to imagine a man of my age, someone whose age shows, who is not glamorous, who's got wrinkles, but who's got a sexual presence and an authority of personality. I imagine him in a group of people, sitting there quietly, not making a fuss. And I think, if *he* can be attractive, *so can I.*

———

In the car with F and M, last night, tired and crabby, I began to see my secret new fantasies as silly and pointless. How long does it take two people to slide into *being a couple*? But then F gave me a garden spade for Christmas. In my fatigue I had forgotten all the nice and lovely things about him, how funny he is, how on the drive home (he drove) we sang together, with M, for miles.

———

A two-year-old girl has been stolen from her bed (the person cut through a flywire screen) and 'sexually assaulted'. She was found 'crying and wandering' in a street ten kilometres away at 1 am. Doctors have had to operate on her to repair 'internal injuries'.

———

Cried and bawled by myself in front of the Mediaeval Mystery Plays on TV. Abraham and Isaac, what a terrible story, it made me hate God, the jealous God who demands appalling tributes, but then at the end when he tells Abraham he may spare his son, and says, '*I* am going to sacrifice *my* son, later on,' I was pulled up short.

———

Mum brought to Christmas dinner some very old photos of us four girls as kids, outside the house at Ocean Grove. I saw myself at nine or ten looking so tragically plain that I lost heart for twenty minutes. Dad picked out the one who in the photos looked the most 'cute' and 'timid', then showered her with affection for the entire day. The rest of us craned sideways from a couch in the next room to watch him hold her, with his arm around her waist, while she stood beside his chair. Later she came up to us and said, 'I think Dad loves me.' We went into convulsions of embarrassed laughter.

———

T mended my pink trousers and then we lay on her bed and sofa and shrieked about fucking young or boring men. She fancies a bloke in a pub where she goes to play music. I said, 'Is he a murderer?' 'I don't know,' she said. 'He's boring and has no sense of humour. But every time I see him I feel all stirred up on the way home.'

———

Dreamt that somebody had a baby but it died. A great deal of sobbing. The father was terribly distressed. I was trying to be of use but did not know how. In a paved courtyard I lit a fire in a metal container with a lid. Smoke poured out of it and I went back into the house and forgot about it.

———

Looking around this room I realise I'll only be sleeping in it two or three more times.

1987

A hot, dry day on the Hume, a sky full of detailed, small clouds. Saw
two or three dead wombats, a couple of dead kangaroos, and a live
brown bird on the gravel with half a dozen live brown chicks. In
the dunny at Tarcutta a Vietnamese woman was washing a baby's
trousers in the basin. I smiled at her. She said, 'How—to Sydney—
how many?' 'Four hours.' '*Four hours!* Very far!' She showed me the
child's clothes, made a spewing gesture: 'My boy—*vomit.*' I entertained myself with songs and sexual fantasies. What will become
of me? What if he's already thought better of it? Important: *do
not wait.* Flying through an outer suburb of Sydney I saw a boy
crouched on the footpath with one hand on the side of a dog that had
apparently been hit by a car: the boy turned up his face to a standing
man. A car was stopped at the kerb. The sheepdog, glossy, long-
haired, brownish-yellow, was panting violently, its tongue lolling
right out. Oddly matter-of-fact expression on the boy's face. I may
have misread the situation.

———

Leaves working hard in a coolish wind. Nobody in Sydney knows
I'm here. There is no food in this borrowed house and I'm not
hungry. How lucky I am to be a grown-up (or trying to stay one)
in an empty house in another town. I could go somewhere, or visit

someone, or call one or both of the men, but I don't want to lose this period of non-existence. Incognito, incommunicado. I feel powerful. As soon as I announce myself my freedom will be over.

———

I'm thinner. Dressing, I see muscles move in my shoulders and upper arms. Swimmer's muscles.

———

In Bernard Crick's life of George Orwell (about Cyril Connolly? Or did Connolly say it about Orwell?): 'And he was emotionally independent with the egoism of all natural writers…'

———

Dreamt of a battered house, a central bedroom with doors opening off it in all directions. The room was dirty, dusty, papers strewn about. Other people and I were busily cleaning it and putting it in order. Someone had tucked a clean white sheet very tightly over a pile of different-sized mattresses, so that what looked orderly was in fact chaotic. I had to take it apart and start again. No resentment— rather an excited happiness at the enterprise of it all.

———

In L's backyard. His tanned face, his habit of smiling and laughing. He talked at length, vehemently, about his annoyance with friends, especially couples with children, who took the liberty of asking him close personal questions of a patronising kind. I wasn't sure what he was getting at. I sat there squinting with my hands around my face against the sun and listened. I pieced together a subtext: that he is still deep in at least one unresolved relationship with a woman. His friends are urging him to choose.

I put my arm round his shoulders (two holes in the top seam of his white T-shirt). '*Do* you want children? Are you going to have children?'

He looks down, shifts in his seat. And it hits me that I'm a protection for him, against a full-on relationship that might lead to his *getting married*. He tells me his father saw his fear of it and said, 'Sooner or later you have to touch that hot thing, and see what happens.'

I felt like saying, Marry someone. Have some kids. I should have said, In my life you are a happy sub-plot. But I only said, 'Don't choose me!'

We laughed.

'You're calm, aren't you,' he said. 'How did you get like that?'

'I'm older.'

'Not that much.'

'Enough. I got sick of being ratty.'

'It'd be ridiculous, at fifty.'

(*Thinks*) 'It'll be ridiculous at forty, baby. You've got two years.' (*says*) 'Also, I've spent a year on my own.'

But I don't think he heard this, the most important bit.

————

The other one calls. His terrifying dry voice. Almost a drawl. I feel shy, almost rebuffed, awkward. I don't know if I can handle this.

We sit under the trees in the garden of the borrowed house. He puts his sunglasses on the table and the wind is so strong that they move across its surface. He says the proofs of his novel have come, and they make him feel sick. We make the kind of conversation about nothing that clever people make when they are too shy to be silent. In the living room I point out some large patches of mould: 'If you had a wall like this in your house, you'd do something about it, wouldn't you.' 'Yes. But I can't help admiring the fact that they don't. Pretty soon that surface is gonna look like expensive French wallpaper. Brocade.'

————

In the gallery he shows me 'the best picture here, maybe the best picture ever painted in Australia'. 'The Sisters', by Hugh Ramsay. 'Why is it the best?' 'Oh, because it's so funny. Because…' He trails off. He shows me a Picasso. It means nothing. I fall behind. Then I pull myself together, detach myself from him, begin to look for myself. 'See this guy?' he says. 'He made his own teeth. Out of wood. His wife used to wear long white gloves. Even in summer. Did you know Lloyd Rees' mother was a leper?'

————

We notice a woman gardener, young and slim with brown legs, shorts, a thick bob, a regulation-issue broad-brimmed hat. An old Chinese woman in a pink, soft, pleated dress, slip-on wedgies and little white socks passes, and we admire her as well.

————

'Can you cook?'

He is astonished: '*Course* not.'

————

On New Year's Eve I call home. 'You should see the dining-room table!' says M, her voice bright with excitement and happiness. 'There's at least twenty-five beer cans on it!'

————

Coming away, with my friends, from the terrible play at the Opera House. The air by the water was creamy. This wonderful city. Every night here, when I turn out the light in my borrowed house, I put on Glenn Gould playing the French Suites and fall happily to sleep, hearing their beauty, intricacy and order.

————

The monolith of his marriage, and my own solitariness and flimsiness by comparison. I feel very small, slight, impermanent. It is not too late for me to save myself.

One Day I'll Remember This

Diaries

Volume II

1987–1995

'But evidently I had not understood enough, or rather, as I was slowly finding out, everything that one thinks one understands has to be understood over and over again, in its different aspects, each time with the same new shock of discovery.'

MARION MILNER, *An Experiment in Leisure*

'What do you write in your diary?'

'Everything. I try to write all the worst things. That's the hardest. The temptation to gloss it up. I force myself to put down the bad and stupid things I do, the idiotic fantasies I have.'

'And do you read back over it?'

'All the time.'

———

Lunch. The company of women. This is what I need. Light and silly conversation about how to keep canvas shoes white. 'People think the world is full of couples,' says E. 'In fact it is made up of triangles.'

———

V's quite a frumpy bloke, really. His body is neglected, his hair is going grey. The pale skin of his arms and shoulders is thickly freckled, those childish freckles you see on boys in primary school, a starry sky of freckles, densely packed.

———

Being in love makes me selfish and mean, puts blinkers on me. I get tunnel vision. I want, I want, I want. That's all that happens, when you're in love. Okay, I've said it. I'm in love.

———

O and I took a turn around the park near his house. Muggy night. A flea bite on my left side. A moon one-third full, some faint stars, a scarf of cloud drifting across the Centrepoint Tower, large fruit bats flapping between church steeple and Moreton Bay figs. We convulsed ourselves by saying '*andiamo*' in posh English accents. In a second-hand shop window I saw a pretty nightie I wanted to buy. Always, under whatever else is happening, a level of thought and fantasy about V and what is possible. I try out the idea of a *mistress*, some long-term thing running parallel to his marriage. I know my ego wouldn't accept this. When I've been with him I feel fed, and anxiety dies a little. Like a junkie after a hit, I am able to contemplate giving him up.

———

My story appears today in the *Sydney Morning Herald*. On the front page: 'A new story from Helen Garner, plus how to avoid cholesterol.'

———

On the ferry V has brought a yellow plastic bag. He pretends it contains sandwiches but actually it's his bathers and a book on Wagner by Thomas Mann. 'I've got very strong ideas on individuality,' he says. 'I reckon the further you get from that, the less you are yourself, the more you blur.' I say nothing, but think, 'How does that sit with being married?' 'Course,' he says, 'that means anyone can do anything,' and gives a short, dismissive laugh.

———

At the beach O's wife teased him and he flung sand in her face, a lot, and hard. She sat up, brushed herself off and said, 'I suppose I asked for that.' She walked down to the water to rinse it off. O said when she was out of earshot, 'That wasn't very nice, was it. What can I do to make reparation?' I wanted to say, 'Get down on your knees to her, for openers,' but remained silent. He shook out her towel and rearranged it. She returned and lay down on it, looking ordinary, and we continued our conversation.

———

Dinner with the retired academics. I made a big effort and stayed with the conversation. Spare me from old men's calm assumption that anything they say, no matter how dull, slow or perfunctory, deserves and will have an audience. Their wives are still real, warm people, compared with these old blokes frozen in their own importance. The jerky little tales of eccentrics and their drinking. Sly innuendo about famous women they have known, one of whom was said to have had 'sixty-four lovers'. I sat quietly, thinking, 'You call that a lot?' Is this what V means when he says women never understand that men want to be with other men? Dread: he too will turn out to be *manly* in that way—looked after by a woman, no longer alive to her yet still drawing full benefits from her love and sacrifice…Is there hope for women and men?

I called home. M's lovely bright voice. Thank God I had a daughter. She tells me she's got a job as a cleaner in an office building. 'I started on Friday. $9.50 an hour. It's hard but I'll get used to it.' I was pleased it was a rough job and she had got it through her own contacts and not mine. She'll learn the connection between work and money.

These two men. I could say 'I love you' to each of them. To L in the most direct, old-fashioned and simple way: I know him, I like him, *he is like me*, we know each other without effort, two greedy, cheerful, sexy, sociable people, takers of foolish risks. To the other, how? A thinker, intellectual, contained, cautious, measured, hard-working, private. And *married*. This will have to be lived. It can't be walked away from.

'How greatly one needs declarations in love, and how greatly one fears them, as though they *used up* something that would otherwise survive longer.' —Elias Canetti, *The Human Province*

Awful evening at L's kitchen table. His attacks on me, the truth in them, but the way he strengthened their force, and ultimately weakened and undermined their truth, by the use of irony, or rather sarcasm. 'You're silent,' he says. 'I'm not like that. It's a powerful position, the silent one.' I put my head down on the table and cried with shame. Sadness, soreness, regret; relief.

———

M calls, laughing and high-voiced with excitement, to report her exam results. 'I knew the mail'd be there early. So I made myself some breakfast and strolled to the post office as if there was no hurry. I got two letters and I even made myself read the other one first.' I shower her with praise. 'Don't feel you have to move out as soon as you get back,' she says. 'It'd be good to spend some time with you in the house before we part. People have been staying over a lot. Some in your bed. But don't worry, I always make it nice again.'

———

V reads me some of his new novel. It's very good. Dry, completely *competent*, full of fancies that make me burst out laughing. He reads badly, in a stubbornly unemotional voice, as if gritting his teeth to do it.

———

Very, very hot day. I thought I was fine on the highway till I stopped at a motel in Yass and got out. Found myself almost unable to speak to the woman at reception. When she asked if I wanted dinner I just stared at her wildly. Trucks passed all night. Single bed, white cotton sheets. I was terribly thirsty. Drank eight cups of tea and a jug of orange juice. Wanted a beer desperately but was too stupefied to go out and find a pub.

———

At Albury I bought a Ry Cooder tape. Played it over and over, those instrumental songs, the leisure and sweetness of their hesitations. The quality of his music is goodness. Absence of straining ego.

———

Today I own a house. Got the key and rushed over. Hated it of course. No sun to show its many light sources. Phone went bung after one call. All windows seem to look on to brick walls. Plants in the garden ugly and neglected and worthy of euthanasia. I began to panic till I stood in the backyard and felt its space. Went again in the early evening, to water. Extreme quietness of the street, darkness beginning to cluster under the plane trees. In the backyard I stood holding the hose on yellowing grass. Sky in the west a paling orange. Above, a colourless clarity.

————

Moving house. One carload at a time. My room looks on to thousands of leaves. I lie on my bed and rest, looking up into the foliage. The dog lies in the hall and gazes out the front door. Back at the old house M's three friends are moving in. Their different types of bed. Nobody there looks at me. I have ceased to exist.

————

I feel, and have to force myself to write, that for the first time in my life I am able to stand up to, or with, a man of my own age whose strength of purpose and self-discipline are at least as great as mine. I'm prepared to behave with respect and patience.

————

Our father twists his head, red-faced, shouts, 'What I want to know is—what are you going to do with my money when I'm dead?' They've been drinking. Mum puts her head back against the armchair and laughs out loud. 'I think that's really funny! We won't *know*! 'Cause we'll be *dead*!'

————

At Manly V wouldn't take off anything but his sandals. He says that men don't like being looked at when they're naked.

————

Boy, can he write! Can he sling verbs around!

————

Paralysis, since I no longer live with M. Everyone I tell has a different analysis. 'It's a lack of structure! What you people all need,' says J, the Christian, 'is original sin. *That* gives you form and structure!

You won't be happy, but at least you'll know there's *shape*.' 'It's the abyss,' says R, the Jungian. 'A brand-new abyss. I envy you. Don't fill it up with old things.'

———

Me: 'This house is full of ants. But single ants. You look at a square foot of floor, and there'll be one ant just walking along vaguely. I think they're Argentinian ants.'

My sister: (*looking bored*) 'Long walk.'

———

Wind blew in the night: I thought I heard doors being opened and shut. Rain poured down. The house was waterproof. In the morning I hired a one-tonne flatbed truck to move the rest of my stuff. The pipsqueak at Hertz demanded incredible details from me—he rang the publisher and asked her to *describe* me. I told the guy who runs the Paragon that my old friend P is going to share the house with me. 'You women!' he said, handing me my coffee. 'You get together again, late in life! Have you noticed?' I was silent with shock. *Late in life?*

———

The black kitten that F palmed off on us is clawing up and down my leg. P accepted the offer of a cat eagerly, sight unseen, though when she did see it she was not *quite* sure about its colour. 'You can't go back on it now,' I said. She consulted one of her spiritual advisers, and returned saying black would be fine.

———

A letter that comes straight towards me with open arms.

———

Dreamt an old auntie told me that a woman 'always needs a good pair of stout brown lace-up walking boots'.

———

Sorted books for hours. At first I was ruthless, and culled, but as fatigue took over, all my decisions acquired a tone of angst, until I had to stop. Found an old literary magazine containing an interview with

V. His sentences were so dry as to be starchy, perfectly constructed in a way that made me feel exhausted and slightly panicky. He is married. He is an intellectual. He is only messing with me. And I have dropped my guard. Reading at random in Canetti: 'It seems that one cannot be *severe* all of a lifetime. It seems that something takes vengeance in one, and one becomes like everyone else.' Is this the sort of stuff V would write? Painful speculations, sometimes grinding, always trying to tackle the worst, the least attractive, what cannot be made beautiful?

————

The cheeky waiter at Notturno is the brother of a wildly erratic and endearing Italian boy I used to teach.

'Tell me, how's your brother?'

'He's gone.'

'Where?'

'Up there.' Points north. 'Carlton cemetery.'

'You're pulling my leg.'

'No. That's where he is.'

Pause.

'Are you having me on?'

'No.' He is calm, but his smart expression is gone. The freckles round his eyes are standing out. 'No. He died.' Looks at his watch. 'On the eighth.'

'*Why* did he die?'

'Heart attack.'

'*Heart* attack? How old was he?'

'Twenty-nine.'

'Did he have something wrong with his heart?'

'No. He had weak lungs. He smoked too much. He loved a bong. His wife came home and found him on the floor. They took him down to St Vincent's and the doctor said he'd be all right. But he said to my mother, "Take me jewellery off, Mum—I'm gonna die." And he died.'

At least I am not bound to anyone, hurting him with my obsession. Examination of fantasy state: it is not a series of clear pictures. Really it is more a stupefaction, a state of suspension.

Lunch in Fitzroy. The way friends, men and women, sit around a table, eating, drinking, telling little stories, making each other laugh. I dislike, and am shocked by, the spiteful sallies of one of the older men. I'd forgotten it. I'm used to living with teenagers. They have no bitterness.

My sister calls, the counsellor. 'How is it, living without M?'
    'Awful. I'm paralysed.'
    'Classic,' she says. 'Classic symptoms.'
    'What of?'
    'Grief. Starts with blankness, then that clears and it hurts more. It gets worse.'
    'And guilt?'
    'Yep. *Huge* discharge of guilt. Also—idealisation.'
    'Have you heard her HSC results?'
    We almost laugh.
    'Crying helps,' she says, 'if you can do it.'
    'But what should I *do*? My friend R says, "Go into it. Don't be busy. *Use* it."'
    'She's right. The sacrament of whatever's necessary.'
    'Who said *that*?'
    'Me.'

Agitated, stunned, in distress, all at once. Sobs won't form. I trudge about the house, hating the colours, ring up and order a deadlock, wait like a rabbit for *Cinema Papers* to call about my review. The cat has decided on a corner of my workroom as its lavatory.

Her first day at primary school, her eagerness, the way she gazed up at the teacher, my *jealousy* of the teacher. The heavy surf of guilt: times when she wanted my company, my attention, and I gave it but not with a full heart, or gave it briefly and soon let my mind wander in boredom with her childishness. I ran away from her. Once when he and I squabbled in the car she punched herself methodically in the head, she punched herself for some time *before I noticed*. I'm ashamed of feeling these things, it's an affliction I have to keep secret from her. Dull sky, cool wind, the side gate keeps banging. Voices in the street speaking another language. This state is like a second labour. I'm struggling to let her be born.

———

A Tchaikovsky piano concerto, on my own. The idea of it made me yawn but soon my skin began to crawl and various thoughts came to me with the music as background. If I go ahead with this, I will be spending a lot of time alone. That's something I am already good at, and often prefer. I will spend a lot of time waiting. And when I'm old I will be alone. How strange these thoughts are. They are serious thoughts. I am contemplating a course of action which at my age will have certain repercussions, important ones. Have I got, can I find in myself, the courage and strength to live like that? Would I want to be 'married'? I am notoriously bad at it. It does not suit me. The wife envies the passion her husband feels for the mistress. The mistress envies the steady companionship...'The world is made up of triangles.'

———

H: 'I'm old-fashioned too.'
  V: 'Oh you are not.'
  H: 'You'd be surprised.'
  V: 'Name one respect in which you're old-fashioned.'
  H: 'I believe that children should be strictly brought up.'
  V: 'Good. What else?'

H: 'Uhmmm…tablecloths. I like them, and I don't mind ironing them.'

———

My first cheerful day since I 'left home'. F called me and we went out to dinner. We spoke mainly French. I can still understand almost everything and can chatter away, but I get words wrong and sometimes a blankness occurs. We had fun, drank a bit of wine and made ourselves laugh. On the way home we stopped at our old house— now M's and her friends'—to pick up my TV, a few pot plants and a ladder. The kitchen was full of the girls plus the law student and a debauched-looking, dense-faced boy I didn't know. They told me M was 'feeling ill' and had gone to bed. They were all stoned, staggering with it, especially the law student, whose face was puffy. He stumbled about in a red baseball jacket, hopelessly bombed, his eyes like eggs. He looked like a pampered, adolescent, middle-class boy and I hated it. He barely greeted me. We collected what we'd come for. A lot of jolly noise, loud wisecracks in US accents—they were waiting for us to be gone so they could stagger out to the Prince of Wales. The law student asked me if I was coming to M's party on Saturday night. 'No. I'm going to the country. Anyway she hasn't invited me.' 'She hasn't *invited* you?' 'Oh, it's all right,' I say, without looking at him or meaning it, already halfway out the door, full of sadness, shame, anger, a burst of disagreeable feelings that still ache with a light persistence. When I got home I looked at myself in the mirror. My top lip had twisted, higher on the left than the right. I looked bitter. Older and wiser. I suppose when your mother is 'old and wise' you have to be very tough to break away. You must have to *show no mercy.*

———

Dreamt that the married man was washing up at my sink. I came and put my arms round him from behind. He turned and wrapped himself around me *like a child*, twining, so that his feet were off the ground. I felt his lightness and smallness with amazement.

'Is *The Fatal Shore*,' says V, 'the kind of book you'd rush out and buy?'

'Course not. I've got no feeling for the past at all.'

'You've got a pretty strong sense of the present, though, haven't you.'

A character with no sense of the past but with such a sense of the present that she can be used as a gauge in any situation: 'What's going on in there? Send in the radar.'

I asked M out for coffee. She agreed eagerly. When I called for her the boys' dorm was still all over the lounge-room floor. The law student took me into the laundry and showed me a bong in a bucket of water. He explained its workings. I was bored, unimpressed, slightly shocked, basically contemptuous. In the cafe I told M about my ten miserable days. She was aghast: 'You should have come over!' She listened to my psychological account. I noticed she had tears in her eyes. 'I came home from work,' she says, 'and found them all bonging on just inside the back door, with the door open and fumes pouring out into the street. I walked straight through and went to bed.'

When we got back from the cafe we found the boys gone and one of the other girls, the opera singer, finishing a major clean-up. She told us she had put the kitchen radio on classical music and started the dishes. In the living room the boys put on one of their records so she closed the kitchen door. The law student burst in, turned off her radio with a violent movement, and shouted, 'Stop acting the martyr! *I'll* wash up later!' Telling us this, her face flushes dark red and huge tears spill out of her eyes and pour down her face. Boys who batten off girls, use their sense of order as something to sponge off and then desecrate. Girls who let them do this.

'I considered nothing. It happened. What will become of us?' At Primrose Gully, in the place where last year I painfully taught myself the discipline of solitude and learnt a kind of freedom, I recognise that I have given up freedom again, willingly let it go, exchanged it for *this bondage*, to time and another person, which is called LOVE.

———

Me: 'Oh, I wish I was an intellectual. But I'm not.'

My sister: 'You're doing a hell of a lot better than me. Or is it I.'

———

An unpleasant, scorching day with dry winds, then a cool change. I drank some beer and ate at the born-again Christian's place in St Kilda. We walked a long way in the dark and the south-westerly off the water, out the pier and on to the groin or whatever it's called. Coming back, we walked with our arms round each other. I said something and laughed and looked up at him and he kissed me, with open lips. I was stunned, thinking, 'This is *the wrong man*.' That thought did not even scrape the surface of the event. We walked on. I said, 'We never could walk in step,' and he said, 'That's how it is.' He told me that at work he had seen a beam of light pass through a concrete wall. 'Were you hallucinating?' 'I've heard the devil can appear as light, so I don't know.'

———

The flight to Sydney lasted only five minutes because I was reading Marguerite Duras' *La Douleur*. When her husband comes back after the war I cried so much my face twitched, I had to wipe my eyes on my skirt. 'I remember the sobbing all through the house, the tenants lingering on the stairs, the doors standing open.' Her writing is so physical. The movement of her sentences captures the movement of emotion and thought—it's real *women's writing*, shameless but never sloppy. Maybe she's what I'm looking for—to show me how to control emotion without being false to its power, how to be absent and fully present at once.

———

Reading in French slows me down, which is good, but there's always that veil, the absence in me of the complex vibrations that one's own language sets up. Vibrations of the past in the words and expressions, the echoing field of meaning in which one and one's own language can *play*. And yet the slowness makes it rich in another way.

———

From the hotel window I can see water, ferries in at the quay, but mostly asphalt and metal. The feelings I get from waiting are like an echo from the future. What is the technique for not waiting? Clearly it is not possible to develop one, while in a hotel room, taskless, homeless, workless, backyardless, carless, bikeless. This trip then is an aberration. From now on, discipline.

———

A letter to the law student. 'Also you are drinking too much and smoking too much dope. It is my prerogative to point this out. We shared a difficult year. Don't act like a fuckwit and spoil everything.'

———

What I miss about L is the sight of him at the Cretan's place, all brown and colourful on the sofa, talking practical talk about gardening.

———

V often fades out, halfway through a sentence.

———

When I sign my name, my first name, on a letter, I look at it and like it, and feel lucky to have been given it.

———

On Bondi Beach the moon, like a slice of lemon or a hunk of cheese, went down fast behind a peculiar tower. I thought about things I want to write. The healing sessions at the born-again church, the ragged doll at Primrose Gully, the bat, the rats, the Christian who wants to drown the cat, the sister planning an abortion, all the things I slid away from writing last year because I was scared.

———

One of the painter's favourite themes, said V, was mother and child. And yet he hated his own mother.

'There are other mothers in the world, aren't there.'

'Other than what?'

'Other than your own.'

———

I try hard to examine him, and him and me, for weak spots that might destroy my respect once the obsession wears off. Mostly I find areas of inadequacy in myself—mental laziness, ignorance, sloppy habits of mind, self-indulgence, while for him my respect grows as he shows himself to me. He is a knower of things. I know things too, but different things, and I know them differently. He loves to tell me things and sometimes I get bored. Why? Because it's a monologue. I have nothing to offer but my attention.

———

I can't stop crying, I'm so tired, and the building noise outside this room is making me crazy.

———

From a chaise longue outside my back door I survey my backyard, its complete stillness, the fine element of damp in the air, the stars thinly sprinkled above the shed.

———

Rosa Cappiello calls me from Sydney. I can hear her panting with the effort of speaking English. I am almost scared of her, she is so violently trying to be herself.

'Elen. Are you with a man?'

'No. Are you?'

'No. Because all the men I know are sick, and dirty. I want someone who is *clean inside*.'

———

Watched the Kundera doco on SBS at my sister's. She slept right through it. I walked home: light was leaving the sky, air clear, streets empty, air and sky perfectly empty. Walked along feeling overwrought, strange, as if some rusted mechanism in me were beginning, after a long stillness of disuse, to turn over again.

———

While the gynaecologist is examining my cunt she tells me that her old dog got cancer and had to be put down. 'I still cry when I think of it,' she says, doing so, burrowing away inside me. 'I've cried every day for two and a half months. He was like a child to me. Life is so empty without him.'

———

Great love I feel for T, her stubborn face and stubborn ability to laugh at the moment before despair. She's recovered from black lung, and is now convinced she's got MS. 'I keep bumping into things,' she says, heaving chairs in over the tailgate of the EH. 'And I've got a weakness which is TOTAL.' I diagnose a hangover. She's been on holiday with her bloke. 'We were together for several days. We were careful with each other, like two actors performing a play.' If she left him she would flourish as an artist. Easy for me to say.

———

The story about looking. I want it to have a curve in it. To come right back and tie itself to the very beginning.

———

P is very exercised domestically by what to me are minor matters: which kitchen table? She weighs this possibility against that, trotting from one room to another or standing in a thoughtful posture, finger against cheek. I adopt a good-humoured but blanked-out patience, like a man in a Maupassant short story with a garrulous wife whom he nonetheless loves. P is adorable, and faithful, with a delicacy that I completely lack.

———

The old journalist in an interview talks about her husband, how they lived a life of intense companionship along with surprising independence. 'So we both lied. I had twice been blindly and hopelessly in love, and I knew that he'd had two love affairs, but they were never discussed. I think the worst thing anyone can do to someone you love is to confess all, because I did love him more than anybody in the world. He was such a marvellous friend and he never bored me. We really suited each other down to the ground.' So even 'blindly and hopelessly in love' can't stand up against 'we suited each other down to the ground'.

————

What am I doing? He has been married for more than half his life on this earth. Why should it be any different from any other love affair? Why shouldn't it run through its phases, wither, and die? I'd better work if I want to survive this, and if I want to play my full and proper part in it. Who wants a lovesick, lazy drip, obsessed with her own emotions and full of resentment against fate?

————

Bad news. The owner of Primrose Gully calls to say he is putting it on the market. I have no money. I thought I could detach myself… but a moment ago, at sunset, the pinkish-gold light on the opposite ridge was so thick we might have been in Tuscany. Oh well. Kookaburras burst out in choruses from the gully. A full moon rises. P surveys it from the veranda couch, sitting yoga-style with her elbows propped gracefully on her knees. I have known her so long that I don't know any more where I end and she begins. I have been friends with her for more than half my life on earth. Like V and his wife. This simple thought is comforting. A corrective. Then she left the kero lamp on all night and burnt out the wick and mantle.

————

Schopenhauer is bracing. Things are about as bad as they can be, for humans, so we might as well recognise this and behave with 'tolerance, patience, forbearance and charity, which each of us needs and which each of us therefore owes'.

————

The born-again quotes Corinthians at me: 'Love seeketh not its own.'

'What's that mean?'

'*You* ought to be able to work that out.'

'How about "Love hath not an eye for the main chance"?'

He seems impressed, but perhaps is not.

———

Warm night, squashed moon, smell of dry grass as if from a plain. I read Kuznetsov's *Babi Yar* with bated breath. My story seemed paler and paler, its tiny thoughts, its peaceful world. All my mechanisms creaking and groaning. Doubt thins everything out, shows the void that always lies behind. Doubt that calls itself realism.

———

The law student and his dippy friend turn up very late at my door: 'We're tripping, Hel.' The friend is a talker, a joker, very tiring. The student's face is a screen on which waves of emotion are projected. I take them into the kitchen and devise small challenges: to get off on a plain white plate, and so on. Soon I'm getting a contact high. I begin to contemplate the flower pattern on the teapot spout, and a sound like distant music that is made by the motor of the fridge. I worry about being old and plain—then I think, 'They're probably seeing only light where I think I am.' The law student works hard at being courteous: 'The minute you feel like going back to bed, Hel…' He is meticulous about emptying the ashtray, but is waylaid by 'all these ants in the bin'. I rush to look, expecting an invasion, but find only two.

———

P and I drove to Albert Park for a swim at 10 pm. Dark water. I waded in. Wherever I moved there was a boiling light under the surface: phosphorescence. I cried out and she was scared—she thought it was pollution or radioactivity. I wanted to swim and gaze at my boiling accompaniment—off my hands came streams of it, in dense bubbling clouds—but the water smelled dirty and I was afraid of sharks. Out on the pier (lightning kept stabbing randomly behind the city) we sat in the breathless stillness and the air began to pour from the north, a wind *grew* as we sat there. P's towel, which had been hanging from the rail, was lifted on an angle and sustained it without flapping. People everywhere in the dark. We drove home yawning and as we walked in the front door it started to pour with rain.

———

After the movie, which I thought was sentimental, I got quite punchy, and mad at P for not arguing and for saying things like 'What's wrong with ending on a positive note?' As I Expounded My Views I felt (a) how *clever* and *articulate* I was being, then (b) disgusted with myself for priding myself on (a). P in her delicate and well-mannered way said that when a film makes 'one' furious it must be because it has touched on some sore point in 'one'. I was suddenly deflated by the truth in this. I was furious because *I'm* sentimental. Because in *my* work I am guilty of striking the sweet note when it should be sour.

———

I want to write a novel about the born-again. Shadow games. Premonitions. Where does the murder trial fit in? A helicopter passes, hovers, unremarked upon, during an important scene. I am a very *unlearned* woman.

———

The only way I can sit still for long periods is if I read and take notes. Maybe loneliness will save me after all. In these states I can listen with profit to music by Bartók, Schoenberg, weird and scary stuff. Except for Bach, other things seem too pleasant or even easy. Scared the shit out of myself by playing several times Bartók's 'Music for Strings, Percussion and Celesta' and his second quartet, and reading the *New Grove* entry about him. The spine-chilling impersonality of those biographies, it actually frightens me, I don't know why. And I can't help noticing the cold note: 'he divorced his first wife in the autumn and married his pupil Ditta Pásztory…' Oh hell. What will become of me?

A couple of beers at Little Reata with the law student. Loved his company, such a tenderness for him, his eager interest in life. He can't bear to think what might be in store for me. He puts his head on the table, holds my hands, groans. I laugh. One day I'll remember this.

If I write a movie I will be forced, by working with other people, to come out of my fantasy world and deliver the goods.

At Primrose Gully with R. Gas lamp hissing. Sky has cleared and is star-sprinkled. 'If I were you,' says R, 'I'd sell my soul to get hold of this place.'

During the wedding ceremony I asked myself why the simple hopes of these promises are so impossible when the complications of life fall on them like a collapsing wall. I do not understand marriage. V is always talking about *symmetry* but we are not symmetrical at all. I am offering everything and he is offering everything except the final thing, which in effect means that he is offering nothing. Is this true or is it just a smart crack? It is quite understandable to be stunned and even sick with fear when you're heading for a brick wall at 100 miles an hour.

'These soul things,' said R, 'they're on another level. They can't be legislated.'

'A girl at the supermarket gave me free coupons,' I said. 'She looked like Dolly Parton.'

   'Like who?' says V.

   'Like Dolly Parton.'

'Who's Dolly Pardon?'

———

Out to hear Washington Wives. I enjoyed moving, and staring at people. While dancing I fantasised what John Shaw Nielson called 'wonderful frocks' of a feminine style—big skirts with little socks—mutton dressed as lamb perhaps but I refuse to be middle-aged.

———

V quotes Degas quoting Delacroix: 'An artist must have no passion except his work and must sacrifice everything to it.' Privately I consider this to be bullshit.

———

Fantasy: I arrange to meet him in the US at the end of the writers' tour. He comes and we meet: but in the meantime I have met *a free man*. I see V coming towards me and I do not know him or want him any more. He is already in my past, a stranger, a finished phase.

———

A man with a habit of giving less information, and in a less coherently organised form, than one needs in order to be able to understand what he is talking about—almost as if he is trying to provoke one to ask puzzled questions so he can accuse one of not paying proper attention.

———

Alone at Primrose Gully. Sun pours in. Wind cool enough for a jumper. Stove quietly working. Could such a place be mine? I look at the cabin with a more critical, demanding eye: this must be cleaned, that painted. I walked along the road with the dog. Trees in their many dimensions flickered, like a Fred Williams painting. Intense beauty of the sparse bush. I tried to sing the Nielson song: 'And in that poor country, no pauper was I.' Floods of emotion passed through me: anticipation of work, ideas about a born-again novel, memories of the Mighty Force and its visitations. Walking on the road I felt my spine to be taller, more vertical. I thought, 'I will never be like V, or write like him, or use his methods. My value, to him and to the world, in fact my JOB, is to work as I know how, as is natural to me.' Terrific exhilaration of this.

———

A scene for a movie: two girls, young women, students, walk along a road in the middle of a dry summer night. They take off their blouses and walk bare-breasted. Wind blows on them. 'Do you remember,' I say to P, 'the night at Merricks when we took our blouses off, walking along the road? It was so hot!' 'I remember the walk,' she says, 'but not the blouses.'

———

Last night I decided to 'sell my soul' to buy Primrose Gully. Today I arrive home and find a cheque from Queensland for the exact price of the property. I had not told her, or anyone, anything about it. '*That*,' said the Jungian, 'is synchronicity.'

———

The healing session at the born-again's Pentecostalist church. 'What's your need, sister?' 'It's my back.' He shouts over his shoulder, 'Get her a chair.' A plastic chair is rushed up behind and I sit on it. The pastor crouches in front of me, straightens my legs, seizes my ankles: 'Make sure you're sitting right back in the chair. See how this leg's shorter than that one?' 'Yes.' He—what *did* he do?—pulls them, I think, equally towards him, says, 'Feel that in your back? Thank you, Lord! Thank you! Now see? They're the same length!' Grabs my hands. 'Up! Now—run on the spot.' I do: 'It doesn't hurt.' I can feel myself grinning. He's still holding my hands. 'And there's a fair bit of tension, too,' he says, 'that makes the back sore.' He put his right hand round my waist and presses it quickly against my lower spine, exactly where the vertebra bulges out, and says, 'It's that vertebra there, isn't it.' 'Yes.' I don't recall whether he laid his hands on my head—but out of him bursts the word 'PEACE!'—hands catch me behind and I'm on my back on the floor. I feel completely ordinary. My face is turning red. I turn my head and see an old woman roll over, scramble on to her hands and knees, and crawl out of the line of bodies back towards the pews. I turn on to my side and lie there staring. Throughout all this there is a complete and total lack of ritual—no music, no set prayers, no *silence*—people chat quietly, the two catchers are laughing and talking in low voices about buying a secondhand Mazda only inches away from where the pastor is laying hands on one person after another and praying loudly and urgently. It's extremely casual, practical and relaxed. Small children are strolling about yelling to their mothers. I get to my feet and walk back to our pew. We leave before the end. In the lobby three little kids in Catholic primary-school uniforms are staring in: 'He's dead! See him push them over? The one in the red jumper's dead.' We walk away along the sunny street and speak of other things—about how he would like to marry, the puzzle of how to meet *girls*.

————

F showed me the bill from the Hôtel de la Plage at Fréhel in Brittany where we first had a holiday, in 1978. We laughed and laughed, in a fit of cheerful memories. 'That was back when you used to be nice,' he said. 'What? I still am!' He urged me, with hints, to recall the name of the next village, the last one on the road: PLURIEN. Laughed till we had tears in our eyes.

————

V: 'What'll you do tomorrow?'
  Me: (*genuinely surprised*) 'Work.'

————

M's been invited to join a theatre company and given (without having to audition) a part in *The Cherry Orchard*.

————

On the drive to the airport he has a cigar but no matches. I pull into a 7-Eleven.
  'What's this?'
  'The match shop.'
  He smokes the disgusting thing and talks like an American.

————

Rode lightless through the Fitzroy Gardens. Men on beat heading for the lavatories, I nearly knocked one flying. Home along Brunswick Street on the footpath. Wonderful summer night, half a moon hanging casually halfway up the sky, thick dry air, people out in the streets.

———

The pencil, and furthermore, it wore down. In another three months it'll be gone. There'll be nothing left of it at all.

———

'Called or not called, God shall be there.' —Above Jung's door.

———

I wonder what he thinks his rights are, in this? Has he the right to be jealous, to make demands? Have *I* got any 'rights'? What *is* a 'right'?

———

We open the front door at midnight. Someone's been here. The plastic box on the hall floor, the cheap jewellery spread as if at leisure. The living-room window's wide open, the blind still flapping over the sill. What's gone? TV still there: video, ghetto-blaster, stereo. In the hall my blue beret and a striped belt on the carpet. My basket's gone, the big light basket I bought in Vanuatu. *That* thing? Broken and torn? To carry away loot? But nothing that *big* has been taken. Ah, behind my bed a missingness: my CD Walkman. My wooden box with brass corners is open on the mantelpiece—oh, my pretty antique rings! But I never wore them. Nothing else missing: M's baby teeth and my wedding ring no. 2 still there but they've taken my first wedding ring. How did they choose? Come back and show me how it looks on you! On the floor where the Walkman was, a cheap gold pendant: a heart containing a pearl. I pick it up. Like a payment. Must've been girls. Dear girls! You've stripped me of a weight: take my things and wear them on your young hands and bodies.

———

Falling in love at this age is terrible because it makes you fear death.

————

'So this poor bitch,' says V, 'in glaring white shoes and a purple jumpsuit...' I flinch. He's one of those old-fashioned men who divide up women into poor bitches, molls, free spirits (Mirka Mora), and then their own women. Let's stop now, before I get so far in I forget where the exit is and have to blow up the building to get out.

————

Everything that can be called A SUBJECT he knows about. And I know about the rest.

————

The game I invent to entertain V when he's sick in bed. I put an object against his back under his T-shirt and he has to guess what it is. A hammer, half an apple. Aching paroxysms of noiseless laughter. When I put a candle there he thinks for ages and says uncertainly, 'Is it your watch?'

————

A savage taxi driver. His anger seethed out of his pores, he was sick and mad with it. 'Sydney's a dump. A bloody rubbish heap full of greedy sick pipple. Town Hall—in there's the biggest bunch of idiots. Wanting to change everything. Pedestrian malls in the middle of the city. Make everyone turn around and go the other way. Newtown. That's another bloody dump. If I had to live in Newtown or Erskineville I'd rather live in a *tent*. In a bloody *paddock*. The houses've got only one wall between 'em. You can hear the bloke next door talkin' to his missus. Where do *I* live? I've lived in plenty of places, lady. King Street—a dump. One lane of traffic. Blocked up for miles.' Battered by his bitter monologue. You only need a couple of thousand people like him to poison the entire population of the world. Considered saying, 'What happened? Why are you so angry?' but I knew he would massacre me.

————

'The first time I ever got into bed with a girl, starkers,' says V, 'I was staggered by the softness. I was absolutely *staggered*.' I thought about the three women I've been in bed with. The astounding softness of their mouths and skin. I decide not to say, 'I know exactly what you mean.'

I say, 'I'm no good at marriage. I think I'd be awful to be married to.'
   'Why? What makes you say that?'
   I look at my bare foot on the bed-end and think, 'Is it even *true*?'

The biographer sent me a copy of her letter to the subject's family, dropping the project because of not wanting to 'hurt' them. She's chickened out. I felt a roll of scorn. Then guilt. R and I discussed possible reasons, and found plausible ones, which lowered my tone. R says, 'She's closer to the precipice than most of us.' Once again I see in myself an impatience with the suffering of others, an unpleasant briskness.

Fear, at three in the morning after a storm, that I'll never write anything again.

I weigh myself on the big machine at Coles. 'Eight stone four,' says the man in charge of the scales. 'That's a good weight. You hang around that weight and you'll be right.'

F tells me about a TV program he saw, about AIDS—junkies as well as gays. Sudden rigid horror—what if I caught it in Paris in 1978? Staring at the chair leg I imagine the blood coming out of my arm into the tube: 'You're positive.' I must have looked panic-stricken. F says, 'I didn't mean to frighten you.' 'Should I get a blood test?' 'You have to be careful, that's all.'

   David Bowie announces cheerfully that he has an AIDS test every time he 'changes partners'.

At Mum and Dad's I sat sideways on my chair, staring out the window. Dad said, affectionately (for him), 'What are *you* thinking about, Helen?' 'Oh,' I said, 'just the meaning of the universe.' A true answer would have been, 'I've found the love of my life, and he's married to somebody else.'

———

I admire and want to imitate the way he looks at, say, a picture, and walks away. He shows me something and doesn't expect me to comment. He gives me time.

———

Kafka's letters to Felice. Struck by their dailiness, the intense detail he goes into about circumstance and feeling—and sometimes by a slicing sarcasm which makes me afraid of him.

———

The men on the excavation site next to the hotel arrive quietly, and go quietly about the tasks of preparation for work. I don't know what they're doing. Checking the huge pieces of equipment. Looking at gauges. Putting oil in things. Not seeming to communicate with each other, in their dark shorts and boots and socks.

———

My beautiful little indigo leather bag is not on my bed when I go to get a stamp out of it. I search my bedroom, the house—I go to search the car but the keys to it are in the bag. A hollow feeling. Where is it? $600 in cash, that P owed me and paid. My pen, my keycard, my bank book, door key, car key, PO box key, *my black notebook*—my notes for my movie, play, novel. I acknowledge it's gone, I call the cops. Two boys and a girl, all armed with pistols. Friendly, courteous, efficient. I wish I had a decent-sized teapot to make them all a cuppa. They leave, full of advice about security grilles, window bars etc. The robber must have taken the bag through my bedroom window, which was wide open to catch the breeze: it is a balmy night, the air is sweet with grass. I cursed and swore. I drank a glass of vodka.

How pretty U is, her clean cheek-line and small nose, her clear eye-whites, her thick curly forelock. She is upset in her self-esteem because a man she went to bed with last week subsequently behaved opaquely and then ceased to contact her. She rang him, left notes. What a terrible tactician, her ego all up-front and undisciplined. 'It's unfortunate,' I said, 'but you have to fake indifference until it becomes real; and then he'll be eating out of your hand. And you don't even *want* him, anyway.'

Are you comfortable, in me? Do you need a window opened, or cleaned? A night-light on your balcony? Are there enough bedclothes? The doors don't lock. The garden is endless and full of vegetables and flowers. Are you happy?

I will get only $4000 in royalties. So much for my fucking Subaru. Stop complaining and start working. Anyway the law student says that a Subaru is 'kitsch' and 'has no style'.

Pleasure of sitting by the fire. P was sewing, I was reading. We were silent for an hour at least. We know how to be silent. We are civilised.

'His Crockery'. First she stood in line at DJ's sale with half a dozen Arzberg plates in her hands. The queue was long. She lost patience and walked away, leaving them on the wrong display counter. Back at the house he said, 'You're a great little shopper, aren't you.' 'Not great enough. I was too mean to wait.' 'I don't care,' he said. 'I'm cooking. Sit down and read the paper.' Then he went away to Italy. Then she went to Grace Brothers and bought a whole set of the plainest white Australian china. She carried it on foot to his house. The other man there let her in. He was on his way to work. 'What's in the parcel?' 'Nothing. Just some stuff.' He closed the door behind him. She put the parcel on the kitchen table, went out to the shed for an axe, and started the job. I want it to have no particular *meaning*. Wherever there is a sign of character development, plot, explanation, I want to stamp on it.

———

An old man presents himself at my door: he found my Medicare card and licence in a neighbour's front garden while 'talking about roses', and returned them to our old house, where the dog attacked him and tore a great piece out of his jumper. He showed me the rip: 'Pure wool it was, and everything.'

———

Before the woman he was going to marry came back from New York, G told me, he understood then 'the black power of love'. Nightmares from which he woke sweating and stammering, mornings when he sang for joy.

———

I've kept myself for decades in a milieu of people younger than me.

———

Sun streams in. Stillness outside. Beans and potatoes boiling on the stove. Dog asleep nose to tail on the matting. Treetops open to air and light but their trunks deep in the darkness of autumn. Outside the window the koala is asleep in the crook of the branches. One foreleg grips, the other hangs loosely by its side. The great black shining claws.

———

I worked on my story. I pulled things out of thin air. I dragged stuff out of chaos. The moment when, working off diary material as a basis, I begin to invent: like the first moment on an unsupported two-wheeler, or ice skates, letting go, doing it on my own.

———

Dream of trying to help a briskly pragmatic old woman with her work of hostliness. The fish in the pond that she declines to notice. Her ostentatious refusal to remark on the fact that I am hopelessly, unstoppably weeping. Maybe R would say: the refusal to attend to the fish—what swims in water—the unconscious.

———

A beer takes the edge off this peculiar low-level...I want to write *suffering*. I worry about being mad, or unbalanced. Being 'brought undone'.

———

Final scene in *The Trial*: the two executioners who plunge the knife into him and then stand, cheeks together, watching him weaken and die; the attic window that is flung open, the figure that leans out with both arms extended in a large mysterious gesture. Both these images must have come straight out of a dream. I love this thought and feel freed by it.

———

There's stuff I *should* be reading, but I don't know what it is, and so I read just anything, and feel all the time that it's the wrong stuff.

———

What if the Mighty Force came back and stood behind me again, and this time demanded that I let V go? The Mighty Force never demanded anything. It stood. That's all. I knew that if I turned and acknowledged it I would not *be able* to continue with F. The thing with F was killing both of us, but I clung to it. The Mighty Force was offering me life. No, not offering. It offered nothing. It stood.

———

Lunchtime break from the Literature Board meeting. I eat then walk round the streets of North Sydney or sit in a park. In two days I'll go home, I'll work, I'll work in the garden with P, we'll go to Primrose Gully, I'll cook meals, paint the kitchen, I'll read, swim, see my friends. I have been neglecting my friends.

———

'Do you ever find,' says R, 'that someone's company, even though you love it, can completely exhaust you?'

———

The urge to blame V. To say, 'He is selfish. He wants to have everything, for the world to revolve around him. He will never choose me. He should never have begun this.' The cowardice of this urge. The old longing to play the victim. What's required here is a bracing of the self. After all, 'we' 'love' 'each other'. These hackneyed words. Who's we? What's love? Do we *know* each other? Or is each of us only a screen for the other's light show?

———

A warm night in Sydney. I don't belong here. A dog ran past in the street. It was sobbing—a voice like a man's—a lost creature, running and sobbing.

———

Taking the train to Central with R, I was shocked by the condition of Newtown station: Londonish, bombed-out, neglected, tumbledown. She says that when as a girl she would come up to Sydney from her small town and see these devastated house-backs, blackened chimneys and factories, it all seemed wonderful to her.

———

We talked about how men love to tell stories about *the famous*. 'They aren't really interested in hearing *our* stories,' she said. 'They can't even listen to what *we* think is poignant, or funny. Like that Down Syndrome woman saying she was 104.' 'But we give them our total attention.' 'Yes,' she said. 'That's the thing that turns women to feminism. Because it's intolerable, not to be recognised on that level.'

———

It doesn't matter how good a man is, he is not guaranteed love.

———

A letter that ends: 'Thanking you in anticipation and oblige, Love Dad.' We laugh and laugh.

———

Weird effect of Thomas Bernhard's blackness—the arrogance of his statements of despair, meaninglessness etc. Sometimes I feel impatient, as with a child in a tantrum or a 'depressed' person wallowing—sometimes want to laugh out loud—but all this is ultimately swamped by the high quality, the *brilliance*, of the writing, and by respect for the way he is able to confront and report the horrors of his childhood. I feel forced by his hopeless conclusions, however, into the area of myself I am most afraid to enter or to give credence to—the crack-up dept., the mind-skids, the blank-out, the flicker of madness. I don't know who I can talk to, about this. After Bernhard everything that's got lightness, beauty, humour in it seems almost wet—even self-indulgent. Bernhard's iron chords.

———

At home, P and I talk by the kitchen fire about the necessity to lose innocence in order to regain something for which innocence is the wrong word.

———

I call Mum. A high-pitched voice answers. I think I've dialled a wrong number. But it's her. She's sobbing. Dad has accused her of having 'something going' with their old, old friend—her best friend's husband.

'But—that's *mad*!'

'Yes! It's mad!'

'Do you want to talk about it? Or is he standing right there?'

'I don't care if he's "standing right there".'

'Where is he?'

'Oh, he's skulking around somewhere.'

She says she'd thrown a handful of cutlery across the kitchen at him at the exact moment I rang.

'I didn't recognise your voice when you answered. I thought it was a stranger.'

'I can tell you, I *feel* like a stranger.'

This is the saddest, cleverest, truest thing I've ever heard my mother say.

———

Y came over to see my house. Showing it to her, I saw only its shabbiness, its temporary arrangements of furniture, its devastated backyard.

———

Reading an old diary. I cannot remember, even in the thinnest or most fragmentary moment, how it felt to 'love' the man I was in love with, back then. All that hideous torment, everyone suffering, and for WHAT? What would I remember of NOW? This one works, steadily, quietly. His mind does not take the easy way out. I can only live the thing to its fullest extent. This is what life is. It's not for saying no.

———

The weird silence of Easter Sunday. Beautiful autumn morning. A wind in restless gusts, sun comes and goes, I take photos of its patterns on the wall above my desk. Sick, been sick for a fortnight, a ghastly cold, coughing up yellow stuff. I can't seem to get better. Phone never rings. I get up and stand at the window staring out between brown slats. Sometimes I feel I should be lonely but I'm not. I wish someone would bring me an Easter egg, or that P would wake up and come in with a cup of tea so I could say, 'He is risen.'

———

Fantasy: V's dead. No one close to him, of course, thinks to tell me. Finally, a day or two later, R calls: 'H, I've got some very bad news…' Odd feeling that he may as well be dead, he may as well never have existed. His existence is purely intellectual. I can't even write him a letter. Because he doesn't exist.

———

I heard on the radio that Primo Levi died last week and maybe on purpose. I got out *The Periodic Table* and turned its pages. Listened for his voice.

———

V: 'If you didn't like my new book, would you say so?'
    H: 'I'd *want* to tell the truth. I want to be able to be blunt.'

V: 'I'd expect you to tell me what you really thought.'
(What if I don't think anything?)

———

His being married is saving me from my own worst faults: he is a perfect example of the kind of man I could go to water for—clever, harsh, super-critical, remote; and once the thrill of it wore off I'd be fighting (myself) to remain myself. I depend on his marriage. For balance, and for my freedom.

———

Ripped through Joyce Johnston's *Minor Characters*. What a bunch of windbags, mamma's boys, manipulators!

———

How F used to read English poetry to me—Keats, Shakespeare—stumbling, putting the stresses all wrong. It was electrifying. The power of the work came bursting through—his utter lack of pretension, acting, expression—nothing there but WORD.

———

A letter comes from L, a dear, friendly one. Just sticking his head over the wall, to see if I'm still here. And I am.

———

At Primrose Gully, a night of the most perfect stillness, hardly a sound, colossal wheeling fields of stars, and very late a small bright moon, lying on its back.

———

Reading Judges 5, a murder story with wonderful repetitions: 'At her feet he bowed, he fell, he lay down: at her feet he bowed, he fell: where he bowed, there he fell down dead...'

———

Woke slowly from a fading dream. It seemed that what woke me was a long, calm, sweet note, as from a bell. I lay there, still, in a state of perfect calm, joy, wellbeing.

———

Two Frenchmen chattering about sausages. One says he knows a

butcher who makes andouillettes. The other jumps in the air and
runs for his pen to write down the address.

'I'm not sure…'

'I'll find it. I'll find it if it takes all day.'

First time I've ever heard French people talking about food
without getting cranky.

———

After seeing M in *The Cherry Orchard* I woke up wanting to write
Chekhov a tremendous and humble fan letter. An excruciating love
for the play: its moods, its changes of tone, the appalling funniness
of its non sequiturs.

———

There must be something seriously the matter with me, that I go
on and *on* being sick. I finally went to the STD clinic and asked for
an AIDS test. Spent hours there, saw a doctor and a counsellor and
was comforted, then a skilful girl jabbed me. I watched. The blood,
surprisingly liquid, like ink, filled the tube. I saw all my prominent
veins. Away I bounced, with new virtue.

———

Windy day, ragged grey clouds flee across a denser grey ceiling, no
sun. Still sick. Made a soup.

———

Reading V's new book. I find it quite mystifying—much less 'funny'
than the earlier one—I don't know what the hell he's doing in it.
And as I read I get the weird feeling that one day I simply won't
know him any more: not that we will 'part', but that he will go
back to being him and I will go back to being me, our contact will
cease to exist; thus, that it has never existed except in our separate
imaginations. Thoughts neither pleasant nor unpleasant. *Do* I know
him? It's all mutual simultaneous projection. I've never seen and
will never see his bed, his table, his chair. How strange.

———

But the bright freshness of his writing, its muscle, its dazzling turns. Carved free of cliché. Scrubbed till it hurts. There is nothing spontaneous about it. Everything is worked, tense, intense; compressed, packed hard. 'Evidence of struggle', he calls it. His incredible detachment. I'm the opposite: I'm close in all the time.

———

'People who are scared of going into therapy,' says S's husband, 'have an image of all their repressed stuff as volcanic—as if it would explode out as soon as they took the lid off. But really it's geological, like those diagrams of rock formations we had to draw at school. You have to dig your way in.'

———

The *Sydney Morning Herald* reports that 'two yellowing envelopes containing the dusty remains' of Dante have gone missing from the National Library in Florence. No one seems to remember having seen them since 1929.

———

I suppose that in my work he doesn't really understand what I'm talking about.

———

At the library I worked for an hour and a half. Every few minutes I felt an urge to bolt but I gritted my teeth and slogged on. After a while the stiff brain began to move, and to produce ideas.

———

Puzzling in the car about a woman we know who left her small children and ran away with another guy. O says, 'I don't judge her for it. I think that one's first duty is to oneself, but—' 'But with children that young,' says R, 'they're still an extension of oneself.' In the back seat I am quiet, but astonished again at people's ability to say things like 'One's first duty is to oneself' or 'I've got very strong ideas about individuality'. I suppose I too live according to certain beliefs, without ever stating them clearly to myself or to others.

———

Hard to remain in *integrity* while waiting.

———

He fell asleep with his face almost touching mine: face to face on the pillow: the little cool wind of his breath.

———

'I've realised,' said R, 'that everything that's beyond the physical world, all those moments of illumination or insight—*that's* God. That's what God *is*. And dogma gets in the way.' The born-again would say that some of those moments were the devil.

———

I got off the plane at 5.15 to find a perfect autumn evening. I feel like a wayward woman who returns to her normally grouchy husband and finds him charming, after all and for no apparent reason. I mean Melbourne, this place I seem to be tying myself to with *property* when all my real urges push me north to where he is.

———

I dinked M home after lunch. We laughed at memories of my dinking her to kinder as a very little girl—singing behind me about witches and 'a very dang'rous frog'.

———

'By soul I mean, first of all, a perspective rather than a substance, a viewpoint towards things rather than a thing itself.' —James Hillman, *Archetypal Psychology*

———

The panic of starting a piece of work. I can't sit still. Any distraction will do.

———

At my kitchen table G talks at length about a young woman with whom he is about to have an affair.

    'What do you want?'

    'I want to own her.'

———

Men sweeping the street. The plane trees drop immense drifts of large, brown, twisted, claw-like leaves. The men sweep without speaking, but when the truck comes they all begin to yell and roar.

———

There's no laughter between lovers that's as precise and deep and full of genuine mirth as that between two people who are no longer a couple.

———

My new black lace-ups. One man calls them 'gumshoes', another says they look like 'two little Cadillacs'.

———

Back to the VD clinic where I'm told that my AIDS test was negative. Felt less elation than I did upon skipping down the clinic steps after the blood had left my arm.

———

Dreamt that a man came and sat opposite me in a cafe booth. He handed me his very small child. It sat peacefully on my knee.

———

Review of V's book: 'a triumph'.

———

On my way up the stairs to the party in Brunswick I heard someone sloppily playing an acoustic guitar and a girl singing a Beatles song. Reached the top and found that the player was G. He is a wonderful guitarist but was too drunk or stoned to use his fingers, also what on earth was he doing at this academics' jamboree? When I left he came with me. Rain was pouring. He was on a roll, raving unstoppably. In Lygon Street I picked up two hitchhikers. The girl was 'a beautiful blonde'. I saw G register her appearance. The air pressure in the car palpably changed. The two kids hopped out but G continued to rave: what bar should we go to, what club? I drove on with a scornful grin: 'I'm not going to any fucking club. I'm bored. I want to go home.' 'Oh yes, but you're in love,' he said crossly. At my place I put on my hideous flannelette nightie and crawled under the doona. He tucked me in and lay down beside me on top of the bedclothes in his suit and shoes, talking non-stop, laughing and making me laugh. 'Ah, Hel. I love the way you remember things. When I was last in Paris,' he said, 'I went to look at that street you used to live in, back in the 70s, rue du Docteur Heulin, remember when I came and visited you there?' He kept stroking my forehead and making much of me and saying, 'Don't *frown*.' Just as I was slipping off to sleep he sprang up and said, 'I'm gonna call a cab.' Next thing I knew it was morning and his wife was ringing from Sydney and he was nowhere to be seen.

―――――

Dreamt I met some black people in a sloping garden. Women made me welcome, but in a reserved manner. We all got out our scissors and sewing gear and began to perform small stitching, snipping and mending tasks together. I felt honoured to be accepted by them.

―――――

These ridiculous interviews V's doing about his novel. *I* should interview him. I'd ask him, 'What is an idea? What is a large idea and what is a small one? Which are the structural ones and which ones is the structure carrying?'

―――――

Awake in the early morning, fears about this movie—that there won't be enough *events*, that my idea is only a framework, that it lacks *flesh*. I love tiny little scenes, barely a paragraph on paper but on screen an image of power and meaning: the sky through the struts of the Harbour Bridge, or in *Heimat* the soldier's fine hair flying up on the wind of the explosion, or Maria riding towards the camera on her bike. Small, small, small. Irritation of not knowing who I am aiming the outline at makes it harder to do. I am tempted to pull back all requests for funding and to write it quietly on my own—so I can shape it as I like, and as *it* wants. To do this I will have to be poor or else grab some journalism. 'You could write something for the *Age*, couldn't you?' says V. 'Yes,' I say, 'except I only like doing journalism that involves dead bodies.'

'Give me a lecture on structure, quick.' 'Structure. Right.' I feel him go into his favourite mode: advice. 'Structure should be like a birdcage. Light, strong, big enough to hold everything you need to put in it. But you have to be able to see straight through it.' The elegance of this image conceals its lack of practical instructiveness.

M did not introduce the boy to me but I was struck by his friendly manner, frequent eye contact etc. He is a very Teutonic-looking boy. Or rather *man*. The other girls arrived, great shrieks, I faded out their back door and rode away, the superfluous mother. A bit painful, but I have other fish to fry.

Three women in the kitchen, a long conversation about hair, should P have hers cut or not? I broke into our engrossment and said, 'Is this neurotic?' 'No!' said P. 'It means something. A circle means something different from a triangle. The shape of your hair affects the outline of your body, where it connects with the rest of the world.' I would give large sums for a tape of that conversation, its movement, tones, pauses; our concentration. Could I ever invent it?

I am labouring with groans, tears and blank spots on this screenplay. The father offers her the tank water and she gracelessly refuses. Less afraid, after a morning's work. In the street, looking at ordinary people working, driving, going about their business, I thought, 'This is my job. This awful, painful struggle is *what I do*, it is my part and I must play it, it is the price I pay for months of *not* working, the luxury of freedom. No one can give me orders. I must do it all myself.' The loneliness of this.

A happy and cheerful day visiting my parents at Ocean Grove. Dad and I chopped wood and went for a '2.5 km walk'. M and dog and I drove to the beach, dark sky, strong cold wind, long waves breaking and throwing back huge manes of spray. We sang all the way home. Felt blessed, fortunate, optimistic.

———

In a book on intimacy and marriage I read remarks on affairs. The introduction of a lover, unbeknownst to one partner, gives the ailing relationship a short breathing space…then, if the affair is serious, it either repairs the marriage or pushes it to dissolve.

———

A walk in a country town. The quieter the place and the happier the day, the softer our voices when we speak. Man: 'I won't live as long as you. I just know I won't live to be old. I'll be lucky to reach sixty—' Woman: 'Oh, look! Rollerskating! And they've got *music*!'

———

Daydreaming is necessary. In float the objects, the patterns and thoughts. Peculiar material rises to the surface. I see where I can use my dreams. I'm surprised by what appears on the page: it's like poetry, coming from somewhere my thinking mind doesn't know about.

———

At R's house I take a mandarin and go out into the yard. A child's voice somewhere above me: 'Hello!' I look up and see a small blond boy high in a sapling that looks hardly strong enough to bear his weight. He says he is waiting for his brother and R's daughter to come back from the library. I hand him the mandarin and say, 'They're already back. They're inside, reading. How come you didn't go?'

'I don't like Tintin books. I'm going to stay up here and wait for them to come and find me.'

'I won't say a word,' I reply, but I think, 'They won't come looking for you. You are a gooseberry.'

———

A very sexy, very good-looking woman strolls past, in cowboy boots with metal trimmings. Women like her walk *really slowly*. Whereas women like me walk as fast as they can, with the aim of becoming a blur.

R shows me an account of philosophy's 'moral man', whose qualities (according to Kant and Schopenhauer, she says) include the
belief that women are unable to make moral judgments but act
only according to what pleases them. It is quite clear however that
men who espouse these stern views *would die* unless women did
their emotional living for them. Is this why some men go berserk
when their wives leave them? Because they are unable to perform
for themselves certain functions of living?

Lindy Chamberlain is pardoned.

A fresh, clear morning: pink light on buildings: an edge on the air.

The producer came to talk with me about this movie. I find her useful
in that she is not ashamed to ask the really obvious questions—the
kind of necessary, grounding questions that I don't ask myself for
fear of *losing height*.

The bus to the city wound its slow route along streets full of trees,
and up through the Cross and down William Street, on which it
picked up a young couple, dark, curly-haired, foreign-looking,
cheerful, liking each other, the woman holding a small boy of six
months or so. The mood of the bus lightened and lightened, to a
point where '*dans mon euphorie*' I thought it would take off into
the sunny air and roar into the sky on the combined beams of the
passengers' high spirits.

Hearing that my letters have all been thrown away—a blast of
liberation—even *that* past is gone, whisked away from behind me
almost as soon as it happens—everything is now now NOW.

He spoke of himself as only men can: as if he were speaking of someone else. 'The power, the intensity that's in my work…' Would a woman ever speak with such detachment, or use such words, about her own work?

———

Yesterday I felt lonely. I knew that he would not leave her. I forgot that I did not want to be his wife. A failure of imagination. I did not feel beautiful. I longed to be asleep. Woke, heard rain falling quietly outside, felt the desolation of my position. I thought about Primrose Gully, the room with the table, hearing rain there, looking out at rain falling, the healing of it. I need to go home.

———

The speakers in the movie mustn't answer each other. Not directly. There's always a little slide, every time. And a subtext. It's so *hard*.

———

'Whenever I get to a dream in a novel,' says V, 'I lose interest.'

———

Went to Gas & Fuel to order a new hot water service. Girl: 'Is it urgent? I'll see if it can be done this week.' (*Returns*) 'The lady said, "Is it the writer?" She's read one of your books. We can deliver it tomorrow.'

———

Lindy Chamberlain interviewed on TV. We sat forward. Her face is thin, extremely good-looking—a wide range of expressions—a very attractive mouth, pretty nose, good strong white regular teeth—striking eyes—very skilfully made-up—and out of this chic and elegant face issues an Australian woman's voice, flat-vowelled, nasal, harsh, with oddly self-dramatising inflections and aggressive intonations. At times she wept and this moved me. I admired her courage in continuing but it also frightened me. Her eyes show a tremendous power. At a distance they seem to darken and narrow. When she laughs, though, she is just a pretty woman laughing—a lovely sight—and her wrinkles fan out from her eye corners in an attractive way.

P took me to Heide to see a show of paintings about childhood. Mostly Blackmans, but some fabulous Joy Hester ink things, some Fred Williams which I loved, and notably a couple of thick, juicy, dark, frightening paintings by Albert Tucker of his son—on a trike, in a high chair, his eyes lazy, almost evil, his cheeks dark red and puffy, his hair flopping thickly. 'There,' said P, 'is a man who hates children.'

'God, I had a hangover,' says the man in the cafe. 'When I took the dog for a walk I spewed in the gutter. The dog tried to eat it but I kicked him in the guts.'

I heard a gospel song in the car and a rush of Christian moral scruples came over me: 'If I gave him up I would be a more virtuous person, more correct, more calm, more blessed.' This kind of thing, which attracts me at times, is almost a death wish, a nothing wish, a blankness wish—like wishing that we could all *like each other's work*, that there should be no *conflict*. The LIFE of life. No laws apply.

My father strides past the window. I know it's him because of the coins jingling in his pockets.

At Primrose Gully shooting with a visitor's .22. The high-velocity bullets passed straight through a beer can on a post without even setting it rocking. We thought we'd missed. Went to take it off the post and saw three holes in it. Question: who fired the shots that struck it? We go inside laughing. A moon rises. P is driving up tonight. I've left a candle for her in the small window, though the moon is so bright she'll hardly need it.

I would like to know how to give an injection, stop bleeding, deal with snakebite, set limbs. Just in case.

A koala is climbing out on a thin branch not far from my desk window. Pleasant stink of kero heater. Crickets. As evening approaches the sky clears, except for pink and lavender streaks low down over the farmer's place. There'll be a strong moon tonight. Since the visitor got rid of the rat, the mice have returned. Their meek shuffle and pit-a-pat.

———

Think I've broken the back of the screenplay draft. The speed and force of the thing's arrival, when it comes. When will I learn and accept that the anguish phase is a necessary part of the process?

———

I began Bernhard's *Concrete* and to my surprise find it hilarious. The cover blurb says, 'His views on life are fascinatingly introspective, profoundly human and strikingly provocative.' They are also cranky, evil-tempered, pathetic, unstable, choleric, mad, and so exaggerated as to be comical, but no hint of this is given on the cover.

———

P asked me what I thought was the purpose of life.
    'Do you mean each person's life, or life in general?'
    'Any way you like.'
    An answer rose smoothly to my mind.
    'I reckon it's everyone's responsibility to clean up their act. To do some work on themselves. So they won't be an obstruction to the progress of the good. Does that sound…?'
    Astonished, now, by this statement. Is it glib? What's 'the good'? And is it making progress?

———

P comes home from work, her mouth all hard with tiredness. I make a fire and cook a meal. I enjoy 'making things nice' for her. We eat, listen to *Scripsi of the Air*, play a record.

———

I paid for Primrose Gully with a bank cheque. A woman in ridiculous boots stood beside me at a cafe counter and I was so elated about owning three acres that I wanted to kneel down and put my forehead on their pointy toes. Everything I saw was beautiful, the sun was shining in air so cold I was still wearing gloves at lunchtime. I felt berserk, as if I should be very careful. Not to go mad. How on earth can I thank my self-effacing benefactor for this gift? I'll write to her: 'Dear Queensland. The days are sunny, the nights are white with stars. I don't know why you're doing this, but I rejoice, I am ever in your debt.'

A reading last night with Gerald Murnane. He is brilliant: a terrific density of personality. He reads those long complex sentences with a tremendous concentrated energy. The *inwardness* of what he writes. Overwhelmed with respect.

At lunchtime drove M to Dimmey's and bought her a double doona. Adored her company: she had a little hangover, chattered at length, an account of the evening before: 'I don't know how I can be hungover—I only had a glass of red wine and four pots.' She breaks off, after half an hour of rambling, vivid discourse, and says, 'It's not really a story—I'm just telling you what we did.' This seemed a sophisticated remark about narrative and I wrote it down.

Today, or maybe yesterday, was the first time I began to think about death. I mean *my* death: being dead, in a closed box, buried. I did not like this thought at all, and was afraid of rotting.

The strongly and seriously married couple invited me to dinner. I am old enough to be their mother. I belong to a different species—like a wild beast, scarred with loneliness and nasty experiences. I often have to bite my lip not to say cynical things about sex and couples. Perhaps they think I'm a lost soul. Perhaps I am. I lay on their sofa and watched her cooking: her smooth skin, contented sober expression of concentration, her pretty lavender cotton top—felt a little bliss, watching her and being looked after.

———————

The awful attraction of cop shops, those hard-faced men, their comfortless echoing rooms, the lost and disappeared children notices with their tragic blurred snaps. I could loiter there all day, staring and sucking it in.

———————

Dreamt I tried on a beautiful coat with perfect shoulder pads. Into the back of it were set irregularly shaped panels of something red and glassy that shone. I looked fabulous in it. I tried it on with a hat of the same colour, also with a sparkling jewel.

———————

We went up the river in the boat. River the colour of tea. Sound of the ocean on the other side of the bar like the sounds of war.

———————

The wife reports a dream: 'I met a man whom I loved instantly. This man had the power to stop time.'

———————

It's easy for me to get lost. I wander in peculiar minefields of doubt and anxiety, arguing with myself, training and disciplining myself, thinking up worst things and planning how I will assimilate them without bitterness.

———————

The former politician dies in a hotel room, at sixty, of a heart attack. A cop tells *Truth* he died with a 'loaded' condom on: 'he died happy'. On the plane I sit beside an eighty-year-old lady who tells me she's his sister-in-law, on her way to his funeral. A nice, funny, direct old woman. I long to say, 'Listen. I love a man. He's married to someone else. What will become of me?' But why would she know?

———————

Someone showed me how to fax my copy to the magazine. 'How long will it take?' 'It's already there.' I was struck dumb with wonder.

F reads the screenplay. His comments are very frank, very open, a painful picture of me as I was in that marriage. His generosity: 'You know you have my imprimatur, whatever you do or write.' Now I'm aware of sadness under everything, the churning up of old matter, and the realisation that the draft is very rough and that it will need a good deal of hard, concentrated work, both technical and emotional, before it's done.

Uncle Vanya at Anthill. The closedness of the play, the imprisoned characters, the wild despair of Vanya's outburst.

Mild sunlight on grass that's blond in winter, flattened in patches as if roos had been lying on it with their great awkward haunches. Stillness on the opposite ridge when I tramped over it with the dog. Sound of the river getting louder the higher we went. Over the spur to its other curve. The logic that leads you to the river. If I were with V, living together, would I still have this occasional, very powerful sense of freedom? And self?

From a review of Jessica Anderson's short stories: '...we are made to see the futility of trying to prolong an affair beyond its natural limits, and how little an outsider—even an ardent lover—can ever know of what actually binds a husband and wife together.'

When the coffin was brought in at the front of the church the man beside me said in a horrified whisper, 'Is that *it*? Is that the *coffin*?' 'Yes.' He turned paler and paler, in his black coat. 'I didn't know they brought it *in*. Will you stay next to me all through?'

V says he 'doesn't believe in jealousy'. This can only mean that he has (a) never experienced it or (b) managed always to give it some other name.

———

Dreamt that on a big ship, a liner, some rats were a nuisance. A campaign against them, but then, moulting and half stunned, they stood about nonchalantly on the carpets. I threw one overboard. It turned on its back, gave me a calm, insolent look, and was towed away by a girl in a boat.

———

F's notes on the movie give a very disagreeable picture of me: 'the artificial turbulence she needs in order to function'. I see myself as tense, fast, always moving—screechy. How awful. For years I went on behaving exactly as if I *wasn't* married. And then later when I started to try to be married it was too late. I became pathetic. A pathetic creature.

———

A woman calls her sister. 'What are you doing?'
   'Threading a needle.'

———

'Don't drop that on the floor or I'll drop *you*.' Man behind me to his three-year-old daughter.

———

Willpower is required to keep pathos from aggregating around certain symbolic objects: *an open suitcase*. 'I only ever saw her in rented or borrowed rooms, the small suitcase neatly packed, the cotton clothes folded.'

———

Is it possible to develop a voice in writing with such coherence and quiet authority that I can do away with narrative structure? (Plot?) In the dream story, all that's holding it together now is the voice, and maybe the imagery—holding it together against its own tendency to fragment, to fly apart. The pieces want to return to *some other order*—not with each other—but I compel them quite quietly to hold together *my way*.

———

My heart feels too light, as if it were growing too high in my chest. It keeps giving spasms of high fluttering. I wonder if I am ill and about to die.

———

I go to Z's house, it's got a new front door with a mail slot. I bend down and see him sitting there on the couch in the sun, neatly reading—he hears my knock, hops up to let me in. 'I was about to make some coffee and eat an orange.' We do this together.

———

V says every man is a moral coward. He's trapped. Trapped between two forms of partial death. How *fascinating*.

———

Gerald Murnane in a review: 'Of those three distinctively human activities, laughing, crying and thinking, the third is most often ranked highest, and books that provoke thought likewise. I do not agree with these rankings. I even wonder, as Robert Musil wondered, whether the best kind of thinking is only a subtle kind of feeling.' These remarks make me think that one writes only *as one can*, as one's character allows and equips one to…that theories and beliefs are superimposed, almost irrelevant.

———

'I've already told you about Cubism,' says V.

'Yes,' I say, 'but I've forgotten.'

He raises his eyes to heaven.

'I know it's terrible, but think about it this way—you'll never bore me because I forget everything you say.'

He takes a deep breath. 'Well. You know how you *look* at something…'

I can't help it. I laugh out loud.

———

R was awake and came downstairs saying, 'If you think I was waiting up for you, I was.' I don't know how she does it but I always feel, within three minutes of arriving in her presence, as if she's said,

'Here. Give me that *huge bundle* you're carrying, put it down here and we'll have a look at what's in it.'

———

The born-again had an asthma attack at 4 am, very bad, taken to hospital in an ambulance—masks, drips, the full catastrophe. At 9 am, having made a fast recovery, he was sent home wearing pyjamas and a jumper, that's *all*. Bare feet! In this weather! He looked awful when I got there—white, with dopy eyes, lying bereft under his wretched Christian single doona, on his Christian single bed. He said, 'Give us a hug?' I took off my runners and got under the bedclothes and cuddled him from behind for an hour or so while he told me what had happened. We both had our feet on the hot water bottle; it was really quite nice. Every now and then he'd give a sigh and say, 'Thanks, Hel.' At a certain point he dozed off and I lay there thinking, 'What am I *doing* here? Lying fully dressed in a single bed in a furnished room in St Kilda with a born-again Christian at 12 o'clock on a weekday?' His budgie's cage was beside the bed. It kept making its fidgety little noises, ringing its bells, whistling tunes.

———

Dreamt I was in a little country town. Its streets were running and filling with water. 'A flood!' I shouted. 'Isn't it beautiful! I've never seen one before!' Shining water dripped off roofs, the streets were flowing.

———

Went to lunch with a feminist academic. Odd to feel so at ease with someone who proudly declared that she had never read Chekhov, and advised me to 'give Dostoyevsky a miss'.

———

The biographer's falsely courteous, reasonable manner while she's destroying my character: by means of her sweet tone, her disarming smile, she makes me ashamed of the violent emotions her words are provoking in me. She says that if she'd been one of the people I've written about she would have sued me. 'It could be thought that I can't bear your success, but I think your books are outrageous. They should never have been published.' My left cheek begins to burn. I go on listening, nodding, saying 'Mmmm,' when truly I want to upend the cafe table and throw her against the wall. 'Can you listen to any more of this?' she asks, in that sweet voice. 'Are you feeling...glazed?' She moves to the chair beside me, seizes my wrist in one gloved hand and holds it firmly, turning her face away and looking out the window. 'I'm only saying these things because I'm so *fond* of you. I'm feeling *fondness* for you.' A curtain of red descends before my eyes. 'You said that to me once before—remember? On the phone one night, ten years ago? You told me all my faults. That I was a bad mother. That you didn't want your daughter to play with mine any more—that my daughter smelt. And you kept interrupting yourself by saying, "I'm only saying this because I'm *so fond of you.*"' She lets go my hand, stands up, begins to put on her coat, looking down at her buttons as she fastens them. 'That's awful,' she says. 'That was disgusting.' She has had nothing to eat or drink. I pay for my coffee. Out on the street we stand looking helplessly at each other. I say, 'Let's shake hands.' 'Of course.' Her hand in its soft glove is all knobbly, from the arthritis. This hurts me. I turn, she turns, we walk away in opposite directions. As I walk I think, 'She's right. What I do is bad and wrong. I'll have to learn some other way of writing.'

———————

'You are a vulnerable person,' writes the old professor on a postcard, 'to people like her, who need to...who are drawn to HURT others to EASE the pain in their own hearts, who see you as a rewarding TARGET, i.e. you are a CREATIVE PERSON—you are so sensitive that they believe they will get from your response the satisfaction they CRAVE. Keep out of the way. Never reply. Listen to Prelude No. 24 in B Minor of Book I of the *48 Preludes and Fugues* by J. S. Bach. It says everything.'

———

'You've got a reputation,' says O, 'as a bitch and a slob, and a lot of other things. I won't tell you some of the things that have been said to me. Fuck 'em. Just keep going. But don't think your friends aren't jealous of you. *I* am.'

———

The Nolans at the NGV. First time I ever cared about Ned Kelly. Peculiar effect of the clusters of brass buttons on the policemen's uniforms. They glow, and seem to mean something to me.

———

In George's import department with G. We saw a fabulous big stiff black shirt with white spots. H: 'Guess how much.' G: 'Ummm…a thousand?' H: (*triumphantly*) '$3245.' He sat near the window on a curlicued gilt chair and I stood beside him, we looked down at Collins Street, spoke as intimately as if we were in a private living room. No one bothered us. I kept thinking, 'This would be a terrific scene in a movie.' 'I don't remember my dreams at all,' he says, 'at the moment. I feel as if I'm going through all sorts of parallel experiences that I know nothing about.' He confesses to something I don't even want to write down. 'Nobody knows. You're the only one.' This strange connection between us. *Mon semblable, mon frère.* When I let him off with his bag at Bourke Street he takes my face in both hands and kisses me.

———

Radio Days at the Rivoli with my sister. We laughed and cried. The girl comes out of the bathroom with a towel round her head and mimes the Cuban song on the radio. The two men come in and watch, she performs for them, they sing the chorus and mime the actions—how much fun they're having, playing and fooling around. It's true, TV's ruined everything: it's smashed the family, nobody looks at each other any more.

———

At the International, two Italian men stand at the huge window on to St Georges Road, talking quietly. Their voices, bass and baritone, are inflected more beautifully and casually than any Australian's could ever be: our voices are made for explanation and argument, theirs for song. The world outside is dry and bright, as if there were no air—the houses *exist*, in purest clarity, radiant and perfect, as they would exist to someone about to fall down in an epileptic fit, or to die.

———

Reading accounts that writers send to the Literature Board of their promotion of self and of 'Australian literature', I shrivel up, long to disappear and work silently in some unnoticed corner. Will I have to make 'pronouncements' on this flamin' US tour?

———

T's got a job sewing costumes at the opera. 'Five twelve-metre curtains made of some slithery synthetic substance. It was like trying to carry armloads of water.'

———

Couldn't fall asleep for hours last night. I had too many shoulders and hips, my breathing was too noisy and in the wrong rhythm.

———

On the plane a businessman's wife: she is working hard at being with him, dancing attendance—dressed up, anxious, not relaxed, very focused on her husband—wanting to do the right thing, to be an asset, but not knowing how, not being part of his world: afraid of losing his attention, which anyway she has not got. She's there on sufferance, as a favour.

———

The literature professor, before he fell asleep at the dinner table, invited me to be writer-in-residence at Sydney University next year. I have also been invited to ANU, and to the Defence Force Academy.

———

'There are plenty of people,' says V, 'I mean really good, really *top class* people—who won't have a bar of psychoanalysis.' A chill comes over me. Afraid of his mind. Sadly I imagine the deflation of this love, its collapse into something bumpy, discourteous, disappointing, regretful.

———

Up at Primrose Gully O, who has a cold, lies under the doona all day. While I busy myself looking after him, making things clean and nice, lighting the stove to make him a soup, he says in a tone I can't quite describe, 'The story of how you got the money to buy this place is too good to be true.'

———

The mezzo in the Mahler is slim and stately in a strange black dress with a fitted top in metallic material and a long velvet skirt. V: 'Why don't *you* get a dress like that?' He carries on with a joke that all the women present must be green with envy of her. How peculiar men are—they like to sow discontent.

———

Horrible massacre in Clifton Hill. A young man who lives behind the station runs amok with weapons, kills six people, injures a dozen. I see his photo and get a creepy feeling that I know him or once even taught him, though this is impossible.

———

How on earth could he leave her, this blameless, kind, funny, faithful woman?

———

'I love intellectuals who *hesitate*,' says the nun.

———

Will the woman who's meeting my plane in Wellington recognise me? I should have said, 'I'm a small, crabby-looking woman in a cheap black suit.'

———

The old poet's house was at the top of a very high hill. I had to puff and pant to climb the steps. In her pretty living room we drank

wine from pottery cups and looked out over a harbour, a mountain
and a great deal of sky. She was intensely likeable, a grandmother,
very intelligent, very powerful. Tall, a big face with a big mouth
and teeth, lipstick. I felt very lucky to have met her, and glad not
to have chickened out of the visit. Talking about a difficult man
we both knew, she wondered if his solitary and very privileged
upbringing had left him without what most people learn in bigger
families—'the experience of defeat'.

From the plane, broken cloud like blips in hot porridge. Clouds
white but in their folds a fine grey-blue, and on the sun side a delicate pink flush.

Romeo and Juliet. What a play. Bodies strewn about (one of them
my daughter's), huge speeches, and in all that worked language such
simple lines as 'Any man who can write can answer a letter.'

The indignity of a mammogram: one's breasts squashed flat between
two pieces of hard plastic. Upset by it, and frightened.

Ate twelve oysters and went to see *Lohengrin* at the Opera House.
A very clear, very cold evening, a ragged half-moon in an inky sky.
The old professor was in one of his weird moods about sex and
women. 'Look at that pretty girl,' I say, 'sitting on the steps. The
one in the white dress and black pillbox hat.' He looks. Pauses. 'Do
you think she'd eat a man up?' '*Tsk*. No. I think she's a pretty girl.
That's all.'

I'd like to write something with weird time-pockets, layers etc. I
know a bit about children. Funny how when I come to Sydney
my mind works in a different way. I have better, freer ideas. Must
remind myself that this is *because* I don't live here, rather than a
reason for me to move here.

———

Headline: 'Man gets life for strangling musician.'

———

I'm crazy, moving around as much as I do. I must make this a RULE: do not accept invitations to GO anywhere.

———

I won a prize for the *Two Friends* screenplay. The cheque is made out by the Housing Department.

———

Ben Chifley used to say, 'Always make your decisions on moral grounds, and the details will fall into place.' Thus, 'if you go down, you go down on something you believe in.'

———

Awake at 4 am. Somewhere in the street a dog moans and yelps. I want to go out, find it, *shut it up*.

———

The hosts of the dinner party were eager to show me their word processor. I enjoyed this but was horrified to see the *alarm clock* that is necessary so people won't become too fascinated and get RSI— one of them already has it. At the table a woman talked about her sister, a nightclub dancer in Europe, who recently came home for a visit. 'She has a wonderful body,' she said, 'but she can't walk. Her muscles are all wrongly developed, for walking. She couldn't walk up the hill to the Kew Library. She just couldn't.' 'I'd rather be able to do the cancan,' said another guest, 'than walk up the hill to the Kew Library.'

———

I made a speech at P's exhibition opening. I keep thinking about her new paintings, feeling wonderstruck. She left me a note on the kitchen table: 'I think we do such equivalent things in our respective ways, it was so nice having the paths cross as they did tonight; dovetailing together then off again.'

———

I saw at once that the small, exhausted schoolboy in the Fitzroy High jumper was coming to the end of a pretty rocky form-one year. He stood in the crowded tram at peak hour when kids aren't allowed to sit down and kept looking with secret longing at the empty seat beside me. I suffered from appalling maternal pangs, wanted to adopt him on the spot or at least be his foster mother for a couple of months until he grew a bit and got used to being in high school. Finally I said, 'Hey. Sit here.' He shot into that seat like a ferret down a rabbit's burrow.

———

Weird feeling, when I look at a photo of V that I took, that once again he does not exist, I have never met him, I have invented him, he is a FIGMENT. If a long enough silence should fall between us we would forget each other and slip back into our previous lives. Does he exist? No particular emotion accompanies these fancies. In fact it's a breathing space between bouts of reality. I don't miss him. How could I miss a flicker, a quick darkness. It would be easier if we never had any further contact with each other, but left each other's lives alone. He won't leave his wife, they'll live out the rest of their lives together, side by side, without passion but with a strong familiarity, *used to each other*. What'll I do? I'll take up piano lessons again, learn to make plants grow, write novels. Summer will come. I'll grow older. I'll be happy. If I could be this calm, when we're apart, then we could live it properly, honour it, without causing smash-up, pain, grief, humiliation. On the other hand, this state seems unreal to me, a kind of nothing state, an interim—or like sleep, or death. '*First—chill—then stupor—then the letting go—*'

———

Breakfast with M on her eighteenth birthday. She keeps watching for 9.03 am, her 'birth minute', and when it comes we kiss each other on the lips. Later I buy her a strapless linen dress in which she is so beautiful that I gaze. My Mastercard is declined, I burst into a rage, we go for cash.

———

I'm cleaning the house. Even if V doesn't come, the place will be spotless. Coldish night. Scent of pittosporum and other blossoming plants stabs the air.

———

These nights I sometimes wake with a jolt for no apparent reason and lie here with my heart crashing and my limbs trembling.

———

Finally I tell G the identity of V. He says he's not surprised. 'I couldn't finish his book. I didn't care about the character.'

'It took him seven years to write that book.'

'Seven *years*?'

———

While I'm in America, V is going to Africa. My fantasy: he doesn't come back. I find out from someone that he's lost. I fly to Sydney and say to his wife, 'Come on. We've got to go and find him.' She won't come, flatly refuses, but when the me character gets to the airport, there she is. The two women set out. The conversations they could have! The silences, resentments, outbursts. And quieter passages: they have to share a bedroom in some shit hotel, two single beds, they lie parallel, like sisters, exhausted, angry, frightened. One begins to talk…would there be flashbacks? Voice-over? Flashbacks that don't match what's being related in the voice-over because each of them is having to embroider the truth.

———

Seeing V's raincoat on my hall chair. He makes a phone call in my kitchen while I'm washing my shirt in a bucket. I keep looking back over my shoulder through the window. He is holding the phone *in my kitchen*.

———

Early in the morning P and I meet at the open back door. Outside it a bird is singing, very loud. We look at each other happily.

———

Gerald Murnane gives a speech in which he describes an experiment he performed on himself: he takes off the shelf books he's read and sets himself to recall as much as he can of each one. Often his memories are, he says, no more than moods, or what he calls 'the memory not of the book itself but of the experience of reading'.

'That's exactly how *I* remember books I've read,' I say. 'I always thought it meant I was a sloppy reader.'

'But surely,' says V, 'he's only talking about minor works. Think about something really great. Proust for example. I remember all kinds of absolutely specific things.'

'Like a woman changing her shoes?'

'Yes, or Charlus arriving.'

'Or the page whose head's like a tomato.'

'Or an experience of time passing. See? He's only talking about *minor* stuff.'

———

At Abu Dhabi airport. As I emerge from the tunnel into the weird tiled womb of the airport transit and duty-free I wish I had someone with me to whom I could say, 'Look! A stately pleasure dome.'

———

Heathrow. At security a grey-haired Sikh woman turned to go back through the beeper arch. All the white guards, male and female, set up a cry: 'Stay! Stay here! Go back! Stay here!' The one who was holding my bag continued to call out, long after the woman had grasped and corrected her mistake, 'STAY. STAY. SIT. SIT. STAY.' One of his colleagues said affably, 'She's not a collie, you know.'

———

Paris. A knock on door at 7.30 am, three young men looking for my host. I go down the hall to wake him. At his bedroom door I realise they're right behind me in their soft shoes. H: '*C'est pour quoi?*' 'Police,' says the second one, showing his ID. My host springs out of bed, making unconvincing gestures of innocence—rolled eyes, widespread arms. Two of the detectives are pleasant, the other who follows me everywhere and watches me with a dull, aggressive eye is an expressionless thug, broken nose etc. I sit on the couch in my nightie, he loiters by the door, suddenly says '*Vous aussi, vous faîtes l'usage de drogues?*' '*Moi? Bien sûr que non.*' The cute one with the dark brown curly hair tries on my host's hat, admires himself in the big poofy gold-framed mirror: '*Ça me va?*' He asks for my passport, copies details into his notebook. Sense of unreality, yet familiarity. Their extreme Frenchness; except for the broken-nosed one they are courteous in a blunt way. The leader even waves me goodbye as they take my host out the door. '*Mais c'est pour quoi?*' I say. The cute one says, '*Oh . . . des stupéfiants. C'est une affaire.*' All the while, though rather palpitating, I can't wait to tell this to my sister.

———

Terrible Paris. The four-digit price tags at Galeries Lafayette, the overkill of display. One feels one lacks some essential female quality. So much elegance and beauty: fine limbs, perfect skin, hairless legs, massed hair. How plain I am: big-footed, small-mouthed: a sense of having to summon up other resources. I long for Australia, the thinness and modesty of things. I gnash my teeth to be missing the lilacs at Primrose Gully. When I get back it'll be snake season. Still, walking along rue Vieille du Temple last night, tired, sad, lonely, pointless, I heard music from a record shop—a piano, someone playing Bach, the *Little Notebook* pieces, I thought—didn't recognise the pianist, stood in a doorway almost bawling—whoever it was used a lot more dynamics than say Glenn Gould would—asked the woman, she said, '*C'est Dinu Lipatti.*'

———

To Des Femmes, who published *Monkey Grip*. Beautiful office, wisteria trying to work its way in through the window frames. The manager tried to roll us but I couldn't help liking her because in spite of her glamorous and rather good-looking face, chic clothes etc, she had clunky ankles, large feet and bare legs that were dry and peeling.

'Les Murray, for example,' said the Australian politician's wife at the reception. 'He's called a poet. Not a writer, not a novelist, but a *poet*. You read his work, but what do you remember of it? Nothing. You couldn't quote a single line.' Stunned by her stupidity and ignorance.

Picasso Museum. I found the mentions of his many women frustrating because I couldn't know *what really happened*. The sequence of them alarmed me, the painful stories that must underlie the bland facts ('secretly accompanied by Marie-Thérèse'). I liked very much the little drypoint illustrations to Ovid's *Metamorphoses*—especially I loved the tiny sketch he'd put in the frame of each one—a face, an arm, two schematic bodies.

On TV a video clip of Mick Jagger and a beautiful brown girl actually (or apparently) fucking. I found it repellent, his revolting scrawny body, huge wriggling tongue—the attempt to shock in this lâche period of history—I kept thinking, 'He's too old to be behaving like this—it's undignified.'

Los Angeles. First newspaper headline we see: 'Hungry sailors barbecue mermaid.'

Before breakfast the agent and I were walking across the hotel's enormous garden towards the swimming pool when from our right came a loud, harsh, whirring sound—like a helicopter—getting louder and louder—it was the rattling of hundreds of windows in their frames, fifteen floors of them. The garden began to blur, the roses were a shivering red streak, the ground heaved under our feet. We stood still and threw our arms round each other. Sirens began to scream. We continued to the pool, laughing and running. A smiling old Japanese couple in kimono waved gaily to us from the other side of the garden; the woman spread her arms and mimicked swaying, the man climbed a tree and hung from a low branch by his four limbs like a sloth.

———

The poet praised my work. His praise made me ashamed, for I felt it was false.

———

Physical loneliness can derange a person.

———

I try to imagine V and me in New York. Two tiny figures arm in arm at the bottom of 'canyons of steel'.

———

The editor is terribly homesick: his wife has just given birth to their first child. We sit in an Ethiopian restaurant and begin to become friends. We speak of emotional things. I say, 'I've got this man. He's married. He lives in another town. I only see him every few weeks. Sometimes between those times I get the weird feeling that I've invented him, that he's a figment—and then when I see him again I'm shocked by his three-dimensionality, and his warmth, and the fact that he's got colours.'

'Yes,' he says. 'When I rang my wife today I was amazed by how sweet her voice was.'

———

The cab turned into Stanford and passed through a small forest of eucalypts. The smell of them in the dry heat was intoxicating. I hung out the window with a lump in my throat.

———

The kind of artist V admires sets himself up with a wife, a companion who cushions him; he puts his head down and *works*. The awful privileges artists claim for themselves: to be waited on and for, protected, tolerated, and at the same time to be *left alone*.

———

For hours fighter planes have been screaming round in the sky over San Francisco and the water. The tearing noise they make—ripping the air—it makes my heart crash and I go trembly. In the street men look up, impassive; women look up and then at each other—some shake their heads, some smile, or laugh, or frown—meaning, 'They can't help themselves; but I don't like it.' Even when I'm lying on my bed mid-afternoon, their roaring and tearing makes me feel sick, my body seems to shrivel as they pass. In the post office, news passes as dotted letters on a screen: the US has sunk several Iranian ships in the Persian Gulf. Woman beside me in line follows the news with downturned mouth, then nods, as if to agree that *of course* Congress must not make the US Air Force withdraw within sixty days. I get a terrible desire to burst out sobbing with fear and ignorance.

———

I went into the poet's bedroom so he could brush fluff off my black jacket. I stood there in a little daze of luxury as he brushed and brushed. A photo on a shelf: two very young boys dressed for baseball, one plainly the poet himself, a face like a landscape, grinning, looking up adoringly at the other who is older, taller, his face half hidden by the peak of his cap. 'Is that your brother?' 'Yep.' 'What happened to him?' 'Oh, he killed himself. In 1971.' I remain silent. He keeps on firmly brushing.

———

I took hold of V's upper arm and felt the skin, the roll of relaxed muscle, *the bone*. The horror of death came to me: one day *he will die*. Is this why I suffer so stupidly when he is late? Because it's a rehearsal for his death? Is this what being an adult is? To grasp what death is? He will be put in a box, the box in a hole, dirt will be shovelled on him, and his body will become meat. Meanwhile I will be walking around in air, breathing it, moving in it, thinking of him in the dark rotting. Appalling horror of these thoughts, incoherence in the face of them. Dumb, stricken, dazed.

———

When he introduced me to his friend, the adventurous beauty, I felt humble and afraid. People like me, who aren't beautiful, fear beauty because it seems to be a guarantee of love. She and V and I walked together as far as the corner of the street, and she continued alone. Why is she alone and unhappy? I see that even beauty as stunning as hers is no guarantee of anything. Perhaps not even of itself.

———

Before he left he made sure I knew where the hotel's fire exits were. A room now without meaning. I lie awake hour after hour, listening to the ridiculous drama of sirens in empty streets—the classic crying and wailing, then the brusque blurting of the deeper, more urgent, the 'real' emergency horn.

———

Bus trip through the Bronx. Empty streets because of the rain. Great blocks of gutted buildings.

———

Dreamt I put my black jacket on a hanger over a car's windscreen. When I returned, pollen had collected on the jacket so thickly that it looked like gold braid.

———

Middletown, Connecticut. Sitting here in a 'clean, well-lighted place' with a window opening on to masses of turning leaves, the agent sitting quietly reading and smoking at the window; black branches, sky clearing; writing down what happened, trying to describe people. I love, and am loved. 'The sun is up/ and death is far away.'

———

On the Greyhound bus between Boston and Waltham a semi-comatose young man with a plastic hospital ID bracelet on his wrist, foam coming out of his nostrils, his eyes half-closed, crawls on all fours down the aisle.

———

The cab driver ripped us off and we had to hurry along Wooster Street to the theatre. Some boys in bovver boots were yelling *Sieg heil*! outside the building. We thought it was the play itself, then one of them turned towards us a white face crazed with something violent and I saw that it was real. Someone opened a door: 'Come in here.' We did, she pulled it shut and a crashing blow landed on it from outside: '*Fucking faggots*!' The cops arrived with sirens whooping. The audience sat in rows rolling their eyes at each other, and the show began.

———

At the Rockefeller Center skaters were told to clear the rink while a man in an ice-mowing machine moved across the frozen surface in smooth, perfectly oblong sweeps. The treated path looked as I'd always imagined ice would look before I ever saw any: deep, a greenish silver.

———

Rain, in Chicago; and the black worker sings loudly a song about rain as he enters the clubroom he is about to clean.

———

A letter from F: 'Each time I hear the tunes of the *Little Notebook* I think of you struggling with the notes in that attitude of panic and "application" that you had in front of the piano, with your little head marking the beat, and it makes me a bit sad. I could have been more encouraging.'

———

I had my hair cut in Chicago by a guy called Benny Casino. As usual a haircut removed, distorted and replaced askew my self-image. When he finished I said, 'Can I take your photo?' This restored my power as looker.

———

I want to be home, writing.

———

A silver mist rises off the river.

———

I blew $200 on the most beautiful pair of brown boots. I rushed straight into a bar, threw myself on to a stool and ordered a margarita. The barman, Saleem, was from Karachi. Turns out he was a fellow shoe fetishist. He darted out the back and returned with a bag containing a pair he'd bought yesterday. We had a short but pointed colloquium on *heel height*.

———

A muggy, cool morning. Empty streets, the weird clustered skyline, the jade water of the Chicago River clashing with the grass-green of its banks.

———

Waiting, in silence, and in full knowledge and acceptance that what one is waiting for one may never get.

———

At Indianapolis airport this morning I pulled out of my head a single white hair.

———

After dinner the four of us, homesick, watched porn on the hotel room video. All these youthful healthy bodies jigging in fierce, mindless rhythms, faces gaping, mouths emitting stupid grunts or foul words. We laughed most at the dialogue. The sex itself made us sad.

———

'Either sit in the carriage or get out of it.' —Chekhov, *Notebook*

———

The flight home. Occasionally a town or city will appear miles below. One, through broken cloud, gave an impression of being a dozen or so comets, randomly scattered, moving in the same direction. After the Hawaii stopover a pleasant Australian girl called Libby takes the seat beside me. We talk quietly. I say, 'It's my birthday. Nobody knows. You can wish me—' She laughs and does. We both doze. When we wake to eat she says, 'I had a dream. You were in it.' Later I got a blood nose. Three oyster-sized clots ran down into my mouth and I spat them into a paper towel.

———

Home. Rain falling softly. Mad spring growth everywhere. Trees in my street heavy with leaves, a green tunnel. Thick greenness outside my window. I can put on a record. I can walk from room to room. Spent the entire day answering mail. I wrote thirty-nine letters.

How I know I have been to New York. A cold, rude tram conductor refused to change my $20 note. I took it back and sat down. He tried to put me off the tram. I said, 'I've offered to pay. You refused it. I'm not going to *walk*.' He went into a flurry of rule-stating and finger-pointing. I sat tight, astonished to find I neither blushed nor had heart palpitations. Small silence. Me: 'Do you have a system whereby I can give my name and address and pay later?' Conductor: (*still huffy but seizing at straw*) 'Yes.' Thus honour was satisfied.

Don't want to leave my house—sun enters it quietly, on angles which I have forgotten, then retreats to clouds and a wind shifts in damp leaves. I look at old notebooks, feel the freshness and usefulness of their contents: so I *am* working all the time, after all.

Saw M play Irina in *Three Sisters* at Anthill. Oh, its funniness, its awful sadness. She has presence, and power.

Dreamt I saw a line of trees along a fence, on a piece of land that was mine but that I had neglected. The trees fell over, all at once, sending up a cloud of dust and leaving a desolate landscape with little figures running about in dismay.

At the sink, washing up, I glance behind me as wind puffs in through the open back door; some cloth moves behind the table, at knee level, and I think there's a little girl in the room. But it's only the tablecloth, on the breath of air.

The Fatal Shore, about cannibalism in Tasmania: '…also off the thick part of the arms, which the inhuman wretch declared was the most delicious food'. The part of V in touching which I apprehended death.

———

Gardening at Primrose Gully. Sun, but fresh wind blowing. Walked to the eagle's nest carrying spade (snakes) and lump of wood (magpies)—saw none of either, though something whisked itself very fast back into the woodpile when I approached the tank. There's a nest in the hanging terracotta pot near the kitchen window. I climbed on a chair. Three speckled eggs, white with brownish-black markings like brushstrokes. A bird sang and sang in the tree near the veranda: an imitable song that I could almost whistle back to it, though less melodiously—a crude mimicry.

———

A review by Elwyn Lynn of Max Kreijn: 'He can let fractured light flicker across pale stone…The wall of hot rust; the paler ginger of the open trapdoor…' Art critics are obliged to work hard on *colour*.

———

P and I sunbake actively in the backyard. 'I'm going to get brown this summer,' she says. 'I don't care about the ozone layer.'

———

The desk girl says, 'Your friend's waiting up in your room.' The door is ajar. I push it open. He's asleep on the bed. Before I can even look at him he springs up, cheeks flushed, hair on end. I throw down my bag and leap on him.

———

Rain pours down. Lightning. A huge roll of thunder. He's telling me about his famous friend in England and his 'flat-chested, pug-nosed, short-sighted wife, a real sweetheart. She serves him.' I want to say, 'Does your wife serve you?'—not meanly, but because I need to know. I'm afraid that if she does, that this is what he needs and will continue to need so he can work. And before long he's saying, 'Do you think two writers can ever live together?' I hardly know what load this question is carrying.

———

Possibilities: this will run its course and subside. He'll sink back into his married life, its comfort, taking with him whatever he's learnt from this. But what about me? I tend this seed of fear, water it, *want* it to sprout.

———

I walk through shops, I look in windows, I am happy. Maybe this is what life *is*: constant change, constant attempt to balance one's needs with what is possible.

———

I notice that I have a menstrual cycle of about twenty-two days, lately. I do not want menopause to happen to me until it absolutely has to.

———

Dinner with the Little Sisters of Jesus, two French and one American, in their Richmond Housing Commission flat. Hot night, beautiful sky. Small cockroaches in the kitchen sink. Awful wine decanted from a cask into a Schweppes dry ginger bottle; a mound of food. One tells of a bag search at Customs: 'I was *red*! Like these carrots!' Another sang '*Je ne regrette rien*', and we did special dancing. I was wearing my new dress with fishtail, they applauded when I twirled to make the peplum fly out. We had *fun*. By 9.30 we were all yawning.

———

Each time I go to see *Three Sisters* at Anthill the same thing happens: when Masha makes her confession of love and asks rhetorically, '*Is it wrong?*' the audience holds its breath. Everyone wants an answer to this question—even perhaps an absolution—but Chekhov won't give one. *There isn't one.* 'These things cannot be legislated.'

———

Clouds today like a layer of pale grey cream. And a north wind.

———

F's cat gets run over, but not killed. "'E is in pieces. 'E is 'orrible to look at. 'E 'ad no—'is 'ead is in shambles.'

———

In a gutter I found an X-ray of somebody's…knee? A joint, anyway. Its shadowy bones. Painful that such an intimate photo should have been dropped in the street.

———

All V's jokes about men hating 'messes', 'trouble' etc. (Should I let him lend me $1000?)

———

Playing with their baby. His head as billiard ball: ivory colour, perfect smoothness. His alert look and profound, mature expressions.

———

I come home and find the gas on under the pea soup, the house full of a burning stink, back door wide open. At ten P and my sister burst in, hysterical with excitement, wearing crudely printed lapel stickers with made-up names: 'Blue Sapphire' and 'Ruby Rose'. They've been at a meeting of a New Age money-making scheme called the Golden Aeroplane. Blue Sapphire rushes straight to the phone to recruit another friend. Ruby Rose reports: 'There were people there stuffing money into their pockets. Someone asked me if I'd mind standing hand in hand in a ring going *OMMMM*. I said, "Look, I don't care *what* I do."'

———

The only way I can tell that time is passing is by noticing that my hair and fingernails are growing.

———

Women can endure things and keep going because our lives are made up of small practical physical tasks, and no matter how lonely or sad or humiliated you are you *do the dishes*, or wash the clothes, and you come to the end of a small task and see a small result.

———

There's a tremendous weight coming from somewhere, pushing me towards feeling that I'm being short-changed, that there's something humiliating in my situation. I hate it. I think it's wrong. I fight it. Because I'm happy, when I don't think about it in that way.

———

Two tasks: 1) to accept that someone loves me, and 2) to accept that at the same time I can be free.

———

In a *Times Literary Supplement* overview of Australian writing my work is described as 'Mills and Boon for bohemians'.

———

We argue about beauty, what it is. I try to explain my ideas about looking: how men have control of it, how in order to be an artist or a writer a woman has to overcome her sense of herself as an object, has to usurp something. V's opinion is that in visual art, depicted figures 'dematerialise' and become shape, line and form, and that what results from this dematerialisation of the female form is more beautiful than the male. 'Listen,' I say. 'I stand at this window. I look out at the blokes working on the building site, and what I see is *beautiful*.'

———

A man can strip his wife's friends away from her over the years, by teasing or mockery or lack of interest, and leave her nothing but himself. Then one day she might find that even this is not completely hers. Small cold wind of this thought.

———

Driving me back after dinner the husband begins to tell me about a 'numbness' he has noticed in my work. I ask very carefully where exactly *is* the numbness? Is it in the story, the characters, the prose? He says he can't really say. He presses on—the words get worse and worse—numbness, a frozen waste, blasted, devastated—all the way to the hotel. As the car goes under a bridge I remember the last time someone gave his opinion on that same book. *He* said my work was too nice, that it doesn't really say what's bad about people, it always looks on the bright side, is not about real life. We part awkwardly.

———

Dreamt that in Melbourne, in a long street quivering with plane trees in full leaf, a man stands with me outside a shop with a deep Victorian veranda, and says with a shudder, 'Melbourne! This endless peacefulness.'

———

The Golden Aeroplane is about to crash. Ruby Rose and Blue Sapphire are going to lose their money—in Ruby Rose's case, half of the thousand bucks I gave her last week to bail her out of a mess. 'It's a scam,' I say. 'No, it's not,' says P. She is very upset. She had believed she was breaking through barriers of mistrust: that she was freeing something in herself. 'You went into it,' I say, 'with a freight of idealism. But I bet most people are like Ruby Rose and only go in because they *want money*.' As I whack down my points I see her face hardening and becoming sharper, and I realise we aren't even talking about the same thing.

———

'Are you going to *Les Misérables*?'

    'No,' says my sister. 'I hate going to spectacles and enjoying them in spite of myself.'

———

Our sister's coming home from New York. 'Dad's rapt.' 'I know. It means he hasn't lost another daughter to some scumbag or other.' Waiting for her at the airport I turned all red from trying not to cry while watching scenes of reunion. I noticed a strange, intense silence that surrounds the reunion of an old woman and her son. Once the cries of greeting and laughter die down and the touching begins, there is a density to it—no one speaks, it's almost visible, the meaning of *mother and child*.

———

V was awkward in a household of women. He said he had felt left out. 'When we were eating in the kitchen you all kept laughing and putting your heads on the table. Like flowers at night.'

———

I walked into the change rooms at Brunswick baths and came upon two fat women in their thirties, naked, drying themselves. Sun coming down from high windows lit their white flesh and it was like walking into the world of two Picasso women, slow, pale, solid, utterly present.

———

'I have come to like a melancholy tone,' says the young writer in a letter, 'because it softens the embarrassment one feels about being ridiculously well-off and happy.'

———

'I once,' says V, 'introduced her to Fred Williams and Arthur Boyd. Together. She gushed.' 'So what,' I say. 'She was shy. Some people gush to hide their shyness. Others turn into silent, dry sticks.'

———

The law student's twenty-first. All the young men singing, talking, laughing, whispering, heads together, their girlfriends mostly forgotten.

———

Huge train strikes, trams packed solid, a party atmosphere. One young bloke so drunk his face was shining with sweat. Afraid he'd spew on me. The handsome young Greek conductor took his hand to keep him upright.

Conductor: (*in loud, merry voice*) 'I'm not a poof, mate, but I'll hold your hand.'

Drunk: (*faintly*) 'You don't *look* like a poof.'

———

My sister says her first memory of me as an adult was when she and our parents drove to my house 'after you'd had a baby. Mum went inside and Dad and I stayed in the car.' There are things in my past so excruciating that I have forgotten them. No wonder Dad keeps offering to lend me money.

———

We drink some champagne. I put on *Graceland* and we all start to dance. The doors and windows are open and a wind is rushing down the hall, F has the colander on his head and we dance, spontaneously but always trying to form patterns: forward and back in step, arms high and pumping, criss-cross paths through doorways, apart with our backs to each other, back again and pass with inscrutable faces.

———

Kath Walker, to an interviewer in *ABR*: 'When the kids come to me all dewy-eyed I say, "What you look for in a man is mateship. Forget about this love thing. I've told at least thirty-five men in my lifetime that I'll love them forever."'

———

'I shouldn't read as much,' says V, 'and yet I should read more.'

———

Church. My sister is one of the servers. Unaware that I'm there, she approaches the spot at the altar rail where I'm kneeling with my hands out. She stops in front me, carrying the big silver chalice, looks down, recognises me. She rocks back on her heels, her face is still with astonishment, then she smiles and I have to keep my eyes on her black shoes. My lips quiver against the rim of the chalice so hard that I'm afraid I won't be able to swallow.

———

F had prepared for us a beautiful little meal, pretty things arranged in patterns: a lot of vegetables; some prosciutto; mango and red currants; champagne. Everything went cheerfully. When we got up to leave he said, 'I wasn't intellectual enough for you. That's what the problem was.' 'No!' I said. 'You were *too* intellectual, *that* was the problem!'

———

Report from Paris: 'This cop smashed me in the mouth, twice. That's all. Nothing special.'

———

Alone on the Hume I listened to Bach violin partitas and Beethoven's third symphony. The ego that's working very hard in Beethoven, the battle he's waging, while Bach sports impersonally in the empyrean. Is this the difference between Romantic and Baroque? Mind filled, emptied, filled again with brilliant things I'd write if only I were brilliant.

———

The attractive, calm reasonableness of Elaine Showalter in *Towards a Feminist Poetics*: 'It is because we have studied women writers in isolation that we have never grasped the connections between them.' Part of my current unhappiness, frustration, unease must be due to the *absence of mothers* that I feel, in work—uncertainty, fear, a floating feeling. I haven't paid proper attention to what women write, have written. I've been tagging along on men's coat-tails, watching for their approval, and look where it's got me.

———

'Why are you embarrassed about your car?' says V.
  'Because it's new.'
  'That's a hippie way of thinking about cars.'

———

Z lambasts a new biography of Hemingway for its ignorant assumptions and 'psychologising'. Compares Hemingway's photo on the cover ('that terrible face—but *good*') to the biographer's on the back ('isn't he *awful*—so smug—and it's taken by his wife, dear little woman'). 'These bastards,' he says, 'they've never *written* a novel, they don't have a *clue* about the writer's life. They live all their lives safe in a university, with a wife and kids. They've got *no idea* of the risks writers take—I don't just mean the risks on the page but the way we make ourselves *uncomfortable* in life, so we'll *learn* things.'

———

M talks about a 2 am death freak-out she had in the motel at Numurkah where we shared a room. 'I kept looking at things in the room—chairs, a table—and thinking, "What are they *for*?"'

Why didn't she wake me? My punishment for her arms-length upbringing is her powerful independence, her resolute not-need of me. But when I told my friend with cancer this story he said, 'Two things. First, she's able to get through a dark night of the soul without needing to wake anyone. Second, dark nights of the soul are *personal*. You feel you want to go right to the end of it, and afterwards you're proud of yourself for getting through it alone.'

———

Two boys passing, on New Year's Eve:

　　One: 'Eddy, Eddy's not allowed to go anywhere near any girls, whatsoever.'

　　Two: (*voice breaking*) '*Bull*sheet!'

　　One: ''E says girls make you weak.'

———

V: 'You're very good, very sharp at *noticing* things, but don't you have any…beliefs, or thoughts, or arguments that you want to convince people of?'

　　Me: 'No. Not in the abstract. Only when something arises out of a practical circumstance.'

———

People keep telling me I look healthy, fit, purposeful. Must be the shoulder pads, which quite drastically suit me.

———

I met an arson engineer in an art-supplies shop. He smelt strongly of pipe tobacco and his lower lip was yellowed, almost charred. 'I've been on call for a fortnight. Three people burned to death between Christmas and New Year. One had left his deadlock key in the bedroom. We found his body against the front door.' I begin to think of violence, death, burning, what people do to each other, to their children. And to think that I need to find out about these things.

———

In the Leichhardt cafe we ran into two old friends of mine. Their simplicity and kindness made me feel very warmly towards them but V was withdrawn, reticent, not curious, and I wanted to kick him. I thought, I don't even *know* you. Who are you? Do you even *exist*?

———

He reads me a lovely piece of Goethe's conversations with Eckermann. 'He must have cleaned that up a bit when he wrote it down,' I say. 'It's not really the Studs Terkel approach, is it.' He stares at me in silence, even more shocked than he was when I said that a certain pink iced bun at Bondi looked like a Fairweather.

———

A storm was smashing over the Opera House when we emerged at interval. Great wide sheets of sepia lightning, sometimes with a hairline fracture down the centre. The bridge sprang towards us on a burst of light then jumped back into the dark. At the end of the show as we left the building we thought the rain had stopped, until we saw an upward-pointed fluorescent street-light squirting what looked like snow into the darkness.

———

Mending my skirt. Even putting a few stitches in something lightens this feeling of uselessness, of not really existing, which I believe I can identify as homesickness.

———

In the borrowed bedroom in the borrowed house, I felt a slowly growing peacefulness which became happiness and then joy. As I pulled the sheet tight and tucked it in, I remembered R once telling me of a 'bliss' that had come over her, a joy so strong that she had to sit down, cross-legged, on the ground and let it fill her completely—I did this, on her gritty bedroom floor, hands on knees, eyes closed, facing her shelf of poetry; and I thought about the dark column of meaning (behind my left shoulder, where it used to manifest) and I let it step forward and enter me—it became me, I mean it fused with my spine, and I was full of such powerful joy that tears ran down my cheeks. Writing this now I'm still shaking with the force of it.

It was my spine that took the meaning. Meaning entered me and became me. It was the Mighty Force. I wasn't afraid of it, in fact I summoned it, I called it and it *came*.

———

The house on Dangar Island. 'Sometimes in spring,' said the host, 'the light reflects off the river on to this wall, and it's *sickening*, it's so bright and dappled.' We ate, I asked to have a nap, he showed me to a hanging bed under the house, and tucked in a mosquito net around me. I read a few pages of Pablo Neruda's memoir. His first poem. He wrote it to his stepmother when he was very small, in a rush of intense emotion, then copied it out neatly on to a small scrap of paper and, still trembling, took it to his parents and handed it silently to them where they sat talking. The father scans it, hands it back and says, 'Where did you copy that from?'

———

The cat next door is going to have kittens. The little girl hangs out the upstairs window and shouts down to us: 'Mummy, ask Helen her opinion of Ginger's pregnancy.'

———

The ten-year-old boy and I share a room. He is charming, clever, friendly. We talk so much in our two narrow beds that we don't get to sleep till after midnight. 'I've realised,' he says, 'that it's possible not to *like* someone in your own family. For example, I respect my grandmother but sometimes she says cruel and hurtful things about people, and when she does that I don't like her. I like my other grandmother more, but I don't respect her.'

———

At my agent's I signed two contracts. I will get an advance that I can use to PAY MY TAXES.

———

'All the…most important problems of life are fundamentally insoluble…They can never be solved, but only out-grown.' —Jung (in Harding's interview book)

Our attempts to discipline this tremendously powerful *thing*. It can't ever supplant his marriage. If we can't discipline it then one day it will have to be put down. Perhaps there *is* no mode that can integrate this kind of love into a structure. Maybe that's the whole *point* of it: that it blasts structure sky-high; that it's all or nothing.

My old friend, with his wife close behind, enters their kitchen where I am cooking. 'My wife looks wonderfully beautiful,' he said, 'while *you* look—' My fear of what he might say, what *ranking* I might be subjected to—then relief when he doesn't finish his sentence.

Alone in their house. Rain falling quietly, a small choir of crickets. It was still light. Sparrows were hopping about in the branches. Rain collected in curved upturned leaves with frilled edges; and in different spots, now here, now there, a load of rain would become too heavy for its leaf, which would suddenly sag and let the water pour down in a quick stream, as suddenly cut off. I tried to call home. No answer. Played the piano. Got somewhere. Opened the front door, stood by it watching the rain. Remembered M when I picked her up from that crèche in Kew. The lady says, 'Your daughter's sitting on the back doorstep watching the rain.' At *two*. This thought made me suffer. What was I *doing* to that little girl? I was so absorbed in love and escape.

Some bloke reviews *Postcards from Surfers* in an American university magazine. I am taken to task for 'transcribing: it appears that she never invents anything'. Even in *The Children's Bach*, says the critic, occurs this Philip character who appears in so much of my work that 'he is almost surely based on a particular man'. *Pfff.* I thought he was an archetype.

We walk into the ward. A rhythmic moaning, is it an instrument or a human voice? An 'operation', one thinks of it as mechanical, a neat metal process, and can't conceive of the brutality, the violence of metal on bone, the force it must take and the body's frantic fighting back: blood, coldness, temperature up and down, shivering, unconsciousness, sleep—*dreams*.

———

People who can't stop talking. Their monologues work as fences (and they must always ride the boundaries) around things that cannot be spoken of.

1988

Dreamt that a Vietnamese man was torturing me by digging his fingers hard into my back muscles. I was kneeling in front of him in a sparse public room. I was obliged to conceal my pain. When I woke my back went on hurting in the exact spots into which he'd been sinking his fingers. Tonight when I pulled my nightie from under the pillow to put it on I found it was torn right across the back.

———

Tremendous dry heat. Not even a sheet over me, till morning.

———

At his cousin's funeral Dad failed to recognise his own sister. Listening to the priest reading Corinthians on life and death, I felt again quite sure that—well, I even thought 'There is no such *thing* as death.' All right—Cambodia, blue plastic bags, Babi Yar, Anita Cobby. And yet. Even so. All those souls struggling to stay a while in this world…

———

P: 'The heat! How will we get through this *night*?'
　　H: 'It's nearly over. It's already midnight.'
　　P: 'But how will we get through the wee hours?'

———

Ian Buruma on 'Oriental' cinema, for example Ray and Mizoguchi: 'The emotions under the surface, the long spells of apparent calm, suddenly interrupted by an emotional climax: a look of terrible grief, a stifled scream, a burst of silent tears. The image of the woman betrayed by weaker men, biting her sari or kimono in anguish...'

———

This is the hardest thing I've ever taken on, in my whole life. Its huge demands: self-discipline, solitude, secrecy; the frustrated longing to speak about it. I pick up his moods. His wind blows on me and I shiver and tinkle. And yet I like my life, perhaps better than he likes his. I don't have to tell lies.

———

Swam twenty laps. Worked merrily on the movie, shuffling the order of scenes and writing more in—enjoying *making things up*. Gee I'm good at dialogue sometimes. The rhythm of it is my natural element. Worked out what to write for *Good Weekend* ($300) and began it.

———

Dreamt I was in a pitch-dark house, feeling my way around a bedroom. When it got light I realised I must have my period: the room was covered with bloody palm prints. Clothes hanging over a chair-back were stained.

———

Mass in the Little Sisters' Housing Commission flat. A dozen people sitting on the floor. Someone read the Gospel. Jesus said to shake the dust from your feet. Is it a curse? No, said a big woman in a corner: shake off rejection, rather than dragging it along with you to the next experience. Bread was a large scone. Wine was passed round in a wooden cup. At the sign of peace everyone got up and milled about, hugging and shaking hands. A window was half-open and a breeze kept puffing the synthetic curtains into the room. Outside, noise rose and fell: shouts, an explosion, a radio on somewhere, traffic. I thought, 'This is real life, this is better than church, it's not even religious.'

———

'Do you think people can ever avoid betraying each other?'

'No. Because promises can't stop everything from moving and changing.'

———

My sister wants me to give her grammar lessons. We get a couple of textbooks and I tentatively begin. 'Come on!' she says. 'You're the teacher! Teach!' We do nouns, verbs—begin to parse. I feel the terms coming back.

———

Drinking coffee as I write, I feel optimism begin to run quietly along my veins.

———

I keep thinking about the children in *28 Up*, the tension of their faces. The seven-year-old in his boarding-school blazer: 'Mai hawt's desayre is to see my fawther, whoo's in Chaina'—his little face hollow-cheeked from the stress of dancing. The roughness of the working-class kids, their ability to change, improvise, *flex*—their readiness to laugh and give a shrug.

———

In the hotel I work happily all morning on the movie. I order tea, they bring it. Men work outside my window on the building site next door. Rain starts, then stops; clouds form, shed water, part again. Drills, hammers. Clanging of pipes. My self-confidence in work waxes and wanes, but never sinks below the level of function. Later in the afternoons he visits me.

'Don't you ever get bored,' he says, 'loafing about like this?'

'Never. Do you?'

'Not bored, but it does seem strange, to spend a whole afternoon...Do you think it's lazy? Shouldn't we be doing something?'

'We are.'

'What?'

'Reading. Talking about adjectives.'

———

He goes home to his life. I will always be displaced by it. And here I am again in this room, calm, half-sleepy, looking forward to going back to *my* life. We will never be a couple. One day we will find the sexual passion gone and a friendship taking its place. And through it all his marriage will have sailed serenely on. A radio's on, somewhere out there, a woman singing wildly. A train passes. I don't care. Nothing can touch me. The power of *work*. Art, and the huge, quiet power it gives.

———

Sitting on a bench, laughing at the mean wit that is so amusing if one is not the butt of it.

———

My friend's home from hospital. Smaller-headed, hair growing back in a convict's prickles. Like an actor playing him, but they haven't quite got it right.

———

On the dark building site after a night of heavy rain a man in a blue, almost-black boilersuit and leather belt walks across the ground floor carrying a folder and a plastic cup. Now someone's whistling in there, like Dexter, a bright whippy little tune. Someone else begins to whack metal with metal, and the night's over.

———

O and R's vast new fridge. It dominates the kitchen and, like the decrepit one before it, hums all the time as if faulty. It looks anomalous there, with its shining surface and squared corners, its aggressive whiteness.

———

A fantasy: I call his number, his wife answers, I identify myself and ask to speak to him; she says, 'Do you know what you are doing to me?' and I say, 'Do you want to tell me?'

———

Walked with R through Hyde Park at dusk. Bud lights along the boughs. She said, 'Why are people afraid of getting married?' I said, surprising myself with the clarity of the thought, 'Because they're afraid they won't find it in themselves to go on loving the other person once the obstacles to their relationship are removed.'

———

To church. At the peace greeting R and I turned to each other and whispered simultaneously. She said, 'I hate this part—I find it *excruciating*.' I said, 'I love this bit. It's my favourite.' She laughed and said, 'You little extrovert!'

———

The children encounter a flasher/masturbator in the churchyard opposite their house, and flee in disarray, leaving a valued skipping rope behind. They call me into their bedroom and whisper their tale. Later their uncle offers to go back with them for the rope. They decline, then a little while later they ask me to accompany them. Very flattered by this. We trudge over there. The perv's long gone of course, but the old churchyard is very beautiful under the thick grey sky: a creamy wind blows across wet grass; the gravestones are crumbling sandstone, one has a sailing ship carved into it.

———

What about a small short story: the flasher gone, leaving the churchyard in a state of strange beauty.

———

Started the structurally very difficult job of cutting the home scenes into the desert trip. It was hard but I was very happy doing it. I cut with confidence, though some things I sadly miss as I toss them over my shoulder on to the floor. The process of tightening the net is exhilarating. And nutting out ways of putting in pieces of factual information unobtrusively.

———

Last time V was supposed to be coming I cleaned all the windows so that if he didn't turn up I'd at least have clean windows.

———

Why is my torso changing shape so radically? I don't like it—a thickening.

———

'But,' said U, 'I really can't bear what I become as soon as I'm involved with a man—this simpering creature. I like myself much better when I'm with my kids and my friends, just doing practical things and trying to be nice to people.'

———

Anyway, I drove P to the Sydney bus at 7 am—her masses of luggage, her little skirt and jacket, pretty legs, pretty golden shoes. Then I went to F's to pick up my uke, which he had lent to some visiting Tahitians. I played until told, 'Shut up, or else play something with a progression, at least.'

———

The nun talked about a man sitting opposite her on a tram: 'I liked his face because it reminded me of my own.'

———

M and F came over to our place at 10.30 pm after his birthday dinner. We played a stupid game of me pretending they weren't welcome and yelling GO HOME! Pretending to attack them with a carving knife. M hurled herself on to my bed and I dragged her off by the ankles. After they left we were ashamed. I had to call F to apologise and wish him bon voyage to Tahiti.

———

An extremely intense conversation with the nun, no small talk, just a driving urge in each of us to *get to the point*. She tells me about the Jesuit: 'We didn't get as far as actually making love, but we got very close to it, and for the first time—you see—years ago when I was working in a very bad ghetto in Boston, I was raped. I was walking home at night and a black man dragged me into a deserted building. I thought he was going to kill me. He was strangling me, and I thought, "He's gonna have to kill me before he gets my body"—and so I was fighting him really hard—but then I thought, "If it gets out, in Boston, that a nun *with a name like McDermott* was raped and murdered in the ghetto, the Irish—'cause the Irish are the ones that hate the blacks the most—the Irish are gonna come in here and burn the whole place down. So I said, "OK, do what you have to and get out." So he did. And it was a really…revolting experience. And between that day and this, with the Jesuit, there hadn't been—so you see'—she sits forward and brings her face, lit up and smiling, closer to me—'for the first time I felt *my body was a sacrament.*'

———

Sometimes at night, when I'm the last to go to bed and I walk down the hall towards my room, seeing the other doors closed or ajar with sleep or undressing or reading or emptiness occurring behind them, this house seems a mansion to me, full of possibilities and a kind of private freedom. I'm so happy, in this attenuated state, that I barely dream of resolution. In fact I'm afraid of it. Because I might lose this happiness. By being greedy.

———

Fragment of a dream: two people, a man and a woman, in profile, sitting facing one another, as if going along in a carriage, not quite but almost in dark silhouette.

———

Late summer morning. Swam. Pool very beautiful. Sun giving out long, oblique rays of pink and gold.

———

At the kitchen table I ate my solitary chop and lettuce leaves and read Sally Morgan's *My Place.* I surprised myself by starting to sob out loud: ashamed of being a twerp, ignorant, an intellectual snob. What would I know about such suffering?

———

I called the born-again on his building site ('Want me to get him for you on the walkie-talkie?' says a bloke eagerly). He nearly fainted when I revealed that the tickets to the Manning Clark musical were $29 each. When we walked into the old Princess Theatre he looked

around him aghast and said, 'I'd like to run a bulldozer through this.'
I told him that when I went to the nuns' Eucharist the priest drank all
the wine and the rest of us got only bread: 'Is that because it's Lent?'

'No. That's Catholic. Didn't you know?'

'WHAT?'

'That was one of Luther's complaints that he nailed to the door.'

'But that's APPALLING. It's a fucking SCANDAL.'

'Good on you, Hel.'

———

To Primrose Gully with T. We sawed branches off a half-dead tree
and planned a big bonfire for the winter. Next: fill in those stupid
ponds. She said, 'I'm a Baptist. I like hell-like activities. How about
we start now, using buckets?' I said, 'No, I have to finish this thing
I'm writing.' So she began to tear meat off a chicken and stuff it into
her mouth. A mild night, with scented air. After tea we walked for
hours: a thirteen-kilometre 'evening stroll'. I had the little torch that
F gave me but it was easier to walk by the faint light from the sky,
which was quite covered, after having turned on a stylish display
of stepping-stone clouds at sunset. Slept with the tomahawk beside
my bed. In the morning we woke and gardened: a lot of destruction.
Bare lines everywhere. Now I'm burnt, cut, blistered and stiff, and
sore from laughing. That is my idea of a weekend.

———

Out to dinner with C at the Siam, where the beautiful Thai waitress
addressed each of us as 'sir'. Back at C's place we loafed about on
the pillows and gossiped. She remarked on my frequent trips to
Sydney—did I have a bloke up there? 'Yes.' 'Does he ever get down
here?' 'Not much.' (*In very small voice*) 'He's married.' 'Oh.' She
smiles and nods, and the subject is pleasantly changed.

———

Worked for hours, slowly and painfully, on the movie. Fearfully,
slowly, obliquely. Wrote another scene, stitched my squares and
oblongs together.

The boys from St Joseph's go roaring and rending the gardens as they pass.

—————

'I don't want him to die. I'd be furious with him if he died.'

My sister, impatiently: 'He *will*.'

—————

I walked down Brunswick Street and bought a wooden towel rack in a secondhand shop. It's got a little heart carved into each end. Now I'm going to paint it white.

—————

So close to finishing the screenplay that I've been half-stunned all afternoon, roaming round the city. I actually wrote what I think will be the final scene. I don't know whether a camera can do what I want it to but I wrote it down anyway.

—————

My sister, asking for the hinged egg-slicer, called it 'the little harp'.

—————

Dancers' bodies, rehearsing. Their stretchableness, length of neck. Their feet in soft laced shoes. Some have regal bearing, others are chunkier. One man very strong and blocky: he can lift, but he is also graceful and has a well-set head. The choreographer tries to explain certain movements to me. I pay attention but fail to grasp her point. She walks off towards the dancers and I say to the composer, 'It's hard to put into words, isn't it.' He says, 'That's why people dance.'

—————

Washed and de-flea'd the dog.

—————

My sister tells us her son wants his golf clubs buried with him, and he wants 'Hello, Is It Me You're Looking For?' to be sung at his funeral.

—————

Replaced the disgusting shower curtain, painted the towel rack, cleaned the bath, raked the garden, ironed the tablecloths, made a soup, picked up things off my bedroom floor, washed my clothes, and sat down to read the Literature Board papers.

———

Someone stole M's bag, she comes over to tell me about it, puts her head in my neck and bursts into tears. 'When I got a new key cut I had to get rid of that old Lockwood one I've had for *six years*—and now I've got this great big *silver* one.' She sobbed and sobbed.

———

Adelaide Writers' Week. Hearing certain British writers speak I realise how scandalously little I have ever *thought* about my own work.

———

I just received the first fax of my life. A procedural matter about an interview.

———

V introduces me to his friend W: her beauty, and somewhere coming from deep inside her, her lostness. She and I take to each other at once, we can't get away on our own quick enough. H: 'I was looking for you when I came in, but I only had his description to go by.' She: 'What did he say I looked like?' H: 'He said you were beautiful, that your hair was white, and that you wore terrific clothes that you just threw on.' She laughs out loud, with happiness. We talk very fast about our experiences alone in our respective bush dwellings. Hers she can only get to by boat.

———

We hired a car and drove to a beach. He clowned at the wheel, making the tyres scatter gravel and keeping a deadpan face. Swam in flat water. Girl in the dunnies was smoking a joint. Beautiful country, clean-looking properties. We saw a dead snake. He backed up so we could have a look.

———

At breakfast the Cretan's fig was bursting with ants.

I read her story. It had three marvellous moments in it. But driving along later I thought that what was missing from it was something hard, sparse, distant and impersonal. I think that what I'm trying to do is stand back from telling the story *myself*, and let the language tell the story. Is this what poetry does? It doesn't preclude at all a first-person narrative; but it means that all cosiness, all *comfort* must be excised—everything easy, chatty, loose.

J says his wife 'bakes the sort of bread you want to peel open and lie down in'.

Sudden money problems: tax $6000, royalties $1500. I was hoping they'd balance out.

A fox at Primrose Gully. 'It came flying,' said my sister, 'straight down the hill from the corral, absolutely *streaking* along. It saw us, and swerved for a second then decided to go straight on. It flew past us so fast that some of us didn't even see it. It had a *huge* brush, a beautiful russet colour, with a white band around it near the tip. It turned its head to look at me and it had a perfect fox's face—a sharp triangle.'

E in Sydney offers me her spare room this winter. A friendly, un-pressing invitation.

The young woman answers the phone in a soft, dreamy voice.
'I didn't wake you from a nap, did I?'
'No…I've got this lovely little baby on my lap.'

György Ligeti's 'Chamber Concerto'. *Corrente; calmo; sostenuto; movimento preciso e mecanico; presto*. All kinds of weird pluckings, knockings, tickling of strings, and a flowing feeling.

On the tram a strange couple, young, a bit lumpen. The girl had untidy red hair and freckles, and a rather dignified and thoughtful expression. She sat half turned away from the boy, not touching, lost in thought. He kept glancing at her, then after a moment, feeling unnoticed, he gave her knee a firm sideways whack with his. Her eyes focused and she looked at him. He said nothing. She got the message: put her arm through his and sat closer to him so their sides touched all the way down. Then she laid her head on his shoulder. All this without changing the expression on her face one iota. He, on the other hand, looked almost pretty with happiness. His eyes shone. Hard to imagine their future. Or anyone's, for that matter. What a stupid remark.

'Don't buy the jacket,' said my sister. 'It makes you look like a businesswoman.'

To a comedy night with M and my mother. Mum loves to inveigh against 'city drivers' and tells endless boring stories. I'm ashamed of my reaction but I can't help it and I know she's afraid of me. Writing this my eyes fill with tears—a pathetic and useless response. M's terrible beauty: it too frightens me and makes me sad—and with Mum it becomes almost too much. Is Mum what I will become? No—because she's afraid of everything and I'm less afraid. But I'll *look* like her; and right now I'm skating along a middle line between them, slightly further on her side than on M's.

'We meet someone at the right moment, I thought, we take everything we need from them, and then we leave them, again at the right moment.' —Thomas Bernhard, *Woodcutters*
    It makes me feel cold, he's so bilious and splenetic.

The extreme *structural* pleasure I get out of pulling a long interview together: trying to make it move like a real conversation, though in fact I have deconstructed it completely.

———

My mother was in my dream, but stronger, freer, cleverer, more alert and focused—I explained to M that Mum's name had been changed to Paradiffy, 'because it was *Paradise* and she was *Different*'. Won't this *ever* end?

———

And now my nun's got leukemia. Stunned by this news. No emotional reaction.

———

There is nothing I can do to get V into my life, or myself into his. Having drunk two glasses of wine I am not feeling any pain.

———

As soon as she grew some pubic hair, said the woman, her mother explained what it was and told her that men were animals.

———

V showed me a shocking photo of his father as a young man: spectacles, hair cut short and combed back, his face thin, hard, clamped, full of some terrible inward-turned power—like someone who could have died of a broken heart, or of bottled-up emotion.

———

A hilarious evening of play and foolery with R and her kids. V played poker with them, examined a broken billycart. Driving away I say, 'It was fun with the kids, wasn't it.' 'Yes,' he said, 'but they take over. Nothing *happened*. Nothing got *said*.' 'Of *course* something happened. We *played*.'

———

One day, sitting at the table in this hotel with the construction workers battering and yelling away outside, I will feel a big wave rush over me, and I'll pack up my things and go home. I'll ring him up or write to him and I'll say, 'If you want me you'll have to come and find me; because I can't keep this up any more. It breaks my life into small pieces and I can't feel whole.' In other words I will find a place to stand, and I'll stand on it.

———

When in doubt, V heads for a bookshop.

———

'What I meant, when I said I was like a Catholic,' says V, 'was that I'm bound. By some inviolable rule.'

———

What I'm learning from this is how to be a grown-up. That life's not as simple as I thought it was. That people are good at not being happy. And that the kind of selfishness I used to function by is simply *not appropriate* in this situation. I'm starting to understand why it's been necessary for people to invent concepts like original sin, to try to explain why we're so good at making ourselves unhappy.

———

Window and blind open, room lit like a black-and-white movie by reflections from high buildings nearby. Our faces must look smoothed of lines but also dramatic, as if enacting a drama, dramatically boned and planed.

———

On the lunchtime ferry a man of seventy or so who seemed to need a witness directed his discourse at me. He'd left Sydney twenty years ago to live in Tasmania and was here now on a visit. He was in distress. 'See that?' he said, pointing at a sandstone building we were passing. 'That was a pub. I used to drink in there. I dunno what it is now—but they'da done better to pull it down and use the sandstone for something else—don't you reckon?' He had been in the city: 'It's all changed—it's terrible what they're doing.' 'What about the quay? They've spent a lot of money on it.' 'Ah, they've spent money, but it's a bloody abortion.' His voice trembled and he turned away to hide the fact that under his glasses tears were running out.

———

At 6 am the air of the harbour is cool, misty, about to be bright. Ships slide past in silence. I'm floating here in this cheap hotel with its outrageous view, cut off from daily life, watching other people's lives going on around me. In my room I haven't even got a table. When I get back later an old man with a suitcase is standing in confusion in the hall: 'Where's room 13?' 'Over there.' He opens it with his key. 'How's it look?' 'Well,' he says, 'it's got a bed in it.'

———

Greek Independence Day celebrations outside the Opera House. Boys dancing. They slouch about clumsily in their extravagant white-frilled skirts, white stockings and pompoms, then at the moment they form their line they stand up straight and strike out in splendour, turning their whole torsos when they turn their heads. The leader holds up his free hand as beautifully as if he were a woman. One Cretan boy dances wildly and with skill, his arms and shoulders open wide—the music tense and repetitive, about to explode—also the smaller children, the preoccupied girls, one round tub of a boy, 'Spiro', working gracefully nonetheless.

———

The girl standing on her own in the street, watched through the window by the four others, holding the dead cat in the bag. This is the central image of her character and role. If V had written this, would he have worked *back* from that idea? I can't plan. I can only work on feeling. He told me that when he saw *Two Friends*, before we met, he thought, 'This person knows about a world that I know absolutely nothing about.'

———

In Ariel I picked up Art Spiegelman's *Maus* and held it out to him: 'Look—it's a cartoon about Auschw—' and he cut across me, 'Oh, look! Steiner!' I stepped back. He said his formula for these moments: 'Sorry to interrupt'—and to my horror I heard myself utter a sharp and bitter laugh. He stood there holding Steiner's novel, I stood there holding *Maus*, three feet apart and facing each other. He said, 'I didn't mean to be rude.' I said, 'Oh, stop it.' I could have sat down (by Grand Central Station) and wept. Instead we both recovered, and he said something about Steiner's novels being no good, and I listened; and then we left the shop.

———

The superstitiously gloomy beams that one casts on love: as if wanting to smash it oneself so that fate won't have to bother.

———

As if I could change myself in any way, at this age. All I can do is try to know myself and apply discipline.

———

A postcard from G, newly married, so recently ecstatically in love: 'I'm missing being able to talk to you. It seems to be the only way sometimes to get to those things in the back of the mind. At my centre is a lack that I keep trying to fill with women. You included, I suppose.'

———

Strange bright clouds of rain are falling but the colours of everything are as if the sun were shining.

———

A box of old papers. Love letters by the score. And two horrible letters from Mum and Dad in 1967 when I was in London and told them I was going to travel home overland with a man. The coldness of their rejection—I was never to contact them or my brother and sisters again if I went ahead with this—once more I felt my world grind against theirs.

———

P and I talked about men we'd been with, their effects on us. She told me about the one who vigorously undermined her as an artist. He said, 'I don't want you to paint. It feels like competition. Do pots, or something.' She did, made two she liked, and in one fight he smashed her second-favourite one, and in another she smashed her best one. 'I did it to *myself*,' she said, 'worse than he did it to me.'

———

I think I must be insufferable. I feel as if I'm beaming out impatience and nastiness. Everything one may have is lustreless because there is one thing that one may not have.

Collected from the old house several boxes of spirax notebooks in a neurotically regular round hand, and in a tone that fancies itself as *writing*: self-dramatising, taking its emotions very seriously; little set-pieces on the weather—quite embarrassing but no doubt full of information. I could sell them. I could probably pay for fixing my shabby kitchen. 'Do you want to buy the series of notebooks on which *Monkey Grip* is based?'

Our dog, left behind in our separation into three houses, I now have to take with me everywhere I go. She lies in silence behind me as I work and is pleasant company. I feel sorry for her glum sadness. Yesterday I took her to get clipped and felt free, as if she'd gone to kinder for an afternoon.

Cranky at Primrose Gully. Broken hurricane lamp still not replaced.

In the Smith Street post office I was served by a frizzy-haired woman in a hand-knitted pink jumper. The fingers of her left hand had bandaids over their tips. She had a very small, dry smile, barely a change in her features, but it gave a short glimpse into an interior that (I sensed) was extremely experienced and morally unrestricted. She drummed her fingers lightly and firmly on my name on the envelope.

'Is this you?'

'Yes.'

'I've read all your books, many times. That one about the junkie. That's my favourite.'

When the born-again was leaving Primrose Gully we said goodbye under a sky 'weak with stars'. I said, 'What's that white patch up there?' 'That's another galaxy.' A corridor of terror opens and closes. Terror of the cosmos.

———

Two women were talking about a young mother they knew who was furious no one had told her how much it hurts to have a baby. Surely she must have read novels and seen movies? Let alone heard other women *talk*?

———

A night's good sleep at Primrose Gully, beside a window full of stars. Later a strong moon, so bright it woke me and I had to draw the curtain. Towards morning, a mopoke. Drove to the opposite ridge and picked up wood. Saw a large kangaroo crash away between the trees; and surprised two eagles. They blustered up from a tree and flapped away very fast. Why shouldn't I live up here? No TV. Only radio. No piano. No power. Very little water for washing clothes. Would I be lonely? I'd start talking to myself. (I do that already.) The pretty little kelpie that followed me home from the stud—she wanted to stay, refused to get out of the car when I drove her back. Old man comes out in the dark to see who's there: his white hair blows up in a crest.

———

'To die is only to be as we were before we were born; yet no one feels any remorse, or regret, or repugnance, in contemplating this last idea…It seems to have been holiday-time with us then: we were not called to appear upon the stage of life, to wear robes or tatters, to laugh or cry, be hooted or applauded; we had lain *perdu* all this while, snug, out of harm's way; and had slept out our thousands of centuries without wanting to be waked up; at peace and free from care, in a long nonage, in a sleep deeper and calmer than that of infancy, wrapped in the softest and finest dust…' —Hazlitt, *On the Fear of Death*

———

R and I talked excitedly on the phone about prose and 'what moves behind it'. 'It's as if,' she said, 'even if all I write is fragments, I'm getting ready for the moment when I'll have something to say.' 'That's it. That's it exactly. That's what my life's about.'

———

I like this cheap paper because it's got exactly the right amount of *drag*, and because sometimes the point of my pen goes straight through it.

———

In recent literary magazines I see that my name begins to be mentioned in a manner that leads me to believe my 'dream run' is over. I'm glad about the relative anonymity of screenwriting. People watch a movie and never ask themselves who wrote it. I'm tired. I worked. Even if I'm 'not experimental' I can still work.

———

'There are feminine garments so lovely that one could tear them to shreds.' —Cesare Pavese's diary

———

I call G in his recording studio. 'Are you busy?'
    'Yes, but…'
    'I want you to do me a favour.'
    'Of course.'
    'I want to send you a letter for the love of my life, and I want you to ring him up and arrange for him to come and get it from you.'
    'Ooh, I *love* this.'

———

My sister puts on the record of Bartók's *Mikrokosmos* and I see it gives exactly the mood I want for *The Last Days of Chez Nous*: dry, thoughtful, slightly manic, slightly out of whack.

———

Typed up the final draft of the movie. It looks solid, as big as a novel. Walked home with the dog, squinting in autumn sunshine. Lay on my bed under a body-temperature waterfall of fatigue. It's done. I've finished it. It's taken me nearly a year and it's actually quite good.

———

I sat in Marios with the two painters. They talked about materials. 'Medium.' It was pleasantly impenetrable. One of them had a very weird style and presence. Her discourse was a series of collapses and reconstitutions.

———

Dinner in Camberwell with my angry sister. She arrived full of bitterness against the tax department, and against me for having lived on a supporting mother's benefit when M was very small. Went to see Huston's *The Dead* at the Rivoli. She fell asleep twenty minutes in. The middle-aged couple on my other side talked all the way through. When Gabriel sees his wife on the staircase, the bloke said, 'Look at that wallpaper. It's peeling.' And during the great monologue at the end about the snow 'faintly falling' all over Ireland, the woman said, 'Huh. Depressing. Bit depressing.' All the way home I felt a violent hatred for *common sense*.

———

'Jesus,' said my nun, 'must have been the sexiest man the world had ever known. Once you've got your*self* worked out, then you know the most important thing is *relationship*. They had to get rid of him. He was *too sexy*.'

———

V meets G and is very taken with him. 'He's a very worked-out, worked-on person. He's strongly shaped and individual. And— have you noticed? Oh, of course you have—he's got extraordinary oval-shaped fingernails.'

———

Mice on the rampage in the Primrose kitchen. Constant scrabblings, comical gambollings in pairs, and whenever I open a drawer I'm confronted by bright eyes, furry faces and pink ears. I set two traps but they got the Weetbix out without springing them, and now I feel attached to them.

'Thin turquoise and delicious musk pink.' —Elwyn Lynn

I ask G if he had liked V. 'Yes. We disagreed, but we seemed to enjoy to disagree. He twists around in his chair while he speaks.'

While I was washing my face I thought that one day I will say to someone, 'Once I was in love with him. We loved each other. It was a great passion.' I imagined myself speaking of it painlessly and without regret, in the past tense.

Not far from my road at Primrose Gully someone has found the badly decomposed body, in two plastic bags, of a man who had been shot twice in the head. It's been there for about three years. This find, rather than spooking me, confirms my previously unexamined impression that the world is full of the results of secret deeds. The bodies that are found are only the accidents, I mean the ones stumbled on. There must be others, everywhere.

Today they're wrecking my kitchen to make it bigger. Traumatic chaos. I can hear them grinding and gnashing away. As if part of my body were being violently dealt with and altered. Teeth, perhaps.

At my agent's in Double Bay we sat on her balcony and watched the rain on the water, the cloud rolling along the surface from the Heads towards us. The paths wind makes on water—rippleless, uncertain tracks. She was affectionate, pleased with my screenplay. I felt approved of. Someone I love is proud of me.

O cooked the dinner and during his labours such a fit of frustration exploded in him that the frying pan twisted into the air and six small schnitzels flew about the room. He found five of them but the sixth remained a mystery. He even went out into the yard, in case it had sailed through the narrow opening at the top of the window and landed among the bikes. Later he called us and showed us the missing piece of meat resting against the lid of the shopping trolley in the passage between the kitchen and the living room.

———

This terrifying Sydney rain. It goes on all day, all night, always the rattle and hiss. This morning R took me to the front door and pointed out a small bird which had taken shelter on the first-floor window of the flats opposite: 'Look at this image of pathos.' We stood in silence on the doorstep and stared at the bird, and the rain kept on gushing down, running two inches deep across the front garden and pouring away into the street.

———

He turns up at last, in a wet raincoat, looking pale. We spend an hour in the car down at the Point, talking, our eternal conversation which flows solidly on, despite these repeated interruptions. Rain drizzles, pours, thunders, falls steadily again. Lights on singly in the shipyard across the narrow arm of water. A gutter spouting up over an obstruction. Tonight, outside my window, a single cricket is trying to chirp, feebly and without enthusiasm or energy—as if only learning.

———

Lately in my dreams my girl is a child again.

———

A married woman asked me about my life, whether I was content with solitude. 'Don't say yes! Or I might feel desperate.' I searched for something negative to offer. I found this very hard to do. Because I love my room, arranged according to my needs, and the way I'm 'beholden to nobody'. But I came up with, 'Sometimes when I see two people who are going home together I long for some sort of domestic intimacy.'

———

Do I want resolution? So I can stop all this travelling? I keep wanting to start a novel. It's starting itself and the only thing stopping it is me.

———

His whole life he has been cosseted by women. A few years between mother and wife. He can't cook, though he (says he) does the shopping and washing. 'I've never made a salad in my life, actually.'

———

'Men handle money differently from women,' says the film director. 'They're *playful* with money, whereas we have little purses, and we count it out—"This is for the rent, and this for the 'lectricity"—but they chuck it around.'

———

Because they could not live together in the world she knew best and inhabited, he detached her from it, very gradually and subtly, and drew her into *his* world, 'the world of ideas and books'. Superman takes Lois Lane flying, holding her firmly by the hand.

———

Why should he love me, or think of me, when at home he has a 'happy, generous, sometimes very funny' wife who knows him, loves him and wants to serve him? In other words, what's the point of me? But on the quay, walking round the curve of it, for a moment I took his arm and felt proud of him, and joyful in his company.

———

Dreamt I was in the driver's seat of a very large, luxurious station wagon, and in charge of a charming little boy. The car swooped along very fast and I panicked, not knowing whether its expensive sophistication meant it didn't need a driver. I yelled, 'Am I driving this thing? *Am* I?' The adults just laughed.

———

Driving along Racecourse Road near the creek M and I saw a little white foxy veer off the footpath and tear across the road. The car in front of us hit it, paused and drove on. We both shrieked. I pulled over and parked. I could hear the dog crying out, it was lying on the road, no blood or guts, just squealing and thrashing. We ran back to it. A lady hopped out of a parked car and we stood around it keeping cars from running over it, and watched it die. I'd never seen that before—the life leave a creature—no, I've seen fish, and insects of course, but not a warm thing. I was horrified that I didn't know what to *do*, though some sense that everyone must have was informing me that it *was* dying and could not be saved. It stopped squealing, but its body was convulsing, big twitching shudders ran from its head down its torso and into its legs. Its eyes and mouth were open, the shudders became less frequent till I had to squat right down to make sure it wasn't just the wind of passing trucks making its hair riffle, and that's when I noticed that its eyes were quite still, wide open (brown) but not registering any response at all to the trucks and cars whizzing past only a few feet away. All this took about three minutes. When we saw that it was dead I was afraid to touch it. I was revolted by it and scared that it might still be alive, that if I picked it up I would hurt its broken spine terribly, and it might turn in pain and bite me. I thought, 'Am I too cowardly to pick up a little dead dog? How *disgusting*.' I got a jumper out of the boot and rolled him up in it. This was the worst part, because he was as warm as a live animal and yet *completely limp*. I've lifted up sleeping children a million times and thought I knew what limpness was but even a sleeping baby is springy compared with this dead dog. I carried him to a patch of grass and laid him on it. When I drew the jumper out from under him he flopped on his side and his face disappeared into the blades of grass. He didn't have a collar, yet he wasn't scruffy like a stray. We left him there and drove on. So that's what death looks like when it comes. His eyes so quickly lost their lustre.

A man is digging some boulders out of my front yard. Light flickers through the plane leaves and bounces off his faded pink windcheater. The dirt he is digging sends waves of a smell like mushrooms through my bedroom window.

Our dog has run away. I went to the Lost Dogs' Home. Awful pathos of the *sorting* of the dogs: small brown ones in one enclosure, big browns in another, whites and greys elsewhere: they will rush up to any visitor, even tilt their heads as if about to be photographed for a calendar.

In DJ's I found a good black coat for $425. I did not buy it because I can't afford it. Apropos black coats, P came out of *Wings of Desire* and spoke of it as if it had been a treatise on angelic powers, a topic she probably knows more about than did Wim Wenders.

I could write a novel about optimism, though maybe only a scientist could do it, for it seems to be metabolic, like a substance secreted by a gland so far undiscovered. I fall asleep tragic, but wake picaresque and humanist.

He lives in a squat monolith, and I live in an extremely tall, thin and airy tower. I've got a little mattress and blanket up near the top, and some binoculars through which I examine the bunker for signs of his life.

'I have read somewhere,' said the Polish philosopher, '—perhaps it was Jesus who said this—"You would not be looking for me if you had not already found me."'

I moved my bookshelf so I can have the big dictionary beside my desk.

'Illicit love between a married man and a married woman. The man abandons his wife and daughter in order to join the woman with whom he has fallen in love. Yet the deserted wife—a teacher who sincerely loves and admires her runaway husband—refuses to be broken by what has happened. "Not a single day shall be spoiled! They all belong to me. And that is that!'" —Chekhov, *Notebook*

———

Cholesterol test this morning. My arms were so cold that my veins were 'too fine', and the young technician could not draw blood. While she struggled I was afraid I might get an embolism and die in this ugly cubicle. She had to call in the other woman, who filled the tube from my left elbow-crook. I saw the red fill the tube and said, 'Bullseye.' 'Not bullseye,' replied the second technician. 'I had to shift it.' The first kept saying to me, 'Look away! Look away!' 'It's all right,' I said grandly. 'I'm not squeamish.'

———

To church. The best part was when my sister, all vested in white, stood up at the end, threw out her arms and cried, 'Go in peace, to love and serve the Lord!'

———

Such a late autumn that the Armenian lady next door is hitting the branches of her apricot tree with a broom to try to make its leaves come down.

———

The Polish philosopher and I sat in the front row at Melba Hall to hear Yvonne Loriod play (her husband) Olivier Messiaen's *Vingt regards sur l'enfant-Jésus*. She looked 'like any old housewife,' whispered my philosopher—loose, ageing skin, faded hair in a bun, pale-rimmed specs—a frumpish figure in a dress like a translucent Bedouin tent and old-fashioned gold sandals. She sat down with a lot of fussy rearranging of draperies, and placed several folded Kleenex under the piano's open lid: she dabbed at her nose with these between movements. Her hands and wrists showed great power. The music was difficult and rather wild: many times she laid down a grid of severe chords, which were then decorated or even assaulted by unresonant explosions in the upper registers. We enjoyed it very much indeed. At the end Olivier Messiaen himself stumbled on to the stage, a heavy-set, white-haired old man in a huge grey suit whose trouser top came up to his nipples. He kissed Loriod on both cheeks.

———

V's letter consists almost entirely of quotes from what he's been reading—Walter Benjamin, whom he describes several times as 'the true intellectual'. This irritates me, for some reason. I want to shake him and say, 'What does this silly phrase *M E A N* ?' I wish that instead of copying out Benjamin's recherché compliments and examining this amazing new feeling ('love') which I have somehow caused him to experience, he would materialise down here and *be a companion* to me. He's become a figment. I don't believe in him at the moment. I know he won't leave his wife. He would be wrong to, on every count, because I don't know if I want him to, because I may be finally unmarriageable, because I dread the death of sex and romantic love that domestic life entails, and because I don't know if I can handle the strain of our life as we are now living it. Fantasy: I say, 'Look, this is going nowhere. Let's decide to part,' or 'This isn't a life, for me. It's too difficult. I'm alone so much that I feel a bit crazy. Tell me what chance there is of our ever being together. If there's none, I'm saying goodbye, now, today.'

———

'So,' writes G, 'I find myself married and at the same time in a state of jealous panic because my "best friend", M-C, the object of my love, is going to marry her boyfriend. She said that the next night we spend together will be the last. "Why?!" I asked, dumbfounded. "What's different?" "I have to at least start this thing off on the right foot," she replied.'

———

My sister comes home from a day's emergency ESL teaching and tells me about the Vietnamese student who, when she asks the demoralised class to write a paragraph, writes, 'I do not understand the teacher. I damn myself. I feel like a mad and crazy lunatic.' When, distressed,

she shows this to their regular teacher he shrugs and says, 'Oh—
Hoah—he sits at the back. He's always quiet and well-behaved.'

———

A mild night at Primrose Gully. Koalas in the night made a colossal
racket, and something wailed. Mice nibbled patiently at food scraps
on the dirty dishes—a slide and a rustle when I went out to piss.
Many stars but very high, in huge wraiths of milky light, not bright,
not crackling, though perfectly clear. How small they were, how
far away.

———

Dreamt R had fallen asleep sitting on a sofa, her head on her arm.
I called her and like a mother she answered me before she was
properly awake. She was angry. Her eyes had a red glow.

———

Last night P and I quarrelled, perhaps for the first time in our
lives. A painful explosion. My sister overheard us shouting in the
kitchen and made a dash for the front door. We calmed down and
exchanged criticisms of each other's hurtful behaviours. We went to
bed chastened and sore. In the morning I heard her moving around
getting ready for church. Saw her through the venetians, all dressed
in white, hurrying out to her car. On the kitchen table she'd left me
a note, in her beautiful swooping hand: 'This is a new day. (Just
thought I would write something.)'

———

We watched *A Passage to India* by the fire. P told the story of her year
(1960) as an exchange student in Kansas City. She shook hands with
both Eisenhower and Kennedy. My sister very envious.

———

My emotional life is in suspension. The metal of it is dull, it doesn't
ring. Till I can slog my way to where he is.

———

The builder took off the old pergola. Suddenly the backyard is full
of sky.

At the hairdresser a young, plain, thin girl with a lot of make-up covering bad skin said to me as she rubbed away at my head over the basin, 'I love the way you dress.' 'Beg your pardon?' 'That long skirt with socks and flat shoes. It's like something out of a magazine.'

In Neilsen Park the astonishing beauty of Sydney in early winter: tremendous towers of cloud coloured delicately in greys and pinks, boats sliding or toiling, clear cool air. How can that hard-looking mouth be so soft?

After the reading, R and I had a long conversation with a poet about child abuse. The poet ran a very strong line against state interference in families. He said that the family is such a mysterious entity that what one family considers a normal expression of affection another would see as an intrusion on private space. He said that if the high percentage of women interviewed in a recent study who claim to have been sexually abused as children are telling the truth then we need either to redefine the word 'abused' or to realise that some things are simply part of 'the give and take of life' and as such should be accepted and chalked up. 'If all these people have really been abused, or if what happened to them were really psychologically damaging, then the whole fabric of *society* would have collapsed by now.' We tried to tell the poet that a woman or a girl deals with unwanted sexual attention by the unfortunate process of ceasing, during the moments when her body is submitting to the handling, to *inhabit herself.* We said we did not believe this process to be *a good thing.* Later, walking home, R said, 'He's on the side of the abuser, isn't he.'

An expression I heard a man use, in ironic quote marks but I don't know who if anyone he was quoting: 'the corrupt flexibility of women—the *diplomacy* of women'.

Marriage, in O's world-picture, has such a dense constellation of importance around it, such a thick cluster of *idées reçues*, of holiness, that my mind will never penetrate these galaxies of reverence.

Is it a dead end when you lose hope that the other still has the power to surprise you? And what does loyalty require of you, when in spite of this dead-end view you must acknowledge that what you are, what you have become, is to a large extent the outcome of what the other has given you—of their devotion to you, to your growth and your wellbeing?

I think I must *do voices* when I report direct speech: V shouts with laughter, doubles up in a silent paroxysm. I probably describe things in such a way that he feels we are closing ranks against the world.

At the exhibition some pictures that V liked left me completely without response, while a painting by a New Zealand woman of two overflowing vessels, which I 'understood' immediately without even having to think, did not touch him at all. I found it impossible to tell him why the painting meant something to me. Is this because I'm ignorant and inexperienced, or because I'm afraid he'll tease me and laugh at me, or because the language for talking about paintings is formed in such a way (i.e. by men) as to make my thoughts foreign to it? I suppose he doesn't need to worry about these things, since nothing he wants to say is excluded by its awkward form from the established discourse.

The English department gives me a big, pleasant office, but no typewriter. I sit down and write two pages of a story with a pencil sharpened by a machine to a long slender point. I am taken to morning tea and introduced to the famously domineering professor who of course (though I've heard I was not her choice of writer-in-residence) is charming, in a pale-blue fake suede jacket, with a confidence-inspiring handshake.

————

As dark fell, a sharp green evening light seemed to rise and rise into the upper registers of sky, leaving us *struggling mortals* down below.

————

I was about to write, 'This is a bad time of my life' then thought no, it's merely a short period of upheaval. Seeing the eagerly begun but unfinished Hildesheimer biography of Mozart beside my bed I fantasised V reproaching me for starting and not finishing a 'great book' and me bursting out at him, 'How can you expect me to read calmly, steadily, moving smoothly forward book after book as you do? Your life is stable. You sleep in the same house, the same bed every night, your hours are regular—but my life is fragmented, always moving and changing, and can't be otherwise if *yours* is to maintain its equilibrium.'

————

La Forza del Destino. Oh, to write such *fierce* events as are the domain of opera—murders, revenge, divine interventions!

————

I've learnt how to wait, and how to be alone, two very useful skills but which must be constantly and consciously *attended to*.

————

'His father went to jail.'
   'What for?'
   'Theft, I think. Embezzling, maybe.'
   'Embezzling's creepy, isn't it,' I said. 'Worse than straight-out theft. It's the betrayal of someone's trust over a long period.'
   Horrified that he might think I was referring obliquely to his behaviour towards his wife. But he didn't seem to notice, and went on talking.

————

Why are his thoughts so silent and oblique?

Because he is trying to behave loyally to her even while he betrays her.

———

G says his lungs are playing up again. He's giving up grog, coffee, cigarettes etc.

———

A dream of a neglected garden that stubbornly still bore fruit. Did it *belong* to me? I got to work clearing away weeds and grass.

———

Watching the gum trees go black while the sky is still full of light.

———

A dream about a middle-aged man in a boat? The boat capsizes? Then rights itself?

———

Night falls. In my small borrowed suburban flat with its shelves of uninteresting paperbacks (Leon Uris) I finish reading the Bellow and begin to cook a chop. I should think about the novel that keeps patiently presenting itself to me—fear that if I don't take up its offer soon it will give up on me and *go elsewhere*.

———

'Prayer is the contemplation of the facts of life from the highest point of view…It is the soliloquy of a beholding and jubilant soul.' —Emerson, *Self-Reliance*

———

R says that what gives one power is needing people less than they need you. 'Most people seem prepared to fritter away their time in socialising. To me it's always been a matter of the utmost urgency to get away by myself and read a book.' We couldn't stop laughing.

———

We fly in and out of moments of declaration with a kind of terrified speed and lightness.

———

My sister on the phone: 'When your postcard came and I read the last line it made me cry.'

'What the hell did I write?'

'About dreaming of a neglected garden that still bore fruit. I lay on the couch and cried for *hours*. I got slug eyes and everything.'

———

Me and V at the Brasserie with G who is thin and handsome, hair lying in its shining blond curls, dressed in a beautiful suit and a *white* white shirt whose cuffs were unbuttoned. G says, 'I want to be rich by the time I'm fifty-five.' 'Why do you want to be rich?' says V. 'Oh, I don't just want money. I want to get rich through record sales, or ticket sales. Through having done something good.'

———

Feeling ill, V puts his head in my lap while I'm driving. It's surprisingly heavy. The Yourcenar story about the outlaw and the priest's wife: she carries his severed head away wrapped in her apron.

———

The flowers in Nolan's *Boy in Township*. When I stare at them I feel like fainting, and want their colours to swallow me up.

———

By being decent, you only extend your own period of suffering. I said, 'I'm not waiting for you to leave. That's not what I'm doing.' But the truth is more like: 'Tell me whether you ever will, or whether I must accept that the rest of my life will involve this complicated, delicate balancing act. What hurts me is the suspense.' I didn't say this. But I must.

———

Biographies in which artists change wives without apparent outrage or destruction (because the tale is told from the artist's point of view) give the false impression that it can be done cleanly, without the charred flesh and gouged innards.

———

Worked clumsily all morning, fumbling and feeling my way, hating some of it, respecting some, trying to balance the sentences and make them flow.

———

W's small tinny, the dash with which she pilots it across from Palm Beach wharf. She says she has learnt to see in the dark and never needs a torch. I slept on a low, comfortable bed with pale-pink sheets, a dark-pink eiderdown, an ancient wool blanket of the most beautiful dark green. A proper reading lamp. Three well-chosen books.

———

Seeing one of her yoga commentaries on the bedside table and a photo of her guru on the wall, I resolve that I will never be scornful of someone else's spiritual struggles or moments of enlightenment—not even gently dreamy ones like P's or stiff, forbidding ones like the born-again's. I can be sceptical but never scornful. And if I want to write about them, I bloody well *will*. Get rid of the biographer and her threats.

———

A wonderful TV remake of *The Shiralee*. The little girl trotting gamely after the uncompromising man—this is how I dragged my girl through her childhood, paying no attention to her complaints.

———

At dinner the men shouted about 'the regional' in Australian art. One of them ran a patriot's line. The other said that any art had to pass over the barrier between the regional and the universal—he roared about Henry Lawson: 'He drags us down.'

———

'Till you pointed it out to me, I thought people still wore their shirt collar *out* of a round-necked jumper.'

———

This English department office is the wrong place for me to work. Every time I write something on a piece of paper I look at it and think, gee, that's not very sophisticated. I've got to get out of here.

Late in the afternoon a moon (full) bounced in a sky powdered with green and pink. Water like yellow silk, like aluminium. At Bondi some satisfying sand-coloured stones were being picked up in mouthfuls by a machine and arranged in baskets made of cyclone wire, which were then laid in a freshly dug hole against the sea wall. A man welded. His cold spark.

Is it menopausal that (1) I often wake up at night damp with sweat? (2) my period comes six days early and lasts two days and nights, then abruptly stops?

Rang Mum for her birthday. When I heard Dad call her to the phone a heavy sense of their marriage crashed over me. This *arrangement* that has lasted nearly half a century, produced six kids, is indispensable to both of them—but what has it done for them? Crushed my mother and made her spirit weak, and frustrated my father: made each of them less than they might otherwise have been. And yet it has survived many periods of unhappiness and cruelty. By comparison I feel my life to be once again light, transparent, almost gauzy, composed of filaments rather than blocks of concrete.

Five people in a room this evening told me I was 'extremely pale'. I'd been quite faint and wild with pleasure all day long, shaping sentences, juggling the pages, trying to get sense and pace into them without flattening the imagery or becoming even the smallest bit explanatory—trying to trim adjectives without losing the sensuous detail they afford—and feeling the shape of the story changing under my attentions—it expands, becomes richer, more leisured and yet still *packed*. I ate things, cleaned up, walked from room to room, thought, wrote again. In my absences from it I could sense its faults of structure, pace and narrative. Got to stop it from galloping away.

Maybe, if we have to part, what I'll miss most of all is talking with him about what we're reading. Always ready to bear a parting. We compete to be the more stoical, I think.

———

Mooching through the Macquarie I come upon 'ablative absolute', a Latin case. The example given is: '*via facta*—the road having been made.' The blunt brevity and portmanteau power of this two-word clause convulse me with envy and frustration.

———

Dreamt of a sturdy, bright shrub, waist-high, that was growing on the extreme lip of a precipice near which I stood, some feet back from the edge. Beyond this plant was empty air, a chasm I couldn't see but whose presence was palpable and which contained a huge, smoke-blue hum of significance. I was trying in this dream to compose a sentence that would encapsulate the existence of this plant: its flowers were an explosive red, it grew with vigour, its branches sprang out from its stem in a satisfying, meaningful shape. The fact that it grew on the very rim of nothingness was of no concern to it. It grew, it was firmly rooted, it blossomed, it *was*.

———

Mozart and Mahler at the Opera House. I tell Z I've bought us the cheap tickets. He props in the kitchen: 'In the *orchestra*? You'll get deafened!'—as if he were suddenly no longer of the party. The seats turn out to be perfectly adequate. The Mahler I did not know. I liked its stereo effect—cowbells, knocking percussion, terrific horns; but though it carried me away I could see why people make jokes about it—all that torment. A colossal rainstorm exploded overhead as we were leaving. Every rubbish bin we stumbled past contained at least one broken umbrella. Water lashed across the road as if a powerful hose were being played from the top of a building.

———

The jumping force field of *interest* between V and me, both mutual and outward, that makes the world seem so rich and teeming with spectacle. His pen moves fast and light across a sheet of paper. The way he can physically put words down makes my pen seem a log.

———

I am always reminding myself that he is not mine, that he belongs to somebody else, that it's not safe to fantasise being with him always. This is the precipice; but on its lip the bush flowers fiercely, *taking no thought for the morrow.*

———

I know, from my own experience, that people can recover from things. And I can't see the end of a marriage as the end of a life. 'Life goes on,' says R. 'It *must* go on. It can't stop.' 'And it can't go back?' I say. 'No,' she says, 'it can't go back.' In a blighted cafe in Rozelle V and I share a small bottle of mineral water. I feel deeply appalled that he's started the process of extrication. My thighs on the seat feel weak. I'm not seeing properly. Terror of the magnitude of these events. And grief. For *them*, and their marriage.

———

Bartók's second string quartet. Some of those harmonies sound like brown wood.

———

Men's horror of the *unreasonableness* of our emotions, the tidal nature of our moods, the way they expand and explode. Men are afraid of losing the *shape* of things, even momentarily.

———

What am I blithely handing over, here? Tonight, walking to give my lecture, carrying my briefcase and feeling unmarriageable and neutrally solitary, I felt a dropping heart at the idea of becoming half of a middle-aged couple. Comfort myself by remembering nonsense and play with F—how even now, after everything that's happened, we can still *have fun* together.

———

'They that have power to hurt and will do none.'

———

Moments of terrible, groggy shock. And yet underneath it the sense of something logically unfolding. It doesn't feel bad, or wrong, to me. The wake slaps me around but the pain I'm getting is vicarious.

———

What am I doing this evening? A trifling question. Doing the ironing. Listening to some music. Reading. Hoovering white fluff off the carpet. Upstairs, muffled, a choir is singing the Lacrimosa from Mozart's *Requiem*.

———

Chicken pieces (?). Cold Power $3.75. Two chops $1.19. Coloured clouds in a low bank over the city, packed there as if to act as dense padding for the bridge's tough curve. The pretty young woman serving in the grocery shop made me feel her fingertips, to show how cold they were.

———

R calls, I give a shout of joy. My dear friend. It's taken me years of work on myself to become worthy of her. I often doubt that I am.

———

A whole life can be spent quietly and patiently drawing nearer to something important. It can't be hurried. This is why there is no such thing as boredom.

———

Violets grow in a pot on the porch of this apartment. I picked some and put them in a glass. At the moment of picking they have no scent, but half an hour later, sitting here, I notice something faintly delicious and turn around. The violets have opened further, become purpler, are in their small way terribly beautiful.

———

Every morning I wake in a sweat. Where one of my knees has rested on the mattress there's a little round pool.

———

The dying man's shaven head is resting on a blue gauze pad. His wife and I go out to the lift so she can fiercely smoke. She lets tears pour. The smoke bumps its way across the thick curls of her permed hair. I ask, 'Is there any comfort? What are you living on?' 'I believe certain things,' she says. 'They're useful to me. I believe there's a chance of more than one life. I believe this because for there to be one thing in nature which made no sense and contradicted itself would be illogical.' We are sitting in two chairs, talking intently, tears running off our cheeks. Our voices are low, but audible to anyone who cares to listen. A teenage girl comes out of the lift and sits down facing us, very close, her forearms along the armrests of her chair. She sits like a judge or a witness, and gazes straight at us. Neither of us takes any notice. When his wife stops crying, her eyes are very widely spaced, full of life and feeling. I walk out through the huge front entrance. Late in the afternoon. Birds are calling very loudly in the trees along Missenden Road. A quick shot of *being alive*. Their song is so loud, it's as if my lively ears had magnified it. Walk along sobbing and gasping.

––––––––

The Queen's drawing collection at the gallery. Appalled to see the little ER stamp of ownership in the corner of each one—on a *Leonardo*! A *Michelangelo*! What a hide these people have got. An Annunciation: an angel with arms spread and knees still flexed from landing. Glad to have gone alone.

––––––––

I told R that even in a ghastly split-up there are certain moments of truce, where both people laugh freely, as if for that moment seeing each other truly and deeply and without rancour. She said, 'How interesting.'

––––––––

In Melbourne our dog has run away twice. She trotted all the way from North Melbourne to Fitzroy and arrived drenched and dirty at F's front door, behind which he was at his desk reworking somebody's terrible French translation of *Monkey Grip*: 'The rhythm of the French sentence is different from the English and with not enough words to play with it is at times difficult to get the music right.'

————

A teenage girl gets knocked off her bike at a crossing, in front of a bunch of pedestrians. She goes flying. She is wearing a helmet and has only skinned her elbow, but she sobs with anger and fright, sweating, trembling, a dark red flush down one side of her neck and shoulder. The driver, an old man grey with shock, gets out of his car and approaches. She yells at him in a student, self-righteous way, tears and dirt streaking her round cheeks. As soon as he sees she is not seriously hurt he makes as if to return to his car, but an Arab truck driver pulls up and the old man is returned by the combined moral force of the silent group to face the raging girl. 'You don't even *care*!' 'I *do* care!' he cries. 'I care very much! I have two daughters!' He says it was her fault. We all say no, it was his, and he becomes greyer and smaller, mumbling, 'I'm sorry, I'm sorry. Thank you.' 'Those wheels,' she shouts, shaking and sobbing, 'cost *one hundred and seventy-five dollars!*' I keep my hand on her shoulder: 'Don't ride home. You're in shock.' The truckie offers to drive her home. She refuses, and wheels her beautiful (undamaged) bike away. 'It was an accident,' says a man, and we all go about our business.

————

Babette's Feast. The artist's cry: 'Let it be possible for me to do the very best I can!' I went home smaller, ashamed of my agitated idleness, my unfinished story.

————

The officer-students at the Australian Defence Force Academy, their trim heads and uniforms, their marching gait with high-swinging arms: they have to fall into step if they walk anywhere in groups of two or more. The only place they don't have to salute is *in the library*. At breakfast in the hotel my father was the only man not in uniform. I said, 'You want to look out someone doesn't hand you a white feather.'

Watching the TV news my father says, 'What's the point of showing us Israeli soldiers shooting round corners? They see the cameras. They're just putting on an act.'

'You mustn't pity her,' I said to V. 'Your pity will weaken her. What she needs is your respect.'

My mother knitted as we talked, showing the best of herself—talkative, but not droning. V was sweet to her, asking her the direct questions he's so good at: 'Do you like having so many children?' 'How did they let you know your brother had been killed?' She told him things I'd never heard before. She mentioned a childhood friend called Florrie Beanland. He threw back his head and shouted with laughter: 'Nobody's called Florrie Beanland!'

V said that women look 'ugly and old' when they cry. R to my surprise agreed. I protested. I said that once I'd cried for three days and then got out of bed, looked in the mirror, and found I looked 'gorgeous—all soft and young'. They burst out laughing, having expected 'raddled', I suppose. We agreed that the final effect of crying was often relief and that this could take away ageing tensions.

I took Mum to the Opera House, to see *Otello*. We both had to wipe our eyes, loving the music. She said, 'It made me think of Dad. That jealousy of nothing.' Oysters at the quay. On the bus we were quiet, gazing out the window at the city, this spectacle. 'Everything is older, here,' she said. 'I wish I didn't have to leave.' At Via Veneto we ran into L and the Cretan. The Greeks were charming and funny, behaved towards Mum with gentle respect, shook her hand upon leaving.

'Your mother strikes me,' says R's son, 'as as someone who doesn't often enjoy herself. She seemed to be surprised whenever she laughed.'

———

Etty Hillesum's diary. Her father visits. All our good intentions, she thinks, are *as nothing* before the huge negative force of our feelings towards our parents. The best that's possible is intense self-control.

———

'I lied,' said V.

———

We talked at dinner about fights where plates were thrown. I said I'd loved the machine in *The Rake's Progress* that turned broken crockery into bread: 'I wish I'd had one of those when I was married to F.' 'Oh!' said Z. 'Did you smash things? I've always dreamt of that. I've only ever been close to people who sulked.' 'There's a wonderful moment,' I said, 'when you hear the *sound* of the smash, but it's very short, and then you have to clean up the mess. You have to get down on your knees.'

———

On the spare bed at R's in the afternoon I try to sleep, counting my breathing, but wide awake. Something's gone. I know what it is: the necessity for stoicism. A hard jacket's been taken off me. At first what I notice about its absence is a kind of blank surprise—then a fencelessness. My thoughts no longer run up against the monolith. I lie under the cheap quilt, calm, empty, complete, as if at the end of some trial. 'The monolith.' That smashed thing. Full of holes. Air and light now pass through its breached walls. Who's responsible?

———

A novelist gives a boring, shallow lecture. Why don't people say what they have learnt about life and what they believe in? I don't think artists should presume to speak unless they are prepared to say something serious—even if they're obliged to slip it in among the fluffed-up egg-whites like a bitter pill.

———

'One thing your wife's done for you all these years is to create around you a cushion of comfort and attention. Hasn't she.' Staggered to see he has no idea he is dependent on this. Men who will not stoop to teach themselves the domestic skills and talents that women possess (or have had to cultivate): they live in a mess, without attractive comforts, waiting for some woman to arrive in a fluster bearing gifts, ready to set the place to rights.

———

I cooked spinach with butter and garlic. He made no comment and ate it without apparent relish. Perhaps he is going to be discontented and hard to please.

———

It feels like spring, and the shops are full of linen clothes not very well cut.

———

What causes stupidity? And what *is* it?

———

Going along the quay I saw the Opera House sails against a perfectly pure sky at sunset: they were *mauve*, the most delicate colour—such beauty, and soon I might be living in the city where it can occur.

———

A man on the building site sings aloud with a joyful shout—a falling and rising riff, like a warrior singing about battle.

———

R said enthusiastically that Emerson had 'anticipated certain concepts in depth psychology'. V's face lost all expression, like a blackboard just wiped. 'Projection, for example,' R continued, soldiering on. 'The idea that we project on to others what is inside us.' He had no word to say. I laughed and went out into the kitchen.

———

I'm tired. My life's in limbo because he has not told the whole truth.

———

Visited a class at Glebe High School. The usual scornful, bored, closed faces one would expect in fourth-formers but the teacher used his imagination, and we got somewhere. The girls were very retiring. The bell went and the boys scattered; then the girls gathered in a tight group around me and the teacher. A Chinese girl asked, 'Do artists have—strange moods?' Another, packing her books, said over her shoulder to the teacher, 'But teaching's an art, sir, I reckon.' I don't know if it's an art, but I remember that it's hard labour: the cold modern building, the inarticulate kids—I take off my hat to teachers.

———

'You said I was emotionally naïve,' said V. 'What did you mean?'

'I don't think you know much about the fluctuations of emotions that people go through in their relations with each other.'

'But I've been married. And as an artist I've observed.'

'Yes, but your life hasn't depended on it.'

———

I walked a mile along streets near the dilapidated Canberra motel, looking for something to eat. I passed sad, neglected-looking buildings, cheap home units with blankets hooked over their windows. Yards of beaten earth. Arrangements of chicken wire and boxes near the gates—cages, but with no animals in them.

———

Her anxiety, at the meeting. Her super-willingness to grasp my points. Her eager face, the poised pen, the notebook.

———

R says that now is the time when I should consider what giving up my separateness could mean, that if I live with him I will of necessity become 'cook and bottle-washer'. Painfully I consider these propositions. But how could I not live with him? Could I fight him about the housework? Could I make demands and hold out for them?

———

In the cafe R and I agreed that we were probably rather androgynous and that we liked this. I said I felt I was physically made of a dryer, harder substance than some more feminine women. She said she wished in fantasy to be an opera singer, but that she could 'never bear that burden of flesh'. The paradoxical, or contradictory, idea that in order to produce an ethereal, heavenly or superhuman sound one must be even *more* fleshly than ordinary humans.

———

Two sparrows fuck on a twig outside the window. He hops on to her back and off, she flutters her wings very fast against her body, he hops on again—they do this five times within two minutes.

———

The empty apartment, a shell of fantasy, not a single stick of furniture, a long space full of light.

———

The sick man died, at last. By now he will be only a pile of hot ash and crumbled bones. The part of him that suffered has been consumed. But his wife. What will she do with all the love?

———

'At our little girl's funeral,' said the woman, 'I fell over.'
  'Do you mean you fainted?'
  'No, I didn't faint.'
  'Did you trip?'
  'No. I couldn't stand. I fell down.'

———

After the service we walked on the beach. E was very vivid and pretty in her black crepe skirt and jacket and her pink blouse with black spots. The escarpment looms over the road and the town. By four the day is ended.

———

In Bar Italia he looked narrower, paler, with darker eyes. I couldn't look at him enough, the sight of him was so precious to me.

———

U's Englishman went back to Cambridge, where she was meant to join him; but somehow she just never went. I imagine returning to

Melbourne and quietly sinking back into my previous life—as if these recent upheavals had occurred in some opium trance. I know this is a kind of death wish, a slide into inertia. But these fantasies have occurred.

————

The child is doing her homework, making a list of twenty-six things (A–Z) that Captain Cook would have taken on his journey: 'N?'
    H: 'Nibs.'
    Her older brother: 'They would have had quills, not nibs.'
    H: 'I bet they had nibs.'
    Brother: (*smoothly*) 'They didn't invent nibs till 1830.'
    H: 'You just made that up.'
    Brother: 'No I didn't. I read it in a history of calligraphy that came with my italic nib set.'

————

We will learn a great deal about each other now.

————

Fear makes people literal-minded.

————

Dreamt I bought a pair of black high-heeled shoes and wore them with socks. Pleased with my appearance. But when I met my sister in a cafe and asked her if she liked them, she said, 'No. You look about fifty in them.' She hadn't waited for me, had already ordered her breakfast. I crept away wounded, with hunched shoulders.

————

To P's show. I looked out the gallery window through the rain to Government House with its little flag, took a breath, and began. I realised that each picture contains hidden things: a sheep on a globe, two little yachts: you could look at them for a long time and be always finding her secret messages. And best of all is the way she puts on the paint: nothing lumpy or bumpy; nothing *thick*. A svelte surface, sometimes with a golden note or a glimmer in it, seeming to have been built up out of many very fine layers.

———

'V's aged a great deal,' said his friend, 'over the last few years. He's an old-fashioned Australian country man who's passionately interested in modern European culture.' 'He's always struck me,' I said, 'as someone the modern world has passed by. It's as if he hasn't even *noticed* it.'

———

My nun's long, detailed story of arriving at the decision to leave the Little Sisters of Jesus. Of choosing life above a promise. 'I don't know what I've missed and what I haven't missed.' I listened with full attention, fascinated, watching her face as she spoke: her smooth skin, her bones, her curly grey hair in its pretty crop.

———

In the newspaper a list of 'the suits men buy: navy 60%, charcoal-grey 25%, mid-grey 12%, brown 2%, other 1%'.

———

V inveighs against the 'tribal' urge of women to 'rush in' and support each other when one of them's 'discarded'. What the hell does he expect women to do? I hold my tongue, remembering having to lie on the floor with the pain of being 'discarded'.

I ask, 'How are you?'

He replies, levelly and vaguely, 'Oh…all right.'

I feel foolish, reproached for having asked. Maybe he expects me to *probe*, since he is not forthcoming. I start to see what I could be in for.

———

Wonderful spring day, little perfumed gusts of daphne, freesias, the very beginning of pittosporum. Windows rattle in the balmy wind. What a dry city Melbourne is: its winds come in off dry, grassy plains, while Sydney's come off water. I wrote several extremely long sentences, the labour of which afforded me the most exquisite pleasure and satisfaction.

———

At the kitchen table with a pot of tea and a packet of Venetian biscuits I recommence *À la Recherche du temps perdu* (in English). My life now is likely to be filled with change, upheavals, departures, lies, white lies, damned lies, and a host of anxieties and sorrows. I need a large-structured element in which to rest and which I can step in and out of without fear of having lost the thread.

———

A puppy yapping in someone's yard woke me at 1 am and I couldn't fall asleep for ages. Why are night thoughts always so much more pessimistic, sorrowful and panicky than thoughts on the same topics in daylight?

———

The old woman showed me her Kakadu photos. 'See? That thing there's a crocodile. They're brown, and they're scaly, and we've intruded on to their territory.'

———

F calls to ask me a language question. Now it's over I remember how much I *like* him. He must never have had my full attention. I could begin to torture myself about this. Walking to church rehearsing my cruelty, selfishness, neglect, I wondered if there's a way to free oneself of guilt, of finally squaring it with oneself so that the load drops off. The first hymn we sang mentioned 'cancelled crimes'.

———

New kitchen doors and windows are in. Chaos but room full of light. I sit at the table eating my breakfast and gazing out at SKY. Royalties $3000. Can I spin this out for four months?

———

Crazy about the way Proust uses physical objects to keep his huge, billowing sentences grounded.

———

In my freshly painted kitchen I turn on the heating, spread out my papers on the tablecloth, and entertain a treacherous fantasy: a fantasy to protect me from *the fear of failure* which is, I think, what I am 'suffering from': I *wish* for failure so that once again I will be free to spread out my papers on this tablecloth. 'I'd like to retire there and do *nothing*,/ or nothing much, forever, in two bare rooms.' —Elizabeth Bishop, 'The End of March'

———

A doona that's been folded, but flat, so it resembles a worn-out asparagus drooping sadly rather than 'a wafer' or a small clean cloud.

———

I am a woman. I (i) long to be of service (ii) like domestic order (iii) am socially quite skilful—at organising lists of appointments etc (iv) can do basic cooking (v) feel an urge to fill gaps where otherwise chaos, awkwardness, discomfort (physical, emotional, social) might occur (vi) like to make practical demonstrations of love. All I need to attend to is that I keep enough of myself free for my work and the hours of private mental time this requires. I mean that my attention to him and his needs should not outweigh my attention to myself for work. '*All* I need'! This terribly hard thing, for a woman.

———

The perfume of pittosporum cuts the air, sharp as lemons. The form of its foliage—puffed, rounded flounces, each lying on the next layer down—in heavy cascades. The leaves are shiny and the flowers fan out in waxy sprays.

———

'I don't even *like* women. It's terrible to say this but women drive most blokes crazy.'

'I'm a woman too, you know.'

'Ah, no. You're different.'

———

Dreamt I said to the hairdresser, 'I want my hair to be purple, and curly.' She gave me a doubtful, ironic look and I said, disgruntled, 'Oh, all right then, just take off a bit over the ears.'

———

The French woman is sixty but looks twenty-five years younger. Her youthful bounce, her round face. I liked her for having on under her red and yellow dress a grubby old white T-shirt. The spectacle of the grim Anglo-Saxon man softened by Gallic flirtatiousness is comical, he is so unselfconsciously *keen* on her, so impressed by her unAustralian, unmasculine quality. 'She's got a marvellous *spirit*,' he raves later, then pulls himself up and his voice fades: 'Oh, so have you—I've always liked *your*, um, spirit…' 'Oh, for God's sake!' I burst out, in a spasm of embarrassment. 'You don't have to talk about me! *I* liked her, too!' How on earth is it possible to behave with grace in this bombed-out minefield between men and women?

———

I must stop being *passive*. I must work out exactly what I need, and start arranging things so I can *have* it.

———

Backyard ravaged, rubbish gone, my essentials halfway to Sydney. Very shaky inside, afraid, sad, guilty.

———

My brother and his wife say goodbye to me in Lygon Street: their baby in his adventurous blue cap with earflaps; this adorable, reticent child. Whenever he smiles he turns his face away, as if to hide his merriment.

———

My sisters packed my car for me: their brisk, cheerful practicality. It was soon done and I had this neat vehicle layered with a weird selection of my worldly possessions. They spread the tartan rug over the lot 'to prevent distracting glare if the sun shines in'.

———

5 am. Viscount Motel, Albury. Somewhere birds are singing madly—showers and blasts of trills. In the night mother-guilt fell on me like a ton of bricks, memories of M's early childhood, its upheavals. I lay here tired and disoriented. Thought of 'cancelled

sins', of 'absolution', 'forgiveness'. All these manifestations of grace that I long for.

———

At Goulburn stopped for food. A 'Lilac Festival' in a park with no lilacs in evidence. A sign outside a tent, its gist: 'Don't get the idea that to get into heaven you only have to lead a good life, go to church etc—you also MUST BELIEVE that Christ died for you person-ally.' Sorry but nobody's going to tell me what I MUST BELIEVE. How can anyone MUST BELIEVE anything?

———

E's pretty, English-seeming house in Enmore—the heavy old blue-and-white crockery, the white-framed doors opening on to a narrow back garden full of trees. A good piano, and she too is a beginner. I take courage. Very much at ease with her, felt liked and treated with affection. She has offered me the upstairs front room. Two French windows that face east (or is it north?) and let in the noise of distant trains. I have brought two lamps, two kitchen dishes, my enamel saucepan, some rubber gloves, the filing cabinet and my white Ikea clothes rack.

———

He made some ravioli with sauce out of a jar. It was delicious.

———

Swam ten laps at 6 am. Now I feel my stomach muscles. Read some Hemingway, then Carver again. Carver's middle period. Large respect for him, the jagged voices, the catastrophes, the spare language and the striving for spare imagery. In such a landscape of struggle, panic, despair, the old images he uses have a deep and emblematic power. *The hem of the garment.* The simple becomes tremendous.

———

F: 'You seem to have a very powerful influence on people and they tend to find it necessary to break away from you and more often than not they do it the hard way.'

———

I said I did not know the skills of sharing a life with someone. V said I'd be okay as long as I did not 'behave briskly—with brisk independence'. I felt chastened, as if *taught*. 'I'm not a tyrant, am I?' he said. 'I think you're probably the kind of tyrant,' I said, 'who simply assumes things will be done the way he likes them, and if they're not he's surprised and rather hurt.'

———

Thick emotions in conflict. There is always the shadow side of our happiness. The private thought of his wife alone in their house. He speaks of her, but not of it. Perhaps all happiness has its shadow, or has to be supported by the sorrow of someone else. Sometimes the longing to see my girl is *sharp*. I feel it 'in my breast', as poets say. My heart and lungs are obliged to toil at their work instead of behaving with natural rhythm.

———

I went to Grace Bros and bought some cream paint. Stood waiting to cross Broadway and thought vaguely, 'This is Sydney and I live here now.'

———

V's friend W came to his place for dinner. She was tall and handsome in a shapeless, burnt-orange cotton dress pulled in with a leather belt. Bare legs, orange Chinese slippers. In his presence I notice her mannerisms of mouth and face, her persona which is 'open', 'good-tempered', 'intelligent', 'funny' etc. We watched the Ellis–Harkin fight on TV. Two young, smooth-bodied fellows battering at each other's heads. When a boxer drops his head and puts up his big stupid gloves to protect it I feel the kind of rage and pity I'd feel if I saw a child having to ward off a blow.

———

In E's balcony room I slept for eleven hours. Light and air of a clarity so perfect that a gum-tree branch outside my window looks transparent: light coming at it from every side.

'Our desires cut across one another, and in this confused existence it is rare for happiness to coincide with the desire that clamoured for it.' —Proust, *Within a Budding Grove*

In the unfinished house high above the ocean the new widow served three of us a large and delicious meal. She was composed, friendly, ready to laugh; but her face, Z said on the way home, was 'tired, and full of sorrow'. We were all writers. Z talked about the way one can't believe, looking back on a book, that in order to write it one went through gruesome stages of uncertainty, fear, ignorance—because the published book looks like the result of certain smoothly taken decisions, the product of a mind functioning *consciously*. Relieved that this happens even to someone as famous as Z.

Dreamt that V's wife drove up to my house in a car packed with her belongings; it had been arranged that she could store them all at my place. I offered to give her a hand. The house lacked storage space but I saw I could pile her things up against a wall in my bedroom, which was enormous, bare, dim and pleasant, with floorboards and a shuttered window; they wouldn't be in the way, and I could keep an eye on them for her.

V showed me some drawings by a painter with a very big reputation. 'He had a problem with facility. He was lazy. He didn't fight it so it all looks too easy.' 'What's your facility?' 'In writing? I haven't got one. But I have to fight my habit of putting in little jokes that nobody but me will understand for fifty years.'

In Chippendale, a man in thick-rimmed glasses was pulling down the charred remains of a back fence, shed and dunny. He worked grimly, alone and in silence, and his whole face, front and forearms were stained black with ash, like a figure in a vision of hell.

I try to write a letter like someone in a Don DeLillo novel: 'I am doing my best here to dress and groom, by mending things from earlier days, but in my closet there's a chaos that's enormous. I lost my little grey suitcase, how come, which I'm permanently sad and disappointed. This is for the present time goodbye, believe me, your poor sister…'

I thought today that I would like to write a novel in which physical violence would occur.

Walked with V along the cliff path to Bronte. We sat on the grass and surveyed the outrageous beauty of the scene. I began to see why he's spent twenty years inside a house. The ocean was *chirping* with light.

R tells me she is thinking of training as a Jungian analyst. Thinking of this extremely suitable proposition, and after reading a severe article about German literature, I feel ignorant, lacking in intellectual power or organising ability. I'm not and never will be a real intellectual. It's not my nature. I forget things, and am distracted by surface sparkle. I will probably never write anything large, lasting, solid or influential. Is this a proper life I am leading? It is a kind of half-life—living secretly in a strange city, asking people to lie for me and cover my tracks.

I never knew before the difference between sadness and sorrow. Sadness is general, broad, heavy, passive. Sorrow is sharper, more focused, more active, working hard. I could even say labouring. Labouring with sorrow. When I think of his wife's unhappiness, my own 'indignities' almost vanish—because the reason he gives for requiring them is to save her from further pain. He does not see that this is unlikely to work, in the long run.

The 'civilised' world is full of wounded people. I don't know what could alter this.

V showed me a couple of American short stories he likes: Irwin Shaw, 'The Girls in Their Summer Dresses' and 'Mixed Doubles' and then one by Cheever, 'The Enormous Radio'. They brought me up once more against the hopelessness of men and women, the vast chasms between them—the death of sexual love, wandering attention, physical degeneration, men's wide-ranging sexual fantasies and greed. At the market we had a stupid quarrel about a melon. In the car he wouldn't meet my eye, and down I plummeted. I longed to say, 'What happened? What's gone wrong?' but I was scared he'd say, 'Nothing! You're neurotic! You're imagining it!'

R is the only person I know who can make comments on people's behaviour and character—very sharp and accurate comments—without descending into judgment. She is like a scientist.

Peter Carey wins the Booker for *Oscar and Lucinda*. We confess to each other, with shameful laughs, a small sinking sensation. 'He and I started out at about the same time,' says V, 'but he threw it into overdrive and now all I can see of him is his tail-lights.' I realise how differently we think about our work in the world: I see that he is able to imagine his work in that league, while to me it is not even thinkable—it never crosses my mind.

G comes over. V becomes attentive but oddly passive. G drinks vodka with beer chasers and is soon slumping loosely: 'Am I slurring my words?' H: 'Yes, but you're making perfect sense.' He reports that Jane Campion's new movie has a sequence in which a woman goes out into the desert with her father. I feel relieved, as if my film won't need to be made after all. We watch him get into his Merc, reverse down the street at sixty kph and disappear.

———

Hot weather a bit alarming due to news reports of THE GREENHOUSE EFFECT: it's only the end of October but yesterday it was thirty-six degrees, exactly like a day of high summer in Melbourne—gusty winds, dry air, gasping sun, white sky.

———

My lovely bed at E's. Clean, comfortable, welcoming. In the morning, she suggests laps at the Enmore pool. We swim separately, without speaking, wrapped in our separate thoughts.

———

G calls and relates an extraordinary tale, like something by Beaumarchais or from a French movie, about going with M-C to a fitting of her wedding dress, pretending to be 'a gay hairdresser, picking up her hair and saying, "What are you going to do with this?" I saw a little silk slip, you know, really short, and I said, "I'll give you this as a wedding present, you can wear it on your wedding night!"' All the while, telling me this in a melancholy, sighing voice, he is dragging on a cigarette or a joint, breathing in, breathing out.

———

When I reported this to V, he launched a leisurely disquisition on women, beauty, clothes, their responsibilities in this regard. I lost my temper, argued wildly about the injustice of women's position as *regarded creatures* who are constantly obliged to think carefully about their self-presentation—the neurotic obsession with one's appearance that results from this. I tried to examine my physical sensations in order to grasp what was going on—a heaviness and sense of turmoil under the ribcage. V seemed puzzled and surprised by how 'cranky' I got, and as I calmed down I felt ashamed of my intemperance—but I wonder if in the end he was trying to argue me round to the point at which *women can't be artists*. If we reached this point, it would mean either (1) that I am barking up the wrong tree in my life or (2) that I am something *other than a woman*. After this we watched 'Murphy's Law' on TV. Quite horrible how one sits there with one's beloved's legs across one's lap and watches people kill, bash, stab, rape and insult each other on a nasty little flickering screen.

Venetian paintings at the gallery, with R. A small Adam and Eve being driven out of the garden by an angel whose wings are a blur of gold; an Annunciation—angel in flight, in a crushed blue garment, holding a single tall and perfect lily; a Virgin whose cloak, of a profound and mouth-watering crimson, is knotted over her belly in the dead centre of the picture.

V said he needed to buy 'a strong kitchen chair'. I said, with a quick vision of my kitchen in Melbourne, 'I've got a pretty set of four…' and suddenly my heart thumped to the floor. I said, 'I'm homesick.' He laughed. On my way back to E's I thought, 'Tomorrow I will be forty-six. And for a while there I lived in a house which was MINE.' Oh, shut up.

Last time I visited R her son was bumptious with me and we squabbled. Today he was subdued and sweet. He complimented me on my white backpack and said it matched a white hat I'd had on the other day. I accepted his atonement with relief.

V said to me that I had 'an extraordinary mind—you think things right through, by prisming them through yourself. Your mind is ten times as good as mine.' What? Doesn't he see my laziness? My disinclination to *think*?

I turn up at his place on the evening of my birthday, an hour early, wearing heels and a long skirt, thinking he had invited me to dinner. He has no food: 'I didn't know whether you were going to bring it.' He returns to the typewriter. I am completely without resources, standing at the bench in my inappropriate clothes, nothing to do, a non-guest, a non-person. So I leave without further discussion and drive back to E's, and here I am in a *room which is mine*, in comfortable clothes, having abandoned all sense of occasion. I sit here missing my family. I am forty-six and *I exist*. I *do*.

———

A letter from Dad. 'Thank you for the pencil sharpener. I have sharpened every pencil I ever had and the little drawer is nearly full of shavings.'

———

A growing affection for E. Her seriousness and self-discipline. My spirits rise in her house, with its tall windows and slanting light. She says things like this: 'I was the only one in the pool this morning. Sun was crinkling along the bottom.' We like to talk about everything. She says she has femocrat friends who earn up to $70,000. 'What do they *spend* it on?' 'They take taxis. They haven't got time to cook so they eat out four nights a week. They have to look good—they spend a lot on elegant clothes.' She told me she'd met a man at a party who was a psychologist at Silverwater prison. He said that the people in jail who are most 'like oneself', most likely to examine themselves and change, are the murderers.

———

'I'm becoming fussily pedantic in supermarkets or whatever you call 'em.'

　'What you call "being fussily pedantic" other people call "shopping".'

———

We quarrel over his demand for furtiveness. I find it humiliating. He says I've over-reacted to a minor event. I say he doesn't know how minor or major this incident is *to me*. Our wills clash. I feel the toughness and irony in him and I display my own. He says, 'I've suffered horribly through all this, these last few months.' 'I know you have. But you don't *show* it.' 'You only had to *look* at me, to see it.' I begin to be ashamed of myself. 'I love you,' he says, 'without pride.' 'I know you do,' I say humbly; '*I* love *you*, but proudly.' I return to E's, a sobered woman. This terrible pride. Through it I begin to understand the imagery of Christianity—the longing to be washed, to have chains struck from me.

———

Still raining. The air all over Sydney is filled with a deep hiss.

———

Dreamt I was in a play but had not learnt my lines. Another character spoke to me expectantly and my mind was blank. I feigned a collapse, fell to the ground and lay there for a long time. Nobody came to see how I was. I looked up and everyone had gone.

———

Y comes up from Melbourne: a wonderful day of talk at E's kitchen table. Nourished by the company of women.

———

A writer announces in a powerful voice that his new novel is the most important book that's been written in Australia in the last decade, that it must be published in hardback, and that if this means other writers have to forfeit their publishing subsidy to cover this, he does not care. E and I appalled by this, but when I report it to V he approves: a writer should do everything in his power to get his book well published and noticed. Echo of Stendhal: 'Neglect nothing that can make you great', a sentiment that V quotes with fiery approval but that makes me shudder with embarrassment. Women artists, I think, are more modest, but also more passive. Did Stendhal become the Good/Great Writer he's acknowledged to be today because he forced himself into the limelight, or because he wrote good books?

———

At the photo shop a brown and bouncing Greek girl said to me, 'I got a new neighbour yesterday! And they like the same music I do!

This morning they put on a really old record that I love—I can't wait to get home and make friends!'

———

I want to write things that push down deeper roots into *the archetypal*. Things whose separate parts have multiple connections with their own structure. Dawning awareness of the point of art, and the limits of my work so far. I can't learn *anything* through my intellect alone. I do it first, or it happens to me, and the mind catches up later. This is why I could never be argued into becoming a Christian. *Do* some people join up because of an argument? Pascal's bet?

———

V reports evening calls from various interested women who have heard he's left his marriage. What have I done? Opened him up and now all the women in the world push past me and rush in. One phones to tell him she loves him, that she always has, and that she expects a letter from him within two weeks. Another turns up and stays till midnight—I remember meeting her outside a gallery a year ago: in her thirties, very good-looking, an aggrieved vibe, something *un-light* about her, a little cross face, unsmiling, expecting the worst from the world. I ought to step back on to my own turf and let whatever happens happen. If I were in Melbourne I'd go up to Primrose Gully and stay there.

———

At E's place she and I watched a doco about Jung in which some old analysts were interviewed. One of them said, 'You have to be *lonely*, in order to experience the unconscious.'

———

Reread my screenplay. The last section is dreadful—a post-mortem feeling. R came over to E's for tea. Her light presence. We talked about standards in art, what it means that her mother likes Pro Hart, whether aesthetics is separate (as a study) from ordinary life. Whenever she's with me I feel cheerful, curious, hopeful. In the evening I wrote out a series of system cards for the screenplay, one for each little scene. Gloom rolled away. I called F and we spoke affectionately of this and that. Woken at 6 am in my balcony room by crackling thunder and a steady flood of rain.

———

'One completely overcomes only what one assimilates.' —André Gide, *Journals*

Thus I must assimilate my jealousy. By what process is this to be achieved? What a cold writer, what a cold *man* Gide is, for all his talk of passions—trembling while reading Shakespeare and so on. In his thin-lipped French way he tries to find and tell the truth, but he has no humour, no sense of laughter. I go cold all over, reading him.

———

Melvyn Bragg interviews Saul Bellow on TV about *The Dean's December*. Bellow grandly puts shit on sociologists, psychologists and criminologists for their failure to cure what's wrong with society. V gives an admiring cheer. I am disappointed and say little. 'I think,' says V, 'you weren't very interested in what he was talking about.' I realise I am withholding so as not to rock V's boat. So I say, 'I'll tell you what I really think. I think he's a windbag.' To my surprise when we discuss this V comes a long way towards my point of view. So we are not dug in. Our egos are not in charge of our ideas. We try to list writers who became windy. Hemingway. Henry James. Faulkner? (I haven't read him.) We agree that windy-ness is a male failing on the whole, and that women's failing tends to be wetness. 'Your mate Carver,' he says, 'is not windy at all.' Is windy-ness to do with ambition? Is it also an American failing? Chekhov, we agree, is never windy. We decide to go away for the weekend. To have 'an adventure'.

———

At E's I opened the balcony door. A wind rushed in and blew my screenplay system cards all over the floor. I saw at once that this was *a sign*: that having used the cards to show me the order of the (hopeless) third draft, I had been allowing that order to dominate my rewrite.

R says that the topics and language of social discourse, with men and women, are set by men. We tailor ourselves to their demands. It would be absurd, she said, to make crude demands: 'Okay, now it's our turn.' We start to laugh, imagining them sitting there biting their lips until 'we' had had 'our' go. Maybe, I say, we're behaving wisely in conducting our discourse among ourselves where it can develop its own organic freedoms. R jumps on this: 'But that's an argument for separatism. Aren't there witty, steady, womanly women who succeed in altering the discourse, when men and women are talking together?' 'But aren't those "witty women",' I said, 'the ones who've absorbed the male modes, and who are competitive with men on *their* terms? Have you ever seen it happen?'

Dreamt I stood at a fence and looked at a house. One corner of it crumbled and collapsed. Out of the rubble were brought four dead babies: very small, homunculi, in fact. They were laid in a line across the garden, half under a tarp. A man and I looked at them. Was there a form of verbal rite we had to perform? Later I came back and found that rats had chewed their faces away. The emotional tone of this I have forgotten.

V is reading Robert Craft's biography of Stravinsky. Driving up the highway he tells me in an awe-struck tone that Stravinsky used to come in to lunch with his wife and children and forbid them to speak not only to him but to each other. I said that this was egotistical and unreasonable. V admitted it was 'tyrannical', but claimed it was justified by Stravinsky's need to maintain in his mind, while eating his lunch, the architecture of sounds that he'd been creating all morning and would return to in the afternoon. I kept my temper by imagining beautiful *napery*, a tall window with closed shutters and a hot day outside, a tiled floor, thick glasses. Clean hands.

I notice hard, square calluses on the backs of V's heels: 'Look. As if you'd once had wings but they've been surgically removed.' 'Mercury treatment,' he says, without missing a beat.

The smile a man gets when he's about to come out with something he wants to say but feels he shouldn't: a smile of *daring*—the look that accompanies an act of irreverence, disloyalty, insolence, cheek.

'His mother and his aunt were seated opposite one another on two brightly painted chairs...They had bought the chairs that very morning and were consequently feeling light-hearted and festive. When the children arrived they were singing a little song together.' —Jane Bowles, 'A Guatemalan Idyll'

My beautiful old Mont Blanc shorthand pen rolled off the table. I caught it but its nib stabbed right into the meat of my middle finger and left a blue mark like a tiny jail tattoo. I had the pen repaired but it's lost its silky, flexible quality. Its strokes are not *inky* any more.

The end of the movie. Who can *help* me with this? I groaned all day and then at 5 pm something happened. Strange power and freedom I experience, when I start to invent. It has its own logic. I feel my way along some kind of dark thread.

During dinner at R's place a colossal storm burst above the house: sky white with lightning, a crackling so violent that we feared to be roasted where we sat. Rain fell in steady floods, even entering the house at certain points. At the storm's height came a great knocking at the front door. We exchanged looks of Shakespearean apprehension. The boy ran to open. It was not a panting messenger or fleeing princess but his sodden schoolfriend bringing a Comedy Company record he had won in a raffle.

———

V showed me the first eight pages of the notebooks he is going to
publish. He went on at such length about its severity that I was
afraid I wouldn't like it, but half a page in I was riveted—his sharp
eye, everything fresh, tough and surprising—and the ideas for his
weird stories forming in the gaps. Felt impressed, respectful. When
I tell him this he writhes and looks away, begins again to criticise
them and make little of them.

———

A movie actress in an interview speaks about 'the important daily
obligation of endearing yourself to someone, the daily confirmation
of love'. This is where I have always failed, in the past.

———

I went to dinner at my agent's. The other guests were Patrick
White, in savage mood, and Manoly Lascaris. 'Patrick, we should
perhaps send Manning some flowers in hospital,' says Manoly. 'I
don't *want* to,' snarled Patrick. '*I've* had artery problems, *I've* had
a clot. When the Writers Against Nuclear Arms people invited me
to Canberra I said I couldn't, that I'd been told I mustn't go—and
Manning said, "*I've* got a clot, and *I'm* going."' I cried on my way
home. With terror, and shock at his trembling thinness. I couldn't
fall asleep till after midnight, then dreamt I had written a poem
about the evening's events and wanted to type it on V's typewriter.

———

An old man on an escalator, with six small children clustered round
him. The youngest one is holding his hand. At the bottom she
pulls away and he leaves his hand stretched after her, it stays in the
air as a large gesture of farewell. Intercut the escalator scene with
the action. Each time there is one child fewer. And each time it's
darker, and the child's dress is whiter; and when the last one darts
away, he is waving to her from the gathering darkness.

———

E says she has vivid and blissful memories of being a child, with her mother. She urges me to read Alice Miller's *The Drama of the Gifted Child*. I do, and begin to see why I have no memory of ever being held by Mum, and no memory of the birth of any of the younger kids except one, and that one only because when we were taken to see Mum and the new baby a nesting magpie swooped me in the hospital grounds.

———

I scrambled to the end of the movie. Now I daren't even open the folder.

———

Christmas Eve in Melbourne. P's new house: it suits her. Shoes off and on to a rack inside the front door. Little furniture, very orderly—everything light and white. A meditation room. Her new housemate resembles, in a softer way, her former husband: a kind, intelligent face, with none of her ex's blunt, laughing masculinity.

———

M's father called to tell me that his old friend had killed herself. Yesterday morning. A drug overdose. I started shaking. Tried to speak and only babbled. Opened the back door of my empty house (the 'tenants' have gone home for Christmas) and saw a forest of weeds higher than my head—only recent rains can have saved the roses and the lilac bush—dry blue rags dangled from the jacaranda. Thick mats of creeping weed had grown right across the hose, up the wall of the shed and along the clothesline. I threw myself at it bare-handed, tore it out root and branch, hacked around the lavender bushes, then with a mattock wrenched up great coarse thistles and dandelions, all the while sobbing and raging—how can she be dead—the time we drove across the Nullarbor and up to Exmouth with the Maoists, starting each morning with the tape of 'Mr Bojangles', stayed in remote caravan parks, she thought stealing was politically justified, she stole a battery from outside a service station and it was a dud, then the drugs and how she sort of disappeared, when I'd knock at her front door she wouldn't come out, her junkie boyfriend would stand with one arm across the doorway meaning *Don't come in*. A long, slow process of self-destruction. How men were drawn to it, to her intent. Intent upon dying. Her pale skin, thick hair and delicate fingers, her slender little body and heavy breasts, her laughter, her *cleverness*. In an hour my hands were wrecked. Huge weeping blisters had broken on both my palms.

―――――

V made a big effort with my father, who returned the courtesy though at first he was aggressive and competitive: 'I dunno if you've ever ridden a motorbike; *I* have.' Wilcannia is mentioned. 'Been to Wilcannia? *I* have, and…' V held his own in a relaxed but energetic manner, and the two men became the main event. My brother's toddler, his busy crawling, head down, like the dog in V's notebooks: 'on a specific errand'.

―――――

At Primrose Gully too there is neglect and disrepair. Heavy rains have filled the tanks but caused the mud-brick veranda to collapse, and the chicken-wire back gate is barely holding out of the garden a flood of sand. I see now that it's irresponsible to *lend* a place to someone and expect them to care for it. Low clouds filled the sky, covering a good moon. The dog clawed at fleas. Frogs struck loud, ringing notes in the bottom dam all night long. A beautiful, chill morning, and very still, after the rats' night scampering. Kookaburras, frogs, crickets. A pure sky. Two koalas, five kangaroos, crimson rosellas, several rabbits. I suppose I'll have to sell it. 'It's served its purpose,' says V, 'but it's over.'

―――――

His manly dreams. 'I dreamed I was bowling to Don Bradman. I dreamed I shot a policeman.'

―――――

Back in Sydney I feel uprooted all over again. I tell V I want to rent myself a place up here, a flat of my own, an office with a bed in it.

He thinks this is a terrible idea—I would be paving the way for 'bolting'.

———

I squabble with O about rigor mortis, how long it lasts. I say it goes on forever. He disputes this, due to what he has seen in fish. To settle it I call an undertaker. He says that it 'drops out' after three or four days: 'Limbs can be straightened with a little bit of pressure.' O as always is gracious in victory.

———

Do people burn in hell for telling lies? Do they burn in hell for hurting people to whom they have made unkeepable promises? Do they burn in hell for breaking promises?

———

Summer evening at Bondi. The curved scoop of beach and bay is filled with a light haze which as darkness comes turns into a mist and wets the grass, flips the ends of my hair into pagodas.

———

All these women coming out of the woodwork. I feel like a dusty old piece of carpet. There must be some childhood chasm of disappointment and rejection that is the paradigm. I am terrified that he will lie to me. That I will have handed myself over to him and he will betray me. 'If we fuck this up, if we spoil it,' he says, 'we're not worthy to be on this *earth*.'

———

I do not want to sell Primrose Gully. That's where I taught myself to be a self-respecting woman. A lesson that has to be relearnt every day.

———

G invited V to see *Tosca* at the Opera House, and afterwards took him to 'some damn bar in Darlinghurst where there was a tableful of very young, very good-looking, very well-dressed people who all knew him. The girls were models, I think, maybe they were photographers' models. They were very *sweet*, rather like children.

And completely empty. Two of the girls came and sat with us. They were both wearing very short skirts, one with a torn-off edge—do you know what I mean?'

———

Dreamt I was dancing with my mother.

1989

New Year's resolution: to read about something in a very orderly and purposeful way; to know about something other than myself.

———

A visit to Darling Point, a high apartment with a staggering view of the harbour. I rush to the windows. Ships gliding behind a headland then their upper parts reappearing fleetingly between houses and pine trees: unsettling conjunction of vessel and vegetation. Changing light, the bridge, the Opera House, between whose eggshell sails light slid delicately sideways. Way, way down, the carefully shaven lawns, clipped shrubbery, a pool in which a young woman in a V-striped costume swam alone, suspended in aqua jelly, her limbs working like a frog's.

———

South African movie, *A World Apart*. The tortured man's face, bruised, caked, aghast. He gulps and gulps, staring straight into the camera with wild eyes, while the police take the wet whips out of the bucket.

———

They like my screenplay. A lot. Maybe they always flatter the writer at the beginning?

———

I try to tell V about the visits of the Mighty Force. I suppose he's embarrassed. He closes it down. 'Did you turn around?' 'No.'

'Because if you had, there probably wouldn't have been anything there.'

———

Elizabeth Jolley's new novel *My Father's Moon*. She re-uses and reworks images from her earlier work, brings forth experiences that she'd often hinted at but never fully expressed. I can learn from this. I used to think that if I'd said something once I could never say it again, but in her book I see how rich a simple thing can be when you turn it this way and that and show it again and again in different contexts.

———

I'm so sick of lies. The lying is making me sick.

———

Read in the *Times Literary Supplement* a review of Mallarmé's letters. The account of his life, personality and thought caused in me an eruption of powerful disgust—to the point of philistinism. I wanted to fart or belch, to yell crudely, 'Oh, come off it. Go to the shop and buy some butter, or a lolly, you exquisite thing.' The first line of one of his poems, '*Ses purs ongles*', made me feel quite frenzied. Fingernails that have never scratched, dug, become grubby, broken.

———

'The stars glitter with the same rhythm as the grasshoppers' chirp.' —Camus, *Carnets*

———

The woman who's typing E's manuscript for her rushes into the kitchen with a hanky over her face, crying over the death of the mother's lover. E is delighted. We stand grinning while the typist blows her reddened nose. We agree it's the best review she'll ever get.

———

Ayatollah Khomeini announces a reward of seven million dollars to any Muslim who murders Salman Rushdie, and two million to a citizen of any other kind. V (who is personally acquainted with

Rushdie): 'I reckon he's a dead man.' I can't compute it. If I think about it long enough I get a crazed feeling, a spasm of mad laughter. These *men*. They think they can make a law to stop words they don't like being said, and when that doesn't work they say, 'I'll *kill* you.'

Three women and V argue at the dinner table about the Stravinsky's lunch phenomenon. E and I take a firm stand against domestic tyranny. V 'trusts' that Stravinsky needed what he said he needed. As in any forceful argument, at a certain point I was obliged to ask myself, 'What am I actually saying, here?' I realised I was saying that *I* would not have tolerated being told to shut up at the lunch table by my father or my husband, no matter what mighty thoughts he was entertaining, or hatching, or endeavouring to keep unsullied in his head. Why didn't the maid take him a tray, in his studio?

V announces that two well-known journalist friends of his, a man and a woman, are coming to his place after work for a drink. Plainly I am not invited and it is assumed that I will make myself scarce for the evening. Keeping a rein on myself I say vaguely that I might call L and see if he wants to go out to eat. V pretends to be outraged. Later, when I laugh at some witticism of his, he says, 'Does L ever say anything really witty?' Our crude manoeuvrings. I hate this. All the resolutions I make. They cause an extreme sense of strain; as if I had a rubber band stretched across the inside of my chest cavity. Next day I hear that the journalists didn't turn up.

I write a letter to the Iranian ambassador. 'Your Excellency: as I am (no doubt like you, Sir, and like many other sincere Muslims and Christians trying to live on this earth together) a believer in a God of mercy who does not require us to murder each other in his name, I beg you most urgently to use your influence with your government to reverse the call to Muslims to put to death on account of his book the writer Salman Rushdie. Yours respectfully.' I show it to four friends. They ask me to change 'I' to 'we', and we all sign it.

————

Autumn, suddenly, is here. Angle of light more oblique, air dryer and gentler.

————

He does what he calls 'old man things': before the start of a TV show we're going to watch, he sets out the teacups with milk and biscuits. I am not used to this and find it endearing.

————

I think I might burn all these diaries. What if I died and people got hold of them and read them? Their endless self-obsession, anecdotes, self-excuses, rationalisations. Meanness about others.

————

A visit from Mum. Terrific strain I'm under, when she and I are with other people. When we're alone I can submit to this vast, slow, stunning stream of monologue and apply as little of my concentration to it as I need to (about fifteen per cent) in order to remain calm. Yesterday she talked so much—on the drive in from the airport, meeting E, shopping at Leichhardt, having coffee at Via Veneto, driving to Manly, walking on the beach—that by bedtime she was hoarse. She never asks a question, or listens. She starts every anecdote days, months or even years before its proper starting point. Her only liveliness in speech comes when she can criticise: idiot skateboard riders, lunatics on motorbikes, men unloading trucks in narrow streets, stupid dills who drop rubbish or leave security doors ajar. A film of the world as she sees it would be always swelling, blurring, lurching, swivelling—sparkling and looming *with danger*. At moments, while she drones on, there comes over me a painful tenderness. This 'tenderness', which if I told the truth I would have to call pity, has to do with my dread of becoming like her. V asks her straight out which of my books she likes the best. She says, shyly, '*The Children's Bach.*' I am embarrassed and don't know where to look. I always give them copies, with a loving message written in the front, but she has never told me whether she's read any of them. *And I've never asked.*

———

V tells me he's going to work at 'having more goodness'.

'What do you mean?'

'I want to be kinder. More open. Less selfish, less severe.'

'What makes you want to change?'

'These notebooks I'm publishing. This dreadful person who wrote them: severe, pompous, humourless.'

He says he thinks of 'getting a job at the hospital, as a porter'.

———

Z and I enrol in a German conversation course at the Goethe-Institut. We're surprised to be put in Intermediate. We'd thought lower. Since I left school I've suffered colossal loss of German vocabulary, though sentence structure is still burnt into my memory. Others in the class are miles worse. Z says on our way home that he wanted the teacher, a gentle, pretty girl, to correct every mistake he made, in speaking. He thinks she's 'too soft'.

———

S's husband tells me that since his father died, last week, he feels 'as if blood's oozing through my skin—no pain, but energy's draining away, downwards'.

———

Dreamt I looked at myself in a mirror and saw the face of a good-looking, smiling young man of mixed race: light-brown skin, brown eyes, black curly hair just washed and flopping in wet, heavy locks, large mouth, perfect teeth, pink gums. At first I was thrown off balance by this new reflection of 'myself', but soon I rather took to it and began to examine it with a happy admiration. I moved the lips, showed the teeth, practised different expressions (mostly smiles), and said aloud, 'So *this* is what it's like to have a big mouth!' Later, R was very impressed by this. 'What a wonderful image of integration!'

V presses me to read a symposium in *Salmagundi* magazine called 'Art and Intellect in America'. He is sombrely impressed by the contribution of George Steiner, who makes a slashing attack on any American pretensions to a culture able to hold a candle to that of Europe. My hackles go up. Where does Steiner get off? Hasn't he heard of jazz? Contemporary art and literature produced under any but totalitarian regimes, he says, are 'an embarrassment'. All right—the horror of the Holocaust is unanswerable. *But we are still here.* What about the losses, griefs and sacrifices, the small heroisms that occur each day, often unnoticed, in people's relations with each other? What about death, and cruelty, and fear, and children, and love? People suffer. Don't we still have to find the meaning in our lives that only art offers? I try to put these thoughts to V: 'Where does this leave us—you? If you agree with him, how come you haven't given up trying to write novels? That'd be the only action consistent with his argument, wouldn't it?' I had a weird feeling that V was seeing the argument only distantly, as a brilliant performance by a man he admires for maintaining excoriating standards—'taking it right up to the Yanks'.

There's a big a cappella gospel choir singing tonight at the Paddington RSL. I long to go. But can't think of one single person I know in the whole city who'd go with me.

Doing my German homework it dawns on me that this is how it must feel to be a 'dumb' kid at school. I keep coming up against words I don't know, hitting and re-hitting a brick wall; dense darkness in front of me; stomach pains, restlessness; a blocked sensation, shame, irritation, boredom, fear. And physical rage—I want to jump up and start smashing things.

Dreamt I went back to our empty family house in Geelong. It

was in beautiful condition, polished, swept, orderly. M was with me and I needed to find a room for her to live in. But in the first bedroom I entered stood two small alarm clocks, both ticking like mad. Couldn't sleep here, with such a racket going on. The second room was locked. I found the key. Its floor was heaped with rubbish, garbage, shit from some animal. But plenty of light was coming in through the window. Just inside the door, on the floor, stood a second pair of little alarm clocks, ticking fast and wildly, making an almost hysterical noise: sharp, small, crazily fast. I was amazed that they'd kept going in there, all those years.

———

On the Hume Highway, a ute containing four black sheepdogs and one very subdued sheep.

———

Things I had forgotten about Melbourne: 1. Cold autumn nights. 2. The way the air in shadow, even mid-afternoon, is chilled while the sunny air is warm to hot. 3. Condensation on a car by 10 pm. 4. How casually excellent a quite ordinary restaurant can be. 5. The clarity of the air. 6. A dewy stillness in the morning: air still capable of biting, though the sky shows a warm day coming.

———

Alice Munro is deceptively naturalistic. All that present tense, detail of clothes, household matters, then two or three pages in there's a gear change and everything gets deeper and more wildly resonant. She doesn't answer the questions she makes you ask. She wants you to walk away *anxious*.

———

V reports Z's 'outburst' against 'women's writing' with its 'domestic nuances' which he dislikes and is not interested in. V tries to get me to pick up my lip but without success since he doesn't hide the fact that he agrees with Z. Later R says, 'To me it's an absolute rule, psychologically, that if someone frequently inveighs against something in another, it's to do with something they hate in themselves.'

———

The director calls to say how much she liked my screenplay. But she can't do it, because she's about to start a year's work on a three-part television series, and after that a movie of her own in New Zealand. I say, 'We can't think of another director who could do it.' 'Oh,' she says with a light laugh, 'I think it's pretty director-proof.' But it's not. Nothing is.

———

These terrible long sentences, in my unfinished story. How could I have gone so far off the track? They have no natural rhythm or inner syntactic logic. Ugly, clumsy, a stupid grid.

———

I'm sitting on the floor in my room at E's, reading old dreams in a diary, when she comes in and gives me four new 3B pencils.

———

If I report a dream to V, the comments he makes are aesthetic rather than psychological.

———

The old artist in his huge, damp-smelling house on the harbour. Broken venetians, dark outside, only thing visible on the water a lit-up tourist boat. Once he addressed me by V's wife's name; no one seemed to notice. V pointed out a spot of foxing on the edge of a faded old painting: 'What's this?' 'Oh, I don't know how that got there. Must've come through from the back. Oh, it doesn't matter. Let it change.' That's when I started to like him. He talked about the way his ex-wives dispose of his early works carelessly: his current companion went to visit one of them in New York: 'She'd let one of my things slip down behind a radiator.' A wicked laugh. He drank quite a large glass of neat gin, to fight a cold he thought was coming on. The folded-paper parcel of Chinese herbs he takes for 'general health': strange twigs, roots, stems, flattened hunks of dark rubbery or waxy substances. These he boils up in a ceramic pot with a spout, into an evil-looking black decoction with a taste like cough medicine. We enjoyed remembering old commercials for cough cures: Buckley's Canadiol, Bonnington's Irish Moss 'with pectoral oxymel of carrageen'. His companion is a sculptor, very likeable, strong and energetic, and graceful, with narrow feet and calves—maroon shoes with low heels, AA fitting (I asked her).

———

R says she sees in V's face 'signs of nervous suffering'.

———

V speaks about his wife with sorrow: 'She's completely gone from my life.' 'What do you miss most, about her?' 'Her cheerfulness. Her generosity.' I'm sad for him, for her. And I thought painfully of F, his merriments, our games and laughter, our outings with dogs to the Maribyrnong—how the removal of daily French, with its possibilities of hilarity, verbal invention, mimicry, was like a door shut in my face.

———

I've put the bloody story away. A vast and sweet relief. Into my head at all hours flood ideas (or are they fantasies?) for a novel. I madly make notes. No anxiety about it—only excitement, optimism, a sense of boundlessness. Whenever one of the characters gets too close to my family I get a faint reluctance, a tinge of emotional nausea, feeling the tug of that maelstrom.

———

Z says that what writers need most of all is patience. We have to learn to wait till we're ready.

———

Royalties came yesterday. I got $1206. V owes money. So gloomy that we can't help laughing. Queensland sends me five tiny violets taped to a sheet of paper: 'So small. So early. Too delicate to pick and yet I did on my way back from the chooks. A harsh, unsympathetic, ruthless wind.' Her letters are long, rambling streams of consciousness, never demanding a reply, but I pick out the eyes, paste them in my diary, and answer them on a postcard.

———

At the Cat Protection Society op shop near E's I find a New Testament in Modern English, translated by J. B. Phillips. It reads like a great yarn, with good cross-headings: 'His strange words to the fig-tree.' 'Jesus puts an unanswerable question.' Memory of the terrifying dinner with Patrick and Manoly. I wish I'd had the nerve to say, 'How can you sit there talking like that about other people with that great big cross hanging round your neck?'

———

Dreamt that someone gave birth to a baby that had muscly little feathered wings high up on its back. It lay there on its belly, naked, while we looked at it—with admiration, but also a slight anxiety, as if at something that had been allowed to *go too far*.

———

'I sometimes think the world is divided into people who survive from their own inner strength and those who have to latch on to others to survive.' —Elizabeth Jolley, interview in *Good Weekend*

———

Reading Luke's Gospel I see why Steiner is so terribly wrong when he says that only people living under totalitarian regimes can produce art worthy of the name. *We all live under the totalitarian regime of the world's evil.* And it's in the terms in which our own culture manifests it that we have to express our struggle against it, or our longing for glimpses of *good*.

———

Driving to town with a big bag of field mushrooms on the back seat, we saw an astonishing sunset. It secretly reminded me of a long orgasm: pulsing, wide, vivid, generous—the whole sky filled with clouds of every kind—wide slivers of gilt and blazing orange, then delicate grey scooped veils, then tiny bright scallops high up—to the north a tender, apricot-pink, melting wash. For a while we drove towards it, along a curving up-and-down road, and at each new rise or corner a further splendour presented itself—we gasped and cried out. The clouds would lose vividness and become pearly, dappled with pink scales—then we'd sweep round a bend that gave us a view lower down towards the horizon where a whole new band of blazing brass and orange would have been lying in wait. I looked over my shoulder, and the entire sky, as far as the eastern horizon, was stained, tipped, scaled, looped, and daubed. It seemed to go on forever.

———

At the boring literary dinner the famous writer's wife takes a quail from a platter and offers me one. When I look doubtfully at them she picks hers up and makes it trot across the plate on tiny legs, saying 'Hello Helen!' in a squeaky voice. I think we will get on. Late in the speechifying a man in his fifties cries, 'None of the young women are speaking. Why don't the women speak?' I ran my eye round the room and saw that the women were slumped, glassy with boredom, humouring the men in their game of being intellectuals of wit and style—their lumbering playfulness. Another bloke sings out, '*Young* women? I don't see any young women here!' An older man calls, 'You get *very* poor marks—for ungallantry.' It was sad, and yet I was free of it, a stranger dropped in from another planet.

———

'The man who raped me,' says my nun, 'nearly killed me, but because I went to a Catholic doctor four hours afterwards instead of three, he wouldn't wash me out.' '*What?*' 'According to Catholic law, to wash someone out more than three hours after a rape counts as an abortion.' 'Where's *that* written?' 'Oh, in some Catholic bullshit somewhere.'

———

Start with the dog. The only member of the household who can't accept its demise.

———

To R and O's for dinner. A sweet evening. I mended a rip in their boy's primary-school shorts, which (to V's dismay) he removed in the dining room and handed to me, then asked if he could put on an old record he'd found in an op shop. He lowered the needle. It was 'Shine On, You Crazy Diamond'. Even the adults stopped talking. His younger sister, who was lying on the couch beside me reading, laid her bare feet across my lap and I stitched away on top of them, full of nameless emotion.

———

Feel a strong urge to go out and buy a chain and cross to put around my neck—to make a declaration, to spend the rest of my life on my knees. Something! *Anything!*

———

Someone has stolen my good denim jacket and both my street directories, Sydney and Melbourne, out of the car.

———

On the plane to Melbourne I sat next to a Catholic bishop on his way home from a policy-making conference. Thin bloke in his fifties with well-formed features, one of those hard, serviceable faces that his generation of Australian men have: dry, tough, gives nothing away unless you can shock it into a reaction. I longed to ask him about spiritual things but was too shy—felt it would not be his area. I asked him about his work, his diocese, what he did when he visited a parish. His answers gave me a picture of the church as a vast bureaucratic edifice. At the baggage carousel he wished me well and said (as I had hoped), 'God bless.'

———

E at the lunch table, telling me about a friend's collapsing marriage, got upset and shouted, 'She handed him a loaded gun! So he *shot* her! Why do women *do* this to themselves?'

———

To church at Pentecost. The Holy Spirit is the only part of Christianity I've got any actual personal experience of. I don't understand 'God' or even 'Jesus', but the Holy Spirit has stood behind me on many different days, even though for a long time I was too frightened to acknowledge it or 'call out to it'. It has visited me and comforted me and become part of me. We sang 'Come Down, O Love Divine' and tears ran down my nose, I had to keep blowing it. When the server put the little cube of bread on my palm I saw it, in huge close-up, expand back to its full shape after the pressure of his fingertip and thumb was removed from it; and yet it consisted only of holes, or of porousnesses, of pale brown threads of matter existing only to keep the porousnesses apart. The vicar said, 'The blood of Christ which was shed for you...' and handed me the cup. I drank from it.

———

I've sold my books. I've let my house. I've agreed to sell Primrose Gully. I've changed cities. I've got no home. I am not to answer the phone at V's, or be present when certain visitors come, or leave my stuff lying around. I am forty-six-and-a-half and I am humiliated. V is unable to resolve the thing by telling his wife the truth. I say to Z that I wish V would deliver the coup de grâce. 'The trouble is,' says Z, 'that to do that, which I agree he must do, he'll have to admit, to himself as much as to her, that his leaving her had something to do with you. He seems to need to keep the two things separate in his mind. He's still *saying* they're separate—as late as yesterday he was saying it. What I think he should do is tell her that your existence hastened the end, but that he'd felt it was over for quite some time already.' 'And did you tell him that?' 'Oh *no*.' 'Why not?' 'Oh, I couldn't do *that*. That would be to deny the whole way he sees himself and his situation.' 'But Z. You're his *friend*. It's the responsibility, the *duty* of friends to help each other see what they're doing. How else can we find out what we're like?' Z seemed very surprised and put off by this definition of friendship.

———

M phones. Our dog. 'I got home from work at midnight and called her. She didn't come. I went out into the yard and saw her against the fence. Her head was up high on a funny angle and the rest of her was sort of collapsed. Her collar was caught on the back gate.

She must have been trying to get out. I knew straight away she was dead. I rushed back inside, I panicked, I couldn't go near her or touch her or anything. I shut myself in, I thought someone was out there, someone had killed her. I rang up F and he came straight over. He was terrific, he did everything. He unhooked her and dug a big hole and buried her, and then we both cried a lot. I wanted to bury her with her ball but she lost it yesterday.' Her boyfriend (an ex-Catholic sceptic) also came, and said a prayer: 'God, please take this dog's soul…'

———

The unusual colour of her fur—a silvery grey that almost shone in the dark. I got out my photo albums and looked for her. Not many where she was the star, but often a corner of her was visible in a picture of something else: a nose, a paw, a length of silvery back. Cried for her terrible faithfulness, her loneliness and confusion when our household broke up, how she would escape and trot the five kms to F's, missing death on the roads. And the way she used to flick up her hind legs in a gay little gambol when she set out with us on a walk.

———

I love it here at E's. Every morning I sit at my table and plough forward in the Old Testament. Stories in Judges full of savagery and horror—then suddenly comes Ruth, a tale of gentle fidelity, courtesy, correctness, generosity, happiness. After reading this book I will never be the same.

———

Work offers come and I take them. I don't want to go over to V's. What if his wife comes visiting and I'm there? Maybe a terrible explosion of truth is exactly what's needed. I said, 'She needs you to tell her the truth. Somewhere in herself she knows you haven't told her everything.' He will not accept this screamingly obvious fact. He decides to invite two friends to dinner, and casually assumes that I'll cook. I say I won't: he can't expect me to turn on wifely service and then when it suits him pretend I'm only a casual acquaintance. He's furious. We slug it out. He says he objects to the way I make flat pronouncements. I say he makes assumptions that aren't even acknowledged by him as assumptions until I challenge them. I can't see he's got a leg to stand on here. We reach a truce, the passionate kind still available to lovers. But there's a reserve between us. We both feel it.

———

Reread my movie. I think it's good. I think it will be made. I can stop worrying about money.

———

Evening at E's in Enmore, already dark at half past five, sound of trains, sky clouded, a chill. Memory of being a wife, of being the one who's in the house when the man comes home.

———

In the gallery V and I run into two people he knows. One, a sagging-faced, white-haired fellow with a glass of red in his hand, tells me he had sat next to a man on a flight to Hong Kong, who saw him reading *Postcards from Surfers* and said he was my father. 'What did he look like?' 'Oh, I don't remember. But he told me some very interesting things about you.' 'What did he tell you?' 'I can't recall, but I wrote them down in my notebook.' Next, his companion, a woman in her fifties, begins to question me: am I living up here now? 'Yes,' I say, feeling relaxed, smooth, and rather dangerous. 'I've still got my house in North Fitzroy, but I'm staying with a woman friend over in Enmore.' Her greenish-yellow eyes give a cold flash: 'And how long have you been up here?' 'A couple of months, now.' I feel so calm and powerful that I know I can deal with anything she says or does. Put a foot wrong, my good woman, and I will splatter you all over the map.

———

I walk into V's. He hugs me and I smell perfume on the neck of his jumper. Cigarette ash on the carpet. Over his shoulder I count with my eyes the number of dishes waiting to be washed. I keep my mouth shut. He drives me back to E's and remarks that I become livelier as we approach her house.

———

Imagine not crediting the Apocrypha when Tobit contains a line like 'The boy left with the angel, and the dog followed behind.'

———

The army has entered Tiananmen Square and machine-gunned students. 'A tiny girl with a plait hanging down her back' whose body 'comes apart'. The boy whose 'guts are fanned out like a crushed cat's'. Stupefied. Only later do I 'feel' anything. It comes in small, dull punches. This, and the scenes of maddened crowds of men swarming up on to Khomeini's throne and kissing it, jumping up and down, howling and beating at their foreheads with their palms—I want more and more to believe in God, though I don't know why. It's certainly not for comfort, specially while reading the Old Testament, whose violence is as shocking as anything I read of in the papers or see on TV.

———

'When I come to Sydney, Helen,' says M on the phone, 'will you cook me hot meals?'

———

A friend of V's has left his wife. Tells V he's had 'lizards crawling in his stomach for seven years'; that she was 'a very, very difficult person'. Foolishly I ask if I am 'a difficult person'. Yes, he says, I am 'the most hypersensitive person, in moods,' that he has 'ever known'. I retort that he is a difficult person too—that his tendency to resist even minor change (e.g. suggestions to buy something, to ring someone up) means I'm always having to drag him out of his rigid negativity. Both of us are ruffled by this, but allow our feathers to settle, and turn on the TV.

———

I ask R if she minds my having used something she once said to me in an essay I'm writing. 'It's not even an issue,' she says. 'The way *we* talk, where everything that's said leads on to the next thing, how can any lines be drawn between what I thought and what you thought? Or where one idea ended and the next began?'

———

Dinner in a restaurant with V and a bunch of other writers. Everyone laughing and at ease. The door opens to admit the solitary figure of G, white and thin-faced from work, looking for a place to eat and read on in Anthony Powell. He joins us and all is merry. He murmurs to me, 'I'm terribly happy, except when I look at my wife.' I report this to V later. He groans and says, 'Oh, is *that* how he feels. He's a goner.'

———

I'm only really afraid of one thing, namely, that something should happen to hurt M.

———

A movie on TV about John Waters. I laughed till I was weak and grateful—I've been missing that angle of life—shit and fart jokes, the utter refusal to be in any way serious, intellectual or polite—and what *is* the quality Divine has, that 'puts everybody in a good mood all the time'? I said to V, 'There's never any little *treats* in your fridge. And there's not enough light and fresh air.' He hates light and likes to keep the windows closed against the cold, though the place is a box in which he smokes cigars. He won't ever stay a night with me over at E's: 'If I've slept somewhere else I find it really hard to get started on my work the next morning.' I say briskly, 'I used to be like that in primary school. But I got over it.' He is delaying to infinity the duty of levelling with his wife. He is permanently lying doggo: 'I don't know why I have to tell her.' Dumbfounded, I say, 'You're thinking of *not* telling her?' 'I don't see why I should have to,' he says, in a lightly defensive tone. I let it pass, in sheer astonishment. As if he thinks of himself as having simply walked out of her life.

———

From Queensland come two lines of Richard Lovelace's poem 'The Grasse-hopper': 'Oh thou that swing'st upon the waving haire/ Of some well-filled Oaten Beard.'

———

G's smashed marriage. His white face, racked, its deep vertical lines, in the coffee shop at 9 am, Victoria Street. 'Last night I stayed in a cheap hotel in Darling Point. $28 a night. So cold. The coverlet was so thin'—he separates thumb and forefinger—'that I didn't get warm enough to sleep till 8 am.' His long, detailed story of betrayal, lies, lust and helpless love. Driving home I saw a couple on a zebra crossing, in their sixties, grey hair, in comfortable, well-worn clothes, holding hands, their faces lit by a gentle happiness. Up the stone steps to the museum they went, smiling, not looking at each other—going out to enjoy the world together.

———

Dreamt Dad handed me a cheque for $1000. In a box on it, to show the purpose of the cheque, he had written, 'For music and lost friendships.'

———

The little aloofness that beauty needs.

———

Magpies are warbling. A pink sunrise.

———

Late in the evening at Mum's seventieth birthday Dad asked me to dance with him and I said no. 'Want to have a dance, miss?' 'I'm double-parked, Dad.'

———

'It's mad,' said Z, 'to think that only what lasts matters. How can that *be*? If we lose *everything*? It *can't* be. And we *all* lose everything. Everything.' I asked if he found the ephemeral enough; I said that so far I thought I did. He said yes. I said that what he'd been saying reminded me of the end of Ecclesiastes. ' "In the day when the keepers of the house shall tremble...And those that look out of the

windows be darkened, and the grasshopper shall be a burden..."'
He went very still, looking right at me. 'That passage,' he said, 'is
the centre of my book.'

―――

This morning when I was sitting on E's outside lavatory, two small
birds flipped, perched, whirred right in front of me on the wisteria
twigs. Fat little ones with pale brown bellies, darker wings patterned
like their heads with rows of evenly-spaced round white dots, as
perfect as an Aboriginal painting; and on their backs, under their
wings, just above their stumpy tail feathers, a flash of red. Their
movements never fluid. A bird moves sharply from one posture to
the next, holds it briefly, then shifts to another—snap, snap, snap.

―――

A slow peace comes from just lying in each other's arms.

―――

In my admiring essay for *Scripsi* about Elizabeth Jolley's *My
Father's Moon* I said that Stendhal's book *On Love* was 'charming if
somewhat juvenile'. V hit the roof. How dare I make this 'tossed-off,
impertinent' remark? Glumly I contemplate replacing 'juvenile'
with 'unhelpful'.

―――

I saw a little gold cross in a pawnshop window and bought it for $39.
With chain. I wore it for two days under my T-shirt. I imagined that
when I was asked what it meant I would reply, 'It reminds me of a
possibility.' This morning I took it off. It seemed a burden somehow,
or too clear a statement of something I am unsure about. Relief of
putting it into the little wooden box with M's baby teeth and my
second wedding ring. Another day I will take it out and think again.

―――

I am too narrow. Always turning over the same ground. (Morandi.
Patiently turned and turned.)

―――

Search for the feeling that came *before* the anger and deal with that:

it's usually hurt, fear, embarrassment.

———

'Herbert alone can say, *My Lord*.' —Peter Porter, 'A Clumsy Catechism'

———

Out walking, I'm cheerfully telling him about something that happened today and he changes the subject, cuts right across me mid-sentence. I protest. He digs in. I go over the top. Oh, how I hate to be told that it's 'not worth having all these feelings', that we 'shouldn't have to talk about this rubbish'—as if the real, proper, reasonable behaviour is always his, and mine is aberrant, my protest a stupid, hysterical temper tantrum that 'at nearly fifty' he was 'too old to have to deal with'.

———

'The love problem is part of mankind's heavy toll of suffering, and nobody should be ashamed of having to pay his tribute.' —Jung, 'The Development of Personality'

———

To dinner at Antipodes with G and his new girlfriend, M-C. G had had a haircut that made him look harrowed and old, like George Orwell. The girlfriend engaged V in conversation. When she turned away he leaned over and whispered to me, 'It won't last. She as much as told me so.'

———

V took me (with, as cover, the adventurous beauty, who's just published her first novel) up the coast to visit his and his wife's friend, the widow of a famous painter. On the drive he kept telling us what a 'great reader' she was. I was prepared for a little old librarian in a tweed skirt. I thought maybe we'd get on. She turned out to be a grandly beautiful old woman with a helmet of silver hair, a high-class accent and a carefree, laughing manner. I had to suppress an urge to address her as Ma'am, a word I've never in my life thought of using. The wall of windows overlooked air and bush, and the huge room was lined, packed, strewn with books. The table was so close to the shelves that when a point was disputed during lunch she could reach an arm behind her and produce Fowler's *English Usage*. She treated me and the beauty with charming courtesy, but had trouble meeting my eye. Several times she summoned up all her grit and praised my work, but around her head crackled a static of muffled anger. I went mousy and quiet. I could see from their playful teasing that she and V adored each other, so, since he could do no wrong, she bounced her anger about me off the adventurous beauty and her new book (which she had already read). Under her intelligent, benevolent, lightly bullying critique, the adventurer floundered. After a while I took her over to the fireplace and brushed her hair. She submitted with bowed head. Her hair was fair and springy, a wonderful thick mass of it. I worked away with the brush until she recovered her equilibrium.

When we got home, V went for me. It took me a moment to grasp that he must have been trying to conduct the visit according to some secret timetable of revelation, and that I, having failed to read his mind, had thrown a spanner in the works. Why the hell, he shouted, had the beauty and I been so ridiculously hypersensitive and unsociable? He was upset, not making sense: 'As I've said before, she loves to talk, and she's generous. I know her fifty times better than you do, and I—' 'Of course you do! I don't know her at all!' Under his stream of reproaches I started to flag. Finally he ran out of steam. We sat on the couch. In a little while he said, humbly, 'Did you like her, much?' 'Yes,' I said, with aching heart, 'yes, I did. Of course I did. She's fabulous. I've never met anyone remotely like her. But it couldn't have been anything but difficult, the first time.' I did like her very much. I wonder if she might come to like me. Anyway I sent her a thank you note. The following morning he gets a phone call from W, also an intimate of the great reader. Turns out the great reader had been under the impression that *I* was pressuring *him* not to tell his wife the truth. I explode. 'I hope someone straightened her out on *that*!'

———

Just as I'm wondering how I can get someone to tell me about building sites, one of the old junkies calls up for a chat and tells me he's working as a builder's labourer. This story is growing, in spite of me. I couldn't stop it now, even if I tried: I'm only a channel for its unformed mass. I come at it in small darts and larger rushes. 'I put on once more with joy the hateful harness.'

———

In Ariel bookshop V shows me Tess Gallagher's tribute to Raymond Carver. A quiet, modest testament to their happiness.

———

Close to midnight in the little street behind V's building a phalanx of Aboriginal boys emerges from the dark behind us—their soft, spread-out advance. I hear one murmur, 'We'll take *that* one.' I hunch against the grab for my backpack but they part around us as if we weren't there and cluster round the driver's door of a parked white Impreza—a sharp thump—V raises one arm in protest—the car starts with a roar, its lights blaze and it surges away from the kerb.

———

Writing has become a pleasure that I nevertheless postpone, for some reason. Connections make themselves of their own volition.

———

Three days of Lit Board assessment. The usual blood on the walls but, also as usual, I left feeling justice had been done, if by a process too organic and fluid to be described as logical.

———

A card (one of her husband's photos) comes from the great reader. 'I am telling you the naked truth when I say I am your devoted fan. You are wise and diplomatic and will be good for our *thick* mutual friend.'

———

V goes out to dinner with some art-world friends and returns scowling darkly: the wife of one of the painters had stated with confidence that Scott Fitzgerald is a better writer than Proust.

———

Repeatedly struck by his old-fashionedness. He's never heard of anything. He didn't know, till I happened to mention it, that women's shirts button right over left. 'How on earth did you manage it? To stay buried for a whole generation?' His friend the old sculptor, too, has been dug up out of some remote bog. An endearing man of fine aesthetic sensibility who seems never to have found it necessary to examine himself. Measures all human behaviour (in which he is hardly interested at all) from a point of view of innocent self-interest—is surprised that other people (especially women) should exhibit needs, thoughts or emotions which don't fit in with his daily work and thought patterns. And yet a strange, almost child-like attentiveness: he notices that the light in the room is bothering my eyes—limps out and returns with a red eye-shade, which I wear for the duration of the visit. He wears one himself, plus sunglasses, while working, he says. V loves to quote the sculptor's dictum: 'When the chips are down, women don't give a fuck about art.' I laugh, but privately expand the word 'art' to mean 'what blokes need in order to go on producing art without tedious emotional interruptions'.

———

The opening pages of what I'm writing feel false and stiff. I've gone in at the wrong point. I want either (a) to get myself right out of this book, as in *The Children's Bach*, or (b) to write everything from an innermost point of myself that I have not yet discovered.

———

What I love on my desk is the notebooks I've typed up, their freshness, their *un-public* tone, their glancing quality and high sensuous awareness. Nothing 'serious' I write can ever match these—exactly as my accounts of dreams, scribbled before I'm completely awake, contain more blunt truth of feeling or observation than I can ever produce when I'm sitting up at my desk telling myself I am 'writing a novel'.

————

I was throwing the I Ching. It told me to pay attention to 'the shadowy'. V, pretending scornful reluctance, asks it a silent question. It replies: 'Even with slender means, the sentiments of the heart can be expressed.' 'What did you ask it?' 'Whether I was a bad person.'

————

I need to free myself from the hierarchy with the novel on top. I need to devise a form that is flexible and open enough to contain all my details, all my small things. If only I could *blow out realism* while at the same time sinking deeply into what is most real.

————

The old professor, after we'd been to dinner with him at R and O's place: 'How pleasant it was. There was no master of ceremonies.'

————

My publishers, both women, are fighting for their lives in a brutal economic climate. I heard Y being interviewed on the radio. The broadcaster lectured her very slowly, restating what she had already said as if she had not said it. He pointed out that their company was probably about to be squeezed out of business by the multinationals. 'Why,' he said, 'don't you just lie back? And take it?'

————

Work stalls. I reproach myself for not 'thinking', 'studying', 'reading' about this state of drift while I am in it. But the point is to *be* in it, not to examine it.

————

Dreamt I saw a photo of myself sitting alone in a cinema, asleep, with my head resting on my bent arm. I wake, spring up and look around. I am young, wearing a beautiful pale-pink dress in a material both light and heavy: like muslin stitched with pinkish-white sequins. It falls gracefully against my body when I move. I step forward and walk with purpose out of the photo. As I leave the frame I see that I am wearing, with this dress pink to the point of shimmering into silver-white, a pair of *red shoes*.

———

Country motel. For hours, from the next room, we heard the cries of a woman being fucked. Repeated bouts of it, for twenty minutes at a time, the head of the bed thudding against the wall. The man was totally silent throughout, and there seemed to be, for her at least, no orgasm, no release or rest, just these rhythmic, bestial cries. Once she said, 'Oh, sorry.' Later, 'No—no, please.' Later again, in a cross, warning voice: 'Get off me. I said get *off* me, Kevin.'

———

Dreamt V and I were in a flotilla of dinghies. To our right, as high as an apartment block, a vast wave was forming, a colossal wall of water, and on its very summit the first frill of breaking foam.

———

R has deeply offended V by telling him she doesn't think much of the work of a certain New Zealand painter he admires. He comes home in a towering rage. Everything she'd said was 'crass' and 'banal', she 'has no credentials'. I argue for her right to have an opinion. He calls her on the phone and says he's sorry if he's 'upset' her. She replies that she hadn't been at all upset—that he must have been projecting. He renews his attack. She stands up to him, she won't bite, so he drops her and swings it around into a tremendous rolling argument between him and me. It goes on for three days and nights. He can't seem to put it down. His incredible, obsessive stamina—as if he's fighting for his life. It seems to be about the ownership of the culture, about who shall speak. I get him on the ropes about this, so he narrows and narrows his attack until it becomes about R's 'tone', in a conversation at which I was not present—and I should not, he says, discuss the matter any further with her. When we fall out like this I am painfully aware that the apartment belongs to him. I get an urge to hide in a corner, and find myself standing in the doorway of the tiny laundry, without turning on the light. He roams about, stands with hands in pockets between lounge room and veranda. When he turns and sees me he laughs: 'You look as if you're standing in a punishment cell.' He claims to have had to 'correct' me when, the night before last, I'd raised my voice and spoken 'harshly' as we argued. '*Correct* me? You objected. I corrected myself.' He accuses me of having 'cross-examined' him. I point out that he's starting to use courtroom terms, as if I were at fault and not simply disagreeing with him. He clicks his tongue irritably: 'Oh, don't pick me up on individual words—just listen to the general flow!' I begin to think less of him and this hurts me, but I'm not stopping now. 'You accuse R of demolition,' I say, 'but what about your demolition of *her* work? Poetry? You've swept it away—you've declared that what means the most to her is beneath your notice. And when you make a running joke of it, she goes along with it, because as a woman she's used to having this done to her—she's used to having to back off and conduct her most intense interests in secret.' 'Yes,' he says, 'that was awful, I shouldn't have done that, even if it was just a joke. But...I often talk to her... about poetry...' His voice slows down and becomes magisterial. 'Yes, I often speak to R...about poetry...I give her books, I show her articles...' 'Yes, but you don't *listen* to her about poetry. You don't want to hear what *she's* got to say—what she *knows*.'

Night after night he wheeled in the heavy artillery, and I dug in. Each bout lasted hours. 'It says here,' he said, 'that Graham Greene prays. Do you pray?' 'Yes, but not to ask for things.' 'What do you pray for?' 'I try to submit myself to something, so I can stop being angry, or frightened.' '*I*,' he said, in a mocking tone, 'don't have to pray in order not to be angry.' He accuses me of disloyalty because I wouldn't 'give him the benefit of the doubt' about the disgraceful nature of R's tone, this toe-hold of territory I had driven him on to and that he would not abandon. I became stunned, slowed-down, capable only of careful physical movements. But I stuck to my guns. Finally I ask him, 'What is it you *want* from me, that I can't seem

to give?' '*Nothing*,' he says savagely. 'I want *nothing*.' I get up from
the table and put on my backpack. 'Are you leaving? I wouldn't
advise you to.' He stands in front of me, barefoot, shirt unbuttoned,
waistband of boxer shorts showing over his trousers. I go into the
laundry, he goes into the bathroom. I stand there in the dark with
my forehead against the dryer.

I begin to wash the dishes. I'm so tired I'm hallucinating. I can't
sense where in the tiny flat he is: I see a shape dart in the corner
of my left eye, and think he's crouching in the dark to jump out
and frighten me. I put down the dishcloth and step sideways to
check. Nothing there. He has gone into the bedroom. I lie on the
couch. 'Are you coming to bed?' The married person's question. 'In
a little while.' I wash my feet, put on my nightie, get into bed. 'I'm
aching like a bastard,' he says. 'It's those bloody typhoid and yellow
fever shots. I feel hollow behind the eyes and in the chest—as if hot
winds were blowing all through me, down my arms and legs.' I say
nothing. He lays down his book (*African Discovery*) and turns to me:
'Forgive me, if I've made you unhappy and angry.' I'm amazed that
after all that madness he can lay his weapons down. H: 'I'm sorry
too.' V: 'You haven't done anything to be sorry for.' We lie side by
side, wrung out. 'It's astonishing,' he says, 'and I'm mortified by
it—how I wanted to go on and *on* with it, even when I could see it
was making you more and more unhappy. I never got bored with
it. I wanted to *keep going*.' He was speaking almost wonderingly, as
if about something he'd never experienced before. I said, 'We had
to get to the end of it.' He said, 'I love you more, for your toughness
and your seriousness.' I don't remember now what I said.

———

The old leftie academic told me that her ancient mother's need
for constant care was showing up quarrel-points between her and
her sisters. 'Yes,' I said with sympathy, 'caring for old parents—
I'm not looking forward to that, much.' 'Yours,' she said, with a
narrow, sidelong look, 'might be so rich that everything will work

out harmoniously.' I'm always rocked by these sideswipes she seems driven to make. After her first visit to my place: 'Of course, my house isn't nearly as big and beautiful as yours.'

———

A letter from a young woman university student: do I try to write with a female voice? Do I consider myself a feminist writer? Hard to answer but I come up with this: 'Whenever I'm writing badly I almost always realise, after weeks of pointless struggle, that I've been trying unconsciously to write like a man, i.e. at too great a distance from myself. So I stop telling myself "I am writing a novel" and I sit quietly and wait for images to present themselves, and then I follow. I stop trying to be ringmaster and whip everything into shape by cleverness and willpower. I *am* "clever", and I *have* got "will". But these attributes invariably lead me down the wrong track.'

———

V leaves for Africa via Toronto. I cook, I eat, I iron, I watch Buster Keaton on TV and laugh till tears come to my eyes. W calls, suggests we go to a Japanese movie she says is described as 'a breathtaking puzzling thriller about a psychotic nightmarish maze of delusions'. We're going to be friends, I can tell.

———

R comes over to V's. While we're talking she looks past my head at a painting on the wall. 'Gosh,' she says, 'that McCahon really *is* something, isn't it.' I stare at her: 'You mean to say I had to go through all that for *nothing*?' She shrugs, and goes on gazing at it. 'I saw it at night. I never noticed the elephant's-breath grey of the sky before.'

———

Wrote another page of 'Recording Angel'. And another. When I look into my folder I find whole passages dashed off that I have forgotten writing. And as soon as I start a story, images come to mind and there is a place for them. This mystery. A novelist in the *TLS* says his writing consists of 'small acts of war'. I don't get that.

For me it's confrontation, then reconciliation, then integration, then release.

———

Air tonight very still, and smelling strongly of warmth, of air itself. Began *Beloved*. Full of wonder and respect.

———

In California an earthquake. A freeway has collapsed. 'Throughout the long evening, a heavy silence was occasionally pierced by a cry.'

———

To church with R. From the sunny garden, voices of children at play while the quiet rituals are observed.

———

The Mahabharata on TV. I watch with eyes out on stalks. 'What? Those stinking bogs? Those gruesome forests?'

———

I have to swear an affidavit for F's and my divorce. I went to the university bank and asked if they had a JP. A shy young man with gold-rimmed spectacles dug out from his glassed cubicle a tiny, battered, green New Testament. There we stood at the open counter, in full view of customers and tellers. I wanted to say, 'This is for a divorce. It's rather personal. Can we do it in your cubicle?' But I thought I should discipline myself to do things wherever I am presented with them. I kept my palm flat on the little green book and he asked me to swear. I swore, and read out the highlighted words: 'So help me God.' The solemn moment of the oath rushed past me, like the moment of communion at the altar rail. I didn't prepare myself. Is that why it flowed past me without ceremony?

———

Three good reviews of V's book. I experience a mixture of pleasure and pride, and a tiny lemon-drop of envy.

———

At church a baby girl was baptised. She lay quietly in the vicar's arms, absorbed in contemplation of things around her, her eyes very wide and bright, her hands spread like stars. During communion a man played a long and beautiful piece on the piano. I asked him later what it was: Beethoven. He played correctly, and with feeling, but he is not 'a good pianist' and that's why I enjoyed it so much, because it was hard come by and humbly offered.

————

G's stories about his girlfriend. She sounds like a version of what I used to be: an anima figure on the loose, rolling wildly across the deck.

————

V must be in Mali by now. I think of him with affection, as he is in our common life here—drying himself, reading—his well-shaped legs and high arches, his scowl. His loosening neck skin that reminds me deliciously of my grandfather.

————

Swam. The pink light that swarms on the surface of a green pool.

————

Dad talking about a bloke from Hopetoun called Parsey Trewin: 'He was terribly agile and strong. People said he was the best wheat-lumper in the country.' 'How big were the bags?' 'Three bushels of wheat per bag, and a bushel weighs sixty pounds.'

————

Dreamt of a guy in a band who was youthful, vigorous, cheeky, healthy. Feel bored even at the *thought* of dreaming about him.

————

E is editing the introduction to a famous Australian novel that's being reissued: 'I need a *crowbar* to get some air and light into his sentences—huge, clonking great subordinate clauses back to back.'

————

A wind blows along the street under the balcony. Dead leaves hiss, sirens whoop in a choir on Parramatta Road.

————

Ran home to catch the Melbourne Cup on TV. I'd forgotten how excited I always am by the race—the tension, how *long* it seems, and the marvellous beauty of the horses—all mythology seems to be packed into those profile shots of their stretched necks, powerful bodies—I could *cast myself* before gods so tremendous! I remembered standing at the rail at Flemington and hearing the roar come rolling round the track, keeping pace with the horses as they ran— the colossal creatures when they surge by, unimaginably tall and alive—then the weeping jockey with the microphone shoved in his face—pausing and pausing, turning away his eyes to control his sobs of joy—the stupid questions, his rush of words—'and then, and then I—I knew I was on the right horse...'

———

I love Thea Astley. Today she said to me, 'I just want to write like Raymond Carver. That's all I want, and it'll never happen.'

———

Got to get this angel story finished before V gets back. At least a draft to a possible full stop. I can't work any faster or smoother because I don't 'know' what I want it to 'say'. I'm finding out as I go.

———

Lunch with G at the Bayswater Brasserie. I am spectacularly plain with greasy hair hooked off my neck with a pink plastic clip, while he is wearing a suit and elegant tortoise-shell glasses. He asks if we can change tables: I'd chosen one in a comfortably dim corner, clearly unfashionable. He explains that he was being stared at, in a way that made his back 'prickle', by a very successful TV producer who had been 'hanging round' his wife since he left her, visiting her and offering her expensive presents: 'A mantel clock' (a brand I'd never heard of), 'an Italian writing set, made of wood. Things he brings back from his trips.'

H: 'What was the payoff?'

G: (*offended perhaps by the naïve crudity of the question*) 'Payoff?'

H: 'I mean what did he want? Blokes don't give presents like that without a reason, do they?'

G: 'Well, he's a suitor, I guess. He told her she ought to divorce me for a lot of money and use it to set up a gallery.'

————

Have stopped wearing my watch. Enormous reduction in pointless anxiety level.

————

R lends me George Herbert's poems. O and I dig out archaic spellings—'grones', 'choak'd'—and become quite hilarious.

————

Y calls. They have had to sell the publishing house to Penguin. Her voice is quiet, as if weakened. They've been wrecked by high interest rates. 'It's like losing a child,' she says. She spoke for a long time. I felt shaken by the news. This must be how kids feel when they're told their parents are getting a divorce: the shock of it shows how little you know, how much you've taken for granted, and how strenuously and with what generous self-command you have been protected.

————

To lunch yesterday at the great reader's. E and Y came too. The great reader is very taken with both of them, and everybody sparkles. Y tells us that very late one night before *The Children's Bach* came out, the biographer had called her and told her the book 'must be stopped—Helen must be *stopped from publishing it*.' I was so jolted by this that I instantly forgot it. For twenty-four hours. It came back just now, bringing with it a (short-lived) spasm of amazed anger. During the lunch I began to see what's lively, energetic, iconoclastic, experienced i.e. *lovable* about the great reader. I've met her too late—she's old, she'll die, I'll be *sad* when she dies.

————

People are sitting on top of the Berlin Wall. They're chipping chunks out of it with chisels, for souvenirs.

————

Eyes troubling me, rolling bars of blur. Thunder is tearing the air into strips outside the balcony, rain is pouring down, making the air silver.

———

Talking with R about original sin, which she doesn't believe in and I do (I think), I realised that my mind is troubled by much darker and more gruesome thoughts than hers is. 'What sort of stuff do you mean?' 'Oh,' I said, 'fantasies of murder, blood-letting... When I look at Peter Booth's paintings I don't see things there that are unfamiliar. The very bottom layers of my mind, the real vile murk of it, are like his paintings.' And saying this to her I thought, 'I need to get this stuff into my work, and *I will*.'

———

Lunch with the Cretan. I tell him about my pointless struggles to work my stuff into the shape of a novel, and my determination to write only what it's personally urgent for me to write. As I speak he leans forward smiling, smiling, and his eyes shine so brightly that I think they're about to overflow with tears. I pause, and he says with joy, 'I can't tell you how good it is to hear you say these things. I've been through exactly the same process. I had this story to tell, but I thought about theory, I thought, "I have to have a multi-vocal narration" and so on—and it became *impossible*—till I realised that all it needed was to be told simply.'

———

Raymond Carver's impersonal 'I'.

———

Two junkies in Andiamo, at the table next to ours. Girl on the nod, her head falling in a slow vertical arc, her face dull, a lump of meat under tangled hair. I long to feast my eyes on her depravity. The attraction of the disgusting, of a public loss of self-control.

———

V returns. Our reunion. He has brought home a book of Morandi paintings. So beautiful, so quiet. We sit close together on the couch and turn the pages, not needing to speak.

Immediately his presence here is normal. I can hardly remember his absence. He quietly reverses minor changes I'd made: moves the fruit bowl back to its former position, takes the pink cleaning cloth out of the bathroom and drops it in the laundry. This place is very, very small. He is worried about *where we will eat in winter*, since I suggested (where does one write a letter, or one's diary?) that I might use as my private spot a corner of the indoor table. His desk, which was mine for five weeks, is the airy one near the north-facing window. In London a famous agent took him on; he can't wait to get started. I have moved my daytime operations across the big road into the Fisher Library. I can work there all right, as long as I don't need to type anything. Somehow, without a word having been spoken, I seem to have accepted that my presence in the flat is superfluous to requirements during his working hours. In the mornings I feel him waiting for me to leave.

I gave 'Recording Angel' to E and am anxious that she will find me somehow monstrous. A monstrous detachment. But this morning she said, 'I think it's fabulous. Keep it quiet till you've got a whole collection done. It's going to depend on what sits around it, and on how you pick up the ends that are hanging. It's brave.'

H: (*uncomfortably*) '*I* think it's *brutal*.'

E: 'I thought it was brutal the first time I read it, but then I read it again.'

I'm wondering whether perhaps I am a monster. Not whether people will *think* I'm a monster, but whether I *am* one. She speaks further about it, though, and I lose my panic and feel an optimistic technical interest in the challenges it presents.

V to someone on the phone: 'Since I've been alone...'

E's balcony room is still free. I can walk there in forty minutes, across the university. The possibility of tea, of a salad for lunch with a hard-boiled egg and a potato, somewhere to wander around without disturbing anyone—me and E working away all day in our little factory, a women's world to balance against the rest of our lives where men and their demands make it hard to avoid becoming objects to their subjects.

———

Maybe we could sell everything and move to the country. An Elders man at Berry shows us a house in a beautiful valley. V in full flight (cricket on the radio) as we drive home. We begin to fantasise an isolated life. (I'm scared.)

———

Ate at the Brasserie with G who spoke of his work so interestingly that V was impressed and later remarked on his 'intelligence and experience'. The bill was $94.50. I seized it before V could see it, and whacked down $65 in cash, which he didn't notice. Felt proud of G as he spoke of these musical matters we know nothing of.

———

Terror stabs me at the idea of country life. What am I afraid of?

———

I've been deceiving myself into third-person writing again. Yesterday I picked up Naipaul's *Enigma of Arrival* and read the opening sentences: 'For the first four days it rained. I hardly knew where I was.' A quiet and dignified first-person voice: instant calm. The struggle went out of me.

———

A friend of V's calls him, wanting to hear about Timbuktu. 'I've ruined the dream of it,' says V, 'now that I've experienced it.'

———

After the service a little boy of four or so sidled out of the church alone, his hands clasped at the waist. He went up to a bored, crabby-looking bigger girl, and asked in a tone of suppressed panic, 'Have you seen my dad? Or my mum?' 'No,' says the girl, and skips away. I took him in charge. I was careful not to rush it; didn't offer my hand till we'd been searching a good five minutes. We found his parents at a meeting in the hall. I led him back into the church garden. 'Have you been drinking a cold drink?' 'Yes,' he whispered. 'What did you have?' 'I had some cordial.' 'Do you know how I knew you had a drink?' 'No.' 'Because you've got a little bit of orange on your top lip.' For the first and only time he looked up, with a crooked smile, and met my eye. 'It wasn't orange,' he said. 'It was red.' He plodded beside me on his square feet in square sandals, holding my hand. 'It was the same colour as—' He pointed at the reddish-brown gravel we were walking on.

———

V went on so long about the 'appalling' and 'mediocre' ABC books program he was interviewed on that I told him to stop grumbling or shut up. He's the first bloke I've been able to argue with to the shouting stage and still feel solid underneath—moments later we're walking arm in arm, pretending to sulk, asking each other for a kiss. Each evening we watch TV in silence, struck with awe at what's happening in East Germany. These millions of people who have *had enough*. The top party members who not only lived in luxurious guarded apartments but were creaming off money and stashing it in Swiss bank accounts.

———

In the middle of the night, hearing the rain still steadily pouring, V mumbled, 'There's definitely something strange happening to the climate.' In the morning he flew away to Christchurch with two art guys to look at the McCahons. Being alone here is very pleasant. Lately I've been snappy, easily angered, bossy. V continues to be loving to me, in a puzzled way, trying to steer round my incomprehensible moods.

———

A letter from the Polish philosopher: 'Now the sky is filled with clouds of delicate colour, and the land below is an outline of human lodgings.'

I wrote another page of whatever it is I'm writing. Trying to flatten the boy's affect: hard to write in a way that gets his dead quality but at the same time creates the sensual world he is dead to, while also giving hints of something untapped in him which will painfully grow, much later.

A perfect, calm summer night in Melbourne: dry air still warm from the day, music from cars with windows rolled down, groups of people in loose clothes walking along the dry, warm, flat streets to places where they will dance. Alone in my borrowed car I feel *the loss of youth*—the stiffening of my spine, the over-sensitivity of my ears, the disappearance of whatever looks I once had. I remember the hours of dancing, the cheap clothes we wore with style, the laughter and the sweat. Thought of Sydney with indifference, even dislike.

At M's I lie on her bed while she sews and irons, muttering instructions and comments to herself. Her astonishing, rewarding beauty. I gaze at her, mystified. Often I see her father's face surfacing in hers—his jawline, his fine nose; but never my own.

A cool, grey day at Primrose Gully. On the murky pond, two brown ducks that F bought at the market are peacefully cruising. Little finches everywhere. Vegetation around the house is all overgrown and out of control. I start to snip off aggressive shoots and runners, then see it is pointless and no longer my business. How wildly birds twitter, up here. A small eucalypt in front of the house has grown three feet and sprouted new, brightly gleaming, reddish-brown leaves. The movements of its foliage are relaxed and slow, like loose sleeves. By nightfall, when I stand outside, I can hear a soft, persistent, ubiquitous whirring, a light nervous tapping made by thousands of insects working among the leaves of the trees within earshot. Did I really spend all those nights up here on my own? Over the back ridge, in a sky not yet quite dark, the evening star.

———

At Y's. V still asleep. I'm noticing an obscure feeling of shame, as if at dinner last night I'd done something gross or hurtful, though I'm pretty sure I didn't. Y is always courteous and hostly, but sometimes her glances unnerve me: distant, or preoccupied, even hostile. It's easy to be here with V, though. Open expressions of affection are possible, even in public. A sense that we're in league together, socially. Relief and pleasure of this, after more than a year of dissembling.

———

Last night I was sorting ironed clothes on the stereo, with the iron and board still set up behind me. As I worked I gradually became aware that I was moving my mouth sympathetically with my hands, in the manner of an old person; and when I glanced up I found that V had been watching me, obviously noticing my 'old' expression too for instead of smiling at me as he normally does when caught in contemplation he flicked his eyes away, almost furtively, then looked back. I smiled broadly. I said nothing. Nor did he.

———

V is reading *The Double Helix*, by James Watson, the DNA guy. He relates with relish how the American Pauling, 'a giant in chemistry', was also working in that field, and how Pauling's son came into Watson and Crick's lab with a letter from his father that contained his discoveries about the structure. 'They grabbed it eagerly,' said V, 'and read it, and within a few minutes they both realised that he'd made a blinding, fundamental chemical error. He'd already sent his paper to a magazine and it was to be published in six weeks. They saw that the roof was going to fall in on him. They could have told him in time for him to withdraw it, but they didn't. Because it would give them more time. Instead they went down to the pub and toasted his failure.' 'How awful!' I said. 'I thought people were supposed to work together to understand our world.' 'Bugger that! If you're on the brink of a major discovery you don't let some poor bastard from *America* get in first! It's a competition!'

———

Dreamt I was going to let my house. A man I'd never heard of applied. I was about to let it to him, but when I asked M and her friends who he was, they said he was horrible, a real creep and dickhead, and not the sort of person I should let my house to.

1990

When I pulled the cloth cover off my typewriter a moth flew out.

———

The light entering the painter's studio through its sawtooth roof windows was very even, so that nothing seemed to cast shadow, and when I sat at the table watching people talking to each other in groups, I wished I had brought my camera (though I would have been too shy to use it in this company), because of the smooth, agreeable definition given to people's features by this light that did not seem to have a source but existed in the room evenly, calmly, without favouring one object, one surface above another: there was light in front of people, beside them, behind them; they seemed to float evenly in light.

———

The fireworks I liked best were the big blossoming ones that seemed to move towards you, giving the impression that you were travelling fast into an exploding area of deep space—heading into a galaxy. Also those that blew out into a puffball, then each atom of the explosion drooped like a lily.

———

Artists' wives who have a gritty ambition, who manage their husbands' affairs. V, I notice, will always, while criticising them for their 'stupidity' and 'greed', maintain the need for them to exist and function as they do. Over and over I see that he is used to being cossetted. He is helpless, bereft-looking, when I don't swing automatically into a maternal role. He does not possess a wallet, but keeps a few notes screwed up in his pocket. 'Have you got—? I've left my card at home.' If there is a task to be done that he sees I don't particularly want to do and that he has no desire to do either, he will say 'I can do it'—not 'I will' but 'I can'. He likes to put things back in order, but does not notice dirt.

———

Back at E's, all morning contentedly alone in her house. Not ready to open my folder. I've been reading too many literary reviews. The paralysis they provoke in me, a brick wall in front of my face, blankness where previously I saw corridors of narrative possibility opening out on to landscapes of what I know, remember or can invent.

———

'The immense beatitude of loving and being loved.' —Anthony Burgess in a BBC interview

———

The letter I wrote V in Mali, confessing envy of how seriously his work is taken in the British literary world, never reached him. And I never told him about it. Why should he have to carry this sour little load for me? When I do touch on the matter of envy, at dinner with him and E—very lightly, making mock of myself—his mood darkens. When men refuse to admit what they are feeling, women must either dance attendance or devise a neutral mode—or withdraw into our private thoughts till the coast is clear.

———

Further hours of struggle. Apparently I had seemed 'sceptical' when he brought home his report of the painter's 'idiotic' wife who'd claimed that Scott Fitzgerald was a greater writer than Proust. Well, I said, it *was* hard to believe that anyone could really think such a thing. But *why wouldn't I take his word for it?* Because he has a tendency to caricature people he disagrees with: he never remembers the name of a 'stupid woman' who has made an offending remark. When I ask 'What was she like?' or 'What does she do?' he can only say that she had a very pointy nose or wore too much lipstick. On this basis, even if I agree that her remark is silly, I don't think I'm being disloyal to him if I don't agree that she is a moron. This sends him into orbit. When I raise my voice he snaps, 'Oh, behave yourself! I shouldn't allow—I mean, it shouldn't be allowed that we speak sharply to each other.'

———

After the ridiculous argument I carried downstairs to the rubbish bin, wrapped in several layers of newspaper, the remains of the Christmas ham, which had gone slimy and begun to stink. It was roughly the size and weight of a new-born baby.

———

Later I thought that I should destroy my description of our fight. Our *naked struggle for supremacy*. But that would be…destructive. So I went to work. I was alarmed by what I was writing. I hardly knew from what squalid dream world it was issuing.

———

Constantly surprised by strands and echoes of other stories that return—as if the thing were knitting itself and I were no more than the dummy holding the needles.

———

At Neilsen Park we sat peacefully together looking at the ships, the green water, the grey sky with high strips of pink that ended in complex boiling curls—like Maori carvings, V said.

———

Dreamt of watching M, at twelve or so, in her little bathers, diving and frolicking neatly in a huge brown African river.

———

A boat with forty-nine people on board, capacity twenty, sinks off Port Stephens. Five small children drown. The parents, in the water, see them through the cabin windows: they'd been 'resting' in there when it sank.

Sick for my house. With many windows and rooms of my own. How have I allowed this narrowing to happen to me? If I want to be truthful and clear I must always be ready to be alone. What are the compromises I will not make?

With V to the great reader's. Hours of quiet, each of us with a book, then eating, drinking, laughing and comparing notes. Her style and stride in conversation. Pale spreads of lightning for hours, and the occasional fork that stabs the horizon. A wild-eyed, rearing, strutting, thieving raven. A magpie which utters, from the ground, a light, liquid gush of song as casually as—a god, perhaps.

At E's a little blonde English girl of ten, with a London accent. We were magnetically drawn to each other: we gossiped, provoked, confided, teased. I was besotted with her. 'Do you learn music?' 'Well…I've got a recorder I can play. And a trumpet.' 'A trumpet! Can you get a note out of it?' 'I wouldn't call it exactly a *note*. But a *sound*.' We laughed so terribly that tears ran down our cheeks. Each time my paroxysms would subside she would turn her pink, sunburnt face full on to me and utter a bursting gush of giggles that would set me off again. I'd forgotten about girls' giggling—that orgasmic collapse of all inner resistance. My life here lacks certain dimensions: kids, dancing, noise in the house, loud music.

Our moving to the country fantasy has been nipped in the bud. By Dad. I learn the hard way that the North Fitzroy house they 'helped me to buy' does not belong to me at all. Even with one's parents one ought to read the fine print. Dad writes V a letter of such brutally blokey insults that I throw myself on the bed and bawl loudly for ten minutes. V is amazed and disgusted. By everything. And I don't blame him. Secretly, though, I know it was a dumb fantasy. I toil for days to boil my rage down into a letter of eight terse lines to Dad.

V: 'Good on you, sweetheart. It's a little masterpiece. It shows you think he's being an idiot, and yet it's *jolly*. Well done.'

———

The luxury of rewriting. There is always something there, forgotten, waiting for your attention.

———

J is here from Western Australia to do publicity. I introduce him to V and they get on. Great bursts of talk in the noisy cafe with rain pouring down outside. 'When I first read your short stories,' says J, 'I thought, now, if I can just get past *this* bastard—' We all laugh. Watching V's pleasure at the younger man's compliment I try to think whether I have ever looked at an older writer of either gender and *pitted myself*. Perhaps if I had...

———

Read *The Aspern Papers* with joy. Its beauty, its drive, its seriousness but its lightness of touch. It didn't frighten me into dropping the pen forever, as Proust was doing several months ago.

———

Whenever I have pace or verb problems I get out *Kidnapped*. The intense *practicality* of Stevenson's prose. Nothing there but 'muscle and blood and skin and bone'. And he shifts it along using semi-colons. Forward movement in smooth surges rather than the staccato effect of full stops.

———

Tristan und Isolde with V. We took a little picnic for the intervals and ate it sitting on the steps with O and R. All of us excited and thrilled. At last the penny dropped about Wagner. Swept away by the music—in Act 3 I realised, sitting forward open-mouthed, that for long stretches of time I had not even glanced at the surtitles. I was completely *listening*.

———

W has gone away and lent me her house, on Pittwater, for a couple of days. Not only did I leave my watch at home but the power is off. I'm here alone with no stove, no fridge, no radio. Somewhere a crow, *hark, hark*. From time to time a great NUT crashes on to the roof and bounces once or twice. I lie on the bed reading Walter Benjamin's *Moscow Diary*, his record of the so-called love between him and Asja Lacis who sounds a frightful piece of work. Relief when I read of hopeless love-journeys made by others: I am not the only one. During *Tristan* last weekend, when the king discovers the lovers' treachery, great waves of shame went lurching through me, betrayals I had perpetrated, especially of F: I must have had the glazed eyes of someone possessed.

———

Mum writes: 'Dad thought he had cancer and they'd just stitched him up and nobody was game to tell him. It was a twisted small intestine, which the doc just disentangled. He has lost a lot of weight and don't tell anyone I said so, but he really looks his age and a bit more.'

———

When V went to the toilet in the restaurant I said to Z, very fast, 'Z—my father's been sick. He was in hospital. I thought he was going to die, but then he got better, and I felt awful—almost disappointed.' 'When they do die,' said Z, 'you'll probably have all sorts of feelings you could never have foreseen.' I saw V approaching and changed the subject. He's heard enough about my father to sink a ship.

———

Since I've been 'happy', my openness to what my senses can observe has lessened. Beauties of nature are less piercing. They strike me less *personally*, I mean with less meaning that's personal to *me*.

———

On the ferry this morning, when I sat on the top deck with M and her boyfriend and the boat moved off towards the next stop, a strange sensation came over me, to do with the blue and sparkling water, the clear sky, hot sunshine and a fresh breeze moving in steadily from the open sea: a memory of a happiness from so long ago that I couldn't even locate it in time. Maybe this is my first day of being old.

———

After they had gone on up the coast with their friends, V grumbled at length about the 'terminal informality' of 'young people in Australia'—apparently the boyfriend had *played his guitar* while V was speaking on the phone. 'They could've stayed in a motel. They're on holiday, aren't they?' He doesn't seem to remember that when you're young you don't have any money. 'You don't really understand, do you,' I said to him, 'that if I haven't got a place for my kid to stay when she visits me, there's something wrong? In my life?' 'Is it me,' he asks, quietly, 'or is it the apartment?' We talk about how hard it is to show each other the deepest parts of our separate lives—e.g. the first visit to the great reader. We try to work it out. Because we love and respect each other.

———

William Styron in *Darkness Visible*—how hearing Brahms' 'Alto Rhapsody' had hauled him back from suicide. A day when I'd been struggling with V and was dully washing up: the radio was on, and they played a Brahms string quartet. For the first time I knew what the word 'grace' meant. It came dropping gently on my head, through the music. My anger and sadness flowed out of me and were gone.

———

'…stretched out his hand. She pricked it, and he did begin to laugh, and she laughed too, and drove the pin quite deep, and kept glancing into his eyes, which ran helplessly in every direction.' —Turgenev, *First Love*

   All those *and*s. I should worry less.

———

The famous British writers at the Wellington festival. We've read them, we're drawn to them, they interest us. V is confident and gets a response, but I sidle up to them so self-effacingly that they don't notice me. James Fenton describes to me how to make stuffing for a chicken, but doesn't meet my eye. Ian McEwan and I talk about piano lessons, we've both tried to learn Bartók's *Mikrokosmos*, but we don't make any real contact. What *is* contact, anyway, and why do I need it?

Last night at sunset, the incredible purity and emptiness of the pink sky, the bony flanks of the hills—how close we are here to the bottom of the earth. Something terrifying about such clarity. Is this what McCahon's on about?

Jan Morris was at the dinner. When she entered the room the world was a warmer place. Thick, dry, wavy, grey hair, a face both mannish and feminine, cheeks of a rosy ivory above the faint shadow as it were of five o'clock. A sweetness of expression—attentive, intelligent, warm—a terrific listener. At 10 pm, in a pause, she straightened up and said in a firm, cheerful tone, 'Well. I must go home to bed.' I felt melted by her, somehow, and blessed by her company.

When we got home from New Zealand, V looked for a place to hang a tiny orange McCahon he had bought in Wellington. The only possible place was already occupied by a picture I'd brought with me from Melbourne, a pastel drawing by T of a road at night; after he came back from Africa and didn't like where I'd put it, I'd moved it to a spot over my corner of the table. Now he took down T's picture from that spot and replaced it with the orange McCahon, which looked very good and right there, and I said so, but I was sad, not knowing where I would be allowed to hang T's picture with its meaning personal to me. I went into the laundry and started to do some handwashing. He came in after me and said, affectionately, 'What's going on in here? Is something wrong?' I said, 'Oh, I feel a bit sad about my picture.' He burst out: 'Oh, I'm not going to put up with this! You're sulking in here as if I'd taken your picture down without asking you! I *said* we were only trying it *out* in that spot, that if you didn't like it there we could put the other one back!' I said, 'I'm not sulking. I came in here to do the washing. I didn't want to parade in front of you the fact that I felt sad.' 'Yes but you *showed* it.' 'Do you mean I have to pretend not to feel sad so you won't be uncomfortable?' 'Of *course* I don't mean that!' He rushed out of the laundry, whisked the McCahon off the wall, put the T back, and whirled out of the flat, slamming the door behind him.

There is of course a highly developed aesthetic behind all this, against which my sentimental tastes can gain no purchase. It's not worth stating them. I haven't got the stamina to face the blowback.

Later I took down T's night road. Later still he put the McCahon back up.

———

He said that I was very 'touchy'. I said that this was true. He asked what he did, or was, that made him hard to live with. After a lot of thought I said it was his tendency to enjoy stressing the negative in everything that came up; that it made me very tired, as if I were dragging behind me a heavy bundle, 'the vibe'. I notice that since this conversation he's stopped snarling, whenever the phone rings, 'Oh, who the *fuck* can this be?'

———

Shakespeare's fabulous verbs: 'If you hide the crown, even in your hearts, there will he *rake* for it.'

———

I propose to V that I should have the bedroom walls as my picture territory. He agrees at once. When his friend the painter comes to visit I overhear V telling him all about it, with comic grimaces, conspiratorial glances, apprehensive shrugs and so on. I resolve not to bite.

———

The great reader's had a heart attack. I keep suggesting V should get his arse to the hospital but he grumbles and fulminates about 'all the bloody women' who are 'flapping around like headless chooks' and 'speaking in dark and sombre tones'. I suppose he is scared of seeing his wife. She ranks me and of course I can't go, but I long to say to the great reader, 'I've only just had the good fortune to meet you. Don't you go and die on me.'

———

A good day's work. My mind moved freely, as if all its windows were open and air could blow through. While I was writing and rewriting, with intense curiosity and pleasure, the dream Maxine has of 'the tiny sad monarch with his orb and sceptre', my old dream title from years ago, 'Cosmo Cosmolino', came back and strode into place as the title for this story but also perhaps for the whole book.

———

R called to me across King Street: 'How fortuitous! I've just been working out my whole position on life with the help of a dream I had that you were in.'

———

Letter from T: 'Some pastels are drawing themselves as I hesitantly run along behind.'

———

I sent 'A Vigil' to J. He wrote back that he didn't like it. It's 'too awful and unrelieved. Am I missing something?' I saw at once that he's right; and that the angelic nature of the two men at the crematorium has remained, through my cowardice, hidden inside my head. Had to lie on the couch for fifteen minutes in my desolated pride. But lying there I began to see ways to shine light beams into the unrelieved mass of misery: only the bird shrieks, not the boy; cut out references to shit...

———

Fish and chips on the grassy slope at Bondi last night with V, R and O. Happy foolery and merriment. Admired once again the way O never bears a grudge: his extraordinary clarity of soul. Driving home down William Street we saw a 6'2" creature striding along

in nothing but a G-string and minimal bra—stiff blond wig—
wonderfully creamy white skin—skilful make-up—and carrying
a very long, very slender whip.

————

'I was taught as a child,' said J, 'always to be polite to strangers, in
case they were angels.'

————

V's gone to New Zealand again, about the *catalogue raisonné* they
want him to do. Bereft without him at the end of the day but kept
working. Later he called to say he had food poisoning, sick and
wretched, alone except for a guy who brought him three bananas.

————

Flipped through the old typescript of *The Children's Bach*. The
extreme simplicity and shortness of the sentences. My work is very
minor. It will never be noticed by the world at large. But this does
not excuse me from the responsibilities of any artist.

————

V is home, and sick again—bad headache, nausea, the shits. I tiptoe
about. 'Can I get you anything? Would you like a herbal tea?' He
rolls away with a groan: 'Aw, I'm not drinking *that* bloody muck.'
Later, when I sit on the bed next to him, he says, 'What are you gonna
do about your hair? Didn't you say you were gonna do something
with it?' 'Why?' I say, alarmed. 'Does it look awful or something?'
'No, but it's getting a bit sort of *thick*, isn't it?'

————

My sister and her friend and I met at the Caffe Troppo the other
night. The waiter brought us some bread and my sister said to me,
'When I left the church you wrote to me, "Doesn't he say *Whenever
two or three are gathered together in my name?*"' She held up her
piece of bread and said, 'This is the body of Christ.' Her friend did
the same, and I did too. Then we ate the bread and drank a whole
bottle of wine.

————

V and I walked round Glebe late in the afternoon. Still warm enough for a T-shirt. Beautiful houses. Dark gardens, each with its solitary cricket.

———

At the Balkan, tired after a day's work, I told V I was going to have a coffee tomorrow with W. He was surprised and disapproving: 'What are you seeing *her* for? We're already seeing her at the weekend.' He talked about Bloomsbury Publishing, who have signed my book (at his instigation, through their publisher, whom he knows). He said Nadine Gordimer had recently moved to Bloomsbury: 'They need people. Their list is *hopeless*. They've got almost nobody.' Stung, I foolishly said, 'What about me?' 'What *about* you.' 'Not that I'm suggesting I'm…' 'What *are* you suggesting?' The rest of the meal passed in awkward small talk. Back at his building, I followed him along the hall. What am I doing here? Cheek by jowl in a narrow flat with a man who scowls when I say I want to go out with a friend?

———

Dreamt I was in a courtroom. The great reader was to give evidence about the value of one of her late husband's paintings, and V was an expert witness. The great reader began to address the court in a wildly agitated manner: 'I'm scared! I've no idea *why* I'm so scared, but I am! I'm scared!'

———

A weekend with V and W up at the great reader's. She is thinner, more subdued; has given up smoking entirely: 'There's nothing like suddenly not being able to breathe, darling bird, to make one see reason.' Sometimes while the rest of us chattered and laughed she sat at the table looking quietly into the distance. The sharpness of the air, up there, its cleanness. The high gum trees streaming in the wind. W and I dyed a T-shirt pink and then washed and waxed the cars. While the great reader rested, V and W and I went down to the beach and picked up beer cans, stubbies and other rubbish. In half an hour each of us was hauling a couple of bulging white plastic bags, and our self-righteousness had given way to a simple hunting spirit: we no longer conversed but progressed bent double along the beach, fossicking in piles of driftwood and dry seaweed. Two little girls ran after us to join in. All this on a cold, clear afternoon with a wind blowing.

———

Today I wrote a page and a half about someone called Janet—name chosen for its briskness, dryness, lack of feminine grace or charm. I am probably cranky and distant lately. It's to do with the blank, contemplative state I'm in when work goes well. Uh oh. The Stravinsky's lunch syndrome. When the piece of work exists, I can almost live in it. V is patient and continues to express love for me. I am ashamed of my absentness, and determine to be sweeter to him.

———

I filled out a questionnaire. Under 'Who (known or unknown, living or dead) has had the greatest influence on you intellectually?' I wrote R's name. But I didn't tell anybody.

———

I keep waking earlier than V. The second or third time, I realise this is a way of achieving a short period of privacy, the way I did when I was a mother.

———

We saw de Kooning on TV wearing two tartan shirts at once. This morning I stopped at the Cat Protection op shop and found a beauty: blurry pinks, greys, blues, greens, yellows. Fifty cents.

———

I think of my characters now as actual people. Their 'paltry experiences' have actually happened. I long to continue the slow, deliberate hacking of stone which will allow me to know their futures.

———

Pentecost. As the service progressed I became aware that all the imagery of the invocation and action of the Holy Spirit is in my story. Light, fire, wind, breath. I leaned forward with my head on my arms and whispered, 'Help. Help. Help.' (Is that praying?) I need help to *keep it up*. And if I can, the book itself will take me where it wants to go.

———

Once they find the clock in the locked room I was at a bit of a loss. Then I wrote about the way the twig cradle sweetened the room, and about the season of winds, but I don't know how to fit it into the narrative, which must keep moving forward, in its looping way. I have forty-two pages in my folder.

———

Ran into the old leftie academic on my way back to V's. She asked if I ever got homesick. I said I did. And then she asked me in a very delicate way whether V had ever considered moving down to Melbourne to live. At that moment, a fantasy of our living in my house got hold of me, and I can't shake it off. Today, washing my knickers in a bucket, I said to V that I was homesick and home-less: 'Why don't we live in my house?' Pause. 'There's something about Melbourne,' he said, 'that I find—I find that in Melbourne I get really depressed. And don't forget that in Melbourne you'd get tangled up with your family again.' I went on washing, and he became very interested in a stray piece of metal that was lying on the laundry floor. He walked away with it, and began to try it out on various parts of the fridge.

———

The book rolls forward at its own rate, acting as a black hole that sucks into it everything I think, witness, overhear and see on TV. Today, instead of trying to perfect each paragraph before I moved forward, I thought, 'Fuck this! I'll keep barrelling on.' Hours passed in big bursts and I ended up with seven pages of stuff I could never have foreseen or invented. Reeled back to V's with sore eyes and an empty head. This must be how it's done—take your foot off the brake, unpurse the lips and see where it takes you.

———

'I think I've got a mother problem,' says my sister, 'rather than a father problem.'

Me: (*astonished*) 'How do you mean?'

Her: 'I *never* have any good moments with Mum. With Dad at least you can have a laugh occasionally, but Mum's so boring.'

Me: 'But don't you find a lot of Dad's horrible characteristics in yourself? A tendency to bully, and to be impatient and angry? *I* do.'

Her: 'It's better to be him, to have those characteristics, which you can learn to channel, or to rein in, than to be like Mum—a bloody *doormat*.'

———

Steel-grey Melbourne skies, a cloud at 5 pm the colour of gabardine behind the bare elm branches in North Fitzroy. Ground dark and damp. Can't think how I could have left this city.

———

To St Kilda marina with T who has bought a small yacht. A new version of the eternal dilemma: the bloke she lives with has a captain's ticket and so, according to the law of the sea, on board her own boat he is master. Her aggrieved account is split by wild laughter. We talk with our usual brutal frankness. The yacht: its ingenious layout, the clever storage and sleeping arrangements, but I was scared of its masts and stays, their tension, a hard professionalism. I'll never go to sea. Not even with her.

———

After dinner in their new 'townhouse' in Kew, Dad offers to play me something from a CD he's just bought—Pavarotti singing 'Caruso' from *The Fortunate Pilgrim*. That voice comes pouring into the room. We listen to the end without looking at each other. Dad: (*shyly*) 'What do you think of it?' Me: (*sincerely*) 'It's beautiful, Dad. It's a really lovely song. The arrangement's brilliant. And his voice is magnificent.' Gratification all round, hostilities forgotten, oiled by a very large scotch he had poured for me, but also by the fact that earlier, snooping upstairs, I'd discovered that my photo was not among the display of family pictures enshrined on a bureau near his desk, but was in his bedroom, on the dressing table, alongside his photos of Mum and his father. I want to say but don't dare, 'Dad, don't you want me to be happy? I am, with V, for the first time in many years. Can't you stop being jealous, and let me be happy?'

———

Gave a copy of my story to Y, and to the Polish philosopher.

———

This is what I miss in Sydney: messing around at somebody's house on a winter afternoon, sharing a bottle of crap pink champagne, working through the ukulele songbook ('Melancholy Baby', 'On Moonlight Bay'), reminding ourselves of stories from the past. Somebody knocks up a batch of drop scones. M plays the piano. We even sing a round. I miss V down here, especially at night. But the singing would have been too much for him.

———

In the *TLS* someone quotes Virginia Woolf's dismissal of R. L. Stevenson's 'dapper little adjectives'. Ooh I was furious! She's a goddess, but at that moment I wanted to kick her flabby Bloomsbury arse. Into the heather.

———

Dreamt I was with a bunch of men who were about to be put in prison. All the women had gathered for the parting. Music was played. The women had to dance, and we did, merrily and with great springiness, leaping high into the air. But when the music stopped and we turned around, the men had been rounded up and hustled away by brutish guards. Men and guards moved across a rainy paddock.

———

V was looking glum. I tried to pester it out of him with teasing and affection, but all he'd say was, 'I'm changing. I've changed. I've lost my edge. I'm not as sharply defined, when I'm with people, as I used to be.'

———

I've always thought that Glenn Gould was my all-time favourite and best, but last night I heard a CD of Sviatoslav Richter playing Beethoven's Piano Sonata No. 17, 'The Tempest'. When he laid down the opening arpeggio, as gently and self-effacingly as if only checking that the piano was in tune, I wanted to prostrate myself.

———

V woke and related an astonishing dream, teeming with imagery— a sleeping woman, a bull, 'two pelicans waddling down a road, black and white, like bloated magpies'. I sat there with popping eyes. It was like some fabulous painting—a Picasso—I don't know. And then he says, 'Now, I defy *anyone* to make any sense out of that.' I bit my lip and remembered what Jung used to say to himself before he approached anyone's dream: '*I do not understand this dream.*' But I felt so tenderly for him, showered with these treasures that he doesn't know what to do with. I wanted to reassure him, and encourage him, but I didn't know how.

———

The sky-blue shirt! I could never have planned it! It came from wonderful nowhere-land, like a brilliant blue tile, an Isfahan mosque tile. I couldn't believe I'd written it! I feel as if I'm a reader too, only more hard-working than the rest.

———

Me: 'I've got no idea what that "Uncompleted" story of yours is about. Not the faintest idea.'

V: 'Yes, but hasn't it got a sort of *austere beauty*?'

We shouted with laughter; and I thought, I must read it again.

———

The writer from America told me she was 'involved with a married man'. We spoke warmly about the difficulties of this. 'Why is it,' she said, 'that when you love someone you always want *more*?

You think, "Once a week will be enough", but it never is.' Later I thought I should have said, 'It's because you want to get past "being in love" and through to an ordinary peaceful life on the other side, if you can.'

———

Out to eat with G and his four younger brothers, all guitarists. I got there early and had a vodka while reading on in Ratushinskaya's prison-camp book. G told me the producer hopes to cast Bruno Ganz in my movie; and he is interested. Having written this I stare at the words in silence.

———

My sister is in charge of our parents' credit card account while they're travelling in Europe. 'In one month,' she tells me on the phone, 'they spent $500 on lunches. And the awful book they gave me for my birthday cost *fifteen bucks*. I also noticed they donated $25 to the Guide Dogs.'

———

The producer told me Bruno Ganz was eager to get the part. 'Eager' was the word she used. In my euphoria I pretended to bite the table edge.

———

I think the point of my story has come to me. I don't dare to write it down in case I scare it away. As usual it presented itself 'twixt sleep and waking'.

———

The blunt candour R and I are capable of, in conversation. There is nothing that may not be said.

———

Dreamt I was in charge of quite a small baby. I carried it about with me, holding it in my arms, wherever I went.

———

After *Lulu* at the Town Hall, we went to eat at Antipodes. Some of the cast were drinking there. A waiter brought out a slice of cake with a sparkler stuck in it, the group broke into 'Happy Birthday', and in the last few notes Lulu and die Gräfin Geschwitz let rip in harmony, at full operatic strength. Plates and glasses jostled on the tables.

———

The whole time I'm writing I'm nearly exploding with the tension of making myself sit still.

———

V, puzzled, shows me a photo in *Women's Weekly*. 'Look. That's not a very good baby, is it? It looks like an old man.' 'It doesn't always look like that, I imagine. It's probably just got a little expression on its face.'

———

I got to the end of *Cosmo*. Where is this stuff coming from? The weird state I'm in. I have to apply my intellect but at the same time keep my instincts wide open. I need to hover between these levels.

———

The Aboriginal activist at dinner. Her tales about clashes with politicians had a swashbuckling quality that made us laugh but I felt slightly cowed by her. Late in the evening, though, she talked about Aboriginal beliefs—death, the return of spirits—in a way I could have listened to all night. Her face softened and lit up: she spoke with loving reverence.

———

Y sat down with me and talked about my stories. As always she was able, with her extraordinary delicacy and skill, to point out the potential in what was still sketchy and clumsy. So grateful, so relieved. 'You don't have to publish a whole *lot* of stories, you know,' she said, 'just to prove you've been working.' I showed her my possible epigraph, from Mother Julian of Norwich: 'After all this, I became more serious.' We laughed. Her husband passed through the room and told me I should 'marry V. He's terrific.'

———

At E's book launch everyone was happy. The young editor was wearing stockings with little golden fleur-de-lys on them.

———

M's twenty-first. A rocking party in a Fitzroy pub. F's speech brought the house down—perfect comic timing, full of hilarious wit and affection. M stood listening at the front of the dense crowd: her face was a vision of wild delight, almost unbearable to look at, she was so illuminated and joyful. I felt humble before her, irrelevant, shaken by the ending of this twenty-one-year stage of my life. I begin to understand my mother.

———

V brings in the *Herald*: Patrick White is dead. Stunned, and vague. Our agent wept on the phone, telling me how when she was putting his wooden cross in his pocket, in the coffin, she'd found they'd put a tissue in there: 'We took *that* out!' I said, 'You'd think at *least* a linen handkerchief.'

———

Things have turned rocky between me and R. An awful feeling that I've used up her affection, that it's drained away. She must be fed up with me and my neediness. I'm always turning up at their place and squabbling with O and bashing their ears. Am I inflated, when I walk in? They both seem to want to puncture me. V takes a certain grim pleasure in the spectacle. 'It's much better this way. It's more *realistic*. You used to talk about her as if she was the Virgin Mary. Touching the hem of her garment.'

———

The difficulty of being in a couple, the long haul, the struggles for freedom within it, the demands for support and love, the disappointments, surprises, angers, the secret contempts. I used to feel things better. When I was on my own, in spite of my sometimes bitter loneliness, I used to notice things intensely. My senses were sharp. Now I'm dulled and ordinary. I plod from day to day.

———

V turns to me upon waking and says, 'We wouldn't have a *destructive* love, would we?' I laugh. There's something weirdly virginal about him. He can't have read Yeats: 'All true love must die/ Alter at the best/ Into some lesser thing./ Prove that I lie.' I say, 'I find living with someone very hard, sometimes.' 'Yes,' he says, 'you *have* got something hard, or indifferent, in you. A hard centre, an indifferent spot in the middle of you—very small, but hard.'

———

To *Lohengrin* with a very musical woman who'd never seen Wagner before. At interval she turns to me and says, 'This is *weird*.' The strange metallic rigidity of the knights in their forest, the inhuman quality of the characters and their dilemmas. The *swan*. We try to stifle our laughter, but soon become absorbed, and at the end agree that it was somehow marvellous.

———

Dreamt that V and I walked past a rubbish bin out of which stuck the hindquarters of a brown dog that was foraging in it. V tried to take hold of the dog to help it out, but it turned on him and sank its teeth into his left forearm. V, though he must have been in pain, kept an expressionless face, and staggered away from the bin with the snarling beast dangling from his arm.

———

At W's fiftieth birthday party I got talking with a very clever four-year-old boy. He asked if he could tell me a fairy story. Away he went, with gusto: 'And so…she skipped along at the huntsman's side…and the stepmother was *ac*-tually FYOUrious!' He bared his teeth and rolled his eyes and clenched his tiny fists.

———

I tell V, trying not to sound 'hard', that we can't go on living in this tiny flat. We need to live in a place where I can have my own room to work in: a room with a desk, and also a bed. He is not happy about this. He replies that I've 'got a problem'; that 'independence is all very well, but deep independence is a dangerous bore'.

I delivered the screenplay again, after reworking two scenes that the producer came and collected from me at E's. When she'd left I lay on the bed. In a while I turned on the radio, and into the room flowed a saxophone and a piano, very melodious and quiet. I lay there on my back, hearing the patterns of the music, the way the instruments moved with and against each other. I thought that I had been behaving like a 'creedless puritan', driving myself in work until the feeling side of me had almost died.

Just as I'm heading out the door to work, V says, 'Listen—do you want to go back to Melbourne?' 'Don't tease me, sweetheart.' 'No—really—if you did feel you'd be much happier there, we could…' I had to rush out, but as I drove past Central I began to notice something tight inside me loosening. I thought of my bike. My kitchen. The *area* of the place. The loosening of things I hadn't known I was holding so tight.

Dreamt I marched into a bottle shop and announced in a grand, resolute voice, 'Stand back. I'm going to BUY something.'

At E's today R told me what's wrong. My whole nature is 'too sensitive, hypersensitive'. She wonders why I'm not exhausted all the time, from being 'so aware, and alert'. She says I bend over backwards too far, with V, in an attempt to get it right; that I ought to learn to switch off and let things go past me. I asked in a small voice if she could explain to me more exactly *how* I was 'hypersensitive'—I hoped that at last somebody might be going to tell me something useful about myself, that I could get a handle on, and apply. But she became vague, declining, I suppose, to get further involved. I tried to be light about it: 'I guess I'll have to change my whole nature.' She laughed: 'I don't think so.' On the doorstep she said, 'Gosh, you look exhausted! I wish I'd kept my mouth shut!' I closed the door and looked at myself in the mirror. I looked white, and older, with dark rings under my eyes.

―――――

'Do you think people can change, at our age?' I said to V in bed. 'Oh…no, not really. Only round the edges. Why? What happened at lunch?' R must have spoken to him on the phone. I burst into tears and gave an account. He made it clear he agreed with R's opinion. But after a while he said, 'Does it help that somebody loves you?'

―――――

Dreamt that a tiny little girl came up to me in a dark, cyclone-fenced concrete enclosure and asked me in a trembling whisper, 'Excuse me—how many pairs of pants do I need to wear, to go and do wee, in here?' I picked her up and carried her on my arm, saying, 'Only one—and do you want me to help you? It *is* a bit spooky in here, if you're on your own.' She relaxed against me with a sigh, and as I carried her in towards the lavatory I could hear her whispering to herself, 'Safe. *Safe.*'

―――――

V keeps saying that Sydney is more 'exciting' than Melbourne, that Melbourne is 'suburban'—what if 'suburbanism' gets into his writing? I'm remembering the freshness of the air there, the chill of even a summer morning, how delicious its water is. I think about my house with a delirious daring. I see myself walking from room to room: an act of indescribable luxury.

―――――

'On some days,' wrote the Polish philosopher, 'any contact with others makes me feel afterwards depleted, as if I lost a chunk of myself, spoke too much or not enough—some mismanagement of self and energy…Panic, panic, it can be a little thing, a sudden heaviness that accompanies a reluctance to look up a word in the dictionary, a little death.'

―――――

It's as if I'd been totally and uncritically in love with R for ten years, and now she's driving me to back off and return her to her status as another person and not a glorious icon of perfection and omniscience. 'It's a good thing, I suppose,' I said, 'but I miss the way we were.' '*I* don't,' she said. 'That kind of intimacy is very seductive, but I think it's rather dangerous.' Fantasies of sharp retorts, of escape from all intimacy: a bare room, a table.

———

Up at the great reader's V and I saw a marvellous bird. It sprang up from behind some rocks and perched on a branch, staring at us with fierce, yellow, large, almost-human eyes. An owl? Not square enough. Must be a hawk. A small eagle? Got feathered legs. But the eyes are so big. Don't owls sleep all day? V was fascinated by it, moved: 'It's not scared of us at all. It's absolutely fearless.' I notice how deeply he responds to nature. He becomes fully absorbed, while I experience it as a background to my private thoughts.

———

At Christmas dinner Mum isolates me in a corner and behaves in a very emotional manner, holding my hand, hugging and kissing me many times, saying how glad she is that I'm 'coming home'. Dad can't meet V's eye or shake his hand but tells a couple of very funny stories. Later V said, 'He's clever. He really knows how to tell a story—how to show the awful part of a story.'

———

A perfect, pure summer's night in Melbourne. At sunset, a long pink cloud, ridged as neat and fine as salmon flesh. People in another garden talking quietly. Every now and then a burst of laughter. The sky very clear, as if the air were finer and clearer than in Sydney where it's always thickened by moisture, perfume, a great warmth remaining from the day's sun. Out the front, now, beside the plane tree, a small three-quarter moon.

C has let me the room above her office on Brunswick Street, a small, pretty space overlooking foliage. Relief of this *immense*. I set it up, and worked smoothly and productively for hours on the screenplay rewrite.

———

V: 'I feel as if I'm not really here, as if I don't know *where* I am.' Meanwhile I know exactly where *I* am—back in town: I've lent one sister $5400 to pay her Visa bill, and another bit me for $600 'till the end of March'.

———

I bought an old piano. I have forgotten almost everything. Except Small Prelude No. 1 and Prelude No. 1 of the 48. I stagger and limp through them.

———

Easter, and E came to stay. She and I spent a day and a night up at Primrose Gully. Terribly dry, the ground cracking. The farmland beyond the valley has a short silver hide on it. Birds sang. Koalas in the trees. A full moon shone all night. We walked over to the opposite ridge. Vast skies streaked and webbed with cloud, tiny wrens wherever we looked.

———

At dinner people talked about sex with strangers on planes. For once I was entirely innocent. One man said that his work colleague claimed he 'always got a fuck on an international flight. But he says you never have anything to do with the person sitting next to you, otherwise over the remaining hours of the flight you have to develop a *relationship*.'

———

Dew-soaked, glittering mornings, long warm dry days. Gardened all afternoon with V. We dug with mattock and spade, we shifted soil about in a barrow, planted a solanum rantonnetii, chives, parsley and thyme. We are now very slowed down and feeling our muscles. And reckless enough to say we are happy, though he refused point-blank even to consider coming out to hear my sister's band.

———

I realise that Dad will forever see everything bad that's happened to me as *my fault*.

———

In a Chinese restaurant in Kew V breaks open his fortune cookie: 'The world is always ready to receive talent with open arms.' He shows it to the waiter, who laughs scornfully and says in a loud, firm voice, 'Bullshit!'

———

Rajiv Gandhi has been assassinated by a bomb in a bunch of flowers.

———

Cold morning and I was up before six. Light comes as a brick-pinkness on the plane leaves, which are still only half down. Out the back the broad beans we planted have popped up like rows of tiny soldiers. Someone's rooster crows; then I hear the magpies. Standing in my own yard I feel almost relieved that my friendship with R is over. Maybe she's right: 'Opposite types threaten each other simply by existing.' V comes to the back door. We walk together to the shop to buy the paper, talking and laughing all the way.

———

The old professor has died. At home, in the afternoon, 'in his wife's arms'. One thing you could be sure of, if you died in *her* arms, is that nothing you did would disgust or dismay her.

———

I have so nearly finished this book that I can hardly make myself leave my office at the end of the day.

———

I call a married couple to invite them to dinner. The husband answers: 'Well, that would be very nice, but there's a problem—we've split up. She's left.' Thunderstruck silence. I ask what happened. He outlines his bewilderment in such a steady, bright, laughing voice that I also begin to feel bright and gay, as if we were discussing the odd behaviour of some other species.

———

The born-again and I meet at the gallery. He says he would like to marry, but because he works only with men, building the Harbour Tunnel, he never meets any women, and doesn't know how to.

———

I saw a fine cut of *Chez Nous* today. *Cosmo* had driven it right out of my head, so that as the plot unfolded I got shock after shock of narrative pleasure—at the *deepening* of the narrative. I kept thinking, 'Oh yes! There's this! And this! And this!' I snivelled a bit and shouted with immoderate laughter. I was shameless about laughing uncontrollably at things that others present found only mildly amusing.

———

I dyed two pairs of white trousers from Esprit, one a beautiful dark green, the other a dusky rose pink. Dyeing is wonderful. One feels original, and satisfied with oneself for being frugal, and resourceful. Waiting for the dye shop to open, I skimmed a few pages of V's first novel. His colloquial tone, so funny and controlled; the powerful visual images; and his splintering of sentences by the use of colloquialism—I felt by comparison a prim classicist. Tonight he's gone out with my sister to see Lester Ellis fight Attila the Hun or some such. Home alone I cook spinach and receive faxes from the

Chez Nous people demanding further dialogue for post-synching. I feel put-upon, but ultimately competent. The director says she asked Bruno Ganz, on the way to the airport for his flight home, if he thought he'd ever come back to Australia. He replied (she *said*), 'If there is another script as good as this one, then I will come.'

———————

I delivered the *Cosmo* manuscript to Y on Borsari's corner as she zoomed through Carlton on her way to Footscray. I opened the door, slung the fat photocopy on to the seat beside her, and slammed it shut. On the plane to Sydney now I'm still listing useful words I come across, with notes as to where they might beef up some passage or other. A 'brooding' sound passes from Patrick White's pine trees to the extra cello in 'Recording Angel'.

———————

V rings me at E's: a 'bitumen-coloured dog' ran at him as he pedalled my bike home from the bread shop. He crashed to the ground and broke three ribs. In casualty they gave him a hit of pethidine and wanted to keep him in—'over-servicing, as usual'—*of course* he said no and came straight home. And no, he does *not* need anybody to look after him. I take this at face value and go about my Sydney business. Next evening I call him. He's been lying down all day because it hurts so much. At 5 pm he drove himself to the hospital and asked for another jab. No, he *hasn't* taken his clothes off and got into bed with a hot water bottle. No, he *hasn't* had anything to eat, or called anybody—who on earth could he ask for help, during the daytime? He doesn't *know* anybody in Melbourne! He doesn't want any bloody women coming round making a fuss! No, *of course* he doesn't need me to come home! I lose my temper and shout at him. Then I call my sister and she says she'll rush round there and make sure he's all right. Oh, I could bloody *strangle* him.

———————

Y's editing as always tough, thorough yet somehow painless. In fact, exhilarating. We laughed a lot over the thing. Vast relief.

In the pew sheet at church they had a Leunig cartoon. 'There was once a man who could no longer believe things that were said. All he could trust was sighing, sobbing, swearing, screaming and singing. If you asked him why he no longer believed he would sigh…He would sob…He would scream and swear…And then he would start to sing like a bird.' I suppose he too was told he was hypersensitive.

We heard 'Death and the Maiden' played twice in one evening. Some Canadians played first, a very melodious interpretation, free, sweet and large; but then the Russians threw themselves fiercely into the drama of it, burning and brooding away, a tight ensemble, always leaning in. The tall cellist swayed so much in the second movement that he was almost dancing. I loved both versions but V wouldn't have a bar of the Canadians: too young, he declared, too ignorant of Europe.

'Last night the stars keenly glittered and sparkled with frost till the sky was all ablaze with them, and the night was strangely light, almost as bright as if there had been a moon. There seemed to be something that we did not know of giving light.' —*The Diary of the Rev Francis Kilvert*

V's gone to New Zealand. I miss him and his stern naval haircut.

I've reviewed David Marr's mighty biography of Patrick White. My parents read the review in the paper. Dad said to me, 'I think the writer of that book will be…*enchanted* by what you said about it.' Watching him struggle for the word I felt like bawling.

Labour of rewriting *Cosmo*. I see its hideous overwrittenness, its laughable clogging with adjectives. Strained, self-conscious, affected, over-ambitious, too complicated. By 4 pm I lost heart completely and rode home in the cold. Ate carrots, mayonnaise. Could have devoured the whole *house*, furniture and all, in my discomfiture.

———

Dinner with some painter friends of V's. A lot of roaring about art critics, how terrible they are, how nothing can be done about them and in the end they don't matter. Someone asked me if I had ever had a bad review. I said, 'Of course!' He looked incredulous. I did not pursue the matter. As we were all leaving, he said to me, 'I'm reading *Monkey Grip*. I'd never read it before. I'm enjoying it.' I smiled and said, 'Thanks.' His expression stiffened: 'I'll leave comments till I've finished.'

———

Out walking as it was getting light, V and I passed a blackbird singing on a wire. A very beautiful song, melodic, generously paced, sweet. V laughed: 'I build good nests. I find many worms.'

———

Y's become a grandmother. 'My women friends,' she said, 'have divided into two distinct groups: those who think it's simply wonderful news, and those who ask me carefully how I "feel" about it, as if I mightn't like it. But I find it doesn't touch on the area of vanity, or anxiety about age, at all.'

———

I'm scared that with *Cosmo* I will come a cropper.

———

The pregnant woman showed us a tiny singlet. I asked: 'Is it double 0?' 'Triple.' Even V laughed at its ridiculous smallness.

———

J interviewed on TV. I notice that his chin is high, all the time, as if nerving himself to do it, or defying something.

———

When V says he's finding it very hard to work in Melbourne, the novelist from New York makes some trenchant remarks. What happens, he says, traditionally—that is primitively, or in our instincts—when a man and a woman decide to marry or live together, is that the man takes the woman on to *his* turf. He proceeds to detach her from her family and her friends, and they continue to live, together, in the area of life he's carved out for himself. V, though, has left his own territory and come entirely on to mine. He has no family and no kids, he's estranged from his wife of twenty-four years, he has sold his piece of property, and he's here.

————

In the company of my parents V is generous to a degree rarely seen. Dad is courteous to him but still can't seem to meet his eye, and yet V goes on *working*, socially, with grace and ease. When he feels it's right, V will always go the extra mile, and more.

————

We planted two climbing roses near the front veranda. Cold wind, grey sky. Scrabbled in the dirt, panting. Brought buckets of good soil from the backyard; dug; clawed with both hands. Erased signs of struggle. Rain fell, heavily but briefly. Now the sun is out, among torn and fast-moving clouds. Rose stubs are standing up to all this, quivering a little. The reddish tinge of their stems.

————

Sometimes I wonder if this whole part of my life—including the book—is menopausal. A kind of lament for the children I didn't have.

————

I can't space out the last section. It *won't space out*. After an hour of struggle I got on my bike, rode up to Carlton, bought myself a white raincoat, and came home to bed. Lay there with a hot water bottle and let my mind roam destructively over the book. Saw nothing but its faults: puffy, hollow, false, affected. Thought of giving back the advance and crawling into a hole. Longed for the cold comfort of minimalism, the bone and sinew where no fat clings.

————

'Mount Pinatubo sunsets' every evening. People say it's dust from the distant eruptions—the sky a bizarre, alarming, metallic, brownish-pink behind wild, ragged clouds.

———

The visiting conductor's patience with our daggy suburban *Messiah* choir, a brilliant teacher, people sprang to obey and to learn. He put the tenors in the front row. One bloke, whenever he went for a high note, visibly clenched his buttock muscles. When the sopranos sang, one lone voice, very thin and feeble and hopelessly off-key, tried to take part. The conductor's eyes contracted, then he carried on as if it weren't happening.

———

Dreamt that in a seaside town I was standing with a man on a pontoon under which the ocean heaved. As we gripped the rail, two immense dark-green glistening swells rose and passed under us, tilting the pontoon like a matchbox.

———

The ousting of Gorbachev, tanks rolling on the streets of Moscow. The failed coup. Young soldiers' funerals, great posters of their faces, weeping crowds, a Jewish violinist playing at a grave, Orthodox priests in golden vestments swinging censers. A toppled statue of Lenin, dangling from a crane, sweeps through the air horizontal, a huge black angel. These colossal events unroll before our eyes. We sit gaping, silent. A head-shot of Yeltsin, sour-faced and squinting, one fist clenched high. 'I think it's terrific,' says V, 'how they don't *smile*. Behind that face there's a lot of deep, hard experience.' V has a tremendous respect and admiration for power.

———

At dinner a woman talks about how her mother had recently tried to confide in her about her past sexual experiences, or affairs. The daughter had been unable to accept it, and had turned away: 'I felt it as a fault in me, that I couldn't let her confide in me.' 'I don't see why that's a fault,' said V. 'Why should you be expected to listen to that kind of thing?' Pause, while everyone registers this. 'I'm her daughter,' says the woman, quietly and patiently. 'She needed to confide in me. She needed to tell me some things about her life.' 'I don't think,' says V, leaning back with his hands folded behind his neck, 'that you should feel that as a failure.'

———

My sister reports that her disagreeable mother-in-law had said to her, 'Goodness—you're looking more and more like Helen!' When the mother-in-law had gone home, my sister's husband said to her, 'She didn't mean that as a compliment, you know. I was impressed by the way you handled it.' Driving home, V and I become quite weak with laughter, though actually it's rather sobering.

———

No matter how I kick against them, all the things that Y told me I'd have to do to this bloody book I've ended up having to do. Or rather they end up doing themselves, because she was right. Every day I think it's still the day before. I'm exhausted. I conk out at 3 pm, my neck and shoulders ache, my fingers are clumsy and sticky. I look around and see that the room is dirty. I turn off the typewriter, the lights, the radiator. I put on my coat, walk down the stairs, wheel out my bike, and ride home. I'm so tired that I can't tell how far away things are. Thoughts about the outside world arrive thickly and are unsubtle.

———

A short, light, friendly letter from R: 'I regret the gracelessness.'

———

Y and I sat by her fire and worked through the remaining problems. She had an idea that in one stroke untied a knot that had been driving me insane for a week. It was such a brilliant inspiration that my mind went blank and I sat there with my mouth hanging open.

———

I ran into the law student at Notturno. We talked about *Thelma and Louise*, which for obvious reasons I had liked more than he had. I said, 'I felt gratified by it, as a fantasy.' 'What, of going on the road?'

'No. Of killing someone.' His eyes snapped into focus: 'Oh! I see what you mean!'

Alone in the house in the early evening. It's getting dark. Cars passing are already lit up. Only a bit of pale sky showing between the bare plane branches. A dog is barking. A bird sings sweetly and tunefully. Sounds like spring. My cramped spirit starts to relax and spread through the rooms.

While V's at the fight I watch a fabulous doco about Mstislav Rostropovich. His terrifying, diamond-dripping diva of a wife, his daughter in a huge fur hat that brilliantly suits her. In a hush between movements a woman's voice rings out in the packed audi-torium: 'Slava is Zeus!' Cut to the green room. Slava staggers in, someone strips off his jacket, his white shirt is soaked with sweat, they fuss around him, mopping and dabbing. He collapses on to a couch, holding his head. In whirls the daughter, shining bright in a silver-plated evening gown, and flings herself on to the couch beside him: 'My sweet daddy! That bitch will not leave this place alive!' The wife strides in and announces in a tone of blood-chilling calm: 'They *caught* her.'

I desperately miss sleeping alone. I long for it, I crave it. I don't think I'm a very nice person. Not cut out for this.

'In every work of genius we recognise our own rejected thoughts: they come back to us with a certain alienated majesty.' —Emerson, 'Self-Reliance'

V called and called to me from the backyard but I was busy cooking and would not come. 'Hel. Come out. It's serious.' At last I stamped out there, scowling. He pointed to the broad bean plants, which are chin-high. I leaned over, expecting a pest, and saw that the flowers had begun to turn into *actual beans*.

———

Hot flushes, several times a day, and sometimes in the night.

———

The great reader in the bar. 'A good hostess,' she says, 'should kill the guest.' I adore the way she speaks, I can't resist pulling out my notebook. 'His attention span to women, darling bird, was so short that it made me *haiku* everything.' Seeing me writing she laughs, takes a swig of wine and cries, '*Beeeee mai Boswell*!'

———

At the third dinner for V's fiftieth birthday one of the painters began again his diatribe against domesticity and its adverse effects on men, especially artists. 'We've got to be *very, very careful*. We have to express our *dark* selves.' The women laughed scornfully, and the hostess fell asleep in her chair. On and on the men ranted, about the dreariness of the *Age*, the ugliness of Melbourne's architecture, the hopelessness of its galleries and theatres. I 'went to the toilet' and slid into a room where one of the children was watching *Animal House* on TV. I leaned on a cushion, 'just for a moment', and next thing V was shaking me, saying in a shocked voice, 'Come on! You can't go to sleep *here*!' I dragged myself up, put my shoes back on and reported for further social duty. The hostess was still out like a light, sitting upright at the table.

———

After the cast and crew screening of *Chez Nous* in Sydney, a woman I once worked with came up to me and said, with a strange, slow urgency, 'Helen, I'm in *pain*. What did she do wrong?' People who think about behaviour in terms of innocence, crime and punishment, instead of as a constantly changing swarm of almost chemical events. I loved lots of things about the movie, felt doubtful about others, and am still numb about the rest.

———

R came to E's for lunch. She looked exactly the same. I was nervous beforehand but her company was as always: lively, quick, gentle, intelligent, funny. When she was leaving she said, 'I've missed you.' I said, 'Me too.' I could have let out a sob, but didn't, and the moment passed.

———

Before I left for Sydney V asked with elaborate casualness where my *Cosmo* proofs were so he could read it while I was away. In a similar tone I pointed them out to him on the shelf. The infant in me secretly longed for a phone call at E's saying, 'I've read it! It's wonderful!' Instead I obliged myself to behave as if he weren't reading it and I didn't care. He met my plane, greeted me affectionately as always, but did not mention the book. I too avoided the topic till the following morning. H: (*with hard-working breeziness*) 'Did you manage to have a look at *Cosmo* while I was away?' V: (*driving along beside the river to the Botanic Gardens*) 'Yes, I did. I was planning not to talk about it till tomorrow.' H: (*heart sinks. Why the delay? Did he find it too awful?*) 'Oh. Do you feel like telling me now?' V: (*pulls up at intersection; without looking at me puts hand on my knee*) 'It's very good, sweetheart. I'm proud of you. It's beautifully written, in places. Yes, it's very good.' I was so keyed up for criticism that I was at a loss. Everything he went on to say about it was technical, intelligent and to the point. A couple of minor things 'needed attention'. At home he showed them to me. His suggestions were subtle and good, and I knew I could use them.

———

Very warm day. I lay on the kitchen couch dozing and reading old copies of the *TLS*. Late in the afternoon V came and sat in a chair and told me about an idea he's got, based on something the great reader's husband told him years ago—about an Australian man who lived in the south of France, and planted a stand of eucalypts. Each tree bore a metal plaque naming its type. But during the war the Germans came and commandeered the plaques for scrap metal, and he lost his classification. Ever afterwards he hung about the village cafe waiting for Australian tourists to pass through, and asking them to come and identify the trees. 'So I thought,' he went on, 'I'd make him have a marriageable daughter…'

I sat up. He had a sudden urge to rearrange the furniture in his work room. He wanted his table to face a bare brick wall. We pushed and shoved, I vacuumed dramatically. He was so casually blank, or 'level', as he would say—'level' is his desired state of being—that I didn't know how to express my excitement, or where to put it. So I swallowed it.

———

Our friends' ultrasound. The recognisable shape of skull and nose, the tiny raised hand. We all gazed at it in wonder. V's face was soft. 'Isn't it miraculous!'

———

Dreamt I searched the piano in vain for the key of S. My teacher instructed me to play a gold ring that one of us was wearing.

———

'Once we lose our sense of grievance, everything, including physical pain, becomes easier to bear.' —Germaine Greer, *The Change*

———

Breakfast at Marios for my birthday. Y came. We discussed the drowning of Robert Maxwell, and the appearance on TV of Kerry Packer who is making a bid for the Fairfax empire. I said I had found Packer repellent, a huge toad-like bully. Y said, 'I fell in love with him on TV. I fell in love with his *power*.' And V spoke with a shining face about Maxwell: 'Just imagine him, striding the world!'

———

In his car O said, 'I've heard that in your new book there's a brain tumour story, and that Y wanted you to change it.' H: 'It's true that there's a brain tumour in it. It's not true that Y asked me to change it.' He started the motor, and said in a calm, pleasant voice, 'Well, I'll just have to be patient, and wait.'

A heaviness, around the heart. A heaviness in breathing. I keep running through details of the story, trying to 'be him' and 'see it through his eyes'. Is it a vengeful story? Not as far as I can tell, in my present state of awareness. Does it give a *complex* picture of my relationship with O? Yes. Very. It goes through the worst of both of us, and the best of him. It was necessary for me to write this story. I remember asking Raymond Carver if there was any line he drew round parts of his life, or people he's been engaged with, across which he would not go. He thought for a moment, very carefully, and said, 'It's my job to write down life as I see it.' Pause. 'It's a jungle out there.' Patrick White's savagery. His utter ruthlessness. Chekhov, the women in *The Darling* and *The Butterfly*: do people imagine that he made up these terrible characters, from thin air?

I gardened, on my own. Spitting with rain. Sang to myself and thought.

V is seriously getting started on his book. From the door I see the plans spread out all over his desk. He really means business. Strange how differently we approach writing. I blunder in blindly and scrub-bash my way through a trackless forest, but he stays well back until he has laid out the route, created a fundamental map. He has an *aim* in mind.

J is taking his young son to Paris because he's writing a book about 'a bloke travelling with his son'. I thought about M and me, our travels, how I put her on trains alone, sent her to a *colonie de vacances* in Brittany that I'd never even heard of, let alone seen.

Now that it's V's turn to start a big piece of work I sense an obliga- tion to remove myself from the premises during the day. How did this come about? By an osmotic process. Something in the air. That

I instinctively obey. I rode around on my bike, looking for a place to be. The library was closed. V has not mentioned any aspect of my book or remarked on it at all, since the proofs went back. I have no idea whether it affected him, whether any of its ideas interested him. I don't expect him ever to say, and I don't dare to ask. I'm scared his face would go blank.

———

As soon as we had ordered our food at Toki, V said, 'Right. Now. *Insurance*.' Couldn't I see I was squandering money? That insurance companies calculated the odds and then slugged people exactly where their deepest anxieties lay? I flailed away about fire and flood. Next he said I had been intractable about his suggestion of a row of pittosporum trees in the garden. I said they would have made a wall of darkness, and that anyway he dominated the house's interior aesthetic, even in my own room. What, he asked, did I want aesthetically that I didn't have? I said curtains on the big kitchen windows and a little bit of caneite above the phone to pin things on. *Caneite?* He poured out a diatribe against people who stick things on fridge doors or kitchen walls—it was 'unconvincing'—it would be fifty times better to have the little black McCahon on the wall beside the fridge. I fired up and said that a kitchen was the working heart of the house, an organic room where things constantly changed, rather than a space for art to be contemplated. He got sarcastic, using words like 'art gallery' and 'museum' and 'mausoleum'. I said I hadn't used any of these words. He said I'd spoken 'with contempt'. I said I felt dispossessed and did not think it was fair that I had to go out all day—why didn't we make the shed out the back into a studio so he could work there without the house having to be kept empty all around him? I said I needed somewhere to *be* during the day when I wasn't working. He said I was neurotic: that I'd come home yesterday miserable because a *library* was closed.

———

In the morning I thought that if I couldn't stay home I could take a mattress to my office so I could be comfortable there all day and read. This is awful, and boring. If I could argue calmly, without losing my temper or acting out a victim role, I would have a...better life. Is it my manner that's the problem? Or is it the content of my demands?

———

I think he fights for ART and its HIGHER VALUE because, having no children and never having wanted any, he resents the high moral tone I apparently take when I assert the value of what one learns from domestic and family life, and from the company of children. 'I don't know,' he says, 'how people who aren't artists can keep going, not making a shape of themselves. I s'pose they do it through children.' He really sees them as alternatives.

———

Y came to Marios bringing bound proofs of *Cosmo*. I think it's all right. Even quite good. But I also noticed its anxious perfectness. I made up my mind, next time, to blast that aspect of my writing to kingdom come.

———

'Dear R and O, I had planned to give you a copy of this book next January when the hardbacks will be printed, but since rumours have already begun to circulate about its contents, I am sending you the first holdable copy that has reached me. With love always, no matter how hard it gets.'

———

I'm trying to become a more practised questioner, to listen patiently with full attention and real curiosity, and to stop using people's answers as triggers for a monologue about *me*. I ask, and I keep my mouth shut and my eyes on the other person's face. In this I'm copying V, who is brilliant at it.

———

V invites my father to come with him to see some paintings that are to be auctioned. Dad accepts, but says to me, 'I don't know anything about paintings. I'm only going for one reason—to see what a bunch of ster-youpid bloody pricks they were.'

———

Driving back from Primrose Gully we hit an animal. It was a very solid, lethal thump and V kept going, but the other man called out, 'Hey-hey!' V pulled over and they walked back. It was a rabbit. V delivered the death-chop with the side of his hand. 'Ooh, ooh,' whimpered the pregnant woman. They put the rabbit into the salad bowl in the boot and we drove on, comparing notes on how to cook rabbits. V skinned it skilfully over the sink. He called me to watch while he slit open its belly: the tightly packed, beautifully designed guts neatly filling their cavity. I put the pieces into a marinade of red wine and onions, and we went to bed. I said, 'When I saw how perfectly its guts were arranged I thought, "All that brilliant evolution, just to be slit open and eaten."' 'You could say that about the wine in the marinade, too,' he said. 'All those grapes.'

———

Dreamt that O stepped out of a hallway into a lobby where I was waiting, and approached me with his arms wide open, and a big smile. He looked young, healthy, cheerful; dressed in light-coloured clothes. He took me in his arms and said, 'That's a very, very beautiful story.' I told the dream to the Polish philosopher. I said, 'I don't want to hurt him. I want him to see that I needed to show our friendship in the most complex way I could. I don't want him to take it as an attack.' 'But it's not an attack. You've shown the friendship on a deep level. Look—could you perhaps consider the dream as his actual response, I mean his *eventual* response, even if it doesn't happen immediately? Even if you have to wait quite a long time?' Her delicacy of manner. Like Y, she knows how to couch a challenge in language that seduces, relaxes and exhilarates.

———

G and M-C, have come to stay. Suddenly he and V are like a pair of schoolboys, cackling with hysterical laughter at the breakfast table. Sometimes I feel like kicking them, two giggling ninnies putting on Pommy accents, a copy of Wisden always at the ready, but when M-C and I join in it becomes fun for us too. I think G is *good* for V, dragging him back to some neglected stage of himself, before he became harsh and solemn.

———

Dreamt I looked at myself in a wall mirror and I had another woman's face. It was me, but I looked like someone else. Movements of 'my' muscles produced expressions on this face that were unfamiliar and did not correspond with 'me'.

———

R writes that I have been 'punitive' to O in my story. The word keeps appearing in my thoughts. Is it true? I snap at V. He takes it quietly, and stoically. I get down on my knees in the dirt. Plant beans, capsicum and basil. Grey sky, cool wind. Hear myself panting and grunting. As the light fades the sky takes on a lurid tinge. A faint pinkish gold glimmers on the undersides of leaves. 'Punitive' floats in and out. I keep on working.

———

I was about to buy a washed-out denim jacket in Chapel Street when V came in and pointed out, correctly, that the darker one the salesgirl was wearing was a more attractive colour. She took it off and sold it to me. Later I found in its pocket a used tissue with lipstick on it and many drops of dried blood, as if from an insect bite or a pimple. I didn't mention this to V, who was already alarmed at my having donned a garment still warm from a stranger's body.

———

Now Paul Keating is PM. He says, 'I feel the poignancy of the moment.' Bob Hawke, ousted, surges out into the brutal light of the media. He is smiling, but looks smaller, and the camera flashes are like a splatter of pockmarks on his face.

———

I did a mammoth bout of ironing, everything I own plus fifteen shirts of V's. I *love* ironing. I sing away, or think. While I was gaily working he opened the fridge and grumbled, 'The place is stripped. There's nothing here to eat.' I went to inspect and found it contained: tomatoes, eggs, carrots, a large plastic container of home-made soup and, right in the front, three beautiful French cheeses. I remarked in what I hoped was a neutral tone, 'There's some cheese in here.' 'Is there? Where?' It's not self-control I need to study, but detachment. This morning he kept returning to the annoying disappointment of finding 'an empty fridge'. I suggested we should change our house-hold organisation so that food-buying was shared and he could have all the things he liked. He thought for a moment, then said he didn't really care about the fridge.

———

V tells me he called his wife for her birthday. She reported certain adventures abroad, then asked him, 'And what have *you* been doing? What's been happening in your life?' He replied, 'Nothing. Nothing much.' I was surprised. 'You didn't tell her you'd started a new book?' 'Listen,' he said. 'She's been in *Africa*, and *India*. Dealing with *elephants* and *tigers*. And you want me to say, "I've started plan-ning a novel and been to the cricket a few times"?'

———

A letter comes from O. It is restrained, decent, deeply generous, deeply offended and hurt, and still attempting a literary response as well as a personal one. I'm sad. For having hurt him. I examine myself for guilt and don't find any. I find a hard nut of something in the centre of my heart. I find sadness but I do not find regret. I suppose this is a friendship lost. Destroyed. By me. How will I answer?

———

I don't know what angels are, but this book I've just written is full of them.

———

A five-year-old English boy came to dinner with his mother and stepfather. He was supposed to be watching TV and eating a chocolate frog but after a while he came creeping out to the kitchen. I set him up at the coffee table with a paintbox and paper and a glass of water. He began to work. Watching him dab his brush in the paint and sweep his upper body sideways towards the paper, V had to cover his mouth to hold in a rush of laughter, then he looked at me with an expression of astonishment and said, 'He's really *absorbed*, isn't he!' When the other adults left the room, the boy paused in his work and said to me, 'V's funny, isn't he.' 'Yes. He's very funny.' 'Why did you choose him, for your husband?' 'Oh…because I loved him. Because he's kind to me, and he makes me laugh.' The boy turned back to his painting, restraining a smile of embarrassment. I heard later that he has an IQ of 135.

———

Chez Nous is going to Berlin. I have to find, before Monday, German equivalents for 'moll', 'dago' and 'fair go'.

———

V thinks parents should speak to their children as Canetti's mother did to him. In an orchard she screamed at him, 'You know *nothing*!' Imagine the bumptious, opinionated creep the little Canetti must have been.

———

G's first wife outside the fruit shop. We embraced. She's been working in Vientiane for two years. 'It was beautiful. I lived in a house next to a rice field. I got around on a little motorbike, or a pushbike. I'd look around me and I'd think, 'This is *good* for me. It's good for my soul.' Pedalling on to work, I realised the point of this meeting: she was an angel to remind me that *things pass*. Ten years ago she shoved a tarot card at me through my car window—a body face down with seven swords stuck in its back—because of a story I'd published about G. Now we kiss when we meet, and talk quietly, using the word 'soul'.

V reports a call from Z, who spoke to him about my book. 'Did he seem to, um, like it?' 'Aw, he said it was "rich", or something.' On our walk to the coffee shop he speaks disobligingly about the Polish philosopher, to whom he had taken quite a shine until last week when she apparently expressed to him several unacceptable thoughts after having read his first novel. Trying to exercise my new mode of detachment and self-command, I merely acknowledge with a friendly murmur that he has spoken. Short silence.

V: 'What's the matter?'

H: 'Nothing. I'm just practising not being "argumentative", "rude", "touchy" and so on.'

V: 'Oh.'

Short pause.

V: 'But I'd really like to know what you think.'

H: 'Well, I wasn't there. But she's so clever, and so sensitive, that I find it hard to imagine her saying anything stupid or offensive.'

V: 'Sometimes I can't be bothered summing up someone else's argument with as much nuance as you seem to want—I just sum it up.'

H: 'But if the argument *involves* nuance, isn't that a distortion?'

V: 'Look—I don't think her ideas were much better than hackneyed.'

And on we walk to the coffee shop, under our little cloud of trouble.

What the Polish philosopher said to him, she told me later, was that in his conversation she finds warmth and sympathy that are missing from his work. She suggested that what's blocking the access of it into his work are his severe theories about what art is or is supposed to be. I agree with this. So does the great reader. But he won't listen. He reads Canetti with immense admiration, and my heart sinks. But also—relief: that I'm not alone in my famous refusal to '*be told*' what's wrong with me and my work.

————

'...We live only with what we do not love, with what we have brought to live with us only in order to kill *the intolerable love*...'
—Proust, *The Captive*

1992

E's pretty new hat: a darkish lavender, of heavy but flexible straw. She didn't want to swim in the waves, and went back to sit on the sand. I dived and floated on my own. Once I turned back to glance at her sitting on her towel. I raised one hand and instantly she waved back: like a mother. She told me she'd seen O. Although he had been very hurt by my story, she said, he fully endorsed my right to have written it.

———

Fantasy. Someone asks me, 'Why do you write such terrible things about O?' and I say, 'Because I love him.' Then they ask O, 'Why does Helen write such terrible things about you?' and he replies, 'Because she loves me.'

———

'He worked a great deal from memory, using everybody he knew.'
—D. H. Lawrence, *Sons and Lovers*

———

I toil over a reply to O's letter. I try to express my admiration for his generosity, grace and sweetness of spirit. I point to the depth and power of his shaping influence on me over our long, long friendship. 'It was with you that my whole outlook as a young adult, my early attitudes towards literature, study, drinking, politics, football, films, music, people—even my sense of humour—were formed.' I say my dearest wish is that one day he might find in the story the love and respect I believe are in it, as well as the struggle and anger and frustration.

———

Z told us how he'd had an audience with the Queen, for winning the Commonwealth Literary Award. 'But Z,' I said, 'you're a republican!' 'Commonwealth,' he replied smoothly. 'Even if we were a republic, we'd still be in the Commonwealth. She's head of the Commonwealth.' Everyone laughed.

———

The characters that people I know become when I write about them are, to me, almost totally separate from the people themselves, once I've finished the piece of work and put it aside, or published it. It's as if I've extracted or borrowed from the real person the aspects of them that I needed to struggle with, and the character consists only of those aspects. I can return to the real person with no sense of overlap. Cold comfort.

———

Hot sweats wake me through the night. I'm so touchy—on a hair trigger. Everything makes me angry and I don't know why. I'm cooking a pasta sauce, V comes and stares into the pot and says, 'There's not much there. There's not enough.' I fly off the handle and we eat wretchedly (there *was* enough, it was rich and there was plenty). Can I find any kind of excuse or reason in the fact of menopause? Yanking weeds out of the grass after dinner, we try to speak reasonably to each other. Am I discontented? I say it bothers me that he has taken over the house, that I can't be at home during his working hours without feeling I'm trespassing, and there on sufferance. He says, 'Everyone needs a clear space, to work.' 'Yes, a room that's theirs. But a whole house—that's an immense luxury.' 'What about Proust?' he said. 'Flaubert?' He says I should come and go as I please, that he will try to adapt. Then I am filled with guilt, as if my claim were unreasonable. Also, I know he doesn't mean it.

———

O replies. 'Amicably and equably' he sends his good wishes to both of us. I read his postcard as a justified dismissal, a farewell. I think I will also choose to see it as a blessing, the sort that might come from an exhausted father who finally throws up his hands, stands back from the complaints and attacks of a daughter, and says, 'Go in peace.'

———

First time alone at Primrose Gully since before I moved to Sydney. Crows, to the south. A wallaby sat up on its haunches, holding an apple to its mouth with both front paws. In the evening a koala began to snort and rumble. Kookaburras. Rain in the night, though I slept so deeply I hardly noticed it. Magpies when I woke: the morning birds of childhood. I swept the house and polished the windows. Everything I saw through them was distinct and glossy, moving in the cool air. I'm happy up here. A better person. My movements are slower and more leisurely. My whole *rate* slows down.

———

A clear, hottish summer Sunday. After breakfast at Marios we walked in the Botanic Gardens. V, smoking his weekly Havana, discoursed with sombre pleasure upon the naivety of the Anglican women deacons who had *actually believed* that the Bishop would ordain them, who said they were 'devastated, stunned and in pain' when the court injunction was granted. 'They're utterly naïve,' he said, 'about *power*. I've realised, from my reading over the last few years, quite a lot about power. It's what makes men unpleasant, but it's also what they *are*. It's what they've *got*. Perhaps it's all they've got.' I suggested tentatively that perhaps women who've been at the mercy of power had as good an understanding of it as did the men who were wielding it, since in order to survive under it they'd had to learn about its ways. He flatly rejected this, and restated his thesis. I floated the idea that if all men had was power, it was not surprising that when they were about to lose it, they panicked. 'I don't see much panic around,' he said superbly, puffing away. 'It's in art, too, in a slightly lesser way. Now that painting's no longer important, anybody at all can have a go. More women are…accepted.' I kept trying to listen analytically—I mean, I tried not to get lost in my dismay. I wanted to be sure I wasn't imagining it. The Havana he was smoking was a prop in a performance: as if some unmodulated male principle had come to inhabit him. He was a mouthpiece to an archetype.

———

The Latin American kids dancing cumbia: blankly single-minded on their fluid legs.

———

A visitor went out our kitchen door and said, 'What a beautiful back garden. It's full of air.'

———

I'm reading *Jane Eyre*, adoring it. V tried to make me get off the bed late in the afternoon and come for a walk along the creek but I clung to the mattress edge with my free hand, saying, 'Wait. Wait. An anguished cry has just rent the night in twain.' I was only half joking but he doubled over.

———

The first capsicum appears, a firm green shiny lump as big as a walnut.

———

It was a warm summer night and we talked for a long time without quarrelling. V said he had to have 'an asbestos suit on' in order to criticise my work. We came at this vexed topic from several angles, lying on our bed beside the open windows. I said, 'I know I'm hypersensitive and unpleasant. But I've been trying hard lately to be more reasonable.' 'Well, it has got a bit easier, but I'm very wary of it.' I tried to explain that I would readily accept his criticisms if only he would preface them by telling me whether the work had affected him, whether it had touched him in any way. He said he'd told me something in the book was 'quite moving'. I think I would have remembered that, but maybe I'd had a moment of deafness; anyway I privately seized on 'quite moving', knowing it was all I could ever hope for. I said that I had a very high regard for him as a reader, and deeply respected his literary opinion, but that after his technical comments he'd never mentioned the book again. He'd dealt with it briskly, like an obligation, and buried it. I said that I kept hoping he might mention something that had stuck in his mind or made him laugh—but he never did. I said I was disappointed that he hadn't been more...comradely. He listened, without interrupting. Then he said, '*I* would never expect you to respond to *my* work in the way you're describing.' 'But I did. Didn't I? When your book came out? I talked about it a lot. I said how much I liked it, I quoted lines from it, I remembered turns of phrase and things that were clever and funny—I *enjoyed* talking about it.' 'I do remember you being very nice.'

Oh, what's the point of all this—saying it in the first place, writing it down later. I don't know how we'll be able to live together as writers. I can't see a way, unless I drop all this craving for...what? These grudging crumbs he'll drop in front of me if I pester him? I long for him to let me see how my work affects him. Maybe it doesn't. Maybe it leaves him cold.

————

Whenever I lie down to sleep, night or day, tremendous hot flushes pour over my torso and limbs—not tremendous in temperature so much as in stiflingness, as if all my body's pores were blocked, a disagreeable sensation, like being trapped in a blanketing force that precisely moulds all my contours.

————

Last night, V sat beside me on the kitchen couch and took my bare feet on his lap and told me what he really thought about 'Recording Angel'—that it was 'a very strong story', but that O would have been shocked to read a description of himself at his lowest, in hospital after that dreadful operation: to be revealed and scrutinised while in that state. I began to feel the horror of what I've done. I heard myself jabbering the same old justifications, how I thought I'd done this and what I'd meant was that, and it made me sick. I broke off mid-sentence and got up and walked over to the sink. He said, 'What's up, sweetheart?' I said, 'I'm sick and tired of myself, that's all.' He came and put his arms round me and gently kissed me. The awful truth is that no one can help you carry the consequences of your behaviour. You are required to carry them on your own.

———

As I rushed down Lygon Street, the biographer came walking up it, all in white, smiling and strolling on her own. I called out her name. When she turned and saw me her face broke into her familiar sweet and beautiful smile. We kissed. I babbled out my destination and ran on. Today I got a note from her: 'That was a moment of pure love and it's still with me. Dear old Lygon Street on a sunny day, dear you, and dear me!'

———

The producer told me that when *Chez Nous* was screened in Berlin, they laughed. Out loud. And at the end they stood up and applauded. And people said to the director, 'What have you done to Bruno? He's so *warm*!' Maybe I'm not such a dog after all.

———

Woman after woman, five of them in a few days, came up to me to say they liked 'Recording Angel'. And each of them said a version of 'It's full of love.' I'd better get used to this. Men see it one way, women another.

———

V has a cold. He's outraged that he's ill: 'How did I *catch* it?' 'Same as everyone else. A germ was flying along and you got in its way.' I make an unobtrusive fuss of him, clean sheets, an extra blanket, vichyssoise, but he insists on getting up at the usual time and sits all morning at his desk with bowed shoulders, honking and groaning.

After lunch he lies on top of the bed with his shoes on and one hand over his eyes.

———

Got knocked off my bike on the footpath up near Natural Tucker by a middle-aged woman in a Volvo that came surging out of a lane. I sailed sideways through the air towards the gutter, hearing myself emit a long cry of protest, and landed comfortably on the pad of muscle of my left upper arm and shoulder. My front wheel was all twisted and buckled. Thoughts passed thickly through my head. The driver was very upset. I said in a clear, authoritative tone, but with a dream-like slowness, 'I'm not hurt. Don't worry. I shouldn't have been on the footpath.' She gave me her phone number, apologised over and over, and drove away. That's when I felt like bawling with foolishness and shock, all forlorn on the pavement with my mangled bike and nobody to help me. Trundled it to the bakery and bought a casalinga.

———

Mum and Dad came to the literary lunch. I went down to say hello. Dad called me 'dear' and introduced me proudly to several strangers at their table. When I was called to speak, he took my wrist and said in a soft, good-natured tone, 'Don't criticise me too much, will you.' I could have howled and laid my forehead on his shoe. I said as many respectful things about him, and Mum, as I could think of. I even thanked him for his 'strong character'.

———

Morning streets so quiet, all we could hear was a dove calling and calling. V polished off a terrific piece about boxing, and then we went for a walk along the Merri Creek in the autumn sun. He smoked a cigar. We collected eucalypt wood for barbecues and chattered away merrily as we scrounged.

———

G and M-C here to stay. He vagues out on her, she is sharp with him at the table. G confides in V, M-C in me. V says they're about

to part. Out in the yard G says to me, 'I want what you've got, Hel.'
'What?' 'I hear you two talking and laughing in bed, for hours.
That's what I want.'

––––––

Reviews of *Cosmo*, some excellent, others bilious (I am 'pretentious'
and so on). I have recovered my equilibrium; V and I read the bad
ones out loud and laugh meanly. I really hardly care at all. Must
have attained satori. The Cretan called: he wanted to 'rush out in the
street and kick its critics right up the bum, so they'd have an orgasm
and then *die*.' The young guy in the bank told me the balance of
my account, then added, 'But it'll be a few dollars more by Friday,
because I'm going out today to buy your book.' Meanwhile I keep
my copy of *Paradise Lost* in the outside toilet. Staggered by its *worked*
quality, the beautiful placing of the feet, their weight and balance.

––––––

While I was cleaning the bathroom basin V came in and we had
an interesting discussion. Leaning against the door jamb with his
arms folded, he advised me that it was time for me to stop writing
'about the 70s'. Oh? Why's that? Because the 70s was a 'period of
bullshit, of clapped-out theories that Victoria is now bearing the
brunt of.' Apparently G shared his opinion; indeed he had told V
that he'd already had 'a little talk' with me about it. I said we hadn't
spoken about this as far as I recalled. Shifting my energies to the
bath, I pointed out that certain social changes had occurred in the
70s that people had been deeply affected by—that this could not be
scrubbed out of either my characters or me, and that to attempt it
would not make sense. I said that his work was coloured by different
assumptions because his ideas were formed in a different era and
through different experiences. I said that whenever I read him I
felt that I was in the 50s. He said that much of his work was set in
no-place and no-time. I said that it was in the relationships between
men and women, and in the underlying assumptions about these,
that period still made itself felt. He asked me what I thought about

what he'd said. I said, opening the toilet lid and attacking the rim
of the bowl, 'I don't think anything in particular.' He pressed me
harder. I said, 'I understand the point you're making. But I can't
say how it will affect me, until I sit down to write the next thing.' I
forbore to point out that in the simple fact that I was on my knees
scrubbing the porcelain as we talked, and in the fact (which he had
only the other evening admitted publicly without shame or remorse)
that he has 'never cleaned a lavatory in his life', resided a thundering
piece of…whatever it is we were talking about: a whopping great
assumption about men, women and domestic labour which dates
him, and judges him, as accurately as does any misplaced nostalgia
that I have been reproached with.

———

Some mornings in our street I hear a birdcall that I can't identify:
a liquid sound, like a string firmly plucked under bubbling water.

———

Went to a general yoga class last night. Much harder than the begin-
ners, different in tone: people were calm, silent, ready to work, a
sense of organisation and purpose in the room. They fell quickly
into lines, certain basic things were taken for granted. I followed
awkwardly but I *followed*. Riding home in the warm dark I thought,
I'm nearly fifty and I *kept up*.

———

I proposed to the *Age* a piece about autopsies. They're lining it up
with Coronial Services. V said he'd like to come too. On the phone
to the professor I talked him in as 'a colleague'. It won't be just
me and the situation. Well, it can be, if I make it be. I've got that
female habit of filtering everything through what I imagine my
male companion's responses are.

———

Today we saw a dead man's body cut open, and his organs stowed
into a plastic bag and sewn back into his abdominal cavity. We
saw the corpse of an old woman slit from neck to pubic bone,

disembowelled, skinned; her scalp peeled forward over her face like a hairy cap and her skull sawn in half as one halves a hard-boiled egg.

———

When we got home I found a message from the *Age* to call the Coroner. He was furious that we had been allowed to go into the mortuary when work was in progress—when *detectives* were there. He said severely that I was to come back to the mortuary at the first available opportunity, 'put on mortuary clothes', and watch an autopsy from start to finish, with a pathologist present to explain each stage of the process as it was done. 'Yes, Mr Hallenstein,' I said meekly, biting back a shout of joy. 'I can come tomorrow morning.'

———

I hardly know how to write what I was shown. A young man with a narrow, dark red trench where the ligature took his weight. A little boy who had fallen out of a ute, his slender body and huge swollen half-shaven head. A woman in her sixties, as if asleep, her expression of patient resignation. A tiny baby on a metal shelf, perfectly swaddled in a pink cotton blanket. The demeanour of the people who work there, their quiet efficiency, their respect and modesty, made it possible for me to witness these things without fear or revulsion. I felt such affection for them. I can say, here at least, how calm and grateful, how *happy* I was in their company. Almost as if I belonged there.

———

At Queenscliff I slept all night beside two enormous open windows. Magpies sang in a particularly ornate and leisurely manner. Huge skies covered in thin pale clouds.

———

'I think you should learn the second Czerny,' said my piano teacher. 'They make a pair. You've been on the first one long enough.' 'Okay. I love boring exercises.' 'I've noticed,' she said. 'You must be looking for something deeper in the music. Something spiritual.' We laughed but I wasn't *quite* sure whether she was teasing me.

———

I've been offered a job reviewing movies for a monthly magazine. Out of the depths of my ignorance I take it. The editor, gossiping about a certain journalist, says, 'Like all bullies and authoritarians, he's very easily wounded.' Later I report this to V. 'Yes,' he says, 'that's good, isn't it. Did you, um, think it might apply to you? A bit?' 'Yes, I did,' I said, hanging my head. And the more easily wounded one is, the more bullying and authoritarian one becomes. To protect the shivering chasm at the core.

———

At dinner V fed Dad questions and played the eager listener; Dad blossomed. In fact he talked without stopping for the entire evening. Not one question did he ask, not one hint of interest in anyone else's views of life or experience. To hear that slow voice grind on and on, hour after hour—I had to keep getting up and 'going to the toilet', for relief from the voice. I could have torn out my hair.

———

Easter morning. He is risen. A steady quiet, outside. A dove calling. All those bodies down there, in the House of Death and Justice and Science, the House of Patience, are only remains. Their spark has fled. The wind gets up. A mild shifting of the plane leaves. Sun comes through in patches. Dry bitumen.

———

At Wilcannia my nun and her friend (girlfriend? I don't ask) live for free in a tumbledown, abandoned old house with walls a foot thick and an immense yard that backs on to the Darling River. From the kitchen door you can hear its soft flow. Last night when I staggered out to the dunny, fighting my way past the three dogs that live in the yard, the Milky Way crackled overhead in a huge arc.

———

I called home. V has a bad cold. Why does he get sick whenever I go away?

When I sit on the outside dunny the brown kelpie pup, Tex, shoves his front legs under the door and madly rummages with them, like a burglar going through a drawer. He likes me. I dream of turning up at home with a dog. For V. To put life back into him. The guy who's minding him said I couldn't take him because I live in a city: 'I wouldn't do that to a dog.' Crestfallen, I hide in the bottom of my suitcase the blue leather collar and webbing lead I'd secretly bought at the store. But the nurse says, 'Of course you can have the pup. We need to get rid of him. No, I won't take any money. I'd love you to have him.' I practise teaching him to sit and stay. He learns fast. He is beautiful and clever. My wrists are covered with bite marks from our wrestling bouts.

The women are busy all day with the overwhelming bureaucratics of their work here with the Aboriginal people. They don't look after themselves, so I do the washing, I iron things, I cook, I do the dishes, I fix broken gadgets, sweep the yard, scoop up puppy shit. I cut an apple and make the nun eat the peeled and cored quarters. She looks up surprised when I place them on the arm of her chair. She eats them obediently.

Out here they pray for rain. The drought is shocking. The land is degraded. It's blowing away. 'When Kidman built his mansion on the Darling,' a farmer tells me, 'he had forty-seven Chinese gardeners.'

I've got a cage booked at Broken Hill airport, the space booked at Ansett Adelaide, and three Dramamine pills from the priest to keep him calm en route.

Rain at night brings the Merri Creek up a foot or so. V and I happily walk Tex along the creek path and watch him frolic and gambol. He likes to race up a rocky outcrop and pose on its peak, gazing nobly into the distance. We call it 'Tex's Look-Out'. He sleeps calmly on his blanket on the back veranda. He has a merry, patient nature. He never complains. But he needs two *enormous* walks each day.

———

J's won his second Miles Franklin. That's a prize I know I'll never win.

———

The great reader's old school friend paid tribute to the great reader's mother: she said that during the war, when they were young women, they used to ask each other, 'Who would you tell if you had a black baby?' The great reader's mother was the only name that came up. This made V laugh terribly. So, the following evening, did F's imitation of Pompidou. V laughed so much he couldn't get his breath.

———

Dreamt that every time I turned over in bed, $400 was added to our electricity bill.

———

'Dear Mr and Mrs Watson, here is the card from the Lost Dogs' Home vet, where we took Tex for his shots; also the worm pill packet, so you'll know what he's had. I'm very sad to give him up, but I know it's the best thing for him, and I'm sure you'll be good to him and he'll be happier in the country. Thanks for taking him. I felt very down in the dumps about him last night but today I cheered up. We ate the carrots and the silverbeet last night, they were delicious. It was really nice to meet you. I hope your CAT scan results are good, Mr Watson. Thanks again for everything. Yours sincerely, Helen.'

———

We read about a kelpie cross called Trixie who, when her master had a stroke and lay paralysed in his bed for nine days, kept him alive by soaking a towel in her water bowl and the toilet and draping it over his face so he could suck the moisture.

V pointed out again, as we walked along the creek, that I had an obsessive interest in 'death, rape, murder and so on'. I wonder if it's true. And if it is true, what it means. Is it wrong?

We hear that Tex is happy. He runs about the farm collecting items for a museum of objects that he likes to toss and catch—old bones, cow horns etc. One day they saw something brown among his treasures. 'That's not a piece of horn.' It was a dead tiger snake. I felt a pang. But life without him and his mad working-dog energy contains less guilt.

Sometimes we talk about getting married.

Two letters from people who hated my articles about the morgue. 'I sincerely hope, Ms Garner, that when I die, my body will be free from your perverted gaze.'

I like the prayer that says, 'Forgive us all that is past.'

I planted a little daphne bush, dug out the old herb patch, composted, mulched, moved the sage plant. V came out with two coffees. Proudly I showed him my handiwork. He glanced in its direction, blank-faced. I tugged at his sleeve. 'Doesn't it look terrific?' He put on a voice: 'Yeah! It looks groovy! *Cool*!' I soldiered on: 'And we'll still go to the tip this Sunday, will we?' 'Oh, *I* don't care.' He trudged inside with the cups. I stood in the shed among the kindling, looking down at my muddy boots and controlling my 'melodramatic', 'hypersensitive' 'overreactions'. Then I went to have another look at the broad-bean patch. Every morning for weeks I've been rushing out to check and there's never anything there. I stared at the line where I'd parted the mulch for them. I was about to walk away when I saw a pale green dot slightly off-centre in the lumpy dirt. I crouched down. It was a bean shoot. Curved over on itself like a bent wrist. Struggling up to the light, shoving aside the clods.

———

Brett Whiteley has been found dead in a motel room at Thirroul. Whisky, needles and drugs nearby. The owner had heard nothing from the room for twenty-four hours, except the TV.

———

My nun's therapist told her that her right hand was stiff because she 'wanted to punch someone'. My nun believes her daily migraines and even her leukemia are due to this frustrated desire, to a lifetime of suppressed fear and rage.

———

The people at Coronial Services invited me to the opening of the Donor Tissue Bank. They said they'd liked my articles so much that they wanted to frame them and hang them on the wall in the building. I blushed bright red. 'Oh! I'd be proud! I'd be honoured!' The Coroner approached me with his hand out. 'Hello Mr Hallenstein!' 'Hal's the name,' he said genially. When I told this to V later he cracked up. It was my happiest day in journalism. On my way home, standing on the cold tram stop dreaming of my hour of glory, I had a wonderful fantasy of being allowed to follow the Coroner around the bloody, violent scenes of his daily work, and when anyone asked him who I was, he'd say, 'She's the Coroner's Poet.'

———

Y asked me what my nun 'gave' me, i.e. what was the point of being friends with her. Her idea of nuns as pinched-lipped straiteners surprised me. She got crisp with me because I didn't understand the difference between the mass market and literary arms of a publisher.

———

My sister and her band had played with some Colombians, who to their joy told them they had 'soul'. 'Playing with Latin Americans,' said her partner, the trumpeter, 'is so different. They don't have any cynicism, the way Australians do. They're not ironic. They just want to laugh and dance.'

———

V marched into my room and without a word banged down on the desk a bundle of typed A4 sheets. He was already gone by the time I'd turned them over and realised it was the opening of his new novel. An impressive density and complexity of texture. And a kick of curiosity at the introduction of the man, Holland, arriving in the town and standing like a tree in the middle of his paddock.

———

I met G up in the Cross. His father has died. Everything in his own life before this death, G said, now seems frivolous, unserious, a waste of time; and he realises there's not much time left. We wondered if the death of V's father when V was twenty-four might have had the same effect on him—turned him into a serious, severe person at an early age.

———

At the Sydney International Piano Competition I sat in the second row where one can see the sweat splashing off their noses and chins and soaking the hair on the backs of their necks. I'd been in a mood for never hearing Mozart again, but a Frenchman played a rondo with such airy clarity and creamy smoothness that I nearly passed out. People in the audience become intimate friends with strangers. By the next session they have completely forgotten each other.

———

Dreamt of a climbing rose that was flourishing gaily, its leaves glossy green with reddened edges, and tiny white buds everywhere, ready to open.

———

Alone in the great reader's small, sunny flat in Double Bay. V will be here tonight. I'll be glad to see him. But one day I'll live on my own. It holds no fears. I even long for it. Maybe I can only have this fantasy because of the emotional stability, the safety, of being loved.

———

In the queue for the last piano concert V reports a conversation with R. 'I told her that everybody from Tolstoy down wrote about real people. She said, "Yes, but he finds it hard, out there in the open." I asked her about you. She said you went through her life like a breath of fresh air. But you're very strong. She said it was part of her growing up—she felt she had to move on.' I was grateful to him for asking. I imagined they must have said much worse things about me as well. Let it be what it is.

———

Alone at home all evening, polishing my rave review of *Wayne's World*. A brilliant, high, cold full moon in an inky sky. Watched a wonderful TV doco about the history of Australian vaudeville. Some of the acts threw me into fits. One of the old stars regretted the passing of entertainment that could make whole families laugh: 'I remember a man who had to be taken to the doctor. He laughed so much he hurt his neck.' Wiping away the tears I thought of O—it was the kind of foolery he loves. Now I've slashed him out of my life I've lost thirty years of shared laughter.

———

The story about going to Wilcannia. It has no *motor* to drive it, no reason to exist. The dog brought a rush of energy, but it faded. I'm giving up.

———

My editor called to say *Cosmo* hadn't been shortlisted for the Victorian Premier's Award. I was surprised that she'd even thought of telling me. I said cheerfully, 'Oh, I don't care! I've decided never to give a prize another thought.' A short pause, then she said, hotly, 'Well, *I* care!'

———

V and I went out to Mum and Dad's to tell them we were getting married. I didn't raise the subject until I'd cooked up a series of excellent spinach and ricotta crepes (unremarked upon: Dad, after guzzling his share, went out into the kitchen and started to make himself some toast). I said, 'Actually we came out to tell you some news—we're getting married. On August 14. And we're inviting you to come.' Mum said, 'Oh! That's nice!' Pause. V said, in a light, jesting tone, 'It's usually the role of the bride's father to provide a tremendous banquet.' '*Huh*,' said Dad. 'Not for the *third* time, *thank* you very much.' Pause. I said, 'It's at the Registry Office. So far, apart from you, we've only invited M.' 'When did you say?' said Mum. I repeated the date and time. Pause. Still possessed by the idiotic hope that one of them might say something, the sort of thing that normal people say on such an occasion, I sat stiffly on my chair at the end of the table. Pause. Dad said, 'We had a lot of really good food, on our trip. Specially at Brissago, and in Nice.' Mum showed us her photos of Hong Kong. And so the topic was dropped. At the door Dad said, 'See you on the 14th.' I wanted to scream and smash things and shout, 'Why don't you ever MAKE A FUSS OF ME?' I seem to have no resources at all to deal with the parents I've got. All the way home I yelled and cursed. This morning I woke up ashamed, as if after a tantrum.

———

V cheered me by reading from Nathaniel Hawthorne's lost notebooks: 'The Abyssinians, after dressing their hair, sleep with their heads in a forked stick, in order not to discompose it.'

———

We walked along the creek this morning. Wind very sweet and balmy, a drying wind. High, creamy clouds, burst through by sheets of sparkling sun. The first spring-like morning. The green shoots clearer on every tree, and everything seems in motion, standing up to the wind in good humour.

———

V wakes from 'a terrible dream. I was on a huge ladder, against a twenty-storey building. The whole things swayed, it all began to go. I grabbed hold of a gutter. Someone I knew who was above me wasn't helping. Could be a dream about getting married, do you think?' 'Are you sure you want to go ahead with it?' 'Yes. 'Why?' 'Because,' he said, 'it'd be conservative not to.' He's off his own turf, down here. We'll end up back in Sydney, I know.

———

The Master of Ormond College is up on a charge in the Magistrates' Court. He's accused of having 'squeezed a student's breast at a dance after a vice-regal dinner'. It went to *court*? Crikey. Isn't that overkill? Aren't courts for rape and violence and murder? I wrote the guy a letter. Hope I won't regret it.

———

Lancelin, even in winter, the presence always of light. Life is organised with the power of light in mind. Trees are full of it, they flash and flicker. A yard without a tree is ugly and shelterless. High fields of cloud in the morning. Each dab of cloud has its own pearliness as well as its top of fierce brightness.

———

Flu. V waits on me kindly. He brings me some Cyril Connolly to read, then goes into his room and bashes away on the portable type-writer he got in a swap with Shiva Naipaul.

———

Gardening, a slow, plodding, dogged state. You don't stop, or think of anything more than the task at hand. I used my hands rather than a tool to loosen up the soil round the beans and lettuces. I dug in the compost with my fingers. I stopped caring about keeping my wedding ring scratch-free.

———

The Polish philosopher reports her conversation with Dad at the wedding.
    PP: 'And so, you are happy that Helen is married?'
    D: (*pulls a face*)
    PP: 'What? You are *not* happy?'
    D: 'It's the third time.'

PP: 'In Powland we say, "The third time is lucky."'

D: (*shrugs*)

PP: 'But *she* is happy, they are happy together—don't you think?'

D: 'They're both writers, though.'

PP: 'They will understand each other.'

D: 'But one day one of them will write something that the other one doesn't like—and there'll be trouble.'

PP: 'They are together already several years. Don't you think they have already read each other's work?'

D: (*shrugs*)

PP: 'Anyway, you like V, don't you? Don't you think it would be nice to show Helen that you are happy for her?'

D: '*She* doesn't care.'

'At that moment,' said the Polish philosopher to me, 'the official speech started, so I could not continue.'

He thinks I don't care. Once I would have got upset. Now I put it down and walk away.

———

The Jungian psychoanalyst James Hillman says on *Late Night Live* that Eros strikes always so that one falls in love with 'the wrong person'.

———

V no longer tries to dissuade me from going to Primrose Gully. We make each other laugh a lot, lately. He chucks a hunk of plastic into the creek for Tess, the blue heeler we're minding for M's boyfriend, and she bombs in after it with a splash as colossal as if someone had dropped a washing machine off a bridge.

———

Dreamt I was a teacher. My class was unruly. In vain I shouted abuse. A boy stood up from his desk and walked forward to where I stood. He was wearing a headdress of great delicacy and beauty: a shimmery concoction of silver wire and pearl drops that seemed barely attached to his head and hovered around it, quivering.

Three writers came to dinner. V was talking admiringly about something European. Absorbed in what he was saying, I asked, 'Do you wish you were European?' He swung round at me: '*No. No, I don't.*' My question was sincere but he was offended and I didn't know why. I started to stammer out an explanation, but the American poet spoke across me in a dreamy tone, 'What do I wish *I* were?' The sting went out of the moment. I looked at the poet's droll, pugnacious face and thought, 'You've got manners.'

The writers' festival. It's like being barbecued. The New Zealand novelist and I drank glasses of water in her forty-fourth-floor room. Outside, dark, rain, thousands and thousands of lights in street patterns. We agreed that at such a height we entertained thoughts of jumping. On my way home, buskers were playing jazz outside Flinders Street. A little boy threw himself into the space and galloped to the music in joyful turns and rolls. His father spread out the kid's parka and coins rained on to it. Everyone was laughing and shouting.

My favourite scene in *Strictly Ballroom*: Barry Otto seen through a window, dancing by himself under a harsh, ugly white light— something fluid and Hispanic—absorbed in his own movement. The secret dancing-life of men.

A day in the Magistrates' Court. The Ormond Master's appeal.

C told me about applying to become a member of the synagogue. She had to fill in a form: two Jewish families who'd vouch for her, the Hebrew names of her children. 'I looked at the form and felt *lost*. I felt as if I'd got lost a long time ago.' She began to cry. 'We used to think we could do without the family. But now I believe it's all we've got.'

Four men and four women entertaining themselves round a table. Someone posed a question: 'What change would you like, to your physical self, if you were granted one wish?'

'Thinness.'

'Yes. Thinness.'

'Thick, long, black hair.'

'Smaller ears.'

'A bigger mouth, with voluptuous lips.'

'Thick black hair and a thick black moustache.'

Then the oldest man at the table said, 'A body that was completely adequate, so I never had to think about it and could appear in a bathing suit without a thought.'

The last of us, a woman, said, 'Same as him.'

———

Reviews of *Chez Nous*. So various that except for the plot details you'd hardly know they were all talking about the same movie. 'Lugubrious.' 'The fine, stern edge of truth.' 'Fatuous.' I stop reading and shove them into the filing cabinet.

———

The trial of the guy who beat the toddler to death. The little white body garlanded, festooned with bruises. On day four the tough, tattooed journalist beside me took her glasses off and burst out sobbing. I hung on till I was riding home. Every outbreath made a weird moaning sound. I crawled along the vegetable patch and pulled out weeds, yanking and weeping, making a lot of noise.

———

It started with one young woman in the jury box. She leaned forward, opened her mouth, and let out a stream of loud, tearing sobs. It ran along the front row in a wave, five women crying and a man too. Their sobs echoed off the walls. They can't reach a verdict, and are dismissed.

———

Time magazine wants to run what I've already written, but V firmly urges me to hold out for the retrial. He is generous, patient and right.

———

I cut up a Christie's catalogue V gave me and made fifty postcards. Messing around for hours with scissors and glue—straight edges, crooked edges, torn edges against the white rectangle of the card. Is this what they call 'a hobby'?

———

Mum and Dad here for dinner. They drank a fair amount of red wine. V made a little wire barbecue and cooked chops. Pleasant evening. Mum mentioned several members of her family and Dad said, 'Your family had a rather tragic history.' He listed their losses. Her youngest brother, barely nineteen, shot down in a flying battle in 1944 near the border of Holland and Germany. 'He was a ter*rific* bloke,' said Dad. 'He was like your *twin*.' A cousin lost in a blizzard, her body not found till the spring, and *her* brother had some sort of crack-up after the war. 'I went to lunch with him one day,' said Mum, 'and he was in a terribly jittery state. He couldn't sit still.' An uncle fiddled the books of the family firm and when found out gassed himself in his car. Another cousin caught polio as an adult, they took him in his iron lung to the football at the MCG, he caught a chill, got pneumonia and died. These stories, several of them news to me, seemed drawn from them by V's presence, the quality of his attention, his ability to ask for a detail at the right moment.

———

My piano teacher quotes Wilfred Bion: a psychoanalyst must embark on a session 'without memory, desire or understanding'. I can't even mention this sort of thing to V. He goes berserk.

———

The imagery V uses in ordinary speech, loaded with reluctance. 'I'll dump you off at work.' 'I said I'd cart her round the bookshops.' 'We'd better get rid of' (i.e. eat) 'those potatoes.' 'I suppose I'll drag m'self into town.' As if the ideal were stasis.

Michael Ondaatje came over, after his publicity tour in Sydney. The
Herald journalist had interviewed him without either tape or notebook, and had invented all kinds of things for Michael to say. He
laughed about it. A very warm, quiet bloke, with a gentle manner.

The two young complainants in the Ormond matter don't want to
speak to me. 'Without them there's no book,' says Y.

Storm clouds formed. Thunder ran absent-mindedly round the sky,
like deep thoughts not yet focused; then it chose its topic and began
to crackle more narrowly. The air was a sharp blueish grey, yet very
clear. Fat, flat drops fell in a rush and with regret I ran inside.

At the painter's place two of the men were scathing about
'religion'. The painter roared that it 'should be stamped out'. I
lost my temper then sat in a gloomy sulk. Tried to pull myself
together and construct an argument but lacked the energy (or
skill) to heave the discussion on to a territory where I could say
what I thought. The men (except V, who tried valiantly to create a
civilised ground) drank and shouted. Y fell asleep in her chair. The
painter's wife was attentive but mostly silent. On the way home V
rebuked me for my lack of interest in politics. I said there was a
hierarchy of topics at any dinner table, and that politics was always
at the top; that people not interested in politics had to sit through
aeons of shouting and table-thumping without protest because of
this unspoken consensus. V: 'Why are you so angry?' H: 'I don't
know.' I did know, but it was too late in the evening to open that
can of worms.

'It seems,' says my sister, 'that women go mad and men have heart
attacks.'

H: 'Would you say that most of our difficulties are basically due to me?'

V: 'Well...I do think that for the most part I'm pretty...blameless.'

———

I asked V what he 'really thought' of my work. He said he thought it was very good but that I should get beyond the subject matter that limited me, 'those households, what are they called? That you always write about?'

———

'Marriage,' said the Polish philosopher, 'is a very powerful symbol. Perhaps your sadness, and depression, might stem from an unconscious fantasy of what marriage could do, or be—for example, that you will have total approval and support. Perhaps you need to locate this fantasy and replace it with a more appropriate idea of marriage.' When I got home V suggested we should see a movie and eat out. We did. I looked at him with a kind of shame and a new affection.

1993

Federal Election. I voted, with clenched teeth, straight down the Labor ticket. V as always destroyed his vote by writing on it a protest against compulsory voting.

————

My nun's leukemia has become acute. The platelets they are giving her twice a week are being destroyed, by the cancer, within fifteen minutes of each transfusion. I feel the first stab of fear.

————

My lovely cheap new sprinkler. On low pressure, a bud of water, then as I open the tap further, a hollow onion; then a wide fountain.

————

A visitor speaks about having brought her ageing mother to live with her and her family. 'It's hard, yes. Hard. If anyone else came in and said, "I've made a cake. Sit down and I'll bring you a cup of tea", I'd love it. But because it's my mother I sort of can't accept it. I won't allow her to do any cleaning. No, none at all.' 'Why not, if that's what she'd like to do?' 'I won't have my mother being a servant.' Next day she calls and says she'd felt as if she'd been 'expertly interviewed'. I was dismayed and began to apologise. No—she didn't regret anything she'd said—it was rather that she'd said things she hadn't known she thought, or felt.

————

Dreamt of a large house in whose garden were discovered thirty-five buried typewriters.

———

I called a tutor I knew at Ormond College and asked if she'd speak to me about the events there. She blew up! She ripped shreds off me. She was so furious, rapping out accusations and challenges, that I started to laugh. After she'd slammed down the phone I had to lie on the couch to get my breath back. Is there something crazy in this story? I think I'll slog on.

———

'Now listen,' said V. 'Your father's got cancer.' Multiple family ring-arounds. The two nurses say that ninety-nine per cent of men over sixty have prostate trouble and he'll probably die of something else before the cancer gets him.

———

It's nearly O's birthday. I wrote to him and said I missed him, and that I was sad that I'd broken our friendship, and lost him. I said I hoped that one day he might be able to forgive me for what I'd done, for having offended him and made him angry, and hurt him.

———

I don't want to go to New York and leave my vegetable garden, and my mulch and compost.

———

Dreamt I was dancing with a gay man from my French class, on an enormous timber floor. We danced in perfect accord, firmly clasped with our whole fronts touching, arms high in classic ballroom position. A thrilling sense of power and mastery. At first I was so dazzled by his grace and confidence that all I did was follow. Then after a while I ventured to press my leg against his as a hint to change direction. He picked it up at once and smoothly incorporated it. I realised with joy that we really were *a double act*.

———

O replies. A restrained letter of such subtlety, generosity and readiness to laugh—and to make *me* laugh—that what was left of my huffy defences dissolved. He even used the term *'folie à deux'*. He opened all the windows and let the breeze flow through.

A big lumpkin of a Down-syndrome boy is lying on the concrete path outside my friends' kitchen window while I wash up. He peeps up just as I'm glancing out. Our eyes meet. We both dart back to shelter, then slowly inch out for a checking look and clash again. I hold up a soup ladle where my head was. He lets out a gurgling shriek. Next time I look he's holding up one fat bare foot. I start to let out operatic trills instead of making appearances. He mimics them in a surprisingly warm, true voice. Thus two strangers entertain themselves through a hot autumn afternoon in Murray Bridge, late in the twentieth century.

Reading Richard Holmes and then Camille Paglia. Comparing their tones is like matching against each other the two intellectual and stylistic influences of my life: the restrained, formal English and the brash, funny, noisy Americans. Maybe the tension between them produces whatever I've got that's mine.

Paglia momentarily takes away my fear, and replaces it with a kind of over-excitement that is almost defiant. What am I scared of? Going out on a limb. Arguing against feminists. Antagonising women. No, that doesn't go deep enough. I feel a weird dark anxiety. Distraction and fear. I told my nun I had night panics. Her immediate practical response: 'Babe—have you got a little Gospel?' 'Yes.' 'Well, Jesus said, about fifty-eight times, "Fear not". Look it up.'

I rush home from a critics' film screening, carrying a box of vegetables and fruit, and propose fresh broccoli for lunch. Alas, V is sick of 'grass and bloody boiled carrots'. Seems I cook in a bad spirit and he often feels guilty when he eats what I've cooked. No, not guilty that *he* hardly ever cooks—it's a fault in *my* attitude. And it's mean-spirited of me to want him to share the work of cooking. In his opinion cooking isn't 'work' in the way that drudgery, like washing dishes, is—it's more 'a kind of giving'. He says he's basically pretty pleased with the way he is, with the shape of himself, and he doesn't want anyone to require him to change—for him to start learning to cook, he says, would be an alteration in his *shape* and *nature*—it would make him less himself.

Still, this evening he cooked the dinner. He served, without eye contact and with disdainful flicks of the spoon, arranging it as unattractively as possible, a delicious rack of lamb with potatoes and capsicum. Why the hell was I sad? I'd got what I wanted, hadn't I? What more did I want?

———

A ten-page letter from G, in his minuscule hand. He is in the thoracic ward at St Vincent's with a collapsed lung. He'd been drinking way too much; M-C finally got fed up with him and the mess he was making of everything. She said she wasn't going to stay with an alcoholic, and moved out of their apartment and into her studio in the Cross. But then the studio burnt down and she had nowhere else to go, so she came back. Now she's pregnant. He feels 'like a plaything in the hands of fate'. He tells me to show the letter to V. I decide that this would be a mistake.

———

Late on a work day V called out under the window of my office. We went up to Lygon Street for a coffee. He said he was going out to play snooker with one of the painters. Hurray. House to myself for a couple of hours, and when he gets back from a blokes' outing I'll be really pleased to see him.

———

Q met a top curator at the National Gallery who told her that V was 'the best writer on art in Australia'. At home, adopting a 'level' tone, I pass on the tribute. He acts as if I hadn't spoken. I'll never understand this guy. I suppose it doesn't help that Q is a woman.

I wanted to use the word 'blowhard' so I called Mum. She was very pleased and interested, and made several fine discriminations that were useful to me. Hung up happy, feeling that for once our minds had connected.

I had a cold and V brought me breakfast in bed. I must slow down and remember him more.

Freycinet Peninsula, on my own, for a travel magazine. Dashed off the piece and faxed it. A roaring black night with a high sprinkle of stars. In the morning big gulls dive-bombed for fish. They soared into a tremendous wind, turned to let it push them over to the fish-field, then plummeted, wings half open, folding them only at the moment of entry. The *work* of being a bird.

Dreams of a river? A baby? A fire?

Got to get myself a Walkman so V won't scowl and say, 'What are you playing that loud, clashing music for?' (It was only Lenny Kravitz.)

I've got this NYU teaching gig coming up. Four months in New York. V presses me to fight the university for a flat that's big enough for him to work in all day but small enough to prevent visitors, particularly my family.

Midnight call from my sister in Bali: her husband has died in the surf, she is about to board a plane. Third sister and I drive across town to tell their daughter. We stand outside the dark house, exchanging looks of dread. A clear, cold, still night, sharp stars—a beautiful night.

Our sister wheels her trolley out of customs, her face distorted and flushed. We rush to engulf her, all weeping loudly, howling and wailing. I open my eyes and see a line of Japanese men staring at us, their mouths sagging, shameless in their shock and curiosity. Outside it's morning, not quite light. I put my big black scarf around her. She's babbling, sobbing, stumbling along between us. We'll take you straight home. *Don't leave me alone!* We'll stay with you, we'll look after you, we won't leave you alone. Between bursts of racking sobs she speaks with a sudden coherence: his car's in the long-term carpark, how much will it cost? I promise to deal with it. Moved by her, deeply impressed. I feel *proud* of her. The crying rolls through her house in waves. I hear someone in another room strike up again, sobbing and keening, but crying is now *what one does*, it doesn't occur to me to go and investigate or comfort. Soon it subsides. Stupor. Someone tells you something—a name, a task to do—you say carefully, 'Yes, right, okay, got that, I'll do it'—you turn to do it, you've already forgotten the entire conversation and you're in a chair by yourself in a room looking through the window at a bare tree branch moving in the wind. It was afternoon, the sun was low, she saw him coming down the face of the wave, she thought, it's too big, and dived under it, and surfaced, but he didn't come up. The sun was in her eyes. The water he died in was only waist-deep. She sits bowed forward with her head on the kitchen table. Under her cheek a cushion wrapped in a towel soaks up her tears.

———

Never before has it been so important that birds sing at the end of the night.

———

I said to Mum on the phone, 'I don't think I've got any tears left.' She was silent for a moment, then said, 'They'll come back again, when they're needed.'

———

V has to drive to Sydney. 'Not a mile passed,' he says to my sister, 'when I didn't think of him.'

———

A dear letter from V's mother: 'Try to carry on and look forward.'

———

If you sit in a garden, you see that life goes on. It doesn't *end*. How could it end?

———

Manhattan. Another planet. There go the sirens, wild and determined—wailers, then the harsh hooters—get outa my way. Eighty-six degrees. In Woolworths 6th Avenue, everything disordered, plastic, cheap, dusty.

    H: 'Let's get one of those ice trays.'

    V: 'Ice? What for?'

———

My borrowed office. Under the desk a dead mouse, its feet stuck to a square of superglue.

———

A tall blond man with hair clipped short walks into the English department cocktail party wearing a striped, reddish-yellow sort of pyjama suit. An obscure Russian tutor beside me mutters, 'My Gahd. It's Yevtushenko. He's a national joke.'

———

Why should I write anything? The world is huge and stuffed with books, and my mind is very small and stiff.

———

Very late in the hot night, a quick smatter of explosions that sound like gunfire, followed by a shuddering echo, a brief silence, then a chorus of screams. We go back to sleep.

———

How well-mannered the students are, so confident and relaxed in their approach to me, not at all shy. I can do this.

———

V and I watched a show called *Seinfeld* that one of the students told me about. Something about a puffy shirt. Laughed. A lot.

————

The Institute for the Humanities has an electric pencil sharpener. You shove your pencil in, it whirs hard, you pull it out and return to your office to push the magnificent long sharp point fruitlessly across the paper. I can't find the spot at which to start this book. I've got to write it dashingly—use the rip and slash that surrounds me here—drop the self-righteous provincial poor-me-scorned-by-feminists tone.

————

At some people's place I got points for knowing who Kinky Friedman and Beavis and Butt-Head were.

————

In the Hassidic computer shop a man with a grey beard spreading all over his chest caught my eye in a friendly way while he was saying to his customer, 'There's a four. There's a five. Soon there'll be a six. *C'est la vie*.' I had no idea what he was talking about, but the beat between his last two sentences was so exquisitely timed that I had a little moment of ecstasy.

————

I want to write charmingly, using 'I' but without becoming grandiose.

————

The lower down the hierarchy the person is, the more likely they are to befriend you or to make efforts to put you at ease.

————

Even V, as the ferry surged away from the Ellis Island Immigration Museum, had a small red line above his upper lip, as if he'd been biting it with his lower teeth in an attempt to maintain its stiffness.

————

V slaps down in front of me, with relish, a big *New York Review* piece by Frederick Crews about Freud. H: (mildly) 'Why do you show me articles against Freud?' V: 'Because I think most of that stuff's *rubbish*.' Neither of us knows much about psychoanalysis, but I am by nature receptive to the idea of it while he is by nature repelled by it. And, for some reason, he feels an urge to attack and destroy. Anyone would think I was 'a Freudian', the way he goes on.

———

At the 92nd Street Y, Shostakovich's 24 Preludes and Fugues played by Tatiana Nikolayeva—a round ball of an old lady in a voluminous silky dress that billowed pleasantly, bringing to mind a breezy bedroom. She played with immense power that rolled down her hard, muscular forearms. The music, which I knew only as recorded by Shostakovich himself in an awkward, harsh, ugly performance, surprised me by its frequent sweetness and beauty. Susan Sontag was sitting a couple of rows in front of us. She applauded seriously but with enthusiasm, holding her large, dry-looking, dark-skinned hands high above her head.

———

A new hang at MoMA. For the first time I get why V is so crazy about Cézanne: a bather, modest, even quite small, and at the same time stupendous, elemental. I stopped dead before it. Twisted face, eyes downcast as if in thought though perhaps he is being careful on the stones. Hands on hips; great big buniony feet.

———

I sat in on the well-known poet's three-hour masterclass at the 92nd Street Y. He was trying to make them think like poets, not fiction writers. They resisted, one sulked, but he prevailed. In a neighbouring room, for the first hour, someone not much more able than I am played over and over Bach's first prelude from the forty-eight. The poets were too absorbed to notice it, but to me it was terribly moving and beautiful, the way it dipped and plunged. Imagine having a good piano in an empty room and no reason to stop—a piece of Bach not too monstrously difficult but always resisting your efforts to master it. It doesn't matter how clumsy you are, it is not possible to make that music sound ugly.

I've reached the point in the Ormond book where all I can do is start paraphrasing and arguing. I don't know how.

Janet Malcolm's big *New Yorker* essay on the biographers of Sylvia Plath: boom! She shows me that the things I'm too timid to write *can be written*—that I should trust the stuff that my inner censor has been telling me to scrap. Meanwhile, in the *New York Times* someone reviews a book: 'a model polemic, full of autobiographical detail, conversations with friends, family and colleagues, and debates the author has had with himself and critics.' Is that what a 'model polemic' is? I think maybe I can do that.

G writes. He has been present at the birth of the baby, a girl with 'long, splayed fingers: I think she could manage a tenth already, on a proportionately reduced piano. I'm dizzy with exhilaration and lack of sleep—exalted, absurdly happy. Is there a plan, Helen, or is it just women carrying on with life, civilising through that peculiarly feminine self-abnegating and unselfconscious love? In awe and wonder, your respectful friend.'

John McGahern's short stories. He goes in very deep, broaching a vast reservoir of sadness, passivity, hopelessness, despair. It excites me that he is so carefree about using 'I'. One guesses 'I' may be McGahern himself but what if it is? It's *not the point*.

I don't think I've got anything you could call 'an argument', in this book. But I do see how a thought can curve around and connect with another in a graceful flourish.

My story about the little murdered boy has won a Walkley Award.

Wrote myself off, accidentally, two nights ago, in various bars with my students after our final class. Poisoned myself with vodka and tequila and God knows what else on an empty stomach. Don't know how I found my way back here. In the bathroom I passed out. When I came to I was face down in vomit. Staggered into a metal shelf in the dark and drove my front teeth into my bottom lip. Blood and vomit everywhere.

———

I am a pariah. V incredulous, revolted: how could I let myself get that drunk? He says it's because I change myself and my behaviour when I'm with 'the young'—I alter my way of talking to be more 'groovy'. Too sick to defend myself. Asked him to go out and buy ten packets of chicken noodle soup. That's all I could eat for days. In bowls handed to me on a very long arm, face turned away. This morning he's gone up to Hartford on the train to visit the Australian art critic. I got out of bed and looked at myself in the mirror. Bruise along my chin like a five o'clock shadow, another under left eyebrow, one across bridge of nose. Mouth swollen, a half-inch open split inside my lower lip. I put on my coat and took a cab to the nearest emergency room. 'What happened?' asked the nurse. 'I got drunk and fell down.' She pursed her lips, raised her eyebrows. The young doctor, to whose blond crew-cut clung a shred of Christmas tinsel: 'Why didn't you come in sooner? It's too late now for stitches. What happened?' 'I got drunk and fell down.' A long, ironic look. I took a breath to explain, then thought, I'll never see them again, it doesn't matter what they think. So I stood still and said nothing, in the desolate freedom of a great city. Antibiotics $30 so I had to walk home. At least it wasn't snowing.

———

On the New York–London night flight we slept. Dreamt I sat on an open veranda where mosquitoes landed on the backs of my hands and stung me, with sharp, fine, very painful stabs.

1994

New Year's Day. We're both culture-shocked. V very snaky. Everything I do irritates him. I may not remark on the weather, what would *I* know about London weather? I'm like a bloody terrier, going on about buying two newspapers! *Nobody* buys two newspapers! I don't dare to ask what's wrong. Is it because he can't forgive me for getting drunk, or because he used to live here with his first wife when they were young and happy? Is he sad? Is he scared? I keep my mouth shut. Near Piccadilly we turn a corner and come upon a parade, people in strange uniforms, a band with drums and silver helmets, the thrilling gold of brass played softly. V turns aside into Simpson's sale and I stay on the street to watch the marching girls go by—a squad of them, long hair pulled back hard, in severe little black fitted jackets with sparkly silver belts, and long skirts with a top layer of black tulle—and each girl wielding a flag on a long, flexible pole. They march double time with tiny rolling steps, and twirl these blue and white flags, no smiles, just serious concentration and always the chins held high. Once they all, in perfect unison, drop into a dramatic pose, front leg bent, the other stretched sideways and back—and the flags are swung head down and laid for a beat or two on the pavement—something stabbing about the proud flags drooping and allowed for a moment to trail on the ground.

———

A great British publisher shows keen interest in V's novel-in-progress. I hope it might make him happier. No luck so far.

———

I say I want to live more merrily, with more spontaneity.

V: 'Do you think we should part?'

H: 'No.' (Was it a serious question? I couldn't tell.) 'You're disappointed in me, I know. What is it about me, that disappoints you?'

V: (*reluctantly*) 'Oh…your street-fighting qualities, and…'

I waited a few moments for him to ask me the same question, but he didn't, so I let it pass.

———

British Airways messed up our flight to Madrid and our English friends had to go on ahead without us. V handled the desk staff so brilliantly, never losing his cool, that he got us a refund for the whole trip, including the hotel, and we even still *went*, at BA's expense, though not arriving till dinner time. Astonished and impressed by the patient charmingness of his negotiations. H: 'We've really had a nice day, haven't we, in spite of our visa troubles.' V: 'Yes, and it's because *I* was in charge.' I laughed; but we're locked in an endless power struggle. When we see couples who are cheerfully loving we exchange sad, wry glances. I suppose he thought we would always be 'in love'. My next task: to pick up at speed enough Spanish to handle the weekend here, without threatening his need to be seen as running the show.

———

Prado. *Las Meniñas*. Thunderstruck. But my favourite is Goya. His speed, force, despair, horror, blackness. *Fight with Cudgels*. A series—an armed bandit threatens a monk in brown, who offers him a pair of shoes then wrests the gun off him and shoots him in the bum—the posture of the bandit as the shot strikes him—his knees sag, his arms fly up and forward, his fingers splayed with shock. Some too terrifying to be looked at. Execution by firing squad. In a park we saw a puppet show, an old woman with a foolish chook in a tutu, a wolf came, the old woman dug a hole and the wolf fell in, children mad with joy, their shrieks and warning cries.

———

What V needs, *en voyage*. At the breakfast table in Madrid: 'Have I had one croissant or two?' When I don't know, he is surprised and cross. He has a throat infection and a nasty cough, but walks about the winter streets with his shirt collar open and his coat unbuttoned. Unable to stand it any longer, I take off my woollen scarf and without asking wind it round his neck. His face softens and he says, 'That's very sweet of you. A rendition of love.' In Kew Gardens. Grand vistas and prospects. The rodent flowing of squirrels. We've brought the old Pentax K1000 only so he can take a photo of the famous eucalypt in the gardens, but once he's got his shot, he expects me to lug the heavy camera all day in my little backpack in case someone mistakes him for a tourist. Unless I'm mothering him—carrying his gear, taking responsibility for his health, his food intake, the state of his clothes—everything about me gets on his wick. He tells me that my way of interrupting him with 'sharp questions and urgings comes perilously close to trimming'. Ouch. All right. I resolve to get off his case.

———

Is this what marriage is? I mean, I need to know: *is* it?

———

My front tooth is dead. I have to have root canal. But I swam eight laps of the Fitzroy Baths. My arms were heavy. Tomorrow I'll do ten.

———

Since my drunken fall in New York I have hardly any sense of smell. I read in Janet Malcolm about a patient of Freud's whose sense of smell went away while she clung to unrealistic fantasies that her employer would return her love and marry her. I ask myself what my 'unrealistic fantasies' are, or rather, what I am declining to say bluntly to myself. And out it comes: 'I regret having got married.

I regret my loss of freedom.' Okay. I regret it. But I also accept it, accept my regret, and decide consciously that I'll try to stay married, and will make serious efforts to be more generous, less angry, less controlling, less *reducing*. I state to myself, too, that for all the faults I find in him V is a clever, funny, decent man who puts up with my craziness and tries to be kind to me. And that while there are thousands of 'wrong' men out there, there is no such thing as the 'right' man.

Of course there is an alternative diagnosis, the one given by my GP: that a nerve has been damaged and could take eighteen months to heal.

———

G, M-C and their baby come to stay. They are calm, smooth, gentle. All his panic, all her reproaches gone. The baby is a tiny, dainty button of a creature with blue eyes and a shock of black hair. In our kitchen, after work, I lie on the couch and contemplate her on M-C's lap, my head resting beside them on a cushion. I'm not hungry, not thirsty, not anxious. Her presence bathes the room in peace.

———

The book is coming round in its curve. I wrote an image of a fireplace that came straight out of the collective unconscious. Thought of the sax player who said, 'When I play badly it's my fault. When I play well, it's got nothing to do with me.'

———

A photo of a young soldier with his beaming, frothy, off-the-shoulder bride, who turns out to be already married to two other soldiers from the same barracks. Everyone's furious. She gets a two-year good behaviour bond. Maybe she just liked weddings. Having a reason to put flowers in her hair.

———

Delivered a rough draft of the book to Y. Now I don't know what to do with myself.

———

My nun's been talking about suicide.

———

On the train to Murray Bridge I think that my fantasies of a solitary life are possible only because I'm resting on a solid base of companionship. I see V's stability and how I've come to depend on it. I remember too that one day he will die. Full of gratitude for him, as the train rolls along.

———

I drive my nun to the hospital for her transfusion. Four bags. On the way home I wait outside the convent while she goes in for one of the consecrated wafers that the priest leaves there for the nuns. She emerges and produces from her pocket a single wafer, which she snaps in two. 'This is Jesus,' she says. 'All good things. Health, hope.' We ate the wafer. I was still chewing as I put the car in gear and pulled out on to the road.

———

At Mount Barker I met a five-year-old boy called Maurice Chambers. I asked him if I could take his photo. He sat very still, looking straight into the lens with a serious, slightly strained expression.

———

The woman in her eighties '…was always gentle, eager to please and prepared to disguise her own keen intelligence and sharp memory if these were to interfere with the general harmony. She had never married, never known the control a wife and mother exercises, the unsimple compromises a man and a woman make with each other.' —Colm Tóibín, *The Heather Blazing*

———

On the station platform waiting for the Overland home I remembered the days when train windows used to open. It was a beautiful mild summer night, soft, with half a moon and the air thick with the smell of dry grass and sheep shit. And I was going to spend it in a plastic box.

———

A friend called: 'Listen, the shit's really going to hit the fan with this book. The street word is you're running the line that women who get raped are asking for it.'

———

In DJ's I found for my nun a beautiful white Italian nightie, in heavy cotton verging on the flannelette she had specified, but with swirls of flowers embroidered on the bosom. I loved it so much I longed to keep it for myself. I walked away with the parcel in my arms fantasising saying to her, 'And when you die I'd like to have it back.' Is everybody greedy and selfish and hard-hearted in secret? I hope so, otherwise I'm a monster.

———

In the hospice she couldn't seem to die, she was out of it, in a coma, the Aboriginal women had seen the message bird out on the lawn, the willy wagtail swinging its spread tail, but she gasped on and on. Her girlfriend called the old priest in Wilcannia: 'Is there a prayer to let her go?' and he said, 'Listen, you have to ask her to forgive you, and you have to tell her that you forgive her—doesn't matter what for.' The girlfriend went down on her knees and whispered to her, stepped out on to the balcony and came straight back in. Two minutes later she gave a big sigh, and died.

———

V didn't know why I'd even gone. He asked me what I'd found in her that attracted me. I stammered and stumbled. I said that when I was with her I laughed a lot and was happy, and that she had the God stuff worked out in a good way. He said she was melodramatic, and mentioned other dying people he'd known who'd behaved with more restraint and dignity. If I want to cry properly I have to hide in the yard, or wait till he goes out, or drive somewhere in the car.

———

I think he must be anxious and a bit wretched—struggles with a gallery about a retrospective catalogue he's to write—scared because his novel won't roll—I feel so sorry for what he's going through but

I suppose he would take it as unmanning if I expressed this. Years ago I stopped trying to comfort him with tales of my inability to write after the end of a marriage. One can't comfort a person who won't admit there's anything wrong. If I could just quietly be nice to him. But I've got my own anxieties and fears to get past. We're both battling, and our battles clash, as well as our two natures. I cooked a brilliant lamb casserole with capsicum, carrots, red wine and a lot of onions and garlic.

———

I'll shred this fucking book if things get too tedious with the law. The journalist was dying to tell me his sources. He was having to *bite his lip*. It was almost funny.

———

I hit a low point today. I felt I could not go on. It was like knowing that a free garden, calm and full of rest, lay on the other side of a wall. I knew where the gate was, I could walk through it whenever I felt like it. I was withholding release from myself. Then I had a coffee and a cake, went back to the desk, forced a solution, and kept going.

———

Gieseking playing Bach makes Gould sound like a brilliant machine. He makes mistakes, at times his beat is bumpy, but this makes the grandeur of the music less awesome, more…enfolding, I don't know. One feels that complexity and beauty are within human grasp. In V's workroom half a dozen superb Fairweathers are leaning against the walls. I wish I could go in there and sit among them for an hour or two.

———

My brother's little boy passionately wants M's boyfriend to come and visit him. He describes the house so he'll know it when he walks down their street: 'There's a tree out the front, with round things on it, it's a green, round-thing tree. And there are walls, and then things like *this*, and they're the roof.' The patient openness on the young man's face as he listened seemed very beautiful to me and in my heart I hoped he and M might marry and have children. I would love to be related to him.

———

V wants us to let this house and move into G's flat in Rose Bay for six months, while they're in Italy. Here we go again.

———

The podiatrist sat on the floor and made me walk barefoot up and down the hall. 'You're hollowed out here,' she said, 'and here. These bones are extremely prominent. Your left shoulder is higher than your right, that's the scoliosis. You swing your left arm more freely than your right, to balance the curve of your spine.' So I am twisted, imperfect, a prisoner of inherited forms—but also shaped and saved by my body's own silent, inventive history of adaptation, its ingenuity, its urge towards balance.

———

E's visit. I love having her in the house. 'When you get to this stage of a book,' she says, 'the knot of anxiety here, in your chest, goes away and is replaced by a sort of warmth.'

———

I am getting more cunning. But there are people out there who are a hell of a lot more cunning than I am.

———

I must learn to let V rant about things. He needs to rant. He should rant, and I should detach from his ranting. I hate to see his face go cramped and dark. A knot of contempt between the eyebrows. I remember what F used to say when I scowled and swore: 'Don't be full of hatred. It's ugly.'

———

At Piedimonte's the checkout girl hits the wrong keys and gives me a bill of $184.20. Seeing this vast sum on her screen she mimes horror and says, 'Don't show *this* to your husband—if you're married!'

———

A warm, dry, autumn wind sped over the landscape. Leaves seemed to change colour before my eyes. Worked well, reinserting the good bits that got lost in the ferocious cull, polishing the curves and slotting in small shiny details. Things will interleaf with each other, quite smoothly and appropriately, if I am patient and do not panic. After work saw a movie with V, then he walked and I pedalled along beside him all the way home. He still loves to reminisce about Tex. We laugh and sigh at our memories of his brief reign. At such moments I feel I am 'happily married'.

————

A phone call from a woman I was friends with at university. I recognised her voice before she even said her name. She's heard around the traps that there are plans to take out an injunction against the book. While she spoke, the room and everything outside it seemed to be slowly darkening. I cursed the day I had first heard about the case. My regret lasted about ten minutes. Then I got back on the horse.

————

V has read the book in manuscript. He said in a brisk, offhand tone that he 'couldn't be less interested' in the feminist aspects of it. The people I have interviewed he compared unfavourably with the ones in Janet Malcolm's book—Ted Hughes's sister, for example—and he discoursed for some time about how 'boring' 'young people' are. I maintained a faultless detachment. Having established the pointlessness and tedium of my project, he made several very sharp and useful editorial suggestions, which I incorporated.

————

We go for a walk most evenings at dusk, along the creek past Tex's Look-out. We walk briskly, sometimes arm in arm. Trees completely bare now. Tonight a yellow sky faded to the purest grey-blue. A moon almost full. Dogs, ducks, a few people.

————

How and when will he write his new book? The wonderful idea of it. What's stopping him? *Is it me?*

Yesterday I made a brick incinerator and burnt quite a lot of my early diaries. 'Felt' nothing in particular. Saved about fifteen pieces of paper, most concerning M. I'll make a small salvage book, perhaps. Very sad, ill-tempered, troubled by thoughts about the book and whether it will be published; about my false position with Y who is so terribly ill and with the publishers and lawyers, everyone is backing and filling and having secret meetings, nobody will tell me anything, even my agent can't get any sense out of them; and about my family and their unlikeable characteristics which, V points out, I too am disgracefully displaying. Not to mention anxiety about moving to another small apartment in Sydney, where V's right to our shared living space he will once again assume to be primary. He hates this subject but we manage to discuss it. He offers, with a stiff, unreadable expression, to be the one to rent an outside office. I accept. And at once feel guilty. This is why feminism had to be invented. This morning I ask him if he's still angry with me. 'Well... not really...but it does seems a bit odd that when I make a serious complaint about your rudeness and unpleasantness I end up having to move out of the house.'

E: 'Men's needs are *like air*.'

Drank a pernod with U in a ridiculous bar. She wore an ink-blue hat pulled right down over her thick curls. Its brim cast a stylish shadow across her pretty little giggly face. I admired this look immensely. We talked about angels and devils. We had both seen them.

A *journalist* called and told me my book had been put back to February next year. I finally spat the dummy.

J's in town with his new book. M is away but her boyfriend, with his dog, brings us calamari and swordfish from the market. J springs

up to meet a fellow-surfer, hand out, face earnest. The four of us
and the blue heeler walk for miles along the creek. The dog applies
her knowledge of physics to fetch a branch out of a pool and drag
it up a steep bank, scrabbling madly backwards for a purchase on
the crumbling lip of the drop. We applaud and she grins up at us,
dripping and spiky.

———

'Four Beds'—a story with no characters in it, only rooms, furniture
and light.

———

On the back veranda G and M-C's baby hears a birdcall. Her eyes
snap into focus and she tilts her head with a shrewd expression.

———

The mighty poet publishes a gratuitously sneering crack about me
in his magazine column. V maintains that it is not offensive. G and
M-L sit gaping at him. Under their incredulous pressure he goes so
far as to say it 'might be discourteous'. 'It *is* offensive,' says G firmly.
'It's an *insult*.' Since I am trying to cook an over-complicated meal for
eight I don't take part in the discussion but work on at the stove. V's
response stings more than the insult, but comes as less of a surprise.

———

V has sold to some mysterious tycoon two paintings I know he
greatly prizes. I ask him, several times and with sympathy, how he
feels about selling them. He replies with what he thinks. I wonder
if he does 'feel', or whether he has achieved complete dissociation of
heart from head. He says his book is going so slowly that he thinks
he ought to give it up. I say, 'Oh no! Keep going, sweetheart', but
with a pang of guilt. As if it were my fault. I try to examine this.
How *can* it be my fault?

———

Watching V's face soften and flush with laughter while he talked
with G on the phone, I thought that people need friends they can
adore, not ones they're afraid of and have to be false with.

V gets out of bed at 11.50 pm to answer the phone. Listens, then slams it down. 'It was some bloody journalist. Wanting you to comment on the closing of the Fitzroy *pool*.'

As a farewell present the old Armenian guy next door passes over the fence to us a small soda-water bottle of ouzo. We break out the glasses and throw back a couple of shots. After this we spend the morning packing in hilarious spirits, laughing and cracking jokes.

A red brick building on New South Head Road, a long, narrow, old, shabby apartment. Out every window a sunny stretch of water, silk-blue and riffling, or else a terracotta tiled roof and large palm fronds. Somewhere a power saw. Crows call, melancholy and harsh. Constant clinking of masts. A mile or so away the Manly ferry goes sliding.

At E's dinner I met R. I said to her, 'I want to talk to you about envy.' 'I,' she said, 'want to talk to you about everything.'

Y speaking on TV about the government's cultural statement. Yes, she looks thinner, paler, but terrific—more dramatic, handsomer, sadder, more knowing. The face of someone who has suffered.

Two magazine editors, women, invited me to lunch. They were fresh and clever and interested in people and the world, and they want me to work for them.

The harbour. I can hardly comprehend its constant differentness from itself. Today wide slow ridges, ten feet apart, move towards me at a slant and softly collapse against the low stone wall. Taking notes—this little discipline—is a defence against the blank word-lessness that overcomes me when I stand at the window and look at the water. Why do I feel I have to conquer this state, subdue it, flail away at it with my vocabulary? In fact it is a tremendous gift. A chance at the soul.

———

The lawyers see the book as defamatory on five points. V keeps saying, as if checking, 'You do feel it's worth publishing, do you? That the general subject is important enough to warrant the effect on him? To me it's a much less interesting and important subject than it is to you.'

———

A photo in the paper of Edna O'Brien, hand on bosom, eyes raised to heaven. V deeply impressed: 'She's all woman.'

———

Thunder like someone running across the corrugated iron roof of a shed.

———

I lay on the couch after V had gone to bed, and watched the Queen's Christmas message. Her ghastly rigid hairdo, the big spectacles, the stream of dull clichés, and worst, at the end, her heart-breaking little attempt at a smile.

———

At last I got to talk on the phone with the defamation lawyer. He was flexible, lively, imaginative. He said at the start that he 'couldn't put the book down', had started reading in bed at seven last night and stayed awake till eleven, 'reading on and on'. After this of course I thought he was the best lawyer in the whole wide world.

———

This morning on our walk we got to within sight of the Watsons Bay lighthouse. I was excited and said, 'I reckon that by the end of this week we can get all the way there.' 'Why would you want to get to the lighthouse?' I must have an eager beaver quality that causes blokes to dig their toes in. I *will* get to the lighthouse. It's only a mile further on.

A plumber came to fix our blocked shower: a boy with dark curls who shook V's hand at the door. We stood outside the bathroom marvelling at his industry. I said, 'You're the first tradie I've ever seen clean up after himself.' He said he would feel embarrassed to leave a mess, that he liked working, in fact preferred work to everything else. He wanted to make enough money to buy a house. He squatted by the plughole pouring water down it from a bucket. I said anxiously, 'Is it fixed?' 'Oh yeah,' he said, 'it's sweet. I just like to see the twirl.'

During the auction E and I waited for V in a bar. An hour and a half later he came briskly walking in and sat down. His face was rather pale. 'Did you get it?' He leaned back and gazed off to one side, with an ironic smile. 'Did you? Did you get it?' At last he replied: 'Yes.'

My agent calls: 'It's on. I'm going to the TAB to place a bet.' To tell the truth I felt not only deflated and slightly drab, after all the adrenalin of waiting, but also a kind of dread about the next mountain, the outcome of it, what publicity I'll have to do.

Y has left publishing. Apparently people are going round saying I 'abandoned her when she was dying'. Oh, for God's sake. No defence is possible against this crazy shit.

1995

New Year's Eve fireworks off the Harbour Bridge. People called out comparisons. Chrysanthemums! Lilies! Tapeworms!

———

Our new neighbour one floor down is a hilarious China scholar with a massive mop of extensions. She says she and her flatmates, young musicians, play a lot of Scrabble—any time we feel like a game…On my way up the stairs I hear them laughing. She drops in to model for us a hat she's found in an op shop: a tiny black cowpat with a curving line of green sequins on the front and a little puff of black veil over one eye. After she leaves, V expresses gloomy concern that this building might be 'too young for us': he says he is planning a serious, quiet life.

———

The first journalist who interviewed me was very skilled. He knew how to present an opposing viewpoint in exactly the right tone of disinterestedness to make me examine my own thoughts more critically.

———

V has, of course, never again mentioned his offer to be the one to work away from home. And I lack the mettle for the fight. My agent borrows me a friend's flat in Bellevue Hill for a month and away I pace each morning, in my runners and straw hat. When I get home he's lying on the couch in the cool, watching the cricket. Home.

What is home. Home is the place one may enter and leave whenever one needs to. Since 1988 I have not had one of these. I don't know by what means I am able to be in such good spirits, to be spontaneously generous and efficient, shopping and cooking and serving, while the little virus of displacement nestles itself more deeply into my vitals.

————

The Pope's in town and the drought has broken. On Channel 9 News they showed a meteo map of a moving rain cloud in the shape of a cross. Even I let out a burst of scornful laughter.

————

The owner of the borrowed flat is back. Over in Bondi Junction a hot little sex bomb called Ronnie showed me a tiny north-facing room above a pharmacy on the mall: 'For $50 a week the owner'll paint it any colour you want and put in a new carpet.'

————

The adventurous beauty tells us about her lover in India.
    V: 'What are his good points?'
    AB: 'He's deep, serious, moral...'
    V: 'What are his bad points?'
    She hesitates.
    H: 'He's deep, serious, moral?'
    She laughs.
    AB: 'Exactly. He doesn't much like to *play*.'

————

Our London friends are going home. I helped them move out of their flat. While we were doing a final clean the husband began to sing in the bedroom and his wife joined in. They had ordinary, tuneful voices. I rushed in and we all warbled away merrily, remembering the words of 'It's Only a Paper Moon' and 'Buttons and Bows'. Something wonderful about this—something I've lost without even realising it was gone. Imagine—cleaning together! *Singing* together!

————

Cool morning, with clouds. Our new flat is calm, with leafy windows and plenty of space. The only thing missing is being able to step out a door and stand near some plants. H: (*eagerly*) 'We should open the windows.' V: (*levelly*) 'What for.'

———

He flopped a new short story on to the table in front of me. Within a few lines I could see it was good. It was beautiful. All the weirdness of his early stuff but also a warmth, I could almost say a tenderness. I went to congratulate him. He writhed, turned his face aside, strode out of the room.

———

In Bondi Junction mall I bought a 70s disco compilation and Steely Dan's *Greatest Hits*. Skipped home, crouched in a corner with the headphones on and played my best tracks over and over. Can't wait for him to go out so I can DANCE.

———

The Cretan's had a little heart attack but he's home. His wife, who has the pretty freckles and dainty feet of an Irish dancer, is a woman you know would be brilliant in a crisis. He looks smaller, paler, thinner. His dark-brown eyes glow fiercely.

———

Dinner out with V and a couple of journalist friends of mine from way back. The white-haired one turns up without his wife. 'It's got nothing to do with *you*,' he says cheerfully. 'She just couldn't stand to go out with *me*.' V: 'Do you and your wife have many arguments?' 'Yep. Lots. All the time.' V: 'How often?' 'Oh…we'd have a major argument about…once a fortnight.' V: (*shocked, fascinated*) 'But those aren't *arguments*, if they're once a fortnight, are they?' The other journo, the husband's close friend, leans in and says, 'Oh, they fight all the time. It's a Jewish thing, maybe. It's not embarrassing or anything, if you're there. Someone'll rush out of the room in tears, and ten minutes later come back in and sit at the table as if nothing had happened.' The white-haired husband laughs and shrugs, and we all reach for the menus. I notice V flicking him furtive looks.

—————

Dreamt I drove past a big square two-storey house—had I once lived there?—that had been gutted, its insides stripped away and burnt. The block of land on which it stood was bare, not a blade of grass to be seen. The house was only a shimmering framework, still erect, but fragile.

—————

I bought a phone/fax/answering machine, a Brother, for my office. $870. It has functions beyond my wildest dreams. I don't even know what they are, and am almost afraid to find out. In case I don't need them.

—————

The daughter of a family who befriended M when she was working in France—she hung out at their house, went on holiday with them—is coming to Australia next month. M writes to ask if she can bring her to Sydney and stay two or three nights. First, the shot of happiness at the thought of their company, and of returning the family kindness; then the clenching gut. Looking out the kitchen window from the sink I see a small, sunny motel on the other side of the lane. Perfect. I'll book them a room there. They'll be out all day, and they can eat with us in the evenings—I won't have to do that nerve-racking juggling of guests' sleeping and waking and tiptoeing around V's work. When he comes back from a cigar-smoking walk I tell him my brilliant plan. He flips. From his position on the sofa he starts to shout, throwing back his head and clutching his temples. 'This is *mad. You're* mad! *Mother*-mad! This is the kind of thing that drives men *crazy*! It's completely *insane* for you to contemplate *paying* for their *motel*! There's something weird about your relationship with M! Why do you go peculiar and behave in these exaggerated ways when she's about to visit, and when she's here?' And so on and on, rolling his eyes and clicking his tongue and groaning when I try to put my case, until he's completely drowned me out. I drop it mid-sentence and say in a dull, exhausted voice, 'Why does this make me feel so awful?' Silence. I get up and go into the kitchen and start preparing the meal. After a while he comes in, puts his arms round me and says, 'Don't be unhappy. There isn't a problem.'

_____

The GP calls. 'There *is* something on your ovary. I'd like to send you to someone who knows more about ovaries than I do.'

_____

The Ormond complainants are going for an injunction. And they're requesting access to my interview tapes, notes, and working journals. Lying in bed in the dark, remembering the journals, the record of my labour, the extreme *personalness* of what's in them, I feel grit start to harden inside me.

_____

The wary, carefully blank face of the defamation lawyer when he's listening. If the complainants succeed in getting access, he says, he sees no reason why they should need to be shown anything other than the book itself, since that's all 'we' plan to publish. He says that in the last few years five journalists have been jailed for refusing to reveal their sources. Privately I resolve to become number six if I have to. They are not getting those notebooks.

_____

The gynaecologist, someone told me, is famous for being a former captain of the Wallabies. I am not a hundred per cent sure who the Wallabies are. He looks to be in his late sixties, with a pleasantly wrinkled face, and the slight remoteness of the old-fashioned doctor. He tells me that my right ovary is enlarged. There's a cyst. Probably been there for a long time. He doesn't think I've got cancer, but he would like to take it out. These things can be bilateral, he says, so he'd take the other one out as well. 'What about the uterus?' 'Well, it's no use to you any more, post-menopause. It's a site for trouble. I'd like to take *it* out as well. You'd be in hospital for a week.' I sit there in a stupor. So it's going to happen to *me*: 'a clean sweep from the waist down,' as women of Mum's generation used to quote their gynaecologists saying; and we'd all laugh. He said, 'We'll put you into George V.' This also meant nothing to me. I took the train back to Bondi Junction and sat in my office. After a while I called V and he came and got me.

———

The publisher calls. 'We won. With costs.' Two hours later: 'They're seeking leave to appeal to the Full Bench of the Victorian Supreme Court—tomorrow.'

———

Our lawyers had to work till late into the night, work wasted, for in the morning the complainants withdrew. Maybe somebody said to them, 'What are you *doing*? There's nothing in this book that identifies you! You haven't got a case!' Maybe now they'll hold their fire till the book's out, and then go for me. Maybe this hysterectomy is rather well-timed.

———

I was buying *Remembering Babylon* in the Tullamarine bookshop and spotted my book on the Picador rack. Heart got smaller and sank into my ankle boots. I walked away from it and sat reading a *TLS* at the departure gate.

———

The doctor gets out his leather-covered pocket diary and I get out my spirax. I propose a date. 'Yeeeees,' he said, 'I'll be around then. I'm babysitting that weekend.' 'Who are you babysitting?' 'Two grandchildren,' he says with a proud smile. He says that the removal of the uterus doesn't make the operation more serious. 'If I made an incision and just sewed it up again, your recovery time would be exactly the same as if I took out your ovaries and your uterus.' So it's the abdominal wound that's the trouble. I go downstairs for a blood test. While waiting I read an article in a magazine about a Californian girl who fought off a serial killer. He raped her and she talked her way out—asked him to *kiss* her (he was someone she knew), talked to him for hours, faked emotion for him, talking and acting and persuading—this against a six foot four man armed with a big kitchen knife. Eventually early the next morning she persuades him to leave because she has to go to work. This ghastly story—but what a woman! 'I remember saying to myself, *Think*!' I was filled with awe.

———

Days of media interviews, back to back. In the boardroom the publishers drink beer and I, timid in my fatigue, stick to orange juice.

———

Dreamt that on a street a young woman came walking towards me. She passed me without a greeting. I saw she was weeping, holding one hand up to her face as she hurried along.

———

At Mildura Writers' Festival the mighty poet was surprisingly friendly to me. No doubt he had forgotten having fanged me in his column so I forgot it too. After the evening session he asked me to walk back to the hotel with him. We paced along slowly. He said he had lost three stone and had to lose more. And that he had always hated feminism. I made a few awkward jokes. We both laughed. He said, 'Well, I've been seen with you, and you've been seen with me.' Over our heads, wonderful desert stars.

———

I met a glorious short-haired pointer on a bridge.

———

I estimate that last week I received about fifty letters about the book. They kept arriving in bundles, forwarded by the publisher and *Good Weekend*. They are mostly favourable, but more interestingly, they are often many pages long—accounts of confusing sexual or semi-sexual experiences that the writers have had, that they long to understand ethically and psychologically. I sat on the floor last night ripping open envelope after envelope, taking out stories of sexual and moral bewilderment, many of them beautiful and touching in their candour.

———

A middle-aged woman came up to me at the Edgecliff Centre and said, 'I haven't read your book yet, but I'm going to.' I said, 'Thank you. I hope you'll like it.' 'It doesn't matter whether I like it or not. I congratulate you for having opened up the debate.'

———

A rather wet radio interviewer gave me nothing to push against, and I found myself charging out into the space she was leaving. I spoke with aggression about certain of my critics and their intellectual dishonesty. Afterwards I felt I'd behaved foolishly, like a boxer all kitted up and dancing around shouting, 'Come on! Hit me!'

———

Breakfast radio with an eminent feminist historian of my generation. The young interviewer screeched at me: the techs in the booth had to turn her down. She seemed to be almost manic. The historian registered this and sat back. I did the same. Like two tired mothers we withdrew our energy and let the girl pour out her spleen: I had set feminism back twenty years, and so on. I must have said something but I don't remember what it was. Time was up and she dashed away to 'the launch of a new T-shirt'. Out on the street I got one of those scary stress attacks I used to have: my mind raced and swerved, I didn't know what country or city I was in, whether the stuff that surged through my head was real or imaginary. I came home very carefully on a bus, crawled into bed, and passed out for a couple of hours.

———

In a cafe in Bondi Junction four or five young women, maybe students, pass my table on their way to the register. Moments later I get a feeling someone's looking at me from outside the door. I glance up. One of the women is facing me foursquare through the big street window, right up against the glass, glaring at me with cold loathing. She sustains the death-ray full blast till I turn back to my food. Which has slightly lost its savour.

———

The hostile letters are coming now. Many of them are from university students with big heads of steam and a lot of women's studies jargon. Some of them loved *Monkey Grip* and feel I've betrayed them. The huffy ones are sort of sweet—sanctimonious and very young. They're going to get rid of all my other books off their shelves. They aren't going to buy my book, they don't want me to get their money, it really shits them that it's on the bestseller list, it's not my story, I've stolen it, I'm making money out of other people's troubles, anyway they haven't read it and they aren't planning to, but they know EXACTLY what the book says and they're outraged. I think I'll try to answer all of them. It's a calming exercise, trying to visualise the person and slide an answer round her shield of righteousness. One older woman calls me 'an immature "bloody" idiot' and abuses me for three pages, then adds, 'You are welcome to respond.' I want to vomit insults but instead dash off a card thanking her for her 'courteous and thoughtful letter'. Turning the other cheek. It gives a small but very enjoyable rush of power. Over myself.

———

The magazine asked me if I wanted to cover the backpacker murder trial. Two pieces, or more if the trial lengthens. I went down to the court. It was almost empty. Preliminary proceedings. Down at the front the accused, in a dark suit, sat beside his barrister with his back to the body of the court. How harmless and respectable a man in a suit can look. I took a seat ten rows behind him and sat watching him for fifteen minutes. When he turned his head to speak to the lawyer I saw the sharp line of his cheekbone and brow. How much of that cold shock was I projecting? I knew right away I did not want to find out.

———

I had prepared for Radio National's *Books and Writing* by rereading the book on a famous 1955 university sex scandal that the academic who was to interview me had published. I was imagining an energetic discussion of both our books, but not until I'd sat down alone in the Sydney Tardis and put on the headphones did I realise I'd been ambushed, that it was going to be only about my book, and that she was on the warpath. The sleazy, story-stealing book she was deploring did not sound like the one I had written. I was on the back foot throughout, shaken by her aggressive, carpet-bombing style. My rational arguments deserted me. At one point my voice trembled. Silences fell. It was a rout. After the theme music played I sat in the Tardis, appalled at myself. A pause. In my head-phones the host of the show spoke softly to me from Melbourne. 'Are you still there?' 'Yes.' 'Are you all right?' 'No.'

———

This morning I sat down to a fresh pile of letters. As I began to answer the first one, it occurred to me that the furious Ormond tutor was probably getting lots of letters too. I almost laughed. Two skinny little ladies, writing away like mad.

———

Easter. I went to St John's Darlinghurst. Hundreds of people. Someone told me that the vicar 'conducts at least three funerals a week, for the boys with AIDS'. At the first hymn, a frightful squawk behind me: a very old lady, trying to sing. I think this is going to be my church.

———

Nearly Anzac Day. A fresh, bright morning. On the bus I sat next to three jolly old blokes with sun-wrecked skin. They told me they were brothers. 'What? I don't believe you! Show me your licences!' Laughing, they dived for their wallets. The eldest, Henry, said he had been in Changi, 'but I weigh fourteen stone now'. Another said he was a farmer, and would march in Cootamundra. They rattled on about themselves as the bus chugged along. Halfway up William Street Henry said, 'But we haven't asked about you! What's

your name?' 'Helen.' 'Helen!' he cried, and struck a poetical pose:
'"Helen, thy beauty is to me—"' I chimed in with the second line:
'"Like those Nicean barks of yore…"' and they all cheered. 'Is that
Wordsworth?' asked one. 'More like Shelley,' said Henry. 'Where
do you live, Helen?' 'Elizabeth Bay. I'm getting off at the next
stop.' I went to press the button and he said, 'I've already pressed it
for you.' I scrambled out over their legs. They waved, and the bus
keeled round the corner. As I walked home along Ward Avenue I
dredged my memory for the rest of the verse, and found it: '…That
gently, o'er a perfumed sea/ The weary, wayworn wanderer bore/
To his own native shore.'

———

Turns out that not only will the transcript of the *Books and Writing*
massacre be run in the next issue of *Australian Book Review*, but
guess who has reviewed the book for them? The carpet-bomber
herself. The editor calls and in a subdued voice tells me the issue is
about to be posted out—do I want her to fax me a copy of the review,
'just so you'll have read it before everyone else sees it?' My mind
scampers over the terrain. 'Oh, that won't be necessary, thanks. Just
send me a copy of the magazine, if you wouldn't mind. But it's good
of you to make the offer.' Spew spew spew. I'm so terminally *nice*.

———

V has found someone in Melbourne who wants to buy my piano.
He's worked hard to persuade me that I won't be needing it again,
that there's no room for a piano here, where on earth would I put it,
a piano in an apartment building is an impossible thing, it would be
outlandish, and imagine how much it would cost to truck the bloody
thing up the highway. I listened, my arguments dying on my lips. I
know that what he's really saying is, 'You're not a pianist, you don't
sound good when you play, it's not really music, and I don't want to
have to listen to it any more.' I can hardly mount a case against *that*.

———

The review. Isn't the editor of the magazine her *friend*? Shouldn't she have persuaded her to lose the embarrassing first third of it, the clunky accounts of our meetings in coffee shops, not to mention the way she sarcastically refers to me as 'the famous novelist'? I'd expected better from her, something coherent, not these insults and distortions. When she wheels on the phrase 'vagina dentata', about my admiring description of one of the complainants, a beautiful young woman in a low-cut evening dress, I was more than anything mortified for her. 'Madam. May I correct one point in your contributor's review of my book? The coffee I drank at our meeting was not a short black. It was a short macchiato.'

––––––––

'Of course, Helen's motivation was purely commercial.' Somebody I know actually *said* that to someone else I know, who repeated it to me. Is that what people really think, or is it just a mean thing to say? Scared I'm so overloaded that I might make a serious tactical blunder. Main thing is to keep my temper. And drink a lot of water. Walking up the hill with V, I saw a page of the *Herald* lying blown against a wall. On it my face, very small, and my name in white caps: 'Garner faces her critics'. Kept walking.

––––––––

Finished my article about the cruise ship. I laughed so much, writing it, that I had to walk around the room and put on lipstick. Then I knocked over my movie review, and filed both stories. V teases me when I say 'file'—he says it's like in old movies when the reporters in the news room shout 'Copy boy!'—but I like 'file', it makes me feel I'm the real thing, and not just 'making a guest appearance as a journalist', as another of the feminist academics wrote in her scathing review. By Wednesday when I hit George V I'll have cleared the decks.

––––––––

I'm not exactly scared. To lose what's left of my reproductive organs. I'm ready. But from time to time I imagine with a cold thrill the scalpel blade slicing through the muscle of my abdomen.

———

I've stopped vomiting. Time passes with surprising slowness. Night-times I wake, trundle my drip to the dunny, piss, trundle back, press the button that delivers a hit of pethidine, sleep, wake, trundle. Towards morning I look in the mirror. The shape of my nose has changed. Flattened bridge, like a boxer. I must be imagining it. Over hours it gets worse. Sun comes up and I've got two black eyes. Must be from tubes the anaesthetist put in yesterday morning after the staples popped out of the wound. The nurse was sponging me, one of them pricked her, she panicked: 'Have you got hepatitis?' 'No, and I haven't got AIDS either.' Her voice went up the scale: 'I'll have to get a blood test.' The Wallabies guy had to come back and put in a new lot of staples, in theatre, with a second general anaesthetic.

———

Very bright, dry morning. Warm. Quality of light in the room makes me think I'm in a country town. The nurse checks my pethidine. 'You've hardly used any of this!' Proud of myself: I thought I'd used heaps and would be addicted. Lower abdomen a glory of bruise, a railway track of metal. Left hand purple, and puffy as a toad. Rather happy. Can't read, too dopey.

———

People come, I don't remember who, I guess I fall asleep because when I wake no one's there.

———

V brought me a brown paper bag. Oh, boy—mandarins! O made me laugh so much my stitches hurt. E came, and R, and the Cretan. The born-again brought me a C.S. Lewis book from his brother.

———

Something in a dream, something about my mother, made me cry hard and woke me. I came to, with my head turned towards the window. 5.45 am. I got up, just to move my body, and shuffled out on to the balcony. Still dark but the air soft and the city moving. Light entered the sky like a pink hem on stage curtains. A woman screamed. I hobbled to the rail, another scream, someone on the floor below, a muffled window with yellow light, someone's having a baby. On and on she screamed, over and over: Aiii-ah! Aii-*ahhh*! I leaned my chest on the rail and the tears kept quietly running out, something hard and stoic in me dissolved, I tried to pray, to *be* with her, I had no technique for this, it was only an idea, but I felt very close to her and somehow satisfied—a feeling of deep rightness and gratitude. I crept back to bed. Even with the window closed her cries and long howls reached me until the day of the ward began and there was too much other noise for me to hear her any more.

———

When I woke it was full daylight, and a middle-aged deaconess in a green shirt was sitting by my bed. She was earnest and humourless. She questioned me about my life and my family. I gave dutiful answers. 'Would you like me to pray for you?' she said. I thought she meant 'when I'm back at the church' and in relief I said thank you, I would. But she took my right hand between her small, dry, ridged palms, and began to address Jesus here and now, on my behalf. I was rigid with embarrassment, afraid some sceptical friend would walk in and laugh at me. She told him who I was and why I was there, how far away my family lived and why my parents couldn't come to see me. 'She is your child, Lord,' she said, and some further barrier in me went down. She blessed me and left the room. No one else came. I cried for a long time, and then I fell asleep.

How to End a Story

Diaries

Volume III

1995–1998

'…betrayal and shame and rage, the great teachers one is forced to share the world with.'

SARAH KRASNOSTEIN, *The Believer*

'The love problem is part of mankind's heavy toll of suffering, and nobody should be ashamed of having to pay his tribute.'

C. G. JUNG, *Civilization in Transition*

Home from hospital, minus various worn-out internal organs. Flat-bellied and sore. Strange nerve-shootings in my legs, as if there were a tightly yanked electric wire between anklebone and groin. Any sudden movement and *zzzzzt*—it flashes—a hot (yet cold), dry (yet liquid) jolt.

———

My widowed sister comes up from Melbourne for a week to help V look after me. She says I look 'pale' and 'washed out'. She shops and cooks and washes and irons, urges me with her nurse's severity to get up and move every hour or so. One night she washed my feet in a bucket of warm water, buffed them with a towel on her lap, then massaged them with skin cream. She has opinions on world affairs (and on the 'claustrophobia' of our flat), which she expresses in a carrying voice.

V can barely endure our presence here in daylight hours: 'Bloody fussy women!'

I *need* fuss. She's gone home. I miss her. I'm still too weak to go to work. He shuts himself in his room, and I shuffle about by myself, up to the Cross, down to the park.

———

My agent says *The First Stone* has sold 40,000 copies. Letters pour in and I answer them. A librarian tells V she was so appalled by the way a 'feminist in long dangly earrings' attacked me on TV that she resolved never to wear dangly earrings again. To think that my book might affect fashion!

———

V's gone to Canberra. I had two thick slabs of fresh pineapple and five cloves of boiled garlic for dinner, and slept under an extra blanket.

———

Fresh attacks in this month's *Australian Book Review*. Now they're claiming I 'invented dialogue' and wrote 'hypothetical meetings with imaginary characters'. I permitted myself the luxury of a quick and savage retort.

V and I were invited out to dinner. I was so crazed by the accusations, and by the panic of not having finished writing the Sydney Institute lecture, that before we set out I shut myself in the bedroom, sat on the edge of the bed with my fists over my ears and silently *freaked out*. Pulled myself together, of course, and it turned out to be a hilarious evening with six clever and delightful people, including a quiet Chinese couple whose stories V drew out of them with his subtle, icebreaking questions.

We walked home merrily, hand in hand. But this morning I woke sad, guilty and confused. I will probably never know 'what I have done' with this book. Whatever it is, I'll have to live with it forever, an outcome made not altogether painful by the income I am earning. *For my work*.

———

At the Bartók concert a woman told me she'd had a dream about me in which I gave her a whole lot of buttons.

———

Perfect winter day. In my office I sat at the desk with my chin in my hand and stared out at the tiny slice of harbour between the buildings.

Towards dark it turned to a silver ribbon. Then disappeared.

———

Church early at St John's. Hardly anyone there. The acting vicar said to me casually, 'Will you do the first reading? Just stand up where you are.' I did. It was from Kings: Elijah casts his mantle upon a young ploughboy, the boy leaves the oxen, runs back to kiss his mother and father goodbye, and follows the prophet.

I walked home along Darlinghurst Road, a fine morning, pavements washed, the doors of the sex bars open to the sunny street. On a bench near the fountain a young gay man was offering to a woman his opinion of the film *Priest*. 'I,' he said, 'have been out with lots of really repressed guys. And they wouldn't *do* it like that. They won't *do* it. Specially not in a car. Being a Catholic's fucked. Religion's fucked.'

———

E and V never tire of arguing about whether women painters will ever be as good as men. E constructs a case about women in society and in art, about men's universalising of their own experience, how a Rembrandt self-portrait in old age is thought to say 'universal' things about getting old, whereas a painting of a woman in old age might be saying quite different things. In the end V always comes back to his question: 'What's stopping a woman from just getting canvas and paints and *crashing through*?' E laughs, and backs out the door mimicking the posture of an exhausted but dogged fencer.

———

In the street we ran into a Labor MP I vaguely know. She teasingly asked V if he was giving me 'plenty of support' since my book came out. V passed it off with a quip but at home later he launched one of his rants against stupid, cliché-ridden, impertinent, presumptuous, offensive women. A heavy vibe filled the flat. After careful thought about my wording I asked whether there was any reason why her question had so violently got under his skin—did he feel perhaps that I hadn't properly acknowledged how much support he *had* been giving me? My attempt at humility didn't cut much ice. He said this hadn't even crossed his mind, and that he was furious because I 'didn't give a shit' about his opinions of her; I hadn't even looked up from the paper. Finally I said, 'All right. Next time I'll pay more attention.'

The bad vibe is still hanging around, hours later. I don't know what this is about; and I'll never find out by asking V, because he doesn't know either. He truly believes it's about the politician.

———

I heard that at the first meeting of the judging panel for the New South Wales Premier's Award, a woman judge made a very strong statement: if my book even got on to the long list she was going to—do something drastic, I forget what. I couldn't stop laughing. It was almost as exhilarating as winning.

———

At a street market I bargain with a tough-looking bloke for a bunch of battered pencils in a rubber band. He wants five bucks.

'*Whaaaat?* It's only some dirty old pencils.'

He draws one out, reads the legend on its side, and says, in a strong accent, 'Zese pencils come from *America*.'

'So? Three bucks.'

He looks at the pencils, hits me with his hard Eastern European gaze: 'No. Five.'

I shrug and walk away, defeated.

———

Worked on my film column. The better the movie the harder it is to write about. It's lazy to take refuge in telling plots—too cramping at eight hundred words to get my teeth into proper analysis. So I end up falling clumsily between two stools.

The *Age* calls my agent, offering me 'six figures' for ten pieces a year, on anything I fancy. I say I'm happy at the *Independent Monthly*. The editor of the *Australian* summons me to his office. I go out of curiosity. He lolls behind his desk, I perch on a chair. Sums of money are mentioned, and a carrot: one day, he says smoothly, I 'might even get to interview *the prime minister*.' I stare at him, too amazed to say, 'Is there anything in my work that makes you think I might be interested in interviewing the prime minister?' Walking home I think, 'He hasn't read your work, you idiot, and he never will.'

A letter from M: she and the biographer have been playing cello and piano together. 'We got down to business straight away. Vivaldi and Massenet.' The biographer, my bitter ex-friend. I thought I would never be able to forgive the ugly things she said to me. But now they have been redeemed for me, through my daughter.

A stoush breaks out over which newspaper shall run an edited version of the lecture I'm giving at the Sydney Institute. My agent accepted a deal with the *Australian* weeks ago, and though Fairfax is offering more, 'we are women of our word', as she puts it. But the guy at the Institute wants Fairfax to have it and goes into a frenzy; even his wife calls me: 'But Helen! If it goes to the *Australian* we won't have any *publicity*!' I give the lecture. Next morning the *Australian* runs the short, agreed-on version. Okay—that's done. Then I pick up the *Herald* and there I am all over the front page: unable to bully or bribe me, Fairfax sent a reporter to the event with a tape recorder and they've run a huge, ragged, clumsy transcript, full of illiterate mishearings: 'shake the dust of this from your feet' becomes 'the dust of your self-defeat'; 'the dancing force' becomes 'the dancing horse'. Thus they've shafted the *Australian* and got what they wanted for nothing. Shell-shocked. I don't care about the money. A deal's a deal. In fact I got such colossal coverage that I'm probably going to have to emigrate. I sit here flinching, waiting for the counterblast. At 8 am the first phone call. Kind friends. People I barely know. Virtual strangers. I'm not alone.

———

A flustered-sounding *Canberra Times* journalist contacts me. She has been on the phone 'for three hours' to the Ormond tutor, no doubt getting the dirt on me and my 'fictionalising' of the story, my 'distortions' and so on. 'When I read your book,' said the journalist, 'I thought what bitches these women must be—but now I've spoken to her I realise that she's a true believer too, like you—just in different things—I don't know *what* to think.'

What on earth was she talking about? A true believer, *me*? Believer in what? In 'what bitches these women must be'? Where in the book did I say any such thing? And I never thought my version of the story was definitive: I'm the first to say it's full of holes. There's a phantom version of the book out there. People can pin on it anything they want.

V was out to dinner. I crawled into bed and lay awake with a heart like a lump of stone, lost in shame and sadness. I thought I had brought worse disaster to people already damaged and wounded; I had betrayed my own principles by making a speech full of injured vanity, playing to a gallery of people who delighted in my smart cracks at the expense of something they feared and misunderstood and were ignorant of.

In the morning I told V about it. He listened, and then he told me something that an old woman he knows, a painter, had said to him about me: 'Success often brings with it unbearable guilt.' Still. I know I have to keep on examining this landscape of destruction, for my role in it. Accept that I have enemies, and be robust about it.

Having stolen my lecture and run it bristling with moronic typos, the *Herald* calls my agent and offers me a column. 'I didn't even mention the theft,' she says to me, 'but I was dying to say, "Sir. You are a *thief*, a *bounder*, and a *cad*."' We laughed till our faces turned red.

'Then will I sprinkle clean water upon you, and ye shall be clean...A new heart also will I give you, and a new spirit will I put within you; and I will take away the stony heart out of your flesh, and I will give you an heart of flesh.' —Ezekiel 36:25–27

In Port Macquarie, trying to have a little sanity holiday. (V wouldn't come, wanted to keep working.) In the estuary (ruffles like grey-blue silk) a dark thing splashes—a bird? It surfaces again and blows air out of a hole in its back. A black fin. It dives again, skims, blows and vanishes. A surfboat smoothly passes, rowed by four men, the sweep standing in the stern. Bliss of the soft air, the sky flushing and fading, wind and temperature dropping. I had a sudden wish to be wearing a soft and blowy skirt. I wonder if it's spring—or just a drought winter. I went to the museum and spent an hour looking at strange objects from past lives. They've got a suitcase in there from World War I, made out of the tongues of soldiers' boots. In the Country Women's Association Tearooms I joined a table of happy old people who sat squawking and murmuring. We conversed shyly. The lady who served us our tea and scones referred to me as 'the lass'. I could have stayed near them all day.

On TV in the motel: Serbs and Croatians tearing each other apart. Refugees on tractors being stoned. Women 'giving birth in gutters'. Aerial shots of mass graves which, when guards are questioned, are passed off as places where 'roaming animals' have been disposed of. The world is a brutal power struggle forever mutating. *And I am part of it.* I have to acknowledge this. There is almost relief in acknowledging it. How is it possible to stay out of it? It's naïve—or dishonest—to think of oneself as 'above' it, or 'to one side', or even 'simply commenting' on it.

————

Reading Camille Paglia, *Vamps & Tramps*. Short, blunt sentences, broad vocabulary and strong imagery. She pounds in her argument like a carpenter hammering in nails: 'My libertarian position is that, in the absence of physical violence, sexual conduct cannot and must not be legislated from above, that all intrusion by authority figures into sex is totalitarian…The ultimate law of the sexual arena is personal responsibility and self-defense. We must be prepared to go it alone, without the infantilizing assurances of external supports like trauma counselors, grievance committees, and law courts. I say to women: get down in the dirt, in the realm of the senses. Fight for your territory, hour by hour. Take your blows like men. I exalt the pagan personae of athlete and warrior, who belong to shame rather than guilt culture and whose ethic is candor, discipline, vigilance and valor.'

Yikes. I have to keep reminding myself of her caveat: *'in the absence of physical violence'*. In the scenario of her movie *Lolita Unclothed* she proclaims in her shouting style that today the mighty *David* of Donatello would 'get Donatello *arrested* and taken off in a *paddy* wagon'!

————

My sister sends me a press cutting about 'busts of mysterious corpses'. Despite the sophisticated techniques that police forensic investigators use to make them, 'busts are an imperfect aid to identification. They are bald, and thus they all tend to look the same. More than once an unknown victim has been identified as the Midnight Oil pop group's lead singer, Peter Garrett.'

———

I didn't know the poet Philip Hodgins well but I liked him very much. They told me today that he'd died at last of his leukemia, and that he'd said to a friend, 'The trouble with dying is that it's so bloody *boring*.' I sat on V's knee and cried, and he comforted me.

———

Spring in Sydney. Currawongs call all night outside our windows. The letters keep coming, and coming. I wish life would empty out for a while. The book's shortlisted for two prizes. I know I won't win either of them. I'm exhausted. This will never end.

———

A fresh scandal takes the heat off me: Helen Demidenko turns out not to be Ukrainian after all. (Also, she doesn't know how to attach an adverbial phrase.)

———

Dreamt that in a public place I noticed I was wearing dark brown shoes with brogue punchings—men's shoes, and a size too big, somebody else's. I did not know why was I wearing them, and was not pleased that other people would see me in them.

———

A guy from the New South Wales Premier's Department calls. Will I be coming to the awarding of the prize that I haven't won? Thank you, no. He says he's only asking because Peter Singer is going to deliver the address, and it contains opinions 'not unduly flattering' to my book. He sends me the speech. I skim it. Singer dismisses my book as nicely written but really only saying what was common sense; the whole thing's a media beat-up. When this is reported in the paper the morning after the ceremony, V agrees with him.

———

Over the Blue Mountains to Orange in a tiny plane, and home again from Cowra in an even tinier one. Lots of people came to my talks. At a dinner I sat with a bunch of wonderfully entertaining locals. We were reduced to helpless laughter by the tales a pig vet told—how she had to crouch beside a boar as he was mounting the sow, seize his dick before it could enter, and redirect it to a flask for artificial insemination. A scientist explained to me that a watertable is actually porous rock. And a midwife who drove me back to the airport told me she'd moved out there because Cowra's got the best telescope, the blackest skies and the least light pollution in New South Wales. In the minuscule aircraft home, with its sheepskin seat covers, I could crane my neck and see over the pilot's shoulder how he lined the plane up with the runway and dived straight for it. I was scared I might be sick, but I had arranged in the seat pocket two bunches of flowers my hosts had given me in Cowra (freesias, stocks, sweetpeas, diosma) and their fresh perfume saved me.

———

The playwright Jenny Kemp is interviewed about her new play, *The Black Sequin Dress*. 'A woman walks into a nightclub, slips and falls.' This is the basis of the work. I was electrified—I nearly shot into the air. The thrill of an image whose meaning and direction are completely unknown.

———

In Melbourne an old lady who had enjoyed my book invited me to afternoon tea. She told me stories of her marriages and of the men in her life, one of them quite eminent. She didn't seem to require anything of me but an ear. The part I liked best was her appearance at the divorce court in the early 60s: 'I wore a black suit, high heels and a beautiful big black hat'—making a large circular gesture at the back of her head—'and when I got to the lawyer's office he was *horrified*! He said, "You can't go to court looking like that! Go home and change! Take off that *hat*!'" Afterwards, as I walked away, I felt as if I were waking from a dream, or had witnessed a scene from a long-ago novel.

————

I read in the *New Yorker* that during the Bolshevik massacre of the Romanov family in 1918, bullets bounced off the chests of two of the daughters because their slips were so 'closely sewn with diamonds'.

————

At her fortieth birthday party our neighbour X, the painter, sat on a sofa at a low table and opened the presents her friends had brought her. The guests gathered in an arc, to watch. It was a quiet little ceremony, touching and endearing. She thanked each giver by name, with a nod and a sweet smile. She uses her body expressively, in ways that are un-Australian—turns of the head, graceful arm and hand gestures. She comes from a culture where women are different from men, and don't try to resemble them.

————

M's postcard from Rome: 'Do you remember Italian policewomen? In dainty court shoes and their hair cascading down their backs. Make-up and jewellery. How do they manage in an *emergency*?'

————

Getting that nervous-breakdown feeling again. Between now and any conceivable rest, I've got (1) Penrith Hospital piece (2) film column (3) two fifteen-minute panel talks for a festival (4) introduction to my essay collection (5) cutting the crap out of those essays.

————

V has gone fly-fishing up near Bathurst. Two whole days and nights alone in the flat. I wallow in the luxury—stand in one room, then in another, put on a boppy record, try on all my clothes and shoes, practise applying and removing eye make-up.

————

In the street this morning I ran into X the painter. We paused to say hello. I said, 'I loved seeing you open the presents at your birthday party—it was almost like watching a little play.' Her smile faded, and she said stiffly, 'It was *not* a performance.' I was amazed. I took a breath to explain myself, but she hurried on.

————

Slaved all day over the hospital story. Inside a labour ward you could be anywhere in the world. I seem to have lost my nerve as a writer. I feel guilty and nervous all the time. I can only transcribe small scenes involving people—can't comment, generalise, editorialise. But I *will do* it.

————

My elegant friend and I broached the new Armani shop. It's a shrine to glorious, simple, unspeakably expensive beauty. The staff, young and good-looking and chic in plain black Armani suits, are still breathless with their good fortune at working there. While we were swooning over a garment they would tiptoe up behind us, lean in over our shoulders and sigh deeply right along with us. My friend and I stumbled away to a coffee shop and sat there trembling and awe-struck. 'What would *you* buy,' I said in a small voice, 'if you were really rich?' 'That men's coat,' she said, 'the long cashmere one.' 'Their men's clothes,' I said, 'are better than their women's, aren't they.' 'Yes. Softer, and more flowing. And less sort of *dressy*.'

————

The Cretan's father has died. He is thin-faced, darkened. He showed us old photos of his parents in their youth. The wonderful formality of the black-and-white portraits: the composed, unsmiling faces, their serious gaze.

————

Maybe my right place to work is down a fissure between fiction and whatever the other thing is. Down a crack.

A very small girl watches the Melbourne Cup on TV. 'Those people have all gone mad. I think I'll leave the room.'

Listening on my Discman to Glenn Gould playing a Mozart sonata—tearing up magazines and pasting things on to postcards— sun and wind outside—ideas and fantasies start to seed and swarm, no focus, no desire to write anything down, just the pleasure of remembering that this process exists.

A *New Yorker* cartoon: two snakes lying on the ground in a rural landscape. One says cheerfully to the other, 'I thought I saw you by the lake this morning, but it was a stick.' No one I've shown it to finds it particularly funny, but I go weak with laughter every time I think of it. I'm especially enfeebled by the fact that it doesn't say '*just* a stick'.

Down on the south coast E and I walk through bush to visit an old couple she knows. The husband, once a sweet-natured and clever historian, is now huge, slumped, dull-eyed with Alzheimer's. Saliva runs out of his mouth whenever he opens it: he has to wear a bib. The wife, thin and small and bright, is now his prisoner: she can never leave him on his own. If she stays out of the room too long he comes looking for her, follows her everywhere. He sits without speaking for most of our visit. She chatters valiantly and we try to do the same. When she mentions one of his respite carers, a young woman, he sparks up and speaks of her with a heavy sexual jocularity. When we leave, the wife comes with us as far as the gate. E whispers, 'It must be hard.' She looks at us in bursting silence, starts to speak, cuts herself off before she gets to the horror of it. Hugs us both very hard. We walk away, unable to look at each other.

———

I think I am in the classic position of a woman artist who in order to maintain a marriage is obliged to trim herself so as not to make her husband feel—what? Something a man is not supposed to have to feel? This must be one of the reasons V is so against it when I have to do publicity. It's also perhaps why he is encouraging to me about doing journalism. He is as generous as he can possibly be about my book and its success, but if I had success like that with a novel there'd be serious trouble—I don't know what trouble exactly, but life would get tougher. Why are men so fragile? If he were getting more attention than I was, everyone would be at ease, it would be seen as normal and appropriate. Tilt it, and everything gets unhappy and shadowy. Maybe it's true then. A woman artist who wants to develop as far as she can needs to live alone. He is a better *novelist* than I am—he can handle broader ideas, more characters etc—this is not the problem. The problem is that my success seems to get in his way. It somehow stops him from working.

What to do? I could accept without further complaint his demand for uninterrupted occupation of the flat. Work harder at cooking. Do less publicity. Pull my horns in. How *dismal*.

———

E talked to me at length about how her father's second wife had never accepted his daughters—E and her two sisters. Not long before he died he told E that his greatest regret was that he hadn't made her acceptance of his children a condition of their marriage. E said that the new spouse is the only one who can make the necessary gesture. I told her how sad I am that V is so mean about M. She said she would talk to him about it. I wonder if she will. And if it would have any effect.

———

I am planning to take the whole of January off. Bludging. Going swimming. Maybe teaching myself to sew. I'll be out of the flat as always but I won't go to work. Boy Charlton Pool, laps, Bondi, surf. And if I want to have M to stay, I will. Imagine marrying a woman with a child and not letting her have the child to stay. What have I been thinking of, to let this be the state of affairs?

1996

Night after night I wake up at two or three and fight through a fit of anxiety about republishing in *True Stories* the piece about the high-school lesson I was sacked for. I tried to cut out a couple of sentences, in the edit, but without them of course the whole thing collapsed; and I felt dishonest and cowardly. Who am I scared of? Dad, the old tiger whose teeth have been removed. V, who still lives in blissful ignorance of that period of my life.

———

Bought myself a sewing machine at Grace Bros, a demo model which, the Brother consultant earnestly assures me, 'only Vicki and I have ever sewn on'. Vicki (big hair, raking red false nails, missing side tooth, gold-rimmed specs) tells me the shop runs classes. 'You learn to make a skirt with a zip, and a shirt with a collar.' I lug it home, dizzy with ambition.

———

A letter from Queensland about the funeral of her old friend, a life-long rider. The woman's horse was led, saddled and riderless. The guard of honour: 'twelve patient men in their oilskins, mounted, waiting in the light rain'.

———

The play was 'splendidly written', in that Irish style that half of me wants to relax and swoon into, while some drier, more English aspect of me draws back in scepticism: Look out, you are being *seduced.*

———

Letter about my book from a stranger, a woman in her forties: 'My inability at times to protect myself, to establish my boundaries, to stand guardian at the gate of my own core, has possibly been the source of most of the pain I have experienced as a woman.'

———

A big wind in the night blew a tall vase of roses off the window-sill and spilt its water into the couch. I woke at 2 am to the sound of V cursing in the living room. I staggered out. He declared in a disgusted, angry voice, 'The wind's blown it off into the *couch*. There's water *everywhere.*' Stunned with sleep I heard his tone as blame. He had picked up one of the wet cushions, but as soon as I arrived he dropped it and went back to bed. I set about dismantling the couch, pulling the covers off the sodden cushions, up-ending a wooden chair and hooking the soaked part of the kilim over it, thinking all the while, 'How on earth can this be *my* fault?'

In the morning, when I described to him this nocturnal labour and my feelings about it, he was amazed: 'But why on earth would I think it was anybody's *fault?*' Why else would he just walk off and leave me to clean it up?

———

My sister and I drive up to Primrose Gully together. It's hers now. She and her husband have launched the big job of dragging it back from neglect. He has begun, skilfully, to line the cabin with pine boards, and I see their camping history in many unobtrusive ingenuities: a wine cork replacing the knob on the kettle lid; a tin cupboard to keep out the rats; clever ways not to waste water. 'Doesn't the fridge work any more?' 'Its insides,' she says without apparent reproach, 'were chewed out by rats.' I'm ashamed. They've got a sort of logbook in which visitors have written accounts of their stays and the work they've done on the buildings and the land, their responses to the beauty of the place. My heart aches. With jealousy, and terrible sadness for everything I've lost. *Given up*.

After lunch we lay down for a nap. While I was falling asleep I remembered the essay I wrote about the place, 'Three Acres More or Less'. And when I woke up I thought, 'I may have sold it, but it's still mine. Even if I never come here again, I own it, in my heart, and I always will. Because I've *made* it in art.' I've never had this sensation before, of *possessing* something because I had made it, or remade it, in words.

———

Dad writes to tell me that all Melbourne phone numbers now start with a 9.

———

Last night I took delivery of some nice big shelves for 'my' room (i.e. the spare bedroom) in the flat. I don't have to work today and I'd like to be messing around at home arranging things on them; and cooking, and doing loads of washing and ironing. But in our cool, quiet flat with its couches and our reference library, V is battling to write his novel. He will not consent to close his workroom door. So once again I find myself wandering the streets, or back at Bondi Junction in my small, hot, noisy room, sitting at my desk, fiddling with unnecessary papers.

———

I've been reading the *Times Literary Supplement* and the *New Yorker*, with sinking heart as to my chances of ever writing any more fiction. My cupboard's bare. I have nothing to say or rather nothing to invent. It's frightening. My future looks blank. I don't know anything. My mind has no grip. I'm just floating.

Worrying about the photo of me on the front cover of *True Stories*. What if I lose anonymity? How will I be able to watch strangers discreetly?

Dinner at X the painter's place, down on Ithaca Road. A small, pleasant flat with bare timber floors, a round table prettily set for five. X's mother was working in the kitchen. When the guests went to greet her she kissed us on both cheeks and said, 'Welcome!' but she stayed in the kitchen, cooking, for the whole evening. She never came out at all. No one remarked on this; it was accepted. When the cheese and fruit had been served, she walked quickly across the entrance hall and into her bedroom, closing the door behind her. (I envied her.) X was a hardworking hostess, always on her feet, serving, checking our plates and glasses, while the other male guest bashed on and on about artists and critics. I was the only person present who didn't know any of the people they were talking about. I was toiling all evening to keep abreast of the conversation. When I flagged I got washed up on the bank, and had trouble not glazing over.

A young journalist came to my office to interview me about *True Stories*. He produced from his bag a much-folded letter, clumsily typed on two foolscap sheets, dated early 1973, from two members of a parents' and teachers' organisation (I could hardly bear to look at it), protesting against attempts by the teacher's union to have me reinstated at Fitzroy High. I ran my eye down its stumbling, distressed, outraged argument, its quotes with the rude words represented by dots, its accusations that teachers like me were foisted on to poor high schools and would never be accepted by, say, Ivanhoe Grammar. They accused me of 'emotional blackmail'. They said

I had broken the bond between parents and children. I sat there, silent, sick with horror, thinking, 'They were right to be enraged. It's a wonder I wasn't lynched. I *should* have been lynched.' The journalist, very worldly wise at thirty, remarked loftily as he folded the letter and put it away, 'Liberals act on good impulses, but they can do a lot of damage.'

I told my publisher about it. He was quiet for a moment, then said, 'Helen. So can conservatives.' There was no one else I could speak to about it.

A night of the horrors, while V slept peacefully beside me.

————

M called. In her calm way she said, 'AB and I have just had our ninth anniversary, and we thought that a good way to celebrate would be to get married.' I was excited, I poured out congratulations, we laughed happily together. I wanted to share this joy. Late in the afternoon I went to the door of V's workroom and quietly told him. He sat there at his desk. I stood at the door. He glanced up at me. His face was blank. A silence. I said, 'Won't you say anything at all?' He burst out: 'You think men are *negative*. They're *not* negative. They're *sceptical*. They're sceptical and they weigh things up. And *that's* why they rule the world.'

————

'Where other people are inscribed with the desire for parenthood,' said a man who is fond of both of us, 'V has a blank.'

————

V said he thought AB had 'a sort of macho attitude towards older men'. 'Macho? AB? What on earth do you mean?' He said, 'I can see what he might be like when he's older, and without the ponytail.' In the Fish Cafe I tried to describe to him AB's character and his talents, what's stable and kind and clever and endearing and hard-working about him; and to explain why it meant a lot to me that they would marry. He replied, 'You've always said they were like an old married couple already, so—if M's happy, I'm glad.'

———

I try to behave with some sort of grace. I try to be pleasant and generous. But I actually feel I'd like to give up this draining attempt to be married, to go and live somewhere high and sunny, on my own. With the windows open. Yesterday my fantasy was to ask him if we could each write down a list of good and bad things about being married to each other, and try to talk about them and work them out. But I haven't mentioned this idea because I know what his response would be—one of his incredulous laughs: 'Why the hell would we bloody well do *that*.'

———

My sister called. When her daughter had heard about M and AB getting married, she said, 'she screamed for thirty seconds'.

———

At Boy Charlton I asked the pool guy if the public phone took coins or a card. He glanced to left and right, dropped his voice, and said, 'It's the secret of the pool: it works whether you put money in or not. Now you know.'

———

V and I watched Melvyn Bragg's interview with Martin Amis. A gripping conversation but there's a grinding quality to Amis's scepticism, or do I mean pessimism, or determination to entertain not a single illusion—or do I mean cynicism? When he said 'If you don't think you're the best, you're not really doing it', I wanted to dong him with a bat. Later, though, we saw a Marcel Ophüls doco in which Jimmy Cagney tap-danced on a 'wharf' as a 'ship' slid out to 'sea' behind him. He threw himself into the dance, in his tight-fitting little suit and hat, and we were spellbound by his speed, the contrast between his chunky manliness and the lightness with which he could spring, fly, turn—it was anti-gravity, the labour of it transcended, invisible.

———

A close friend of M's I'm fond of, the opera singer, asks if she can stay one night (out all day) in early March. Such a simple request plumbs the depths of us. Horrible bitter arguing. Spoke of parting. Slept. This morning we were careful with each other and made light jokes about whether we still loved each other.

———

Dreamt I was looking for a house to rent. I was taken to see one in a grassy, leafy suburb. I had to sneak in through an overgrown garden. I glanced into a dark room off a corridor, saw an eye: it was a horse, patient and powerful, standing quietly in the darkness.

———

Sewing class. The anxiety of using the teacher's big shears. When I thought I'd cut my skirt too short, the cheeky girl at the machine next to mine said, 'Line-dancing, Helen. Boot-scootin'.' All I really want to do is listen to Linda Ronstadt's *Boleros y Rancheras* and sing and dance and flip my hips.

———

Checkout girl at Edgecliff Farmers' Market asks for my autograph: 'My ambition is to become a writer. One day perhaps *you'll* be reading *me*.' 'What's your name?' 'Molly Hutchinson.'

———

Dreamt that at a retro '70s event in Carlton I ran into a woman I used to share a house with back then, when we were single mothers. We shrugged at the retro show. 'Not like the real thing, is it,' she said, and walked away. A younger woman sat down beside me and said with an intense, challenging curiosity, '*What's* not the same? What's different?' I sighed, weary at the thought of having to talk about it, and said, 'The households. The households are gone.'

I get home from work late afternoon, loaded with food for tonight's dinner, and find a note from V. He's down in the park having a coffee with X the painter, do I want to come down? I conquer a surge of female martyrdom—How hard I work! How much money I spend! How little thanks I get! I get a grip, put on a record and set about cooking the meal. By the time he comes in I'm cheerful. He reminds me of a short trip we've been planning to the Flinders Ranges. His tone is so reluctant that I say, to let him off the hook, 'You don't feel like going, any more?' 'Aw, it'll be all right, I s'pose.' Does it come from his family, this tendency to take all the joy out of something in advance? Or is he just being 'level'? Is it the weary struggle of writing his novel? Or is it me? Am I a bore? Am I distracted? What am I doing wrong?

'We are prepared to misuse…anyone, in order to rescue ourselves from some dreadful mood that is tormenting us, some mood we have gotten into without knowing how.' —Thomas Bernhard, *Extinction*

The bookmark in his copy of *True Stories* is still right up near the front. It hasn't advanced in a week. He hasn't said anything about it. It hardly hurts at all, now. In fact whenever I pass the book with its stationary marker I feel like laughing.

W invited me to bring M and AB up to Pittwater. They took a shine to her and loved everything about the place: the wharf, the tinny, the steep bush track, the little timber house open to the elements. We ate, we slept, we drank and played games for hours, Categories and Dictionary—fooling around, singing, not needing to tiptoe or tone it down or account for ourselves. When we were back in town

W sent me a fax: 'M has that lovely stillness and openness that comes of being well-loved.' V did his best to be hostly, he really did, until they went home.

———

A formal letter from AB's parents: 'Your beautiful daughter will be welcomed as a precious addition to our family.'

———

I took Mum and Dad a copy of *True Stories*. 'Errr,' they said, looking at it with peculiar gingerly expressions. Dad said that the cover photo made me look old, and 'didn't do much' for me at all. Then, while explaining to me how to sharpen a knife against a stone, he demonstrated with his blade across the smooth surface of my book's cover, this chancing to be the flat object closest at hand. My niece and I shrieked about this later, but once more I'm winded by their ignorance of social forms—I mean, doesn't one learn from life to say 'Congratulations'? Whatever one might feel about the quality or significance of the achievement in question? Less and less do I understand them. They become more mysterious to me, with every passing year.

———

Daylight saving ended last night. Fresh bright earliness. Tiny breezes move through gumtrees and in at our bedroom window. We walk across Rushcutters Park and up into Darling Point. The water glossy silver, boats quite still in breathless air, clouds pinkish-grey. Liquid magpies, currawongs scooping and wolf-whistling.

———

X the painter called and complimented me warmly on *The First Stone*.

———

'One likes to hear what is going on, to be *au fait* as to the newest modes of being trifling and silly.' —Jane Austen, *Persuasion*

This is why I love *Who Weekly*. I can rip through it on the train between Kings Cross and Bondi Junction.

———

Stayed a night with Mum and Dad. My widowed sister gave an afternoon tea to celebrate the coming wedding. Both families were there. It was a very happy day. After most people had left I heard two men singing together in the kitchen: it was AB and my brother-in-law, starting to clean up the mess. And when I went to bed I found a letter on my pillow: 'Dear Helen, just a note to say I am so proud of and so lucky to have such a wonderful bunch of kids. I really enjoyed today just watching you all. Sleep well. Love Mum.'

———

A taxi driver told me he had been laid up vomiting for three weeks with peptic and duodenal ulcers. He was so determined not to acknowledge his condition that when he was throwing up pieces of his stomach lining he convinced himself they were cherries.

———

Lately V is telling me and others that he feels he's going to die soon. When I question him he goes vague: he's not ill, and he's not *afraid* of dying—he just has a certainty that he *will* die in a not too distant future. I could say, but don't, that I too have often wished to die when something I'm writing is going badly. He has spoken about this feeling to various people (all women, I think). Each of them expressed the kind of interest that made him wish he hadn't mentioned it. One of them, he told me, diagnosed anxiety about his novel, and called him again the next day with urgent advice: he must bring the novel to an end *within a week*. We laughed so much that things between us became harmonious.

———

I set up my machine after tea and sewed for hours. I've got the hang of it now. It's so calming and absorbing.

———

Wakeful these humid nights, I hear birds singing down in the park. I read about a soldier from Queensland who at the front in World War I heard the first nightingale of his life 'singing in the apple tree just above our tents'.

———

A journalist told me that several weeks after she married her husband she started having asthma attacks. When she parted from him, they stopped.

———

Walking in Paris with M, how easy it is—I drift along, invisible, but attached to her little bubble of beauty. This is the state I've been longing to be in—no anxiety, no obligations, just tired and free and calm and vaguely curious.

———

At 4 am I tried to call V, and got a long silence broken only by a sound like breathing.

———

My dear ex-junkie ex doesn't look well. He's terribly thin, the back of his pelvis bonily visible even through jeans and two layers of shirt. He shivers, feels ill in the morning after five of us have shared a bottle of champagne. His lover, a man of imperturbable calm, asks me when we're alone, 'How do you think he looks?' I try to be frank: 'He's a lot thinner. And there's a shadow in his face.' I am starting to admit to myself that he's going to get full-on Aids, he's going to die. When he feels sick he just keeps working on his movie. In their flat I glance up from the sofa where I'm half dozing and see him watching me through the glass door of his office. Our eyes meet and he smiles at me, tenderly.

———

French schoolchildren on a train. Sure sign of a high position in a pecking order is the ability not to acknowledge that someone is repeatedly calling your name.

———

The sharp stab of saying goodbye when M left for Cannes. And walking away from the Metro, suddenly not having anything to do, any tasks or routines with which to blunt the pain.

———

Vienna. A beggar in the cathedral porch: as soon as he's set himself up he starts to shiver, and when I come out an hour later he is still shivering vigorously. A short black here is called *ein kleiner Brauner.* A banknote has a picture of Sigmund Freud on it. The toilet seat in the Cafe Anna is decorated with a silver pattern of barbed wire. A box of pansies in the street, their special Austrian way of nodding. A woman limps up the step into the streetcar carrying a basket of trembling white lilac; its perfume fills the vehicle.

———

All this jabber I carry on with lately, about how I'm heading for non-fiction, leaving fiction behind, never been any good anyway at 'making things up'—suddenly it strikes me that what I'm doing is vacating the field.

———

For my menopausal symptoms I see a Chinese Western doctor cum herbalist. She sells me three paper bags a week of weird, chunky, dried-out bits of bark and tree. I boil them for an hour until a cup of dark, licorice-flavoured fluid can be poured off, which I drink. I haven't noticed any improvements in the first week but she looked at my tongue this morning and said it had a *much* better amount of FUR on it than it did a week ago. Apparently last week it wasn't furry enough. I hope she knows what she's doing.

———

After the festival screening of his second movie, the young film director whose first film I had reviewed approaches me in the lobby.

H: 'Congratulations!'

YFD: 'Could we perhaps arrange to have dinner some time, so that we can resolve our differences?'

H: 'Our differences?'

YFD: 'Helen, you don't understand. I was *devastated* by your comments.'

H: 'What? But I thought I was so diplomatic!'

His girlfriend: (seizing his arm, laughing) 'He was prostrated. For three weeks.'

H: (speechless)

YFD: 'You see I'd just come out of film school—'

Woman Film Producer: (butting in) 'Where no one had ever criticised you. You should be grateful. Because now that you're successful, no one will ever tell you the truth again.'

———

I got home from work an hour earlier than I'd said I would. The flat was empty and dark. This is unheard of. I searched the rooms for a stark corpse. Messed about cheerfully on my own. Eventually he came in. He'd gone to meet the art critic and X the painter at the Vinyl Lounge, but the critic hadn't turned up.

———

I miss my nun. I miss her no-bullshit, sunny nature. Her loud laughter, the way she called everyone 'babe'. And I wish my sister would come up so we could put on accents and mimic people cruelly.

———

V still dying. He says he has 'persistent difficulty in swallowing'. I force him to see a doctor, and he does so on his way to Perpetual Trustees to make a proper will, for we are about to fly to Adelaide for his mother's eightieth birthday and a side-trip to the Flinders Ranges, thus incurring the risk of two flights and some country driving. He makes a list of 'gifts' to various people and insists against my protests that I do the same. We are to leave them on the dining table, just in case.

———

We walked right across Wilpena Pound and back. Plenty of kangaroos, but what really entranced us were the marvellous birds. Galahs, their raspberry pink and silver grey. Brilliant green parrots with long tail feathers that turned blue at the tips, and little yellow ruffs. Eagles got away too fast for the dainty binoculars that I'd bought at Vienna airport. Crows with smooth, in-curved backs and wings that gleamed with a sinister, brilliantined blackness. On the drive down to Hawker the ranges were always on our left, pinkish tilting rock masses, a cloudy sky.

———

Opened the door of the silent flat and saw the two 'wills' lying neatly side by side on the clean wooden table.

———

In a magazine's personal columns, this humble seeker: 'Hoping to find a lovely man who wants an ordinary woman, 45, single, no children, non-smoker, on carer's pension, enjoys conversation, food, arts, when you have some spare time.'

———

An old journo friend in Spain: 'Sorry I missed you,' he writes, 'when I rang from the airport. It was good to chat to V. He always sounds so *calm*! And he asks you interesting questions—like a good journalist. You only realise later that he's interviewed you.'

———

The First Stone has won what I suppose is a sort of consolation prize—for 'the book that Australian booksellers most enjoyed selling' this past year. Very touched by this comradely gesture. Jeffrey Archer (who has a limp handshake) presented me with a fax machine wrapped in brown paper and a cheque for $1000. I made a thirty-second speech. Trying to present a small target.

———

Right on cue comes a letter from a woman whose name I remember from an insulting one she sent me last year, in which she declared she would not buy a copy of *The First Stone* so as not to swell my coffers. Now she's read *True Stories*. 'I remain amazed at your arrogance and smugness. The moral victory is the students'. Your self-interest rode rough-shod over them, and by association, rough-shod over all sexual harassment survivors.' Everything around me goes quiet and dark. A physical sensation of losing heart.

———

I wish I could 'become a poet'. Fat chance. But I fantasise escaping plain narrative into some wonderful freedom of LYRICAL UTTERANCE.

———

Bach's fugues with the headphones on, up loud—their form and the way he plays with it excite me so much I just about burst.

———

We spent the weekend in the country with G and M-C and their little girl. They squabbled in the car and at the table, we had to look into our plates. V adores G and won't hear a word against him; in our room he seethed against M-C. On TV they ran some footage from the late 70s of G on stage in his famous band, beaming and prancing with his guitar, thick blond curls flopping; then a head-shot of him as he is today—lined, almost crew-cut, against a black ground, speaking intelligently and in syntactically sophisticated sentences about how hard it is in Australia to find an *adult* way of performing popular music. M-C and I loved his 70s look and razzed him about it, but V couldn't even grasp that it *was* G: 'Why the hell is that bloke jigging around?'

R says she's going into full-on analysis in October. She asked if I'd ever considered looking into it: 'When we were first friends I used to feel very angry with your mother—you were so hypersensitive to the small pains and slights of life, it was as if no one had ever given you enough love.' I said I had considered it but I was scared. She said she was scared too, but had 'an almost sinister urge to understand everything'; that she wanted 'to be relieved of unconscious dread', to be 'free to feel'. We talked about our mothers. I asked her if my mother's repetitions of the same phrases, over and over in the same tone of voice, was something she remembered from the early stages of her mother's Alzheimer's. She said that the onset, in her mother's case, had seemed to be a slow intensification of what she'd always been like: 'You work so hard to keep reality at bay that after a long time reality ceases to exist, and you sort of *die*.'

V and I merrily washed our bedroom windows. Made them shine.

Rain falling steadily. Birds call at dawn. Does the rain bounce or slide off their feathers? Do they try to shelter, or don't they care?

I ask my sister if she is having to deal with much about Mum, in therapy. 'Lots,' she says. 'Mum's what it's *about*.' My insides go faint with dread. 'It's necessary,' she says, 'to get Dad out of the way first. And then behind him there's this...*void*.'

In the middle of the night, at my widowed sister's house, I woke to the sound of strong wind and rain. I stood peeping through the slit of the bathroom window into a narrow strip of garden. It came over me that there was nothing out there, there was nothing inside, that everywhere was nothing, and I was in the nothing, the past and future were nothing, and all there was to do was to keep on dully living forward into more nothing. It was horrible. I was frightened. I crawled back into bed and fell asleep. In the morning I wondered if I had absorbed that desolation from my sister, from her suffering, from the air of her house.

———

At the World Symposium of Choral Music, when the huge choir sang the final chord of Berlioz' *Requiem*, the young man sitting beside me very softly hit the bass note, deep in his chest, and held it right to the end.

V and I liked best the Hungarians, whose conductor displayed a body language so extravagant, expressive and hilarious that we kept having to muffle laughter—capering, standing rigid with military arms, then rising on tiptoes and bounding and swaying—and his choir responded exuberantly, the women's faces lit up as they sang, their heads moved suavely, their eyes shone—all the young singers full of a springy joie de vivre. The audience went wild. Next morning we woke in good spirits. V didn't seem to be dying. He remarked at breakfast that one major aspect of choirs was that the women loved being *managed* and *directed* by the conductor. 'What about the men?' 'Oh, no,' he said, buttering his toast, 'not the men.'

———

R gave me the name and number of a therapist she recommended: 'a strong, warm, complicated Jewish woman' of our age whom she liked and respected. I called her. Her voice on the phone was very calm and attractive. I can start next Monday. $70. So sudden, I was dizzy.

———

A woman with a racked, pointed little face tells me that her husband has fallen in love with one of his students and 'it's been hell all year'. They're talking about selling their house, trying not to wreck things for the kids. Apparently he doesn't want to leave, though: 'He says he's stopped seeing her, but he weeps and wails and says he can't bear it.' 'Kick him out,' I said. 'You can't live with that.' The man wreaks havoc but lacks the guts to give the coup de grâce, so *she* has to do it.

———

I bought a diaphanous black skirt at a sale.

———

Coldest Sydney day since the 60s: max ten degrees. I got to the therapist's early and shivered on the veranda till she came out. A slim, serious, dark-haired woman with shadows under her eyes, dressed in black wool pants and sweater; something metal round her neck. We faced each other in cane chairs padded with cushions. She sat very still with her hands clasped, while I writhed and fidgeted and gabbled. She said that what happened 'in this room' would be as important as the things I would tell her about my life 'outside'. In the corner of my eye was a sort of day bed with a folded rug at its foot. *The couch.* I want to lie on it. I want that rug over me. I want to break eye contact so I can stop jabbering and let silences fall. What if I go to sleep? Would she let me use up my hour by sleeping?

———

I didn't tell V where I'd been. I don't want to have to work my way past his hostility, disapproval, wary ironic curiosity and horror that it costs $70 an hour.

———

The floor between the clothing racks in David Jones seemed very pale and glossy, and there was a lot of it. Hanging clothes too were pale, almost airy. And the idea that had been trying to get my attention since I walked to the station this morning crawled out of its sheath, fluffed up its wings and stood there fresh and fully formed. Could I write about my sister the widow? About death, in its full radiations and explosions?

———

V read late and slept late so I went walking by myself, further into Darling Point. The windows of an old cream waterfront apartment building were open and I thought how it would be, living close to water—to wind and light. A fresh stillness in the harbour air as I strode along.

———

'He began to believe that people could, in fact, be used up—could use each other up, could be of no further help to each other and maybe even do harm to each other. He began to think that who you are when you're with somebody may matter more than whether you love her.' —Anne Tyler, *The Accidental Tourist*

———

As I walked down the hill to her house my mind began to rev and race. For everything I thought of to say to her it produced an instant 'interpretation', as if some defensive part of me were leaping and springing ahead of the rest, ahead of *her*. 'This.' 'Ah, *this* means *that*'—leaving me nowhere to move that was pure, or clean, or uncontaminated by dry, grinding *brain*.

———

Noticed today for the first time, very happily, that above her couch hangs a framed picture of Ganesh, Remover of Obstacles. She said that I'm in competition with her, interpreting my own dreams. My sister says, 'Don't try to write down the session afterwards. Trust it while it's happening, and let it be.'

———

'He was a good dancer, Robert,' says the journalist, when I tell her that Robert Haupt has died. 'He could waltz. There's not many men you can say that about.' V wasn't sure about going to the funeral; he would lose a morning's work. I talked him into it.

The establishment of journalism had turned out for Haupt.

People cried, you could hear them, and the blowing of noses. I cried too, but tried to keep a lid on it because of V, who after all was his friend, whereas I'd only met him twice, and was more of an admirer really. On our way out of the church, when V introduced himself to the two daughters, their poor little tear-swollen faces broke into smiles, and one of them said, 'Oh, we've often heard *your* name!' And he kissed them.

————

I took one of the ancient, wealthy bohemian ladies who adore V to see a show at the Powerhouse. In the crowd she became impatient, bristly, even rude. But at the cafe table we talked for an hour and I liked her. She's as sharp as a tack, a dry observer. She asked me whether V was 'hard to live with'; she said she had never known (or liked so much) a person whose habit was to denigrate himself and others so thoroughly and so often: 'He lives with the lights turned down low. He's an introvert.' When we got up to leave and I was helping her to put on her top layer (a shirt over another shirt), I said, 'It's quite hard, isn't it, putting a shirt on someone else.' 'Oh!' she said, with a sly smile, 'I thought that with V you'd be pretty good at it.'

————

V puzzles over the differences between us. 'I'm like an ocean liner,' he says, 'levelly forging along. And you're a smaller boat that swerves and flitters here and there—a bright little thing.' He tells me he's noticed that my nature is 'split', and that he's been making a list of some of the splits he's observed in me.

    H: 'Like what, for example?'

    V: 'For example, you like both high culture and popular culture.'

    Pause.

    H: 'That's—a split?'

————

Walking through Darling Point early this morning, he told me that I had been too 'emphatic', much too forceful and sure of myself, while he was debunking the high position that Robert Hughes on his TV show had accorded to Edward Hopper: 'Hopper,' said V, 'was too much of an illustrator to be a great painter.' Also, he said, he was not happy that, although he had spent years looking at pictures, I had challenged his memory of the usherette's posture in a particular Hopper painting, as well as what he'd said the painting was about—'female wistfulness'. My disagreement about 'wistfulness' he had experienced as 'correction'.

I don't get this. Is it my tone?

———

When my office lease at Bondi Junction runs out I will look for a little studio to rent, maybe in Elizabeth Bay, with bathroom and kitchen and a bed where friends can stay. Because otherwise I'll wither away with loneliness and disconnection from my roots.

———

After lunch I took a bus to Bondi and spent an hour and a half in the Icebergs pool. The air temperature hit thirty but the water was very cold. Beach wonderfully beautiful: dark green water, a warm dry wind flattening the waves.

———

A grapefruit tree hangs over a lane we walk along each morning. We pick up the fallen fruit, so much now that we have to bring a bag. The flesh is thin, pale and pippy, but when I squeeze them at home the juice fairly spouts out, thick, dark yellow, both sweet and sour, its consistency almost viscous.

———

I tried to talk to V about loneliness. He said that if I was lonely it was probably a side-effect of my 'thing on Mondays'—that nothing, compared with that, could possibly match up, for attentiveness to me and my feelings. He launched a criticism of the whole idea of psychotherapy and of my doing it. He said I was 'too smart', that I would 'run rings around any of them', that perhaps it was useful to 'damaged people', but that I was already 'working and unravelling', that I didn't need anyone to do it for me or to accelerate it, anyway how did I know what *she* was bringing to it, did I know anything about her and *her* father? Maybe she was 'giving it a nudge' here and there, nudging it away from my mother and back towards my father because *she* had father problems. I trudged along while he poured out this stream. I made a couple of stabs at defending my decision to do it. I started to say, 'Couldn't you say something different? Couldn't you say, "Look, Hel, I don't know why you're doing this and it gives me the horrors, but I can see it means a lot to you, and you must have thought about it before you made up your mind to go ahead—so good luck with it, and I hope you get out of it what you want to find"?' but I don't know, somehow I got derailed and couldn't make my point. I used the word 'reproach' and he said, 'It's *not* a reproach. Every criticism's not a reproach. Maybe you could ask her why you always do *that*.' Then we came round the corner and saw the fresh fall of grapefruit and the subject was changed. Walking home he added, 'These objections aren't original, you know.' He produced the names of Musil and Canetti who had criticised Hermann Broch for going into analysis: 'They thought it might affect his work.' He told me that I was 'an artist' and that my 'family unravelling' was part of the basis of my work.

———

Talking to me on the phone, my sister looks out her window and says she can see 'a whimsical sky'.

———

R and I sat at her backyard table and, well, *bitched*. But bitching with R is really something else, something drier and classier and more analytical. She doesn't revel in it, or wallow or find unpleasant gratification in it. She is tough, dry, harsh, accurate, and funny, but not for the sake of amusing herself or me—rather, she's funny because she's so serious, and so acutely aware of the absurd. She's been reading Bion, and speaks in terms of things 'leading to death, or to life'.

———

I note that I have transferred this diary to my office. I brought it here one day for a purpose I've forgotten, and gradually I've let it establish itself here. I didn't mean to. It just sort of stayed. As if the centre of my private thoughts belonged here, now, instead of at the apartment.

———

At 8.30 this morning, on my way to work at Bondi Junction, I stopped for a coffee at the little cafe further up our street, where I never usually go. I was sitting on the bench outside when two people walked up the street: V and X the painter. They didn't see me and passed barely inches away, deep in conversation. They walked around the corner, as if heading for the leafy bus stop on Onslow Road, and disappeared. Several minutes later a bus surged out, and V re-emerged and headed back down the hill. He saw me on the bench and stopped short: 'I didn't see you there!' He said he'd been giving X an article about Bernhard's translator, which she was going to photocopy for him. I thought, 'But you never see anyone or do anything or even speak on the phone before lunch—isn't that why I have to go out to work?' Unworthy speculations filled my mind. Would I care if he was 'seeing' her? I would, I realise—going by the trembly feeling I got at the moment when he passed me, almost brushing against me, without seeing me.

———

I don't think I ever really said goodbye to my piano teacher in

Melbourne. I remember walking down the side of her house and across the garden to her teaching room. How it felt to knock at the door and be let in. And one day I played some piece I'd been slaving over, and she seemed to have an emotional response to it. Vicki was her name.

———

V's fifty-fifth birthday. I gave him a beautiful leather skipping rope with wooden handles. So he can be like G, and skip like a boxer.

———

V has been stewing over a remark the minister made at Robert Haupt's funeral: 'We should be glad that his tribulations are over.' V said it was a ludicrous misrepresentation of Haupt's whole approach to life. I agreed that it was a misrepresentation, but suggested it was an attitude integral to a Christian's beliefs, which in his own church a minister has a right and perhaps even a duty to express. A fierce argument broke out. I retreated to the closed-in balcony where we eat (which V has from the day we moved in referred to, for some reason, as 'the sewing room'), and sat at the table to sew a button back on my nightie. It's nice in there, the cheesecloth curtains that I made puff and drop on a breeze. V walked through the room. Seeing me stitching away there he said in a soft voice, 'Good room for sewing, isn't it.' I realised that to see me sewing, by hand or with the machine, releases in him a flow of feeling. While being touched by this I also secretly resolve to make use of it, if and when things get rough. I mean that I could sit down with a needle and thread, and bring about a lessening of tension.

———

My sister says that sometimes when she's leaving her analyst's house she feels 'tiny—so small I don't know if I'm big enough to drive the car'.

———

I bought a new pen.

———

He says he's sick of the way I 'nitpick' in arguments, e.g. when I pointed out and found fault with (I thought 'analysed') his use of the word *audience* in his criticism of the minister at Haupt's funeral. I try to explain that I picked up on this word because it revealed how he conceived of the minister's role, which was what I thought we were talking about. Unresolved. We go to bed and fall asleep.

When we wake it's a warm spring morning, bright and dry: sun on trunks and leaves outside our window. I say, 'Let's try to make a fresh start.' I'm not sure how he receives this proposal, but things go cheerfully enough at breakfast time.

———

Reading, on V's recommendation, Michel Tournier's *The Erl-King*: bursting with ideas of the sort that men adore and that I find diverting if rather head-trippy—but what does bowl me over is the freshness and crispness and accuracy of his physical world. The way he can show in a couple of brief strokes the posture of a child dragging something, the relation between the size of a skull and the angle of the eyes set in it, the sound of an animal brushing against a closed door.

———

To Singapore, to give a 'distinguished author lecture'. Its tiny audience was composed mostly of academics; my speech must have sounded very naïve and theoretically threadbare. But the second gig was a different story: me, a young Singaporean writer/architect, a tough old novelist/journalist from Manila, and a hilarious, loose-cannon Sikh, who was the most relaxed and skilful moderator I've ever seen at work. It was fun. Everyone was thoughtful but there was plenty of laughter. We wound up drinking and cracking jokes in a karaoke bar. I was sad to say goodbye. Towards midnight I crossed the lobby of my hotel and heard Sam Cooke singing 'Twistin' the Night Away'. I followed the song to the bar and found five or six Chinese couples dancing—expressionless, but graceful and energetic, very young and quick and light on their feet.

———

In my absence poor V has pulled a muscle in his back, after endless hours of typing. I tried to massage it and only made it worse. But while I'm trying he becomes sweeter and more open—his skin is soft, his cheeks kissable. I like looking after him and he so rarely responds to it—quite a luxury, really.

———

His novel is picking up speed. He actually tells me things about how it's going, instead of just groaning and skulking and tearing out his hair. I have resolved to make more of an effort, to be kinder and more generous. It works, and we are both happier. I cooked a splendid roast chicken for our dinner, and received several compliments, not just the usual blank, dutiful 'Very nice'.

———

A professional clash with E. We sulk in our different parts of the city, and write each other stiff, defensive letters. I force myself to call her on the phone. The surprise in her voice and its familiar timbre bring up in me a rush of affection. We negotiate our way out of it, point by point. 'I always find it rather a shock,' she says, 'being angry. Admit it, and it seems to go away.'

———

The China scholar's flatmate downstairs has invited me to have a game of Scrabble with them on Sunday afternoon. He's going to buy a new set and we're going to christen it with champagne.

———

A sense of dread all morning, faint and flickering but always present. When I try to locate it I realise it's *her*. My session with her this arvo.

I lie on my back, writhing and sighing. Long silences fall. Behind me I feel her quiet presence. Sometimes she'll say something. Occasionally her remarks are so obvious I feel impatient and irritable. Others surprise and relieve me. She seems to think I can't tolerate remaining in a state of *not knowing*. There's a lot of truth in that, but I don't even know what the topic is. *Is* there a 'topic'? And for this I pay $70 a week.

———

'Don't sit around and wait till you have the story; just start telling the story.' —Henry Louis Gates, *Inventing the Truth*

———

I make a list, for her. 'Afraid what I tell you will leak away and be forgotten. Afraid to trust you. Afraid of swamping you, that you'll fade out and disappear. Afraid you'll be too weak. Afraid I'll be too strong.' She pointed out my 'foetal position' when I lay down, and the way I had rolled up my scarf as I spoke, turned it into a small pad or bundle, 'like a comforter, or a bottle', and held it up against my face (I was smelling it). Something about 'all the times you've had to go to sleep alone, or comfort yourself'. She seemed warmer, kinder, more open and expressive.

———

In Melbourne, cramming visit after visit into ten days, I miss V and think hopefully of our new plan to go to Vienna together next year, when his book is finished.

———

AB's band on the river at Southbank last night. I hadn't drunk a drop but they were so funky and the crowd so tight-pressed and happy that I couldn't help moving with them. People around me shouted and sang and danced—all these open-faced, relaxed-looking boys in their early twenties. Times *have* changed, things have got better.

———

A technique: whenever someone does something that causes me pain, I instantly think, 'But *I've* done that to him/her/somebody else. I've got no right to object.' This acts as (1) a deflection of pain, (2) a spreading and evening out of bad deeds and unhappiness, (3) a sort of numbing or muffling, (4) a sense of control and simultaneously of *guilt*. I've often been aware that my mind was performing a tricky little side-step manoeuvre, but just now for some reason it unknotted itself.

———

Reading *Seven Nights*, lectures by Borges, who must be the most charming, seductive, modest speaker the world has ever known. Is this kind of modesty really a persona formed to deflect parasitic admiration? 'I am almost incapable of abstract thought—you will have noticed that I'm continually propping myself up with quotations and memories'—'almost' here must be carrying a heavy load. 'It is truly awful that there are mirrors'—for this I'll love him forever.

———

In the *Australian* a reviewer says my story 'What the Soul Wants' is 'soulless and contrived'. Ouch. She's probably right. On the same day comes a letter from a stranger, enclosing a money order for $12. He has bought a discounted copy of *True Stories* and declares that its introduction alone—'what a cracker!'—is 'worth a damn sight more' than what he paid for the book: '$7.95 for thirty stories. That's roughly 25 cents a story. From the end of the week, I'm out of a job. I have twenty bucks. $12 is for you and $8 is for me. I reckon that's fair. Now I'm going to crack a bottle of something and finish your book. Cheers.'

———

Since I got back from Melbourne I've had to stay in bed with a horrible cold, coughing up brownish-yellow stuff. V's gone to the gallery with X the painter. He mentioned with elaborate casualness that they'd had 'a few coffees' together while I was away. I realise that by getting sick I'm encroaching on his private daytime social life, which he so often and so strenuously denies the existence of. Yesterday he kept remarking on how 'much better' I seemed, and when I announced early today that I was going to stay in bed again he seemed surprised and taken aback. I suppose he'd already arranged the X outing. No suggestion that I might go. Oh hell. Should I pay attention to my instincts here? Can I be bothered letting jealousy develop? If you're a man's second wife you know for a fact that he's capable of anything.

———

A manuscript by the music critic John Clare is studded with moments of electrifying power and beauty: Sydney's 'brassy, mari-time light'; 'a ferry walked on tiny spines of light'; two drunks wrestle in the Cross, and one stretches the other's 'cardigan a yard at least'; a man frenziedly about to fuck a girl in a dark lane sees over a fence, through a kitchen window, 'four people gravely playing cards'. *Gravely*. I take off my hat to that.

———

V finishes and hands on to me Gitta Sereny's huge biography of Albert Speer: 'You're gonna love this, Hel.' Her marvellously human voice. The immensity of her research, her narrative always intimately planted in people's personal lives and immediate experiences. How she makes little bridges between one person's account and the next. I read slowly, and re-read to make sure. We talk and talk about it, admiring and moved.

———

Opening at random Lichtenberg's *Aphorisms* I note that V has put a mark in the margin beside this: 'To excuse one's own failings as being only human nature is, provided one has meant well, every writer's first duty to himself.' It is? I flip the pages, seeking more clues to his thoughts about himself. Feel as criminal as if snooping on a diary. A page corner has been folded: under it I read, 'It is very charming to hear a foreign woman speak our language and make mistakes with her fair lips. Not so in the case of men.'

———

This morning we read in the paper about local socialites' flurries of self-presentation for the brief visit of Princess Diana. We laughed about their anxious extravagances. V loved the detail that some women had taken their jewels from safe deposit boxes, and added that X the painter had told him she too had some jewellery in a city bank. He gestured with his fingertips round his left wrist. 'A bracelet?' I said. 'Wow! Has it got diamonds, or—?' 'Maybe sapphires,' he said. He put on her little accent: 'My mother received it from my father.'

———

I suppose X is exotic. She *is* exotic. One compares oneself, fruitlessly. One is nearly fifty-four, with an Australian voice, wrinkles, mannish taste in clothes, and a recent haircut which, one has been informed only this morning, is 'a bit short'. X, it must be said, is a tiny creature with a waist, who trips about in high-heeled, strappy, unusual shoes, and long, very feminine garments tightly cinched with original belts, all in clever and beautiful colour combinations. Her hair is fair and wavy, her face is smooth, pale, pretty. She wears glasses that make her eyes, which are skilfully made up, seem deep, large and rather wild; and in the presence of men she has a way of fluttering her lashes that I've never seen before, except in old movies. She radiates an intense European femininity, is charming, intelligent and likeable. She is very keen, says V, on Thomas Bernhard and Ian Fairweather, and loves to converse at length on these and other favourite topics of his. I suspect she is keeping out of my way.

———

Peter Porter called in, carrying a can of Passiona. We gazed at it with respect and affection: it was an iconic object from our distant youth, or would have been, had it been a bottle rather than a can. At one stage in a long and juicy conversation Peter remarked that envy is an emotion felt by many more people than jealousy is. It occurred to me that all children displaced by younger siblings know both jealousy and envy. Right to the bone.

————

Dreamt I was surfing. I caught a big wave. It was a dark, tall curve, very powerful and unbroken. I got my balance under its lip—I had no board, I was standing barefoot on the water. Below me in the dark green I could see many other surfers submerged. I swept over them with no fear of collision. By the time I reached the shore I was travelling at tremendous speed but the wave, when it finally broke, dissolved into froth and dropped me neatly on to coarse, gravelly sand.

————

She pressed me about what it had meant to me that she'd been unavailable over the fortnight's holiday. I said I hadn't thought about her in Melbourne, and that on the second missed Monday I'd got sick and gone to bed and stayed there for most of the week. 'You *got sick*,' she said. Light dawned: '*Oh.* Yes, and I read, and I hope this won't offend you but I read a book about the murder of the Jews.' I was appalled at what I was letting myself say. But at the same time a stream of associations presented itself and I thought, This is what I'm here for, this is what she's after, I'll go with it. In the end, a sense of having moved forward.

————

V and I drove up to W's place for the day. I made pancakes. Four people sat out on the veranda eating and talking and laughing while I cooked and served. I was so happy—that's how I'd like to live.

A rainbow lorikeet landed on the decking, swaggered towards us on its ungainly legs, came right up to me, and poked its stickybeak into the mug of tea that was standing beside me. We held our breath: the dusty yellow and rose-pink breast, the grey-flecked lavender of its head.

———

It seems to be about my lifelong habit of hiding the pain of parting, of being left; of soldiering on, pretending I'm not hurt. While I was reading out a dream to her someone knocked at her front door. She had to go and answer it. Ten minutes later, another knock. I lay there squashed, humiliated: what I was reading had no value, it was silly and pompous, I'd been taking myself ridiculously seriously in writing it and in expecting anyone else to be interested in it. I gritted my teeth and forced myself to tell her this. That's when she suggested I start coming twice a week.

———

I was doing the ironing when V's friend rang him: the old sculptor wasn't answering the phone to the emergency service that calls him several times a day. V was strangely vague: for minutes he was unable to make it clear to me what on earth he was talking about. Then I couldn't understand why he was so slowed down and stunned, instead of jumping into his shoes and sunglasses and diving straight out the door into a cab. I began to hustle and pester him: 'Aren't you going to call someone? Aren't you going over there *right now?*' He made no response but sat on the chair by the phone. After a few moments he said, 'Trouble is—how will we get in? He's got the whole place barred and locked, in case of robberies.' 'Call the police. They'll smash the door down.' He kept on dreamily moving from room to room. It dawned on me that this is why he's good in a crisis: instead of rushing off in all directions, as I would, he slows down and thinks clearly from one point to the next, visualising in advance. Two more phone calls, and he headed out at a reasoned pace. As soon as the door closed I switched off the iron and began to try on clothes and shoes in a way that's impossible in my life, usually, for he almost never leaves the flat when I'm here. My relationship with my own appearance, body, clothes etc has had to become rather furtive. I folded the ironing, put on a Herbie Hancock CD that G had lent me, cooked a Thai curry and cleaned the kitchen. While doing these things I thought on and off about how the old sculptor might be feeling. Is he injured from a fall? Has he had a stroke? Did he lie on the floor all night? Did he swim in and out of lucidity? Was he angry? Was the night cold, down there near the water in Balmain? Do all men get ill when their partners are away?

————

The Polish philosopher calls. V had sent her a copy of *The Drover's Wife*. 'My *God*! It's so rrrrre-*veal*-ink! For one moment I had the temptation to be devastated!'

————

Running for the bus in the Cross I glanced into the hallway of a strip club as the spruiker opened the street door for business. A warning sign hung over an inner door: 'IF NUDITY OFFEND...' It brought me up short—the subtle beauty of a subjunctive, the tiny shock it administers of apparent grammatical wrongness, which cracks open into depths of 'wish, doubt or supposition'.

————

'Lily Briscoe watched her drifting into that strange no-man's-land where to follow people is impossible and yet their going inflicts such a chill on those who watch them that they always try at least to follow them with their eyes as one follows a fading ship until the sails have sunk beneath the horizon.' —Virginia Woolf, *To the Lighthouse*

————

I think I'm searching everywhere for a model, someone to show me how to write a book about my widowed sister and her rage and grief. I don't know where to stand, to write the story. Is it even 'a story'? Where to grab hold of it. Whether to build this not-knowing into the story, or to blast a way through the uncertainty and *pretend* (to myself, or to whoever I fantasise as reader) that I know what I'm doing and how to do it.

———

'It is true that we are unaware of the particular sensibility of each of our fellow-creatures, but as a rule we do not even know that we are unaware of it, for this sensibility of other people is a matter of indifference to us.' —Marcel Proust, *The Fugitive*

———

Fresh morning, water satiny, cloud cover still low but breaking up along the horizon into cauliflower clouds through which light soaks in long beams.

———

A stupendous dream packed with meaning. Going to her is dismantling something stiff inside me. The hard box of everything. I don't like the feeling. It hurts. And it frightens me. But I have to keep going now.

———

A letter comes, printed in a clear green parent's script and scribbled over childishly with orange texta: 'Dear Helen, My name is Eloise and I'm two and a half years old. I really like your photo on the back of Daddy's book and I talk about you a lot. Would you mind writing me a letter. Love, Eloise.' I send her a postcard with red shoes on it.

———

At the old man's funeral, in Canberra, I sat near the front between the two men I'd come with. After the service we went back to the house. It was packed. In a bedroom near the toilet I found a tiny baby in a car capsule, revving up to cry. I unbuckled its straps and was getting up my nerve to take it out when a man and a pair of little girls came in. They said the baby was theirs, that she was six weeks old and that I was welcome to pick her up. So I did. She stopped crying. I wrapped my big wool shawl round her and went out into the garden, passing the row of bouquets on the back doorstep (one was of big dark crimson roses, almost black, and murky with deep perfume), and along the narrow paths. I remembered the widow, on my only previous visit, showing me the vegetables and herbs—her careless gestures, brushing at the leaves with one hand in passing. I strolled around the garden with the baby in my arms for an hour or so, murmuring away to her, pointing out trees with little hard green fruits clamped close to their leaf-sprays. I chattered in every language that I knew, and she rested against my chest in her tiny snail-curve. The sky was grey, all the trees were in fresh leaf, the air was cold and clean. On the drive home one of the men said, 'Let's sing hymns.' The old words came back to me, verse after verse.

———

On Saturday morning V didn't know why the hell I was going to G and M-C's daughter's third birthday party in a park at Bronte. I said, 'I'm representing both of us. We're her godparents.' He went to his desk. At the party G rocked up to me with a grin: 'So! V went out to dinner last night with X the painter!' This was news to me: I'd gone to bed early, thinking he was eating with G and the other guys he'd gone to the boxing with. I acted cool and shrugged. M-C shot me a puzzled look: 'Is it true they hang out together in Elizabeth Bay in the daytime?' I managed to say casually, 'Yeah—they're quite good friends.' My insides began to tie themselves in knots. I walked round the cliffs to Tamarama. I didn't know any more how to be happy or to enjoy, for example, the glorious beauty of the ocean and the summer sky. I took a bus home. V was reading on the bed. In a small voice I said, 'V? Can you tell me whether I should be worried about you and X the painter?' He flew at me: 'Who's given you *that* idea? All I did was—'

I told him what G and M-C had said. He was furious. 'I went to dinner with her because she'd just won a bloody prize and she wanted to thank me! Anyway *you* go to dinner with *your* men friends!' 'But I always ask *you* to come,' I said, 'and you won't.' And so on, and on, and on. Through all the density of this surfaces the thought that it's really about the terrible struggle I'm being dragged through in therapy—a process that reaches right down to the very bottom of my guts and churns everything up. A horrible, sore and shameful sensation. My heart weighs a ton. Everything's out of joint. I can hardly stand it, but I can't stop now.

———

Today I bought a computer. A second-hand Mac. $800. It was *traumatic*. I got it back to my office and sat there looking at it. What do I do next?

———

Dreamt I was in Paris with V. We got jammed in the exit of a Metro station. Scores of people were stuck in the doorway, gently jostling—nobody could get through—then out in the darkening street someone started to play chunky chords on an acoustic guitar. The music made it possible for us all to relax and move and surge out on to the street, in a large free flow. I had no shoes, and the pavement was covered with tiny rose suckers that were sprouting up through the concrete: they pricked me when I walked.

———

The great reader pressed on me Enid Bagnold's autobiography. Oh, I love it. 'In those days I slept all night. In those days I got up every morning made perfect by sleep.'

———

V quoted to me, while we were standing up on a train, what G had said to him about his X the painter clanger at the party. 'He said, "Don't worry—if you *were* giving her a length, I wouldn't have dobbed you!"' He laughed, watching me. I tried to smile, but my mouth went glassy and I had to turn away.

———

'In physical suffering, at least we do not have to choose our pain ourselves. The malady determines it and imposes it on us. But in jealousy we have, so to speak, to try out sufferings of every shape and size, before we arrive at the one which seems to fit.' —Proust, *The Fugitive*

———

The wastepaper basket beside her couch is usually empty. But today it contained half a dozen screwed-up tissues. I said, 'Gosh—*some-one's* been crying!' She made no response. I was embarrassed, as if I'd been trying to joke her into disloyalty to another client. And writing this now, I see my smart crack about the tears of the absent stranger as a childish attempt to curry favour with Mum: 'One of the others has been crying, but *I'm* not crying. *I'm* not going to make a nuisance of myself by crying.' You great cake. Pick up your lip, before you trip over it.

———

This morning on the packed train to Bondi Junction a little girl of nine months or so, all fresh in nappy and white cotton, lay in her pusher and cried and cried. Her mother, a very young Islander of extreme beauty, with a calm, rather sweet expression, and a tattoo of a bleeding cut on her left arm, did not pick her up but simply stood rolling the pusher forward and back in tiny movements. Another girl, of four or five, stood beside the pusher, holding a bottle, trying to put the teat into the baby's mouth, but the baby went on and on crying, inconsolable. Everyone in the carriage was excruciated. A young thug with tatts and a tough, scary face twitched his bare legs this way and that, pressed his running shoe against a metal pole, folded his arms, and closed his eyes. A tall man beside me looked up from his paper and flicked me a wry glance. Every woman's head, no matter what her age or station, was turned in the direction of the baby. Our faces were strained. We were paralysed. An old Italian woman in black sat with her arm round the chubby torso of her little grandson. Her mouth was drawn in, her eyes slanted sideways and down towards the crying baby. She looked up and our eyes met. She glanced down at her relaxed-looking charge, and her face opened in a smile: *my* boy is content. The train approached Bondi Junction. A heavy, oldish woman in thongs and loose trousers came down the stairs from the upper section, approached the pusher, grabbed the baby's foot in its bright white sandal, and gently jiggled it. The crying stopped. The baby's mother watched, in her genial passivity. The train pulled in to the platform and everyone rushed for the doors. On the escalator I lost the baby and her mother and her sister, but as I went through the turnstile and out into the sunshine and the fresh breeze, I heard her crying start up again.

————

The Friday night feeling begins: I want to stay home on the weekend, as other people do. I want to do things around the flat in a leisurely way, hem the curtains, take in my linen trousers, play music loud, cook something that takes all day. But he wants to work. How long can this go on—the closed blinds, the hopeless old stove that we can't replace (though I offered to pay) until the tiles behind it are replaced, and we can't have *them* done because because because—*why?* Because nothing can happen, nothing can change or be disturbed till V finishes his book. It could be a year. Two years. Then what?

————

A photo of Mum holding a baby. The baby is clutching the front of her blouse with one hand, and glaring at the camera. I get a weird feeling off the baby's face: its slightly mad eyes, its square head that contains the brain with which I now contemplate it.

––––––

An evening with the Polish philosopher. Afterwards V and I were calm and sweet with each other, laughing gently about the philosopher and her generosity and warmth. He said, 'I think I'll leave her something in my will.' She exudes a quality of optimism, a sort of universal *yes* that affects everyone in the room and makes life more enjoyable and hopeful. In conversation with her one says things one hardly knew one felt, or thought.

––––––

My friend gave me a marvellous book called *Macs for Dummies*. The minute I saw a page headed 'Mindlessly opening and closing files' I knew it was the book for me.

––––––

'The world,' announced V at the breakfast table, 'is contaminated by a creeping tide of psychiatry.' To say, 'Don't you mean psycho-analysis?' would have been correcting, so I bit my lip. A rant began that lasted on and off for twenty-four hours. When I tried to speak, my voice sounded unusually slow and dopy. I asked how else a person might manage to change deep-rooted emotional habits that were making them miserable and helpless. He said that intelligent people could examine themselves and work it out. I said it wasn't an intellectual process—that a lot of what needed changing was unconscious—that one needed outside help even to *notice* uncon-scious behaviour. He said plenty of people had been able to do this. I asked him if he knew anyone who had. He said, 'Well, yes. Me, for example.' He raised his chin and looked at me down his cheeks: '*I* had an unhappy childhood. *Most* people's childhoods are unhappy.'

I tried to get him to think about whether he's ever been surprised at himself: 'When was the last time you got a shock about yourself? Saw something in yourself that you didn't know was there?' I gave as an example a jolting realisation I'd recently had that I'd been patronising O because of his illness. He didn't seem to want to admit that this meant anything much, or to be keen to compare notes on such discoveries.

When I got home from work, towards 7 pm because there were no buses, and lugging food for dinner, half the Christmas presents for Melbourne, and his English brogues which I'd picked up from the repairer at Bondi Junction, he said to me, 'M rang. The wedding's off.' Dumbfounded, I gaped at him. Something must have been visible, because he hastily added that it was postponed so they could go to Sundance together, with her movie. When I sat down at the phone to call her, he put a glass of wine in front of me, and awkwardly offered to cook the pasta.

How Elizabeth Jolley ends a letter: 'Dear Hélène, I must iron my blouse.'

E reports that she has 'met' someone. 'It's a shock to realise that you've still *got* a heart, that blood *does* still flow in your veins.'

At my office, having one of those stress attacks: most of my mind is functioning but I keep getting a sensation of confusion, as if I'd just forgotten something terribly important—not a fact, but an entire situation I may have been in, the moment before I forgot it—was there something I was doing? In England or America? Am I actually here and if so how did I get back here? It's a barely controlled panic. Been arguing with V since breakfast when I foolishly asked him if he'd feel like kicking in for the Christmas presents we're taking down to Melbourne tonight. He said I'd refused his suggestion to make a list, and had cornered the entire task. I said he'd been so hostile and irritated about the very idea of taking presents that I'd veered off on my own, out of a desire to preserve the pleasure of the task. He said I was giving larger than necessary presents to my family out of guilt at living in Sydney instead of Melbourne; that if we'd made a list we could have got rid of all the books we don't want, that we stash in the corner of his room. I said I'd found a pretty lavender linen shirt at Country Road for his old bohemian lady. How much was it? $140. He hit the roof. 'But we *agreed* we'd give her a linen shirt—and she's been so generous to you.' 'I had no idea it would cost that much!' He said my family showed no interest in him at all, that they were all completely self-obsessed, that I was the least self-obsessed of 'that whole bunch'. He said he could only spare three days away from his work to see everyone *he* wanted to see in Melbourne, and that I should come with him to his friends' place on Christmas Day instead of going to M and AB's. I sat on the phone chair and sobbed. He came over to me and put his hands on my shoulders. I wept on, not caring that he hates to see 'women crying'. I could feel my face swelling up, getting 'ugly'. I said that I loved him and loved my family, and that what was unbearable, *unbearable*, was the relentless pressure he puts on me about my family, always speaking badly of them, resenting the phone bills, never wanting any of them to come and stay.

I think I'd better lie down on my mat and go to sleep.

———

Downstairs on the mall four young girls with sensitive, eager faces, dressed in long black skirts and little white T-shirts, were set up on chairs in a doorway, surging through a Mozart string quartet. I sat on a ledge with my sandwich, and stayed till the end.

With a friend who is married to a painter I compared notes about our respective husbands and their demands. In his determination to deter visitors, hers has disabled the buzzer and made adjustments to the heavy street door of their house that make it impossible for her to get in, even with her key, without putting down everything she is carrying. Like me, she is expected to run the house, do the shopping and cooking, and keep the home fires burning, all this without being permitted on the premises during work hours. I saw in her face my unhappiness. We did not know whether, or how, we could go on tolerating their regimes, or what we could do to change them. When I was leaving she said, 'I'm beginning to experience it as violence.'

1997

We're both sick, a horrible flu. My nose keeps bleeding. I went over to Edgecliff and bought food, cooked up a storm to stockpile: two soups, sauce for pasta—so I can get into bed and we won't have to live on eggs. The great reader called. V gave her fifteen minutes of details on his condition then passed me the phone. Her questions showed he hadn't mentioned that I too am ill. I slept in the spare room. At midnight he came in, kissed me, and wished me a happy New Year. I woke up stunned, and touched. In all the time I've known him he's never made such a gesture.

———

'Personality…is the repertoire of strategies that siblings use to compete with one another, secure their place in the family, and survive the ordeal of childhood.' —Robert S. Boynton, reviewing in the *New Yorker* Frank Sulloway's book about birth order, *Born to Rule*

———

H: 'Let's take out hospital insurance.'

V: 'Why.'

Pause.

H: 'I've got an idea. Let's agree not to ask each other *why* in that aggressive way. Could we avoid that tone? Do you think? For the New Year?'

V: '*Why* is one of the most important words in the language. It's an absolutely *crucial* word. It's a *much* better word than *Let's*.'

Short silence.

H: 'Do we have to be in competition all the time?'

He makes out he doesn't know, can't imagine what I mean. I point out his placing of *why* and *let's* in opposition. He acts as if he's amazed by this ridiculous suggestion.

————

I got to the Wharf restaurant early. A tremendous orange container ship from Trinidad was sliding under the bridge, so vast that it blocked the view with its freshly painted side, so tall as to seem two-dimensional, and right up on top a rim of clear, sparkling white. One little tug behind it, another right in under its ribs: how do tugs work? They're so small and sturdy and determined, puffing out black smoke in vague little wisps, and the water beside them riffling, riffling tightly with bright gold tiny tips as the sun goes down. People at tables stop talking and gaze. The girl selling theatre programs turns from her podium and stands in reverie, her translucent white blouse floating around her torso like a mist.

————

We had tickets to a play at the Seymour Centre last night but V was still really sick; he wanted to go to bed early. I went by myself. The play was old-fashioned and dull. I nicked out at interval and came home on the bus. The flat was in darkness. I crept in so as not to wake V, went to my desk and started writing a letter. Half an hour later a key was thrust into the outside door. It burst open and in he rushed. I laughed in shock: 'I thought you were asleep in there!' He was flustered: 'Look at my eye. It's all red. I've been over at X's to do some paper punching for her.' 'What—did somebody punch you?' In this spontaneous question resided my sense that the floor I was standing on had just disintegrated. I went quiet. I thought, 'Shut up, don't start saying things, just clean your teeth and get into your bed.' In the bathroom I looked at myself in the mirror and thought, 'If I don't say something I'll poison myself with faking.' So I went to the bedroom and said quietly, from the door, 'There *is* something between you and her, isn't there.' He reared up from his pillow in wild, angry denial: '*What?* Are you *serious?* What the hell do you *think* is going on? Do you think I'm *rooting* her or something?'

———————

In the morning he came into 'my' room early, got into the spare bed with me and, cuddling me from behind, began to talk in a charming way. He told me about some beautiful clothes that X's mother, 'who's a lovely woman', had saved from *her* mother—things to whose cuffs she had stitched extra pieces of velvet, 'to strengthen them, or something'. He told me that X 'squanders her teaching salary on clothes', mostly from 'some shop called Zambesi'; that he's given her a list of questions to put to her tax accountant this morning; that she didn't even put her prize money in a cash management account—it was in an ordinary savings account. I said, striving for a civilised, interested tone and succeeding only in sounding sucky, 'I used to do that. Till you pointed out that it was irresponsible.' 'Actually,' he said, 'I rather envy that sweeping attitude to money.'

———————

I think he's lying to me. I said, 'If you don't *tell* me you're seeing her, if you sneak behind my back and I find out accidentally, it makes me feel mad. It makes me crazy.' He appears to take my point. But in a darker area of my thoughts I'm remembering his declaration, made to me several times over the years, in various contexts, and always with a note of defiant eternal-verity-ness which I would have to describe as smug: 'All men are moral cowards.'

———————

I asked him why he never invites X to our place. 'Oh,' he said, 'she's not interested in you.' I imagine how pleasant it must be for him to leave the scene of his struggles with his bolshie Australian wife, to stroll in the evening down the hill to that shadowy little apartment, and to be welcomed by two tiny elegant women with European accents and feminine manners; to sit in a room with them and their two cats and their pot plants, and to be served tea in a delicate foreign way; to be shown the strange, beautiful old home-sewn garments from the 20s and 30s, and to admire the handiwork; and at a certain point the old mother retires discreetly to her room, and V and X turn to each other and talk intently about their shared passions—Bernhard, Fairweather, McCahon, Cézanne; and then my imagination applies its brakes and I choose not to force it further.

———

'Now that you're starting to *go to things*,' he said, on our walk this morning, 'I was thinking that'd be a good time for me to see X. In the evenings.' Whereas he once used to think, he said, that it was 'ridiculous and wrong' of me to get up in the night and sleep in the spare bed (*because he snored*! which is not mentioned), he has now begun to see that 'separateness, for adults, is a natural and good thing'. If it weren't for X, I'd be fine with this. But somehow I feel manipulated, roughed-up by him. As if he's turning me against myself. You want separateness? I'll show you separateness!

———

'Listen—I'll go with you some other day, if you like, but I'm going to see the Beyeler exhibition this afternoon with X.'

———

I seem to have an unlimited quantity of tears inside me—they tip over the edge and start sliding out. Yesterday afternoon, while I was doing the ironing, they dripped and dripped on to the board, they wouldn't stop. It was relieving but also tiring, and sort of endless. While I was unpacking the shopping in the kitchen he asked me

what was wrong. I lay on the bed and bawled. I said all the things
I've been bottling up—how he refuses to do anything with me any
more, how G's become *his* friend instead of mine, how he spoilt my
hopes for a trip to Europe when his book's finished by saying I'd be a
bore as a travelling companion. He listened. He didn't say much, or
if he did I've already forgotten what it was. I just offloaded, and he
rubbed my back, which was turned towards him to hide my shame
and 'the ugliness of bloody women crying'.

———

W said, 'He's been trying to crush you into his mould ever since
you've been together.'

———

Went to the Opera House by myself this arvo to see *A Comedy
of Errors*. I laughed many times (sometimes I was the only one
laughing), and at the reconciliation scene another overflow of
tears occurred. The early scenes about the jealous wife stung:
'Self-harming jealousy! Fie! Beat it hence!' Coming away from
the theatre I resolved to kiss V when I got home and say, 'I'm sorry
I've been jealous and a pain.' But he had an art dealer friend visiting
and they were talking about Fairweather so it wasn't the moment.

———

The wedding invitation arrives, AB's beautiful design: an explosion
of pale green foliage on a cream ground. They're having it in a park,
and a church hall.

———

Whenever my thoughts tilt towards X the painter, I turn them
firmly in another direction.

———

A long letter from my very first friend in childhood, the girl who
lived next door to us in Geelong. We've had no contact in nearly
fifty years. She lays out a chronology of her life. She too had a

hysterectomy in 1995. A chequered career with men. Things have
not ended happily with the latest, who makes her laugh but 'dislikes
my kids—competition. Blending my kids with him does not work.
Please don't get the notion I wallow in self-pity.' In fact the letter is
tough, factual, dry, impressive.

———

On the couch I describe dreams in which various men (M's father
and others even further back) surface from my past. What 'happens'
in these dreams, if anything does, vanishes in the moment of waking,
but the *feeling* of each dream remains: a good-tempered calm, a
sense of a deep, old connection that has spontaneously come back
to life, like a gift, encouraging and comforting.

———

Late in the afternoon at Bondi Junction station a bloke in shorts,
carrying an airways bag, dropped or threw something down on to
the tracks, and jumped down to retrieve it. People watched half-
heartedly. He seemed young and strong and competent; but when
he came back to the edge of the platform and placed his hands on
it, to climb back up, he was shaking so much that he couldn't get
a grip on its edge: twice he tried, but his forearms and hands were
trembling with a wild flamboyance. People started to take notice,
turned their bodies and faces to him. No train was in view or to
be heard, but on his face was a grin of fear. He didn't call out but
two men hurried forward and reached down for his upstretched
hands, heaved him up in a rush, and stepped away. He stood on the
platform with his airline bag beside him, still half-smiling in relief
and foolishness. A boy of ten or so near me said to his father in a low,
fascinated voice, 'Did you see that? How much he was shaking?'

———

My sister's in town. We went for a swim at Boy Charlton. A perfect
high summer day. Dripping swimmers lined up along the pool's

chin-high wall to watch two grey naval ships reverse out of Woolloomooloo Bay, attended by tugs; a bosun's pipe shrieked. We dried
off and sat under an old tree, admiring a view of dark, green-blue
water under thick foliage.

I felt happy and confident for hours after we'd parted. I went
home and chattered away to V about the ships, and the pool, and
about my sister's father-in-law who used to race against Boy Charlton. He seemed friendly, and made a cup of tea. I rinsed out my
floppy flowery dress, and as I laid it on the rack in the 'sewing room'
I thought, 'If I was hanging this in my backyard in Melbourne,
it'd be dry in ten minutes.' This sent an absolute bolt of happiness
through me. I lay down on the bed for a nap, but instead, fantasies
gushed up. One day I would go back to Melbourne without V. I
would live not too far from M and AB and all my family. I would
have a bike and a car. I'd work. I'd swim. I'd plant things. I'd visit
people. I'd go to hear bands, and dance. People would drop in. I'd
come and go as I pleased, and sleep with the windows wide open
winter and summer. I'd have music on, loud. I'd have the sewing
machine and the ironing board set up permanently. And when M
and AB have children, I'll be their nanna and hold them and mind
them and read to them and love them. In this huge rush of imaginary future I got back some more of my soul.

———

'Your responses to V,' she said, 'are like your responses to your father.
Panic, rage and flight. Flight, now, is your burst of fantasies about
Melbourne.' Cranky, deflated, I tied my shoelaces and glanced into
the wastepaper basket beside the couch. It contained nothing but a
fresh, pale-yellow banana skin. 'Look! A banana peel!' She laughed,
but quickly recovered her professional mode: 'What does it make
you think of?' 'Oh, just funny.' Stood up, took my bag from the
table, added soberly, 'A banana peel is what you *slip* on.'

Still. I'm going to find a place in myself to stand, from which I can engage better with V. I would like him to know that I don't see him and his inflexible regime as my only possible source of happiness.

And I'm determined that I'll give this marriage the best I've got, without thinking about 'flight', till he finishes his book. I'm going to work hard at not wallowing and being abject. I'm going to tell him what I feel, and not in an accusing tone. I'll keep on inviting him to 'things', and going to them anyway whether he comes or not. Plus, I'll try not to turn X the painter into the mule to carry all this anger.

At the wedding of V's old friend's daughter, in Taree, the women and girls ran outside to dance in the soft summer darkness, laughing and singing. In the corner of my eye V stood under a tree, jerking his head at me: come on, let's get out of here. I turned my back and went on dancing.

Dinner at the Verona last night with my niece and her boyfriend, both choral singers. In a pause the boyfriend said, 'Do you two like each other's work?' A jolt, a short silence. I said, 'Well, *I* like his!' V said, '*The Children's Bach* is very good.' Awkward pause. The boyfriend said, 'I was just wondering if it was a problem.' To save the moment I said, 'Do you two like each other's singing?' We all laughed. I went downstairs to collect our movie tickets.

This morning V told me that in my absence the boyfriend had apologised. 'He said, "I hope I didn't put you on the spot!" and I said, "No, of course not! It was perfectly all right."' I asked him, in the least 'emphatic' tone possible, if he thought we *were* in competition. He seemed surprised by the question, and said very firmly that he didn't think we were. I said I didn't *feel* competitive with him, but that it would be quite weird if there weren't some degree of rivalry. I said I had wondered at times whether I hadn't adapted my work, 'to get out of your way'. 'What do you mean?' 'I mean by moving over into non-fiction.' 'There shouldn't be even the slightest *hint* that you adapted your work in that way!' 'Yes, but what if it happens unconsciously? What if that's why I'm a bit paralysed at the moment? You only ever encourage me to write journalism. You never say, "Come on, Hel! Try some fiction!"' He said, 'It didn't even occur to me to mention your non-fiction last night—and I must say if you'd said you liked the Fairweather book best, I'd have been devastated.' We laughed. It wasn't a quarrel or even an argument. It was something, but I don't know what.

————

Rain. It will never stop! It came down hour after hour, bringing its comfort. The air's heavy with dampness. Before work I went to Boy Charlton. Pool flattened and pocked by rain. The rain fell and *fell*. All there was to do was stay in the pool and keep swimming. Breaststroking, there are two sounds in alternating rhythm: hiss of rain on surface, then booming silence under water. Freestyle, there's the slap of arms striking water and the hard peppering blows of raindrops on one's tight rubber cap. I got out and stretched my arms up over my head, like a hippie or a religious nut. I felt glorious and free. I said out loud, 'We worship you, we give you thanks, we praise you for your glory.' The sky was a thick dark grey, and *low*. Dried and dressed, I stood under the roof for fifteen minutes holding my briefcase and gazing out at the rain. My body was warm and loose, extended lengthwise, strong.

————

V has raised again the possibility of my buying a little flat, as a work space and for visitors to stay. (Renting is anathema to him: 'money down the drain'.) Tried to stay calm. Asked him if he could see any other way of resolving our situation about the flat. I can't remember what (if anything) he said. I have a pathetic, unspoken hope, or fantasy, that one day he'll say, 'Look, we can solve it all in one simple stroke: *I'll* rent an office.' So many times this suggestion has been blasted away that I know it's never going to happen. He offered to speak to a real-estate agent for me, to a tax accountant. I'm being very firmly pushed. Horrid little spurts of fear.

———

I tell her I'm angry with her, that she's shoved me off a cliff and is watching me flounder. I say I'm drowning, and she just *sits* there. I tell her she's ripped all my scabs off and I'm exposed. I say I don't know how long this will go on, I can't bear it, I've become stupid, I can't concentrate, I can't understand or remember anything I read. She says I sound as if I feel very small; that the thing I used to tell her about, my 'cleverness', is no longer in play; that perhaps my 'cleverness' in the past had been stopping me from 'feeling like this'.

———

Only a man distracted by love will get up from the dinner table and return with a single glass of water; will barge first out the heavy front door of the building and let it slam in his wife's face. The sick power of knowing something he thinks I don't know; of knowing that he's lying to me. The clumsiness of the lies, the humiliation of being clumsily lied to.

———

A visitor from France. When I served the dinner she did something I will never forget: she looked down at her plate, then up at me, opened both her palms in the air near her shoulders, and said with a smile, 'Hélène—*merci*.' I took her for a walk, down to the park. She questioned me very discreetly about the difficulties of living with a man. I was feeling so rotten, so unscabbed and frightened, that (leaving X the painter out of it) I sketched our domestic struggles.

She touched the tip of her nose: 'I smelt it.' She herself, she said, at one stage of her life had to wander the streets of Zürich until nine each evening. 'Who owns the apartment?' she asked. 'He does.' 'Do you still love him?' The unanswerable question. Today I think I hate him. 'You need two things. You need a long holiday. By yourself. Go to Prague. Just walk round and look at things. And then you need to find yourself a place of your own. Something small, but with a bit of a kitchen, so you can invite people. You're good at cooking.'

———

In my fantasies of flight I see myself taking the bed, the sheets, the pillows; the stereo, the music. All the things that I brought with me, or paid for: things that are mine.

———

The morning after the Frenchwoman's visit, as we walked, he took up his railing against 'self-obsessed people'. His particular bugbear is people who never ask him questions. I asked him whether he'd always found himself surrounded by such people, or if it was a recent development. 'Oh, there've always been some, but there are more lately. And when I went to live in Melbourne and met your family, I really started to become aware of it.' I said, working at not being 'emphatic', that I'd had a bit of an idea about this problem. I said I'd noticed that when he met someone new he would soon begin to ask them quite intimate questions. They, surprised, would reply; and then he, rather than offering corresponding information about himself and his own life, as most people do in the give-and-take of conversation, would push on with further questions (always intelligent and sensitive) into the other person's territory. In this way the other was drawn into revealing himself, while V remained veiled, and thus, in the end, more powerful. This made him furious. He said I'd 'shifted the blame' on to him. I said I didn't think I was blaming anyone. I said I was trying to examine the dynamic of the phenomenon that bothered him so much. He battered away, declaring that men's way of conversing is 'better and wiser' than women's, because it doesn't 'depend on subjective anecdote'.

―――――

I stayed a night with friends at Mona Vale. V wouldn't come. Ashamed to be sleepless, to be in this much pain. And yet this is life. The toughness of life. People's utter, bottomless selfishness. This is *what people do.* The fact that I've been faithful to V for ten years has no weight, in the big scales of what will become of us. No 'virtue', no 'self-control' can save us, or protect us from each other. We can't make room for each other. We push each other into the most extreme versions of ourselves, and then with a gritty determination we fight.

―――――

But the sea booms patiently all night long. Light comes, and kook-aburras start to shout with laughter. Magpies stream forth their ecstasy.

―――――

Twenty bucks for an hour of nakedness in the Korean bathhouse: spas, saunas, hot and cold pools, the sleeping room. Chestdeep in the ginseng bath I got talking to a wiry little blonde-permed woman from Ulster, here visiting her son in Bondi. He had bought her a bathhouse voucher as a going-home present. Startling contrast between her fiercely tanned limbs and her creamy torso. In the Omagh hospital's X-ray department she'd had to deal with so many injuries caused by 'the bombs and the bashings' that she'd recently retired. 'I've never even had a massage before,' she said. 'We don't have places like this in Ireland.'

―――――

A loans officer at the bank says I'd be up for repayments of at least $350 a week. A dim light bulb goes on. I could cover that with (1) the rent from my house in Melbourne plus (2) what I pay the therapist, if I stop seeing her. You want escape fantasy? I'll give you escape fantasy!

———

'Your jealousy,' said R at the Botanic Gardens kiosk, 'seems disproportionate. I wonder if it mightn't at least partly belong to V? He is jealous, but he won't acknowledge it, and so somehow it all gets sheeted home to *you*.' As for the matter of X the painter: 'He needs a secret. And he needs to have someone who's more interested in him than she is in you.'

———

Mum and Dad are moving into an eighth-floor city apartment, opposite the Treasury Gardens. They sound happy and excited, and that's how I feel, too—symbolically, it's a reconciliation between the Mum and Dad in *me*. For years they've lived a weird, separate 'Fort Knox' existence in two tiny flats beside each other—a madness of inconvenience and internal division, always the carrying about of keys, the locking and unlocking of doors, the anxiety about theft and intrusion, the dull grey walls with their prison-like aspect. Now they're going up high, into air and light, into one unified dwelling. When I talk about coming to see them, Dad says grandly, 'Well, I think we can accommodate you *very nicely*. We'll roll out the carpet.'

———

Without turning a hair I swim a masterful kilometre. I am fit and strong. I have a light tan. X the painter and my fears have receded into a distant spot on the horizon. Occasionally they go *booga booga booga*, but I can subdue them with a little flexing of personal muscle, or by simply turning away to something more interesting.

———

Two work offers: the *Herald* offered me $1000 a week for six pieces a year; the *Australian's Review of Books* a dollar a word to review movies. I told them I'd think about it.

———

When she speaks about my anger, I feel it start to boil inside me, like Les Murray's 'black kelp'. But in my belly, not my head. She urges me to feel it towards *her*; and I see that if only I could, it wouldn't keep oozing out into the rest of my life, spoiling everything; and I could put the effort I devote to hiding it to some better purpose. Is that how this thing is supposed to work?

———

'The late Dame Peggy Ashcroft, hailed by many as the greatest Shakespearean actress of her age, was promiscuous to the point of nymphomania, a biography is expected to claim next month.' V reads this out at the breakfast table. I silently curdle with rage on her behalf—but of course it's on my own behalf, for I, as a younger woman, could have been (and probably was, behind my back) described in exactly those terms. V points out, with approval, Harold Pinter's retort: 'She was a wonderful person and a dear friend. I don't know what the hell this biographer thinks he's doing.' My thoughts of myself as 'promiscuous' I keep quiet about. They belong on the couch. Peggy Ashcroft in that TV movie I once saw, hunched on the edge of a bed in a holiday hotel, crushed in her cheerfulness by her bullying husband—how, watching this movie in *my* hotel room twelve years ago, knowing in every nerve that something at home was terribly wrong, I saw in her cowed posture first Mum, then *myself*. And I called home, and said I couldn't live like this any longer; and the very next day my whole faking world collapsed.

Peggy Ashcroft stands at important doors in my life. One of those angel figures. Not saying anything. Just *being*, in a certain significant way.

———

Everything fine in our bodies, but no emotional contact. No eye contact, no sound, not a word spoken. He turned his head sideways on the pillow so as not to look at me. In a small rush of courage I took hold of his chin and gently turned his head towards me: 'Hello? Are you there?' He opened his eyes. I said, 'Hello? It's me. *I'm* here.' 'Eh? What's the matter?' 'I had a feeling things were happening only from the neck down.' We both laughed. He said, 'Of course they weren't.' But they were.

———

To Guerilla Bay with E. She drove confidently through endless rain, and we talked in our long, looping lines. In the cold house she lit a fire. Rain in the night, steady and faithful. The dropping and splattering, and the trickling of the gutters, obscured the occasional boom of surf two hundred metres away. In the morning I open the blinds. The trees are dark with rain, and every flat surface bright silver, including the sea, over which hangs a low, whiteish mist of spray.

———

On the couch I produced my Peggy Ashcroft promiscuity-to-the-point-of-nymphomania story. She said she wondered if, going on the pattern I seemed to have, of not being able to be myself in close relationships, of cutting off pieces of myself as the only way to sustain closeness, I may have kept moving on as a way of avoiding the intimacy which would have led to the cutting-off-of-pieces, the inertia, the unbearability and so on. This was a description innocent of moral judgment, so the sting of it was the sting of truth, rather than the usual boring cataract of shame.

———

From the balcony at my parents' new place. A soft dawn over the cathedral, Parliament House, the huge trees in the Treasury Gardens.

———

I told my sister I couldn't write about her and her grief over the death of her husband. I said I was still shocked by the depths of anguish she had reached since he drowned. I said I couldn't find in myself, as a writer or as a person, anything large and deep and competent enough to contain it, either emotionally or formally. I said that in the face of what she had gone through I felt completely inadequate. I said I hoped she would forgive me. I expected anger, but she looked at me with a sweet expression and said, 'It's all right. I understand that it's too hard. I'm really touched that you even thought of doing it.'

———

Maybe I can write some *very* short stories.

———

My mother's fearfulness and timidity. Dad goes to bed at 8.30, she sits on the sofa and puts on an Errol Garner CD. I come in and find her sitting in the dark with her feet neatly side by side. I say, 'How about we go downstairs and have a cool drink in a bar?' She looks up with a blank, slightly bewildered expression. I can't tell if she doesn't feel like going out and can't bring herself to say so, or if she can't compute the suggestion, or if she hasn't been invited out for a drink in a bar for so long that she's forgotten how, or if she's scared to go out in the city at night without Dad, or what. So I repeat the invitation, and she says vaguely (or is it obediently, or timidly?), 'Oh, all right.' She tiptoes into the bathroom and puts on some lipstick, then turns to me, in her neat green skirt and stripy blouse and sandals, with an open-handed gesture of helplessness that means 'I haven't got any money'.

    H: 'I've got money—let's go.'

    Mum: 'What if the phone rings?'

    H: 'Hmmm. That would be bad. I know—I'll take it off the hook. And I'll leave us a note so we can put it back on later.'

I lay the note on the floor and we step over it. Mum points to it and says, 'What's that?'

H: (patiently) 'It's a note to remind us to put the phone back on the hook when we get home.'

Down we go in the lift. I press the red button for the heavy street door; it swings shut behind us very fast, pushing us out, and she glares at it, offended, as if at a personal insult. On the street the night air hits us, hot, dry, stifling. 'Take my arm, Mum. We're going out drinking!' We parade down Collins Street to the Sofitel. At the table she relaxes, and looks around: 'Nice here, isn't it!' If there's one thing my mother's familiar with, after all these years of being dragged around the world by my restless father, it's a bar in a big American-style hotel.

———

At 5 am, fumbling around in their kitchen to make myself a cup of tea, I notice a small single-sash window above the sink. A flash of my mother painfully scrambling up to it and throwing herself out. Sick jolt. Where's this coming from? Is it me picking up on her despair, or am I projecting my wretchedness on to her? Yesterday morning before she woke up, Dad spoke to me about her increasing vagueness and depression. 'She's so *touchy*. F'r instance, we'll be sitting there in the TV room, having a talk about something or other, and she'll start crying. I s'pose it's something I've said. I get up and walk out o' the room, and twenty minutes later she's still *sitting* there, with her head down—I've got *no idea* what's the matter with 'er.'

Speechless at this unconscious statement of what the problem is, I stand there by the toaster listening with what I hope is an expression devoid of dismay. 'She forgets things,' he says. 'Can't seem to *grasp* things, like dates—she can't seem to get them into her head. And she repeats things, over and over, the same story about her brother and how he got out of the Air Force and went into the family business—

I don't know *how* many times I've heard that.' 'Yes,' I said, 'she's told me that story three times in the two days I've been here. And always in the same words, too—do you notice that?' 'Yes! I don't say anything. I just listen. But it's getting worse and worse.' I suggested she might have the beginnings of Alzheimer's. 'I don't really know what that is.' I explain. 'I forget things all the time too,' he says. 'So do I. But you've still got a basic grip on things, haven't you. Mum seems to be losing hers.'

———

I heard V on the phone describe my father as 'a barbarian'. I think he would have stopped at 'peasant' if not for last night, when he took me and my parents to dinner at the Hyatt and witnessed Dad's inability to control his haste and greed: how he rushed straight to the buffet, before we'd even settled ourselves at the table or made contact with the waitress, and returned with a bowl of soup which he gulped down, blind and deaf to the social nature of a meal, even leaning back and raising the bowl to his mouth with both hands to slurp the last few drops. It's ugly, and shameful. But also somehow pitiful—childish, bereft.

———

Even at 10 pm the temperature was still in the high thirties. The breath desiccated as you drew it in. Strolling home from dinner, we passed some expensive shops. Mum stopped in front of an elegant boutique and said happily, 'We bought an outfit in there for your sister, when *she* got married.'

———

Just as I was about to set out this morning, rather flustered, on the day's preparations, Mum said, 'What a fuss! Pity it can't be like *your* wedding!'

'Oh well. That's all in the past now, Mum.'

'I'll never forgive your father for that.'

I let it pass and hurried out the door.

———

On the road all day with M, on wedding business. Everywhere we went the shop people were friendly and generous, even the ones who knew nothing about our mission. At Bunnings, where we bought metal buckets for flowers, the checkout girls were sneakily cooling themselves with green icy-poles. The girl at Hardware House gave us the use of her phone. The heat was so extraordinary that everyone was excited about it—united in suffering.

———

Back at their house, M and AB found to their alarm that they had gone way over budget. I said, 'Look. Your father and I had a wretched little hole-in-the-corner wedding. We both want yours to be done properly. I've got some money and I'm happy to spend it.' AB got beers out of the fridge: 'What do you mean, hole-in-the-corner?' I rolled out the story: 'Dad went to the minister and tried to stop it.' 'What? How old were you?' 'Twenty-five. Anyway, the minister liked me. He'd taught me at school. I don't know what he said to Dad, but he said to me, "Your father is the most stubborn person I've ever met in my life." Dad forbade the others to go. He told my sister that if she went he wouldn't let her go to uni. Mum defied him—I suppose she paid for that later, I never heard. The only people there, apart from us two and his parents and Mum, were the minister, my sister who'd already started nursing, and a schoolfriend of mine who happened to be walking past the church and saw us going in.'

I told this (as I always do) for laughs, but AB's face went blank with shock, and I decided not to add the remaining details. One bottle of champagne was enough for the whole party. As we left the Carlton Hotel, my new father-in-law took a photo of us against the railings of the ANZ bank, but later when he went to have it developed, he found that he hadn't put the film into the camera properly. So there's no visual record of the event.

———

A scorcher. Dad wouldn't lend me their car so I had to take the train out to St Albans to decorate the wedding cake with AB's mother. She is visually very alert and daring, and superbly competent in the kitchen; I was content to follow orders. AB's young twin brothers came in, blindingly handsome blonds with huge white smiles and a shy demeanour.

———

At 10.30 last night I washed two linen tops and a pair of silk knickers and hung them in the bathroom. By 6 am they were so dry as to be stiff and crackly. The sky at the eastern horizon is streaked a dramatic bluish pink. Jackhammers are battering away, eight floors down and across the park.

———

Dreamt I was watching a film acted by Muppet-like creatures. A close-up of 'a mother': her head was out of shot and her breasts were showing among her loosened garments, as if she'd just been feeding a baby. Beside her, near her lap, sat a capsicum. It was hard, red and hollow, and squalling wildly, desperate for food. Still with her head out of shot (though somehow I knew she was amused by the capsicum's antics), the mother picked it up and put it to her breast. A slit opened in the capsicum's side and it began to suck voraciously. Appalling hunger, redness, hardness, an inner-ridged hollowness.

———

Q has made me a silky, fitted, moonlight-coloured dress, buttoning from neck to calf, with long sleeves and a lot of skirt.

———

I took a wad of cash to my brother's restaurant. He was so calm, I knew there was nothing I needed to worry about. 'This wedding,' he said, 'is paying for my divorce.' The waitresses suddenly rushed to the windows and threw them open: the cool change had come.

———

After the speeches, Mum grabbed my hand behind Dad's back, leaned towards me and covered my face with kisses. I was shocked, I didn't know how to accept them. The capsicum squalls to be fed, but when the breast is offered, it can't make a big enough split in its hardness and hollowness to let the food come in.

———

'It was a robust, solid celebration,' said AB happily on the phone, the day after the wedding. 'The bands, the bridesmaids in their dresses, the speeches, the dancing, the throbbing muscle cars…'

'Thank you, Helen,' said M in a tiny, blissed-out whisper, 'for helping to make our dream come true.'

———

After I'd put V in a taxi to the airport, I plodded back to the apartment so depleted that I was beyond speech. Mum ran me a bath. I crawled on to my bed and crashed into a deep and dreamless sleep. I woke at 6 pm and said I was going to my brother's to settle the final accounts. My father appeared at the other end of the hall, one hand against the wall, and started to bellow at me: 'What the HELL are you going over to your brother's for? It's absssssss-olutely ri-*dic*-ulous! Why on earth don't you ring 'im up? You don't need to go *over* there! Just ring 'im up and do it over the phone!' For the first time in my life I see through the roaring to the feeling behind it: I see that he is worried about me, that he cares about me and loves me. I answer in an ordinary voice: 'Okay. That's a good idea. I'll do that.' The roaring cracks and falls off like a thin coating.

———

I said all I could think of, on the couch, then my mind drifted. After a few moment's silence I said, 'I'm bored. Everything that comes to mind seems pointless.'

'It's as if you think,' she said, 'that most of your thoughts aren't worth saying.'

'I do. I've got a hierarchy of thoughts. Below a certain point they seem trivial.'

Pause.

'The unconscious,' she said, 'works in strange ways. Why don't you say them?'

'Say them?'

'Yes. Say them. Free-associate.'

'Oh! All right!'

And, almost immediately, out poured a stream of images—a woman at the wedding breastfeeding a baby; the Greeks whacking down on the tables great platters of juicy lamb; AB's mother squaring off in front of the wedding cake, running her eye over the crowded tables, and attacking it confidently with a big knife, showing me that it's easy to cut a big cake into 150 small slices and have lots left over. Images of giving, of giving and giving and there still being plenty left.

———

Overnight, it's autumn. A slant to everything, a mildness to the light even late on a hot morning; and very early, when we went out walking round Rushcutters, the air was drier, less weighty on the skin.

———

I told V how the newlyweds had had to go back to the church hall on Monday and clean the forgotten, congealed lamb fat out of the oven. We laughed—not a bad image of marriage, we thought.

'The people running the hall,' he said, 'should make a list of everything that has to be checked by hirers.'

'That's exactly what M said to them. You and M are both Virgos.

Orderly people who like making plans and working out details in advance.'

V: (protesting) 'But I'm *creative*!'

———

G wants to set to music a wonderful series of tiny Chinese sketches that Pierre Ryckmans sent to V.

H: 'What a good idea!'

V: 'It was mine, actually.'

V does have good ideas for other people, often *very* good, the sort of idea that one is surprised not to have had for oneself, the sort that shows his perception of one's imagination.

———

Paul Hasluck's *The Chance of Politics*. Most of the men he's discussing are dead, and his notes about them were made many years ago. How rare it is these days to hear someone firmly, soberly laying down character judgments, assessments based on old-fashioned criteria such as decency, learning, tendency (or otherwise) to vengefulness. Maybe today the very concept of 'character' has been undermined or dismantled—all these theories one hears about the ceaseless construction of 'self', the idea (extremely irritating to me) that there's no such thing as 'stable character'. Everything Hasluck says rings with a very masculine, almost Shakespearean seriousness. It's a gaze I'd dread to be exposed to. Scornful of laziness, falsity, narrowness. I can't put the book down.

———

A woman's voice called my name in the street: X the painter was crossing the road towards me, smiling, tiny and fresh, in high heels, trousers, a little knitted top. We kissed on both cheeks. As we walked up the hill we compared notes on work spaces. She said that if her mother wasn't with her ('but I'm glad she *is*!') she'd sell the flat and buy a place in Surry Hills where she could both live and work. She said her mother needed a place near trees and gardens. At the station we said goodbye, and went our ways, to work.

————

Reviewing a production of *The Seagull* for a new magazine. God, what a play. I started rereading it on the train and was soon in muffled fits of the unique kind of laughter Chekhov provokes—close to tears but at the same time airborne, a light hysteria. The ghastly vain mother, the tormented son, his frightful play and his anguish and rage at her teasing; the person at the lake who remarks casually, 'The angel of silence has flown over us!'

————

A fan was whirring in the room. I had a sudden fear that she wasn't behind me. I twisted round on the couch, to make sure, but yes, there she was, rather closer to me than I'd realised, leaning forward on her chair with her chin resting on her hand, gazing thoughtfully across the room to the opposite corner. 'You were afraid I'd left you,' she said. 'That no one was there to hold you, and to look after you. To feed you.'

I say things now, instead of bottling them up and censoring them.

————

Two American naval ships are berthed at Woolloomooloo. One is immense, its decks thickly packed with helicopters. At each end (like parents, she said later, when I described them) stands a really big chopper, its rotor blades neatly folded in a clump behind, like a bird's wings. After I'd swum twenty laps without stopping I crawled out of the pool, stood on the wooden seat and looked out at the ship. It lay calmly on the water under thick grey clouds. I stood with my stomach and chest up against the sharp bobbles of the concrete wall and my arms along its top, and tears ran down. It was a relief to cry. Not that bottomless wretchedness I've been stuck in for the last few months (which I'm beginning to realise was a stage in therapy—learning to feel things I'd been stoical and blocked about for nearly as long as I've been alive—feelings I had to be helped to stay in, to be held in, until I'd bloody well *felt* them) but a more pointed sort of crying. My daughter, my girl, is a married woman now. And my father's a helpless, motherless barbarian lost for his whole life in a terror of not being fed; and my mother's…whatever she is, if I can ever find out.

———

A letter about the wedding from my first mother-in-law. 'I loved the dancing. I danced with my son. M will always be your and his child.'

———

The Chekhov review was the first thing I'd written in months. I was rusty and creaky, but God! The miracle of the computer! What once would have used up hours of retyping I dashed off in no time at all, inserting my changes briskly, with a pleasant soft clicking. On the way home I had a craving for a brandy Alexander. In the Bayswater Brasserie I watched, in stunned reverie, as the waiter laid the two straws across the rim to make his little pattern with the nutmeg. A dozen glamorous young women were sitting at a nearby table. As they drank they became noisier. I looked at them and tried to imagine being a man: how does one choose a woman from a bunch of strangers? First I chose a sharp-looking girl in black, with an excellent short haircut and a fine neck; then I lit on a softer-looking blonde, with cushiony lips and curved cheeks. Then I got bored, and returned to my private thoughts, such as they were.

———

Swam a kilometre at Boy. I needed a new pair of goggles. The girl at the desk said shyly, 'Buy the non-fogging sort. They're *unreal*.' Funny how guilty I feel when I go swimming early in the morning. I sit at the bus stop churning away: 'I could go to work with my bathers on under my clothes—even if I haven't had a shower—it's already nine o'clock and I shouldn't be out on the street at this hour—I should be at the desk'—all this in spite of the fact that I have nothing to say at the moment and do not know when I will. Everything improves as soon as I get into the water.

———

Some old and dear friends from London (whom V and I both knew, separately, before we met each other) have invited us to spend a few days with them in a borrowed holiday house at Pearl Beach.

H: 'Let's go up for a day and two nights.'

V said no, he wouldn't take time off from work.

I *went* for him. I yelled that he'd become an appalling fanatic, that this might be the last time our friends ever came to Australia— was he too bloody mean to spare them a few of his precious hours?

V: 'Fanatic? Do you think I'm a fanatic? But it doesn't feel fanatical to *me*. *I* don't feel wrong about it.'

H: '*Of course you don't!* You're *inside* it! You *love* it! It's other people who suffer from it! Me! Your *friends*! We don't *see* you any more!'

V: (in bewildered protest) 'I see G.'

I hammered away and eventually, looking almost pleased, he consented to take the train to Woy Woy, stay Tuesday night, and come back with me on Wednesday morning. Next, the phone call to CityRail for timetables. This gave him an opportunity to fulminate against recorded messages, delays, stupid muzak. At last it's all arranged. 'But I'm not leaving the house,' he says 'till I've finished the next chapter.' 'You will finish that chapter,' I say, stabbing him in the chest with a pointed finger, '*by lunchtime tomorrow*.'

———

He's working happily on the book now. He's been sweet to me lately. When the American copies of my book arrived he brought me a bunch of red roses. Later that same day he came into 'my' room and saw that I'd casually propped a collage that my friend had made, and a Renaissance postcard in a tiny frame, against a little Klippel work on graph paper that he'd made me buy, back in the 80s. 'What've you got the Klippel underneath *these* ghastly things for?' I went ballistic: 'You may be in charge of the aesthetic in the rest of the flat but this is *my* room and in this room I will have pictures any way I want.' He said it was 'about *art*, not about whose room it was or whose aesthetic was in control.' I said this was bullshit. By this time we were both in the front hall, shouting. He told me to lower my voice. I told him not to sneer at me. '*That* wasn't a sneer. If you want to see a sneer *I'll* show you a sneer.' He went off to his desk, and I went back into my room and threw the Klippel behind the filing cabinet. I replaced it with a photo of M and AB, and leaned the Renaissance postcard against some books. Then I went into his room and said, 'Still got the shits with me?' And we both cracked up.

———

Baby Ruby in our building, four weeks old. In the lobby I held her while her mother unfolded the pusher. Ruby went on squalling in the crook of my arm, her hair on end, her face red, her tiny socked feet pedalling. I hung on and kept murmuring; she stopped yelling and gave me a long look. Her eyes gently closed. She was asleep.

———

A letter from Elizabeth Jolley, about her bush house that burnt down in the fires: is she at seventy-four too old to rebuild? 'I guess I'll live a bit to see something grow out of the deep black ash—yesterday I was at the one-time orchard and there in all the blackness, an illumination of little pink lamps, were the Easter lilies faithful in every possible way.'

———

Won the Kibble Award for *True Stories*, twenty grand. A new stove! Proper tiling in the kitchen! A trip to Vienna and East Prussia!

Wrote my first movie review for the *Australian's Review of Books*. Typed it straight on to the computer. It took me three hours. Or a bit less, because I went out for a sandwich.

———

X the painter, walking beside me up the street, tells me about her ex-husband. I ask what sort of man he was. 'Oh, he told lies. He could not seem to tell the truth. Not in a *purposeful* way—but yes, he would lie to me. This is one of the things I most hate. People who tell lies.'

———

A colossal American aircraft carrier comes to Sydney. Sailors in white, hands behind backs, stand in a single line along the rim of the deck, a frill of white lace round the huge dark mass that moves grandly up the harbour. The streets of the Cross swarm with sailors. Some of the white ones are raw-looking boys, guzzling Coke, carrying bags full of boomerangs; others, especially the black ones, are young and slender, their skin smooth and gleaming under the brilliant white of the gob caps. They stand about in twos and threes, murmuring to each other: 'Yo. Yo. Hey, man. Wassup? Wass happnin'?'

———

The nakedness of strangers. Every time I go to the Korean Bath-house I feel more free. I can gaze at the perfect, and *differently* perfect, bodies of very young women without envy. May as well envy a tree, or a rock, in its perfect 'thing itself'-ness. And the older bodies flabby or scrawny—marked by child-bearing or overeating or heredity, or just the attrition of gravity—they move me too, with a comradely feeling of respect.

———

V puts on his new Armani jacket and goes out to dinner with X the painter. 'Are you meeting her there?' 'No. I'm picking her up. Bye.'

The door closes. Picking her up? We live between her place and the restaurant. She should be picking *him* up, surely? New customs apply. I continue to file receipts in my tax folder. When I get hungry I go down on to the street. It's warm, getting dark. I walk up to the corner. Don't know what to do. The streets are full of young people, sailors, black and white men. The Bourbon and Beefsteak is hung all along its terrace with large American flags. Everything looks festive, balmy, exciting. I buy three nori rolls with various fillings, and carry them back to our intersection. I don't want to climb the stairs and go inside. I sit in the dark on the low wall of the next-door flats and eat my food. Then I go to the corner shop for a Magnum, gnaw the chocolate coating off it, and throw the rest into a bin.

———

Our neighbour, the Scrabble champion, novelist and China scholar, has been taken apart in a 'profile' by a notoriously savage woman journalist. The week before it came out, having been warned by the magazine editor that it was unfavourable, she sat on our couch and shook with fear. I did my best to prepare her. But when I saw the profile this morning, oh, it was a hatchet job. More vicious, more spiteful and cruel than I could ever have imagined. Nowhere in the article was the sense I have of the China scholar, gained from hours at her kitchen table over the Scrabble board, as a witty, sweet and rather gentle person, clever, thoughtful, full of kindness and laughter. At 4.30 I tapped on her door with a comforting Leunig cartoon and we played a round. She beat me, as she always does, but the words we laid down for each other were elegant and poetical: *mealy, totem, infinite, silky.*

———

I heard that Clive James, in London, has taken up with a woman twenty years younger, with whom he is learning to tango. Imagine! A passionate dancer hidden all these years inside that brain on legs, now unexpectedly set free. I think happily about this when I play Astor Piazzola CDs on my Discman. I've got half a dozen of them now.

———

V says that women's writing 'lacks an overarching philosophy'. I don't even know what this means. Also, I don't care.

———

A pretty little black and brown dog in a studded collar loitered between the tables outside the cafe. A young Japanese couple strolled past, the girl in a childish get-up of pigtails and shorts. The dog darted towards them, and she went into a shrieking panic. We all looked up, astonished. Gibbering and sobbing she dashed sideways and crouched behind a table at which a man in horn-rimmed glasses sat reading a newspaper.

———

I spent several hours, alone and in phone consultation with F, translating a 1983 interview with Thomas Bernhard from *Le Monde*. Translating is good practice: it revives moribund areas of my English vocabulary. I gave the draft to V. Soon I heard him eagerly reading it out to someone on the phone. He hung up and said, 'That was my little friend down the road. She's desperate to have a look at it. Is it okay if I give her this copy?' 'Sure. It's on the computer.' Away he rushes, holding the article in two hands. I remain behind, singing 'Thine Be the Glory' while I scrub the bath. This is better than the other stuff, madness and jealousy. He returns cheerfully. 'She thought it was terrific. But that bit about the wall—she didn't think that sounded like him.' Internally I give a little bristle; but I keep the dog on its leash. She's right—I'd strayed a bit far from the literal meaning of the text, but that part of the text didn't sound like him in French either, because it had been translated from German; there was nothing I could do to fix it. Except call F again, but he must be feeding his kids, so we'll all have to wait. I realise I was hoping to *impress* X with my skill as a translator.

_____

Looking out the window at the two big gum trees, as it gets dark, I think: the only way I can go on keeping a diary—the bits about myself, anyway, i.e. most of it—is to conceive of it as a record of soul. As it were in the presence of God, who is never fooled.

_____

Easter Day. I went to St John's Darlinghurst. Open graves and rolling away of stones and letting all that has been buried be set free. I had furnished myself with a large clean hanky. On the way out I stopped in the porch to flip through the book in which people are invited to write requests for prayers. One of the American sailors must have dropped in, for there was a request that we should pray for the mother of 'a boy from San Antonio Tx: she's been through divorce and stuff. Pray for her and that I get through my service till my time is up.' I stayed for morning tea in the church garden. We had buns with pink icing.

_____

I told her about the two abortions I'd had when I was a student, how, though I see them now as killing, I don't regret them, and remember feeling at the time nothing but relief. And *why*, I asked her, why on earth did I have my tubes tied in the 70s, when there was good contraception, when it was completely unnecessary? 'You wanted to stop yourself, somehow,' she said. 'But *why*?' 'You couldn't stop your mother from having baby after baby; but you could stop *yourself*.' I talked to her about the imagery of the open grave at Easter, the earthquake, the angel in white raiment rolling away the stone. I felt the tears starting and for the first time in her presence I let them come. I lay there and wept and told her that she was, to me, an angel who had rolled away a stone.

There's something dry and tough about the Freudian stuff that I greatly respect, but sometimes I miss the poetic nature of the Jungian approach. 'The Freudian thing,' says R, 'acknowledges that what happens to us makes us what we are. We're stuck in it. We keep re-enacting it, over and over.'

I told her about the crying.

R: 'I've never cried there. I'm scared that if I started I'd never stop.'

H: 'I think what I'm afraid of is getting angry.'

R: 'I've got angry with my guy. Once I got up, grabbed my bag and barged out without even saying goodbye. I slammed the door after me.'

H: 'You slammed the door? I could never do that! She's always pointing out to me that I'm scared of my anger. Often I'll say, "I'm scared So-and-So is angry with me," and she'll say, "I think you're scared that *you're* angry with So-and-So."'

R: 'Okay—I've got a fear of bottomless grief—but what would happen if you got angry?'

H: (flailing blankly) 'Oh—I'd wreck the room or something? I've got no idea. I have no idea whatsoever.'

Days glide past without my *doing* anything. Vague ideas for a hysterectomy story told from the points of view of the medical people who dealt with me. So far only an opening sentence: 'She came in here for a routine check-up.' The mean nurse who stabbed her finger on my faulty staple and asked me in a panic if I had hepatitis: how to give her fear full value while showing how offended I was.

Saw the *Beavis and Butthead* movie last night. It's not as good as the TV show but I loved its utter grossness and moronic stupidity.

———

She wondered whether I could imagine anger without having to act it out. Being angry but just allowing myself to be angry, to *feel* it without doing anything about it.

———

The Polish philosopher is in Sydney for a few days. Dinner out, just the two of us. The remarkable quality of her attention enabled me to talk about the therapy in such a way that there was a loud and continuous sound of pennies dropping. She helped me to grasp what happens on the couch: I'm being held in confrontation with things that in my ordinary life I barely glimpse and then run away from, as fast as my legs can carry me; I'm held there, facing them, with firmness but also in safety.

———

A still, autumn afternoon with low sun. The room too seemed still. An interpretation that she offered was so penetrating and audacious that I lay there with my head spinning. 'I hate you for doing this, for making me stay here when I'm humiliated and hurt. But I also love you for it.' I heard these words come croaking out of my throat, and felt that, at last, after all this time, just fleetingly, I *got* it.

———

An old journalist has published a book about the Easey Street murders, the still unsolved 1977 Melbourne crime that made every share-house-dwelling woman I knew say, 'There but for the grace of God…' It relieved something in me to read that the single mother, Suzanne Armstrong, for all her sexual adventurousness, was someone liked and respected by people who knew her. They told the journo that she was 'clean', 'decent', 'a real straight-shooter'.

———

V announces that he and X now have an arrangement to dine out together 'bi-monthly'. I can't remember if this means twice a month or every two months, and decide not to inquire. They're out tonight. Not a twinge. May this state be sustained, and not by force. I saw an Indian movie, had sushi in the Cross, and answered letters with the headphones on, listening to Errol Garner, *That's My Kick*. Life could be a LOT worse.

———

He came home in good spirits and found me in the same. At bedtime, when I was taking off my watch and earrings, I took off my wedding ring as well and put it on the bedside cabinet, with the vague thought of taking a rest from always having something on my hand. Next morning on our walk I noticed it was gone—'Hey! My ring!'—then remembered where it was. Haven't put it back on yet. Don't want to. Have fantasies of buying myself a different ring, one with coloured stones set flat.

In the evening V wanted to watch *Conan the Barbarian*. I wasn't interested. I went into 'my' room and called an old journalist friend in Melbourne, a guy I used to work for. We gossiped pleasantly for a while. When I emerged V said, 'Who've you been talking to?' I told him. '*What?* All that time?' I looked at my watch. Forty-five minutes had passed.

Of course I 'know' that these behaviours are pathetic punishments for V's regular dinner date with X the painter. I suppose they're petty. They *are* petty. I don't plan them, or intend them, but there they are.

———

On the couch I report the bit about the ring. 'So,' she says in her quiet voice. 'You were sulking.' All my symbolic superstructure collapses. I slink home and put the ring back on. V hasn't noticed anything. The whole drama is being played out inside my head.

———

After communion a parishioner walks to the front and holds up a laminated A4 sheet with flourishes of handwriting on it. 'During the service,' he says, 'one of the Kings Cross bikies came into the back of the church and handed me this. It's a kind of an award.' He reads from it: ' "To St John's Darlinghurst, for services to the Kings Cross community." And it's signed Animal, Steptoe and Feral.' He lowers the paper and looks out at the congregation with a pleasant, ordinary expression. Everyone sits quite still, then there's a faint rustle of movement, and very soft laughter. He steps down and returns to his seat.

———

Astonished again by the intense fatigue that hits me after I've written a piece of journalism, even just an 800-word review. Today I filed a book review, and slept on my office mat till home time.

Towards evening the China scholar knocked on our door and asked me over for Scrabble. She vanquished me once more but I played on in dreamy unambition. *Doubt, pith*. I put down *knee*, and while she pondered her turn I softly sang to myself, free-associating, 'Knee-oh, knee-oh, knee-oh Nazi.' We both collapsed in spasms, heads on the table. I had to run to the bathroom and blow my nose on toilet paper. Then she said earnestly, 'Is *quib* a word?' and we were off again, howling and gasping. This is why we play. For that ecstatic state.

———

Last night and this morning V said that he hated and deplored the thought that I wrote about him in my diary, and worse, that when I died it would be read by M and 'given to a library for people to pore over it'. It was a very vehement statement and although I understood it immediately and saw its truth, I was taken aback and disturbed, also angry in a stunned sort of way—not that I hadn't known about his feelings before, but this time he was taking it right up to me. We talked for a long time. It was awful. It came to a head-on smash between my lifelong habit of recording and analysing my private life, my need and right to do this—and his revulsion against being recorded in *his* private life: both tenable positions, which cannot be reconciled.

I offered to go right back and expunge all—or all unfavourable—mentions of him. He looked sceptical. I said it would be a distortion, but that I'd do it if it was necessary. I also offered not to mention him any more, except procedurally. I said it was the first time I'd had to make a decision between being a writer and being married. He laughed and said I was overstating it. I said I didn't think I was. This morning we spoke further about it. He expressed his revulsion again, but said he felt 'awkward' about seeming to 'demand self-censorship' from me. He said I should write an account of this disagreement, and then continue to write as before. This to me is not quite right. But I don't know what I ought to do instead.

It would be a ridiculous distortion not to write about him at all. There's no way he'll ever understand that writing about my life is the only thing that makes it possible for me to live it. I can't (or won't) give it up. And I won't burn the notebooks or leave instructions for them to be burnt when I die: this last is where he's putting the pressure on. Actually I feel real sympathy for him. It must be awful to know his life is being reported through my eyes. It would be awful to be married to me.

———

From now on I determine not to write about V except in passing.

———

Publisher says that *True Stories* is selling 'eighty to a hundred a day' since it won the Kibble Award. Why so gloomy, then?

———

Gripped by a dumb fear about three lectures I'm to give in Townsville. What on earth can I talk about? I know plenty of practical things, but I don't have a subject, or a line to run. Anxiety so intense that it leaches meaning out of everything, leaves me staring at nothing, empty inside.

———

In Bondi Junction, the building next to the one that contains my tiny office is about to be demolished. I have to keep the window closed all day to block out the sound of the chainsaws. They've lopped the top off a big eucalypt. Went down to the bank and saw the remains of a beautiful plane tree that used to shade the hideous corner of the mall. Now I look out my window and see them savaging a huge, glorious old jacaranda.

———

A letter from Queensland. Her cat: cancerous ear, a burst abscess, blood all round it in the morning. 'I knew I could ask my daughter but I thought if she could shoot a sixteen-year-old cat to put her out of her misery so could I. She mewed for milk and went outside. I went over and over in my mind how I would do it, practised loading and unloading my .410. Went in search and soon found her curled up in a thicket of cannas. She looked at me. I couldn't possibly shoot her face to face so I squatted down quite close and weeded for quarter of an hour. She purred and turned her back to me and fell asleep. I quietly placed the barrel of the gun behind her head and pulled the trigger. A brief limb-jerk. Stillness. Cremation in the incinerator. I miss her. I'm glad she is no more. I rejoice to see fairy wrens and a willy wagtail outside the kitchen and know they are safe from her.'

———

Townsville lectures went all right, I thought. But what I'll remember is that a woman took me snorkelling off Kelso Reef. We went out on a big catamaran. It rained. It was cold. The other passengers stayed in the closed, stuffy lounge, watching nature videos. Two hours out from shore she and I put our togs on and got masks and flippers, and sat in lashing rain on a thick wire platform just submerged. A throng of large pale fish rushed at our legs—gaping mouths and goggling eyes—I squealed but she touched one as a land-person would a cat, saying, 'Hello, beautiful!' Her ease with things marine: in the water she was graceful and fearless, and *hostly*, showing me how to do it. I was anxious about air, kept feeling my mask leaking, had trouble controlling my urge to use my arms in breaststroke; but I tried to copy and follow her. She moved in smooth surges, arms along her sides, hardly seeming to use her feet. Like a little mermaid she rolled on her side, swooped, glided, plunged down to touch something, hung quite still, then twisted and shot away. Because it was raining the water wasn't lit with halls of brightness, like in the commercials, but the fish were extraordinary: minute ones of the most intense blue, smaller than the palm of a hand; and clams, their velvety flesh starred with tiny circular points of iridescent orange, rhythmically gaping and closing inside their crinkled shells.

———

Today, on the couch, as I was relating to her the tale of two little nameless chickens that G's daughter told me had died, there occurred without warning an explosion of meaning, a series of insights that came in a ripple, then an unstoppable current—vital connections that *made themselves* in me, that flowed straight into my mouth from the unconscious, not even passing through my intellect: a dense electric current that ran right through my body. The world spun and went blurry. I was giddy, I thought I was going to faint. I lay there, emptied. She said nothing. She just kept *being* with me. Moments of quiet. The room was tranquil. I thought, 'The room is clean.'

———

The pressure cooker feeling I've had, ever since deciding I wasn't going to write about V any more. A source of consolation and

understanding has been blocked off. But surely I can write that
on Tuesday he showed me the latest fifteen pages of his novel. It's
beautiful. I was moved and impressed, and said so. I said, 'If I could
write anything half as good as that, I'd be thrilled.' He went all
wooden and solemn, and gave a brief lecture on writing 'in and out
of a woman's point of view, which isn't often done'. He asked me if
I was sure it wasn't 'drifting into—*you* know—*mush*'. I reassured
him on this point. Next morning I went for a walk by myself and
thought a lot about the pages he'd shown me. It struck me that this
new writing contains or manifests the exact thing that's been missing
from his previous work—all of it, in fact, except *The Drover's Wife*.
I came home and delivered this insight. It didn't go down too well.
I meant it as an admiring compliment, but he appeared to feel it
(quite stoically) as only criticism. Which it was, I suppose—of the
past—but only in comparison with the new glories of NOW.

————

I'm knocking back work offers, mostly journalism. What I need is
some large project that will push me past *The First Stone*.

————

The Morandi show, with V and his old friend, another painter,
who's the perfect person to look at art with: 'See that white stripe
of road, slanting across? If it wasn't for that, you'd hardly be able to
read the picture at all.' Lovely, calm still lives. As we walked down
the steps V said to him, 'Well—does it make you want to rush home
and grab the brush?' 'Actually,' said the painter in a dreamy tone,
'it doesn't make me want to rush to do anything.'

————

Our friends from north of the harbour here for dinner. So much
fun, I looked at my watch and found with amazement that it was
gone midnight.

————

Letter from a woman I know whose husband had an affair but came back. 'It failed. Transpired he was in contact with her the whole time we were meant to be reconciling. He always wanted isolation, and over the years I kept my family and friends at bay for his convenience. His friends and colleagues became my only friends. Now I feel I have lost everything.'

———————

Algerian taxi driver at Bondi. He remarked gaily on the beauty of the weather: 'a morning like such as this!' We spoke French. He said his family was still in Algeria and couldn't come here: 'They're very poor—and then there's the civil war...' When I got out he said goodbye and something I missed. *'Pardon?'* *'Je suis ravi de vous connaître!'* He was delighted to know me!

———————

Dreamt I visited two journalists I know, a couple, and tore some pages out of a notebook with a decorative cover. They discovered my theft, were offended and upset, and reproached me for having taken liberties with their precious life-records. I was shocked at myself for what I'd done, and sank into a state of disconsolate shame, which soon began to seem to them disproportionate: 'Come on, Helen, cheer up! It's not *that* bad!' I refused to be reassured, and sat in silence with my head down, all achy inside, but also aware that I was sulking, to pay them back for being cross with me.

———————

To the Valhalla with V and G, to see Buster Keaton's *Our Hospitality* accompanied by a live band called Blue Grassy Knoll. The queue and the band consist largely of young, student-looking people; V glares at them suspiciously.

    V: 'One of those musos has got *red hair*.'

    G: (puzzled) 'What's the significance of that?'

    V: 'Aisle seat?'

G looks blank.

H: (interpreting) 'He wants to be able to get out fast, if he doesn't like it.'

G gives V an uncertain smile. We file in and sit down. V points out to us the man with 'red hair'. It's a particularly screaming dye job. The movie is wonderful, the band good-humoured and melodious, with passages of mad racing in the chases. A tremendous river rescue scene; a pretty black sheepdog that runs behind the train, all the way from the city to the mountains. I wished O had been with us: it was exactly his kind of thing.

———

I had so much fun writing my movie review (*Volcano*) that I faxed it to V. When I got home he praised it. 'Really funny. You get this rollicking thing going. Best yet.'

———

Some sort of gastric attack. Had to stay in bed all day. V disappears into his workroom with the cordless. Swimming in and out of nausea I hear him murmuring away, on and on and on. Later in the afternoon I hear 'If you miss Padua…' and 'Why not take the night train, and sleep?' It must be X the painter. They're planning the itinerary of her trip to Europe. It occurs to me that her need to be organised is deeply attractive to him: I tend to resist his offers to direct my life, trips, tax returns, reading matter etc, whereas she asks for it, values it, can happily spend hours in conference with him about it.

———

In order to write freely in here, all I need to do is decide that the book is *for me* and not for 'some bloody archive'.

———

5 am. A night of struggle: apparently X the painter has complained to V that I was 'rude, and cold' to her when she called him the other

morning. In fact I was so surprised that someone was allowed to phone him in his work hours that I just said, 'I'll call him', handed over the phone and went out to work. I wind up on my own in the spare bed. Finally I make a cup of tea and take down Proust's *The Guermantes Way*. He's the king of jealousy: 'It is better not to know, to think as little as possible, not to feed one's jealousy with the slightest concrete detail.' Funny how relieving it is to start reading something beautiful and great. I've laughed several times, and experienced rushes of gratitude.

———

I left for V a note of apology and of promises to be more generous and trusting: 'I've been reading Proust most of the night, about jealousy. I'm ashamed, and see I am being ridiculous.' And I wrote X the painter a letter: 'I am sorry if I seemed cold on the phone. V tells me that the reason you never call in here is that you're not interested in me. I can accept that. I have no trouble understanding why V values his friendship with you. What makes me unhappy is his habit of secrecy and exclusion.'

———

On a bright, cold platform at Central, early on a winter morning, I wait for the train down to G and M-C's in Kangaroo Valley. A young man approaches me: 'Got a lighter?' 'I don't smoke. Can't help you.' We smile at each other. He walks away. I glance down and notice how sparkly the gravel is at the bottom of the gap between train and platform. At the same moment I think, 'I didn't say sorry.' Hurray! I managed an exchange with a man that involved not giving him what he asked for, *without the urge to apologise.*

———

'As soon as jealousy is discovered, it is regarded by the person who is its object as a challenge which justifies deception.' —Proust, *The Guermantes Way*

———

Outside Bomaderry station I tore up the letter to X and chucked it in the rubbish bin.

———

How happy G and M-C and their girl are, down here, in this valley! Bright air. The treetops sparkle. M-C and I went for a walk in gumboots this morning, scrub-bashed down a steep creek bed above which vegetation strove in an arch to blot out the sky; our clothes were torn at by long thorns on slim, bouncy shoots. The German shepherd pup slunk and slithered along beside me. 'These bad times,' said M-C, 'seem to go in three-year bursts. Then you break through into five or seven good years.' At bedtime she brought me a hot water bottle. It was still warm at 4 am.

———

In the evening V calls. Speaks about how terribly tired he was after our wakeful night, but said he had worked all day and finished a new chapter. Strain in his voice. After three forced minutes he started making about-to-hang-up noises.

   H: 'Is it over?'

   V: 'What?'

   H: 'Aren't we going to talk any more? Didn't you get my note?'

   V: 'Yes, I got your note.'

   H: 'I thought you might have mentioned that you'd got it.'

   V: (irritably) 'Yes, I did get it. Of course I got it. It was a sad note. I wasn't going to start talking about all *that*—not while you're down *there*.'

———

'Such are the revolving searchlights of jealousy…Despair at having obtained fidelity by force: despair at not being loved…Here I mean by love reciprocal torture.' —Proust, *The Guermantes Way*

———

M-C and G talked about the garden they've made, hacking out a space, planting, growing fruit: 'It's saved our relationship,' said M-C. 'Living in a flat is a recipe for insanity.' *Living in a flat.* A factor I had forgotten. We invented a little caravan somewhere on their property—laughed about it. Further fantasy, in private: get out of the flat. Get my own place to live and work in. Not in his suburb. I don't want to see them together in the street. I want my bed, my stereo. What's stopping me from doing this? Reluctance to 'bolt', to wreck something that still has life in it.

———

I told V (leaving X the painter and my jealousy aside for the moment) that our marriage was so close to dead that if we didn't get some air and light back into it soon, it *would* die, just from the normal attrition of marriage, the inertia and casualness and laziness that everyone slides into. He said he couldn't stand the way I refused advice, or help—my 'refusal to *be told*'. I said we lived alongside each other now, barely engaging, barely even looking at each other. Even sex had lost any emotional contact. In the middle of this quiet talk, my nose began to bleed.

———

I rang up X and said I was sorry if I'd seemed 'rude and cold' to her on the phone. She was puzzled: 'I didn't think you'd been rude and cold?' 'Oh. That's what V told me you'd said.' We didn't know what to say next. But wished each other well and hung up. This must be what G meant when he said he thought of V as 'a manipulator; a spider in the middle of the web'.

———

Walking down Mona Road at dawn yesterday we heard raised voices. A couple on the footpath—man in a tracksuit with his back to us, obscuring everything of the woman except her arms, which were flung out from her sides in a wild gesture. We got closer, heard the woman (late thirties, short blond hair, tight dark pants and high-heeled boots) cry out desperately, 'Why don't you put me out of my misery and *tell* me?' while over her the man was shouting, 'Listen! You're not *allowed* to follow me round!' His hair was still ruffled from the pillow, he was carrying two takeaway coffees. We walked away down the hill without a word. This morning as we passed the spot, now empty, V said, 'I wonder what happened to that bloke.'

———

Jeff Buckley has drowned in the Mississippi.

———

V tells me he is now the executor of X the painter's will, and of her mother's.

———

I told V that the matter of my daily banishment from the flat is like a little stone that lies in the bottom of my heart and never goes away; it only shrinks occasionally. He replied that if he rented a flat outside and I worked at home, it would simply be a reversal—that *he* would then be the unjustly treated one.

———

He shows me a new chapter of his novel. It's *very* good—warm and touching—I loved it, and admired it as openly as possible without frightening him. 'It's not mush, is it?' he keeps asking. I reply again and again, 'V, there is not the slightest tinge of mush in it.'

———

He's made a proper will at Perpetual Trustees. He tells me about his bequest to X: $20,000 and the little black McCahon painting of a hill—a painting I like very much: when he brought it back from New Zealand he would often say, fondly, 'How do you like your McCahon?'

V: 'You're getting the flat, though I have to say—and I hope this won't be taken the wrong way—it's occurred to me that when *you* die, the flat will go to M and AB.'

H: 'Oh. And—you'd prefer that not to happen?'

V: 'Well, they won't *need* it. Anyway I hardly know them, AB anyway, and I'm not close to M at all.'

H: 'I hope you don't think I'm secretly going, "Oooh, great! When I get this flat off him I'm gonna give it to my daughter!"' (Making clawing motions with both hands.)

V: 'No! I don't think that at all! Not for a moment! Because you're not *like* that! There's not even a hint of that in you. It's one of the most attractive things about you.'

H: 'Listen, why don't you rethink the flat? I don't want you to leave it to me. Leave it to someone you *want* to have it. Someone who needs it. Why don't you leave it to X?'

V: 'Why on earth would I want to do that?'

H: 'I dunno. Same reason as the twenty grand? Actually I am a bit sore that you didn't ask me about the painting, though. You always said it belonged to both of us.'

V: 'But she's a painter. And she's mad about McCahon. Obsessed with him. And when I lent it to her, you didn't even notice it was gone till two weeks later. Also, you haven't left me anything, have you. You've left everything to M.'

H: 'I haven't got anything to leave. What do I own? My parents own my house. Everything else of mine is already yours and mine— the books and the stereo and the bed and the fridge and a couple of filing cabinets and some CDs.'

V: 'And a computer.'

All this was quietly and harmoniously spoken but to me it was rather ghastly. At one point I said that his leaving me the flat empty of its meaningful items was an image of what I'm afraid is happening to us lately: I've still got his physical presence, but everything alive and emotional and personal inside him is being directed elsewhere—to his novel, and to X. To this he made no response.

———

He says that when I die, boxes of my diaries will be delivered to M and AB's house, and that they and their friends will 'sit around the kitchen table reading bits of it out loud'. I was staggered: 'They're not like that! They're not that sort of person!' He says he will bet fifty bucks that seventy-five per cent of the mentions of him in the diary are unfavourable. I don't dispute this, since it's probably true, but I try to argue that I'm not just whingeing, that I'm making an attempt at analysis, of myself as well as of him. This is no comfort.

———

J's in town with his new novel. He came to church with me this morning. We skidded into the front pew just in time to say, 'And also with you.' The vicar spoke about a murdered girl whose body had been dumped in the lane behind the rectory. 'What are Christians supposed to do when things seem hopelessly black and despairing? What is "faith" under these circumstances?' He says Christians have to live as if there were no God—no God 'jogging along behind our shoulder whispering messages of encouragement or instruction'. He said that the opening words of the Bible were useful: that God spoke out of chaos and darkness. 'We just have to stumble on.'

———

J came back to our place for lunch. When V opened the door, J seized him in a huge, full-frontal hug. V mortified but perhaps pleased somewhere under his stiff manly exterior. J teases him roughly, makes him laugh.

———

V complains about my 'sadness'.
    H: 'It won't go on forever.'
    V: 'How do *you* know.'

———

A tree hangs over the street from inside her fence. As I come down the street I notice for the first time that it's completely bare. Thin black branches and twigs. I say to her that I feel 'pretty leafless myself at the moment'. She points out that I seem to see only two extreme possibilities in my relationship with V: capitulation or departure.

'What do you feel you have to do, in order to be in an intimate relationship?'

H: (abruptly) 'Shoot myself in the foot. Cut bits off myself. Become abject. Because if I don't, I won't be loved. I'll go to Europe and he'll have an affair with X the painter. I'll go to Europe and someone else will take my spot with you. Someone with *perfume*.'

———

A postcard from M: 'Today there's a man working under our house, restumping. I have to write an essay on Hugo, Baudelaire and Mallarmé; he has to dig holes lying down. And it turns out he was one of those refugees who stowed away in a ship container, and lived on tomato sauce for weeks.'

———

The matter of V and his will took several days to work itself out from under the concrete. The jackhammer was wielded by a friend I ran into at a book launch: during the speeches we moved to one side and started talking. I swore her to secrecy and told her that my husband had 'a woman friend' to whom he had recently, without first consulting me, willed a painting I'd believed belonged to both of us. She stared at me with her mouth hanging open: 'He *what?*' In return she confided in me certain painful recent events in her marriage, which astonished me in that I would never have suspected them from her husband, though they were routine betrayals. We stood against a wall in the gallery, looking into each other's faces. A pause.

She said: 'Do you get angry?'

'Yes. Very, very angry.'

'Do you yell?'

'No. Mostly I bottle it up, and keep trying to argue.'

'I yell,' she said. 'And I've got a filthy mouth.'

We had to look at the floor to control ourselves. I said, 'This'd make a great scene in a movie.' We decided to have dinner soon and get drunk.

———

V and I went to the Verona to see *Swingers*. It was very funny. There weren't many people in the cinema, and by a curious acoustic quirk the reactions of a man sitting behind V and one seat further along reached my ears so clearly that I kept thinking it was V himself letting out little breaths of laughter. Several times I glanced at him in surprise, only to see the Mount Rushmore profile, grim and resistant, while beyond him the other man's teeth and eyes shone in the light from the screen.

———

In the restaurant we argued fiercely, in low, furious voices. I knew that the idea of fighting in a public place, even one as ill-lit and music-dominated as the Verona, would be his worst nightmare; but I'd stopped caring. Inside me seethed a La Brea Tar Pit of rage. I said what I really thought and kept on saying it. 'Without consulting me you left her that painting, that you said again and again was mine, and ours? Now I learn in this crude legalistic way who the painting always belonged to. All the things you said to me about it were just bullshit.'

We walked home, quarrelling bitterly all the way.

'You don't want me to see her at all, do you?'

'I want you to level with me. I want you to be open to me, and not to have a secret from me that frightens me and makes me jealous. If it's "just a friendship like any other", as you say, why does it have to be behind my back?'

In the flat we fought on, drinking glass after glass of water. I kept pushing. I lost all restraint. I shouted and shouted. He sat leaning back hard against the cushions, with his legs stretched out and his feet on a chair, a posture that looked in its lines like relaxation but was a desperate attempt to appear in control. He kept his head tilted back and stared at me down his cheeks with eyes sardonically half-closed. He stared me down again and again. I had to drop my eyes against the cold power of his stare. He kept saying, 'Stop shouting. *Please* stop shouting. It agitates me. It agitates everything. You don't have to shout. Be *nice*. Be *polite*.' I almost laughed. I stopped shouting. I lowered my voice. But I spewed out the stuff: how he'd expected me to recover from serious surgery much too fast, how I'd been given a week at home and then had to get up and get out of his way and soldier on—how I'd needed to be looked after, but my weakness was nothing to him but a nuisance. He blasted me again for going to a 'shrink', for 'starting to use shrink-talk'. In the middle of this assault he asked, 'Do you think *I'd* get any benefit from analysis?' He asked this aggressively, as if he knew he wouldn't and that for me to say he might would be further evidence of my having been brainwashed. I said, 'Yes, I do. It's almost impossible without help to see yourself, your emotional and mental habits.' We swept on past it. The old central homelessness stone was heaved up again, and again rejected: 'You knew I was like that when we got together.' 'Yes. It was made clear to me the day after you got back from Africa and I was *out on the street*.' I said that in his obsessive struggle to write this novel he'd systematically stripped us of shared endeavours and activities—no car, no garden, no children welcomed, no holidays—there was nothing left.

I said he'd better decide what he wanted—a proper marriage with trust and openness, or a continuation of this moribund charade with his secret life running along underneath it. I said that if he chose the latter I was leaving.

We fell asleep exhausted. Scared and chastened. Next morning was calm, but doomy. He looked resolutely on the blackest side: I was probably leaving; he spoke of this with resignation, as if he had no feelings about it. I said, and he seemed to agree, that it wasn't surprising we clashed like this: we'd got together as adults, and since we were writers, each of us had a horror of being engulfed by the other, and had to fight against it.

———

Next evening he announced bluntly: 'I called Perpetual Trustees. The painting's yours.' Did he really think this was about me *wanting the painting*? Awkwardly I thanked him. An hour later he added, 'But I've still left her the $20,000.' 'Yep. Okay. It's your money. And did you leave her the other little McCahon?' Up comes his chin, his eyes narrow: 'Yes. Is that all right?' 'Of course! It's yours.'

I wanted to add, 'But why didn't you just tell me? Why did I have to ask you—even after all that, last night?' I kept my mouth shut. He has a powerful need to withhold information from me—tiny, crucial pieces of the jigsaw—so that my picture of what's going on is always incomplete.

'And listen,' he said. 'When you decide to pack your bags, can you wait till I've finished this bloody book? Do what you have to do—but can you hang on till it's done?'

'As if I'd dream of walking out at this stage. Of course I won't.'

In the morning I did a load of washing and he helped me hang it on the rack. I asked him to make me a coffee, and he did. As I was leaving for work he said, 'Have you taken an apple?'

Small acts of kindness. I'm not used to this.

———

I'm coming to see that he has no conceptual equipment—nothing that would help him to analyse a mess like the one we're in. All he can do is repeat his statements of will and purpose. But when I calm down and start taking things apart, he listens to me and almost always agrees. Or appears to. Because what I say lets him off the hook. Of 'right' and 'wrong'. Neither of us is a criminal. At those moments I have a powerful sense of myself as *working*.

———

We're engaged in a bitter struggle to define ourselves, each against the other. He sets his face against things that have meaning to me; and my urge is to split hairs and demand exactitude. I suppose I'm just as unbearable to him as he is to me.

———

Good Weekend asks me to go on an Antarctic cruise in December.

———

'I know this mightn't sound very good,' he said, 'but why do you imagine that anyone would be interested in reading your diary? Reading about your life—about our lives?'

We discuss diaries as a literary phenomenon. Eventually I say, 'Look—how about I put a hundred-year embargo on them?'

'A hundred years? They wouldn't want to do that.'

'I can put any length of embargo I fuckin' well *like* on them.'

He brightens. 'I s'pose you can. Yeah—maybe that's the thing to do.'

———

V's sick, diarrhea and vomiting. He's in bed, fully dressed but minus shoes. I stay home from work to look after him. He rejects my care in his surly way. The phone rings halfway through the morning. I answer, someone hangs up.

———

Drank cocktails in a bar with G and M-C before a play at the Opera House. (V wouldn't come.) It was so bad that halfway through the first act we fought our way along the row and rushed out into the rain. We took a cab to the Landmark and sank a few more martinis. Poor G with his hep-C liver had to content himself with a hot chocolate. Cracking jokes and shouting about the terrible play, we gorged ourselves on biscuits and then a platter of sushi. A thunderstorm burst, with lightning. At 12 I said goodnight and trotted home in torrential rain that gushed so wildly down Greenknowe that the tyres of parked cars sent up rows of little fountains eighteen inches high.

———

Janet Malcolm has reviewed *The First Stone* in the *New Yorker*. Exhilarating, a critique by someone who wouldn't know me from a bar of soap. Her concentration on the *process* intrigued me: as if her cool mind had been gazing down from a height while I went through my contortions. I thought, 'How conscious *can* one be, while thinking about something and writing about it? How conscious is Janet Malcolm, for example, writing her review?' I was dizzy, thinking of the eternally receding layers of unconsciousness on unconsciousness, peeling back for ever and ever. Then I felt thrilled to bits: she has *read* me. Even her disagreements don't sting, because she writes as if *I* had written almost unconsciously. How mysterious this is. (Also, she used the expression 'this extraordinary book'.)

———

At the Korean bathhouse with M-C. We scrubbed each other's backs. School holidays, a lot of young women there. When she was called for a shiatsu I lay back in the ginseng tub and went into a trance of gazing. It was like being inside an enormous painting: women's frank postures, in the absence of men—they sit naked on the low stools with knees wide apart and buttocks spread under their weight, almost squatting. Some, with long hair, sit with both arms raised to deal with the mass or the length of it, head tipped forward, lengthening the spine. These postures were so unaffected and graceful that my eyes blurred and a lump came into my throat: a sort of euphoria.

———

Dreamt I was in bed, in a squalid student house, with a scrawny, pale, red-headed, very young man who was pressing me for sex. He was inexperienced and excited, but I sensed that under all his bravado he disliked me, and probably disliked all women. When he'd finished, with a great deal of noisy triumph, I saw there was blood on the sheet. I grabbed his shoulders and forced his attention to it: 'Look. One of us is bleeding.'

———

We were invited to Bryan Brown and Sam Neill's birthday party at the Passenger Terminal, Darling Harbour. It was a *grand bash*. I'd never been to one like it. V wouldn't come, though he's the one who knows Sam Neill. M was in town and he gave her his ticket. We went in a cab with an elegant journo friend of mine. We danced and *danced*. I didn't think I'd feel like keeping on dancing, but I did, and it was fabulous. By 2 am M and I were whispering at the bathroom mirror, taking off our make-up. She kissed me goodnight. At breakfast V asked for an account of the bullet he'd dodged: expressed the usual horror, disgust, amazement etc, and relief at not having gone. We pressed on and eventually got a few laughs out of him. I think he was sorry he'd missed seeing the haka.

———

The other morning V and I headed up the hill early to La Buvette, for a quick coffee together before I left for work. But its espresso machine had broken down. As we walked glumly away, trying to decide on a substitute cafe, he said, 'You could come back to my place.' Shocked by the slip, I laughed. He was abashed. He is now floating the idea of our living separately: he won't 'discuss' it, because he doesn't 'want to think about anything but the bloody book', but occasionally he mentions it, pointing out that 'other writers have done it successfully'. On a rational level I see it's a good idea ('people who get on each other's nerves') but my stomach drops with dread.

————

At the Byron Bay festival a screenwriter spoke about the theme of her latest movie: 'the fact that romantic love must die'. Several women near me bristled at her blunt statement. 'Thanks very much!' said one of them under her breath.

————

The woman driving my cab told me that she had lost three babies to cot death, then had to have a hysterectomy.

'Why?'

'Cancer.'

Her husband 'couldn't cope with it', and left her. Her one surviving child was now a teenager: 'He means everything to me.'

'Gee. You've had a rough time.'

She shrugged: 'Everyone has bad stuff to deal with.'

'Not that bad. You've had it tougher than most.'

'Oh, I stopped making comparisons a long time ago.'

At parting we shook hands.

————

I read in a tabloid paper about a young woman who went to Bateman's Bay and with 'two men for company' gave birth to a baby. They left it on the beach and went away. Later she went to a hospital. The men led the police to the spot where the baby had lain all night. It was alive. 'After a bath and a feed, the little girl was doing fine.' On the couch, telling her this and the story of the taxi driver, I started to cry. Not wild sobs, or any sort of sobs, really. Just deep spasms, trembling voice, tears running into the cushion. Grieving at last. A generation later. For my two dead ones. The babies I killed before they could even become babies. When I was barely twenty. The enormity of it opens and closes inside me like a door. 'I think you're talking,' she said, very low, 'about the life force and the death force. In yourself.'

————

Since this, I've been lighthearted: as if I'd excavated right through a whole planet's worth of buried sorrow and broken out into air on the other side: like the mountains I saw from the beach at Byron, a low band of them, going back and back, layer upon layer, paler and paler, with tops of curly complexity.

————

V is being unusually charming, sweet and forthcoming. He keeps offering to *do* things. Today we went shopping for food together at his instigation. I did wonder if this might have something to do with a letter he recently showed me from his enormously admired correspondent Pierre Ryckmans. In it Ryckmans took up the matter of a *New Yorker* piece V had sent him about Nabokov and the incredible devotion of his wife: Ryckmans remarked that he had always found in Nabokov's work a certain coldness or lack of humanity, and opined that his wife might have done better to be a little less devoted: *he* might perhaps have 'gone out for the groceries', now and then, for example, with profit. Whatever the reason, anyway, the mood between us has lightened. We are liking being together again. We have conversations. We lie in bed talking to each other. I did not think this was possible. 'The revolving searchlights of jealousy' have switched themselves off, of their own accord. Yesterday X called and I passed the phone to him pleasantly. After they'd hung up, V grabbed me and gave me a kiss and called me 'darling'. *Hello???* 'Do you want,' he said, 'to go out for lunch on Thursday?' '*What?* Are you asking me out to lunch? Oh, I'd love it!' He looked up with a crooked smile, as if he thought I was being ironic, but I must have had a thrilled look on my face. 'Why are you doing this?' He writhed his shoulders: 'Aw...y' going overseas, 'n'...' Next, he announced casually that he would come to the airport with me on the bus. This was so utterly out of character that I nearly keeled over.

———

V reported a dream while we were walking up the steep part of Yarranabbe Road: 'We were in a station wagon, and there was a bear in the back. It was dead, and yet alive. I got in the back next to it. It was a beautiful bear, liver-coloured. I thought it was dead, but then it yawned.' I said, 'Mmmm,' not wanting to scare him. 'Well,' he said in a provocative tone, 'what does *that* mean?' Subtext: 'It doesn't mean anything, and you're deluded if you think it does.' I played it with a straight bat: 'I wouldn't presume to interpret someone else's dream. What do *you* think it means?' 'I wouldn't have a bloody clue.' I asked a few questions: was the car moving? Who was driving? And so on. He replied with increasing vagueness, so nothing came of it, and I let it drop. But secretly I thought, 'That bear is our marriage. It looked dead but then you paid it some attention and found it was still alive.'

———

Several journalists call me from London about *The First Stone*. An hour of lively but nerve-racking talk. After this V and I go to dinner at the Brasserie with a couple of his art-world friends. 'So!' says the man. 'I didn't realise you were going overseas next week—that explains why you're so jumpy!' 'Jumpy? I'm not jumpy!' 'Yes you are,' he says. 'You've been jumping and twitching in your seat all evening!' V chimes in: '*Yes*! You're *jumpy*!' I burst out: 'Oh, get fucked. Both of you.' V turns away with distaste: 'Why talk like that? It's coarse, and rude.' The woman speaks up in my defence. The man withdraws, smiling. V gives me scorching glances of disgust and disapproval. I try to sit still, full of angry shame at having lost my temper and shown my ugly side. Soon I go upstairs to the toilet. When I come back, the vibe at the table has changed. At my approach, the woman sits back as if interrupted while talking about me, and says with a friendly look, 'I've been sticking up for you.' 'Thanks.' V's glance is less hostile. I say, 'I'm sorry I was rude.' The man replies magnanimously, 'There's nothing to be sorry about. You weren't rude.' 'Yes, I was. I'm sorry.' He offers his hand. I take it and kiss it. We all laugh, rather awkwardly. On our way out of the restaurant the woman and I walk on ahead and she murmurs to me, 'Funny, isn't it, how they can't stand anger.'

I have to act in a clean stroke, not hedge my actions with little requests for guarantees and reassurances. I have to decide what I need, and act on that. Fantasy of a sunny flat. Up high.

The foundation-rocking demolition in Bondi Junction mall has let me out of the lease. A magazine journalist neighbour has offered me her spare room, a hundred metres up the hill from our flat. Restful and private. I dashed off a thousand-word piece for a magazine in a morning: it shows, but I don't care.

To the opera with Z. *Giulio Cesare*. A wonderfully pure and elegant production. So long since I'd seen Z, I'd forgotten how much I like him, and what generously knowledgeable company he is.

A visiting American woman, hearing I was about to go to London, said, 'It'll be summer there—do you know?'

London. 2 am in my publisher's spare room. A cramp in my left leg. Half awake I did the worst possible thing, pointed my toe. A wrench of pain threw me on to the floor. My calf was rock hard, twisted

into a square block. I had to clench my teeth so as not to wake the
whole house with my grunts and whimpers. Gradually it loosened
its grip. I'm sweating. The room is stifling. The window is huge,
but it gives direct on to the street so I don't dare try to open it. What
the fuck am I doing here.

_____

My publisher's husband is learning guitar. While she cooks, calling
out friendly remarks from the kitchen, he shyly plays me the music
his Brazilian teacher is soaking him in. He's got a sweet sort of reverence for what he's learning: 'Listen to this!' Bossa nova, samba, I
don't know the difference but I love it, even when it's only a beginner
playing it. We drink a lot of wine. They're easy to hang out with,
I like them, though there's a tiny part of me that still cringes at an
educated English voice. Maybe Australians of my age never get over
that cringe. It must be a regression to the time a teacher mocked me
for my state-school accent when I first opened my mouth in private
school, but in the company of well-spoken English people I always
feel I'm the youngest person in the room. Not really a grown-up.

_____

I'm pretty sick of talking about *The First Stone*. I can't get excited
about it any more. Like me, it doesn't belong here. Still, they've
brought me here, so I'll soldier on.

_____

At the BBC, in what I suppose was a 'green room', I sat against a
wall with a couple of other unfamous writers who were waiting to
be interviewed. One was a woman doctor, I guess about forty, who'd
published a book—it must have been her first—on some medical or
social matter, and was working herself into a state of frantic terror.
She had a foolscap pad on her lap and was wildly scrawling page
after page in enormous writing. I could hardly bear to watch her.
She looked up at us and said with an angst-ridden laugh, 'If I take

my notes in with me I'll be all right!' Everyone uttered meaningless murmurs. Not a single one of us put a hand on her arm and said, 'Listen—throw the notes away. You know more about your book than any bloody interviewer. You're the world expert on it! Trust yourself!' Why didn't we try to save her? Was it a lack of nerve? A social paralysis of a special English kind? Or maybe we were all faking, and she was acting out the suppressed panic of everyone in the room. I can't *believe* I didn't say anything to her. In my ridiculous accent.

––––––

In a department store I tried on a sea-green sort of raincoat, calf-length, made of soft synthetic material. For a light shower rather than a downpour. When I did up the belt I looked silly in it, waistless and boxy. I could have howled. I pulled the belt out of its loops and threw it on the floor. That's when I saw the point of the coat. It was cut to swing out behind you when you turned. I bought it and walked to the National Gallery. I lengthened my stride to make the coat flow. No one knew me and I was elegant. In the gallery I stood in front of a Cézanne with my hands in my new pockets. An apple in the painting was so intensely green and perfect that I felt its coldness in my palms.

––––––

The publisher threw a little drinks party for me on my last night, at her house. I was mortified with shyness. At one point I sneaked away into another room, to hide. It was dim in there. A woman was sitting in an armchair in the corner. Not doing anything, just sitting with her hands folded in her lap. I looked at her helplessly. She smiled up at me. It was Margaret Drabble. I said, 'I'm no good at parties.' She laughed: 'Neither am I.' If I'd had my wits about me I would have said, 'I loved that book of yours where the character called Rose Vassiliou takes a guy to look at a bombsite with chickens roaming about on it.' But the party was ending and the guests were going home, probably wondering why the publisher had bothered to host such an ingrate. When I get back to Sydney I'm going to write Margaret Drabble a fan letter.

———

The Freud Museum in Vienna. It's in the apartment he and his family lived in, Berggasse 19. You are issued with a catalogue in your own language, which explains each item on display. Many photos. They've used quotes from Freud's writings, very charmingly and humanly, in connection with the exhibits. While most museums are full of people moving in a steady stream past the things on display and only fleetingly stopping to concentrate, the visitors to the Freud Museum stood for a long time in front of each item, carefully reading the accompanying text from the catalogue, then moving on. The rooms were very quiet. The only sounds to be heard were the soft shifting of rubber soles and the squeaking of the parquet floor. I stayed there for an hour or so. I loved looking out the windows. The courtyard had been modernised. The big street windows let in a lot of light. A strange feeling to be in the rooms where his patients used to wait, let alone the consulting room itself. I couldn't help thinking how much anguish must have walked up those stairs to the apartment. The house doesn't look at all grand from the street, but when you go through the heavy entrance doors suddenly you're confronted with a huge marble staircase. The landing over the courtyard has big panes of decorated glass. Didn't one poor woman throw herself down that staircase and die?

———

Travelling alone. I am no good at this. In Vienna a horrible modern hotel, Ibis. Poleaxed by a frightful cold. Been lying here for a day and a night and another day, choking and hacking away.

———

Three days in bed. This morning I'm better. What is one supposed to do, in Vienna? I walk past the Opera House. *Tristan*. The last night of the season. The only name I recognise is that of the conductor, Zubin Mehta. I timidly approach the box office and in my rocky German ask for a ticket. We have one left, says the woman. It's in the middle of the front row of the stalls.

———

Saved again by music. Four hours of it. Oh, it was glorious. In the intervals, here, you can run upstairs to a grand lobby and buy yourself a sweet bun! A ferocious espresso in a little china cup! It was the perfection of solitude. Nothing broke my reverie and it flowed on forever.

———

Six o'clock on a bright Sydney September evening. I emerge from customs, carefully arranging my features into a nonchalant expression. V not in sight. I trundle my case towards a seat. Twenty minutes later a grey-faced, grey-haired man with hunched shoulders drifts past in the thin crowd. He hasn't seen me. An absence of pleasure at the sight of him, a blankness, nothing. I call out, he turns, his face springs into focus: 'The bus was late.' Pecks my cheek. He would have got back on a bus. I say, 'Let's get a cab.' And away we go. Gradually, gradually, as time passes and he cooks some frozen ravioli and makes me have a shower and we drink a glass of wine, feeling seeps back into the occasion. I admire the old sofa that's been re-covered in my absence. I labour to drag facts out of him about the progress of his book. I sleep, we sleep.

———

A brilliant, dry morning. Currawongs are calling near our building; they've been awake all night, in the park. Light so clear and pure and bright that we have to shield our eyes when we walk into it. Up the hill to La Buvette. On the street everyone has that blessed

look, smiling and looking up at the sky and the fresh-leaved trees.
It must be spring.

———

He disappeared all day. I went out for food and made lunch. He
didn't turn up or call. Late afternoon the key in the door. I call
out a greeting. His response is a loud groan: 'My *back*.' I can't help
laughing: it's the same gambit he used on the night he sneaked out
to X's place with the paper punch while I was at the theatre: 'Look.
Something's wrong with my *eye*.' He's like those birds that pretend
to have a broken wing, to lure predators away from their chicks.
Turns out he's taken the train to her studio in Erskineville, where
she is frantically trying to get enough pictures ready for the catalogue photographer. No doubt looking cranky, I cook the dinner.
He comes into the kitchen and asks impatiently, 'What's wrong?
What's the *matter*?' 'You could have rung me.' He blusters away. I
can't raise the energy to say the same old things: 'Why do you sneak?
Why don't you just tell me?' I produce a good meal and serve it with
eye contact and a smile. As usual he eats doggedly, looking into his
plate, as if it were a pile of baked beans, then ten minutes in recalls
himself and makes a perfunctory comment. After dinner we listen
to Derek Jacobi reading the *Iliad*. I think it was Christa Wolf who
wrote, 'To whom can I say that *The Iliad* bores me?'

———

Today I reached the end of his novel. I was filled with admiration
and enjoyment, and said so. My only criticism was that he'd used
the word 'spreading' about a dozen times. I pointed this out very
delicately. We both laughed. I gave many sincere and thoughtful
compliments. He touched my arm and said, 'You're a good person.'
Later he said, 'I care more about what you think of it than anyone
else. Isn't it funny how different we are.'

———

Mild waves of ordinary affection come and go. But the atmosphere of the marriage is stifling and frustrating. He has turned outwards and found himself someone new to spark things up. I suppose I could do the same. If I wanted to. If I could be bothered.

———

'Theirs was practised, undramatic love-making, a set of protocols and assumptions lovingly followed like a liturgy which points to but really has little connection with the mysteries and chaos that had once made it a breathless necessity.' —Richard Ford, 'The Womanizer', *Women with Men*

———

V's birthday. I give him two books (Virgil, Lampedusa) and head out to work. Halfway through the morning I come home to pick up a forgotten notebook and find X the painter at our street door, buzzing. I greet her, she spins around. We kiss in greeting.

H: 'Are you going up?'

X: 'No. He's coming down, I'm carrying too much, I've brought his present.'

V appears, iron-faced. Apparently X and her mother had earlier sung happy birthday to him on the phone. 'Was it silly?' she says, smiling at him with a manic intensity. 'Did you think it was silly?' They go up the street to have a coffee, leaving me on the doorstep.

———

When I get home he's on the cordless. He flaps his hand at me: don't interrupt. I go into the other room.

Turns out it was X, in her studio, completely hysterical, screaming and sobbing, she's been destroying paintings, she's in total despair, if it weren't for her mother she'd hang herself, she's let everyone down who's helped her and given her the prize and so on.

'She depends on you now, doesn't she.'

'Yes, she does.'

―――――

Her birthday gift that morning was a two-volume Schocken hardback edition of Kafka's diaries. He has ditched our old paperback and installed the new ones in its place. Virgil and Lampedusa are already on the books-we-don't-want pile.

―――――

I lie silent on the couch.

'I think,' she says, 'that you might be depressed.'

'Depressed?' I snap. 'I'm not "depressed". I'm just suffering from incapacitating sadness.'

Pause.

'Actually,' she says, 'that's not a bad definition of depression.'

―――――

We lie under the doona quietly talking. He tells me why his friendship with X the painter is important to him: 'She's a good person. She's good when she talks about art—she's *veeeery* good when she talks about art. And about certain aspects of literature. I respect her for her independence. She's not bogged down in any theory or ideology.'

'She's not independent at the moment. She's dependent on you.'

'Yes but that's because she's having an artistic crisis.'

'It's not an "artistic" crisis, V. It's a psychological one.'

'Oh, it's impossible to talk to you without you correcting everything I say.'

―――――

I ask him what he finds hardest to bear about me. He cuts across my question: 'Your *anger*.' He says he can't bear my family, their 'rudeness and selfishness', and their total lack of interest in him. He doesn't want to have any more to do with them. He says I may not like X's mother singing happy birthday to him but *my* mother doesn't even know when his birthday is.

I say I'd hoped the completion of his novel might be a good moment to renegotiate our living conditions: 'Could you contemplate the prospect of my not going out to work every single morning, as before?' 'But I'd hear you moving about,' he says, 'and talking on the phone.' It soon becomes clear that he is not prepared to change anything: 'It's what I *am*. There's a long precedent. When we got together there was a double given—I'd always worked at home, you'd always worked outside. Anyway what would the difference be, between a flat of your own and what you've got now?' I start to laugh: 'The fact that you can ask that shows you haven't ever understood a single word of anything I've said, all these years!' 'But what *would* the difference be?' 'A comfortable bed to nap on, or to lie on and read. A kitchen, where I can cook myself something for lunch, or invite someone for a meal. Music to listen to. *Books*, V. Reference books.' 'What reference books?' 'All the reference books that you've got access to, all day every day, when you're working. The reference books that belong to both of us, that you can use whenever you want to. The encyclopedias. The big dictionaries. The French and German dictionaries.' Surely this might touch a nerve? He makes no sign. About our living separately, he says: 'Of course there is a risk—that someone might find they liked being alone all the time, or someone might get tangled up with someone else.' 'If I moved out,' I say, 'I'd take my saucepans. I'd take the stereo and the CDs.' He goes rather quiet. Do I 'believe in love'? I say I think there are many different sorts of love, including the love of children. He declares that for him love means only love between man and woman. Our discussion of this drifts vaguely here and there, without resolution. I say that romantic love is a kind of madness, which must lose its intensity and turn into something more stable and mundane. 'Don't you love me any more?' he says. 'Yes, I do! I do love you!' We make a weary sort of love, we fall asleep.

At work, when my computer gave trouble, I sobbed and paced up and down, clutching my temples like someone in a Chekhov play: 'I'm a stupid woman and I've done a stupid, stupid thing.' I wonder if I should just pack up and go back to Melbourne. I don't know if I can bear the pain that's coming. The pain of living in this endless struggle, or of living separately but so close by that I have to see him out and about in the streets and cafes with *my rival*. I have lost hope today. I feel completely despairing. When my friend the magazine journalist came home and I showed her my computer problem, she briskly showed me how to fix it. I told her I'd been howling over it. She said, 'Ahhhhh!' and put her arms around me.

In an art shop I heard a girl say to her friend, 'Life's too short to spend it with a wanker.' I let out a snort of laughter. They looked at me and we all cracked up.

Dreamt I was a teacher in charge of a room full of rough but cooperative fifteen-year-olds. I said to them, 'Does anybody else think it's a bit dark in here, or is it normal?' Some put up their hands so I turned on the light.

V goes out to eat at the Balkan with X and their art-critic friend. I make myself a pasta with a powerful sauce of garlic, chilli, parsley, tomato and anchovies, and call M on the phone. She tells me she and AB have bought a battered old house opposite the station in Kensington. It's got a huge crack down one exterior wall, which is why they could afford it. 'You're keeping your Melbourne house, aren't you? When we have babies, I'll want you to be in Melbourne to help me with them! And AB thinks so too!' 'There's no way I wouldn't be there. It's absolutely out of the question.' 'I think I have a prior claim, there,' she says.

———

One day somebody will want me. Somebody will need me.

———

A perfect sunny spring day. A bird calls with a cheerful, plaintive insistence, if such can be.

———

X calls and engages me in a five-minute conversation which I surprise myself by enjoying. She expresses mortification at her 'self-absorption—to have behaved like that on somebody's birthday! I feel so guilty!' 'Oh, you needn't feel guilty.' 'To tell the truth, I am so self-absorbed at the moment that I haven't got time for guilt.' We laugh. She asks me how I deal with deadlines. I describe my usual torment: completely blank, I'm certain I've got nothing to say, and that I never will, I'd better call them and say I can't do it, I hit bottom, utter hopelessness, then I start work. She says that because of her glandular fever she's had to miss one of her deadlines. All this amicable. V speaks to her briefly and hangs up.

———

My workroom at the magazine journalist's place is large and full of sun. I open the window. Dead leaves off a Virginia creeper blow in on a warm breeze. I get hold of a little straw brush and sweep the sill clean of debris.

———

Artarmon friends to dinner. They praised V's novel with warmth and I saw him blossom. We all not only praised it but kept referring to details from it in a spontaneous and natural way—the yellow dress, the Latvian's death, Ellen's high heels and her difficulty in walking in them. Evening of merriment. Even when I was tired I didn't want them to leave.

———

Contest between me and V about what each of us has done to keep the soap from going mucky in the bathroom.

V: 'You may not realise this, but with those soap dishes you have to empty out the water that collects.'

H: '*Derr*. Who do you think used to dry the little wooden racks, before?'

V: 'Excuse me, but *I* used to take the soap off and rest the racks on a tilt on the *windowsill*, to stop them from growing *mould* on their *bases*.'

H: 'Hello? *I* used to take a dirty towel or the bathmat and carefully *dry* the wooden racks so no mould would *sprout*. *And* I used to put my fingernails between the ridges and drag them along, to gouge out all the soap fat that was clogging them up.'

V: 'What *you* don't know is—'

And so on and so on, until feeble with laughter.

———

Since I was last in Melbourne both my parents have become very small. Dad's whole face seems to hang from his nose. Mum has had a lot of skin cancers removed. There are lines of black sutures on one calf, the back of one hand, and her right temple, though she seems to have forgotten the one on her face. Dad is jealous of the attention she is getting, and keeps changing the subject back to his prostate surgery three years ago. Night falls while we're sitting together in the living room. We talk on for a few minutes in the semi-dark, the only light source being the hall light beyond the dining room. Eventually Dad gets up: 'I'm going to bed.' He strolls into the hall. We hear a distant light switch snap. Mum and I are plunged into total darkness. We manage to make each other out in the tiny glimmer of light from the street outside the big windows, and are overtaken by a fit of giggles. To him, any room that he's not in is by definition empty.

———

Early Melbourne spring. Vast clear pale sky, sun dry and unbearably bright, even late in the afternoon, down the broad straight avenues. The whole front of my house is blossoming and nodding with scores of chubby pink Lorraine Lee roses *planted by me*. A perfumed profusion, wonderful to behold.

———

Because of Mum's stitches I gave her a bath. I washed her, shampooed her hair ('I don't mind if you give my scalp a bit of a rub'), then helped her out and dried her with a towel; down on my haunches I rubbed her legs right to the crutch; then I put skin cream all over her body, including her breasts and belly. 'You're in pretty good shape, Mum,' I sincerely said, 'for a woman in her seventies.' As I was bouffing up her hair with the dryer she said, 'Have you got a friend in Sydney who'd do this for you?' The answer is no, but I said yes. Writing this now, though, I recall W, who of course would do it, and without needing to be asked.

———

Home. It's the week between Rosh Hashanah and Yom Kippur so she's not working. At a loose end, I wander around, stuff myself with sweet biscuits.

———

It's nearly Pentecost. My favourite moveable feast! They've put me on the roster at church for reading the lesson. I have to read from Job, and Psalm 34. Better practise.

———

I look at small flats for sale in Potts Point. 'Elegant', 'stylish', 'perfect home for discerning buyer'. They're awful. I mention them to V. He urges me to sell my house. My piece of Melbourne? My only garden? Out of which we ate food that we'd grown? No way am I selling that house, even if it was mine to sell. He has no time to criticise my stubbornness, and anyway he's not listening: he's on the phone hour after hour with X, painstakingly working through her catalogue with her, page by page.

———

He's flooded with local offers for his novel and his backlist. He pretends not to be pleased. In fact his face tells me he's waiting for British offers. The local ones matter to him, he says, 'fifty times less'.

———

Got to my borrowed office this morning and found a fax here for V from his London agent. Honourably refraining from reading it, I called him and he walked up the street to get it. H: 'I can't understand how she happened to have my number—how could she have had it?' 'Aw, I s'pose I should have told you. I said she should fax me at your number if she couldn't get through to me at home.'

———

He showed me the fax. It was full of praise and excitement. Very big names, and in various European countries, are bidding for the book. On all my day-lit levels I am delighted for him. He stands about in my sunny office, looking at the ceiling, one hand holding his chin. Off he goes home. I sit on a chair in the sun, thinking inchoate thoughts. He reappears in the doorway: 'You'll have to let me out. There's a deadlock.' I hop up to oblige. Coming along the hall behind me he says, 'What were you brooding about, on your chair?' 'Oh, just sitting in the sun.' I'd like to understand what's making me feel perturbed and slightly sick. Is it rivalry, envy? What else can it be? But it started when I found he'd handed out my phone number—his casual enlistment of my private working space. He will always put his needs ahead of mine, every time, without even thinking about it. Yesterday, though, when a journalist came to the flat to interview me, he did make a point of serving tea and biscuits in a friendly way.

———

I'm dangling in the space between old customs and new ones I don't know how to establish.

———

G always sees straight through my façade. He must be finding it hard to balance his friendships with me and with V. He loves to talk about their little girl at home, his delight in her endless streams of imagination and fantasy. 'Gee, I miss having kids in my life,' I say. 'I envy you so much.' 'I sometimes feel like telling V he's missed out on something really important,' says G. 'For a bloke who's written a book about a father and a daughter, he doesn't know the first thing about the subject! Of course I know the book's not meant to be real—it's a fairytale, mythological, imaginative version of a father and daughter—that's what he'd say, and he's right, but—' When I get home the first question V asks me is, 'What did you and G talk about?' I rattle out some bullshit answer and change the subject.

———

International publishers are making V big offers. I feel—I was going to say 'sorry'—for him: the difficulty of making a decision while keeping his integrity, which seems to concern not looking money-mad or even particularly money-interested, and yet at the same time wanting the Australian publisher to offer more. He's never had such wild commercial attention before. It must be wonderfully gratifying, but already I can see him becoming bewildered by this embarrassment of riches.

———

This marriage is either breaking up or being exposed to thorough scrutiny and reorganised.

———

I found *Astral Weeks* in a second-hand shop. After dinner V shut himself in his room to make a phone call and I played 'Sweet Thing'. Within three bars, big fat tears of memory and joy were bouncing down my cheeks. I had to mop them with a tea towel. 'I will never, never grow so old again.' I *was* young once, I was adventurous, and sometimes I was happy.

———

This morning I put on lipstick and went out to get myself a flat, to work in and to put a table and a bed in. I trudged from one agency to the next. Surely, there must be a place for me somewhere. I looked at three horrible dumps, then I pushed myself against inertia down to St Neot Avenue, a sloping little street I've always been attracted to, and there I found a tiny north-facing studio with an afterthought of a kitchen and a shabby bathroom, on the second floor of a 1940s building. Outside its steel-framed casement windows, the branches of a tremendous camphor laurel, a view of a corner of the bridge, down the hill half a battleship standing in green water, and a great deal of sky with bits and bobs of cloud. W answered my call; she came for a reality check.

H: 'Now we must be serious and make a list of its bad points. What are they?'

Pause. We turn about and look.

W: 'Well—apart from this built-in wardrobe—there aren't any.'

H: 'Where's the phone jack?'

W: (efficiently) 'Here.'

And so on. In rising elation.

———

Today I went back for another look, dreading to find it shrunken and mean. I opened the door. It was bigger than I'd remembered—airy and sunny, pleasant, *fixable*. I took off my shoes and sat on the carpet, lay down on my back. Quiet. No traffic because it's a dead-end street, only a flight of steps right outside the building, leading down to the harbour. I practised saying it: 'This is my place. This is *my* place.'

These bright mornings! Tomorrow I get my flat. At the breakfast table G and V argue about the economy. Red and pink geraniums blossom on the windowsill.

'X the painter isn't on my mind any more,' I say on the couch. 'He mentions her, I mention her, casually. I hear him talking to her on the phone and it doesn't affect me. It's sort of unclenched itself.' 'Perhaps,' she says, 'it's because the real issue's being dealt with.'

These bright afternoons! I pick up Proust again, *The Fugitive*. 'Mademoiselle Albertine is gone!'

Phone rings, X engages me in conversation, with a slightly determined air but as always courteous and interesting. I pass the phone to V. From his side I gather they have already arranged to have dinner tonight, since I am going to see *The Full Monty* with O and his daughter.

I signed the lease, paid the money, and took the key of 16/7 St Neot. Up and down Macleay Street I strode under thick new plane leaves and speckled sun, carrying minor household objects in big plastic bags: a dish rack, Ajax, a dunny brush, shower curtain etc. In Bondi Junction I bought a bar fridge.

At lunchtime I take V to see the place. He says very little. I notice myself becoming anxious and disappointed: I want to drag a response out of him. I want him to like it. He withholds in obedience to some dark part of his nature. I keep control of myself: whether he likes it or not is COMPLETELY IRRELEVANT. In fact, this irrelevance is part of the point of my renting it in the first place. Finally he says, 'You can bring some of our old clapped-out cups

and saucers down here.' 'Bugger that. I'm not putting anything in
here that I don't really like.'

———

Setting up my place. When V's been there it shrinks, as does my
heart. Later I return to it alone and they both expand. I understand
dimly that he is carrying all the doubts that I'm refusing to feel.
Unfair to him—and yet he is so willing, so eager to see the harm
and failure and mediocrity and disappointment in everything that
comes up that he attracts one's projections of shade as a magnet
draws iron filings. This morning I cleaned and scrubbed, singing
madly. I missed church without a second thought. V carried a chair
for me and when he'd gone I sat on it at my tiny kitchen table and
drew plans of furniture and how I shall dispose it. I will also buy a
CD player, amp and speakers. Tomorrow, the vodka.

———

Perhaps I seem a little pathetic, in my excitement over such an
unluxurious, unspectacular flat? V spoke sombrely today, pointing
out that it was 'really only an office with a shower, rather than an
apartment where people can come and stay'. Perhaps he feels embarrassed that I'm so easily satisfied. Maybe he doesn't grasp what a
comfortless hole that room was at Bondi Junction. Maybe *I* don't
grasp that St Neot is somehow—not good enough?

But *I like it*. I'm in love with its windows.

———

The magazine journalist took me to the Basement to hear the Irish
fiddler Martin Hayes and the guitarist Dennis Cahill. Mild evening.
We wore coats and walked fast through Woolloomooloo, making
nervous jokes about the tomahawk murderer who's on the loose
up in the Cross. The two musicians sat close together and played
with an intense mutual attentiveness and intimacy. The music was
deeply Irish, but sometimes it made me think of Bach, with its

clean, complex purity and glorious speed, always light and sweet but with a developing and at times almost overwhelming power. Their effortless segues from tune to tune made the crowd cry out with joy.

———

An Orthodox Jewish man outside the fruit shop yesterday on Bondi Road was carrying a toddler, a little crying girl. She wept and sobbed on his shoulder. He stood still in his black hat and eighteenth-century frock coat, and rocked gently from side to side. The Asian shopkeeper ran out and pressed a mandarin into the child's hand. Surprised, she paused in her weeping and held it against her father's beard. The orange globe burned against the black.

———

V's friend the wealthy old bohemian has fallen in the street. She is recovering in a hotel overlooking Bondi Beach. V paid her one visit, organised a doctor to call, then palmed off her care on to me. Luckily for all concerned I like her and we get on. Yesterday I spent five or six hours with her. For the first three we entertained ourselves with stories and gossip until the doctor came. While he examined her I sat on her tiny balcony in bright sun. Jackhammers battered down on the street corner, surfers floated on slow clear swells. Away goes the doctor. I am to take her to Bondi Junction in a taxi for an X-ray. She stands up, strips off her stained cotton nightie and stands there completely naked in front of me, with the careless freedom of extreme old age. Looking at her I am not shocked. I think, 'So that's all it is? I'd expected worse.' The frame of her body is still firm and bony, but the flesh in its loose bag of skin has fallen forward and down, very pale and wrinkled and crêpy. I hand her clean garments and she struggles into them.

———

V is being surprisingly kind and thoughtful, since I stacked on a turn about his complete lack of interest in the public thrashing I'm getting in *Bodyjamming*, the book of essays edited by the Ormond tutor: one of them is a malicious personal attack on me as a high-school teacher, the sort of character-destroying lies one could sue about, if one were the sort of person who sues. On Radio National the Ormond tutor, in a revved-up, articulate interview, reduces me to what she says activists like her are up against: 'a woman in her fifties who has a problem with younger women'. For this, one becomes a non-person? An academic I know, who chatted and laughed with me on the two-hour train trip to Newcastle a week ago, pointedly ignores my greeting outside La Buvette. I gulp down my food and hurry away. Passing his table I see that his companion is the Ormond tutor's husband, who also cuts me.

———

Meanwhile, every night while we sleep, faxed offers for V's novel flood in from publishers in the UK, Europe and the US. One German publisher's list groans with the tremendous names of twentieth-century literature, writers V reveres and in whose company he would kill to be seen: Canetti, Borges, Singer, Kundera, Calvino. V's agent's assistant calls to report that the book has been 'the sensation of Frankfurt'. I have to admit to myself that I feel irrelevant, small, hollow, untalented, worthless—and frightened. The energy required to maintain self-command is so great that I am always tired. How repellent one is. If only I were writing something.

———

But. My lovely, tiny, private flat. With its casement windows. It's all set up, waiting for me to take a deep breath, open the door and walk in. Pleasant light all day, windows letting in water breezes. Birds call.

———

I would like to write something, but what?

Dreamt of ice-skating. It wasn't exactly me who skated, but a man in his thirties or forties, tall and slim with strong legs. Somehow the dreaming 'I' was at the shoulder of the skater, close behind him, so that I zoomed along (though disembodied) in unison with him, and experienced his sensations: exertion, exhilaration, power. The river along which we skated was a magnificent world of whiteness. Beside it stood tall frozen verticals, trees coated in frost and ice. The whole landscape was shaped in ridges, everything a sparkling powdery white.

Out at 6 am, sunny and bright, air damp with the harbour morning, we saw a very fat woman walking down Yarranabbe Road with her personal trainer. 'She's twice his size!' said V. 'He looks like her toy.' They were talking gaily together as they strode down the middle of the road, and I don't know why, but imagining the heroic weight-loss struggle ahead of her, I started dreaming up a character: a woman goes to AA, gets off booze, chooses three people from her past to make amends to. Does she pick them at random? Make a list and stab it with a pin? And when she tracks them down she finds that what they were offended by was not what she thinks she did wrong at all, but something way more oblique. She has to rewrite her whole history. From other people's points of view.

V took me to Darley Street Thai for my birthday. Astonishing food. You take a bite, complex flavours flood your mouth, you chew and a new wave comes, then just as you think you know the taste, a note of some other herb or spice breaks through, as clear as a beam of light through a cloud.

To Melbourne, to see M and AB's house: a chunky, yellow-rendered, two-storey, German-looking place in a street lined with plane trees. In a little park between the house and the station stand two huge and splendid eucalypts. A perfect, still, mild, fresh spring night. Air scented by flowering gardens. The odd cyclist whirs past, white helmet glowing, tail-light winking and stuttering. If V becomes internationally known, as it seems he is about to, the gap between him and this family life down here will widen even further. I'm fighting to balance on two rollerskates, each one heading in a different direction: I'm going to be split in half.

———

The Australian edit of V's novel arrives by courier. He bristles: 'There's something on every page! He's flattened it out! He says the daughter's a blur! I *wanted* it to be like that! I'm not going to change it—so many people in England and Europe really like it!' 'But V—you haven't seen their edits yet.'

———

Scrabble with the China scholar, who's wearing a pretty, scoop-neck, faded-to-dark-rose-pink dress. She beats me as usual. We drink red wine. My opening words, *feuds* and *axes*, remind us of *Bodyjamming*, and we riff on this with enjoyable savagery.

———

V tells his old painter friend that he's anxious, now, lest his book, so impressive to publishers and so instantaneously and internationally accepted and bought, might *for that very reason* be 'mediocre', even 'middle-of-the-road'. The old friend's wife, reporting this to me, bends her elbows and knees, clenches her fists, bares her teeth and hisses, 'I hope it's a *bestseller.*'

———

Dreamt that R and I had to carry the body of an old man to the place where it belonged. First we carried it horizontal, shoulder-high as one does a corpse, but soon he began to stir and we realised he was still alive. We lowered his feet to the ground and he managed to stumble along, with his arms round our shoulders. He was a very *sweet* old man, endearing and gentle; we felt tender towards him. As we tramped along he would occasionally become dead again and have to be carried, then would revive and be able to walk for a while. It was hard work to keep going but we did it, and it felt more like a privilege than a task.

―――――

Two hours in church and it didn't seem long. The vicar (who reads everything and knows what's going on) even prayed for me: 'Help Helen keep her dignity.' During a hymn I got deep-down quivers that were beyond control. I pulled out my hanky and sang on, mopping and shaking. No one turned a hair. Watching scores of people go up to communion I thought it was a place where I belonged, that no one there would think me too weird, or not weird enough. I'm part of that strange community, now. Later I told V about it: 'I cried in church, about this *Bodyjamming* shit. I felt better afterwards.' His face loses animation, goes rigid and blank. Five beats. 'Did anyone see you?'

―――――

The young guy upstairs in our building asked me again if I'd take him to church. I said I would. He said, 'I *need* to go.' Later I was cross with myself for not asking him why.

―――――

V: 'X the painter's mother's very nice, but she's a bit like your mother—fading away.'

―――――

Out walking, V asks me if I've started writing anything. I say, 'V. I'm not writing. I haven't got a single idea, not a single thought. I'm starting to wonder if I'll ever write anything again—if I'm not even a writer any more.' 'But you are a writer,' he says at once. 'You *are* a writer. That's *all* you are.' He meant this as encouragement, I know, as a strengthening compliment; but I'm not only a writer. I'm a mother.

———

On the couch an outpouring of horrible images and memories— death, violence, a child hitting a baby, murder, suicide. I lay there and talked and talked this stuff, not knowing why. She said, 'Something in you is only just staying alive. Like the sweet old man in your dream. Only just managing to survive.'

———

> *They built by rivers and at night the water*
> *Running past windows comforted their sorrow;*
> *Each in his little bed conceived of islands*
> *Where every day was dancing in the valleys*
> *And all the green trees blossomed on the mountains*
> *Where love was innocent, being far from cities.*
> —W. H. Auden, 'Paysage Moralisé'

———

V asks me if I would ever stay again in the hotel I chose in Vienna. I say no and explain why. He begins to talk about 'when I go to Vienna in May'. I look up, surprised: 'I thought we were both going.' He becomes flustered: 'I'm going over—*if* I go over— for the *book*. It's *work*.' After dinner he goes to call on X, taking her our copy of Berlioz's memoir. I fantasise hurling heavy objects through glass. Here I sit, neatly writing it all down.

———

In my flat, listening to Hayes and Cahill. A heavy bee flew in at my window. 'Go. Go!' It swerved away and headed north between the muslin curtains. In an instant, bee gone, I'm alone here, with the blank computer, my sore feet and the Irishman's fiddle, the Irishman's suave guitar. I sit on the carpet in my petticoat, threading curtain rings through loops of tape. Everything here seems to be mine, or to have something to do with my life. I read aloud from *The Fugitive*. I can make those long sentences sound graceful and draw out their meaning, if I slow them right down and concentrate.

———

Michael Hutchence has hanged himself in Double Bay. The hotel door, the belt, where did he hook it, oh, poor boy? The chamber-maid: her feet ache, her knees crack and crumble, her hand skin is leather, she taps, she taps again, applies the shoulder and the key, and stumbles into the gasping room, the curtain's white flare, legs clunking against the timber—what secrets, what precious moments of knowledge before she starts to scream.

———

V's gone to Melbourne for the edit of his novel. He calls and grunts in reluctant half-sentences that I can't grasp—I'm straining to read his mind. At first I'm irritated, then with a heave I drag myself off centre stage and apply my imagination: he's tired, he's frightened, he's freaking out. The editing goes on and on and on, he and the publisher are together all day, right through lunchtime, brooding over the manuscript, struggling over it. And here am I, in this calm flat with music softly playing, full of privacy, and all I can do is scrutinise his tone towards *me*. A kinder woman would want to lighten his mood. So I try. I hear my voice soften, rise into a better register. That's when he mentions the card I'd slipped into his suitcase: a knight in armour with two long sharp spikes protruding from his breastplate; I'd written on it, 'Don't be too spiky—a bit spiky—just spiky enough.'

———

A rich friend of V's in Melbourne has bought one of X the painter's pictures. V brought back the money for her in cash. There's a little plastic bag on his top shelf, bulging with folded $100 notes.

The inside of the bag is fogged with value.

———

Walking home from La Buvette.

H: 'These sandals have turned out brilliant. Last year I thought, "Oh bum, they're a lemon," but suddenly they've gone all soft and comfortable.'

V: (glances down; grunts)

H: (mimics his voice) 'Huh. Pity they're so ugly.'

V: (with a cross laugh) 'You bloody women! You always think you know what a bloke's thinking!'

H: 'No we don't! We have to make it up! You won't engage with us! You won't answer when we speak! You present us with a blank face! We have to *invent* a response, out of loneliness and despair! So we won't have to live in an emotional vacuum!'

———

Robert Manne in the *Herald* lays out the reasons why the Howard government must make a formal apology for the terrible damage done, between the late nineteenth century and the 1960s, by the official removal of Aboriginal babies and children from their mothers and communities.

H: (busily snipping out the column) 'It's exciting, isn't it, when something really important's happening in the country.'

V: 'Think so?'

H: 'Don't you? I find it thrilling.'

Moments later he comes in and slaps down a column from the *Financial Review* that runs the opposing line.

———

On my way out to church I went to his desk to say goodbye. 'Gonna say a prayer for me, sweetheart?' 'I will if you want me to. Do you?' He leans back in his chair, tilts up his chin, narrows his eyes and looks at me along his cheeks, with a closed-mouth smile: 'Do you really think prayer has any effect?' 'I don't know.' 'But shouldn't you know? What *do* you think?' Long pause; is it a trap? Finally I say, 'I'll go with Emerson. Prayer is the contemplation of things as they are from a very great height.' Later, at church, I report this exchange to the vicar. He laughs: 'I don't think there's any answer to that question.'

———

After everyone had gone I sat in the sun outside the church door. A girl was in the porch, writing in the prayer folder. I heard her crying softly to herself as she wrote. She goes to the inner door and stands looking into the empty church, crying without drama or noise. She turns and walks out, passes me sitting on the bench, smiles at me. She heads off along Darlinghurst Road. I go to the folder and read what she's written: she thanks God for the love of her family, for her brother Derek, for her two best friends: 'Please help me to be happy here, though I'm so far from home and so alone and scared.' I run after her. There she is in the phone box near the corner. I stop a few yards behind her. She's got a folded page of the classifieds beside the phone. Under the traffic noise I hear her eager, shy voice, 'I'm English, as you can probably hear!' The rest is drowned out. She hangs up and steps away from the booth, hesitates by the red brick wall of the fire station. I rush up and stammer out my story: 'I saw you just now in the church—I hope you don't mind but I read what you wrote—I was worried about you—I wanted to give you my phone number just in case everything gets too much for you.' She's thin, pale, with a pointed chin and glasses. Her little face splits open in a huge smile: 'Oh, how *sweet*! That's so *sweet* of you!' She puts out her hand and we shake. I say, 'I saw your name was Helen and that clinched it—my name's Helen too.' She beams at me: 'I can't belieeeeeve it!' Turns out she has a job but is still in a backpackers' place on Victoria Street: 'You don't know of anywhere I could live, do you?' I say no, we laugh and say goodbye, go off in our different directions.

All day and into the night I fantasise with increasing wildness being in a position to have invited her home on the spot, given her a meal, offered her the spare bed for as long as it takes for her to find a place to live. I try to imagine squeezing her into my tiny office, but it's *too small*, she would have no privacy, it would be hopeless for me and awkward for her. On and on I go, picturing myself in a house, a great big kitchen with a great big table, cooking copious meals, having a spare room, even two, for spontaneously invited wanderers, on and on, fostering freaked-out children and abandoned babies, caring for them and loving them—being free to give, give, give. I fantasise myself into a state of total despair about my life.

And, stitching away at my muslin curtains, I admit to myself that St Neot *is* too small. That once again I've drawn back at the threshold of solitude and freedom, and taken *only a little bit*—as if I thought that was all I deserved.

The Helen in the church is me, of course. The lost and homesick and homeless part of *me*. At fifty-five, in my own country, still without a home.

———

After dinner he wanders in from X the painter's place: 'I gave her the Stendhal and wrote a couple of letters for her.' 'Why doesn't she ever come over to our place?' 'Oh—she feels uncomfortable with you—not at ease.'

———

We talk, lying under the yellow sheet, till past midnight. He lays a lot of our troubles at the door of my 'going to a shrink. You turned away from me. You turned inwards and became self-absorbed.'

H: 'I had to. You were jealous and hostile. You criticised what I was doing so harshly that I had to protect it from you.'

V: 'I was *not* jealous.'

H: 'Don't you remember how you always used to say "he", even when you knew she was a woman?'

V: 'I never for a second felt even the slightest jealousy, not a flicker.'

H: 'You were angry with me for being sad. And your way of dealing with it was to start a close friendship with another woman. I can't help noticing the timing.'

V: 'Well, I suppose it does look a bit odd, but I certainly didn't do it like that on purpose.'

––––––––

He says he can't talk to me any more, that I keep correcting everything he says, that I've got a list of subjects that I don't want to hear about any more.

I say it's because he never has anything new to say on those subjects, and only rants and fulminates—how boring young people are, the worthlessness of popular culture, the tedium of first-person writing. He says he experiences my response to this as censorship, and trimming. I say I can understand why he wants to spend time with someone fresh, who hasn't heard all his opinions yet, who can admire him and be refreshed by him and look up to him, and be advised by him on what to read—the Stendhal, the Berlioz. His love of certain writers is new to her. He seems miffed by this.

––––––––

I say that since we've been together our lives have been arranged in such a way as to facilitate only his work needs: that he's an imaginative writer and needs seclusion in order to write, so we've got things set up domestically to create the best possible conditions for this. On the other hand, I'm a writer who works off and is nourished by the events of daily life, which means that our living arrangements actively work against what I need: 'Nothing happens. There are no children, there's no garden, no noise, no dancing, no flow of people through the house.' He is very taken by my description of him as 'an imaginative writer', and dwells on it for a moment in a pleased way. 'I bet,' he says suddenly, in a flip tone, 'you'll bolt. I've got twenty bucks to say you'll bolt. Yes. That's what you're going to do. You'll make one of your fast decisions, and you'll bolt.' He nods, as if he's produced a chunk of incontrovertible truth and chocked it into place. Eventually we sleep.

———

In the morning the sun comes up and sparkles through the trees outside our window. He recalls my description of him as 'an imaginative writer': he lies on his back and contemplates it with serene pleasure, his hands clasped under his head on the pillow, his eyes out of focus. 'Remember when we left Melbourne and I said I'd get an office? I told a lie, yes,' he says, with a roguish smile, 'but I did it for a reason, and now I'm glad I did! Because look at the result! Right—I'm going down to get the paper.'

———

M and AB move into the house they've bought. I call to hear how the move went. 'Oh, we're so grateful for the removalists you paid for. AB said it was the best thing that had *ever* happened to him in his whole *life*. Not better than our wedding, was it, though, AB?' (Murmured exchange in the background.) 'No—he says the best apart from our wedding.'

———

I went to dinner with two journalists recently back from years in New York. They suggested a swim at Bondi in the morning. I didn't think they'd remember, we'd all drunk a bit of wine, but the buzzer lets out a blast at 7.45 am. 'They've come—they've come!' I rush around throwing my bathers on, towel in bag, tear downstairs, and away we roll to Bondi. They haven't been in the ocean for years: 'It's a perfect morning for re-entry!' Sun out, sparkling, but with a bank of grey clouds slowly moving up from the south. Tide out-ish, water mild and of staggering clarity. Waves of a manageable size present themselves in sets, their surfaces a glossy, silken green. They rise and bulge with leisurely authority, translucent, glassy, so beautiful you want each one to curve forever—*and I catch one!* I push off into it, take a few strokes, and suddenly I'm picked up and sent surging forward in harmony with the force of the universe. I stagger to my feet in the shallows and look back for the others. They're two heads lifting on a swell, thirty metres behind.

———

V and I lie round talking about stuff like Henry James's late style, which we both find almost impossible, and about whether we would accept radical chemo in the case of very late and apparently hopeless cancer. Remembering (but not mentioning) my nun, I say I'm pretty sure I wouldn't. V is not sure at all.

———

Dreamt I had a big mop of thick, springy hair. Rain fell on it but didn't wet it right to the roots. Someone said, 'Get it really wet and then you'll be able to manage it.' I soaked it (under a tap? In the sea?) and it became a wonderful shapeable mass that grew back off my forehead quite splendidly.

———

Elizabeth Jolley sends me a *New Yorker* cartoon: two smiling middle-aged women in a plush booth, about to tackle lethal-looking cocktails. The more flamboyantly dressed of the two says, 'I got married once—to avoid writing.'

———

Since I've taken on two magazine deadlines (shoes; second-hand photos) I start to notice things more intensely as I go about my business on the streets, on buses, in shops—things are very bright, and force themselves on my attention in a way they haven't for a very long time. There's so much around me to be noticed and absorbed that two little articles won't be big enough to hold it all.

———

V came home and said he'd seen a man having a heart attack on the footpath outside McDonald's in Darlinghurst Road. He spoke with intense interest about how the paramedics had worked on him: they ripped his shirt open to reveal his huge bulging gut, his grey track-suit pants, white runners—H: (urgently) 'What brand?' V: (recoils) 'How the hell would *I* know?'—and gave him electric shocks that caused him to sit up and then flop back down. 'He was pretty grey, getting darker all the time.' V wanted to go to the police station to find out if he'd died but I said they probably weren't allowed to tell.

When we first lay down in bed he suddenly and without a word, as if joking, made several strange movements: a jerky sitting up then a collapsing on to his back. I was bewildered, and laughed; then it dawned on me that he was mimicking the movements the man had made in the street. God, he really is scared of dying. He is able to *imagine* dying. How terrible to die like that in the street, in front of everyone, having pissed yourself, without dignity or privacy.

———

Don DeLillo, interviewed by David Remnick in the *New Yorker*: 'Between books,' he says, 'what happens is, I drift. I feel a little aimless. I feel a little stupid, because my mind is at odds. It's not trained on a daily basis to concentrate on something, so I feel a little dumb. Time passes in a completely different way. I can't account for a day, a given day. At the end of a day, I don't know what I did.' The work, when it starts, 'comes out of all the time a writer wastes. We stand around, look out the window, walk down the hall, come back to the page, and in those intervals, something subterranean is forming, a literal dream that comes out of daydreaming.'

———

V slides out the door at 7 pm, delivering a Judas kiss in passing, to dine at the Balkan with X the painter. I eat some soup, watch a bit of TV, read my stars in *Who Weekly*, always worth a look: 'There's a lot of confusion around. It may be that too little is known about a situation or that someone is not giving out the whole truth. Proceed cautiously.' Then AB calls: he's in town with three guys from his band to see Teenage Fanclub, they saw them last night and tonight they're going again: why not come? I put essential things in my pockets and hail a cab. I bowl up to the Metro, pay $25, get a stamp on my wrist, and plunge into the darkness. It's packed. A double Stoli at the top bar, and a spot on the side stairs, with a good view of what's going to happen. I don't really expect to find the guys but I keep an eye out and here they come, surging up the stairs to the bar. They see me and jam on the brakes: 'You've come? You've come out to rock?' I've chosen the exact spot they'd stood in the night before. They hand me a joint. I take a couple of drags. Five minutes later a tremendous wave rears up and crashes over me. My knees go weak, my head spins. I get a grip on the cold metal banister and I do not let it go, except to lean down and stand my vodka glass on the floor, because one thing I do not want to do is be sick. The curtains sweep open grandly to reveal five guys and some equipment. Is that all? Everything the same as it always was? It's only a band, it's only a hugely loud and good rock-and-roll band and I'm a woman of fifty-five who never listens to this sort of music any more but who is now too smashed to move and will have to stay hanging on to this rail for the next two hours. 'They're so LOUD!' says AB right into my ear. 'Twice as loud, three times as loud as they were last night! Somebody must've told 'em to turn up!' We are standing under a powerful current of fresh, cold air that's being pumped downwards from the ceiling. I have to remind myself, over and over again, to *breathe* this air, that if I breathe it properly I won't panic, the dope won't make me spew, I won't fall over or have to sit down. My mouth dries up. I know I need to drink a lot of water but I daren't let go the banister, let alone climb the many stairs to the bar. I hang on and suddenly the music stops being an undifferentiated wall of sound and divides beautifully into distinct streams: without effort I perceive what each instrument is playing, and can follow them all at once. I am wonderstruck by this. And then my mind slips its moorings and goes swerving and zooming away through the world and the centuries, making colossal swoops across Europe and England and America, and I plan all the books I will write in future years, I recall every house I've ever lived in, every backyard I've ever stood in, every song I've ever heard or sung, every garment I've ever worn or washed or hung on the line or ironed or borrowed or lent; and every now and then my mind comes back in a huge curve and focuses on NOW, and I think in stupefaction, 'My God, I'm standing on the stairs at the Metro holding on to a cold metal banister and listening to a band.' Somewhere out on the edges of this mad scary glory a little voice is saying calmly, 'This will eventually wear off. You are not doomed to be in this state for the rest of your life. It will go on for hours *but it will come to an end.*' One of the men I'm with pushes his face right into mine and mouths, 'Can I get you another drink?' 'Water!' In the twinkling of an eye it arrives and I guzzle it, thank God, this will save me, and in another twinkling the hours pass and they play one last song that's so loud I can't hear a thing and it's over. The men are going to kick on, they kiss me goodbye, I stagger down the stairs and into the lobby, weirdly alone in that there is absolutely no chance of seeing anyone I know. I'm wedged into a crowd so thick that it's scarcely moving. Everyone's in a good mood, we flow along in a peaceful stream. I cross the street by means of a miracle of concentration and jump straight into a taxi. It's a summer night. I roll the window down and the soft air pours in. On the radio Elvis is singing 'Kentucky Rain' and I feel a huge helpless grin forming on my doughy features, thinking of the day I phoned my sister's radio show and put on a voice and asked her to play 'Kentucky Rain' for all the girls down here at the factory and she wouldn't because her show was a *funk* show. V and X the painter have of course been dining and laughing and talking and kissing in the furthermost reaches of my mind throughout the evening; I have tried by means of loud music and dope and booze to blot them out, to 'be in the moment', and have for a while succeeded. I creep into the flat. V has left the bed lamp on and is sound asleep. I undress and get into bed. I am tormented by the questions 'What time did you get home?' and 'How long can anyone spend in the fucking Balkan?' and 'What did you do after you left the restaurant?' but I grind them to powder and force them into a bottom drawer and kick it shut. The room begins not exactly to spin but to waltz about, to tilt and expand and swoop. I lie in a pleasant opium swoon that continues until dawn.

G comes up from the bush for a couple of days. He rings to say he'll have to call off a lunch date with me. On the day in question V tells me he's going out to lunch. With G. After their lunch G calls me and suggests he might 'fit me in' when he goes to have a haircut. Thanks, but no thanks. A friend calls. I tell her this little story and mention V's claim that he has never been jealous. 'Pfff,' she says. 'He's making sure he never needs to feel jealous.'

'How's that?'

'Most husbands would be unsettled if their wife had a close friendship with an attractive man. He's dealt with this by taking over the friendship.'

———

I told an old friend, a film producer, that I'm going to Antarctica. He looked at me in surprise: 'What'll you write about?' In a flash I see why I'm not excited about going. In unison we say: 'There are no *people* there.'

———

I have had to expend a great deal of energy persuading V that he should read his proofs. He says it's not necessary because they're on computer, and anyway the European and UK proofreaders will be 'fifty times better' than the Australian ones. I say everything's on computer now and that I always find mistakes in everything I write. I offer to help him and we set aside several afternoons to do it. In the British edition I come across a mention of a famous regiment called the Royal Welsh Fusiliers. 'V—the Royal Welsh Fusiliers?' 'Yep. Robert Graves' regiment,' he replies briskly. 'Well, I've got a feeling it's one of those words that are spelt funny. Shouldn't it be WELCH?' To humour me he reaches out an idle hand to the encyclopedia. 'You're right! The Poms have missed it!' He faxes the corrections to London, pointing out the military clanger with glee. I decide not to ask him if he told the publisher that his wife was the one who spotted it.

———

A man from the Jewish Film Festival calls and asks for a copy of my review of *Un Vivant Qui Passe*: he says that 'Claude' wants to read it. 'He really liked the review you did of his last movie.' 'What—you mean he's *read* it? He's read what I wrote?' 'Oh yes. It was one of the reviews he liked best from that festival.' I am staggered by this and fall silent. *Claude Lanzmann has read what I wrote.*

———

We are both putting on a performance of normality but there's a thick cloud of stubbornness and unhappiness and resentment hanging over us: a black cloud of silent struggle. To the death, I sometimes think. We sleep beside each other, we eat together, we kiss goodbye when one of us goes somewhere, we kiss goodnight before we go to sleep. But we're turned away from each other, inside.

———

V admires a pair of grotesquely high heels that Marilyn Monroe is wearing in a photo. I look at them and see two instruments of torture. He speaks at some length about how women who wear high heels are showing that they like men, that they're prepared to 'put up with a bit of discomfort' to please a man. They are much more feminine than women who wear flat shoes or runners.

———

He questioned me about why I was 'a jealous person', and what I thought jealousy was. I said it was a panic, a terrible fear of being rejected or replaced. I said that one of the things I loved in Proust was his brilliant, hilarious accuracy about jealousy and his intense interest in it. V said he thought there was far too much about jealousy in the book, and that what he liked was the 'overarching' shape of the book and its interest in time. He said that if he were a jealous person like me he would try to get control of it. I said I had worked hard to get control of it. He said, 'What's the evidence for this?' I said, 'The fact that you're still walking around, for instance.' He half laughed. I said I sometimes thought that if I were a man I'd be in jail. 'What for,' he said. I said, 'For violence.' This irritated him, and he said so. He said that I 'despised the rational' and 'worshipped feelings'; that I 'used' feelings. I asked him if he thought there was anything about his personality that might also be contributing to our troubles. He went vague. I asked him what sort of person he thought he was. He replied that he thought he knew himself pretty well, that he had a clear view of what he was like; and even though some of the aspects of this were 'not very good', there was no point in trying to change them now, since there was little hope that people could change their basic nature. He said he thought he had a tendency to meanness, that he could be generous but that he tended towards the mean. He was ignorant about some things, disinclined to forgive, impatient. 'I know I can be charming, but sometimes it's a con job.' He asked me once again, tipping his head back and staring down his cheeks, whether I thought *he* should 'see a shrink'. I said that I would never try to persuade him to do it, that it had never occurred to me to suggest it to him.

I don't know what look is on my face, during these horrible low-voiced conversations: on his, a blank stubbornness, mouth tight, chin up. He's fighting me for his own survival, just as I am fighting him: for respect, and for self-respect, for a place to stand.

———

Up at Palm Beach with W I bought a calf-length skirt of heavy, flower-patterned Indian cotton, crinkled and weighted with an extra layer at the hem that makes it swing out wonderfully. I asked V which top I should wear with it. As always his advice about colour and form was good and I followed it. But we might have been talking about a box of rubbish. 'Do you like the skirt?' He looked at it grimly: 'Aw…I quite like it, I s'pose.' I wore it when we went to a friend's place for lunch, and afterwards, out on the street, one of the other men present said, 'What a beautiful skirt.' *This is not about the skirt.*

———

I thought I would make a list of V's generous impulses, of the good things he brings to our relationship.
- He buys bottles of mineral water at the supermarket, though he disapproves of the drinking of mineral water, and leaves them by the door for me to take to my office.
- He bought a large quantity of toilet paper and left some for me by the door.

- He buys excellent wine at considerable expense and we drink it freely.
- Every morning he makes a good espresso and serves it to me.
- He offers me the best seat on the better couch, to watch TV from, whenever I sit down for a moment while cooking the dinner.
- He says, 'Put on some muzak, sweetheart'; and though I am always privately irritated by the word *muzak*, I like it when he asks me to make the choice.
- He advised me which shares to buy when I suddenly had money, and organised the buying of them for me.
- Every year he pushes past my pride and bad temper, and gives me advice about my tax return that saves me hundreds of dollars.
- He has said several times that I read aloud better than he does.
- Once, ten years ago, he said to me humbly, 'Am I getting any better?' which shamed me then, and the thought of which shames me now.

———

Occasionally it occurs to me that he might be suffering as much as I am, when we go through these endless struggles. His refusal to express or to admit to emotion has, despite my vehement attacks on it, succeeded in its aim: to convince me, as well as himself, that he *does not feel things*—these things I feel that he says are 'not *worth* feeling'.

———

The ferry ride last Sunday from W's place at Coasters to Palm Beach: at the first stop a large slow crowd enters, mostly parents with young children. They pour on, relentless, endless. The boat fills up with bodies and the rain pours down outside. Everybody's soaking wet. The way a small child sleeps on his mother's lap: seated facing her chest with his parted legs dangling outside her thighs. I'm scared. What if the boat sinks? The windows are fogging up with the humidity, surely no more people can fit on board, yet still they come, steady and slow and on and on. At last we move away from the wharf, slowly, slowly, and plug on towards Patonga. The boat's riding low in the water. One man slides open a window, but the mugginess is awful. I ask a man near us to open another, but he and his wife struggle in vain to shift the stuck pane, and subside. Their little girl, of eight or so, cries out, 'Where's my ten dollars? It's gone! It's gone! Mummy! My money! Where is it?' She begins to sob wildly. She pushes her hands into the pockets of her cotton trousers and pulls them out empty. She is a plain child with long fair hair tied in a bunch behind. She sobs and weeps aloud. Her mother remains calm: 'Do you think you could have left it in your other shorts?' But the child is away, inconsolable. 'I want another one, Mummy. I want another one.' 'You'll get one,' says the mother peaceably, and lifts her daughter on to her lap, in the same chest-to-chest posture as all the other mothers and children. The girl sobs to her heart's content, till she can cry no more and her poor little face is white and her eyes puffy and pink-lidded. Then she lies there against her mother's bosom, her cheek hooked over her mother's shoulder, though she is leggy and growing fast and soon will be too big to be cradled. Her swollen eyes are open and her gaze is blank and faraway. The boat ploughs on through the rain-pocked, silver water.

—————

I tell this to her on the couch and its meaning becomes clear as I tell. The girl is me. She is the boat/the mother. I am afraid she will sink under the weight of all the anger and sadness I need to load on to her. All this done in fleeting dabs and hints. The fogged windows remind me of the tiny plastic bag full of money that V brought back from Melbourne for X the painter. Money. Mummy. Oh, it's so excruciatingly obvious that it hardly needs to be spelled out. How

will I say goodbye to her for the summer, next week? I lie there
wondering if it will be acceptable to put my arms round her and
hug and kiss her; then I think no, I'd better just put out my hand;
but that would be manly, and I don't want to be manly. I told her
all this, and as I spoke I felt tears come into my eyes and my voice
began to tremble. A few feeble spasms went through my chest and
some tears squeezed themselves out. That was all.

On my way home, loaded with briefcase, supermarket shopping,
and food for dinner, I stepped on to the kerb in front of our building and tripped—I don't know, I was suddenly falling. I landed
on all fours, skidded forward, bags everywhere. Scrambled up.
A passing man with grey hair smiled: 'You right?' 'Yeah—what
happened?' Picked up my affairs and climbed the stairs, shaken,
with scratched knees and palms; came in, put down my load,
said to V, 'I fell. In the street.' He was surprised and nice to me,
took the groceries. I sat on the edge of the spare bed, all trembly
in the diaphragm. Wanted to let go and make a racket, but was
constrained by V's presence in the kitchen. Went and lay on our
big bed and got a clean hanky and bawled. He came in and lay
on his back next to me: 'Why are you crying?' 'I feel silly. I hurt
myself in front of people.' 'Why would that make you feel like
crying?' 'Oh, don't interrogate me. Let me have a howl. Don't
you ever feel like just having a good howl?' V: (very crisp and
firm) 'No.' And it all dried up. He examined my knees and I felt
how trivial it must seem to him, as a physical wound. I got off the
bed and went to have a shower. Why didn't I put my head on his
shoulder and *ask* for comfort?

———

A train to Dulwich Hill where the born-again is camping and
building for his sister. A loud chirring on the pavement. A passing
man looks down and picks up a 'ci-cahda' as they say up here. Its

wing is torn. He lifts it to a shelfy spot on the nearest tree trunk. We exchange brief courtesies and pass on.

The born-again has fallen off a ladder. His arm is in plaster. We sit in the small, weed-choked backyard, with its corner dunny and exposed tree roots. Overhead, a perfect clear summer evening sky, an almost-full moon still low, and the occasional winking, roaring jet. He calls over the fence and the neighbour lends him a corkscrew. We drink white wine and talk, harmonious and absorbed. I tell him about the wounded cicada. He says he digs up lots of them in the yard while he's working: 'They live in little sort of caves. For seven years. Then one day they come out and start whirring.' I remember his particular wit, its slyness and modesty. We recall our religious battles in 1986, at Drummond Street. We laugh at the way we were. 'But it was a wonderful time,' he says, 'sort of shimmering.' I mention Psalm 55 and he goes for his Bible. 'Read it out?' He reads it in a simple, slow, beautiful, ordinary way. In the last sentence, 'But I will trust in thee', he puts stress on the 'I'—as if others would not. I cook, we eat, it gets dark. He is going to a party. His plaster incapacitates him: he needs help changing into clean clothes. I stand behind him and pretend I *am* him, so I can tuck his shirt in properly and button his fly; then I kneel down and put his shoes and socks on him, and tie his laces neat and firm.

———

In the 'sewing room' mid-afternoon we talk again about our future. Should we buy a house or get a second flat? The outcome is (1) that 'a lawn and a dog' (two things M-C has sensibly said she thought we needed) are not at all what he wants, (2) that I feel our domestic arrangement is intolerable, and (3) that I will buy or rent a flat and move into it. 'It might be difficult,' he says. 'Yes,' I say, 'and more difficult for you, perhaps. Because you can't cook.' He walks into the bedroom, lies down and falls asleep. I return to my attempt to make a silk pillowcase. When he wakes I call out, 'There's too much struggle between us.'

'There certainly *is*.'

'*Between* us. It's both of us.'

'That's what I meant,' he says. 'And I'm *not* a nasty person.'

'Yes you are. You've got a huge nasty streak, right down the middle of your back. It can be seen for miles. You can't contain your nastiness.'

We're both laughing. I go back to my amateurish sewing. He comes in and starts rummaging through the table drawer: 'I said I'd change X the painter's washers, but I don't think I've got the right ones.' *Change her washers?* I carry on pinning the soft fabric, holding back an urge to crack a coarse joke.

H: 'I didn't think you were much chop with washers.'

V: (rummaging) 'Huh. Anyone can change a washer.'

H: (pleasantly) 'How come we had to get a plumber?'

V: 'What?'

H: 'The other week. To change our washers. We had to get a plumber.'

V: 'Oh, that was because we had to turn off the whole building's water.' (He brings out a washer.) 'I've changed X's already but it was the wrong one.'

H: 'When did you change it?'

V: 'A couple o' weeks ago. Okay—I'm off. See you.'

His timing. We laboriously arrive at a decision that I'm going to look for a place of my own, and within five minutes he's demonstrating his husbandly devotion to another woman. I'm too tired for this. I've got *cancer* of fighting and being too tired, and of not knowing how to sew a pillowcase. Can't work out how to make the seams smooth both inside and out. So I just sit there looking straight ahead. My skull is full of metallic cottonwool.

He came home four hours later. In the calm of total despair I was cooking a meal. He could not face me or enter the kitchen where I was working, but passed the door at speed, calling out, 'Hello sweetheart.'

———

He says he's always suspected I would leave: 'Because of your restlessness.' He describes again my unpleasant character, my awful family.

'So you think I should be satisfied with my lot?'

'Yes,' he says, 'I do.'

———

For three days we worked on the proofs of his novel. He read aloud, I wielded the pencil. I was once again impressed and moved by the book's sweep, its intricacy, its flow of ideas. And also surprised by the way his imagination seems to dwell forever in the 1950s. His efforts to get inside a woman's head—every now and then a convincing spark, then a weird impression of *his* impression: as if he imagines our minds as *'vague'*, *'soft'*, *'drifting'*, *'spreading'*. Up close to the texture of his work, I realise I understand almost nothing about him, and he understands almost nothing about me. We have no shared experience, it seems.

———

The sun has come out at last. Yesterday a tremendous, racketing storm, thunder crackled among the facets of the apartment blocks, the rain smashed and lashed, the sky a dirty grey, the lights on at 4 pm.

———

At church the vicar spoke about how God finds us, how we find God, 'in the *excluded* things; the small sins, the lying and the cheating'. When we sang 'But in thy dark streets shining/ The everlasting light' I leaned against the fat sandstone pillar beside me. I liked its cold roughness. I looked more closely at it and noticed the thousands of chisel-strokes that marked its faintly dusty surface. The work of it, the labour.

———

I guess I could take a punt on my own nature—the better aspects of it, that is. I could try to be generous and mind my own business.

1998

There's a mysterious Emporio Armani bag, sealed, in V's work-room, on the floor under his desk. I saw it out of the corner of my eye while we were inspecting the old IBM Golf-ball that we had picked up off the nature strip in Darling Point. I didn't say anything. It's nearly Christmas.

———

G calls. We discuss the storm of publicity that V will soon be walking into. 'It's going to be really terrible,' says G. 'He's got no idea how bad. He'd find it easier if he had you there to talk about it.' 'Nah—he doesn't want me there.' 'You're a difficult person, Hel. You're prickly and you're dominating. But I don't think you're the *problem*.'

———

V's old bohemian lady in Melbourne wants to give him her small car, which she can no longer manage. We flew down yesterday to collect it. At her apartment she was cracking hardy, laughing when V teased her and flirted with her, but I didn't think she was in a good way. I went to the toilet and it was smeared with shit, there were blobs of it on the tiled floor. I wiped them up. I don't know who's supposed to be looking after her. This morning he went off in the car to do art-world stuff and I dropped in on her again, with

Ajax and rubber gloves in my bag, and secretly cleaned the toilet. I'm flying back to Sydney this arvo. He's got things he has to do, and will drive home, probably tomorrow.

———

Today I went to a lunch party in Paddington. I got there early and so did Clive James, visiting from England. I was shy but he was jolly in a loud and likeable way. I asked if it was true that he had started to learn tango. It was! And he offered to teach me the basic steps. He seized me and pressed me hard against his torso. It was a terrifically hot day, sweat soaked his sky-blue shirt and he kept apologising for it, but I didn't care; he was a good dancer and a skilful teacher, and I immediately found that if I followed him I could do the steps. We had twenty minutes, before all the other guests arrived, of hilarious fun. Hearing I was soon to pass through Buenos Aires en route to the Antarctic, he advised me to stop there, find a bar and a tango hall, and only *think* about the Antarctic. Later I overheard him saying to another guest, 'She's a natural tango dancer.' Could he possibly have been talking about me?

———

A woman I'd met through V, and who I knew was a close friend of X the painter's, took me aside at the lunch and asked me if anything else, beside the book attacks, had given me a bad year. I stammered, caught off guard. 'Because X the painter,' she said, 'rang me the other day and asked me for advice about underwear.' I let out a laugh: 'What?' She kept looking me right in the eye, put her arm round my shoulder and said, 'Oh, I can see such awful sadness coming off you.' She told me that V had called her on several occasions this past year and said, 'Why don't I bring a broad over for dinner, while Helen's out of town?' Oh, this is like some trashy movie.

———

I went home and wrote him a very short, last-ditch letter. I said I missed the trust that used to exist so effortlessly between us, that I'd like to understand where it's gone and why, and to be able to establish it again. I put the letter on his desk, with his other mail.

———

He gets home, tired and sweaty from the drive up the Hume: 'It was so bloody hot I had to stop at a motel in Gundagai and read for a couple of hours.' He settles in with his usual slow deliberateness. We lie parallel on the couches and he goes through his mail. Passing his workroom door I see my letter open on his desk. Hours pass and he doesn't mention it. He reads the *Financial Review*. Soon after 8.30 he yawns and seems about to drop off on the sofa. In a state of unbearable tension I wait and wait. Not a word. We go to bed and lie side by side in the new white sheets. He takes my hand and reads on in the newspaper. He withdraws his hand to turn a page; then drops his forearm stiffly back across my chest. His wrist lands, bony and un-tender, against my face. In a burst of savagery I bare my teeth and snatch at it like a dog, but miss. 'What's up?' 'I was hoping you might mention my letter.' 'I haven't read it. I started it, and then I thought I'd read it tomorrow, when I'm firing on all four cylinders. Okay?' 'Yes—I know you're tired now. I just thought you might mention it, that's all.' He clicks his tongue: 'I've been *on the road*. I didn't want to start talking about that stuff when I'm too tired. I'll read it tomorrow, when I'm firing on all eight.'

———

2 am. I can't sleep. Wind's been blowing, gusty and restless, since late afternoon. Fruit bats make their shrill screeches outside. I lie here in the semi-dark fantasising escape, revenge, violence. I want to take back my pathetic letter with its appeal to love, maturity, a future. I fantasise tearing it up and shoving the pieces into the Armani bag, or stamping on one of his precious paintings or bundling up the two McCahons and dumping them on X the painter's doorstep. Where

can I go? Where's home? His withholding nature, the meanness, the lies, the sneaking, the self-satisfaction about his novel, the concrete-filled room of 'greatness'. His sardonic smile when I told him about Clive James teaching me to tango: 'Was this before other people arrived, or did you do it in front of people?' 'Both.' 'Was everybody dancing?' 'No. Just us.' He looks at me without speaking, then turns his face away with that smile.

The pain. It's like an invasion, infecting every cell.

———

In the morning I sit on the floor in his workroom, where our shoe polish is kept, to clean my sandals.

H: 'Have you bought yourself something at Armani?'

V: 'No, it's something X got for her mother's birthday, that she wanted hidden.'

H: 'What is it?'

V: 'A hat or something, I think.'

———

I set out for St Neot. I'm so tired, so scared and lonely. My whole body is aching. I'm terrified of the pain. From St Neot I call W. She assures me that he loves me, that he wouldn't have been able to write the novel without me, that he's always had flirtatious friendships, and that one can bring about by one's own behaviour the thing one most fears. She suggests I stay at St Neot for a few days, to take the pressure off. I cheer up and play a bit of Irish music on my little stereo. By now it's lunchtime. I stride home to pick up the things I'll need. He's out. I pick up my nightie and the mozzy zapper, then thinking I need a suitcase I go into his workroom to get one down from the big cupboard. As I cross his room, moving fast, I notice a sheet of paper folded over on the desk. In my absolutely last naïve moment in this history I think, with a little kick of hope, 'Hey! He's started to answer my letter!' I unfold it and read the salutation. Oh, it's years since he wrote that to me—hurray! Then I read on.

———

A blow from a baseball bat.

———

I stand there holding the paper. Then I stumble into the kitchen and go berserk. Soup, coffee cups, butter all over the cupboard fronts. The espresso machine I seize and fling violently to the ground. It splashes dirty water all over my shirt and skirt. I pick up the Napisan and put it in the suitcase with the iron, pepper grinder, bread knife, TV remote. I wrench the McCahons off the wall. Hide them under a bed? Too pathetic. Smash? No, I love them. I prop them on the couch back with a note to X: 'Why wait for the will? Have them now.' I destroy the note. I want to steal the black hill painting but it won't fit into the suitcase. I call W, sobbing and raving: 'I found a letter. A love letter to X. Did you know? *Did you know?*' 'Of course not! I had no idea!' 'I'm smashing things. I've got the hammer in my hand.' 'Hel. Put the hammer down. Put. The hammer. Down.' I put it down. 'Darling. Go to your office. Go to St Neot and stay there.' I hang up and rip open the Armani bag, there's a dark blue straw hat in it with a narrow round turned-up brim. I punch it twice in the crown but it keeps popping back into shape. I throw it on to his desk, and drop two of his big ugly shoes on top of it. I get from the bedroom the Armani scarf he gave me in New York and cut it into pieces with the scissors, and pour a bottle of ink on it. I grab the proof copy of his fucking novel and fling it down on his desk with the shoes and the hat. I wrench the cap off his Mont Blanc fountain pen and stab the proof copy with the nib, gripping the pen in my fist like a dagger. I stab and stab, I press and screw and grind. The nib gives way, bleeding ink, and twists into a little golden knot. I hurl it aside.

———

I stagger downstairs with a load of bags and a suitcase and take a cab to St Neot. The fat driver asks me if I've seen the movie *Flubber*, and what did I make of *The Absent-Minded Professor*. On neither do I have an opinion but I remain polite. I dump the gear and head back on foot, walking fast, giddy and sweating. Back at the flat I seize the blue straw hat and slice it into strips with my sewing scissors. I shove one strip into each of his big ugly black suede shoes. I leave a note on a card: 'Don't you know that being lied to makes people crazy?'

———

I open the humidor. Rows of matte brown cylinders. I grab a handful and rush out to the kitchen. The orange saucepan is up-ended in the sink with the beetroot soup I made for him under it, half run down the drain. I lift the pan off the spilt soup, force the squashed, snapped cigars into the muck, and lower the pan over it, to surprise him.

———

Off I go again in another cab, loaded down with gear. I drop it and walk quickly back, planning to empty the entire contents of the humidor into a bath which I will run specially, or else tear them to bits and flush them down the dunny. On the street I run into the China scholar and her flatmate. I greet them with a manic cheerfulness.

———

I throw open the front door and there he is, barefoot and gaping in his T-shirt and boxers. 'What's the matter?' He rushes at me and tries to grab my upper arms. I barge straight past him, gasping and sobbing: 'What's the *matter*? I read the letter, you liar! You cheat! You lied to me! You lied to me!'

V: 'It's not what you think! I didn't lie to you! Nobody lied to you!'

H: 'Oh don't start again! She was with you, wasn't she! She came back from Melbourne with you in the car!'

V: 'She didn't! No, she did not!'

H: 'You're still lying! I knew you were lying yesterday when you told me you stopped in a motel in Gundagai and lay on the bed and *read*! You would never do that! You're too mean! You lay on the bed all afternoon with her, didn't you! *She* was with you!'

V: 'No! She wasn't!'

H: (sobbing loudly) 'V! I *beg* you not to tell me any more lies! If you lie to me any more I'll go insane!'

———

Eventually he admitted it. She had flown down to Melbourne after I'd left, he'd met her at the airport and they'd set out straight away. When I got home from the lunch party yesterday and found him all hot and flustered, he'd just dropped her off at her place. I flung myself on the couch and wept and howled, doubled up, holding a hanky over my face. He kept trying to get a grip on my arms and I kept shouting, 'Don't you touch me! Don't you dare touch me! You lied! You lied!' 'I didn't lie!' 'You did lie! You lied and lied! You lied *all year*! And five minutes ago you were still telling me she wasn't with you on the drive! In the motel! At Gundagai!'

V: 'I didn't want to tell you.'

H: 'Why? Why?'

V: 'Because it would hurt you and make you upset.'

H: 'For Christ's sake! Nothing is worse than being lied to! No pain is worse than that!'

The bitterness and disgust, the self-disgust for having been a fool. I kept groaning and crying out, 'I can't bear this pain.'

I got calmer. He went out to the kitchen and got a cloth and began to clean up. I sat on the phone chair, slack and stupid, beyond speech.

———

He said he was sorry. He said he didn't want us to break up. He said
he didn't want me to move out. He said he was trying to break it off
with her gently. I didn't believe anything he said.

'Make me trust you again,' I said. 'Do something to make me
trust you.'

'What can I do to make you trust me? It's like the Bible. You'll
just have to believe the bits you can believe.'

———————

In the middle of this, the phone rang. It was Clive James. He
announced himself jovially as 'your tango partner'. He said he was
sitting down with two of my books—'your pellucid prose'—and was
calling to pass on the names of two tango schools that gave group
classes in Buenos Aires. He told me I was a natural and should
follow it up. He said he was sure we would meet again in London.
The timing of this call could not have been more felicitous.

———————

Within twenty-four hours V was off the back foot and almost airy.
Very keen to get the focus off the sex and lies part and back to what
had been wrong before 'this happened'—namely, all the unsatisfac-
tory things about me that had made him want to have an affair.
He's already told X that I trashed the apartment. I shrugged. I must
maintain this shrug: any minute now he will begin to reproach me
for the wreckage. Oh, and he tells me the reason why she 'doesn't
much like' me: because at her birthday party, after she had opened
the presents and thanked people, I had come up to her and said
sarcastically, 'What a performance!'

———————

A night at St Neot. Lay there and lay there and lay there. At dawn
I stuck my head out the window. The city! Painted flat on the sky
out to my left, above the naval ships and the strip of green water and
the finger wharf being dismantled. And in front of the skyscrapers

a blur of cloud, discrete, like a scarf hanging in the sunny air. I put
on my walking shoes and set out on a new route: to Mrs Macquarie's
Chair. Round there it's almost like bush, the smell of gums, the
harbour pale blue and silvery on my right.

———

Yep, here it comes: he grizzles about having to go all the way to
Leichhardt to replace the espresso machine—how could I have done
such a disgraceful, appalling thing? Trashing the place? Tearing up
his proof copy? Pouring ink on a story he was writing? And how
could I have destroyed X's mother's *hat*? He'd promised to reim-
burse X, she went back to Emporio to get another one and they were
all sold out. She called him from a public phone and screamed and
said she wanted to punch me in the face, to kill me, and he didn't
blame her! Why was I so destructive? I laugh in wild glee: '*Destructive*? She's got the gall to stash something where I live? When she's
fucking my husband? This is enemy territory! She shouldn't be
surprised if it gets destroyed!' 'Don't you lecture me! I don't want
to get a lecture from you!' 'It's not a lecture. It's a challenge—I challenge you! Stop dodging and lying and being a sleaze!' Deadlock.
I gather my things and head for the door. 'I can't walk you home,'
he says with a sneer. 'I'm expecting a phone call. From my British
publisher.'

———

Yes, he says at last, it had been an affair all along, though not sexual
till very recently. I don't believe the second part but at least I can
breathe: I *wasn't mad*, all last year. But the following day he claws
back the ground he's given, becomes proud and defensive and cold.
He's back in his concrete bunker and looks out at me through the
slit, with a cool, appraising face. All he wants is to move along, to
get to the bit where I cop the blame.

———

The restaurant was breezy, with a leafy outlook to Hyde Park. He ordered me a glass of French champagne. We sat calmly together and talked about the things we always talk about: certain writers, movies, thoughts we'd had about them. Waiting for the bus in Castlereagh Street we crouched on the threshold of a shop, so exhausted we could hardly speak.

———

'An enormous blip' is what he calls this.

———

A friend called.
    'Is V having an affair?'
    'Yes.'
    'Is it with X the painter?'
    'Yes—how did you know?'
    'I guessed. He took my husband round to her place and tried to get him to buy one of her paintings.'

———

He asked me if I still loved him. I said, 'I *have* loved you, very much. We've been connected to each other in a deep way. But the connection's been uprooted. It's all bedraggled and torn.'

———

I use the word *negotiate*. He begins sullenly to complain that he is now completely without a place to negotiate *from*, that he has lost any arguing position by virtue of 'this bloody nonsense', that he will be 'forced', by this, to make changes that he doesn't want. 'This could be like the Versailles Treaty,' he says. 'Punitive damages exacted, and then look what happened.'

———

It's terribly hot. I suggest a late afternoon swim at Bondi. 'But it's not what I normally *do*!' 'Get your bathers.' The weather changes while we're on the bus. He becomes dead again, looking straight ahead without expression. We wade at dusk into awkward choppy little waves, the water dark green and riffled. Air damp and full of turbulence, scraggy dark clouds moving fast and low, a dull alien light far out to sea. Globe lights along the foreshore stand far apart, like full moons. Bondi is ugly and brutish, dressing sheds primitive, floor clogged with wet sand and the debris of a scorcher. We eat fish and chips in a shelter through which a damp wind tears.

H: 'Remember when we used to pash down here?'

V: (with a defiant smile) 'No.'

H: 'Why do you say no?'

V: 'We only did it once.'

———————

His dreary resistance to everything, his reluctance to live. And *my constant appeasing*. Do I really want to spend any more of my life with this half-dead curmudgeon?

———————

God, I'm bored.

———————

Outside my window at St Neot white cockatoos are eating berries off the huge tree: big, muscly birds with jaunty postures, crunching the fruits that they thrust into their beaks with a deft movement of one foot. Their activity sounds like the first drops of heavy rain. The air is cool, stirring the curtains.

———————

V: 'I feel hardly human.'

H: 'I feel as if I've been fed through one of those sausage machines. I'm made of sausage meat, but shaped in human form.'

V: 'I feel more like an animal. Like a fox, that's been hunted. In its lair, driven to ground.'

I look at him curiously.

V: 'You wouldn't ever feel like an animal, would you.'

H: 'Oh yes, I would. There are times when I feel like a beaten cur. With its tail curved right in between its legs.'

———

R is gratifyingly and totally on my side in the matter of the hat. She keeps laughing, incredulous that a woman could do such a thing as to *hide* the hat. I tell her I cry all the time and he hasn't shed a tear. 'You're falling in with his reality, there,' she says. 'You carry all the emotion, and absolve him from it. He needs to have feeling, and you need to have self-containment.'

———

G calls and tells me he's just written a short story he thought was good, but when he showed it to M-C she flung it back at him, exclaiming that it was so V-influenced she couldn't stand it. We giggle weakly.

———

Various friends of V's and mine who've read his novel have remarked to me, 'He could never have written this if it hadn't been for you.' My bet is he'll declare that the book has come out of his 'friendship' with X the painter. WHAT? I put in seven years breaking rocks, and she frolics in at the last minute and takes the credit? But wait. He would never attribute to the influence of *some bloody woman* a radical warming in his writing, if such there be. If there has been a change, he'll claim it grew from years of serious application to difficult, mighty texts. At this I start laughing. Sick of it. Goodnight nurse.

———

Walking back to St Neot from the drycleaner with my dress from M's wedding over my arm, I spot X a few yards in front of me, in an ink-blue linen skirt and high-heeled sandals. I say her name. She turns, stands still, looking at me.

H: 'What can we say to each other?'

X: 'I don't know.'

We are both trembly-voiced. We walk along together. She is tiny, barely five feet tall. The perfect skin, the unlined face, the pretty lace blouse, the toughness. She gives nothing away. She raps out harsh statements and impertinent questions.

X: 'Your marriage must have been in a very bad state. When did this begin?'

H: 'I beg your pardon?'

X: 'V has told me that you live separate lives.'

H: 'That's not true.'

X: 'You told me he said I didn't like you, and was not interested in you. I asked him. He said he had not said this.'

H: 'He did say it. You must realise he's telling lies to both of us.'

X: (stubbornly) 'I trust what he tells me.'

H: 'He has *told lies to both of us*.'

Her face sets hard. This must be her famous 'independence': she experiences no female solidarity. I see that she means business. I have no resources to deal with such a woman. I'm breathing hard, with one hand over my mouth.

H: 'What do you want?'

X: 'I just want this pain to stop.'

I am supposed to be going to a party. Holding my moonlight-coloured dress on its hanger, I turn and run away across the park.

———

Our friend calls from Melbourne. 'People know what he's like. We're very fond of him. We miss the talks. But we've been watching what he's doing to you. You thawed him at the start, Hel. You did it with your whole heart. And it was very good for a while. But now he's stopped you from writing. He's cementing himself again. Don't let him cement *you*.'

———

The Polish philosopher, on living alone: 'You wake in the middle of the night, to a deep silence. That silence is where the writing comes from.'

Here, that deep silence is panic, worthlessness, jealousy, grief, loneliness, despair. I block it out with earplugs and a Normison.

———

Is it a common syndrome? That on the eve of success, after long struggle, you dump the person who's stuck with you through the hard years of slog? Why? Is it because you don't want to be dogged by the intimate witness to your humiliating battle? Do you want to explode fully formed on to the world stage, as if by pure inspiration and will?

———

What his novel cost. No piano. No holidays. No weekends. No outings. We sold my car. No river, no sea, no garden. No dog. No outdoor clothesline. No singing, no dancing, no swimming. No children. No noise. No fresh air. No sunlight. No wide-open windows. He has never understood what Peter Craven calls 'the deep moral value of fun'.

———

I don't dream any more.

———

Just now, putting out the rubbish at St Neot, I found there was a back staircase leading to the flat roof of the building. I walked right across the roof till I was at the front, above my own flat, and there I stood, gazing out towards the Opera House sails, the bridge, the ships at Woolloomooloo, the green water near those ships. Two vast plane trees overhang the roof on its western side. The sun is shining, the air is fresh and breezy. Someone has pegged washing along an old rope clothesline. I sit on a rusty metal chair and say, in an orderly manner, with clasped hands, 'This is the day that the Lord has made:

I will rejoice and be glad in it.'

———

My sister calls. She tells me I shouldn't make myself 'so available'. I ask her what she actually thinks of V: 'Do you like him?'

A pause.

'I liked him when you lived in Melbourne. I liked him a lot. But when you went back to Sydney he became weird.'

———

'You can either put it down and bolt,' says M-C, 'and leave the field to her, or you can move back in and be the wife, and fight. I don't mean fight *her*, but fight for what you want, with love. In the end that's all you've got to offer.'

———

'You're "going to fight"?' says my sister. 'What are you fighting *for*?'

———

I went to our shared appointments diary, to put in my Antarctica trip dates. Lying on the open page, face-up, was a note to V from X the painter describing our encounter in the street: 'I don't think I told her anything you wouldn't have. If she tells you she didn't run after me, don't believe her.'

———

I am beginning to see that you can't numb yourself and step cleanly out of a marriage. You can't just pack your stuff and walk out the door. There *is* no door. You have to dynamite your way out. Blast, burrow, crawl—and you have to let yourself keep on feeling it, every inch of the way.

———

'Don't think about the future,' says my sister. 'It will form itself, if you're true to what's happening inside you. If you jump over the pain and start making plans, they won't be true plans.'

———

Buenos Aires. I might have loved being here, but as it is I trudge
up and down the avenidas lugging my smashed and bleeding heart.
The amount and quality of pain I'm in is somehow sort of unbeliev-
able. But the city has a loose, good-tempered ease and generosity.
Dirty air, taxis with yellow roofs, big Art Deco buildings like Paris.
I don't understand much but can get by with a lot of gesturing.
People are patient, sweet and generous with smiles. I sit in a side-
walk restaurant with a beer, waiting for a *minibif con fritas* for my
dinner. As always V has given me a shopping list for cigars. In the
coolroom of the shop I had what M as a child once called 'a sudden
feeling of meanness', and bought a pair of five-inch Cohibas instead
of the expensive boxes he had specified. In the last week I have lost
half a stone and my fingernails have split and cracked and peeled
back. Before I left he was going through his charade of what he
calls 'blowing on the embers', 'having another crack at it', while also
stating several times that, 'If all this falls apart, she'll probably be
around to pick up the pieces—I'll probably spend a fair bit of time
with her, yes.' The nights are frightful. There's something with
teeth in the bottom of my heart, gnawing gnawing gnawing at it
like a big black rat. My personal evil rat. I drop a Normison and
pass out till daybreak, when I start talking to myself.

In the street I heard a man singing. A harsh, powerful voice, full of
anguish. I kept walking till I found him. He was busking, sitting on
the ground against a shop window. His face was dark and scarred.
He had no legs. Somewhere further on, an accordion. A man and
a woman were dancing a tango. I forgot Clive James, his friendly
sweaty grace and laughing advice. The melodrama of the dancers'
lowered brows and surly gazes, their strained abdominal muscles,
made me want to shout a curse. But then I looked at their feet. It
was shocking how closely they had to work, how delicately and with

what manic precision; how little space each dancer's feet left for the other's. It was a breathless, intimate struggle for ground.

———

If this has to end, I want to end it cleanly, with honour. I'm not letting go until he respects me. When he stops lying to me, when he tells me the truth, that's when I'll leave. *I will not let you go until you bless me.*

———

Got to get up at 5 am tomorrow for the four-hour flight to Ushuaia, the world's southern-most town. I wish I could have a clean heart. Mine's like an ashtray. Full of Cohiba butts and spit. Antarctica, here I come.

———

A force-9 gale in the Beagle Channel. If I strap myself in and brace my feet against the end of the bunk I can handle the rolling and pitching. It's cold here. It's white. There's icebergs. A collapsing glacier. An abandoned whaling station. Penguins. Zodiacs, whales. Beaches made of big grey rattling stones. Air so clean that the inside of my head is an ice landscape, an element of brutal clarity, like the first snort of cocaine. All I want to do is grip the rail and gaze at these crazy, building-sized lumps of ice. It's too mighty to be crammed into this book of shit and misery. I'll have to keep a separate notebook for the article or I'll go off my head.

———

In the sauna with the ship's doctor. We get naked and talk, red-faced and dripping. She says stress can make your fingernails crack and peel, and your hair fall out. She parted from her husband five years ago. It took them 'six agonising months' to break up: 'I didn't want to live, at that stage.' But once the break was made, 'things started to go right for me. I'd been working against the flow of things for so long, and suddenly I was going *with* it instead.' 'It's amazing, isn't it,' I said, 'how much against-ness you can go on tolerating.'

———

The guy who's running this voyage has climbed Mount Everest and K2. He walks with a wiry bounce and a spring, alert as an animal, very clear-eyed and sensitive, but also calm, a watcher, contained; when he speaks, eloquent; and under it all, a rare sense of grit. When you're near him, you feel completely yourself. I tell him I've been reading a book about a long-ago Antarctic expedition: 'It says the men would let out shouts of bliss.' All his lights come on: 'Yes. That's what climbing mountains is for—those squirts of sublime joy.'

———

On our last evening I ran out on deck looking for stars (of which for ten days I had seen none, due to cloud cover) and stood at the rail in my cotton pyjamas, unlaced shoes and polar jacket. Mild air, a low, smooth, old-looking coastline a couple of miles away on the port side; behind it the last pink flush of sunset, then a layer of apricot yellow, then clear dark-blue night with a handful of fresh stars. I took a breath and smelt something dry and warm, like grass. Land.

———

Hotel Albatros, Ushuaia. Slept deeply in a single bed under an open window. I got up in the dark to piss and the room was tilting. Even after I remembered I was on land it kept swaying and moving. I had to grab hold of the furniture.

———

The waitress's tiny daughter, Yvonne, knelt on a chair next to me at dinner and entertained me in Spanish. I understood barely a word but we drew pictures on the paper tablecloth and made each other laugh.

———

With a woman called Deborah I took a cab to the chairlift, then set out on foot towards 'el glaciar', along a track that climbed and wound beside a loudly rushing stream. Stony ground with clumps of dull and dark green moss. We battled along merrily, up and up. Overhead hung curly-rimmed stony peaks, split by a narrow, not-quite-pristine glacier, and scarved by constantly evaporating thin white clouds. Many fast, cold streams came chattering down. High up, Deborah sat down to rest and gaze out to the Beagle Channel, while I scrambled on, up goat-width twisty tracks and over large bare humps of shaly grey stone, almost crawling, grabbing at the ground with my bare hands. My wedding ring slipped off and I thought of flipping it away into the scree, but strung it on the chain round my neck and kept climbing. The higher I went, the more elated I became. The ground here and there was springy with the matted roots of low, coarse-leaved plants. The concrete inside me started to soften and give way. My whole face quivered. I got down on my hands and knees and pushed my nose into the tight, springy moss-pads, breathed in their woody perfume. I sat on a rock and stared at the stones around my feet: saw the stripes of them, their oldness. I picked up three and put them in my pocket: stones from Tierra del Fuego, the land of fire. I wondered if it was altitude that was making me light-headed, or if these were 'squirts of sublime joy'. I sat still and looked out over the channel. Cloud shadows stood like pale, vague marble pillars, pinkish-cream, on the glossy surface of the water.

I raved out loud as I came down the loose-surfaced humps in a crouch, knees flexed, both hands spread: 'Give me another twenty years, Lord. I swear I'll use every minute. I'll never grow so old again. Give me twenty-five more years.'

———

The dreamy beauty of this harbour, cast away at the bottom of the world. I sat on the wharf. The evening light, warm and gentle and clear, brought out startlingly the red hull of the *Humboldt* from

Peru, whose invisible crew I could hear singing along in manly voices to a radio: it was a Lionel Richie song, 'All Night Long'.

———

Wakeful, I watch a talk show on TV Uruguay. A sad woman in her thirties speaks about the way *el amor de su vida* has turned out to be a *ladrón*. I don't know what a *ladrón* is. But I can guess.

———

Rio Gallegos airport at 4 am. My last air of this continent, between terminal and plane: a waft of dry grass on a small steady breeze, in the dark. Fingernail of a moon, a tiny star or two. Breathe, breathe it, and be thankful.

———

The plane is running ahead of the dawn. The horizon behind us has been flushed for over an hour without ever growing any brighter or extending its area of colour. The curved little moon very high and clear. Under us, an endless layer of pale and puffy cotton. A young woman beside me, from Trujillo in Peru, tells me her story in careful, hardworking English. Glistening dark-brown eyes, gentle smiles. She marries an Australian, after three years in Sydney he leaves her, her mother-in-law helps her to get back on her feet. She works now as a nursing assistant in a hospital and (her face lights up) she has just been accepted at TAFE to study for the next level. We talk quietly about gardening.

'It's a wirtue?' she says. 'A quality? Of Australian women, that they like to make a garden? A wirtue?'

'Yes. A virtue.'

———

I was braced to be stoical, to get myself home and start the final round. But he met my plane. He welcomed me affectionately, with full eye contact and a kiss, his face open. I was completely thrown. He'd made the flat clean and orderly. He'd gone to Edgecliff for attractive food. He made gin and tonics. He volunteered that he had seen X only once, that they'd spoken on the phone, that he had broken it off with her. I was incredulous. He insisted. He said, 'Something in me's been broken, by seeing the misery you're going through, and the misery she's in.' He said this quietly, almost humbly.

I said, 'What did you mean, when you said something had broken?'

'It was a sort of a soft…crack.'

'Maybe it was your heart breaking.'

'Is that what they call a broken heart?'

'I think so, yes.'

Then, lying on his back on the couch, he put out both arms to me, and I knelt beside him, and we held each other without speaking for a long time.

––––––––

V's British publisher called. In magisterial tones he invited me to accompany V to London ('over here in the spring'). I thanked him but said I thought V was planning to make the trip alone, if he made it at all; I said I thought he had serious doubts about doing publicity. Long pause. 'He *has* to come here.' Longer pause. 'It matters im-*mense*-lah.' Tremendous pause. 'People have to hear him *thinking*.'

––––––––

After church I was in my room, cleaning up my desk, when V came in carrying a cardboard carton. He placed it on the floor by the door: 'Here's a box, if you need to recycle paper.' 'Thanks!' It was empty. An hour or so later I approached it with a sheaf of scrap paper and found it one-third full. How did that happen? Did I put them there? Was I jet-lagged? On the top, face-up, lay a couple of my old notes to V, and under them several A4 sheets covered in his

small, rapid hand, messy with crossings-out, like discarded drafts.
I pulled one out.

*Again I told her I loved you, how you had become so important; that
she and I had had the wobbles long ago; that, yes, it was an obsession,
you and I, and good.*

The horrible sick trembling. I heard myself humming and
whistling as I knelt over the carton.

*She asked if I still loved her. 'To some extent' was all I could say, in
truth. I feel such pity for H, her shocking misery. G phoned yesterday. He
has been good, very sympathetic, very understanding of you. We spoke
for more than an hour. He listened. Acted like the good friend he is. Was
all sympathy—he thought living with H could be 'hard going'. Apparently he told H that. He was strangely ambivalent about my history
of expecting silence and solitude from 9 am, in order, as he put it, to
write masterpieces. I know that your love and loyalty were undivided.
A selfless, exemplary love and generosity, without fault. Yet it remained
that I was unable to bring down the knife on H.*

———

'What are these?'

Just notes, he said. Stuff he'd written before I went to the Antarctic. After I'd found the letter and he'd called it off with her.

'I used to respect you. Even when your judgments were too
harsh, I respected you for not being afraid to say what you really
thought. But you're a liar. You've lied to her as well. You never once
told me you loved her. You never told me it was "an obsession". You
always told me she was "just a friend", someone you "really liked
to see", and that I was just "a jealous person". You gaslighted me.'

'What does that mean?'

'Oh, go and look it up.'

———

'The worst thing for me these last few years,' he says, 'was seeing you turn away from me.' He holds up one flat hand, fingers together, vertical, and slowly turns its palm outwards. And it's true. I did turn away.

———

This explosion of Eros. The *arrival* of Eros, in a frozen sea. The groaning of the floes. The *pain* Eros brings. The necessity of pain so that other feelings can flow.

———

How can I believe anything he says? I can't trust my own instincts any more. But whatever happens, day by day, I will not bolt. I'm going to live this out, however it ends. I know I will have to leave him. But first I have to live it through, right to the bitter end.

———

I inspected a place in Edgecliff Road. 'Too far,' he said. 'Much too far. Imagine having to walk that far.'

———

H: 'I saw X in the street. She didn't see me. I realised that she must be sad. And I felt ashamed of myself for having railed against her.'
    He didn't speak, but nodded.
    H: 'And I want to say—I realise that *you* must be sad, too.'
    He just looked at me. I saw that he *was* sad. His face was dark with sadness.

———

He makes a concession. He offers to rent a place to work. 'All I need's a bare cell, whereas what you need is two bedrooms, and it'll cost a bloody fortune. I could rent a place for six months and see how it goes.' So staggered I couldn't speak. After all these years he is talking about it simply as a question of logistics, and not as an attack by me on the very fibre of his innermost being. Later I recall that the last time he made this offer it was a lie. I also know that it's come too late.

———

I repotted the geraniums from the 'sewing room' windowsill. Yanked them out of the old potting mix and found with something like disgust that the roots—especially in the second pot in which two plants grew, very leggy though still stubbornly flowering—were very long, and had been obliged to twine and twist inside the narrow pot, fighting each other for nourishment and space. I squatted on the kitchen floor and upended the pots, scraped out the exhausted mix, replaced it with new, and then with knife and scissors fiercely pruned the three plants. Their stems and roots I cut back hard. Almost grief at this act, trimming back the plants so they'd fit into the cramped space available for them here in this apartment.

———

G: 'You lost your voice under his influence. You absorb influence very fast. And out came high art stuff that wasn't properly digested. Whereas *he* digested *your* influence slowly, over many years, and out came something really different, a deeper change, and a *huge* improvement.'

———

Taxi driver with hearing aid. He asked me how I was. I said I had man troubles. 'Husband?' 'Yes.' 'Fooling around with another woman?' 'Yes.' 'Oooh. People like that should be staked out on an ants' nest.' He gives me advice: 'Don't be too tired. Jump him. When he least expects it.'

I try this. It works.

'Lately,' says V, 'you've been almost the way you were at the beginning.'

———

A woman writes me a letter: 'There's a quiet place in my heart where I'm waiting for your next book.'

———

To Breastscreen, for the results of my second mammogram. Half a dozen women in the waiting room, Greek, Italian. We get talking, comparing notes, no one's shy, in fact we're all probably a bit manic. There's music playing, Tracy Chapman, 'Give Me One Reason'. The door opens, someone calls my name. I jump to my feet. Five faces are raised to me, smiling, but strained. I come out again, with my sheet of paper: 'I'm clear.' Cries of congratulation. Laughing, they reach out their hands and touch me, as if for luck.

———

W remarks on the 'lively' look of the geraniums on the sill. 'I pruned them.' 'Did you cut back the roots as well?' 'Yep. Cut 'em back hard, top and bottom.' 'Good. Now they'll really start to flourish.'

———

I feel as if I've stepped out of a suit of armour. It's still standing there, with all its metal and straps and buckles and visor, waiting for me to climb back in. But I'm not going to.

———

A creature lives secretly in our kitchen. It chewed up a cockroach motel, and while we were down in the park after dinner it ripped open a plastic bag of food scraps, foraged in it and left a mess.

    H: 'It must be a horrible big rat, if it chews up plastic.'

    V: 'It's probably only a mouse, sweetheart.'

    H: 'We've got to get some poison.'

    V: 'We'll get a cage, and take it down to the park.'

    Privately I think of it as X, his feelings for her, her effect on 'our home'. On the couch I describe its ravages. 'Sounds,' she says, 'like the rat you said was gnawing at your stomach in Buenos Aires. You're afraid it will come back, unless you kill it.'

———

This morning I put on my Armani trousers, I'm thin enough now for them to hang off me, but I didn't like myself in them, so I took them off and put on a yellow skirt. I don't want to look like a man. I want to feel and act like a woman. The Polish philosopher, with whom I had lunch at the Queen Victoria Building, complimented me on what she called my 'more flowing silhouette'. She told me how she and her husband had parted: how horribly hurt she was when he took up with someone else, but she 'opened the door and said, "If you want to go, you must go."' He goes. (The flat belonged to her.) Some months later he comes back, 'but I soon realised that our marriage was dead, and I didn't want it any more. I know now that I was right, that the deep part of my life was ready to begin— but that if I hadn't had that man/woman thing with him, I wouldn't have been able to move into it.'

On the way home I bought coffee cups to replace the ones I smashed.

———

The rat. Last night I was climbing into bed when it shot past me in a wide fast curve, heading for the living room and thence to the kitchen where it met V, ran over his bare foot, failed to get behind the fridge, skidded across the floor and vanished behind the stove. I yelled out as it passed me—it was *galloping*—I heard its claws grab the carpet weave. Its body looked about as big as a clenched fist but V insists it's only a mouse. 'I never saw a mouse with a tail that long,' I said. 'If that rat could speak, it would have a Romanian accent.' He turned his head away to hide a laugh: 'Oh, don't talk like that.'

———

A lovely evening: inky sky with stars, fresh breeze after a warm day. We went walking in the dark down to Rushcutters, hand in hand. He told me that my sister had called him, to ask how things were going with us. It was 'very nice' of her to call, he said, but ultimately it had been 'useless', she had moved quickly into 'applied psychology'—and away he swerved into his jeremiad against my family, their rudeness to him, their total lack of interest in him though for several years he had taken *great* interest in them, until he realised how self-obsessed they were, at which point he had given up.

I said sadly, 'Did they hurt you?'

'They didn't "*hurt*" me. They made me angry, and then indifferent. Who do they think they are? What's so special about them, that they can behave like that towards me?'

I said I was really sorry, but that I didn't know what I could do about it. I tried very tentatively to suggest that he might perhaps have opened himself to them more, talked about himself, volunteered information.

'Nobody *asked*!'

'But why did you have to wait to be asked?'

'Other people ask lots of questions!'

'I've moved eight hundred kilometres away from them—what more can I do?'

'Yes, you've moved, but they're still a large part of your thoughts. You're always concerned with what they're doing.'

'Do I bash your ear about them? Do I go on and on?'

'No—but they're always in your head.'

As for his own family, he's simply divested himself of it. They seem to mean nothing to him at all. He rarely mentions them, or gets in touch with them. I don't understand this, and I never will.

———

I ask him what he thinks it achieves, for him not to be seeing X. He twists away, he doesn't want to talk about it. I repeat the question, gently: 'If you're pining, what does it achieve?' 'I'm pining for *everyone's* sadness. It makes things simpler.'

———

I wonder if we drink too much gin.

———

Woke early, heard the wind blowing in the eucalypts outside, lay there feeling I had exactly the right amount of covering, liking the slitheriness of my silk nightie. Thought calmly about where I can live. Where can I afford to live? I tried to make calculations. At that moment none of it was hurting me. I felt sorry for *him*. The chaos that's about to break open his narrow little life. The split library, the vanished stereo and CDs. I liked hearing the wind. I imagined myself hearing it from some other apartment, in a bed that's completely mine, an apartment without a rat.

———

Yesterday I stayed working at St Neot till 6.30. As the day ended I noticed again a quietness starting in me, an increase in concentration that was calm, and happy. I looked forward to going home and seeing V, but at the same time I wanted to stay where I was and sink deeper into that quiet.

———

In a mood of manic confidence I tell him I'm sick of being like Juno, rushing round the countryside hurling thunderbolts at nymphs. How silly it is, I declare, that falling in love should have to mean a wholesale destruction and abandonment of something valuable. And at our age, isn't the idea of going back to square one with someone new a bit ludicrous? If he takes up with X the painter he'll have two little ladies fussing over him, singing happy birthday, serving up special meals, showing him the pretty things they've sewn—and after a while this feminine twittering and fluttering will start to drive him completely insane. He'll start to miss his over-emphatic wife and her boorish, uncaring relatives who leave him in peace from one year's end to the next.

And to think you can replace me, I gambol on, with *another artist*! The hysteria! The tears! The talk of suicide! We are both laughing. I propose a more creative approach. I have vital interests that he doesn't share, and I no longer want to cut them off. I'd like to hang out with other people, hear different music, go out drinking and dancing, hike up mountains with guys like the ones I met on the ship. I don't see why as mature people we can't work out a way to have what we need without having to turn our backs on each other. Does this sound like hippie bullshit? No! It doesn't! He is cheering up. He makes a coffee. We drink it.

Meanwhile, strong gusty winds blow along the sides of our building. Sun flickers in and out, flashes off neighbours' windows. Air fresh, dry, cool.

———————

I bought a rat trap, the killing sort. V set it with a piece of my veal stew and stood it on the kitchen floor. Middle of the night, over the sound of rain and wind, we woke to a sharp snap. Lay on our backs with beating hearts. A soft dragging sound. Oh no. It's dragging the trap to its hole. The sounds stopped. Silence. V got up and went to look: 'It's a rat all right. And it's big.' I got as far as the couch back and saw the dark blob lying still, the mean curve of the tail, and jumped shuddering back into bed. We lay restless waiting for dawn. Listening for its family. 'They'll come looking for *you*,' said V.

———————

In the morning we inspected the dead rat properly. It was female with visible nipples—were there babies somewhere?—and was quite beautiful, its small ears round and shell-like, its eyes alert, dark and wide open. The trap had caught it across the bridge of its nose, not the back of its neck. I imagined with horror the blinding explosion of pain, the cut-off breath, the smashed-forward tip of the skull—the shock, the instinctive struggle and twitch, the closing down of light, then blank.

'It's pretty, isn't it,' I said.

'It's got pretty fur,' said V.

Hundreds of people were at church this morning. On the way out I said to the vicar, 'What a crowd! Were you worried there wouldn't be enough?' He said, 'Each slice I know I can cut into thirty-six pieces. I made a rough calculation and there turned out to be plenty.'

Colm Tóibín at Z's place. His funny, muscular face all expressive and squashed-looking, his confidential way of talking, holding in laughter, dropping his voice to a whisper and pressing your arm for emphasis at the punchline. We shyly praised *The Heather Blazing*. V's face unusually open and undefended.

The wife of V's old painter friend calls: V had lunch with him last week and told him he was worried about my future. *Really?* Meanwhile, each day he brings out the brochures for container ships and spreads them on the table, as if wanting to suggest I come to Europe after all, though he doesn't say it outright. Then, on our walk this morning I say, 'When you go to England for the book—' and he says, 'Aw, I dunno if I'll go to England.' 'What? You're always telling me I'm doing big swerves, but what about you? I've never seen a bloke *do* such swerves.'

On the plane to the Perth Writers Festival I was waiting outside the toilet when the pilot, whose lunch was being delivered on a tray, glanced out through the open door and invited me into the cockpit. Two cheerful blokes, one with acne scars. They told me that airlines run courses to prevent pilots and flight officers from having fights that cause planes to crash. I expressed surprise but they told several hair-raising stories, one about how a flight officer, untrained in ways of overriding a madman's heavily defended mistake, had sat there and watched while the pilot brought down the plane on to a

ploughed-up runway, killing them both plus the whole plane-load
of passengers. 'There've been crashes,' said the flight officer, 'where
you can hear them fighting all the way down.'

———

Luxuriating here in my vast bed with its thick white sheets I hear a
toilet faintly flush in another room: comforting, companionable, as
if the hotel were a large house, where people I knew lived alongside
me. In the morning, busily ironing my clothes, I ponder the fact
that X didn't know why V hadn't left me when I first stumbled
on the letter. That'd be right: you don't hesitate, you administer
the 'blinding explosion of pain' and you *get out* while the rat's still
stunned and staggering. This must be what C meant when she said
on the phone: 'Hel. Don't be a wimp. Take a leaf out of the Eastern
European woman's handbook. Of how to play hardball.' I start to
laugh, thinking of C's tough Jewish nous and wicked grins. Then I
wonder if I've actually gone mad, if V's still scheming away with X,
getting me back on my feet so I'll be able to cop the coup de grâce
they've got in store.

———

Bus to Fremantle, dinner with J and his family. Ate and drank and
had fun. J told me that while I was in the Antarctic he had been
briefly in Sydney, and had a breakfast with V that 'lasted hours'.
V had talked to him at great length about our troubles. I was flab-
bergasted (a) that this had happened and (b) that V had made no
mention of it to me. 'He talked,' said J, 'like a man who felt he'd
fucked up in a really big way and didn't think there was much hope
of fixing things.' 'I imagine he left out the crucial factor of the third
person?' 'I got the impression there might be one, and from his
tone and expression I guessed it wasn't you who was involved. But
he skirted round it so subtly that I couldn't be sure. He mentioned
a painter, but I had no idea whether it was a man or a woman. He

wants to be a reclusive artist,' J went on, 'and to be married. You can't have it both ways.' 'Did you tell him this?' 'Of course. I said the flat should be a neutral space. You should *both* work outside it. He can afford to.'

————

V calls. He says his throat hurts.

H: 'Think you ought to see a doctor? Get her to shine her little torch down your throat?'

V: 'Aw no—bloody doctors.'

H: (gaily) 'When I get home I'll shove a torch down you myself. Right into the belly of the beast.'

————

The ukuleles at Zenith Music in Claremont. Top of the range, at nearly $700, Hawaiian ones of such sweet, chunky, dark, wood-scented beauty, such low action and effortless resonance and volume—'They can really fill a room,' says the salesman—that for a few moments the 'sickness of desire' came over me. I applied stern self-command and bought a German one for $139.

————

Went out for a drink in Perth with V's younger sister: small, fair, slight, with a narrow face in which I saw his, flickering and fading, though hers was lit by a greater animation. She gave me a folder of poems she had written. She said V had recently sent her a cheque to help with her daughter's wedding, and had signed the letter 'with love'. She was touched by the gift and amazed by the word 'love', as if it had never been used between them before. I dived right in: 'Why is V like he is? Why does he have so little contact with his family?' She talked about how V as a boy was 'always in trouble' with their father, who was 'a tyrant and a disciplinarian', though she herself had always got on well with him. (V had told me she was 'his favourite', and 'spoilt'.) If you weren't home at the exact time he'd specified, she said, 'you would get the strap, even if it was only six o'clock.' V left home 'much earlier than people did in those days', and went to Melbourne.

We ordered a second round of drinks and became hilarious, comparing notes about kids and music and work and all the things one talks about in bars. She offered to drive me to my dinner date with Elizabeth Jolley in Nedlands. We sped along the highway with the radio up loud, rocking and bopping and singing along. She told me the terrific stereo and speakers had cost almost half as much as had the car itself, a second-hand Mitsubishi.

———

Elizabeth and I also drank. When I said I had been feeling like Juno, hurling thunderbolts at nymphs, she became weak with laughter and said, 'Have you written about this? You should, you really should.' I took a taxi back to the hotel, under a tall dark-blue sky with a high, round, white, raving moon.

———

Busselton, in a 60s motel of the purest and most endearingly humble stripe. A breeze enters my room from a garden whose trees, foreign to me, cast a dense shade, dappled only at its edges. A gang of magpies on the grass outside the open door jostling pleasantly and letting loose an occasional curlicue of song: they don't seem to be improvising, like our magpies 'over east'; they have their shared melody and they sing it over and over.

———

There's to be an eclipse of the moon, which is blazing now in a perfect black sky. A gentle wind moving in several directions. Big dogs barking half a mile away.

———

A bookshop gig, an evening's work with other writers, a dinner, laughing and drinking and eating with friendly strangers; a whole night's sleep. Kookaburras strike up. I open my eyes, incredulous. Was the moon eclipsed while I slept? I was having so much fun I missed it!

———

And for all this, nature is never spent;
There lives the dearest freshness deep down things;
And though the last light of the black West went
Oh, morning, at the brown brink eastwards, springs—
Because the Holy Ghost over the bent
World broods with warm breast and with ah! bright wings.
—Gerard Manley Hopkins, 'God's Grandeur'

———

Z told R that he doesn't think I can write fiction if I stay with V. Maybe we can't mend this.

———

The publisher remarks that V's habit of judging people according to whether or not they've read Thomas Bernhard is 'the kind of inane snobbery that Bernhard himself would despise. You can tease V about his prejudices, though. I told him he wanted people entering a shop to do an exam before they're allowed to buy his book; and he laughed.'

———

I drove an old friend to a funeral in Maroubra. When we said goodbye he said, 'Thanks, Hel. You're adorable.' He took my face in both hands and kissed me on the mouth.

———

What I want to know—what I'm *curious* to know—is whether he's given her the impression that it's worth her while to wait. Whether their plan is to sit me out.

———

He won't contemplate J's sensible suggestion about the flat as neutral zone. Too expensive. When I point out that it's actually the cheapest solution by several hundred dollars a week, he switches back to the 'breaking of a lifelong work pattern' line.

———

'All the people who should be told *have* been told,' he says. 'Our friends are bored. They're sick of hearing about it.' Turns out he's been going round telling them that we've hit a rocky patch, that I'm unhappy. Puzzled people keep ringing me up: 'What's going on?' In each case, I learn that he has omitted to mention the third party.

———

Baptism of a baby called Monte, who lay back in the priest's arms, so relaxed that his silver-bangled right arm was flung out in a gesture of abandon, while his eyes roved calmly over the priest's face.

———

Domestic peace. I cook, he washes up, there is order and cheerful companionship. I've taken on a couple of little jobs. Writing changes everything. Anxiety drops away, my cage opens. I feel alive again, as if I'd been dead for a really long time.

———

In my filing cabinet I came across the piece of paper on which V had written, in 1994, that I'd lent him $15,000 'towards the purchase of the apartment'. He had recalled the sum as $13,000, whereas I had forgotten the loan completely. (What sort of wimp 'forgets' fifteen grand?) The loan was in fact to help him get the full purchase price together so he wouldn't have to borrow from a bank; and it was also supposed to cover my contributions to running expenses, levies etc at the flat. V says he will give me back the $15,000 minus the contributions in question. As I walked to work this morning I thought, hang on. The value of the flat will have increased sharply in four years. My $15,000, if considered as an investment, must also have grown. I think I'm going to need a lawyer.

———

Up at the great reader's (who knows nothing of what's going on),
I am required to pretend that everything between us is normal. V
keeps a warning eye on me, alert for signs that I'm flagging. Two
other friendly old women were visiting, and it was exhausting,
gruelling, to keep on faking, though I thought I was pretty gay,
really—gossiping with the old dames, trying on someone's sapphire
rings, asking for a recipe. But later at home I found myself feebly
crying in the toilet.

'Why are you sad?'

'I'm scared, and I'm tired.'

'What are you scared of?'

'I'm scared of having to up stakes again. I hate thinking of someone
coming into this apartment and moving my stuff out of it, leaving bare
gaps. I don't know where I'll end up living, and I'm so tired, I don't
know how I'm going to get the energy to go out and search.'

'If this is what we decide to do,' he says, 'we'll do it together. You
won't have to do it on your own.'

———

R says these fluctuations—happy for days, then hours of sadness and
tears—are 'like mourning'. Having it named begins to free me from
it. Walking home I see the freshness of the day. It should be autumn,
and autumn's what the angle of the light and the dryness of the air
are saying, but it's hot, thirty degrees, so one says 'late summer'. I go
into V's room and put my hand on his head. He turns his face up to
me without flinching. I kiss him and smile at him. 'What?' 'Just a
kiss.' 'Like what you see?' he says, mugging. 'Yass! Crazy about it!'
Not crazy, but still linked to it, and grieving over the smashing of
my trust in it. And yet. Something good must come. Say nothing.
Drink the gin.

———

V's got the shits because I told him G said the Jack Nicholson character in *As Good as It Gets* was like him. 'What? An unpleasant character like *him*?' We squabble. He says I think I'm a good person. I flinch and he corrects himself: I am always '*trying* to be a good person', also apparently I have bad breath and have had for some time. Scratching away at each other, irritable and cranky, hurting in small dull flicks.

———

I said, 'Look, V. We're married. We know each other. We know what's horrible about each other. We don't subscribe to each other's myth. And the only way out of being known like that, if you can't stand it, is to leave and find a new person. For a while they think you're wonderful and believe in your myth, but then they get to know you too, and the same thing happens all over again. Anyway, don't worry. I won't be around much longer.'

He scowls: 'What?'

H: 'I won't be around to bug you for much longer.'

V: 'What a thing to say.'

H: (recklessly) 'Well, that's what you want, isn't it?'

V: (indignant) 'No! It's not! If you found a way to stick around, it'd be really nice!'

———

At St Neot. A warm autumn day with a breeze and the curtain puffing and tools banging down at the Finger Wharf. I'm happy because I'm not going to England with V or travelling home on his bloody container ship, and because I boiled some green beans for lunch, and also had a tomato and lettuce sandwich; and because I'm working, knocking out my Antarctica story for *Good Weekend*.

———

With V, G and M-C to hear Ivan Moravec at the Town Hall. Huge power in his arms and wrists—power harnessed and directed and completely under his control. He played some Debussy and I felt I really *got* some of those Preludes for the first time. Then Chopin, the last piece so crystalline—little dropping clusters of notes that called out, called out, again and again, straining after something always out of reach. When the pianist left the stage, G gave a big sigh and said, 'We should gather round him, give him something to eat and a drink, and ask him things—talk with him. It's salon music, isn't it?'

————

Dreamt that V asked me about the progress of the article I'm writing for 'Goodbye' magazine.

————

Y's husband, who is fond of V and greatly enjoys their friendship, says that V is the most ambitious person he has ever met.

————

In my office—sun through huge tree, windows open for warm breezes, clatter from the wharf building site, passersby crunching on fallen berries—I write on merrily about Antarctica.

————

V: 'Have you been talking to a lawyer?'

H: 'No, but I will if I have to.'

V: 'I knew you'd taken a new tack. And do you know how I knew? Because you turned away from me in bed.'

H: 'But you told me the other day that I had bad breath. That's why I turned away.'

————

I dreamt about Siamese twins who had been separated. I woke and told V about it. He said, 'It was about *us*.' And I remembered a doco I'd seen about conjoined twins who were surgically separated. It was shocking to see them, after the operation, lying apart like lumps of meat. When they came out of the anaesthetic and realised they'd been separated, they screamed, they wept, in rage and anguish. One of them had been powerfully dominating. They had only three legs between them, and the stronger, bigger twin had been able to exert control over their behaviour, to dictate where they'd go and what they'd do. The smaller, weaker one would be swept away from whatever she was engaged in doing, she had to knuckle under and be as it were *an attachment,* without separate volition—or rather, her will had been subordinated.

I felt my dream as a gift: 'the handle towards my hand'.

————

I get home from work, the flat is silent, I think he must be out, then I become aware of his voice, murmuring low and intimate. I stick my head round his office door, he looks up from his chair with a face at once surprised and tender. At his feet the bottle of wine he is going to take out to dinner with his art-critic friend. I withdraw and go about my business in other rooms. His voice murmurs on and on. Eventually he emerges. 'Bloody John. He wants to meet at 8.30.' 'Was that him?' 'No.' We have a gin and tonic. He goes to the stereo and puts on a CD: 'Listen to this.' Out of the speakers oozes, for the fiftieth time these last few weeks, the overture to *Tannhäuser*. He returns to his sofa, looking at me with a defiant smile, chin tipped up: '"Too muscular" for you?'

'No. It's only at breakfast time that I object to Wagner. What are you going to do for music when I move out?'

'You'd better leave your stereo here and get a new one.'

'Why?'

'I had these shelves built specially for the speakers.'

'It'd cost a lot to replace it. It's a really good stereo.'

'How much?'

'A couple of grand.'

At this point we both sicken at our nasty tone and sink into silence, parallel on the sofas.

He says he doesn't think X the painter and I will be able to speak to each other 'for ten years at least'.

'Why?'

'Because you hate her, and because she thinks you've been rude to her.'

'Well, what's the point of my looking for a place to live in this suburb? It shits me that I have to move out of this part of town. I like it here.'

V: (quick as a flash) 'She was here first.'

I beg him, I implore him to tell me the truth. Again and again he insists that all he wants from his relationship with her is 'just a close friendship', but that since he hasn't seen or spoken to her for months, and the few notes he's had from her have been 'cold', he doubts whether this will be possible. He describes her as 'a *very* demanding woman, with tremendous pride, which is one of her faults, I think.' 'Why is pride a fault? Maybe it's all she's got. Her only defence. Against you.' He says that women drive him absolutely crazy, but that he 'adores' them.

I take a train to Bondi Junction and inspect a flat: stuffy, noisy, gloomy.

I said I thought his effect on me had diminished my life. He said this was 'a very serious charge', and that my effect on him had been totally good: 'You've softened me. Made me more tolerant, and more psychological, though I've avoided—thank God—*applied* psychology. There's the family thing too. And music.' I said that his good influences on me had been focus, and seriousness; but that he was always leaning towards oldness in a way that cut off the possibility of youthful nonsense, sparkle and play.

———

Who can help me?

———

On Easter Saturday afternoon I went out on my own to see *Boogie Nights*. Got home, he doesn't call out, I go into his workroom, lights on but he's not there. The whole flat is empty but lit—unheard of. I stand in his room. On the table a few sheets of folded A4. Oh no. Another letter. Shaking hands, racing eyes. In the bin another folded sheet. I expect his key at any moment. Bundling up the papers I run downstairs and sit on the hotel fence under the streetlight and read them properly.

Slowly and yet surely the saga continues, enough to try the patience of Job...

...the extent of the damage inflicted by the lack of contact, and the no-mans-land and scorched earth policy between us...

From next week H is to begin looking for a suitable apartment. I'll help her in this. I'm not even sure, at this stage, where she'll be looking. My feelings? They go from interest in trying to help her, perhaps over-trying, to true sadness at her misery, to impatience, to a sort of deadness and embarrassed awkwardness. She is wanting me to pay for setting the apartment up, furniture etc which she thinks might be $10,000+.

Her unusual hard tone during discussions makes me wonder whether she's spoken to a lawyer. Some of her lady friends have perhaps advised her?...

At any rate. That is the position now. I imagine I see it in more positive terms than you. I've simply no idea whether or not you've lost patience or have wanted me to be in contact before I could give this firm, or firmer, news. If I thought it was allowed I would be speaking or writing to you every day, and would be giving all sorts of help and encouragement...

He's still not back. I walk down Ithaca Road and stand in the street looking up at her flat. I glimpse through a lace curtain an old woman's shoulder, in a sleeve, moving slowly across a lit window. I walk on down to the small park by the water. No one there except the mad Korean guy who lives in the shrubbery near the public lavatories: he is strolling home in the dark, letting out his weird cackles and groans.

I go home, find her number and call it.

'I only want to know—is V there?'

'Of course he is not here. I haven't seen him for months.'

I'm jabbering: 'I know now that he's making reports to you of everything that happens between us—'

'Oh Helen, I'm so sorry that you—'

I say, 'I came home and he wasn't here and I didn't know where he was and I thought—'

She cuts across me: 'He has written to me, some of his letters I haven't even opened—'

'I don't want to talk to you or hear this, I'm going to hang up.'

'It is manipulative of you to call me—because *you* are distressed you want to give your distress to *me*—my pain is as great as yours—'

'I'm going now—'

'This is pointless. You have your story and I have my story and there is no point telling them—'

'Yes—and V has all the power because he's a liar, and now I'm going to hang up.'

I put the receiver down. Shaking like mad.

The phone rings. 'Hello?'

'Listen, Helen, it is *not on* that you—'

I put the phone down, gently.

I pour myself a gin and tonic. I sit at the table near the window.

I feel intensely tiny, and flat. Like something run over by a car and left on the bitumen.

Halfway through the gin he comes in the front door, whistles gaily and calls out.

'Don't bother to be cheerful. I read the letter. You betrayed me. You report to her about me. You've been lying to me. Won't you ever stop lying?'

He sits down, white, facing me, takes my non-gin hand in both of his. He appears devastated. He doesn't defend himself. I can't even cry. I sit there and drink and between long silences I say things, horribly feeble, I can hardly push a thread of voice out of myself.

'*You* move out. Why should I be the one to move out? You find somewhere else to sleep. I'm sleeping in our bed. Go to her. Sleep at her place. This is my home and you've ruined everything. I'm trying to think of someone I can stay with. I'm all smashed up inside. I need to be looked after but I can't think of anyone.'

'I'll look after you,' he says, in a small voice. 'I'll be glad to look after you, if you'll let me.'

I lie on the couch in a foetal position: 'I've got no dignity left.'

'I'm the one with no dignity,' he says.

————

'Don't talk to anyone about this, will you.' Normally this would enrage me, but I say, 'I won't. I'm too ashamed. I'm ashamed of my own naivety. I'm ashamed for you. And I'm ashamed because people will say, "*What*? She's still hanging round waiting for that jerk-off?" I'm not going to tell anybody about this.'

And I'm not. Got to the end of what can be told. How do I get past this letter? He's finally managed to silence me. To reduce me to such a point that I'm too ashamed even to ask for help.

————

He jumps awake: 'Oh! I dreamt there were some metal trays that you were looking at, they were covered in tawdry rubbish, but there were one or two things of value in amongst them.'

———

For the first time I begin to understand the women who stay with men who hit them: the shock of violence, the dissolving into grief and shame, the feeling that flows both ways when a deadlock is broken; the passionate, open sex; the nostalgia for past happiness; then the gentle jokes, the teasing; then the man's small vanity about the gesture of apology he made (V's flowers: he's mentioned them twice so far); then the gradual reassertion of normality; the stiffening back into what the problem was; the dullness, the stoicism; the woman 'being good', limiting herself, living hyper-alert for the next incident.

———

A strange mood arises, as if we had frightened ourselves into snapping out of something. We talk, we discuss. In bed yesterday, hearing the flat-minder upstairs crashing about antisocially, we started a game where I 'go upstairs to complain': I 'tap at their door', V plays the flat-minder, his tough response to my polite objections: four, five times I tap and he invents a new reply. We lie here writhing with laughter. Every other day we see a movie. We go to Gowings to buy him King Gees and a pair of the suddenly fashionable Hush Puppies. We eat and drink at Bambini Trust. We order in pizza. We talk about London, who he'll see there.

'Will people ask after me?'

'Of course they will.'

'What will you say?'

'I'll say I asked you to come but you wouldn't.'

'No. You'll say the truth: "I broke her heart and then pretended I wanted her to come"—that's what you should say.'

'Do you remember,' he says, 'how we always used to marvel at how exactly right our skin temperatures were together?'

'I remember the first time we got into bed together and a sort of tingle ran right through my body. As if my body was registering my happiness before my mind could think it.'

————

'As for happiness, that is really useful to us in one way only, by making unhappiness possible. It is necessary for us to form in happiness ties of confidence and attachment that are both sweet and strong in order that their rupture might cause us the heart-rending but so valuable agony which is called unhappiness.' —Proust, *The Captive*

————

My computer at St Neot packed up so I had to work at home all day. He actually brought me a coffee.

V: 'Want me to make you a little snack?'

H: (amazed) 'Thanks! Yes! I'd like that!'

V: (mimes a flinch, as if put upon)

H: 'You did offer.'

V: 'I can do it, if that's what you'd like.'

H: '"I *can* do it." This is what you do! You make an offer, then when I accept it, you withdraw it. That's your *style*!'

It was an illuminating moment. For me, at least.

————

I ripped through the rest of the Antarctica story—loved writing it, remembering with emotion what I saw and learnt there. V read it and made several useful suggestions. The editor is very happy with it. She told me that women are much easier to edit than men: 'If you point out a problem to a woman, she's likely to say, "Yes, I felt myself there was something wrong there", whereas a bloke will say, "Whaddya mean, there's a problem?"'

————

M here for a few days before she goes to France. Everything going

well between her and V. Rain. Humid. Getting towards the end of
The Captive. So extreme I can read only one or two pages at a sitting.

———

'Where life immures, the intelligence cuts a way out…The intelligence knows nothing of those closed situations of life from which
there is no escape…Ideas come to us as the successors to griefs, and
griefs, at the moment when they change into ideas, lose some part
of their power to injure our heart; the transformation itself, even,
for an instant, releases suddenly a little joy.' —Proust, *The Captive*

———

Dreamt I saw a baby, on his mother's lap, nonchalantly puffing at a
cigarette butt. Shocked, I dashed it from his lips and ground it into
the floor with my shoe.

———

'I was in one of those periods in a life when nothing can move. It
is a log-jam, a marsh, a quicksand, you have weights on your feet.'
—Doris Lessing, *Under My Skin*

———

'You see,' she said, 'I think you're in a process of changing modes.
Whereas once your habit was to bolt, to run away, to distance yourself from a painful situation, what you're doing now is learning that
you can stay in it, and tolerate the process of understanding it and
working it right through to the end. You're finding that you can
tolerate the intolerable.'

'I'm scared of living alone. Coming home at the end of the day to
a dark house. Now I know why E always leaves a couple of lamps
on when she goes out.'

'I think,' she said, 'that the house is you. The dark part of yourself.
But perhaps the parts of you that have come back to life, or have
unfrozen, will be like lamps in your house.'

———

V and I are like two punch-drunk boxers staggering around hand in hand. I am right up against the deepest, most impermeable centre of him, his idea of himself as a man and as an artist. I fling myself against this in vain. There's a homunculus crouching inside the monolith but he can't hear through the concrete.

———

G says: 'V's wrong. He's the wrongest person I've ever known, but the success of his book proves to him that his wrongness is rightness.'

———

He says it makes him 'physically sick' to think about my leaving. I can't bear it either; but even less can I bear the shrunken half-life I have to lead in order to stay with him. He clings to his belief that therapy is at the root of our problems: it's made me 'too self-obsessed'. As if without it I would have been able to go on this long putting up with his art-before-life regime! Something I'm learning again, though: sorrow and sadness are different from each other. Sorrow is an active thing, almost a kind of work, while sadness is draining and unfocused and somehow connected to not being honest.

———

I'm dreading the division of books and household goods more than anything else. I mean standing there saying, 'I'm taking this. Can I take this, and this?'

———

I don't know what she would make of this but here's what I think happened: I wanted so much to be loved that I tried to turn myself into the sort of woman I thought I would have to be, in order to be lovable. In the process I falsified myself, lost part of my soul, made myself sick with swallowed rage; I connived, I enabled; and I allowed him to set hard into worse versions of the misogyny he already felt: the little tin god, the artist as superior being whose needs must be met, no matter what it costs or who pays.

In other words, it's not all his fault.

———

The uprooted tree in her front garden.

———

This year (V having as usual fought past my pride and helped me put in my tax return) I claimed all my therapy expenses as professional development *and they allowed it*! So I am getting a large rebate. V could hardly bring himself to tell me this news, it galled him so terribly.

———

'One does not always sing out of happiness.' —Pierre Bonnard

———

W told me she rang R in February and said she was scared I was going to kill myself. R had been afraid of the same thing. This *staggers* me. Don't they know I would *never* do that?

———

In the street we ran into a literary critic I know, a woman.

Critic: (to V) 'I've just reviewed your book.'

V: 'What book?'

———

In a restaurant with V and my journalist friend, we disagree about the Labor party's desire to impose local content quotas on radio stations. In the heat of the argument V tells me sharply that I have 'no beliefs—no centre'. I feel the jolt of it hit my friend side-on. She turns to me with a look of shock, then to V, her mouth open, speechless.

———

The woman from the Antarctic voyage company calls to report that on the morning my story was run in *Good Weekend* they had forty inquiries about trips to the ice.

My short-story collection is in the shops. There's a bit of jostling and fooling when we stand in front of a bookshop window: 'Hey, there's yours.' 'There's *yours*.' 'Yours is in the front.' 'Yes, but yours is standing up.' 'Yes, but there's two copies of yours.' 'Yes, but yours is a hard cover.' 'Yes, but yours is a trade paperback.' 'It's a bloody nuisance, being married to you.'

Dreamt last night that Dad died. Or was dead.

The eminent critic who has just reread V's whole backlist and reviewed his new book praises 'the sheer uncompromising tough- ness of the will towards realising an artistic vision...He has never been willing to cut himself down to national size in terms of aesthetic ambition: his books are absolutely unyieldingly coherent through success and failure. This makes it all the more remarkable that his new novel should turn out to be not only an exfoliating book of stories within a story but a radiant love story in the vicinity of nature...Australian fiction is not likely to produce a book that comes within cooee of [its] gravity and tenderness, as well as its shapeliness and pizzazz.'

Rat # 2 died last night in a trap on the bench beside the toaster. There was a lot of blood. V got rid of the rat, I cleaned up the blood. While I could not have touched the rat, the blood did not worry me at all. I mopped it up with a hot towel from the ragbag.

Another of V's draft love letters appears, face up, in my paper recycle carton. Scrawled on the back of an article in German about his book. *The distance between us is like a Kiefer painting...My grand plan is in tatters...I have trouble sometimes working you out...Still, I love you...*

We should see each other before I go to England... We're not teenagers...
You and I together are not like anyone else. We will never be like anyone
else. Don't you understand that? Und so weiter. In other words, she
must still be saying, 'Sort out your marriage or nothing doing.'

Well, that's a position one could call honourable.

But God. His 'grand plan'. Why not have the guts to 'bring down
the knife on H'? I would respect that. I would even take it as a
blessing, and be grateful for it.

I will not let you go until you bless me.

———

At dinner with married friends, V uses the expression 'a prisoner
of conscience', and adds, 'which is not a bad way of describing
marriage'.

———

I understand why V and G have become such close friends. Listening
to their conversations I am aware of the breadth of their common
interests and matters of intellectual excitement. I feel as if I'm less
intelligent now than I once was. As if V hogs all the intellectual
activity while I commandeer the emotional.

———

Dreamt I stood on a nature strip where a Kombi van was parked.
Through its windows members of my family were gazing out at a
dog that lay on its side on the footpath. My sister stood next to me.
The dog began to go into labour. After two or three spasms (H:
'Have you ever seen this happen before?' Sister: 'No') out surged a
puppy. I'd expected it to be enclosed in a membrane, the way I've
seen kittens being born, but it was all brown and furry and ready
to go. No motherly licking required. I picked it up in two hands. It
was warm and strong, all muscle. I held it up so the watchers in the
van could see that it had been born.

———

Two women I used to teach with at Fitzroy High have written an open letter defending me against the character-assassinating essay in *Bodyjamming*. Their staunchness and their contempt for the slurs against me have put ground back under my feet.

————

In the restaurant I told V about my magazine journalist friend and her trip to Kenya and Tanzania: how she loved going out each day with the guide, walking and climbing, and especially how she'd said to me, with tears in her eyes, 'The animals that thrilled me most were the ones I didn't see.' His face stiffened and went dark. He began to harangue me about my lack of interest in going to Africa and seeing wildlife. He absolutely hammered at me: said that when he'd once suggested we go to Africa I'd wanted only to climb Mount Kilimanjaro. All I wanted to do in foreign places, he said, was to 'exert' myself physically in order to 'experience' it and 'bring it back to *the self*'. My mind whirred and clanked under the pressure. What did he actually see wrong in that? What one did in a foreign place, he stated, was *to remain detached and observe it*. Once again our innermost selves clash. I try to point this out but am met with a further barrage—I've never shown *any interest* in Africa, but as soon as some woman spends a bit of time there I get all impressed because she's *walked*. What is this urge to do *exercise* there? I try to argue from Ushuaia, the path to the glacier—I quote the mountain climber's phrase 'squirts of sublime joy'—big mistake—he explodes: 'Oh, *fuck* the bloody mountaineer.' At the table with the view in the expensive restaurant, the puff goes out of me. I sit there, small and sad and plain—a Mum sensation; a Peggy Ashcroft moment. I try hard not to cry. I'm so sick of crying. He pulls himself together. We share a dessert and walk home the long way, in silence.

————

On the couch I tell her the story. I expect a bucket of cold water,

but she says in her quiet voice, 'It can be hard to recognise jealousy
in someone else.'

———

V at the departure gate: he turned and looked back at me with
a funny, crooked grin, waggled his fingers at shoulder level, and
disappeared. Poor V. Heading for London, via Vienna. London is
his Mount Everest.

———

He was hardly airborne before I'd smoked a joint with the neighbours and rushed off with two other friends to Sean's Panorama.
Home now in ecstatic cheerfulness. Mine, mine, mine, for seven
weeks. As I drove away from the airport, though, I said, 'God bless
V and keep him safe', several times and meaning it. Now the bliss
of sleeping alone. God bless *me* as well as him.

———

On the couch. Why do I find it so hard to be happy? She suggests
that pain is more familiar to me, that I gravitate towards it. We talk
about the 'desert' in me, how V had reached it, no longer found
what he wanted and needed, and turned away to another woman:
how *this* was my part in what happened; and how I'm learning that
there is a spring of water, if I can just find it in myself. Walking
away from her house, I find I don't remember which of us put these
things into words.

———

In the street early yesterday (or was it evening?—her smooth, icy
cheek) a woman I'd once clashed with came to greet me—came
straight up and seized my shoulders and kissed me and looked right
into my face and smiled.

———

Australian Chamber Orchestra—so young! So incredibly good-
looking! Dressed in loose black, they performed standing. Haydn

and Mozart, then Weber's clarinet concerto played on a recre-
ated ancient instrument by Eric Hoeprich, a thin, acne-scarred
Dutchman—his fly-away hair, his gawky neck that seemed to bulge
and contort as he rampaged through the work. At interval I moved
to the front row and the music flooded over me. Alone at the Opera
House I was happy. Not manic or exuberant, but in good spirits,
content, even joyful. Got home to find V's cranky voice from Vienna
complaining about the answering machine. I was pleased that he'd
rung but delighted that I wasn't there to take the call.

———

Heard an art-world rumour that I too 'have had affairs'. Feeling of
virtue. For once, on this score at least, *I am innocent*!

———

V the writer and X the painter. Two childless fanatics. Without
relief.

———

Played Scrabble with the China scholar's flatmate. We drank a
whole bottle of red wine.

———

A man writes to me about my Antarctica story. Says he was down in
the Southern Ocean during the war, in a destroyer. 'I laughed with
you. I laughed at you. I suffered with you and for you. I loved your
words so much I read them aloud to my family after Sunday lunch
and they loved them too.'

———

I know in my mind that all I need to do is write a sentence, then
another sentence, and see where it leads me. But in my heart and
body I'm still scared.

———

Alone in the flat, at a loose end, I begin to understand why people
watch TV. For the comfort and containment of *story*. I watch

Seinfeld, lie here laughing, feel among friends.

———

'Dear X, I know you must be very unhappy. Do you think it might help if we met and spoke to each other? Sincerely, Helen.'

———

Like a hamster in a treadmill, round and round and round I run. Always longing to be told the truth.

———

The Polish philosopher, on the phone: 'Let's say you decided to leave V. What would be holding you back?'

Long pause. I walk through our life, as it were room by room. It is very bare.

'In my heart I know I have to leave. But I'm hanging on. Because I've got this terrible need for him to tell me the truth. And because I'm scared.'

'What of?'

Longer pause.

'Failure. This is my third marriage. Fear of my failure to sustain intimacy. To sustain a relationship.'

'Intimacy,' she says, 'has to go both ways. And the aim of a relationship is not to sustain the *relationship*.'

———

To Bondi, to have dinner with a friend from long ago, his wife and their two small kids. I'd forgotten I was hungry for the company of children—their open faces, the way they use language, the risks they take with it; their stunning beauty, flashes of wariness—their whole lives are risk—skating out on ice they've never been on before. We played the French game where two people hold each other by the chin and look straight into each other's eyes; the first to laugh gets a *tapette*—a slap on the cheek. The boy's face nearly exploded with the strain of self-control. The little girl mimicked her wacky music teacher, her high voice and weird hand movements: doubled over with laughter she kept saying, 'She must of used to be a dancer!'

Later, on the couch, I lay there and howled: '*I* used to be a dancer. I've lopped myself. I've been living in the dark. Starving in the dark.'

———

V called from London. I eagerly questioned him, dragged a few reluctant things out of him—without my dragging there would have been silence. The China scholar asked me over for tea. We drank a bit of wine and tried on all the hats in the house (I ran home for my black pillbox with net), then the guys got out a guitar and a double bass and the Beatles songbook and we sang for an hour, till the neighbours upstairs started knocking on the floor.

———

Late this afternoon X the painter called me on the phone. She was in bed with flu. First thing she said was, very politely, 'I don't know why you think we can help each other.' An hour of conversation followed, a quiet comparing of notes, during which many long pauses fell. Pauses of thought. Of stunned attempts to match up pieces of information. Turns out that right from the start he told her we lived separate lives: 'He told me you are an old hippie; that you had separate friends, that you would not mind his visits to me.' Even before last Christmas he told her we'd decided to part: that we were parting because we weren't able to resolve our disagreements about work and the flat and about both being writers. When I found the first letter (neither of us mentioned *the hat*) she had told him she was not prepared to continue with him until he sorted out his marriage. I said he'd told me that *he* made the renunciation in order to save the marriage. She said she had held out for months, keeping her phone unplugged, not reading his letters; but that on Mothers Day she had plugged the phone in and he'd got through: he'd told her I was going back to Melbourne to live, that I was 'happy' about the decision, that we'd reached it together, that we liked and respected each other and would remain friends. Thunderstruck, I said that I'd thought of going back to Melbourne only because the pain of his lies had become unbearable, that I couldn't stand the pain.

Here, an enormous pause.

Had V really told me that she didn't like me? She asked this in a tone that meant she didn't believe it could be true. I said, 'Many times I said to him, "Why don't you ask X over for dinner?" And he'd always say, "Oh, no—she wouldn't want to come. She doesn't feel comfortable with you. She's not really interested in you."' 'But I *did* like you,' she said. 'I *was* interested in you. Couldn't you tell from the way I was when we'd meet in the street?' 'You were friendly to me when we met, yes,' I said. 'You'd even kiss me. And we'd walk up to the Cross, or ride along in the bus. I liked it. But he told me several times that you weren't interested in me—that you didn't like me. I thought you were just being polite. And I never followed it up.'

'So,' she said. 'He stirred us up against each other.'

I said, 'It's obvious that he's in love with you, but he won't say so. If he'd been able to say to me, "Listen, I love X and I want to leave you and go with her," I would have accepted it. I would have been hurt and angry and sad but I would have *accepted* it. Instead he keeps saying he still loves me, and that he's extricating himself from you and wants us to get through this.'

'Do you mean to say,' she said in a faint voice, 'he never told you how he felt about me?'

'No. I found out by snooping. All he's ever said is that he likes you, that you're a close friend that he likes to see.'

Enormous, endless pause.

At last she said, 'So—all we've learnt is what each of us most feared.'

I said, 'To me, the most destructive part of all this is how he denied and kept on and on denying—and is still denying—what I instinctively knew the truth must be. He's damaged my faith in my own instincts.'

'Oh,' she said at once, 'but that is what men always do to women. And I wonder if they have any *idea* of the damage it causes.'

I said, 'My friend has just arrived. We're going to the theatre. I'll have to go.'

'I hope you have a pleasant evening at the theatre,' she said. 'I hope the play is good.'

Surprised, I laughed and said, 'I hope your flu is better soon.' *She* laughed.

I said, 'Thank you for having this conversation. Goodbye.'

'Goodbye.'

———

Immense relief. Freedom, lightness, clarity. And thinking of V and his manoeuvres, a stunned, incredulous pity, even tenderness, as towards an oafish boy, a yokel, a creature barely evolved.

———

The play was *A Doll's House*. The husband: 'Can you tell me how I lost your love?' W and I talked wildly all the way home about the play, and why Shakespeare is so much greater than Ibsen.

———

C calls from Melbourne. 'I've just finished his book. I wanted to get on a plane to Sydney and punch his fucking lights out. Get that bloke's voice out of your head, Hel. Go back to writing fiction the way you used to, before.'

———

I asked the GP about the frequent brief attacks I've had, over the past few months, of racing heart: *boom boom boom boom boom* then back to normal. She said it was called paroxysmal tachycardia, that it was benign, and that it was due to emotional stress. Freed by X's phone call from unbearable cosmic anxiety I went home, lay on the sofa, turned on the TV, and saw a family of tigers swimming in a river; a close-up of elephants' feet as they trudged to the water (their tremendous pale toenails); two rhinos mating (she has to bear his two tonnes of weight for more than an hour at a time); and best of all a small bird, every part of it a different colour, perching alone on a windy twig: its shoulders kept flexing as the twig swayed, and its long beak was a deep rose pink.

———

On the couch: after months in the doldrums, stuck in endless dull pain and going nowhere, the whole thing's put on a surge. Remarkable physical sensations of internal reintregration, as if my heart and guts have been in shreds but are reshaping themselves into their proper dimensions, and can do their work again.

———

V calls from London. His voice is affectless, dutiful. As I labour away to draw his news from him, I feel something draining out of me. Something that grows in me when he's away.

———

Conversation with a little girl about fairies. How big they are, what they wear, their 'tiny silver slippers', whether their wings are fixed to their clothes or grow out of their backs. 'They grow out of their backs,' she says. I ask what they'd feel like. Her eyes glow: 'They'd feel as soft as snow! But not so cold, of course.'

———

The brilliance of *Seinfeld*: George Costanza tries to call it off with his girlfriend but she refuses to accept it, and simply goes on behaving as if they were still a couple. Turns up at his apartment every evening saying, 'Hi, honey! What'll we have for dinner?' He tries to manipulate her by taking up with a second woman and engineering a 'discovery' in a restaurant, but the two women discuss matters calmly and agree there's no grounds for either of them to leave. So he's stuck with two women who stubbornly go on being his girlfriend and not even particularly resenting each other.

———

On the couch, a memory of a photo: my mother at fifty, smiling, shy, but relaxed, chin propped on hand, sitting at the kitchen table in my share house, and holding lightly by its tips, balancing it vertical, a big black-handled pair of scissors.

Me: 'I've left it rather late in the day to bring up the scissors.'

Pause.

Her: 'I think you know what they mean.'

I tell her my fantasy of bringing home unwanted, lost, abandoned children to look after. They all sit around my table, holding their spoons vertical, and I serve them from a great big pot: I've got the apron on *all day*.

'I think,' she says, 'that you want to make reparation, and receive absolution.'

Can such a state ever be arrived at?

———

'The British reviews of the book,' writes V, 'are of greater interest to me than Australian ones, because they're uncontaminated, and don't crap on about national characteristics.'

———

Jackie Leven at the Basement. A bulky body, dark pants rolled up over great chunky calves, long cream socks pushed right down, guitar across his lap, a tap on the sole of one shoe, a mike bent down to catch the beat he keeps with it. A thin man surprised to find himself encased in fat. 'Never give a sword to a man'—several powerfully thoughtful chords—'who can't dance.'

While V's in Europe, M comes to stay a couple of weeks, for the shoot of a movie. We work, we eat, we sleep. Merrily we carry on our lives.

'Do you miss him?'
    'No.'

Reading history as one of the judges of a literary award I come across an account of Elizabeth Macarthur keeping a journal on the horror voyage to Australia with her angry husband and sickly small son. Their cabin was separated by only a thin partition from the quarters of screeching, foul-mouthed women convicts. An image of my psyche: how thin it is, the wall that holds the foul-mouthed harpy separate from the civilised wife and mother who stays quiet and writes it all down in her diary. How *very thin* that partition is.

A journalist tells me a story she's heard, perhaps 'only' an urban myth. A woman's husband travels a lot for his work. In his pocket while doing the washing she finds a phone number and calls it. A woman answers. Turns out he has a second domestic establishment on the other side of the country. They agree to confront him. When he gets back to whichever house he's due at, he finds both women sitting at the kitchen table. He looks at them: '*Oh.*' Pause. 'Right. Just let me have a shower.' He goes into the bathroom and shoots himself.

Big changes in the flat since V left the country and M arrived. The table, where I can now work and read at any hour of the day or night, and on which we also eat, reminds me of the old white-painted one I had in Melbourne that V persuaded me to get rid of when we left, but which I'd always loved for its size and solidity, and its adaptability to every purpose. *We do not presume to come to your table, merciful Lord, trusting in our own righteousness*. The flowers, the homely mess, M's cello lying on its side behind the sofa. Integrating my severed parts, lately—wanting to do everything under the one roof, not to be split any more.

————

I saw X the painter walking to the bus stop. I waved to her and she waved back. A courteous salute, returned.

————

My friend asks if he can paint my portrait. He loves to work at home, to be close to the place where everything's happening. His partner is hugely pregnant. While I was there the midwife came; the two women talked quietly in the kitchen about the coming homebirth, and the painter worked on his portrait of me in the living room. I had brought my knitting. Their little boy roamed about. He offered to be my 'wool-winder'. His sombre, manly little face and posture, his hazel-green eyes, his intense dislike of *getting wet*, his sweet-natured company and his gradual approach to me until he was on the arm of my chair, then leaning on me, then virtually sitting on me. A game we invented when I took off my two crosses to pluck a thread of wool out of the chain's clasp: he picked up the blue one and I picked up the gold, and we were two people: 'Let's kiss! Let's dance! Let's go to the cave (my spectacle case) and see what's inside! A monster! Wooooh!' I'd almost forgotten the way two minds at play can run side by side, inventing, moving smoothly from scene to scene, each grasping the other's idea and leaping forward with it. Wonderful calm happiness, being in their house, where a baby will soon be born.

————

Still this odour, or perfume, in the air tonight. Even with only one window half-open it keeps coming to me, reaching me. Something good's happening, I don't know yet what, but I can feel it. Went to St Neot this arvo and began to write. It felt natural. Things shaped themselves spontaneously. I was not, in myself, an obstacle to their formation: instead, my experience was their tool. I could smell the air through the window beside me. A naval ship strung with lights lay at the bottom of the street. Something in me has begun to change, is changing. It's to do with the day I spent in the portrait painter's house, the look and feel and sound of it, the woman's huge hard belly, the presence of the little boy, the way when the painter paused to examine his work through his fine rimless glasses his mouth would curve gently upwards while he studied it: not a smile, but an expression of interest and even pleasure. The calm of sitting. Time flashed by: an hour, another hour.

———

Both windows open to the night. Very early, before light, it rained, soft and thorough. The currawongs struck up their watery calls, down in the amphitheatre of the park.

———

Two days in Melbourne. To Primrose Gully with my sister and her friend. I walked to the opposite ridge, surprised two black wallabies, mooched about in a strange, calm mood. Sky clouded, grass clumps oddly lit. Looked at certain trees with close attention: a slim, pale eucalypt whose trunk was covered in tiny flecks. Sound of the Moorabool down in its deep valley. In the evening, a long and interesting talk about suicide as displaced murder. I stayed up till 1.30 am, tidying things, calm, wide-awake, happy. Too happy to want to lose the consciousness of happiness. Even with this haircut, happy.

———

Last night, 10 pm, at Sydney airport waiting for the bus home. Cold, windy, no one much about. Oddest sensation that my entire consciousness was, for once, located inside my head—behind my eyes—powerfully and calmly looking out at the world—rather than a certain quantity of it being split off and floating somewhere outside myself, waiting to lodge itself inside *some man* from whose head it could then turn back towards me and examine me critically. A continuing sense of focus, steadiness and power.

———

A friend reports to me some gossip she has heard around the traps about V and X the painter—a distorted version of the facts, or of what I have been led to believe are the facts. I take a breath to curse the pair of them, but before the words are out the urge drains away.

———

The schoolgirl has cut the laces of her older brother's expensive and cool new running shoes. At the dinner table she is very firmly rebuked, and hangs her head—a twelve-year-old, just entering the painful years. Our eyes accidentally meet and I have to bite my lip to hold back a grin of solidarity. I long to say, 'Sweetheart. I have cut up a straw hat with scissors and drowned cigars in soup. We are sisters.'

———

My first multifocals. The surprise of my eyes' new focus. People on the street seem to look into my face more than usual. I'm not just a powerful looker and seer. I am no longer invisible.

———

In work, though, this shadow of THE NOVEL is still hanging over me. A tyranny. The feeling that I have to have a structural idea before I even start. I have imbibed osmotically V's contempt for 'the confessional first', as he calls it. Why don't I just shitcan all that and follow what moves me? Keep working the territory that I have opened up and marked out and developed—the crossover between fiction and an account of *what happened*?

———

In *Who Weekly*, the thinking woman's gossip rag, I feast on the fate of poor Farrah Fawcett. Drugs and violence and massive cosmetic surgery, and now she's in court dealing with the 'shame' of admitting she had smashed her ex's possessions with a baseball bat. Is that all? *Go Farrah.*

———

V sends a telegram from the container ship: he gets to Fremantle tomorrow; why don't I fly down to Melbourne and meet him when it docks there?

W: 'But what would *you* do, after you'd met him at the wharf? He sails on to Sydney the next day, and you—what?'

H: 'Trudge back to the airport and fly home, I guess, at considerable expense. Nah. I'm not going. I'm staying right here.'

———

Rain, falling quietly all night and day, and still falling now. Pleasant feeling of being benevolently closed in, for my own good. I stayed home, knitting on the sofa, for the whole day. It passed at speed. I looked up from the screen, as *Saturday Night Fever* ended, and it was dark.

———

My anxiety level, even before his ship reaches Fremantle, begins to rise. I'm starting to feel flustered about how I've moved the furniture around, about M and her things in the flat, about being forced to choose between M and V. I don't want to live in fear, but I feel the fear coming back. Occurs to me that X the painter also might be preparing herself for a reunion. What does *she* think the outcome of our phone conversation was? I realise I've been assuming she has withdrawn from the field.

———

I've hoovered the flat, scrubbed the bathroom tiles, put my work stuff back into the room M's sleeping in. He must be in Fremantle but he hasn't rung and I almost dread that he will—the end of my freedom, my social life full of music, young children, Shabbat dinners, dancing at night in this room that's come to feel like mine.

———

With time to kill between food shopping and my appointment, I drove to Watsons Bay. I thought vaguely, maybe this is how people commit suicide. They find themselves driving apparently by chance to a clifftop—they think, 'Why don't I just jump?' Rain. Mist over the harbour. Turned the car near the bus depot and drove back up the hill. Parked near the Gap, got out with my umbrella and walked to the fence. Busloads of tourists wandering in the drizzle. I looked over.

A very narrow area between fence and cliff edge, hardly as wide as this notebook. Ribs of swell moved steadily off the ocean through the heads. Below where I stood, cream smashed itself into layers of lace streaked with pale brown muck.

———

'I think you're talking,' she says, 'about a terrible destructive force in you—the you that thinks of throwing yourself off the Gap.' At those words my whole body booms and fizzes. My eyes go blurry. I wonder if she had to *risk* saying those words to me.

'I think,' she says, 'that the you with the broken heart is very *young*.'

———

At midnight, rain, still, again. Falling quietly and smoothly, and yet one is aware that it is composed of separate drops.

———

Telling M, as we walk to Global Gossip, about what happens on the couch: 'I won't go on and on. There's nothing more boring than someone telling you about their therapy.'

'Actually I find it really interesting.'

'It comes up again and again, why did I have my tubes tied? Why did I do it? God, imagine if I'd done it before I had *you*!'

'When did you do it?'

'I think it was around 1977. The same year I had *Monkey Grip*.'

We both heard it, the subtle chime of the Freudian slip. Stopped dead, staring at each other, open-mouthed.

———

Dinner at the apartment, just around the corner, of a famously erudite Australian art critic. I was nervous because of my ignorance of art, but the only other guest, a French guy from Amiens, turned out to be the most tremendous jazz buff. Both men had an encyclopedic knowledge of music. The host put on a Four Freshmen record. Two bars in I said, 'They sound like the Beach Boys.' 'The Beach Boys,' he said, 'revered them.' 'Oh!' I cried, 'I can't believe—I'm thrilled to hear you like the Beach Boys!' 'Anyone who's musical,' he said suavely, 'loves the Beach Boys.' We moved into jazz standards. With unobtrusive use of a remote he played various versions of 'Lush Life'. At times we all joined in. Well after midnight I strolled home still singing. A passing woman gave me a look but I was too drunk to be embarrassed. M had only just got back. She put on a Xylouris CD and taught me a soft-footed Cretan dance in the living room.

———

On the bus I saw X the painter's mother, loaded down with bags of food. No eye contact. Does she recognise me? Does she know the whole story? What did she think would happen? What did she hope for? Does she blame me for her daughter's unhappiness? Does she, like her daughter, think that 'Australians are the worst people in the world'? Does she know I cut up her blue straw hat?

———

V calls from Adelaide: 'M is to stay. I insist on that. She's to stay.' Some woman must have been hauling him over the coals. Too late.

She's already gone home.

———

The horn player, in Britten's 'Serenade for Tenor, Horn and Strings', had an unusually long neck. Shadows cast on it by his head made him look like a ventriloquist's dummy—as if his jaw were a man-made, articulated joint, carpentered. He stood with his feet well apart, his fist shoved into the bell, his knees slightly bent and turned a little to the left—like someone poised to break into a powerful slanting run. Was his angle of turn designed to show the golden coil of the horn to the audience? Brassy flashes bounced off it and dazzled me, almost as if aimed. *The splendour falls on castle walls.*

———

Sydney water has to be boiled again since last night: giardia, crypto-sporidium. One hardly even curses—just swings the big brown saucepan under the tap and on to the stove. The kitchen fills again with steam.

———

V's expecting me to meet his ship today. For two days I've been calling and calling the shipping company about when and where it will dock. They say they can't tell me, don't know. How can they not *know*? Rage in abdomen. Can't sit still. Pacing back and forth. Heart revs up, pounds faster, subsides again.

———

V calls. He's on the wharf. At Botany Bay. He's about to take a cab home. His voice is big, real, animated. Yes, he's an actual person.

———

He's brought me a scarf from London. 'Thank you! It's beautiful! I love it!'

Watching me try it on this way and that, he says, 'What about all your other scarves?' 'What about them?' 'What does this mean about all your other scarves?'

He's most displeased—perhaps hurt, though he doesn't say so—that I didn't meet the ship. When I wasn't there he had 'thought the worst'. Why couldn't I have met him? In vain I describe my fruitless two days on the phone to the shipping company. He cuts across me—everyone else on board was met, the Dutchwoman's friend, a couple from the north coast—all their people were waiting for them, and on the wharf, too, not even outside the wire. Well, I say, I did my best: they must have had some other source of information. When he hears that I went to my therapy appointment instead, he walks out of the room.

Strange how much smaller he is than I'd remembered.

Up at the great reader's, a pittosporum was coming into bloom. Its sharp scent in whiffs all day, all night. The ground strewn with dark violets. With all this blossoming going on outside the windows and doors I was somehow no longer living in fear. We talked for hours, in the big twin beds. I felt I could say anything. Even speaking about X did not stab me, though I'd seen her on Friday as I swung down Elizabeth Bay Road towards the Sebel—I was actually thinking of her when I saw coming up the hill a small figure in elegant black, pale face, matte lipstick, dark glasses, soft hair waving round her brow—oh hell, it's X. As we drew closer I kept my eyes on her face, ready to smile and say hello—she came closer, and closer, and I realised she was going to pass without looking at me, without a greeting. As we passed I said in a low voice, 'Hello, X.' She gave a small, bleak smile, a tiny glance flicked to me and away: 'Hello.' Her face was smooth but full of an emotion under control—anger? sadness? She must, I suppose, rather hate me, striding down the pavement in my flat suede boots and blokeish haircut; why should he stay with me instead of going with dainty, pretty her, charming and feminine? To be frank *I* don't know why, either—or even *if*. Seeing her reduced my bounce, but in a way that was oddly strengthening. So that when V and I talked at length, in the great reader's giant single beds, I could even ask, without irony or self-laceration, what sort of life he had envisaged with her (he doesn't know), whether she had urged him to leave me (she had, or so he said). It was all rather sombre, though occasionally we laughed. On Sunday morning I put forward the idea that over the last few years, while he wrote his novel, he had got to the lonely central part of me, and that our two bleaknesses had combined into a desert that neither of us had been able to deal with.

———

I asked him if he'd missed me on his trip.

'Of course. Did you miss me?'

'Well, no—or only for the first few days.'

'*What*?'

'No, I didn't miss you. I thought about you, every day, and I was glad to hear from you. I wanted to tell you things. But it was a really good time, for me. I realised I could live alone, if I had to, and that a lot of people seem to like me and want to have me in their lives.'

'But you already knew that, didn't you?'

'Over this last year, no, I didn't. I thought I was ugly and old and past it, and humiliated and sad and crazy. I *was* crazy. Half mad. Being lied to makes people go mad. After I spoke to X I stopped feeling mad. I got my dignity back.'

He said that I shouldn't have contacted X, that we 'shouldn't have had that conversation'.

I let that one lie.

———

He asked me how much I loved him. I said I didn't know how love could be measured. I said, 'I threw in my lot with you. I left everything behind, and went with you. I didn't take it lightly. You were *my guy*, in that primitive way. Is that love?'

———

He's still insisting, always in the same words, like a mantra, that X is 'just a friend. A good friend. That I like to see.'

———

I'm never going to get a blessing from him. He's never going to tell me the truth. It's beyond him.

———

Now I find that I have 'a gumboil'—an infection at the root of a tooth. 'Do you grind your teeth?' asked the dentist. Is the Pope a Catholic? I have to take penicillin for it, and swill out my mouth with very hot salty water six times a day. Meanwhile V discourses on a new theme: how European women are better groomed, sexier, more sophisticated than Australian or British ones. I make no protest, but am sometimes tempted to say, 'You've got yourself one! She's languishing at the bottom of our street! Why don't you go away with her and leave me to be a disillusioned, big-footed, trouser-wearing, short-haired, gumboiled Australian?'

———

The Antarctica people send me a photo of all the 'voyagers' on the deck of our ship, the *Professor Molchanov*, forging past the very tip of South America, Tierra del Fuego. We're standing with our backs to it, to face the camera, but there beyond us it lies, a land of mystery and fear, rocky, shrouded in mist or spray. I am thrilled with the picture, to have been there, a part of it. I show it to V. He studies it carefully, then hands it back and says with a laugh, 'You really have got a small head, haven't you!'

———

Last night we saw a movie of *Washington Square*. He liked it more than I did—another tale of a father domineering over his daughter—but I liked Jennifer Jason Leigh, her muddy skin and awkward gait. Walking to the cinema he grumbled about a seventy-year-old Dutchwoman, a portrait painter, who was on the container ship—how she was in Sydney for two weeks and he dreaded running into her round the cafes.

H: 'You could have a coffee with her, V, couldn't you? Or was it one of those shipboard intimacies that—'

V: 'What? *What?* Intimacy? I suppose you think I was—'

H: 'Hey! Stop! I meant when there's hardly anyone to talk to, so you get friendlier with somebody than you normally would—and then back on land you can hardly stand them! You don't have to bite my head off!'

V: 'Well—all right—but to me the word "intimacy" just means sex.'

———

Dreamt I looked down a steep pebbly hillside to its base where a woman in a brown dress lay on her side, curled up and motionless. A brown linen dress, like the one I wear every day. I know that girl's posture: it's the one in which I lie on the couch, knees bent, enduring the gruelling ordeal of *what we say* in that room.

But on my way out of her house, yesterday, crossing the front veranda, I noticed, on the neglected geranium that I've been furtively watering all these months, the tip of a tiny red bud. Like the point of a sharpened pencil.

———

M-C came to dinner and to stay the night. She's excited and happy because she and G and their daughter are moving down to Braidwood, to a very old house they've bought: 'The ceilings are high, but the doors are low and thick. A huge kitchen. The school bus stops right at the fence.' Around nine o'clock V went downstairs with a bag of rubbish, leaving the front door ajar. M-C and I washed up. No sign of V. She had a shower. No sign of V. We put our nighties on and went to bed. Still no sign of V. A warmish night, still and quiet. I opened both the bedroom windows wide and got into bed, expecting him to come in at any moment. I read for a while. An hour passed. Where is he? Has he had a heart attack in the street? Should I do something? Am I going crazy again? I dozed a little, woke, read, turned off the lamp, fell asleep. I don't know how much later a click, a blaze of light from the ceiling, and in he walks. I sit up, dazed. 'Sorry, sweetheart— I've been with'—he raises his shoulders, bends his knees, bares his teeth—'I've been with X. And her husband.'

'Her husband?'

'Her ex-husband. They just happened to walk past while I was putting the rubbish in the bin.'

I lie back, blinking. He goes on the front foot, starts to rant. 'There's nothing *wrong* with talking to bloody X down by the rubbish bins, is there?'

'No—it's just that we had a friend here for dinner and you disappeared and didn't come back for nearly two hours. I had no idea what had happened to you and I felt an idiot.'

He gets into bed. I say, quite gently, 'Do you feel a bit shaken up, seeing her again after such a long time?'

He stiffens: 'I haven't seen her for ages.'

'Yes, you said that. Do you feel shaken up, seeing her?'

He goes vague. I'm not going to get anywhere with that line of inquiry.

'Does her mother know about everything that's happened? She never seems to recognise me, in the street.'

'Aw, I s'pose so…She might've…' His style of evasion: the trailing voice, the unfinished sentence.

'She does know all about it, doesn't she.'

'Mmmm…I s'pose she does…'

'Did you use to stay the night?' All this very quiet, not an inter-rogation, just slow and mild.

'Oh, why do you need to know that? Why do you hurt yourself by trying to find out details?'

'I just need to understand it. Otherwise the whole thing seems unreal, as if it existed in a kind of cyberspace. You told me she never slept here, but then you said you never stayed at her place, and you never stayed in a hotel except at Gundagai, so it must have happened on some other planet.'

'Well, yes, I did.'

'Stay at her place?'

'Yes.'

'So her mother must know about it. That you were married and that you were sleeping with her daughter.'

'Well, they do live together.'

'There's only one more thing I need to know. When did you actually start having an affair?'

'Why do you need to know that?'

'I need to know how long I was fooled. How long you were sleeping with her and at the same time telling me I was mad for being suspicious.'

'Oh sweetheart, I don't even remember.'

'Come on, V, for God's sake. I'm not going to scream or cry. Just tell me.'

'It must have been sometime in December. Maybe at the begin-ning of December. I think that's when it was.'

Silence. I got up and went to the kitchen and boiled some water to do the mouth-wash for my infected gum. I sat on the edge of the bath in the dark with my head among the damp towels on their rail, waiting for the cup of salty water to cool enough for me to take a mouthful.

In bed I put one arm around him from behind, felt the tiny

twitches of his muscles as sleep crept over him. I was wide staring awake. I thought, 'I'll get up and do the ironing. I'll do all those shirts, and my green linen trousers. I'll empty the ironing basket.' Then I thought, 'No I won't. I'll take a Normison and get four hours' sleep.' Waiting for it to kick in, I picked up Thackeray, *The Rose and the Ring*. I knew its phrases and narrative almost off by heart, from so far back in childhood it was almost pre-memory: the insolent footman Gruffanuff on the threshold makes 'an odious, vulgar sign' at the Fairy Blackstick—and she turns him into a knocker and the screw goes right through his belly and fixes him forever to the front door. I couldn't hold in a laugh, then I thought I'd better turn off the light or I would *disturb V*.

————

We went for a walk, early. Fresh morning: glossy water, tide high, clouds scattered, air spiked with perfumes from invisible flowering plants. We were both yawning. Coming up the steep part of Yarranabbe I said, 'You know why we're always tired? We're exhausted from flogging a dead horse. Can't you see it's time we parted?' 'What? Just because I happened to run into X in the street when I was putting the rubbish out?' I said, 'Things between us are too fragile for something like that to have no meaning.' It was nothing serious, he said, it was trivial; I was overreacting as usual, it wasn't *worth* getting upset about, it wasn't *worth* having all these feelings.

We were on the home stretch, along the Rushcutters sea wall. I said, 'Listen, V. All this year I've eaten the shit you served me. The way you lied to me. I can't get past those letters you wrote her. You smashed my trust. You'd tell me you were sorry and make an excuse and I'd go along with it, I'd gulp down the plate of shit. Last night's plate was a small one but I can't swallow any more. You're never going to be straight with me. I know you can't help it. That's the sort of man you are—you're never going to do your own dirty work. So I'll do it. I've run out of masochism. This is over.'

He didn't argue or defend himself. His face was cramped and lined like a screwed-up paper bag. He started to talk about 'love', the 'love' he still has for me. I said, 'If you love somebody, you don't treat them the way you treat me. Let's divide everything up, and part.'

We walked past the exercise equipment and across the little footbridge. There were dogs, people with dogs. A young man, a derelict bloke we often see who looks like a psych patient turned out on to the street, had slept on a bench under a big overhanging tree, and was sitting up in his dark, filthy clothes, his hair on end, staring out at the water and the yachts.

———

A friend calls from Melbourne. 'He probably thinks you'll just take your clothes and your toothbrush. Get a property settlement. Or you'll get skun like a rabbit.'

———

Two huge, serious young Maori removalists transport my things. One of them is folding and stashing their blankets when I carry a desk lamp past the open back of the truck.

'That your ex in there?'

'Yes.'

He bends on me a kindly gaze. 'His loss, by the looks.'

———

Bellevue Hill. I'm on the fifth floor, top of a rise. Way down in the backyard there's a sea of nasturtiums and *two rotary clotheslines*. My outlook is tremendous. One way the ocean, the other a tiny sparkly strip of harbour. I can see on the horizon the very tips of the towers at Manly. The weather moves across the sky in great surges. Today, misty rain, strange winds.

———

My first night. I walked over to Bondi Junction looking for a place
to eat. The only thing open was something called Sushi Train. I took
a stool. Nobody spoke to me or looked at me. The little carriages of
food choo-choo'd past me on their endless oblong track. I seized a
passing plate and tried to eat what was on it but I couldn't swallow
for the lump in my throat.

———

We fought about money. He raged at me, said he had a tight band
round his chest, as if he was having a heart attack. I cried so much,
I couldn't stop, my eyes were all bunged up. We resolved the money.
Fairly.

———

Actually, my heart's broken.

———

V says his old friend's wife has told him she'd thought all along that
I'd leave him. 'And she said it's because of your restlessness.' Jolted
by this, I call and ask her. 'Yes. I did tell him you'd leave,' she said.
'Right back at the start. I couldn't believe the shit he was giving you,
and how long you went on taking it.'

———

A big envelope from V in my letterbox. No covering note. It contains
a *New Yorker* piece by Paul Theroux on V. S. Naipaul. A line in the
margin beside this: 'He was one of the strangest men I had ever
met, and absolutely the most difficult. He was almost unlovable. He
was contradictory, he quizzed me incessantly, he challenged everything I said, he demanded attention, he could be petty, he uttered
heresies about Africa, he fussed, he mocked, he made his innocent
wife cry, he had impossible standards. But he was also brilliant,
and passionate in his convictions, and to be with him, as a friend or
fellow-writer, I had always to be at my best.'

———

M's come to stay, for a movie shoot. She creeps in so late from work that I never see her till morning. We have breakfast together. I love and admire her *so much*.

———

After all these years in a flat with no yard I'd forgotten about towels that have dried outdoors in sunshine: thick and bristly, smelling of air.

———

Striding into Chinatown to eat with the Cretan and his wife and her brother. His wife squeezes my arm and says, 'It's fun being out, isn't it!'

———

V can't understand why only one member of my family has called him.

'He thinks you've all surrounded me,' I tell my sister on the phone, 'and slammed the door on him. He says if any of you had split up, he would have called you.'

Long pause.

'When my husband died,' she said, 'I used to ring V. He'd be pleased to hear from me and he'd give me a lot of advice; but I can categorically state that he never once called me.'

———

Dusk. Strings of lights come on, down in the gully and along the golf course, chains and filaments, some still, some crawling, some flashing or blinking. Sea a band of blurry blue-silver. Crickets in chorus. A pleasant breeze refreshes. A bus drops into low gear, streets away. My silent apartment: nobody here but me.

———

Yesterday I had a proper look at my brown linen dress. I still loved its sweeping skirt and the funky buttons down the front, but it was too sombre and nun-like, and the cuffs have always been too tight.

So I seized my black-handled scissors and laid the dress on the floor and crunch, crunch, I chopped the sleeves just above the wrists. I put the dress on and rolled the sleeves to the elbows. I put on my sandals and my straw hat and my glasses and walked over to Bondi Junction to bank my royalty cheque. In DJ's cool basement furniture department, where I was as usual the only customer, I picked a path among the little domestic arrangements they've got down there, and disposed myself and my voluminous skirts upon a two-and-a-half-seat roll-arm sofa that I come almost every day to visit. No one else is ever looking at it. It's plump. It's blue. When I sit on it, it embraces me, and supports me.

I am nearly fifty-six years old and I have never owned a sofa.

———

Hideous one-hour phone call from V. Horror of accusation and counter-accusation. His voice shook with emotion, chiefly rage. He said that yesterday he'd been so furious with me that he'd almost started smashing things; he'd gone down to the park and walked along mumbling and cursing to himself like a lunatic. 'I got *no work* done! That's *two days* with no work!' It was my fault that he'd got 'tangled up with' another woman—women drove him absolutely crazy! I refused to see how hard I was to live with! The constant anger! Contradicting him and correcting him all the time! The things he wanted to talk about—I'd glaze over and turn away! Why was I so angry? I'd told him that all women were angry, but he'd been talking about this on the phone with the Polish philosopher— and *she's* not angry! She *said* so. *She's* certainly not angry!

I sat here crying and crying and crying.

He tore strips off M again, accused her of being hopelessly, terminally self-obsessed. He raved at me for having been unhappy: why didn't I tell him I was unhappy? Why didn't we sit on the couch and have a *conversation* about it?

Because he was mad at me for being unhappy! His way of asking about it was: 'What the hell's the *matter* with you?' And when I tried to say, he'd argue me back against the wall! My job in the marriage was to keep the vibe up around him and be his unobtrusive servant, out of the house all day, while he bored his way into that fucking novel, year after year. And then when I got so lonely and numb that I had to go into therapy, he took an unshakeable stand against it. He got angrier and angrier. He kept asking me aggressively how long I was going to *be* like this? Telling me I used to have 'a lovely naturalness', but that now I had 'a forced naturalness'. And while I was trying to go into my unhappiness and attend to it and deal with it, he abandoned me. He left me in it and went out and found somebody else.

At least now he can keep a conversation like this going, instead of closing it down at the first sign of a tear. Now he can tolerate actual loud sobs, and keep going. And it dawns on me that though he drove me out, he's feeling all the rage and pain of having been left; and he doesn't know what it is or how to deal with it because he's *never been left before*.

———

I went over to Bondi Junction and bought myself, on his card, a vacuum cleaner, a mini stereo and a tiny little TV.

———

My left ankle keeps giving sharp stabs, as if I'd turned it, lugging this huge weight. This tremendous load. Of failure, and loss, and sorrow.

———

A gentle rain is falling. I looked up from the sink and saw it start. Sobbing's good for me. Instead of dry stoicism. It takes away the tension and sometimes I lie down and fall asleep.

———

The Lily of the Valley, breathing in the humble grass,
Answered the lovely maid and said: 'I am a wat'ry weed,
And I am very small and love to dwell in lowly vales;
So weak, the gilded butterfly scarce perches on my head...
—William Blake, 'The Book of Thel'

———

The Polish philosopher calls: 'You cannot have an argument with such a person! Because he twists! He *twists*!'

———

My favourite character in *South Park* is the one who's a 'piece of poo'. Its endearing little white gobcap, its heart-rending jauntiness and courage, as it rows its tiny boat along the sewer.

———

How dark the sea goes—a dark blue, *very* blue—on days when the temperature drops and the wind blows.

———

He declares that for a man, 'having to pay' in money as well as morally is enraging, on top of all the other feelings. I say, 'You talk as if you're giving me under duress something that's yours. What's really happening is that we're dividing up our common possessions. You've kept my stereo, and my speakers. The bed. And the spare bed. And what about my library? It was swallowed up in yours when I first moved in, don't you remember? I've hardly taken any of it.' He quickly backtracks.

    H: 'Do you feel I'm ripping you off?'

    V: 'No. Do *you* feel ripped off?'

    H: 'No.'

———

He was very put out when I said I'd heard from the great reader—apparently I am to contact her only through him. And I can see why: everything she said to me in her sad but rather chilly letter shows he must have told her that *I* broke up the marriage—that I left because I wanted 'freedom'.

————

V has always told me he would die early, that his father had died at fifty-two and so on. I used to poo-poo this as a bullshit Romantic death urge, though I always worked hard on him to eat less and better, get regular exercise, lose a bit of gut—but perhaps this explains his inability to deal with *my* deathliness, the desert in me that gradually grew and grew over the past few years. He had no life-resource, he had to draw on a woman's, and when I ran out of it, when I could no longer supply it, in fact needed it from him, he had none to give. He had to go out and find himself some, in another, younger woman.

————

Reviewing *The Oxford Book of Australian Letters*. I love the formal salutations people used in the eighteenth and nineteenth centuries. I could write a whole article about the gradations of affection, passion, despair and humility that you see in the way people sign off. If I wrote a letter today I would say, 'I am, Sir, your affectionate but afflicted friend.'

————

M reports that she and a close friend have been comparing notes on their former stepfathers. They were struck by the similarities: both men endlessly accused them of being self-obsessed, and were angry that the girls didn't *ask them questions*. Neither of them would ever volunteer things about himself in conversation, but would sit there waiting to be asked. And all they had to offer was advice.

————

Once rage acted in me as an anaesthetic. Now it combines seamlessly with grief, and produces the same flooding tears.

————

Dreamt of huge waves crashing on to a built-up foreshore. Strange buildings of concrete render, like old dressing sheds, with hollow passageways that opened on to a narrow beach, and these waves rearing up very close—and yet boys were surfing them. Wonder and fear.

————

Perhaps this is my karma. Not as punishment, but as logical outcome of what happened at the beginning of V and me: the poison of the lies, their slow, long-term, irreversible damage.

————

V's mother calls me. 'Hello dear? I'm so sorry to hear the news. What happened?' This motherly concern, the benign curiosity that I long for from Mum. I reply bluntly: 'Things got tough between us, and he fell in love with someone else.' 'Oh, he *didn't*,' she says, with that crooning note of protest against fate that old ladies use. 'Oh *dear*. Well, I don't want to lose touch with you. Because I love you. Keep on sending me your little cards, won't you.'

————

The incredulous pleasure of staying home all day. A house in the morning. The endless, disbelieving joy of it.

————

I must have been scared of him. I didn't *feel* scared, but looking back I see I *acted* as if I were scared of him.

————

The blue sofa's still there, in DJ's basement.

————

Poor G's come off his horse at Kangaroo Valley and made a mess of himself. I went down to see him in Wollongong Hospital. His wounded, swollen, sliced and stapled leg: when he flexed his foot, bright blood oozed out around one of the metal spikes. He said it was hurting quite badly. He said one of the other men in the ward had died during the night. He said he doesn't know what sort of friendship he can have with V, now we've parted. 'I could cut my tongue out, Hel, for the stupid things I said.' I didn't say anything much, but I thought, 'You'll adapt to V's new regime. Pretty soon the water will close over him and me as if we'd never been.' I sat beside his bed. I liked sitting there. He tried to stroke his foot and ankle where the punctures were: he said it helped with the pain. I offered to do it for him and he let me. I kept on stroking, very lightly, for as long as I could. If I'm not careful I'll forget what touch is.

———

I read in a magazine about feng shui. Unpacking my cartons I go through their clogged energy masses like a winnowing wind. Out, out, out.

———

Two excitable young men deliver my chest of drawers.

'Hi! I'm Ivan, and this is Francis! Are you the *famous* Helen Garner?'

'I write books, if that's what you mean.'

'The *famous* Helen Garner,' he says, with a big smile and a satisfied nod.

They pause to admire the view from my bedroom window.

'Give the chest a coating of beeswax!' cries Francis over his shoulder, as they dash away. 'Leave it for twenty minutes and then buff it! It'll come up beautifully!'

———

A mortified letter of apology from V for having been 'boorishly objectionable' the other day: 'I feel like a malignant tumour that's been removed from you.'

———

W comes down from the northern beaches to stay a night. She

strides in—her tossed Indian shawl, her battered old Volleys—and looks around beaming. 'Everything about your apartment makes me feel delicate. Delicate and fresh.' I mention V's letter of apology. She frowns. 'I'm sorry I'm not more impressed. But at the opera the other night he kept saying "Poor Hel", and it made me furious. I wanted to say, "Poor V would be more like it!"'

———

The way he used to speak to me about his first wife, as if the loss of him were the most majestic calamity ever to befall womankind: 'She's unhappier than she's *ever been*,' he would declare, shaking his head in a ponderous and tragical way. Her unhappiness, he was certain, was final, profound and complete. Nothing made me feel more solidarity with her than that. Now, hearing the words 'Poor Hel', some abject part of me wipes its tears, scrambles to its feet and tries to dust itself off.

———

Titanic mania. My sister reports seeing a T-shirt: 'The ship sank. Get over it.'

———

M sends me a present, *Planet and Glow-worm, a Book for the Sleepless*, compiled by Edith Sitwell. It's long out of print, a battered little thing from 1944, with a torn blue cover and gold lettering on the spine. I keep it on the bed, under the other pillow, on which there used to be a head. At 3 am I console myself with its excerpts from obscure, phantasmagorical works of literature—pearly thrones, worms upon dewy beds, Wolfes behowling the Moone, and an 'Apparition which disappeared with a curious Perfume and a most melodious Twang'.

———

Why is he being so sweet to me? He makes seductive overtures: invites me to lunch in nice restaurants, insists on coming over to hang a heavy picture for me, greets me with warmth and eagerness when I open the door, smiles at me tenderly, strokes my cheek, grabs my arm and squeezes it, calls me by all sorts of endearments he's never used before. But I have been an ex-wife, an ex-girlfriend more times than I can count. I know this premature 'friendship'—hectic, almost hysterical—a rickety bridge that people cobble together in relief after a separation, to hold them above the abyss of unbearable guilt and grief.

———

And I am also learning that there's a kind of man who believes he can have everything. He thinks he deserves both a wife and a girlfriend, and that everything will be fine and civilised, that he can become 'really deep, strong friends' with his wife, once she's been exhausted by the struggle and dropped off, just so long as she doesn't ask whether he's still having the affair that finished off the marriage.

Well, yes, he is. Sort of. 'I spend most of my time alone,' he says. 'I'm like you. I like being alone. I walk from room to room thinking about things. I miss you terribly, but at the same time I think it's good for me to be alone.'

'But you're not alone, are you. You're with her, and you're still trying to make me think you're *not* with her.'

'Yes, okay, I do sleep with her, but eighty per cent of my time I'm alone. Being alone is the *larger* truth.'

———

Woke early, dozed again, and in my sleep saw a snap vision of V, caught in a single-frame shot—standing in the hallway facing me, frozen in a strange posture of furtive, fastidious movement—one knee bent, arms held away from his torso, wrists sharply angled; his face younger and darker than in real life, his expression alert, surprised—sprung! The dawn of a guilty smile.

———

I took the bus to Elizabeth Bay, to vote in the federal election. Mistake. As I approached that part of town my guts turned to molten metal. But I walked to St Canice's, and voted Labor, and then I walked home.

———

In this flat, alone, I can at last see myself as a grown-up. I've moved a cane chair into the bedroom so I can survey my view. I sit there in the early evenings and contemplate it. At certain hours it looks almost Italian. One day I'll be light-hearted again. I swear I will. I will work my way there.

———

I call V on the phone: 'Listen. I've got an idea. How about we say to each other, "Okay. We have parted, and we won't ever be together again." And then we stay right away from each other, and you don't come over, and I don't go over, and we don't call each other or talk any more.'

Pause.

'We should be better than that,' he says.

'I don't care. I'm too angry, and I'm too sad. And I can't stand it.'

Pause.

'Okay.'

'Right. I'll say it first: we have parted, and we'll never be together again.'

He laughs: 'We've parted; and I'm keeping an open mind on the rest.'

'Oh, don't start to fool around!'

Long pause.

'No. Okay. You're right. We *have* parted—yes, we've parted, and I can't see how we could ever be together again, because I've—because too much damage has been done.'

———

For three days I haven't stirred abroad, except yesterday to Spot-
light, to buy about a mile of a creamy-yellow cotton fabric for my
curtains. I'm going to make them long and loose, I want a lemony
light in every room, I want them to puff grandly on the breezes
that stream up the hill this building stands on. On Bondi Junction
mall, at a second-hand stall, I found a single wine glass. The sort of
glass you see in an old still life, half-full of light red wine on a table,
among fruits and chicken carcasses—wide-mouthed yet dainty,
with a little pattern of vine leaves etched around its rim. From now
on, that's what I'm going to drink out of.

On the way home I dropped into DJ's basement, to salute the blue
sofa. A sign was propped against its cushions: '30% off'.

———

Next door to the newsagent there's a flower shop. They've got big
metal buckets outside, full of fresh lilac, dark purple and damp as if
with dew. I stopped in the wave of perfume. A very old lady turned
from the flowers and smiled at me. 'Where I was born,' she said, in
a cracked and quivery voice, 'there used to be *hedges* of lilac.'

'Where were you born?'

'Prague.'

The lilac hedges of Prague. It sounds like a title.

———

Over in Rose Bay, in the early dark, someone is letting off fireworks.
Dull thuds, a brief crackling. I stick my head out the window just
in time to see the sky fill with an exploding galaxy of lilies and an
enormous chrysanthemum, half red and half green, which stains
the low cloud cover, fades and dies.

———

A handyman's here, putting up curtain rod brackets for me, when
two young blokes from DJs stagger in, lugging the sofa wrapped
in thick white plastic. They heave it across the spartan living room

and dump it with its back to the big window. I've only ever seen it in dim artificial light. They strip off the first sheet of wrapping, and the second. Somebody gasps, somebody sighs. It's a dusty, silvery, ethereal blue-grey, shading into pale lavender. The spring morning pours into the room, bathing it in purity, a light in which the sofa levitates, as insubstantial as a cloudbank. The three men and I stand in a line, breathing together, in wordless rapture.

A NOTE ABOUT THE AUTHOR

Helen Garner writes novels, stories, screenplays, and works of nonfiction. In 2006 she received the inaugural Melbourne Prize for Literature, and in 2016 she won the prestigious Windham Campbell Literature Prize for nonfiction. In 2019 she was honored with the Australia Council Award for Lifetime Achievement in Literature. Her books include *Monkey Grip, The Children's Bach, Cosmo Cosmolino, The Spare Room, The First Stone, This House of Grief, Everywhere I Look,* and her diaries *The Yellow Notebook, One Day I'll Remember This,* and *How to End a Story.*

A NOTE ON THE TYPE

This book was set in Granjon, a type named in compliment to Robert Granjon, a type cutter and printer active in Antwerp, Lyons, Rome, and Paris from 1523 to 1590. Granjon, the boldest and most original designer of his time, was one of the first to practice the trade of typefounder apart from that of printer.

Linotype Granjon was designed by George W. Jones, who based his drawings on a face used by Claude Garamond (ca. 1480–1561) in his beautiful French books. Granjon more closely resembles Garamond's own type than do any of the various modern faces that bear his name.